Introduction
to Modern
Information Retrieval

McGraw-Hill Computer Science Series

McGraw-Hill Advanced Computer Science Series

Introduction to Modern Information Retrieval

Gerard Salton
Professor of Computer Science
Cornell University

Michael J. McGill
Associate Professor of Information Studies
Syracuse University

McGraw-Hill Publishing Company

New York   St. Louis   San Francisco   Auckland   Bogotá   Caracas
Hamburg   Lisbon   London   Madrid   Mexico   Milan
Montreal   New Delhi   Oklahoma City   Paris   San Juan
São Paulo   Singapore   Sydney   Tokyo   Toronto

This book was set in Times Roman by Progressive Typographers.
The editors were Charles E. Stewart and James E. Vastyan;
the production supervisor was John Mancia.
The drawings were done by VIP Graphics.
R. R. Donnelley & Sons Company was printer and binder.

INTRODUCTION TO MODERN INFORMATION RETRIEVAL

5 6 7 DODO 9 0

ISBN 0-07-054484-0

Library of Congress Cataloging in Publication Data

Salton, Gerard.
    Introduction to modern information retrieval.

    (McGraw-Hill computer science series)
    Includes indexes.
    1. Information storage and retrieval systems.
I. McGill, Michael J.   II. Title.   III. Series.
Z699.S313   025'.04   81-20843
ISBN 0-07-054484-0   AACR2

Contents

Preface

An information retrieval system is an information system, that is, a system used to store items of information that need to be processed, searched, retrieved, and disseminated to various user populations. Information retrieval systems thus share many of the concerns of other information systems, such as data base management and decision support systems. In particular, it is necessary to choose efficient organizations for the stored records, rapid search procedures capable of finding items of interest in specific cases, and effective methods for disseminating the retrieved data and interacting with the system users.

Information retrieval systems are normally used to handle bibliographic records and textual data. This is in contrast to data base management and management information systems that process structured data, and to question-answering systems that use complex information organizations and inference procedures designed to answer questions in particular subject areas. In an extended sense, however, any information system designed to augment the state of human knowledge and to aid human activities does utilize concepts and procedures from information storage and retrieval.

Today, information processing activities are carried out with the assistance of automatic equipment. Thus, a direct link exists between information retrieval and computer science. On the other hand, information retrieval also takes on aspects of behavioral science, since retrieval systems are designed to aid human activities.

Most practitioners interested in the design and operations of actual retrieval systems are concerned only about applied computer science. However, many topics in theoretical computer science are also of direct importance to information retrieval, including, for example, information theory, probability theory, computational semantics, and programming theory and algebra. Techniques from these disciplines may be used to build information retrieval models and to obtain insights into various aspects of retrieval theory and practice.

Although information retrieval is mentioned in many computer science curriculum proposals, retrieval courses are often replaced in practice by material on data structures and data base systems where attractive approaches have been developed for formalization and abstraction. The study of information retrieval is thus frequently carried out in library science, information science, and information management schools. In these environments, the mathematical foundations necessary to make a substantial impact are often omitted from retrieval system courses.

This text is aimed at increasing the understanding of modern information retrieval by students of computer science as well as by students of information science and management science. The book covers the basic aspects of information retrieval theory and practice, and also relates the various techniques to the design and evaluation of complete retrieval systems. The book is introductory in the sense that no prior knowledge of retrieval methodology is assumed; it is modern because currently active trends and developments are examined. The text concentrates in particular on the description of the concepts, functions, and processes of interest in retrieval rather than on the detailed operations of any one existing retrieval system. In order to keep the material at an introductory level, the more advanced mathematical aspects of retrieval theory have been deemphasized or simplified. The text should thus be accessible to students with only a cursory knowledge of the operations of digital computers and only a superficial exposure to computer programming. More advanced readers can supply the relevant mathematical background by consulting the references given.

The text begins with an introduction and a description of the main retrieval processes incorporated into existing, operational systems based on keyword indexing and Boolean query formulations (Chapters 1 and 2). Chapter 3 contains a detailed explanation of modern automatic indexing techniques with evaluation results and assessments of the importance and practical usefulness of the techniques. Experimental retrieval systems, based in part on fully automatic analysis, search, and retrieval methods, are covered in Chapter 4 with emphasis on the design of the SMART and SIRE systems developed by the authors. The main evaluation techniques used to assess the effectiveness and efficiency of information retrieval systems are covered in Chapter 5 with emphasis on the use of the well-known recall and precision measures. Chapter 6 deals with important techniques usable in the design of future systems, such as automatic classification methods, query negotiation, and reformulation processes used in on-line environments, collection restructuring, and bibliographic citation processing. Language processing methods useful in retrieval, including current syntactic and semantic methodologies, and artificial intelligence approaches to language understanding are examined in Chapter 7. Chapter 8 introduces specialized hardware useful in retrieval, such as parallel processing devices, array processors, and special back-end search devices useful for manipulating and searching large data bases. Also covered are modern techniques used for dictionary searching and for automatic text scanning systems. The relationship between information retrieval and other information systems, such as data base and decision support systems, is examined in detail in Chapter 9, and the current work in data base processing and data base management is described. Finally the expected future directions and developments in information retrieval are covered in Chapter 10, including the importance and likely effect of personal computers, word processing, advanced display systems, and paperless information systems.

The text should be useful for computer science as well as library science and information science students on a junior-senior level in college or for beginning graduate students. The book can also serve the professional reader as an introduction to the design and operations of information retrieval and management information systems. A common core for computer science as well as information science readers is contained in Chapters 1, 3, 4, and 10. Computer science audiences should profit in addition from a complete treatment of Chapters 5, 6, and 8, since these chapters emphasize the more mathematical aspects of the field and the connection to software and hardware implementations. Library and information science readers, on the other hand, should concentrate on Chapters 2, 7, and 9 in addition to the core to gain a thorough understanding of conventional retrieval and other information systems and of the language analysis methods useful for processing natural language texts.

To simplify the reader's task, the material has been graded for technical difficulty:

*Sections marked with a single asterisk contain technical material that may be difficult for some readers. Often a modest computer science background may be useful, or an acquaintance with elementary algebra or basic probability theory. This material is considered important, and the reader is encouraged to read the section and obtain an understanding of the content.

**Sections identified by two asterisks contain technical material at a somewhat more detailed level. A particular procedure may be covered in detail; alternatively, a theory may be introduced requiring some technical know-how. Readers who find this material difficult may wish to skim the section rather than dwell on the details.

Sections not marked by * or ** should be accessible to all readers without special background.

The following sample curricula will provide complete coverage of the principal aspects of retrieval system design and operations:

	Computer science	Information science and management science
Chapter 1 (Core)	What is information retrieval? Functional view of retrieval	What is information retrieval? Functional view of retrieval
Chapter 2 (IS emphasis)	Basic set theory inherent in list processing	Standard Boolean operations Standard retrieval Conventional systems
Chapter 3 (Core)	Theory of automatic indexing Term weighting and associative indexing Basic evaluation results	Theory of automatic indexing Term weighting and associative indexing Basic evaluation results
Chapter 4 (Core)	The SMART system Relevance feedback and cluster searching Weighted retrieval in Boolean systems (SIRE)	The SMART system Relevance feedback and cluster searching Weighted retrieval in Boolean systems (SIRE)
Chapter 5 (CS emphasis)	Mathematics of evaluation Evaluation parameters and computational aspects	Basic definition of recall-precision parameters Cost evaluation
Chapter 6 (CS emphasis)	Term relevance theory Cluster generation and search Pseudoclassification Document space alteration and dynamic file processing	Use of citations in information search systems
Chapter 7 (IS emphasis)	ATN grammars Criterion tree processing Concept representation	Language analysis Syntax and semantics Context-free and context-sensitive grammars Concept representation in information systems
Chapter 8 (CS emphasis)	Basic hardware devices Parallel processing techniques Microprocessors Dictionary search methods String search algorithms	Basic hardware and parallel processing techniques Microprocessors Text scanning machines
Chapter 9 (CS and IS emphasis)	Relationship of information retrieval to other information systems Data base systems and models	Relationship of information retrieval to other information systems File processing, accessing, searching File security, data structures
Chapter 10 (Core)	Future directions Text input Distributed architecture New retrieval theories Advanced information systems	Future directions Text input Distributed architecture Mixed information retrieval systems Paperless information systems

By limiting the coverage to the more basic aspects of the various topics, the material can be assimilated in a one-semester course. A second semester may be required if the various algorithms and techniques—for word stem generation, pseudoclassification, string searching, and so on—are covered in detail, and if additional sources are consulted.

A number of graduate students at Cornell and Syracuse universities have made substantial contributions to the design of the SMART and SIRE systems, including, in particular: Robert E. Williamson, Clement T. Yu, Chung Shu Yang, Anita Wong, Harry Wu, and Edward A. Fox at Cornell and Terry Noreault, Jennifer Kuehn, Judy Tessier, and Matthew Koll at Syracuse. Several readers have reviewed the manuscript and made many valuable comments and suggestions, including, in particular: Professor Richard H. Austing of the University of Maryland, Professor Michael D. Cooper of the University of California at Berkeley, Professor Jeffrey Katzer of Syracuse University, Dr. Michael E. Lesk of Bell Laboratories, Professor J. F. Nunamaker of the University of Arizona, and Professor Linda C. Smith of the University of Illinois. The authors have also profited from discussion with many colleagues and friends. Some early material was typed by Peggy Montgomery at Syracuse. Geri Pinkham at Cornell has typed the complete manuscript over several times with unusual speed and competence; in the process she became familiar with the intricacies of an automated text editing system. Without her help the text would have remained in manuscript form for a long time to come. Edward Fox and Elena Seifrid have also helped to produce a version ready for automatic typesetting. The writers are greatly indebted to all these individuals for guidance and assistance.

Gerard Salton
Michael J. McGill

Chapter 1

Information Retrieval:
An Introduction

0 PREVIEW

This chapter examines the information retrieval problem by considering the social and technological world in which retrieval systems exist. Later chapters
will deal with individual system functions and parameters. To render this discussion meaningful, it is necessary to understand the context in which information retrieval systems operate and be aware of the various types of existing information systems.

    The chapter closes with an examination of the functional components of
information retrieval and a description of a few basic methods for organizing
information retrieval files. The second chapter covers retrieval systems whose
operations are based on one of these file organization methods, the inverted
file.

1 OVERVIEW

Information retrieval (IR) is concerned with the representation, storage, organization, and accessing of information items. In principle no restriction is
placed on the type of item handled in information retrieval. In actuality, many
of the items found in ordinary retrieval systems are characterized by an em-

phasis on narrative information. Such narrative information must be analyzed to determine the information content and to assess the role each item may play in satisfying the information needs of the system users. The items processed by a retrieval system typically include letters, documents of all kinds, newspaper articles, books, medical summaries, research articles, and so on.

Most people are faced with a need for information at some time or other. Typically one might first turn to friends and acquaintances for help, but if that is to no avail, a more formal search might be initiated in a library or information center. A first search effort might then lead to one or more information items that are selected for detailed examination. In some cases these initially chosen items might suffice in satisfying the existing information needs. If not, additional items might be sought. One possibility for extending a search for information consists in using references to previously available information items to find additional items in related areas. Alternatively, the information need could be redefined. For example, a person interested in information about the effect of tetraethyl lead on the environment and on human beings may conduct separate searches for articles dealing first with the effects of tetraethyl lead on humans, and then with the effects of tetraethyl lead on the environment.

To facilitate the task of the information user in finding items of interest, libraries and information centers provide a variety of auxiliary aids. Each incoming item is analyzed and appropriate descriptions are chosen to reflect the information content of the item. Each item is classified in accordance with the established procedures and incorporated into the collection of existing information items. Procedures are established for formulating requests designed to satisfy an information need and for comparing these requests, or *queries*, with the descriptions of the stored items. These comparisons are the basis for deciding which items are appropriate for the respective queries. Finally, a retrieval and dissemination mechanism is used to deliver the information items of potential interest to the users of the information system. These steps are all carried out in conventional libraries where a card catalog forms the principal auxiliary tool used in an information search. The processes and methodologies needed to carry out those tasks automatically are described in the remainder of this book.

It is often claimed that the usefulness of a collection of information items depends crucially on *currency* and *completeness*. The desire to maintain currency implies that new items must constantly be added to the collections. Completeness implies further that the collection contains a large proportion of the items of potential interest, and that obsolete items are removed only when the obsolescence of an information item can be established without doubt. The U.S. Library of Congress which attempts to maintain both currency and completeness, is adding about 3,500 new items to the collections every day [1].

Currency and completeness are obviously impossible to achieve simultaneously in an age of limited resources. Hence it is necessary to compromise by attempting to incorporate into the collections all the ''important'' items. But item importance is difficult to evaluate in advance: many information items attract little attention and are never used; others, such as, for example, Vannevar

Bush's "As We May Think," outlast most contemporary items [2]. In practice, somewhat arbitrary decisions are often made to control the acquisitions and the collection maintenance procedures.

The collection development problem is aggravated by the growth in the available information. In early times, the total available knowledge changed relatively slowly. However, by the year 1800, the amount of scientific publication was already doubling every 50 years [3]. More recently with the impressive growth of science and technology, the rate of increase of available knowledge has vastly accelerated. Between 1800 and 1966, the number of scientific journals has increased from 100 to over 100,000. At the present time, no upper limit is apparent in the rate of increase of available information items.

Consider now the problem of actually locating a particular item included in a collection of documents. Various access mechanisms may be provided, related to either the physical or the logical organization of the items. In a library the *physical organization* is generally controlled by the arrangement of call numbers. In the United States common call numbers in use in libraries of academic institutions are those provided by the Library of Congress classification system [4]. Books placed in order according to these call numbers are clustered on the library shelves by topic area. Thus, books about information retrieval may be assembled under common call numbers beginning with Z699. Unfortunately, the same call number (Z699) may also be used for other related subjects such as library automation, cataloging, and general library processing. Furthermore additional information retrieval items can also appear in various other sections of the library, notably in classes identified by call numbers TA and TK in the Library of Congress system.

A person seeking a given information item may then be forced to outguess the library cataloger who made the original decision about the placement of the particular item. To render this guessing task easier, a *logical organization* of the data may be superimposed on the physical organization. Thus, books published on information retrieval can also be identified by looking in a library subject catalog under the term "information retrieval." In some libraries the correct term might be "computer-based information retrieval" or perhaps "information systems retrieval." In any case, once the appropriate term is found, adjacent cards will identify books related to the topic being sought. These books may belong to various call number locations (that is, Z, TA, TK, etc.); all those locations will provide some reference to information retrieval. Given a particular call number, the corresponding item should be found at the designated location on the library shelves. If the item is not at the designated location, one presumes that it is in use or that it may be lost.

When a subject catalog is available, changes can be made to the subject terms without actually reshelving the books themselves. In particular, the items can be logically reorganized by suitably changing the library catalog without altering the physical arrangement. A large number of different logical organizations can be used to characterize the various items. Thus, the items can be placed in order by author, size, date of publication, date of acquisition, title, subject, and so on. Each logical organization then corresponds to a different set of cards in the catalog.

One problem faced by all users of information systems is the need to reduce to a manageable size the number of items that are to be examined. It is not obvious that the methods currently available for this task are adequate. As early as 1945, the existing methods for information organization were criticized [2]:

> There is a growing mountain of research. . . . The investigator is staggered by findings and conclusions of thousands of other workers—conclusions which he cannot find time to grasp, much less remember. The summation of human experience is being expanded at a prodigious rate and the means we use for threading through the consequent maze to the momentarily important item is the same that was used in the days of the square rigged ships.

Similar sentiments have been voiced by many other observers. In Alvin Toffler's "Future Shock"—a book dealing with society's inability to cope with change—Emilio Segre, Nobel prize–winning physicist, is quoted as saying that "on k-mesons alone, to wade through all the papers is an impossibility" [5]. In other words even in specialized, relatively narrow topic areas, one tends to become overloaded with information very rapidly.

The construction of an effective system of information organization which permits efficient use of the information items is difficult for at least two reasons. First, the volume of information expands unevenly for different topics. Some areas such as computer science, for example, are growing at a very fast rate, while other subjects such as certain foreign language studies may not be growing at all. Future growth patterns of information are difficult to predict and any predictions are subject to large error rates. To take care of future growth, one may want to provide for some expansion in each and every topic area. Ultimately these expansion mechanisms will be overtaxed in some areas while not being used at all for other topics [6].

A second difficulty in creating effective information organizations is the desire to keep related items relatively close together. For example, books on algebra, matrix theory, graph theory, and topology should appear close to one another in the collection [7]. At first glance this may appear to be easy enough, especially when these topics all clearly fit under the more general topic of mathematics. Special problems do, however, arise for interdisciplinary topics such as systems analysis. This particular subject is related to several major topics including computer science, operations research, engineering, management science, education, and information systems, as shown in the scheme of Fig. 1-1. An organizational arrangement which would allow items on systems analysis to appear close to other items in all related topic classes cannot be achieved by placing the items in order on a bookshelf (an organization based on only one dimension). Rather the organization must be multidimensional.

A two-dimensional organization could, for example, take into account shelf locations above and below a given area rather than only those situated

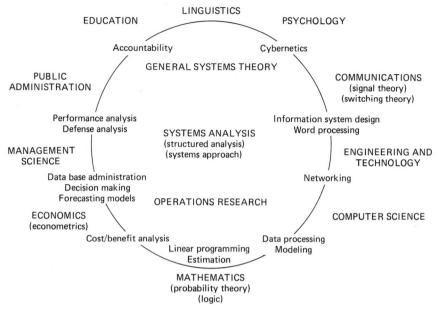

Figure 1-1 Systems analysis: related disciplines, tools, and techniques.

adjacently on the same shelf. Figure 1-2a depicts a one-dimensional organization, while Fig. 1-2b and c represents two- and three-dimensional organizations, respectively. The actual number of dimensions necessary to keep related subjects close to each other must be determined from the number of required relationships. Unfortunately, the physical organization of information stored in computer systems is limited to the few dimensions of the existing hardware systems. Hardware devices and software methodologies are available that may effectively increase the number of available dimensions. These are introduced in Chapter 8.

2 CHANGING TECHNOLOGY

Up to this point a fairly desperate picture has been presented. Barring substantial logical and technological advances, a situation may soon arise where it may not be possible to isolate the useful items from the mass of available information. People may be forced to use whatever turns out to be most accessible and ignore the remainder. Fortunately, computer technology is providing increased capabilities for the manipulation of all types of information. The trend over the past 15 to 20 years has been for computational capabilities of every sort to double every 3 to 4 years. That is, twice as many numbers can be added together in the same time and twice as many items can be stored in the same space as 3 or 4 years ago. The exception is the cost of computing which has decreased. Thus for equivalent dollars one can buy two or three times as much computational capability as was available 3 or 4 years ago [8–10].

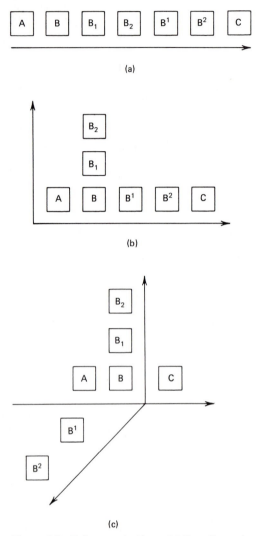

Figure 1-2 Data organizations. (a) One-dimensional data organization. (b) Two-dimensional data organization. (c) Three-dimensional data organization.

Startling advances have been registered also in the capabilities of the physical devices which store information. The amount and type of information that can be retained in storage has changed significantly. The first electronic computers were capable of storing only a few numbers. At the present time, devices are being designed that are capable of storing a trillion characters of information. The growth in capacity of storage technology is such that one should soon be able to store library-sized quantities of information in a cost-effective manner. For the stored information to be useful, the information must be delivered to the potential users. Communication technologies such as the telephone play an important role in this delivery process. Unfortunately, communication devices are still relatively slow and costly at the present time. However, numerous changes are occurring such as, for example, the introduction of satellite communications, the use of optical fibers as communications channels, and the design of sophisticated communication networks. If this technology continues to improve, large quantities of data should be transmittable efficiently in the foreseeable future.

In summary, the existing information problems appear difficult to master without the use of sophisticated methodologies for storing, processing, and transmitting information. The availability of modern information retrieval systems has greatly improved the access to many stored information collections. However, even the current systems are unable to deal effectively with the increasing growth of information. In spite of many efforts on the part of researchers, current operational capabilities remain at a relatively elementary stage [11]. In part, this may be due to the unwillingness or inability of individuals in the information fields to try out and utilize devices and methods which would render the traditional methods obsolete [12]. The present text describes current capabilities as well as promising areas of work and the main research efforts dealing with the information retrieval problem. Before proceeding with a detailed description, it is necessary to place information retrieval in the context of other information processing work. This is done in the next section of this chapter.

3 INFORMATION SYSTEM TYPES

Information retrieval exhibits similarities to many other areas of information processing. The most important computer-based information systems today are the management information systems (MIS), data base management systems (DBMS), decision support systems (DSS), question-answering systems (QA), as well as information retrieval systems (IR).

A Information Retrieval Systems

Information retrieval is best understood if one remembers that the information being processed consists of documents. In that context, information retrieval deals with the representation, storage, and access to documents or representatives of documents (document surrogates) [13]. The input information is likely to include the natural language text of the documents or of document excerpts and abstracts. The output of an information retrieval system in response to a search request consists of sets of references. These references are intended to provide the system users with information about items of potential interest. The users of information retrieval systems have a wide variety of different information needs. They include research scientists seeking articles relating to particular experiments, engineers trying to determine whether a patent covering some new idea has previously been obtained, buyers of vacuum cleaners trying to obtain new product information, as well as attorneys searching for legal precedents. In other words, information retrieval system users exhibit many different backgrounds, and many different reasons may lead them to use the retrieval facilities.

B Data Base Management Systems

Any automated information system is based on a collection of stored items (a *data base*) that needs to be accessed. Thus data base management systems might simply be systems designed to manipulate and maintain control of any data base. In actual practice, data base management systems are concerned with the storage, maintenance, and retrieval of data facts available in the system in explicit form. That is, the information does not appear as natural language text but is available instead in the form of specific data elements stored in tables [14]. In a data base environment each item, or *record*, is thus separated into several *fields*, and each field contains the value for a specific characteristic or attribute identifying the corresponding record. The characteristics used to identify a set of personnel records might be the names of the individuals involved, the addresses of the various people, as well as the social security numbers, and the job classifications. Specific values of these characteristics, that is, specific names or specific social security numbers, are used as identifiers for the individual records.

The processes of concern in data base management include the storage and retrieval of data, the updating or deletion of data, the protection of data from unintentional or deliberate damage or misuse, and perhaps even the transmission of data to remote users or other data management systems. The output of the systems may consist of individual records, portions of records, tables, or other arrangements of the data from the data base.

In order to be suitable for data base processing, each search request must state the specific values of certain record identifiers for the records of interest. A user may, for example, wish to retrieve all the personnel records corresponding to people of a certain age, height, sex, and so on. The retrieved information will consist of all records which match the stated search request exactly. In information retrieval, as opposed to data base management, it is often difficult to formulate precise information requests, and the retrieved information may include items that may or may not match the information requests exactly. The information contained in data base management systems includes a good deal of numerical data, and statistical or computational facilities may be provided to manipulate the numbers.

C Management Information Systems

A management information system is a data base management system tailored to the needs of managers. The functions performed by a manager in a given corporation depend on the availability of many kinds of data. Of particular interest may be information leading to the choice of possible alternatives by the manager presented in terms of ranges of values of particular attributes. A management information system therefore fits the general data base management framework. However, in order to be useful to the manager, the information may be subjected to special processing not normally available in data base management systems. For example, a data base of geothermal dispersion data may be used by a manager to determine the effect of differing equipment configurations in a plant. In such a case, data relating to particular equipment configurations and to dispersion characteristics would be connected to a modeling capability to support the manager's activities. Such special-purpose systems useful for management are known as management information systems.

D   Decision Support Systems

The systems described so far perform specific operations on homogeneous classes of information items. Normally, information retrieval systems do not perform management information functions, and vice versa. However, it is in principle possible to conceive of information systems in which a variety of different components are assembled into a single cooperating structure that includes information retrieval systems, data base management systems, computer graphics systems, and other technical capabilities which collectively provide powerful tools in support of the decision making process. If, for example, the manager interested in the dispersion characteristics of plant equipment were additionally given the ability to match the dispersion effects on a television screen and to use the graphics equipment also to review written materials in this area, the complete integrated system might be characterized as a decision support system. Decision support systems exist on a limited basis for narrow ranges of users employing data bases in restricted subject areas [15].

E   Question-Answering Systems

Question-answering systems provide access to factual information in a natural language setting. The stored data base often consists of large numbers of facts relating to special areas of discourse, together with general world knowledge covering the context within which conversations between persons usually take place. User questions may be received in natural language form, and system responses may also be furnished as natural language formulations. The task of the question-answering system consists in analyzing the user query, comparing the analyzed query with the stored knowledge, and assembling a suitable response from the apparently relevant facts.

Question-answering systems currently exist only as experimental devices. The extraction of meaning from natural language and the determination of general rules of intelligent behavior seem to be major barriers to creating effective question-answering systems for general use. An overview of question-answering systems is provided in references 16 and 17.

Figure 1-3 sketches the relations between the various types of information systems. Although the management information and data base management systems have a great deal in common, this is not apparent for the other system types. Data base and management information systems process structured data, often in the form of tables of numeric information. Document retrieval

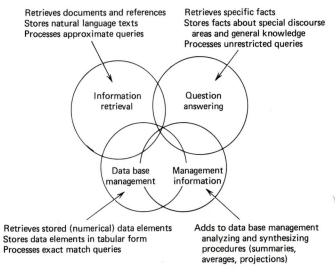

Figure 1-3 Overlap among types of information systems.

and question-answering systems, on the other hand, are concerned with natural language data, the former to retrieve documents and the latter to retrieve specific facts in answer to incoming queries. The users of such systems may have many different interests and backgrounds, and will thus require a variety of services and end products from the systems [18].

The analysis of natural language information is examined in Chapter 7, and the design of question-answering systems is described in more detail in Chapters 7 and 9.

4 FUNCTIONAL APPROACH TO INFORMATION RETRIEVAL

Many different information retrieval systems currently exist. To put these systems in reasonable perspective and to understand the advantages and disadvantages, it is necessary to understand the key functions performed by these systems.

Every information retrieval system can be described as consisting of a set of information items (DOCS), a set of requests (REQS), and some mechanism (SIMILAR), for determining which, if any, of the information items meets the requirements of the requests [19]. Figure 1-4 shows the relationship of these components. SIMILAR represents a relationship operator mapping specific queries to particular items included in the stored document set. In theory, the relationships between queries and documents can be obtained by direct comparison, as suggested in the model of Fig. 1-4. In practice, the relevance of specific information items to particular requests is not determined directly. Rather the documents or information items are first converted to a special form using a classification or indexing language referred to here as the indexing language,

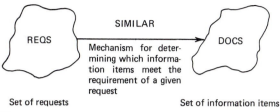

SIMILAR

REQS

Mechanism for deter-
mining which informa-
tion items meet the
requirement of a given
request

DOCS

Set of requests   Set of information items

Figure 1-4   Information system environment.

LANG. The requests are also converted into a representation consisting of elements from LANG. Figure 1-5 exhibits the processing of the information items
and the requests into LANG.

The mapping of the information items to the indexing language may be carried out manually, automatically, or by a combination of the two processes.
This mapping is known as the indexing process. The mapping operation for the
requests represents the query negotiation process. The procedures for determining which information items should be retrieved in response to a query are
based on representations of the requests and information items consisting of
elements from the indexing language. SIMILAR is a relation operator determining the similarity of the various information items to a given request. The
similarity measuring process produces identifications of information items that
are potentially relevant to the request. SIMILAR may also be considered to be
the retrieval function because it identifies the specific items that are to be retrieved. In some instances, the system places the retrieved items in order of
probable relevance to the request; in general, however, the retrieved information items will appear in the order in which they are located in the files.

The indexing language is either prespecified (controlled) or taken freely
from the text of the information items and information requests (uncontrolled).
Sometimes a combination of controlled and uncontrolled elements may be included in the indexing language. Whichever type of language is used, an infor-

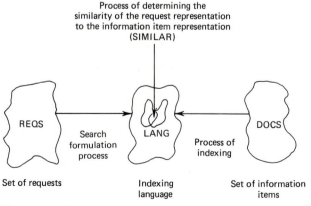

Process of determining the
similarity of the request representation
to the information item representation
(SIMILAR)

REQS

Search
formulation
process

LANG

Process of
indexing

DOCS

Set of requests   Indexing   Set of information
                                   language   items

Figure 1-5   Functional overview of information retrieval.

mation item is usually assumed to be representable by a list of elements from the indexing language. For example, a particular information item entitled "Environmental noise assessment study, Part I" could be represented by using the controlled index terms "noise," "environmental influence," "utilization review," and "resident environment" [20]. To form a unified representation of this information item, a four-element *vector* can be used. For instance, the representation of this information item may be a structure such as

$$\langle 1 \quad 1 \quad 1 \quad 1 \rangle$$

where the first 1 is understood to stand for the indexing language term "noise," the second is "environmental influence," the third is "utilization review," and the fourth is "resident environment." A second document that includes the same topics except for the term "noise" would be represented as

$$\langle 0 \quad 1 \quad 1 \quad 1 \rangle$$

The particular method used to represent the individual information items is less important than the actual choice of the elements of the indexing language made during the indexing and text analysis processes. These questions are discussed in Chapter 3.

Following the choice of a representation for the information items and requests, the item representations must be organized into a *file structure*. Specifically, the item representations must be collected together and organized to ensure the efficiency and/or effectiveness of operations such as file searching or file updating. File structures vary in complexity from those with little or no organization to those structures maintaining various explicit relationships between information items.

5 SIMPLE FILE STRUCTURES

A Linear Lists

The simplest file structure is referred to as a linear list. A linear list is literally an unordered collection of items. Recall that current computer storage devices are largely one-dimensional. Thus, to find a specific element in a linear list kept in a computer store requires that the file items be examined one at a time. The item being sought may fortuitously be the first element examined—or if one is especially unlucky, it may be the last item. On the average, a specific item will appear in the middle of the file. Hence, on the average (n + 1)/2 items must be examined to locate a given item, where n represents the number of items in the file.

A linear list of the kind represented in Fig. 1-6 exhibits many advantages for information retrieval. For example, when new items are introduced into the system, they can be added to the file without concern about altering the order of already existing items. Nor need deletions from the file be followed by any

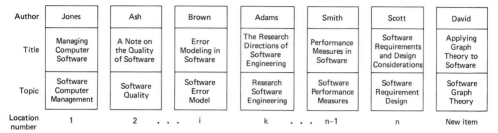

Author	Jones	Ash	Brown	Adams	Smith	Scott	David
Title	Managing Computer Software	A Note on the Quality of Software	Error Modeling in Software	The Research Directions of Software Engineering	Performance Measures in Software	Software Requirements and Design Considerations	Applying Graph Theory to Software
Topic	Software Computer Management	Software Quality	Software Error Model	Research Software Engineering	Software Performance Measures	Software Requirement Design	Software Graph Theory
Location number	1	2 . . . i		k . . . n–1		n	New item

Figure 1-6   Linear list.

file rearrangements. The file maintenance process is therefore largely eliminated.

Since the items relevant to incoming requests are unknown in advance in a linear list arrangement, all items may have to be examined to determine those that must eventually be retrieved. When the file includes only a few items, this is a reasonable process. Unfortunately, for large files the file scanning operation becomes very inefficient. For example, assuming that it takes $1/2$ second to decide whether or not to retrieve a specific item, 83.3 minutes will be required to answer a request for a file of 10,000 items. Thus, on the average the search for a specific item will take 41.6 minutes. If, on the other hand, it takes $1/10$ second to determine the retrieval status of an item, the retrieval time is reduced to 16.6 minutes in all, or to an average of 8.3 minutes when a specific item is wanted. Thus, the usefulness of a linear list is dependent on the size of the file and on the speed of retrieval. Chapter 4 introduces the notion of clustered files that may be used to increase the efficiency of retrieval. In a clustered file, items are grouped into classes in such a way that all items entered into a common class exhibit certain similarities. When a clustered file is used for retrieval, it is no longer necessary to examine every file item; instead the search can be restricted to certain classes of items that appear to be "close" to the request.

B Ordered Sequential Files

In most instances, certain portions (fields) of the records stored in a file prove to be of special importance for retrieval purposes. For instance, the name of the first author of a journal article is often used as the main criterion for finding that article. The fields used to obtain access to the stored records are referred to as *keys*. A given file may be ordered sequentially according to the values of one of the keys, in which case this special order may be used to obtain access to the file. For instance, an ordered file consisting of journal articles may be ordered alphabetically according to the last name of the first author of each article. In contrast, the linear list would store the same journal articles in no specifiable order.

The addition of a new item to a sequential file requires that room be made at the appropriate spot to enter the new item. That is, a new journal article to be placed in the file must appear at a specific location if the order of the file is to be maintained. Other items may have to be moved in order to make room, as

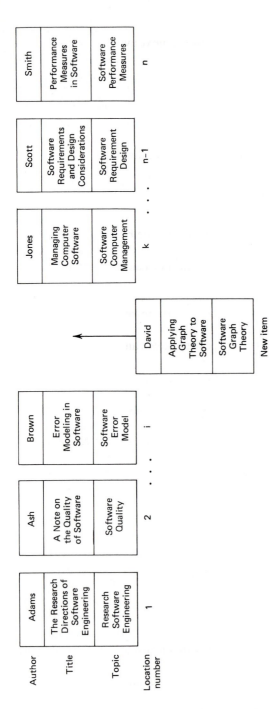

Figure 1-7 Sequential file ordered by author.

shown in the example of Fig. 1-7. On the other hand, in the linear list which is unordered a new item can simply be placed in the next available location.

To locate a specific item in an ordered sequential file it may still be necessary to look at $(n + 1)/2$ items on the average. That is, one can start at the beginning of a sequential file and work through the file item by item to find any desired element. However, the efficiency of search in a sequential file can be increased when the file is ordered by the key values used in the search. For example, a *binary search* can reduce the required number of steps to $\log_2 (n + 1)$. In other words, assuming that the file contains 1,023 items, a desired item can be found in 10 steps on the average using a binary search, but the search would take 512 steps on the average with the sequential scanning method described previously.

To use the binary search procedure the file must be ordered according to the key values and the record sought must be specifiable by citing the value of that particular key. For the example used earlier this implies that all records would be retrieved by citing only the particular author name. Instead of initiating the search at the beginning or the end of the file, the record in the middle of the file is examined first. The key value for the middle record is then compared with the key value specified in the search request. If the key values match, the middle record is the record being sought. However, if the values do not match, it is necessary to determine whether the desired key value occurs before or after the key value of the middle element in the sequential order. If the desired key value occurs after the value of the middle element, the beginning half of the file is ignored and the middle element of the remainder of the file is examined. This process continues until the desired record is located. For example, if a file consists of seven elements with key values A-B-C-D-E-F-G and the search is made for the record with a key value of C, then the items examined in order will be D then B and finally C. The middle element of the whole file, D, is examined first. Its key value does not equal the desired key value, C. The desired element logically precedes the D element; so the last half of the file is ignored for the remainder of the search process. The next comparison is made with the middle element of the first part of the file, that is, B. The desired element C comes after B; so the beginning portion of the file is ignored for the rest of the search. At this point the only remaining element is C, the desired element. The binary search process is illustrated in the example of Fig. 1-8 [21,22].

Compared with an item-by-item search the binary search is very efficient. A file of 10,000 elements in which $1/2$ second is needed for each key comparison can be searched in approximately 7 seconds, compared with the 41.6 minutes needed for the sequential search. Unfortunately, in information retrieval many searches are not conducted for specific items of known key values. Instead items must be located that appear meaningful in some sense to particular requests. Furthermore, the unique key values used to identify the records in an ordered sequential file are sometimes difficult to specify in a search request. In general several different keys are therefore specified to identify potentially relevant items, and simple binary searches are no longer useful in these circumstances.

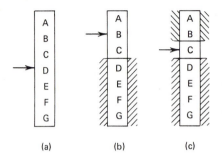

(a)   (b)   (c)

Figure 1-8 Binary search example for search key C. (a) Initial comparison with middle element (D). (b) Next comparison with middle element of upper half (B); ignore lower half. (c) Final comparison with remaining element (C); ignore upper half.

Some simple file accessing methods, including binary searches, are treated in more detail in Chapter 8.

*C   Indexed Files

Another way to speed up a search for an information item is to develop an index which provides access to segments of a file. For instance, an index may be constructed using the first letter of the author's last name for the ordered sequential file of Fig. 1-7. The index identifies the location of records corresponding to the first letter of a particular last name. In Fig. 1-7 it can be seen that the authors whose last name starts with the letter J begin to appear at location number k. Figure 1-9 shows an index constructed for the sequential file in Fig. 1-7. Given a particular author name, it is then possible to use the index to find the storage location of records with author names beginning with a given letter. The search for a particular record now requires only a search of the index and a search of that portion of the file specified by the index. The number of steps needed on the average to find a specific item is reduced to the number of steps required to search the index, plus $(n + 1)/2$ additional steps for the sequential subfile where n is the number of records in that specific sequential segment. As an example, consider a sequential file of one million records. A sequential search for a record beginning with a specified letter will require $(n + 1)/2$ or 500,001 steps on the average. If an indexed file arrangement is used

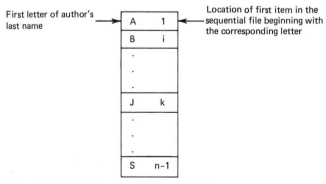

Figure 1-9 Index to ordered sequential file.

instead, the number of records with author name beginning with the specified letter may be equal to 50,000. The index would then normally consist of 26 entries, one for each letter of the alphabet. Thus, the search will require (26 + 1)/2 steps to search the index plus (50,000 + 1)/2 steps to search the records beginning with the given letter, or 25,014 steps. The search has been reduced by a factor of 20.

Indexes are particularly important for certain kinds of computer storage devices such as disks. Disks permit rapid access to consecutive records, but access to particular regions of the disk is slow. An index may then be used to locate the special region of the disk which contains the records of interest for a given query. These records can then be scanned sequentially. By contrast, a binary search requires multiple probes to various parts of the file.

Unfortunately, indexed files carry one big disadvantage. When new records must be added to an indexed file, both the file itself and the index must be changed. This can be an expensive undertaking which may outweigh the gains achieved in the search process. In addition, the previously mentioned disadvantages in updating an ordered file still apply.

On the other hand, if the search process appears most important, and the file needs to be updated only at infrequent intervals, then the index provides a valuable tool. If a record carries more than one key, such as an author name as well as individual words from the title that may also be used to gain access to the record, the idea of an index for a single key may be extended to cover all the record keys. A single index structure may then be built that includes every value for each key for the records in the file. That is, the data organization is turned around (inverted) to create an index for all unique key values in all documents as in Fig. 1-10. The illustration of Fig. 1-10 shows an information file arranged in order by item number, each item being further identified by various topic terms. A file in which the items themselves provide the main order of the file is known as a *direct file*. The inverted index, on the other hand, is arranged in order by topic, and each topic includes the corresponding list of item numbers. When an inverted index is available, each topic term is then usable as a key to obtain access to the corresponding items.

An *inverted file* ensures quick access to the information items because the index alone is examined in order to determine the items which satisfy the search request, rather than the actual file of items. Furthermore, the index is sequentially ordered by the key values. For example, to retrieve all the information items dealing with the "systems" topic, a search is made of the index to locate "systems." Items 1, 3, 4, 5 are then identified as candidates for retrieval in the example of Fig. 1-10. One need not examine the individual records to determine their actual key values, because that information is already contained in the index. It should be obvious that the addition of new items to the file is potentially laborious, because not only must a new item be placed in the main file, but the index entries relating to this new item must also be updated. The effect of adding a new item (number 6) to the file structure of Fig. 1-10 is shown in Fig. 1-11. Note, however, that the new item itself is placed at the end

Related information items

	Topic	1	2	3	4	5
	Computer	1		3		
	Information	1	2		4	
Topic	Retrieval	1	2		4	5
	Systems	1		3	4	5
	Users		2			5

(a)

Item number	1	2	3	4	5
Author	Ash	Brown	Jones	Reynolds	Smith
Title	Aspects of Computerized Information Retrieval Systems	A Survey of Users of Information Retrieval	The History of Computer Systems	The State of the Art of Information Retrieval Systems	Users of New Retrieval Systems
Topic	Computer Information Retrieval Systems	Information Retrieval Users	Computer Systems	Information Retrieval Systems	Retrieval Systems Users

(b)

Figure 1-10 Sample inverted file organization. (a) Inverted index identifying item numbers corresponding to particular topics. (b) Sample information items.

of the file, or wherever convenient, and that no special order is required in the main record file.

In many cases the inverted index constitutes a file of considerable size. This index file must be searched to find a desired key value and changed to reflect the addition and deletion of key elements. To increase the efficiency of the index search, one can build an index to the index. In fact, hierarchies of indexes are often required to render quick searches possible. Unfortunately, given a hierarchy of indexes, the addition of new information items may require changes to the indexes at all levels of the hierarchy.

Inverted files are used in almost every commercially available information retrieval system. Experimental systems may use inverted files, or alternatively a direct file organization may be used, as in standard linear lists or ordered document files. The relationship between the inverted and the direct file structures is surprisingly simple. The inverted file identifies all information items associated with a given term; that is, for each term in the indexing language a list of information items indexed by that term is carried in the index. On the other hand, the direct file includes for each information item the list of terms which are associated with the item through the indexing process. If the presence of a term or of an item is indicated by a 1, and the absence is indicated by a 0, then the example of Fig. 1-12 shows the relationship between the two file structures. The inverted file is accessed using the individual terms, while the individual information items themselves are used to access the direct file. Thus an access to

(a)

		Related information items				
Topic		1	2	3	4	5	6
Computer		1		3			6
Information		1	2		4		6
Retrieval		1	2		4	5	
Systems		1		3	4	5	
Users			2			5	

(b)

Item number	1	2	3	4	5	6
Author	Ash	Brown	Jones	Reynolds	Smith	David
Title	Aspects of Computerized Information Retrieval Systems	A Survey of Users of Information Retrieval	The History of Computer Systems	The State of the Art of Information Retrieval Systems	Users of New Retrieval Systems	A Study of Computerized Information Systems
Topic	Computer Information Retrieval Systems	Information Retrieval Users	Computer Systems	Information Retrieval Systems	Retrieval Systems Users	Computer Information System

Figure 1-11 Inverted file with added item. (a) Inverted index with a new item 6. (b) Sample information items with added item 6.

Information items

		Document 1	Document 2	Document 3
	Term 1	1	0	1
Topics	Term 2	1	1	0
	Term 3	0	1	1
	Term 4	1	1	1

(a)

Topics

		Term 1	Term 2	Term 3	Term 4
	Document 1	1	1	0	1
Information items	Document 2	0	1	1	1
	Document 3	1	0	1	1

(b)

Figure 1-12 Inverted and direct file examples. (a) Inverted file. (b) Direct file.

the inverted file for term 1 identifies information items 1 and 3 for retrieval in the example of Fig. 1-12. On the other hand, accessing item 1 in the direct file structure reveals that the item is indexed by terms 1, 2, and 4. The relationship of inverted and direct files is exactly that of matrix transposition.

The items obtained from a direct file as a result of a search must be processed to determine which, if any, are likely to be of interest to the user of the retrieval system. On the other hand, the items identified through an inverted file access are already known to be indexed by the given search term. Such items are then assumed to be of potential interest. Of course, the searcher may wish to combine different terms with each other to formulate a search request. Such processes are described in Chapter 2.

Differences in the file organizations used for retrieval play a major role in the retrieval process. For example, in the direct file an access to a particular information item reveals information concerning *all* the index terms assigned to that item. Using the inverted file, one obtains no information about other terms that may be assigned to a given information item, unless the item itself is retrieved. As a second example, consider the efficiency of the search process. If one assumes that information items are to be retrieved by citing particular search terms among the item identifiers, then an access to the inverted file immediately identifies all information items to be retrieved. On the other hand, an access to an information item in the direct file simply begins the process necessary to determine whether the particular item should be retrieved. That determination must be made for each and every information item in a direct file.

6 SUMMARY

Some of the principal information retrieval problems have been outlined in this introductory chapter. Several different types of information systems were introduced, and two simple file structures currently in use were examined in some detail. The information retrieval environment is complex. The information to be stored is often available in the form of natural language texts, and the mechanisms used to represent the texts include both controlled and uncontrolled vocabularies which separately or in combination constitute the indexing language. The indexing process transforms the natural language text of the information items into the elements of the indexing language, and the search formulation process converts statements of information need into elements of the same indexing language. The identification of information items to be retrieved then depends on the item representations rather than on the original natural language texts of the items.

The organization of the items in the files has a great deal to do with the efficiency of search and retrieval. Clearly the use of inverted files is more efficient for searching than the use of direct files. On the other hand, the inverted indexes must be stored and updated when changes occur, and these auxiliary operations may substantially affect the efficiency of the retrieval operations [23].

REFERENCES

[1] The Bowker Annual of Library and Book Trade Information, 25th Edition, R.R. Bowker Inc., New York, 1980, p. 97.

[2] V. Bush, As We May Think, Atlantic Monthly, Vol. 176, No. 1, 1945, pp.101–108.

[3] H.S. Heaps, Information Retrieval, Academic Press, New York, 1978, pp. 2–3.

[4] A.C. Foskett, The Subject Approach to Information, 3rd Edition, Chapter 21, The Library of Congress Classification, Linnet Books and Clive Bingley, Hamden, Connecticut, 1977, pp. 359–367.

[5] A. Toffler, Future Shock, Random House, Inc., New York, 1970, p. 159.

[6] F.W. Lancaster, The Measurement and Evaluation of Library Services, Chapter 5, Evaluation of the Collection, Information Resources Press, Washington, D.C., 1977, pp. 165–206.

[7] G. Salton, Dynamic Information and Library Processing, Prentice-Hall, Inc., Englewood Cliffs, New Jersey, 1975, p. 7.

[8] F. Withington, The Changing Profile, Datamation, Vol. 25, No. 6, May 1979, pp. 10–12.

[9] J.M. Gabet, VLSI: The Impact Grows, Datamation, Vol. 25, No. 7, June 1979, pp. 109–112.

[10] S.A. Caswell, Computer Peripherals: A Revolution Is Coming, Datamation, Vol. 25, No. 6, May 1979, pp. 82–89.

[11] M.J. McGill and J. Huitfeldt, Experimental Techniques of Information Retrieval, Annual Review of Information Science and Technology, M.E. Williams, editor,

Vol. 14, Knowledge Industry Publications, Inc., White Plains, New York, 1979, pp. 93–127.

[12] M. Taube, Machine Retrieval of Information, Library Trends, Vol. 5, No. 2, October 1956, pp. 301–308.

[13] J. Minker, Information Storage and Retrieval—A Survey and Functional Description, SIGIR Forum, Association for Computing Machinery, Vol. 12, No. 2, Fall 1977, pp. 1–108.

[14] C. Meadow, Applied Data Management, John Wiley and Sons, Inc., New York, 1976.

[15] E.C. Carlson, editor, Proceedings of a Conference on Decision Support Systems, Data Base, Vol. 8, No. 3, Association for Computing Machinery, New York, Winter 1977.

[16] B. Raphael, The Thinking Computer: Mind inside Matter, W.H. Freeman and Company, San Francisco, California, 1976.

[17] P.H. Winston, Artificial Intelligence, Addison Wesley Publishing Company, Reading, Massachusetts, 1977.

[18] F.W. Lancaster and E.G. Fayen, Information Retrieval On-Line, Melville Publishing Company, Los Angeles, California, 1973.

[19] G. Salton, Automatic Information Organization and Retrieval, McGraw-Hill Book Company, New York, 1968, pp. 210–215.

[20] Resource Directory, Health Information Sharing Project, School of Information Studies, Syracuse University, Syracuse, New York, 1978.

[21] E. Horowitz and S. Sahni, Fundamentals of Data Structures, Computer Science Press, Woodland Hills, California, 1976.

[22] C.C. Gotlieb and L.R. Gotlieb, Data Types and Structures, Prentice-Hall, Inc., Englewood Cliffs, New Jersey, 1978.

[23] M.J. McGill, Knowledge and Information Spaces: Implications for Retrieval Systems, Journal of the American Society for Information Science, Vol. 27, No. 4, July–August 1976, pp. 205–210.

BIBLIOGRAPHIC REMARKS

This text assumes some knowledge of computers and computer science. If the reader has little or no background in this area, any of the following texts may be helpful:

Marilyn Bohl, Information Processing, 3rd Edition, Science Research Associates, Inc., Chicago, Illinois, 1980.

Richard Dorf, Introduction to Computers and Computer Science, 2nd Edition, Boyd and Fraser Publishing Company, San Francisco, California, 1977.

Gerald A. Silver and Joan B. Silver, Data Processing for Business, 2nd Edition, Harcourt Brace Jovanovich, Inc., New York, 1977.

Fred Gruenberger, Computing: An Introduction, Harcourt Brace and World, Inc., New York, 1969.

D. Wilde, An Introduction to Computing, Prentice-Hall, Inc., Englewood Cliffs, New Jersey, 1973.

For a different look at information retrieval the reader may wish to examine:

F.W. Lancaster and E.G. Fayen, Information Retrieval On-Line, Melville Publishing
Company, Los Angeles, California, 1973.

C.J. van Rijsbergen, Information Retrieval, 2nd Edition, Butterworths, London, England, 1979.

The first text presents an excellent overview of information retrieval systems as
of 1973. The second covers research problems in information retrieval and experimental retrieval systems.

EXERCISES

1-1 a Assume that a file contains one million information items. If the file is organized
as a direct file, how many items would need to be examined on the average in
order to locate one specific item from the file?

 b How many items if the file is an ordered sequential file using a binary search?

1-2 Using any programming language take an arbitrary string of text and break up the
text into individual words. Be sure to consider text items consisting of numbers
containing decimal points such as 37.235, abbreviations such as Mr. and Mrs., and
all punctuation marks. Hyphenated words such as semi-automatic should be
treated as single words.

1-3 What extensions are required to the answer to Exercise 1-2 in order to handle a
chemical data base which includes formulas such as H_2O and chemical names such
as N-benzoyl-glycine and di-n-propyl-ether?

1-4 Describe in detail the procedure necessary to add a single new document to a system based on an inverted file. Consider both the case in which the new document is
indexed by some terms not already found in the inverted file and the case where the
new document is completely indexed by terms already in the inverted file. Describe
this process either in a flowchart or as a step-by-step narrative.

1-5 Consider the area of American history. This topic subsumes a number of subareas
such as vocabulary construction, the American Revolution, and the Civil War. Develop a one-dimensional physical organization for books on American history. How
will this change if the organization becomes two-dimensional? three-dimensional?
etc.

Chapter 2

Systems Based on Inverted Files

0 PREVIEW

This chapter covers the operations of retrieval systems based on inverted files. The effect of the main Boolean operators that are used in many information retrieval environments is first described, followed by an examination of adjacency and term frequency operations. Selected features from the available commercial information retrieval systems are then described. Finally enhancements are considered to the basic inverted file design.

1 GENERAL CONSIDERATIONS

It was indicated in Chapter 1 that virtually all the commercially available systems are based on inverted file designs [1]. That is, each system logically consists of a document file and one or more auxiliary directories known as the "inverted index." The inverted index contains the allowable indexing terms. For each term an associated list of document reference numbers is included in the index [2]. Each document reference number uniquely specifies a document to which a given term has been assigned. Thus, the retrieval of the documents identified by an arbitrary term requires a search of the index to find the desired term, and hence the associated document reference numbers. Finally the identified documents are selected from the document reference file. This simple process carries out the functions of the SIMILAR operation introduced in Chapter 1 when single-term queries are processed. In practice, query statements consisting of a single term are rarely used. Occasionally a single term may be sufficiently new or unique to make it a reasonable query all by itself [3]. An example of a term which may fit this criterion is "videodisc." However, by the time this text is published, many thousands of references may already exist even for such a specialized term.

A Boolean Expressions

Normally the searcher has to restrict the number of items retrieved by a search to fewer documents than are found by using a single term. For instance, the terms "information" and "retrieval" may be separately included in the inverted index. The person searching for references to the concept "information retrieval"would like to ensure that the retrieved documents are at least identified by both terms. The assumption is that documents that include both terms may in fact be about the topic "information retrieval" [4]. The SIMILAR function of Chapter 1 is then interpreted as requiring the presence of both query terms to select a given document as potentially useful.

To identify those documents containing both the term "information"and the term "retrieval,"it is necessary to process only the information from the inverted index rather than the information from the document file. Boolean logic is used to construct queries consisting of a variety of terms using the Boolean operators AND, OR, and NOT [5]. These operations are implemented by using set intersection, set union, and set difference procedures, respectively. One query which may be used to identify documents on "information retrieval"may be stated as

INFORMATION AND RETRIEVAL

The following procedure might then be used to find the corresponding documents:

   1   Use the inverted index to retrieve the document reference numbers associated with the term INFORMATION. Call these document reference numbers Set 1.
   2   Use the inverted index to retrieve the document reference numbers associated with the term RETRIEVAL. Call these document reference numbers Set 2.
   3   Determine which document reference numbers constitute the intersection of Sets 1 and 2, that is, are contained in both Set 1 and Set 2. Call these document reference numbers Set 3.
   4   Use the main document file to retrieve the documents identified by the document reference numbers in Set 3.

In other words, documents included as members in both Set 1 and Set 2 (the set intersection) are those that satisfy the query and are to be retrieved.

The query

INFORMATION OR RETRIEVAL

refers to documents which are identified either by the term INFORMATION or by the term RETRIEVAL or by both terms. Set 1 and Set 2 may be determined in the same manner as for the AND operator. These sets are then combined into a new Set 3 which contains an identifier for each document contained in either Set 1 or Set 2 or in both sets (set union). Any document included in this composite set is then retrieved by the query statement.

The NOT operator is usually implemented as an operator which specifies that some particular term is to appear in the retrieved document but that some other term is not allowed to appear. For instance, the query statement

INFORMATION NOT RETRIEVAL

refers to documents containing the term INFORMATION but not containing the term RETRIEVAL. In order to accomplish the negation operation using an inverted file system, the following procedure may be used:

1 Use the inverted index to retrieve the document reference numbers associated with the term INFORMATION. Call these document reference numbers Set 1.

2 Use the inverted index to retrieve the document reference numbers associated with the term RETRIEVAL. Call these document reference numbers Set 2.

3 Remove from Set 1 any document reference number included in Set 2. That is, construct the set difference between Sets 1 and 2.

4 Use the document file to retrieve the documents indicated by the document reference numbers remaining in Set 1.

In other words, the documents that satisfy the query statement have reference numbers contained in Set 1 but not in Set 2 (set difference).

B Order of Operations

The complexity of a query can grow substantially as new operators are added, and a variety of rules are necessary to ensure that queries submitted by the searcher are interpreted correctly by the retrieval system. Consider as an example the inverted index as shown in Table 2-1. A query such as

APPLE AND ORANGE OR BANANA

is ambiguous. If one starts at the left of the query statement and works toward

Table 2-1   Sample Inverted Index

Terms	Document reference numbers				
APPLE	1	3	5	7	
ORANGE	2	3	4	5	6
BANANA	4	6	8		
GRAPE	3	7	9	11	

the right, the items to be retrieved are identified by the document reference numbers

3   4   5   6   8

because the set intersection between the sets for APPLE and for ORANGE produces items 3 and 5 to which are added items 4, 6 and 8 when the set union is carried out with the BANANA set. On the other hand, if one starts at the right and works toward the left of the query statement, then the items to be retrieved are given by the document reference numbers

3   5

because the union between ORANGE and BANANA produces items 2, 3, 4, 5, 6, and 8 and the intersection that follows with the set for APPLE restricts the output to 3 and 5.

The order in which the operations are carried out is critical. The strategy may be left-to-right or right-to-left, or some other method may be used to specify the order in which the operations are to be executed. For instance, one procedure specifies that all the OR operators are performed first, followed by the AND operators, and finally the NOT operators; all equivalent operators are performed from left to right. Parentheses are usually provided to circumvent the strict processing order described above. In particular, operations within parentheses are normally completed first. For the previously used example the left-to-right order is thus equivalent to (APPLE AND ORANGE) OR BANANA, whereas the right-to-left order corresponds to APPLE AND (ORANGE OR BANANA). Each operation or set of operations within parentheses is first carried out according to the regular processing rules. When this is completed, the remainder of the query statement is processed. Consider the query statement:

(APPLE AND ORANGE) OR (BANANA AND ORANGE)

The following process may be used for this statement:

1   The first AND operator on the left side of the query statement combines the document reference numbers associated with APPLE and ORANGE (items 3 and 5).

2   The second AND operator combines the document reference numbers associated with BANANA and ORANGE (items 4 and 6).

3   Finally the OR operator combines the sets retrieved in steps 1 and 2 (items 3, 4, 5, and 6).

The set of documents retrieved by using the parentheses differs from the sets retrieved by rules given earlier. Once the rule for parentheses has been established, it can be applied over and over again. That is, nested parentheses can be used so that the operations within the innermost pair of parentheses will be carried out first. For instance the query statement

(APPLE AND (ORANGE OR BANANA)) NOT GRAPE

is executed beginning with the (ORANGE OR BANANA) portion of the query statement. In order to allow parentheses, it is necessary to keep track of intermediate results. For this reason, some systems do not allow the use of parentheses and others allow only limited nesting of parentheses.

2   ADJACENCY AND TERM FREQUENCY FEATURES

Each commercial system includes certain features that make it unique. This complicates the problem of learning how to use each of the systems. A few of the more interesting and basic operations are described in the remainder of this chapter. Since the various processing approaches are considered to be proprietary information by the system vendors, there is no assurance that the methods presented here are strictly factual. The presentation of the basic methodologies covered in the next few paragraphs is, however, expected to be reasonably accurate.

A   Adjacency Operations

Consider a retrieval system which allows the searcher to formulate queries using words included in the document texts. It may be useful to specify that two words must appear next to each other in a text and in the proper word order. If the operator ADJ stands for adjacency, a query for documents on "information retrieval" may now be stated as

INFORMATION ADJ RETRIEVAL

The searcher is then assured that the two search terms do not appear in unrelated portions of the document but are in fact contained in adjacent word positions.Thus, the probability that the concept "information retrieval" is contained in the document is higher than if the searcher were to use the terms INFORMATION and RETRIEVAL combined by an AND operator.

It is difficult to implement the adjacency operation using the basic definition of the inverted file. The following procedure may be used, however, when only a basic inverted index is available:

1 Use the standard inverted file to identify the documents that satisfy the query

INFORMATION AND RETRIEVAL

2 Use the document file to search specific fields of the corresponding documents by means of a character by character match (a string search) to detect the presence of the characters "INFORMATION RETRIEVAL." The fields to be searched are normally prespecified and may include the title and abstract for each document.

3 Retrieve from the document file those items for which at least one complete match of the given character string is found.

String searching is a laborious task which consists in scanning an arbitrary set of symbols in search of a specific sequence of symbols. That is, the text of a document is examined character by character until the desired sequence of characters is found. String searching procedures are implemented in certain systems but are used only when essential. In particular, the system normally warns the user of the inefficiency of the string searching process, and various restrictions may limit the conditions under which string searching may be conducted.

Another possibility for implementing the ADJ operator consists in enhancing the inverted file by adding information about the location of words within each document. For instance, if the stored documents consist of abstracts of two or more paragraphs, and each paragraph includes several sentences, then the term location information might include the document reference number, paragraph number, sentence number, and word number within each sentence. Thus, RETRIEVAL (345 1 2 5) would indicate that the term RETRIEVAL occurs in the first paragraph, second sentence, and fifth word of document 345. Document 345 would be retrieved by the query statement

INFORMATION ADJ RETRIEVAL

whenever the entry INFORMATION (345 1 2 4) appears in the inverted file in addition to the entry RETRIEVAL (345 1 2 5).

Another way to provide term location information is to add to each term entry in the inverted file a distance indicator specifying for each word occurrence the distance from the beginning of the text in terms of the number of intervening words. Thus, RETRIEVAL (345 13) indicates that the term RETRIEVAL occurs 13 words from the beginning of document 345. Again document 345 would be retrieved by the previous query only if INFORMATION (345 12) were also included in the enhanced inverted file. This procedure does not recognize sentence boundaries and is not therefore completely equivalent to the previous method based on paragraph, sentence and word numbers. In practice, the two methods are probably equivalent in terms of retrieval performance.

A comparison of the methods for carrying out the ADJ operation shows that the character by character analysis of documents requires substantial computational resources but the inverted file is not encumbered with additional word location information. The other two methods are based on an expanded inverted file. When word location information is kept in the inverted file, little extra processing is required for the ADJ operation with the exception of an added comparison between two groups of numbers to determine the appropriate order. The added word location information does, however, take up a great deal of potentially valuable storage space.

To date the tradeoff has seemed clear. The character by character searching, as usually implemented, is so inefficient that the use of extra storage in the inverted file appears mandatory. However, fast string searching operations have recently been discovered that may reverse this situation. These methods will be discussed in Chapter 8 of this volume.

B Frequency Information

Another way of enhancing an inverted file system is to include information about the frequency of occurrence of the individual terms. It has been shown that special usage patterns exist for the words included in natural language texts in certain subject specialties. In particular, the frequency of use of a given term may correlate with some indication of the importance of that term in the given subject area. If word frequency information is to be used in retrieval, it must be stored by the system, and the most practical way to do this is to include the information in the inverted file. In many systems "posting"information is kept in the inverted file for each term. That is, the inverted file includes information about the number of documents in which a given term occurs. This frequency information is referred to as the number of postings for the term. In this way a user can quickly ascertain the number of documents that will be retrieved by using a given term. For instance, the term INFORMATION has 53,504 postings in the ERIC data base available through the DIALOG system at the time this is being written. A query which includes only this single term would therefore retrieve 53,504 documents.

3 COMMERCIAL INVERTED FILE SYSTEMS

A The DIALOG System

The DIALOG system is a product of Lockheed Information Systems of Palo Alto, California. In May of 1980 some 122 individual data bases were available through the DIALOG system [6,7].

The DIALOG system is based on an inverted file design. The system creates sets of document reference numbers by means of a SELECT command.

Thus, the SELECT INFORMATION command creates a set of document reference numbers associated with the term INFORMATION. The system provides the user with a set number identifying these document reference numbers. For example, the statement given earlier would be assigned set number 1 if it were the first SELECT command issued by the searcher. A second command SELECT RETRIEVAL would therefore create set number 2. These sets may then be processed by a COMBINE statement which allows the use of the Boolean operators AND (∗), OR (+), or NOT (-). Thus the statements

COMBINE 1 AND 2

or

COMBINE 1 ∗ 2

are used to form the query statement

INFORMATION AND RETRIEVAL

This query was introduced earlier in this chapter when the document reference numbers associated with INFORMATION (Set 1) and the reference numbers associated with RETRIEVAL (Set 2) were combined with an AND operator to form the new Set 3. The NOT operations are performed first in the DIALOG system, followed by the AND operations, and finally by the OR operations. Parentheses are allowed in order to alter this specified sequence of operations. Thus, a statement such as

COMBINE (4 OR 5 OR 6) AND (7 OR 8) NOT 9

produces a legitimate search operation assuming that Sets 4, 5, 6, 7, 8, and 9 have all been previously defined.

In the DIALOG system a term may be truncated on the right to indicate that any characters following the truncation symbol are acceptable. For example, PSYCH? can be used as a search term to retrieve items associated with

PSYCHIATRIST
PSYCHIATRY
PSYCHOLOGICAL
PSYCHOLOGIST
PSYCHOLOGY

and any other terms that begin with the characters PSYCH. The truncation symbol ''?'' may also be used to specify the maximum number of characters that may appear following the user supplied characters. The number of characters allowed is indicated by the number of "?" symbols immediately after the word followed by a blank and another "?" symbol. For example,

DOCUMENT??   ?

specifies that the search term DOCUMENT may be followed by up to 2 additional arbitrary characters. Thus, documents associated with the terms DOCU-MENTS and DOCUMENTED will be retrieved, but documents associated with the term DOCUMENTATION will be rejected.

The truncation operations can be carried out in an obvious manner using an inverted file. In the first case (truncation without limits), the inverted file need only be searched for the terms whose initial characters correspond to the user input. Using the PSYCH? example, the system need only examine the first five characters of the terms included in the index file. If an exact match is found, the associated document reference numbers are placed in the retrieval set. The same logic is used for truncations with a limited number of trailing characters. That is, an exact match of characters is required between the characters supplied by the searcher and the characters of the term stored in the index file. Once this condition is satisfied, it is necessary to consult the index file to determine if the number of additional characters of the given term in the index file meets the criterion specified by the user. In order to determine that the matching term carries the right number of trailing characters, the characters specified by the ? symbols need not be examined individually. However, characters occurring to the right of those specified by the ? symbols must be considered. If no characters occur in the term stored in the index file beyond the last ? symbol, the corresponding document reference numbers are retrieved.

The truncation character "?" may also be embedded inside a term supplied by the user. For example, WOM?N would be used to indicate both the term WOMAN and the term WOMEN. The process used to handle requests of this kind may be based on methods similar to those described earlier. Note that there is no need to add any location or frequency information to the inverted file.

DIALOG also offers the ability to search for pairs of adjacent words or for terms occurring within a specified number of words of another term. This capability is based on the use of terms derived from the actual texts of documents or document abstracts, as opposed to terms assigned from a controlled vocabulary. Controlled terms are not generally assigned in any meaningful sequence. The pertinent operator used is "(W)," and it must be used with the SELECT operator. Thus,

SELECT PROGRAMMING (W) LANGUAGE

would retrieve the documents from a data base which included the terms PRO-GRAMMING and LANGUAGE occurring side by side in the text and in that stated word order. As in the case of the ADJ operator discussed earlier, the corresponding search can be carried out either by processing the actual texts of documents following identification of items which include both terms, or by adding location information to the inverted file. In the DIALOG system, the inverted file is enhanced by the position number of each word within each document. Thus retrieval is based on the determination of consecutive word position numbers in the inverted file.

When word position information is available, one can also determine if two particular terms occur within a specified number of words of each other in a text. This is done by subtracting the location number of the first term from that of the second one. If the order of occurrence of the terms is deemed important, one may want to insist on a positive difference between location numbers. If the difference is allowed to be either positive or negative, the order of the terms is disregarded. Thus,

SELECT PROGRAMMING   (5 W) LANGUAGE

would find all documents in which the term LANGUAGE follows the term PROGRAMMING within a distance of up to five words; term order is clearly taken into account. If term order is not important, the term LANGUAGE may either precede the term PROGRAMMING by up to five words, or it may follow PROGRAMMING by up to five words. In the DIALOG system the order of the words is important and the system assumes they are to appear in the order specified in the query statement.

The DIALOG system also uses field identification for author (AU), classification code (CC), corporate source (CS), document type (DT), journal name (JN), language (LA), publication year (PY), and update (UD). The latter field indicates when the document was added to the data base. Since some of these fields contain measurable values, it is possible to include the corresponding values in a search statement. For instance, a range of values can be specified for the publication year as follows:

SELECT PY = 1977 : PY = 1979

which indicates that documents with a publication year between 1977 and 1979 are acceptable. The colon (:) designates a range of measurable values to be used.

From a computational point of view such a process seems to present problems. If the publication year is included in the inverted file for each document, then in order to select the appropriate range of publication years one must search for exact matches corresponding to the whole range of allowable publication years or be able arithmetically to compare the publication year. Thus, for the example given earlier the specified dates must include 1977, 1978, and 1979. The number of possible representations for a publication date in a given data base is quite large. For example, 1978, June 1978, 6/78, and '78 may all be used to represent publication dates for the year 1978. If all those alternatives were allowed in a retrieval system, a complicated search would become neces-sary. In the DIALOG system a specific representation is selected, in this exam-ple 1978. This makes it possible to carry out exact matches on specific dates to retrieve documents with date specifications. Alternatively, it is quite feasible to keep a separate inverted index for publication dates alone. Assuming that such a file is kept in chronological order and in a numeric representation, the system need only search for values in the range 1977:1979. Thus, a document may have terms or values assigned from a number of different inverted indexes. A different index may be used for each field of the document such as publication year or author. Different indexes may also help to distinguish identical values for different keys such as publication year 1980 and page number 1980.

Many other features are included in the DIALOG system. In this discus-sion some of the important features have been highlighted to indicate ap-proaches that have been used by the system designers.

*B The STAIRS System

Another prominent system is the storage and information retrieval system (STAIRS), which is a program product of the IBM Corporation. Whereas the STAIRS system itself is available through IBM, no data bases are made avail-able by IBM. Rather the user must purchase or lease the STAIRS programs and apply the system either to commercially available data bases or to private data bases. STAIRS runs on the customer's own computer.

STAIRS consists of two sets of programs:

1   Utility programs for data base creation and maintenance
2   An on-line retrieval system called AQUARIUS, which stands for a query and retrieval interactive utility system.

The retrieval function is a multiuser system which develops an effective dia-logue with the user. This dialogue leads to the search and eventual retrieval of stored data.

A principal difference between STAIRS and DIALOG is that a full STAIRS implementation includes not only a text processing and document re-trieval function but also an associated data base management system. The latter is designed to process formatted (highly structured) information such as numeric data available in tabular format. In the data management context, the retrieval of records is based on the values of particular attributes of the records. STAIRS uses separate modes of operation to handle text and structured data known as the SEARCH and SELECT modes, respectively.

To use the text retrieval system it is necessary to create an inverted file, a text index, and one or more text files. These are illustrated in Fig. 2-1. The text file contains the documents using a special format in which the retrieved docu-ments are presented to the retrieval system users. The text index includes pointers to records in the text file, as well as privacy information and formatted data associated with subsets of records in the text file. These formatted data

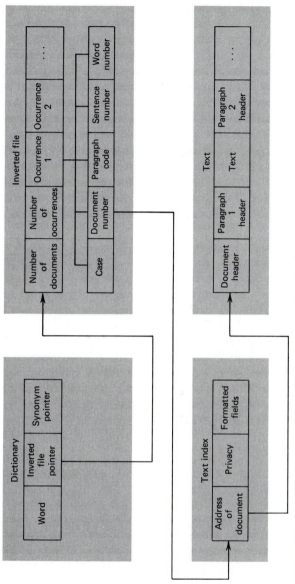

Figure 2-1 STAIRS file organization. (*Adapted from reference 8.*)

include attributes for which a range of values can be specified in advance. Because the allowable values are known in advance, the manner in which the values appear in the files can be prespecified. For instance, the publication dates may be restricted to the format ''1978'' and dates of the form 6/78 or any other format will be disallowed.

The dictionary contains a record for every unique word included in the data base. Associated with this entry is a pointer to a list identifying each occurrence of the particular word in the text. This is of course the inverted index described earlier in this chapter. The inverted file portion of the system may also be used to identify words which are synonymous with a given term. The system accomplishes this by maintaining a separate synonym dictionary. Access to an individual word in the dictionary is obtained by using letter pairs. That is, the first two letters of any word are used to identify a specific grouping of terms which is searched in order to find the wanted term. Associated with the term is a pointer to the list of associated document reference numbers. The dictionary has two levels: the first level contains the information about the letter pairs and indicates where the search must start on the second level to find the words beginning with particular letter pairs; the second level contains the actual words along with associated word length information and synonym information. Thus the dictionary itself is organized as an indexed file (see Fig. 2-2). Note that the location information in the inverted file consists of three numbers (triplets) representing paragraph code, sentence number, and word number. This information is present for each occurrence of each word in the data base.

The STAIRS retrieval system uses the free text of the documents or document abstracts for search purposes. The location information for each term is an important part of the STAIRS system, as is much of the remaining information described in Fig. 2-1. Controlled vocabulary terms may also be used with

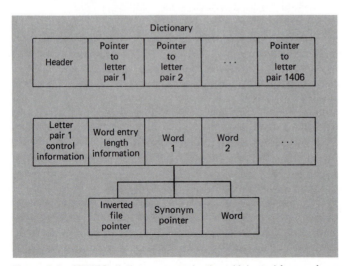

Figure 2-2 STAIRS dictionary organization. (*Adapted from reference 8.*)

the STAIRS system. In that case the location information is not helpful, since the controlled terms are never combined using adjacency or term distance measures.

Documents are found in STAIRS using the SEARCH command. When this command is specified, the SEARCH mode is entered. In this mode the user searches the unformatted portions of the records. Each search statement, normally consisting of a term followed by an operator and another term, is assigned a number of the STAIRS system. For example,

HEART AND DISEASE

is a legitimate search statement in which the normal Boolean AND operator is used. Other legitimate search statements include

HEART
HEART OR DISEASE
HEART NOT DISEASE
HEART$ AND DISEASE$3
(HEART OR CORONARY) AND DISEASE

The "$" symbol indicates truncation and the "$3" indicates truncation with up to three unspecified characters. Other operators of interest are

ADJ

specifying that two terms must be adjacent to one another,

WITH

indicating that the two terms must appear in the same sentence,

SAME

specifying that the two terms must appear in the same paragraph, and

SYN

specifying that the two terms are to be considered as synonyms. The use of these operators is based on a straightforward manipulation of the files presented in Fig. 2-1. Adjacency (ADJ), same sentence (WITH), and same paragraph (SAME) operations use the available location information to ensure that the necessary retrieval criteria have been met. For example, a search statement such as

PROGRAMMING WITH LANGUAGE

specifies that the two terms must appear in the same sentence.

The synonym dictionary is developed by recognizing term equivalences specified by a SYN command. Thus two terms are considered as synonymous when they are connected by the SYN operator. If COMPUTER and MACHINE are both entries in the existing dictionary,

COMPUTER SYN MACHINE

means that the user needs to specify only one of the terms to formulate a query covering either term. Note that a place is left in the dictionary for the synonym pointers. The SYN operation can easily be implemented by placing in the synonym pointer location of each component of a synonymous pair the location of the other component. A query which specifies COMPUTER as a term would then automatically also refer to (be pointed to) the term MACHINE. Document reference numbers for both terms would be retrieved using either term in a query.

The following hierarchy of operations is used to process the STAIRS statements:

ADJ
   SYN
      WITH
         AND, NOT
            OR, XOR

with the ADJ performed first, and OR or XOR (exclusive OR) operations performed last. The XOR operator indicates that a document is selected whenever it contains either of the specified terms but not both. Parentheses are allowed in order to alter the order in which the operations are performed.

The DIALOG and STAIRS operations appear reasonably similar even though the commands actually used are named differently and the underlying file structures differ in many details.

To manipulate structured data, the STAIRS system uses the completely separate SELECT mode of operation. In that mode the formatted fields of data normally containing the values of record attributes are searchable. The SELECT mode provides new search operators and operates on portions of the documents different from those specified earlier for the SEARCH mode. For instance, a special AND operation is provided which acts across several distinct formatted fields (major AND); another AND operator is used to operate within a given field. The same is true for the OR operator. For example, the query

SEX EQ MALE AND HAIR EQ (BROWN OR BLOND)

selects records for which the HAIR field is specified as BROWN or BLOND and at the same time the SEX field equals MALE.

In the SELECT mode special relational operators may be used in a query statement in addition to the standard search operators. These relational operators specify restrictions on the values of certain attributes attached to the documents. For instance, one may wish to retrieve all items described by an attribute called AGE with a value for AGE greater than 30; alternatively all items may be wanted with an attribute called SEX equal to FEMALE. In the SELECT mode each attribute is given a name and the attributes are characterized by particular values in each given document. In other words, a given attribute called AGE may be defined in the data base and the value associated with that attribute may be set equal to 25 in a specific document. A query statement used to retrieve this document might specify

AGE EQ 25

where EQ represents an operator specifying equality. Other relational operations include not equal (NE), not greater than (NG), not less than (NL), greater than (GT), less than (LT), within limits (WL), and outside limits (OL). A query statement such as

SEX EQ MALE AND AGE WL 25 , 35

specifies that the items to be retrieved must have attributes called SEX and AGE, the value of the SEX attribute being equal to "MALE," and the value of the AGE attribute lying within the specified limits of 25 to 35. As in the SEARCH mode, the system assigns numbers to the individual query statements.

Although the search operators may not be mixed between the SELECT and the SEARCH modes, one can use a query number from the SELECT mode as a part of a query statement in the SEARCH mode. Thus, if the earlier query including the attributes SEX and AGE is assigned query statement number 1 by the system, then the corresponding set of document reference numbers can be combined with other sets based on the specification of words in the SEARCH mode. For example, in the SEARCH mode one might use a query statement such as

1 AND INFORMATION ADJ SPECIALIST

to indicate that the items to be retrieved must have all the following properties:

1 The formatted attribute SEX must be equal to "MALE."
2 The formatted attribute AGE must have a value within the limits of 25 and 35.
3 The term INFORMATION must appear in the item.
4 The term SPECIALIST must appear in the item.
5 The term INFORMATION must immediately precede the term SPECIALIST in the item.

Note that the adjacency operator (INFORMATION ADJ SPECIALIST) is evaluated before the AND operator in accordance with the precedence previously established.

The processing of information in the SELECT mode differs from the typical information retrieval processing. Rather it fits into a framework explicitly used to handle structured information. The IMS (Information Management System) data base management system is often associated with the STAIRS retrieval system to carry out the structured data manipulations. IMS uses inverted file structures in the sense that for each value of each allowable attribute a list of associated document reference numbers is stored by the system. Processing of the AND and OR operators is therefore a matter of set intersection and set union as previously described. To handle the remaining operators such as "greater than" and "less than" it is necessary to determine if the specified attribute values meet the desired relational criterion.

Another feature of STAIRS is its ability to rank the retrieved documents according to one of several prespecified algorithms. The RANK command is used to operate in a special ranking mode. In the RANK mode the initial search is carried out using the SEARCH mode of operations previously described—sets developed in the SELECT mode are not available in the RANK mode. Once a document set has been chosen for retrieval using the SEARCH mode operations, a ranking of the documents can be obtained by assigning values or weights to the individual terms associated with a document. The retrieved documents may then be presented to the user in ranked order according to the sum of the weights of all terms that match the terms included in the user's query. The value of a term associated with a document is determined by a user selected combination of:

1   The frequency of the term in the document
2   The frequency of the term in the retrieved set
3   The number of documents in the retrieved set in which the term occurs

One particular term weighting algorithm uses the following formula:

$$\text{Value of term} = \frac{\text{frequency of the term in the document} \times \text{frequency of the term in the retrieved set}}{\text{number of documents in retrieved set containing the term}}$$

Consider, for example, a term such as SALINE which appears in 152 distinct documents retrieved by a particular query for a total of 1,247 times in all. Assuming that this term occurs 16 times in a particular document, the value of the term SALINE for this document is then determined as

$$\text{Value of term} = \frac{16 \times 1,247}{152} = 131.26$$

A final value can be calculated for each document by summing the values of all terms which match the query terms. In the RANK mode, documents are presented to the user in decreasing order of the term value function, the assumption being that this order corresponds to a decreasing order of presumed relevance of the documents with respect to the corresponding query.

STAIRS is a uniquely powerful system. It is designed to offer a great deal of flexibility in the sense that it offers all the power of a free text search system in addition to the formatted retrieval capability based on the values of specific attribute fields. However, the STAIRS system may be expensive to use in that it requires a data base management system in addition to the retrieval system, as well as a large storage capability for the term location, frequency, synonym, and associated information. Furthermore, the user must have a large IBM computer system available for use.

C The Bibliographic Retrieval Services (BRS) System

The Bibliographic Retrieval Services (BRS) system is a system that uses STAIRS as a basis [9]. BRS is a commercially available system operating on about forty data bases. The system had its origins in the biomedical communications network of the State University of New York.

BRS operates exclusively as an information retrieval system and not as a data base management system. Thus, many of the commands included in STAIRS are eliminated. Since no data base management facility is available to the user, there is no need to distinguish between the SELECT and the SEARCH modes. The user may use a LIMIT operator, however, to specify values such as publication year or language. In addition the ranking ability is not present in BRS. Hence the RANK mode has also been deleted. The one remaining mode of operation, the SEARCH mode requires no special identification. The operations used are those included in the STAIRS SEARCH mode with certain added features. One specific extension allows the qualification of a search statement after the search has already been conducted. Thus, one can supply special field designations in the query statements that limit the output produced by an earlier search. For instance, the code TI refers to the title field of a document. A search statement such as

1: PROGRAMMING ADJ LANG$

first identifies all documents containing the term PROGRAMMING adjacent to terms which begin with the characters LANG (such as LANGUAGE or LANGUAGES). The number 1: designates the query number. The initial search statement can be modified by specifying

2: 1.TI.

which implies that search statement 1 is to be modified to restrict the two search terms to the title field only. If a document includes the terms in adjacent positions in the abstract of the document but not in the title, then that document will not be retrieved.

An advantage that BRS maintains over the STAIRS system is its simplicity and processing efficiency. The removal of many of the commands, modes, and functional requirements available in STAIRS produces a much cleaner and simpler processing framework. Fewer decisions must be made and simpler programs are used. Furthermore, users do not need either their own computer or their own data bases, and the system is easier to learn to use than STAIRS. The designers of BRS have thus identified the most used portions of STAIRS and confined their attention to the implementation of a streamlined information retrieval system.

D   The MEDLARS System

Perhaps the most famous of all available information retrieval systems is the MEDLARS system of the National Library of Medicine (NLM). This system was built as a result of activities initiated in 1964 aimed at the publication of an automated form of Index Medicus. Experiments with on-line bibliographic retrieval systems began in 1967. The first system used the Abridged Index Medicus (AIM) as a data base that became accessible through the Teletypewriter Exchange Network (TWX). AIM-TWX proved the viability of an on-line information retrieval system.

Following the construction of the early system NLM in cooperation with the System Development Corporation (SDC) modified the on-line retrieval of bibliographic information—timeshared (ORBIT) system to meet the special needs of NLM. MEDLARS first appeared in 1971, and several revisions have since been made both to the data base structure (MEDLARS) and to the on-line search package (ELHILL). The number of available data bases has increased and the capabilities of the system have been enhanced [10–12]. Unlike the other systems previously mentioned, the coverage of MEDLARS is largely restricted to documents in the biomedical area.

The structure of the MEDLARS system is principally based on the use of inverted files. Three different files actually constitute this system: the INDEX file, the POSTINGS file, and the DATA file. The data file stores the complete information associated with each record; this includes all the data which can be displayed for the user. Each record is identified by a unique reference number, in this case called the computer assigned number (CAN).

The index file contains all the unique search terms, such as author names, terms from a controlled vocabulary, numbers such as dates, and classification codes. Each entry in the index specifies the term and the document field in which it may be found. For instance, JONES (AU) specifies that the term JONES is located in the author field of the document. Following this information, a two-part number is recorded in the index. The first portion of this number is a reference to the postings file. That is, it designates the position in the postings file where information about this term begins. The second portion of the number specifies the number of postings associated with this term. Table

Table 2-2   MEDLARS Inverted Index Organization

Search term	Sequence number address	Postings
ABDOMEN (MH)	527	3213
AGED (MH)	1073	51604
AGEE JW (AU)	1075	4
:	:	:
:	:	:
ZYMOSAN (MH)	10379	62

Adapted from reference 11.

2-2 shows the organization of the index file. The term ABDOMEN occurs in the main heading (MH) field of the given document, information about the term begins at location 527 in the postings file, and 3,213 different postings are associated with the term. The postings file contains the CAN numbers which identify the specific documents associated with each term. Associated with the term ABDOMEN, 3,213 distinct CAN numbers are therefore listed beginning at location 527. Figure 2-3 describes the overall structure of the MEDLARS system and the path of a query through the various modules of the system.

The commands used by the MEDLARS system are similar to those described earlier for the DIALOG and BRS systems. The format differs in that no search mode is selected by the user and no parentheses are allowed. The user must adhere strictly to a hierarchy which requires that all AND operations are performed prior to any OR operation. Thus if a user is interested in ''computer languages'' or ''programming languages'' then

1: COMPUTER OR PROGRAMMING AND LANGUAGE

will not produce the desired result. Rather, the two statements

1: COMPUTER OR PROGRAMMING
2: 1 AND LANGUAGE

are necessary.

The user is allowed to conduct a string search within MEDLARS. A preliminary search is first conducted and the retrieved set of documents is then scanned to find a specific string of characters in the texts. Thus, a given set of documents can be examined on a letter-by-letter basis in the hope of detecting a given word or phrase occurrence. For instance, the command

STRINGSEARCH 1: HEART DI:

can be used to find those records identified as a result of a previously defined

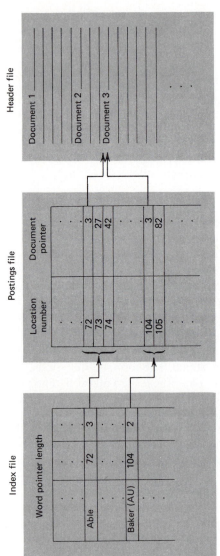

Figure 2-3 MEDLARS file organization. A search statement ABLE AND BAKER would first identify document identifier sets [3 27 42] and [3 82]; the logical AND operator would then be used to indicate document 3 as the only item to be retrieved. (*Adapted from reference 11.*)

search statement 1 which exactly match the string of characters HEART DI. The user may then be increasingly confident that the search results are indeed related to the concept of heart disease. Note that the query HEART AND DISEASE may well retrieve items that have nothing directly to do with heart disease, such as, for example, items dealing with the effects of lung disease on the heart. On the other hand, documents containing the terms ''HEART DIMENSIONS'' will also satisfy the sample string search.

A string search may be expensive to perform when conducted by most available algorithms. The MEDLARS system therefore limits the potential cost by restricting the string search to document sets retrieved by earlier searches, and by allocating limited time slices for the string search operation. At the end of a given time slice, the system informs the user of the number of documents found so far containing the requested character string. The user is then asked to approve the continuation of the string search process. The same procedure is followed at the end of every time slice. The user may be quickly discouraged by the repetitive procedure. In fact, most sophisticated users limit string searches to small sets of documents.

The efficiency and effectiveness of the MEDLARS system have been repeatedly evaluated. Because the system constitutes the first international on-line information retrieval system it enjoys a worldwide reputation. There will be further occasions to refer to this system later in this text.

E The ORBIT System

The ORBIT system provided the basic foundation for the design of MEDLARS. It should not be surprising that the two systems exhibit many common features. The basic operational environment is common in both systems. The existing differences are related to the specific procedures designed to help the user in the search process. For instance ORBIT allows the user to generate a chronological display of various search statements entered by the user during the search effort. MEDLARS does not include such a feature. Both MEDLARS and ORBIT do, however, allow the user to view a hierarchical diagram of the search logic [13,14].

F The Information Bank

The Information Bank provides access to the news articles and editorials published in *The New York Times,* and to additional articles from numerous other publications. The search vocabulary is strictly controlled, and the logical operators AND, OR, and NOT are used to relate the terms included in a search statement. Terms entered by a user for which an entry is not found in the term index initiate a dialogue between system and user. The user is eventually asked to select terms from a displayed list of available terms. Searches may be restricted by specifying fields such as date or type of material. The output may be sorted chronologically.

The Information Bank is powerful because the available data base constitutes a unique source of newspaper materials which is not otherwise easily accessible. Plans are under way, however, to render the data base of the Information Bank also accessible through the BRS system. The Information Bank may be particularly valuable to public figures, university professors, students, and in fact to anybody concerned with current or past public events. The Information Bank significantly contributes to the current popularity of on-line information retrieval systems. On the other hand, the technical design features of the system are essentially the same as those of the other systems discussed earlier [15,16,17].

G The LEXIS System

The LEXIS system offered by Mead Data Central provides a service specifically devoted to the manipulation of legal information. The documents are indexed automatically from the text of the items which is stored in its entirety in the system. The searcher uses the traditional Boolean logic to connect the text words included in the search statements. In addition, word location information may be used by insisting that terms appear in a specific portion of a document, within a specified number of words of one another, and in a particular word order. The search terms consist of text words assumed to have a specific meaning related to the document content. Common words such as "the," "it," and "her" are excluded. The common terms are deleted at the time the document is first entered into the system and are not processed any further or entered in the inverted file. Hyphenated words such as ANTI-TRUST are used as two separate terms in the LEXIS system. Thus, the term DATA-BASE is stored as two entries under DATA and BASE, and is considered distinct from DATABASE. Some special word endings can be recognized by LEXIS and reduced to common forms; for example, the terms CITY, CITIES, CITY'S, and CITIES' all retrieve the same document set. Complex morphological differences such as CHILD and its plural CHILDREN are not, however, recognized as equivalent terms.

The processing of terms necessary to remove common words and to isolate terms with common word stems occurs prior to the use of the inverted file. Thus, the LEXIS input processing is distinctly different from the document input and analysis methods used by the other systems described so far. No other publicly available system stores the full text of all documents and uses it for search and retrieval on the scale of LEXIS. Following the elimination of common words and the generation of word stems, LEXIS uses an inverted file system similar to those included in the other retrieval systems. The inverted file retains word location information which may be used either with or without specified word order information. In this sense, the LEXIS system performs much like DIALOG or STAIRS [18].

4 ENHANCEMENTS OF BASIC RETRIEVAL STRATEGY

The use of an inverted file structure appears to be a prominent feature of the existing commercial information retrieval systems. The main inverted file concepts appear to have been used initially on a computing device by Herman Hollerith, who introduced punched cards to handle the computational work for the 1890 United States Census. Since that time the basic inverted file design has not been radically modified. New term location and term frequency information has been added, as in the STAIRS, DIALOG, and LEXIS systems. But the file organization using individual terms and document reference numbers has remained unchanged. This organization can easily handle Boolean operators by translating the AND, OR, and NOT operations into the set intersection, set union, and set difference, respectively. Thus, inverted file procedures are easy to implement and offer the user a powerful way of expressing information needs.

The use of unweighted term combinations such as

ALPHA AND BETA

implies that the user considers the terms ALPHA and BETA equally important. If these terms are not equally important, some means is required to express term importance. Typically the searcher is asked to specify term importance by assigning numeric values to terms. For instance, values between 1 and 10 could be used to designate terms of little importance (1) as well as terms of most importance (10). The user may also be asked to specify a threshold to determine which documents are to be retrieved and which are to be rejected. Thus, given the weights and thresholds

    ALPHA = 4
    BETA = 5
    GAMMA = 6
    Threshold = 10

a query such as

ALPHA OR BETA OR GAMMA

would retrieve the following document sets in order:

1 Documents containing terms ALPHA and BETA and GAMMA (4 + 5 + 6 ≥ 10)
2 Documents containing the terms BETA and GAMMA (5 + 6 ≥ 10)
3 Documents containing the terms ALPHA and GAMMA (4 + 6 ≥ 10)

This assumes that the terms occurring in the documents are unweighted and that satisfactory methods are available for choosing appropriate weights for the query terms.

The query term weights produce a partial ranking of the retrieved documents which may improve user satisfaction. However, in practical situations term weighting has not produced substantial improvements in search satisfaction. The reason seems to be that a great deal of effort is required on the part of the searcher to determine correct weights and assign them to the various terms. Thus, de facto, most searches are conducted using the basic inverted file system organizations with unweighted terms.

The inverted file process permits a great deal of flexibility in the design of the user-system interfaces. Even though most systems are based on the same fundamental file organization and search strategy, different ways exist for presenting the information to the user. The manner in which commands are presented, the hierarchy of operations, and the different operators allowed in each system render each system unique.

Currently, several hundred data bases are associated with the various systems. These data bases include millions of documents. Thus, an enormous investment exists in systems designed to operate with inverted files. The introduction of changes and modifications to the existing commercial retrieval systems must therefore depend upon not only the technical feasibility but also the economic impact of the alterations. The great expansion in the availability and use of retrieval systems over the last dozen years leads one to expect a continued growth in system development and services in the years to come.

REFERENCES

[1] D. Fife, K. Rankin, E. Feng, J. Walder, and B. Marron, A Technical Index of Interactive Information Systems, Systems and Software Division, Institute for Computer Science and Technology, National Bureau of Standards, Washington, D.C., March 1974.

[2] M.E. Senko, File Organization and Management Information Systems, Chapter 4, Annual Review of Information Science and Technology, C. Cuadra, editor, Vol. 4, Encyclopaedia Britannica, Chicago, Illinois, 1969, pp. 111–143.

[3] F.W. Lancaster, On-Line Information Systems, Encyclopedia of Library and Information Science, Vol. 20, Marcel Dekker, New York, 1977.

[4] F.W. Lancaster and E.G. Fayen, Information Retrieval On-Line, Melville Publishing Co., Los Angeles, California, 1973.

[5] D. Lefkowitz, File Structures for On-Line Systems, Spartan Books, Rochelle Park, New York, 1964.

[6] C. Bourne and B. Anderson, DIALOG Lab Workbook, 2nd Edition, Lockheed Information Systems, Palo Alto, California, 1979.

[7] DIALOG Information Retrieval Service, Database Catalog, Lockheed Missiles and Space Co., Inc., Palo Alto, California, May 1980.

[8] IBM World Trade Corporation, IBM System/370 (OS/VS), Storage and Information Retrieval System/Vertical Storage (STAIRS/VS) Reference Manual.

[9] Bibliographic Retrieval Services, Inc., BRS Bulletin, Schenectady, New York.

[10] National Library of Medicine, On-Line Services Reference Manual, U.S. Department of Health, Education and Welfare, Bethesda, Maryland, January 1980.

[11] National Library of Medicine, MEDLARS, The Computerized Literature Retrieval Services of the National Library of Medicine, Department of Health, Education and Welfare, Publication NIH 79-1286, January 1979.

[12] D.B. McCarn, MEDLINE: An Introduction to On-Line Searching, Journal of the American Society for Information Science, Vol. 31, No. 3, May 1980, pp. 181–192.
[13] System Development Corporation, Highlights and Hints: ORBIT, System Development Corporation Search, Santa Monica, California.
[14] System Development Corporation, Search Service News, Newsletter of the System Development Corporation Search Service, Santa Monica, California.
[15] J. Rothman, The Times Information Bank on Campus, EDUCOM Bulletin, Vol. 8, No. 3, Fall 1973, pp. 14–19.
[16] The Information Bank, Thesaurus: A Guide for Searching the Information Bank and for Organizing, Cataloging, Indexing, and Searching Collections of Information and Current Events, Parsippany, New Jersey, 1977.
[17] J. Rothman, The New York Times Information Bank, The New York Times, New York, 1969.
[18] Mead Data Central, LEXIS Quick Reference, New York, 1976.

BIBLIOGRAPHIC REMARKS

Readers interested in learning more about the use of inverted files in various areas of application may want to consult the following additional references:

G. Wiederhold, Database Design, Chapter 3, Basic File System Organization, McGraw-Hill Book Company, New York, 1977.
C. Meadow, Applied Data Management, Chapter 3, Data Storage, and Chapter 7, File Maintenance, John Wiley and Sons, Inc., New York, 1976.

For an elementary discussion of data structures see:

G.G. Dodd, Elements of Data Management Systems, Computing Surveys, Vol. 1, No. 2, June 1969, pp. 117–133.

The following items relate inverted file systems specifically to information storage and retrieval:

A.E. Wessel, Computer Aided Information Retrieval, Chapter 9, Computer Software and Some Hardware Considerations, Melville Publishing Company, Los Angeles, California, 1975.
C.J. van Rijsbergen, Information Retrieval, 2nd Edition, Chapter 4, File Structures, Butterworths, London, England, 1979.

The operation of information retrieval systems using inverted files is described in the following texts:

F.W. Lancaster and E.G. Fayen, Information Retrieval On-Line, Melville Publishing Company, Los Angeles, California, 1973.
F.W. Lancaster, Information Retrieval Systems: Characteristics, Testing and Evaluation, 2nd Edition, Chapter 2, The Matching Subsystem; Chapter 3, The Application of Computers to Information Retrieval-Off-Line Batch Processing Systems; Chapter 4, On-Line Information Retrieval, John Wiley and Sons, Inc., New York, 1979.

The reader should be careful to distinguish books dealing with file structures from texts covering principally data structures. There is some confusion in terminology between data and file structures and between lists, indexes, and files. In information retrieval, the term data structure normally refers to abstract constructs used to represent the entities and concepts under consideration—for example, documents, terms, and sentences. File structure, on the other hand, refers to the organization of the document files and of the auxiliary files used to access the main document files.

EXERCISES

2-1 Consider the following inverted index

TERM A	1,4,5,6,8
TERM B	2,3,4,6,7,9,10
TERM C	3,5,7,9

Identify the document numbers associated with each of the following retrieval statements
a TERM A   AND   TERM B
b TERM A   OR   TERM C
c TERM A   OR   (TERM B AND TERM C)
d TERM C   NOT   TERM A

2-2 Using the inverted file structure from Exercise 2-1 describe a procedure which will identify the documents in which TERM A is immediately followed by TERM B.

2-3 If TERM A is assigned a weight of 2 by a particular user, and TERMS B and C are assigned weights of 4 and 3 respectively, which documents will be retrieved by each of the following statements, assuming a retrieval threshold of 6:
a TERM A   OR   TERM B
b TERM A   OR   TERM B   OR   TERM C
c TERM B   AND   TERM C

2-4 Using any programming language and an arbitrary text string consisting of more than one sentence develop a routine which creates an inverted index for the words from the text and the associated sentence numbers. For example, given the text: "The objects are processed serially. The first of the objects becomes the representative," the appropriate inverted index will be

THE	1	2
OBJECTS	1	2
ARE	1	
PROCESSED	1	
SERIALLY	1	
FIRST	2	
OR	2	
BECOMES	2	
REPRESENTATIVE	2	

Use the program created for Exercise 1-2 to isolate the individual words in the text string.

2-5 Under what circumstances would it be reasonable to keep term location information in an inverted index? Given the example in Exercise 2-4, develop a routine to create an inverted index that includes term location information.

2-6 Create a routine which transforms the inverted index of Exercise 2-4 into alphabetical order.

Chapter 3

Text Analysis and Automatic Indexing

0 PREVIEW

In the first two chapters of this book the design and operations of existing information retrieval systems have been presented. Of all the operations required in information retrieval, the most crucial and probably the most difficult one consists in assigning appropriate terms and identifiers capable of representing the content of the collection items. This task, known as indexing, is normally performed manually by trained experts. In modern environments the indexing task can be performed automatically. This chapter is concerned with the techniques used for automatic indexing, and with the effect and performance of these techniques.

The basic indexing task is first described, followed by a comparison of manual and automatic indexing. Basic techniques are then examined for choosing good content terms and for assigning weights to the terms according to their presumed value for content identification. A simple automatic indexing procedure is then suggested, as well as refinements consisting of the use of term phrases and thesaurus classes. The use of linguistic and probabilistic techniques in automatic indexing is also briefly introduced. Finally, evaluation output is included to demonstrate the effectiveness of the proposed indexing techniques applied to small sample collections.

This chapter includes some technical material. The reader is urged to follow the difficulty indications in mastering the theories underlying the automatic indexing process.

1 INDEXING ENVIRONMENT

Of all the procedures normally used in a document processing environment, the most important and also the most difficult to carry out are the *analysis* operations consisting of the assignment to the bibliographic items of terms or identifiers capable of representing document content. In principle, a document analysis process is redundant if the document collection is small enough to permit the scanning of the full text of all items whenever a request for information is received. In practice, such a solution is too time-consuming and too expensive. Hence it is customary to characterize each item by assigning a short description, or profile, to the item which can be used to obtain access whenever the item is wanted. In standard library environments, the analysis operations are known variously as cataloging, classification, indexing, and abstracting.

The document profile fulfills the dual role of representing a given document by providing a short-form description, and also of describing the document content; the profile is therefore often divided into two parts consisting first of objective information relating to the data external to the document text itself, such as author name, publisher, and date and place of publication; and second of identifiers specifically describing the information contained in the document. In conventional libraries the choice of objective document identifiers is known as author/title or descriptive cataloging, whereas the assignment of the content information is termed subject cataloging. As explained in Chapter 1, the content description of an item consists of a call number chosen from a hierarchically organized systematic list, and of additional subject headings that may be represented by relatively free language words and phrases. Each subject heading assigned to a given item may be entered onto a separate catalog card, and the resulting collection constitutes the library catalog. In a modern document processing environment the conventional library catalog does not exist as a physical entity. Rather the profiles are collected into a data base. In this case, the content analysis operations are then collectively known as indexing. When the assignment of the content identifiers is carried out with the aid of modern computing equipment, the operation becomes *automatic indexing*.

It would be nice to think that the choice of the *objective* document identifiers presents no difficulties. In fact, elaborate cataloging standards have had to be defined specifying what author names are acceptable and how the author/title information is to be entered into the catalog. The study of existing author cataloging rules presents many challenges which deserve to be critically examined [1,2]. In the present context, however, the most interesting problems arise in connection with the generation and standardization of the content, as opposed to the objective, identifiers. Therefore, this present chapter is concerned with the analysis of document content and in particular with automatic indexing procedures.

The assignment of content identifiers to the information items is designed to fulfill three related purposes [1]:

1 To allow the location of items dealing with topics of interest to the user
2 To relate items to each other, and thus relate the topic areas, by identifying distinct items dealing with similar, or related, topic areas
3 To predict the relevance of individual information items to specific information requirements through the use of index terms with well-defined scope and meaning

The methods used to accomplish these aims depend on the particular indexing environment in which the operations take place.

The first distinction to be made is that between *manual* and *automatic indexing*. Historically, the analysis operations have been carried out manually—maybe one should say intellectually—by "subject experts." To this day, manual indexing is the rule rather than the exception in most operational environments. A variety of aids are made available to the indexer to control the indexing process including terminology lists, instruction manuals, and specially structured worksheets to record the indexing products. "Scope notes" may also be used to define the meaning and interpretation of each of the allowable index terms. Obviously, lists of definitions and scope notes in natural language text form are not easily incorporated into an automatic indexing system.

The second distinction to be made is that between *controlled* and *uncontrolled indexing terms*. Many experts feel that an uncontrolled indexing vocabulary which in principle can include the whole variety of the natural language introduces too many opportunities for ambiguity and error. Hence, a limited indexing language is often advocated in which the terms available for content identification are rigidly controlled. This permits the control of spelling and the elimination of synonyms by referring to unique accepted terms for each synonym class, and by identifying semantically related terms. The use of controlled terms guarantees retrieval of appropriately marked items when the correct search terms are known, but it also normally implies that trained intermediaries are needed to formulate the query statements.

A third problem relates to the type of vocabulary used for indexing purposes. A distinction is made between the use of *single terms* to characterize document content, as opposed to the use of *terms in context* where relationship indicators may be available to connect several identifiers, and the basic units may consist of compound entries and phrases. In the single term mode, the content identifiers, known as index terms, keywords, or descriptors, are represented by individual words used to express the concepts included in each document. Then each document is characterized by a collection of individual terms. The terms are eventually combined, or "coordinated," to form topic descriptions when the search requests are formulated. This process is known as "postcoordination." On the other hand, when compound terms are utilized for indexing purposes, consisting of phrases possibly including nouns, adjectives, prepositions, and a variety of relationship indicators, the process is called "precoordination." For example, indexing this book under "automatic information retrieval" is a use of precoordination; indexing it separately under each term and finding it in response to a query such as INFORMATION AND RETRIEVAL represents postcoordination.

In many manual indexing situations where trained experts are involved, the use of controlled indexing languages using precoordinated compound terms is preferred. Automatic indexing systems, on the other hand, often use single terms because the automatic assignment of effective single terms is well understood; the terms are then combined by postcoordination at search time only. No matter what indexing environment is preferred, it is always necessary to take into account two characteristics of the indexing products known as "exhaustivity" and "specificity." Exhaustivity refers to the degree to which all the concepts and notions included in a document are recognized in the index descriptions. The more exhaustive the indexing the higher may be the proportion of the relevant items that can be retrieved, because all the various aspects of the subject matter are then properly recognized. Specificity, on the other hand, refers to the generic level of the index terms used to characterize the document content. If the indexing vocabulary is very specific, and if narrowly defined terms are assigned to the bibliographic items, a large proportion of the nonrelevant items may be properly rejected when the documents to be retrieved are determined.

In many retrieval environments it is customary to measure the effectiveness of retrieval by using two parameters for each search known respectively as "recall" and "precision." Recall measures the proportion of relevant information actually retrieved in response to a search (that is, the number of relevant items actually obtained divided by the total number of relevant items contained in the collection), whereas precision measures the proportion of retrieved items actually relevant (that is, the number of relevant items actually obtained divided by the total number of retrieved items). These evaluation measures are examined in more detail in Chapter 5. The use of exhaustive indexing and a specific indexing language is believed to lead to high recall as well as high precision.

The dual characteristics of exhaustivity and specificity are sometimes subsumed under the notions of *deep* and *shallow* indexing. Deep indexing implies both high exhaustivity and specificity and hence a good retrieval performance. Shallow indexing, on the other hand, is produced by using a few broad terms to characterize each document. In these circumstances, the retrieval performance may be expected to suffer somewhat, but the indexing task may be performed more rapidly and more economically.

2 MANUAL AND AUTOMATIC INDEXING

Before turning to a description of automatic indexing methods, it may be useful to summarize briefly some of the conventional manual indexing practices. In most situations a controlled indexing language is used in which a single standard term or phrase represents a wide variety of related terms and descriptions. Thus, if the standard entry "oscillation" is specified in the accepted indexing terminology, alternative related expressions such as "vibration," "undulation," "pulsation," "swing," and "rolling" are replaced by "oscillation" when the documents are indexed and the search requests are formulated. To facilitate the interpretation of the indexing vocabulary and the retrieval of relevant information, the elements of the controlled vocabulary may be used in context, through precoordination of terms. Thus, instead of assigning single terms such as "dyes," "solvents," or "spectra," many systems specify complex indexing entries such as "dyes, spectra, effect of solvents" or "solvents, effect on spectra of dyes" [2].

When precoordinated, controlled indexing languages are manually assigned, it is necessary to abide by the rules relating to the degree of desirable context. That is, the number of related terms that should preferably be used; the order in which the associated terms should be listed; and also the type of relationship indication to be used between the components of an indexing entry are all specified. Thus, the indexing products may be restricted to short phrases or may be of sentence length equivalent to a complete document title. The listing order may prescribe that a thing or object be entered before any action performed on the object, which in turn should be listed before any instrument used in the action. Thus, an entry might have to be specified as "coal, production" and not "production, coal."

Among the relation indicators accepted in various systems are the standard natural language prepositions and conjunctions, as well as *links* to indicate connections between two or more terms in a description, and *roles* to specify the function of particular terms in an indexing description. Thus if one were interested in the hardness of copper and the conductivity of titanium, a link between the first two terms and another one between the last two would relate each substance to the relevant property. Typical "roles" performed by index entry components are "action," "instrument," "object," "subject," etc. Prepositions and conjunctions that are sometimes ambiguous could be used with some types of free-language indexing; links and roles on the other hand are normally defined precisely and used with controlled vocabulary indexing.

To solve the intellectual problems of index language design, and aid the indexer in the term assignment and the searcher in the formulation of search requests, a variety of vocabulary lists and terminology descriptions may be used, including in particular thesauruses that contain lists of equivalent and related terms for each standard thesaurus entry. Hierarchical dictionaries may be available containing general term arrangements capable of identifying broader and narrower terms for the various dictionary entries. The following types of cross references are often included in the existing terminology descriptions:

1 "See" references which identify the standard entry for terms not accepted by the indexing language ("aircraft, see airplanes")

2 "See also" references, sometimes also designated RT (related terms), which provide references between groups of related terms ("accidents, see also collisions, hazards, safety, survival")

3 References to generically broader terms, sometimes designated BT ("conversion coating, BT coating")

4 References to generically narrower terms, sometimes designated NT ("cooling, NT conduction cooling, convection cooling, evaporation cooling")

The terminology lists may take a variety of forms, including in particular alphabetical term arrangements in which the entries and subentries within entries are alphabetically arranged (Table 3-1a). Alternatively systematic, hierarchical term arrangements in tree form can be used where indentation on the page denotes the generic level (in the excerpt of Table 3-1b, "traffic potential" is generically inferior to "traffic," which in turn is inferior to "airlines"). In addition to formal vocabulary arrangements, it is often convenient to maintain lists of index entries derived from the formal thesaurus together with references to the documents indexed by the corresponding entries. To facilitate the consultation of these indexes, it is customary in many cases to repeat each entry

Airlines	Airplanes
___ Certification	___ Cargo
___ Depreciation	___ Convertible
___ Economics	___ Light
___ Employees	
___ Fares	

(a)

Airlines
  Traffic
    Traffic potential
  Finance
    Accounting
  Operation
  Equipment

(b)

Peas, deficiency of copper and zinc in
Copper, deficiency in peas
Zinc, deficiency in peas
Deficiencies of copper and zinc in peas

(c)

Table 3-1 Conventional dictionary formats. (a) Excerpt from alphabetical terminology. (b) Excerpt from systematic terminology. (c) Multiple entry articulated term arrangement.

several times by changing the "lead term," that is, the term used to gain entry into the index. Various strategies are used to construct the set of multiple entries, known as rotation, cycling, chaining, permutation, and so on. In each case, the aim is to furnish a separate entry into the index for each standard as well as each related term in a given compound expression. An example is included in Table 3-1c where the various entries (under "peas," "copper," "zinc," and "deficiencies") are all assumed to refer to the same document or documents. A similar strategy is used in the so-called permuted title indexes which are a part of many modern automatic indexing environments.

An evaluation of the performance of standard subject indexes shows that the use of full index term context leads to a much better precision performance than the lack of context exemplified by the use of single term entries. Increased term specificity and a better understanding of the meaning of the index entries may suppress many nonrelevant items that would normally be retrieved if entries devoid of context were used. On the other hand, when the various forms of context are compared with each other, such as the use of rotated entries and of function words to designate term relationships, few differences in retrieval effectiveness are detected [3].

The foregoing considerations make it plain that much can, in principle, be gained by using a sophisticated indexing product in finding useful documents, rejecting extraneous items, and determining the potential importance of the stored information items. These gains are dependent on the quality, accuracy, and consistency of the indexing performance. Not only must indexers be intimately aware of the available indexing vocabularies and practices, but they should also have knowledge of the collection characteristics and of the type of user queries the system may be expected to process in the future. Furthermore, the performance of the various indexers and searchers that must participate in most operational environments ought to be sufficiently consistent to guarantee that similar documents are identified by comparable indexing entries.

In practice one finds that accuracy and consistency are difficult to maintain. The situation demands a good deal of sophistication, training, and experience on the part of the indexing personnel. But more often than not, the resulting index entries are insufficiently exhaustive, omitting relevant entries, or lacking in specificity. The former produces recall losses, while the latter may lead to recall as well as precision deficiencies [4]. A lack of indexing consistency also produces difficulties in detecting similarities among queries and documents [5,6]. Therefore, the potential advantages of strictly controlled, manually applied indexing languages may be largely illusory.

An uncontrolled, natural language indexing system that is applied automatically exhibits substantial advantages. A natural language system, when properly used, can be specific in the sense that the language may provide just the right kind of expression to denote each particular concept. Furthermore, the natural language is the language of discourse. The authors of documents as well as users of information systems are accustomed to the language, and even the human indexers and other subject specialists are likely to feel comfortable dealing with a natural language system. For this reason natural language indexing may be carried out more rapidly, and hence more cheaply than indexing based on a controlled vocabulary and precoordinated terms.

On the other hand, in a natural language indexing system where a controlled thesaurus is not immediately available to make the distinction between acceptable and forbidden index terms, some way must be found to supply the synonymous and related terms that are available in a controlled indexing environment. Various approaches have been used for this purpose. Thus, exhaustive indexing products may be obtained by choosing a wide variety of different index terms for assignment to queries and documents. Term relationships can be added, for example, by constructing term phrases instead of individual terms; and the precoordinated indexing entries available with controlled term systems can be replaced by juxtaposing individual terms when the search requests are formulated. Nevertheless, the generation of effective indexing products remains a major problem in a natural language indexing system.

It has been claimed that automatic, free language indexing products are necessarily inferior to manual systems because automatic systems are *derivative* in the sense that the original document and query texts must serve as principal inputs for the indexing operation. It becomes necessary in these circumstances to wrestle with the peculiarities of the languages used by individual authors, and to worry about unusual terminologies and expressions. Any assertions concerning the inadequacy of automatic indexing can also be bolstered by demonstrations designed to show that the results of particular automatic indexing procedures will fail to pass any rational test carried out by independent human observers [7]. In so doing, one forgets that the results of manual indexing are also influenced by the terminology contained in individual documents, no matter how much control may be provided by the auxiliary indexing aids.

In any case, the justification of any indexing technique ultimately lies in the retrieval results obtained. Substantial evidence now indicates that simple automatic indexing methods are fast and inexpensive, and produce a recall and precision performance at least equivalent to that obtainable in manual, controlled term environments. A wide variety of automatic indexing methods are examined in the remainder of this chapter, and performance evaluation data are given for some of the proposed methods.

3   AUTOMATIC TERM EXTRACTION AND WEIGHTING

A   General Considerations

The indexing task consists first of assigning to each stored item terms, or concepts, capable of representing document content, and second of assigning to each term a weight, or value, reflecting its presumed importance for purposes of content identification. The first and most obvious place where appropriate content identifiers might be found is the text of the documents themselves, or the text of document titles and abstracts. This section is thus concerned with methods for the extraction of content terms from documents and document excerpts and with the assignment of term weights in order of term importance.

Most automatic indexing efforts start with the observation that the frequency of occurrence of individual word types (that is, of distinct words) in natural language texts has something to do with the importance of these words for purposes of content representation. Specifically, if all words were to occur randomly across the documents of a collection with equal frequencies, it would be impossible to distinguish between them using quantitative criteria. In fact, it has been observed that the words occur in natural language text unevenly. As a result of this, classes of words are distinguishable by their occurrence frequencies. To quote from H.P. Luhn, one of the pioneers in automatic indexing [8]:

> The justification of measuring word significance by use-frequency is based on the fact that a writer normally repeats certain words as he advances or varies his arguments and as he elaborates on an aspect of a subject. This means of emphasis is taken as an indicator of significance. . . .

In fact, it is known that when the distinct words in a body of text are arranged in decreasing order of their frequency of occurrence (most frequent words first), the occurrence characteristics of the vocabulary can be characterized by the constant rank-frequency law of Zipf:

$$\text{Frequency} \cdot \text{rank} \simeq \text{constant} \tag{1}$$

That is, the frequency of a given word multiplied by the rank order of that word will be approximately equal to the frequency of another word multiplied by its rank [9]. The law has been explained by citing a general ''principle of least effort'' which makes it easier for a speaker or writer of a language to repeat certain words instead of coining new and different words. The least-effort principle also accounts for the fact that the most frequent words (those with the lowest ranks) tend to be short function words (and, of, but, the, etc.) which are easy to coin and whose cost of usage is small.

The law has been verified many times using text materials in different areas. A short illustration is contained in Table 3-2 [10]. A typical graph showing the cumulative fraction of word usage in natural language texts is shown in Fig. 3-1. It may be seen from the figure that the most frequent 20 percent of the text words account for some 70 percent of term usage.

Using the *Zipf law* of expression (1) as a starting point, it is now possible to derive word significance factors based on the frequency characteristics of individual words in document texts. An early proposal was based on the following general consideration [8]:

1   Given a collection of n documents, calculate for each document the frequency of each unique term in that document. This is the frequency of term k in document i, or FREQ_{ik}.

Table 3-2   Illustration of Rank-Frequency Law
(Number of Word Occurrences N = 1,000,000)

Rank (R)	Term	Frequency (F)	R · (F/1,000,000)
1	the	69,971	0.070
2	of	36,411	0.073
3	and	28,852	0.086
4	to	26,149	0.104
5	a	23,237	0.116
6	in	21,341	0.128
7	that	10,595	0.074
8	is	10,099	0.081
9	was	9,816	0.088
10	he	9,543	0.095

Adapted from reference 10.

2   Determine the total collection frequency TOTFREQ$_k$ for each word by summing the frequencies of each unique term across all n documents, that is,

$$TOTFREQ_k = \sum_{i=1}^{n} FREQ_{ik}.$$

3   Arrange the words in decreasing order according to their collection frequency. Decide on some suitable high threshold value and remove all words with a collection frequency above this threshold. This eliminates high-frequency function words such as those shown in Table 3-2.

4   In the same way, eliminate from consideration low-frequency words. That is, choose some low threshold and remove all words with a collection frequency below this threshold. This deletes terms occurring so infrequently in the collection that their presence does not affect the retrieval performance in a significant way.

5   The remaining medium-frequency words are now used for assignment to the documents as index terms.

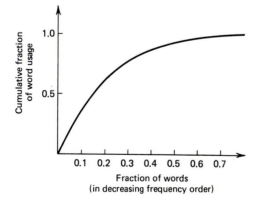

Figure 3-1   Word usage statistics.

Since neither the high- nor the low-frequency terms are good content identifiers, Luhn conjectured that the "resolving power" of the index words extracted from document texts would peak in the middle-frequency range as shown in Fig. 3-2. By "resolving power" is meant the ability of the index terms to identify relevant items and to distinguish them from the nonrelevant material. Among the recommendations made by Luhn for an actual automatic indexing policy, the following may be considered typical [11]:

> A notion occurring at least twice in the same paragraph would be considered a major notion; a notion which occurs also in the immediately preceding or succeeding paragraphs would be considered a major notion even though it appears only once in the paragraph under consideration; notations for major notions would then be listed in some standard order. . . .

There is some evidence that these original ideas are too crude to serve in a practical operational retrieval environment. Thus the elimination of all high-frequency words might produce losses in recall, because the use of broad, high-frequency words for content identification is effective in retrieving large numbers of relevant items. Contrariwise, the elimination of low-frequency terms may produce losses in precision. Another problem is the necessity to choose appropriate thresholds in order to distinguish the useful medium-frequency terms from the remainder. Finally, a question of principle arises concerning the use of *absolute* frequency measures (such as $FREQ_{ik}$ or $TOTFREQ_k$) for the identification of content indicators. The reason is that a useful index term must fulfill a dual function: on the one hand, it must be related to the information content of the document so as to render the item retrievable when it is wanted (the recall function); on the other hand, a good index term also distinguishes the documents to which it is assigned from the remainder to prevent the indiscriminate retrieval of all items, whether wanted or not (the precision function). Thus a term such as "computer" may never constitute a reasonable term for assignment to a document collection in computing, no matter what its frequency of

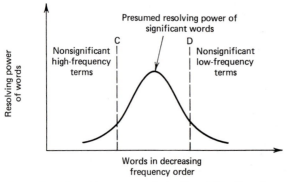

Figure 3-2 Resolving power of significant (medium-frequency) words. (*Adapted from reference 8.*)

occurrence in the documents of the collection, because "computer" is likely to occur in *every* collection item and cannot therefore be used to distinguish the items from each other. This suggests the use of *relative frequency* measures to identify terms occurring with substantial frequencies in some individual documents of a collection, but with a relatively low overall collection frequency. Such terms may then help in retrieving the items to which they are assigned, while also distinguishing them from the remainder of the collection [12,13].

Several term weighting functions have been derived from these basic considerations, including an inverse document frequency function, the signal-noise ratio, and the term discrimination value. These weighting functions are briefly introduced in the remainder of this section.

*B The Inverse Document Frequency Weight

The first possibility consists in assuming that term importance is proportional to the standard occurrence frequency of each term k in each document i (that is, $FREQ_{ik}$) and inversely proportional to the total number of documents to which each term is assigned. Specifically, one counts the number of documents in which a term k occurs. This produces the document frequency $DOCFREQ_k$ of term k, representing the number of documents to which term k is assigned. A possible measure of the inverse document frequency can now be written as [14]

$$\log_2 \frac{n}{DOCFREQ_k} + 1 = \log_2(n) - \log_2(DOCFREQ_k) + 1$$

where n is the number of documents in the collection. For example, in a collection of 1,000 documents, consider the term ALPHA occurring in 100 documents, term BETA occurring in 500 documents, and GAMMA occurring in 900 documents. The inverse document frequency factor will then be 4.322 for ALPHA, 2.000 for BETA, and 1.132 for GAMMA. The emphasis is seen to be placed on the terms exhibiting the lowest document frequencies.

A composite expression measuring the importance, or weight, of term k in a given document i would increase as the frequency of the term in the document, $FREQ_{ik}$, increases but decrease as the document frequency $DOCFREQ_k$ increases. A possible weighting function is

$$WEIGHT_{ik} = FREQ_{ik} \cdot [\log_2 (n) - \log_2 (DOCFREQ_k) + 1] \tag{2}$$

This function assigns a high degree of importance to terms occurring in only a few documents of a collection [14].

**C The Signal-Noise Ratio

A related viewpoint suggests using information theory considerations to construct a measure of term importance. In particular, it is known that the information content of a message, or term, can be measured as an inverse function of the probability of occurrence of the words in a given text. Specifically, the higher the probability of occurrence of a word, the less information it contains. The information content of a word is measured as INFORMATION $= -\log_2 p$, where p is the probability of occurrence of the word. For example, if the word ALPHA occurs once in every 10,000 words, its probability of occurrence is 0.0001, and its information is

$$\begin{aligned} \text{INFORMATION} &= -\log_2 (0.0001) \\ &= -(-13.278) \\ &= 13.278 \end{aligned}$$

On the other hand, if the word THE occurs once in every 10 words, its probability is 0.1 and its information measure is

$$\begin{aligned} \text{INFORMATION} &= -\log_2 (0.1) \\ &= -(-3.223) \\ &= 3.223 \end{aligned}$$

The term information value can be regarded as a measure of reduced uncertainty, in the sense that when terms are assigned as content identifiers to the documents of a collection, knowing a particular term reduces the uncertainty about the document content. Furthermore, the smaller the probability of occurrence of the terms (that is, the greater the term specificity) the larger is the reduction in uncertainty.

By extension, when a document is characterized by t possible identifiers, or terms, each occurring with a specified probability p_k, the average, or expected information (that is, the average reduction in uncertainty about the document) gained by using one of the terms is given by Shannon's formula [15]

$$\text{AVERAGE INFORMATION} = - \sum_{k=1}^{t} p_k \log p_k \tag{3}$$

For example, if the terms ALPHA, BETA, GAMMA, and DELTA are expected to occur with the probabilities 0.5, 0.2, 0.2, and 0.1, respectively, the the average information is

$$\begin{aligned} \text{AVERAGE INFORMATION} &= -[(0.5 \log_2 0.5) + (0.2 \log_2 0.2) \\ &\quad + (0.2 \log_2 0.2) + (0.1 \log_2 0.1)] \\ &= -[(-0.05) + (-0.46) + (-0.46) + (-0.33)] \\ &= 1.3 \end{aligned}$$

It is known that the average information is maximized when the occurrence probabilities of the terms are all equal to 1/t for t distinct terms. For example, if ALPHA, BETA, GAMMA, and DELTA are all expected to occur one-fourth of the time, the average information value will be 2 instead of 1.3 as in the earlier example.

By analogy to Shannon's information measure, it is now possible to define the *noise* $NOISE_k$ of an index term k for a collection of n documents

$$NOISE_k = \sum_{i=1}^{n} \frac{FREQ_{ik}}{TOTFREQ_k} \log_2 \frac{TOTFREQ_k}{FREQ_{ik}} \tag{4}$$

This measure of noise varies inversely with the "concentration" of a term in the document collection. That is, for perfectly even distributions, when a term occurs an identical number of times in every document of the collection, the noise is maximized. For example, if term k occurs exactly once in each document (all $FREQ_{ik} = 1$)

$$NOISE_k = \sum_{i=1}^{n} \frac{1}{n} \log_2 \frac{n}{1}$$
$$= \log_2 n$$

On the other hand, for perfectly concentrated distributions, when a term appears in only one document with frequency $TOTFREQ_k$, the noise is zero because in that case

$$NOISE_k = \frac{TOTFREQ_k}{TOTFREQ_k} \log_2 \frac{TOTFREQ_k}{TOTFREQ_k}$$
$$= 1 \log_2 1$$
$$= 0$$

A relation clearly exists between noise and term specificity, because broad, nonspecific terms tend to have more even distributions across the documents of a collection, and hence high noise. An *inverse* function of the noise might then be used as a possible function of term value [16,17]. One such function, known as the *signal* of term k, is defined as follows

$$SIGNAL_k = \log_2 (TOTFREQ_k) - NOISE_k \tag{5}$$

For the maximum noise case previously discussed (where each $FREQ_{ik}$) is equal to 1 the SIGNAL is equal to 0, since $TOTFREQ_k$ in that case equals n. On the other hand, when a term occurs in only one document, a maximum signal of $\log_2 TOTFREQ_k$ is obtained.

In principle, it is possible to rank the index words extracted from the documents of a collection in decreasing order of the signal value. Such an ordering favors terms that distinguish one or two specific documents (the ones in which the high-signal term exclusively occurs) from the remainder of the collection. Alternatively, the importance, or weight, of term k in document i can be computed as a composite function taking into account $FREQ_{ik}$ as well as SIG-

NAL_k. A possible measure of this type analogous to the term weighting function of expression (2) is

$$WEIGHT_{ik} = FREQ_{ik} \cdot SIGNAL_k \tag{6}$$

It will be seen later that the signal value does not give optimal performance in a retrieval environment.

*D   The Term Discrimination Value

Luhn's early proposals were designed to measure the "resolving power" of a term with respect to a document by using the frequency of occurrence of the term in the document. Another approach is to compute the *discrimination value* of a term. This measures the degree to which the use of the term will help to distinguish the documents from each other [18,19]. Consider, in particular, a collection of documents, and let D_i and D_j represent two documents each identified by a set of index terms. A similarity measure $SIMILAR(D_i,D_j)$ can be used to represent the similarity between the documents. Typical similarity measures generate values of 0 for documents exhibiting no agreement among the assigned index terms, and 1 when perfect agreement is detected. Intermediate values are obtained for cases of partial agreement.

If the similarity measure is computed for all pairs of documents (D_i,D_j) except when $i = j$, an average value AVERAGE-SIMILARITY is obtainable. This represents the average document-pair similarity for the collection. Specifically,

$$AVERAGE\text{-}SIMILARITY = CONSTANT \sum_{i=1}^{n} \sum_{\substack{i \neq j \\ j=1}}^{n} SIMILAR(D_i,D_j) \tag{7a}$$

for some constant [for example, $1/n(n - 1)$]. The foregoing expression reflects the *density* of the document space, that is, the degree to which the documents are bunched up in the "space" of documents. When all n documents are identical, $SIMILAR(D_i,D_j) = 1$ for all document pairs, and AVERAGE-SIMILARITY reaches a maximum:

$$AVERAGE\text{-}SIMILARITY = CONSTANT \sum_{i=1}^{n} \sum_{\substack{i \neq j \\ j=1}}^{n} 1$$

$$= CONSTANT \cdot n(n - 1)$$

The space density can be computed more efficiently by constructing an artificial, "average" document $\overline{D}$ as the *centroid*, in which the terms are assumed to exhibit average frequency characteristics, that is, the average frequency of term k is defined as

$$(AVERAGE\ FREQ)_k = \frac{1}{n} \sum_{i=1}^{n} FREQ_{ik}$$

The density is then computed as the sum of the similarities of each document with the centroid

$$\text{AVGSIM} = \text{CONSTANT} \sum_{i=1}^{n} \text{SIMILAR}(\overline{D}, D_i) \qquad (7b)$$

Consider now the original document collection with term k removed from all the documents and let $(\text{AVGSIM})_k$ represent the space density in that case. If term k had been a broad, high-frequency term with a fairly even frequency distribution, it is likely that it would have appeared in most document descriptions; therefore, its removal will reduce the average document-pair similarity. This case is clearly unfavorable, because when such a high-frequency term is assigned to the documents, the average similarity will increase and the document space is compressed. On the other hand, if term k had been assigned a high weight in some documents, but not in others, its removal would be likely to increase the average similarity between documents.

The discrimination value DISCVALUE_k can now be computed for each term k as

$$\text{DISCVALUE}_k = (\text{AVGSIM})_k - \text{AVGSIM} \qquad (8)$$

Following the computation of DISCVALUE_k for all terms k, the terms can be ranked in decreasing order of the discrimination value DISCVALUE_k. A typical ranking of this type for document collections in three different subject areas appears in Table 3-3. In each case the 10 best discriminators are shown— those whose removal will compress the document space the most—as well as the 10 worst discriminators (other than the previously eliminated common function words whose discrimination values would no doubt be even poorer). It may be seen that the terms at the top of the table are highly specific, whereas the terms at the bottom are much more general. A term such as "flow" occurs in most documents in the Cranfield collection on aerodynamics, accounting for its poor performance as a document discriminator.

For experimental purposes the index terms may be placed into three rough categories according to their discrimination values:

1 The good discriminators with a positive DISCVALUE_k whose introduction for indexing purposes decreases the space density
2 The indifferent discriminators with a DISCVALUE_k close to zero whose removal or addition leaves the similarity among documents unchanged
3 The poor discriminators whose utilization renders the documents more similar, producing a negative DISCVALUE_k

Frequency distributions for three typical terms, one from each category are shown in Table 3-4. It may be seen that the negative discriminator in the rightmost column of the table exhibits a total collection frequency TOTFREQ_k of 527 and a document frequency DOCFREQ_k of 337 for a collection of 450 docu-

**Table 3-3 Best and Worst Discriminators for Three
Collections**
(Cranfield: 424 Documents in Aerodynamics; MED: 450
Documents in Medicine; *Time:* 425 Documents in World
Affairs)

Cranfield 424	MED 450	*Time* 425
	a **Best discriminators**	
1. Panel	1. Marrow	1. Buddhist
2. Flutter	2. Amyloidosis	2. Diem
3. Jet	3. Lymphostasis	3. Lao
4. Cone	4. Hepatitis	4. Arab
5. Separate	5. Hela	5. Viet
6. Shell	6. Antigen	6. Kurd
7. Yaw	7. Chromosome	7. Wilson
8. Nozzle	8. Irradiate	8. Baath
9. Transit	9. Tumor	9. Park
10. Degree	10. Virus	10. Nenni
	b **Worst discriminators**	
2642. Equate	4717. Clinic	7560. Work
2643. Theo	4718. Children	7561. Lead
2644. Bound	4719. Act	7562. Red
2645. Effect	4720. High	7563. Minister
2646. Solution	4721. Develop	7564. Nation
2647. Method	4722. Treat	7565. Party
2468. Press	4723. Increase	7566. Commune
2649. Result	4724. Result	7567. U.S.
2650. Number	4725. Cell	7568. Govern
2651. Flow	4726. Patient	7569. New

Adapted from reference 19.

ments; the term occurs once in 221 documents, twice in 75 additional documents, three times in 19 documents, four times in 15 documents, and five and six times in 3 and 4 items, respectively. It is not surprising that such a ubiquitous term operates poorly as a discriminator.

The second and third columns of Table 3-4 contain examples of an indifferent discriminator and a good discriminator, respectively. It may be seen that the indifferent discriminator term has a very low document frequency of 16 items out of 450. Its assignment leaves the document space more or less unchanged. The good discriminator in the third column has a document frequency of 61 out of 450 and a total collection frequency of 188.

The document frequency DOCFREQ$_k$, total collection frequency TOTFREQ$_k$, and average frequency of each term are shown in Table 3-5 for the 10 best discriminators and 10 worst discriminators in a collection of 852 documents in ophthalmology. In each case the rank of each term in decreasing order of the discimination value is also shown in the table.

The data of Tables 3-4 and 3-5 and related comparisons of the frequency

Table 3-4   Distribution Characteristics of a Typical Term in Each of Three Discrimination Categories
(Collection Size 450)

Number of occurrences of term k in documents	Number of documents with corresponding frequency		
	Low-frequency term zero DISCVALUE$_k$	Medium-frequency term positive DISCVALUE$_k$	High-frequency term negative DISCVALUE$_k$
1	10	26	221
2	3	13	75
3	3	8	19
4	—	4	15
5	—	2	3
6	—	2	4
7	—	—	—
8	—	2	—
9	—	—	—
10	—	—	—
11–15	—	2	—
16–20	—	2	—
21–25	—	—	—
26–30	—	—	—
30+	—	—	—
Total term frequency TOTFREQ$_k$	25	188	527
Total document frequency DOCFREQ$_k$	16	61	337

characteristics of terms with their discrimination value confirm Luhn's original notions that medium-frequency words are to be preferred for assignment as index terms. The discrimination value computation [expression (8)] provides an objective method for determining the frequency thresholds: high-frequency terms with a negative DISCVALUE$_k$ are poor and should not be used directly for indexing purposes; low-frequency terms with a zero DISCVALUE$_k$ may or may not be used—their assignment will not hurt the performance of the retrieval system but may be questioned on efficiency grounds because the storage and manipulation of large numbers of low-frequency terms tends to be expensive; the good discriminators—those with resolving power to use Luhn's terminology—have a positive DISCVALUE$_k$, and they happen to be medium-frequency terms in the collection in which they occur [21,22].

A display of the frequency distribution of good, indifferent, and poor terms in signal-value order [expression (5)] shows that the terms with the best SIGNAL$_k$ values have very low document and collection frequencies. Typical DOCFREQ$_k$ and TOTFREQ$_k$ values for those terms with good signal values are 3, 20; 6, 33; and 2, 9, respectively, showing that the terms with the best "information value" are not those best able to distinguish a substantial number of documents in a collection [18].

Table 3-5 Highest-Ranking Discriminator and Nondiscriminator Terms
(852 Abstracts in Ophthalmology)

| | Nondiscriminators | | | | Discriminators | | |
Term	Document frequency	Total frequency	Average frequency	Term	Document frequency	Total frequency	Average frequency
8672. Patient	201	408	2.03	1. Rubella	10	47	4.70
8671. At	194	292	1.51	2. Capillary	19	54	2.84
8670. Use	179	247	1.38	3. Laser	11	32	2.91
8669. Have	194	257	1.32	4. Collagen	12	40	3.33
8668. Retinal	134	275	2.05	5. Cyst	17	42	2.47
8667. Present	184	219	1.19	6. Cholinesterase	6	26	4.33
8666. Has	171	231	1.35	7. Fiber	16	50	3.13
8665. Effect	150	259	1.73	8. Cyclodialysis	4	12	3.00
8664. Result	179	234	1.31	9. Implant	18	36	2.00
8663. Found	174	228	1.31	10. Uveitis	21	45	2.14
8662. Report	141	172	1.22	11. Vessel	36	82	2.28
8661. Occular	125	194	1.55	12. Spray	2	25	12.50

The term discrimination value of expression (8) can be used to compute an importance factor, or weight, for each term in each document of a collection by combining the term frequency factor with the discrimination value. This produces a weighting expression for term k in document i analogous to expressions (2) and (6) for the inverse document frequencies and the signal values as follows:

$$\text{WEIGHT}_{ik} = \text{FREQ}_{ik} \cdot \text{DISCVALUE}_k \tag{9}$$

The insights concerning the term occurrence frequencies are incorporated into a simple automatic indexing process described in the following section.

4 A SIMPLE AUTOMATIC INDEXING PROCESS

It may be of interest briefly to describe a simple process for the automatic assignment of index terms to the documents of a collection. Such a process must start with the identification of all the individual words that constitute the documents. A problem arising in this connection is the definition of the document to be used. There are many so-called full-text retrieval systems where the full text of the documents is used for indexing purposes. This is true in specialized areas of discourse, for example, law or medicine, where the vocabulary may be specialized and the presence of a particular term, say ''tort'' in a legal document, has specific connotations [23]. However, the computer storage of the full text of documents is expensive and is rarely possible except as a by-product of automatic typesetting operations. For many practical purposes, it is sufficient to use document excerpts for analysis, such as the titles and abstracts. The available experimental evidence indicates that the use of abstracts in addition to titles brings substantial advantages in retrieval effectiveness. However, the additional utilization of the full texts of the documents appears to produce very little improvement over titles and abstracts alone in most subject areas [24].

Following the identification of the words occurring in the document texts, or abstracts, the high-frequency function words need to be eliminated. These comprise 40 to 50 percent of the text words, and as suggested earlier, these words are poor discriminators and cannot possibly be used by themselves to identify document content. In English, about 250 common words are involved, and it is easy to include them in a dictionary, sometimes called a negative dictionary, or *stop list*. An excerpt from a typical stop list is shown in Table 3-6.

The next step, following removal of stop words, is the identification of ''good'' index terms and their assignment to the documents of a collection. It is useful first to remove word suffixes (and possibly also prefixes), thereby reducing the original words to word stem form. This reduces a variety of different forms such as analysis, analyzing, analyzer, analyzed, and analysing to a common word stem ''analy.'' The word stem ''analy'' will have a higher frequency of occurrence in the document texts than any of the variant forms. The generation of word stems, and subsequent identification of common stems, is rela-

Table 3-6   Excerpt from Typical Stop List

A	AMONGST	BECOMES
ABOUT	AN	BECOMING
ACROSS	AND	BEEN
AFTER	ANOTHER	BEFORE
AFTERWARDS	ANY	BEFOREHAND
AGAIN	ANYHOW	BEHIND
AGAINST	ANYONE	BEING
ALL	ANYTHING	BELOW
ALMOST	ANYWHERE	BESIDE
ALONE	ARE	BESIDES
ALONG	AROUND	BETWEEN
ALREADY	AS	BEYOND
ALSO	AT	BOTH
ALTHOUGH	BE	BUT
ALWAYS	BECAME	BY
AMONG	BECAUSE	CAN
	BECOME	

Excerpted from reference 25.

tively easy to do for many languages (including English) and serves as a recall-enhancing device. When the stems are used as index terms, a greater number of potentially relevant items can be identified than when one of the original full text words is in use.

Several well-known algorithms exist for the removal of word endings, generally based on the use of a list of suffixes followed by the removal of the longest suffix matching any entry on the suffix list [26,27]. An excerpt from a typical suffix list is shown in Table 3-7. In using a suffix removal algorithm it is important to handle various classes of exceptional cases. The following list identifies problems in English:

1   It is desirable to remove the suffix "ability" from computability, or the suffix "ing" from singing; however, the same suffixes should not be removed from the words ability and sing, respectively; problems such as these are normally solved by specifying a minimum stem length that must remain following the suffix removal.

2   Several suffixes may be attached to a single stem; thus effectiveness may be shortened to effective by the removal of "ness," which can in turn be shortened to effect by removal of "ive"; multiple suffixes can be handled either by applying the suffix removal process recursively several times or else by including in the suffix dictionary all multiple suffix entries, and removing longer suffixes in preference to the shorter ones.

3   Various examples of morphological transformations exist in English which may alter the stem of many suffixed words; for example, the word absorb is transformed into absorption when the suffix "tion" is added; similarly hop becomes hopping, relief becomes relieving, and so on. Transformational rules can be set up in order to recode various automatically generated stems fol-

Table 3-7 Exerpt from Typical Suffix List

ABILITIES	ACIDOUS	AIC
ABILITY	ACIDOUSLY	AICAL
ABLE	ACIES	AICALLY
ABLED	ACIOUSNESS	AICALS
ABLEDLY	ACIOUSNESSES	AICISM
ABLENESS	ACITIES	AICISMS
ABLER	ACITY	AICS
ABLES	ACY	AL
ABLING	AE	ALISATION
ABLINGFUL	AGE	ALISATIONAL
ABLINGLY	AGED	ALISATIONALLY
ABLY	AGER	ALISE
ACEOUS	AGES	ALISED
ACEOUSLY	AGING	ALISEDLY
ACEOUSNESS	AGINGFUL	ALISER
ACEOUSNESSES	AGINGLY	

Excerpted from reference 25.

lowing suffix removal. A typical rule might state ''remove one of double occurrences of b, d, g, l, m, n, p, r, s, t from the end of a generated stem.''

4   Finally, a number of additional exceptions which depend on the particular word context must be taken care of, using various context-sensitive rules. For example, a rule for the suffix ''allic'' specifies a minimum stem length of three and prevents suffix removal after ''met'' or ''ryst''; another rule applicable to the suffix ''yl'' permits removal only after ''n'' or ''r'' [27].

In summary, it is not difficult to implement a suffix removal algorithm producing usable word stems for the vast majority of existing English word forms. A stored suffix list must be used together with a few contextual rules applicable to certain suffixes. A list of transformations to recode some of the generated stems is also necessary, or a stored full word dictionary could be used for that purpose.

After the word stems are generated, it becomes necessary to recognize equivalent stems occurring in the texts and to choose those stems to be used as index terms. The frequency-based techniques can be used to determine the potential usefulness of the remaining word stems. A high standard of performance at modest cost is obtainable by using the inverse document frequency function $1/DOCFREQ_k$ to obtain a term importance factor. Another possibility consists in using the discrimination $DISCVALUE_k$ or the $SIGNAL_k$. The latter, however, emphasizes term concentration in only a few documents of a collection and should be used only in order to emphasize precision at the expense of recall.

The terms (word stems) with sufficiently high term value factors can be assigned to the documents of the collection either with or without a term weight. When the indexing mode is *binary*, a term that occurs in a document is assigned an implicit weight of 1, no matter what its actual frequency of occur-

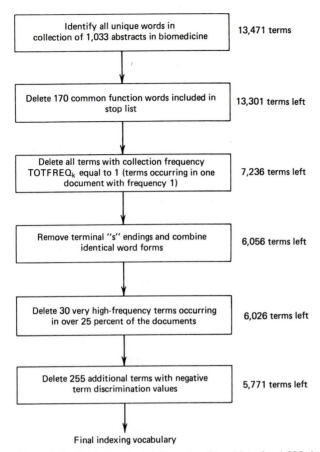

Identify all unique words in collection of 1,033 abstracts in biomedicine	13,471 terms
Delete 170 common function words included in stop list	13,301 terms left
Delete all terms with collection frequency TOTFREQ$_k$ equal to 1 (terms occurring in one document with frequency 1)	7,236 terms left
Remove terminal "s" endings and combine identical word forms	6,056 terms left
Delete 30 very high-frequency terms occurring in over 25 percent of the documents	6,026 terms left
Delete 255 additional terms with negative term discrimination values	5,771 terms left

Final indexing vocabulary

Figure 3-3 Typical term deletion algorithm (data for 1,033 documents in medicine).

rence. In a *weighted indexing* system, a term weight may be used to reflect term importance by using the weighting functions [expressions (2), (6), or (9)] previously described. This produces for each document D_i a *document vector*

$$D_i = \langle d_{i1}, d_{i2}, \ldots, d_{it} \rangle \tag{10}$$

where each d_{ij} is the weight assigned to the jth identifier for document D_i. For example, if there are three terms ALPHA, BETA, and GAMMA, respectively, then

$$D_1 = \langle 2, 4, 0 \rangle$$

means that document number 1 is identified by the term ALPHA with a weight of 2, BETA with a weight of 4, and GAMMA with a weight of 0. The vector length t corresponds to the number of distinct terms assigned to the whole collection, and weights of 0 are assumed for terms not assigned to a given document vector.

It remains to determine what to do with terms whose importance factors are not high enough to make it reasonable to assign them to the documents. In principle such terms can simply be deleted from the identifying vocabulary. A prototype indexing system based on various term deletion methods is reproduced in simplified form in the flowchart of Fig. 3-3. The index term data of Fig. 3-3 are based on the processing of 1,033 document abstracts in medicine. A simplified stemming method was used in which the only recognized suffix is a terminal ''s.'' The indexing vocabulary eventually is reduced to 5,771 stems from the original 13,471 words.

Term deletion methods must be used with caution because the removal of some broad high-frequency terms may produce unwanted recall losses, whereas deletion of certain low-frequency terms reduces indexing exhaustivity and may result in reduced retrieval recall and precision. Instead of deleting the poor discriminators, it may be preferable to improve such terms by turning them into terms with better discrimination properties. This can be done in various ways by using context and term associations, as explained in the next section.

5 AUTOMATIC TERM ASSOCIATION AND USE OF CONTEXT

A Thesaurus Rules

It was seen earlier that some words or word stems extracted from document texts may not function effectively as index terms. This is the case notable for very high-frequency terms that occur in a large proportion of the documents of a collection, and for very low-frequency words which occur very rarely. The question is whether such terms can be transformed into different types of entities that prove more discriminating and better able to reflect document content. The natural language provides a variety of devices for changing the specificity and scope of individual terms: for example, the phrase ''term specificity'' has a narrower, more specific interpretation than either ''term'' or ''specificity'' alone; similarly, the term ''computer'' has a broader meaning than ''minicomputer.''

In the preceding discussion, several tools have been described that may be useful for controlling or changing the scope of individual words or terms. Thus, a variety of dictionaries may be available in conventional indexing situations which allow the manual indexer to choose broader or narrower or related terms in addition to or instead of an initially available dictionary entry. A term broadening step was also included in the basic term extraction methods examined in the preceding section in the form of a word stemming process. The stemming process replaces a full text word by a word stem with a broader interpretation.

The basic idea in improving the usefulness of index terms with questionable discrimination properties then consists in using *associations* between terms in the hope of refining or broadening the interpretation of these terms. Many kinds of term associations can profitably be incorporated into an automatic indexing system. The first and most obvious one consists in imitating the manual indexing process by using a *term thesaurus*.

A thesaurus provides a grouping, or classification, of the terms used in a given topic area into categories known as thesaurus classes. As in the manual indexing case, thesauruses can be used for language normalization purposes in order to replace an uncontrolled vocabulary by the controlled thesaurus category identifiers. A thesaurus may broaden the vocabulary terms by addition of thesaurus class identifiers to the normal term lists, thereby enhancing the recall performance in retrieval. Alternatively the thesaurus class identifiers can replace the original term entries in the hope of improving recall and providing vocabulary normalization. When hierarchical relationships are supplied for the entries in a thesaurus in the form of "broader" or "narrower" terms, the indexing vocabulary can be "expanded" in various directions by adding these broader or narrower terms, or certain related terms, as the case may be.

An excerpt of a thesaurus used in an automatic indexing environment for documents in engineering is shown in Table 3-8. The thesaurus class identifiers are represented by identifying "concept numbers" designating the various term classes. Thus, when a document contains the term "superconductivity" or (stem "superconduct"), that term may be replaced by class identifier 415. The same operation could be used for another document, or for a user query, containing the term "cryogenic." Should the document contain "superconductivity" while the query term is "cryogenic," a term match would result through the thesaurus transformation, but not using the original word stems.

Thesauruses may be constructed manually, semiautomatically, and fully automatically. No matter what process is used, two separate problems arise at once:

1 A decision must be made about what terms should be included in the thesaurus.
2 The terms specified for inclusion must be suitably grouped.

To decide what to include, the various term value models described earlier can be used. The discrimination value model specifies, for example, that the most important terms are those with medium document frequency, followed by those with low document frequencies and near zero discrimination values. Since the main purpose of a term classification is the improvement of the recall performance, one concludes that a thesaurus should certainly include a grouping of the low-frequency terms into classes of higher frequency. In addition, a grouping of the medium-frequency good discriminators might also be useful for some purposes, particularly when a high recall performance is wanted. On the other hand, the high-frequency low discriminators might be eliminated altogether.

The following thesaurus construction principles derived in part from the

Table 3-8 Typical Thesaurus Excerpt

408	DISLOCATION	413	CAPACITANCE
	JUNCTION		IMPEDANCE-MATCHING
	MINORITY-CARRIER		IMPEDANCE
	N-P-N		INDUCTANCE
	P-N-P		MUTUAL-IMPEDANCE
	POINT-CONTACT		MUTUAL-INDUCTANCE
	RECOMBINE		MUTUAL
	TRANSITION		NEGATIVE-RESISTANCE
	UNIJUNCTION		POSITIVE-GAP
			REACTANCE
409	BLAST-COOLED		RESIST
	HEAT-FLOW		SELF-IMPEDANCE
	HEAT-TRANSFER		SELF-INDUCTANCE
			SELF
410	ANNEAL		
	STRAIN	414	ANTENNA
			KLYSTRON
411	COERCIVE		PULSES-PER-BEAM
	DEMAGNETIZE		RECEIVER
	FLUX-LEAKAGE		SIGNAL-TO-RECEIVER
	HYSTERESIS		TRANSMITTER
	INDUCT		WAVEGUIDE
	INSENSITIVE		
	MAGNETORESISTANCE	415	CRYOGENIC
	SQUARE-LOOP		CRYOTRON
	THRESHOLD		PERSISTENT-CURRENT
			SUPERCONDUCT
412	LONGITUDINAL		SUPER-CONDUCT
	TRANSVERSE		
		416	RELAY

earlier indexing models and in part from previously obtained experimental evidence can be enunciated [28]:

1 The thesaurus should include only those terms likely to be of interest for content identification in a subject area (for example, a term such as ''hand'' might be used in a thesaurus dealing with biology, but it should not be included if its frequency of occurrence is due largely to expressions such as ''on the other hand'').

2 Ambiguous terms should be coded only for those senses likely to be important in the document collection (at least two thesaurus categories should thus be used for a term such as ''field,'' corresponding on the one hand to the notion of subject area and on the other hand to its technical sense in algebra; no provision need be made to cover the notions of ''a patch of land'' if the thesaurus deals with the mathematical sciences or related technical fields).

3 In order to obtain good matching characteristics between query and document terms, each thesaurus class should include terms of roughly equal frequency; furthermore, the total frequency of occurrence should be as close to equal for each class as possible, thus ensuring that the probability of producing a match between queries and documents is approximately equal for all thesaurus classes. (If these frequency characteristics are grossly violated—for example, if a high-frequency term such as "computer" is entered into the same class as a more specific term such as "minicomputer"—queries about specific topics will produce general responses, thereby depressing the precision of the search.)

4 Whenever possible, terms with negative discrimination values should be eliminated; even if the size restrictions that control the thesaurus construction do not immediately lead to the elimination of all high-frequency nondiscriminators, the latter are best relegated to thesaurus classes of their own (their classification together with lower-frequency terms would produce low-precision output).

Concerning now the actual thesaurus construction method, a manual thesaurus generation process is an art rather than a science. In recent years, a number of automatic aids have considerably simplified the thesaurus construction task. Thus, given a collection of documents, it is now easy to automatically produce concordances exhibiting the occurrences of all terms in the context in which they occur, arranged in alphabetical order for convenient access. Thus all occurrences of the term "information" would be collected under the letter I, together with contextual information for each occurrence of the term. This makes it possible to determine the placement of each term within a thesaurus class arrangement by collecting in a common class various terms occurring in a given document set in the same context.

An automatically constructed alphabetical arrangement of terms derived from a given document set can in fact function as a kind of thesaurus, and has been widely used in practice to obtain access to document collections. Normally, the terms included in such a listing are the words occurring in the titles of documents. The resulting products are known as keyword-in-context (KWIC) indexes. Alternatively, related term arrangements known as KWAC and KWOC (keyword and context, keyword out of context) are also obtainable. An example of KWIC and KWAC arrangements is shown in Table 3-9. The entries shown in the table are produced by a document (number 3,313) entitled "User Preference in Published Indexes." This title generates four entries: one under I for the term "indexes," two under P for "preference" and "published," and finally one under U for "user."

When aids such as KWIC indexes are used judiciously, and the previously mentioned thesaurus construction principles are applied, the task of building the term classification is simplified. The main intellectual decisions for the actual term grouping process are, however, reached manually.

*B Automatic Thesaurus Construction

A variety of fully automatic thesaurus construction methods are available, based on the use of a set of document vectors of the type shown in expression (10). A document collection is then representable by a matrix such as that in Table 3-10. It was seen earlier that a similarity function SIMILAR(D_i,D_j) re-

Table 3-9   KWIC and KWAC Entries Produced by Document on "User Preference in Published Indexes"

KWIC		
RENCE IN PUBLISHED	INDEXES/ USER PREFE	3,313
HED INDEXES/ USER	PREFERENCE IN PUBLIS	3,313
USER PREFERENCE IN	PUBLISHED INDEXES/	3,313
UBLISHED INDEXES/	USER PREFERENCE IN P	3,313

KWAC	
INDEXES	
USER PREFERENCE IN PUBLISHED INDEXES	3,313
PREFERENCE	
USER PREFERENCE IN PUBLISHED INDEXES	3,313
PUBLISHED	
USER PREFERENCE IN PUBLISHED INDEXES	3,313
USER	
USER PREFERENCE IN PUBLISHED INDEXES	3,313

Adapted from reference 3.

flecting index term similarities can be computed for each document pair (D_i, D_j) by comparing pairs of rows of the document matrix. While the rows of the matrix represent the individual document vectors, the columns identify the term assignments to the documents. That is, a column, j, of the document vector matrix reflects the assignment of $TERM_j$ to the documents of the collection. The vector comparison process previously used to compute the density of the document space [see expression (7)] can also be used to obtain a similarity measure between pairs of columns $SIMILAR(TERM_k, TERM_h)$, reflecting the similarities between $TERM_k$ and $TERM_h$. Given term vectors of the form $TERM_k = (t_{1k}, t_{2k}, \ldots, t_{nk})$, where t_{ik} indicates the weight or value of $TERM_k$ in document i and assuming n documents in the collection, a typical similarity measure may then be defined as

$$SIMILAR(TERM_k, TERM_h) = \sum_{i=1}^{n} t_{ik} \, t_{ih} \qquad (11)$$

Table 3-10   Matrix of Document Vectors

	T_1	T_2	$\cdots$	T_t
D_1	d_{11}	d_{12}	$\cdots$	d_{1t}
D_2	d_{21}	d_{22}	$\cdots$	d_{2t}
$\vdots$	$\vdots$			$\vdots$
D_n	d_{n1}	d_{n2}	$\cdots$	d_{nt}

or, using a normalization factor to limit the computed results to values between 0 and 1,

$$\mathrm{SIMILAR(TERM_k,TERM_h)} = \frac{\sum_{i=1}^{n} t_{ik}\, t_{ih}}{\sum_{i=1}^{n} (t_{ik})^2 + \sum_{i=1}^{n} (t_{ih})^2 - \sum_{i=1}^{n} t_{ik}\, t_{ih}} \qquad (12)$$

When all pairs of distinct columns of the matrix of Table 3-10 are compared with each other, a *term-term association* matrix T is constructed in which the element located in row k and column h equals $\mathrm{SIMILAR(TERM_k,TERM_h)}$. A sample term-term association matrix is shown in Table 3-11.

A variety of *automatic classification* or clustering methods can now be used to construct classes of similar terms (equivalent to thesaurus classes) by collecting in a common class all terms whose similarity coefficients SIMILAR are sufficiently large [29,30]. Automatic clustering methods are covered in detail in Chapter 6. Many different methodologies are available. For example, the *single-link* process collects in a single class all items $\mathrm{TERM_k}$ such that the similarity between $\mathrm{TERM_k}$ and at least one other member of the same class exceeds some threshold. In the *clique* process the similarity between $\mathrm{TERM_k}$ and *all* other members of the same class must exceed the stipulated threshold.

In the single-link or clique methods, the term classes are constructed from the beginning starting from the term assignments to the documents of a collection. A number of classification methods assume the prior existence of term classes, and proceed by refining the initial state of the classification. Various possibilities exist for defining such an initial term grouping:

1 A given term class may be defined as the set of terms assigned to a particular document, or document set; this generates a number of initial term classes equal to the number of documents used as starting sets.

2 A term class might also be defined as the terms contained in the set of relevant documents retrieved in response to certain user queries; here the number of initial term classes is equal to the number of starting user queries for which relevance information is available.

For each existing class, a centroid $\mathrm{TERM\text{-}CENTROID} = \langle \bar{t}_1, \bar{t}_2, \ldots, \bar{t}_m \rangle$ can then be defined as the average vector for the term vectors of that class.

Table 3-11   Term-Term Similarity Matrix

	T_1	T_2	$\cdots$	T_t
T_1	$s(T_1,T_1)$	$s(T_1,T_2)$	$\cdots$	$s(T_1,T_t)$
T_2	$s(T_2,T_1)$	$s(T_2,T_2)$	$\cdots$	$s(T_2,T_t)$
$\vdots$	$\vdots$	$\vdots$		$\vdots$
T_t	$s(T_t,T_1)$	$s(T_t,T_2)$	$\cdots$	$s(T_t,T_t)$

That is, term $\bar{t}_k$ of the centroid is defined as the average value of all the values of TERM$_k$ in the individual documents of the class, or $\bar{t}_k = \dfrac{1}{m} \sum\limits_{i=1}^{m} t_{ik}$ for a class which has m term vectors. The term class refinement now consists in computing the similarity between each term vector TERM$_k$ and each class centroid TERM-CENTROID for all existing classes. Assuming t term vectors and p classes, the process requires the generation of t × p similarity coefficients SIMILAR(TERM$_k$,TERM-CENTROID$_h$) for k ranging from 1 to t, and h ranging from 1 to p. Each term vector is now entered into the class for which the similarity to the TERM-CENTROID is largest. If this involves a switch of a given term vector from one class to another, the centroids of those classes must be recomputed. This process can be pursued until no further class changes occur for the vectors, or until the number of class changes which occur after processing all the term vectors is sufficiently small [31].

Methods also exist for constructing a hierarchical arrangement of term classes, for example, by first building small classes consisting of a few terms exhibiting substantial pairwise similarities, and then expanding these initial classes into large groups. The new term groups subsume the initial classes by adding new terms whose similarity with the other terms already included in the class is successively weaker. Alternatively, large heterogeneous classes can be broken down into small more homogeneous entities by removing terms that have relatively weak similarities with the remainder.

Since the number of terms in a system is normally much larger than the number of thesaurus classes, thesaurus construction methods such as the single-link and clique methods which depend on the availability of all pairwise term similarities may be expensive to implement. Methods based on initial cluster assignments of the terms require less computer time. The available evidence indicates that thesauruses and automatically constructed term associations are quite effective in improving the recall performance provided the items entered into common classes exhibit high similarities. That is, SIMILAR(TERM$_k$,TERM$_h$) should be large if TERM$_k$ and TERM$_h$ are entered into a common class. The high-frequency terms must be excluded from the thesaurus.

C Thesaurus Use

A thesaurus can be used to broaden the existing indexing vocabulary by replacing the initial terms with the corresponding thesaurus class identifiers, or by adding the thesaurus class identifiers to the original terms. A simple term expansion process which requires only the availability of term associations, but not of formal thesaurus classes, is illustrated in the example of Fig. 3-4. Assuming one already has term similarity information such as that provided by a term-term similarity matrix (see Table 3-11), a threshold K is chosen. This is used to transform the original term-term matrix into a binary form by replacing each

$$
\begin{array}{c c c c c c}
 & A & B & C & D & E \\
A & 1 & 1 & 0 & 0 & 0 \\
B & 1 & 1 & 0 & 1 & 0 \\
C & 0 & 0 & 1 & 0 & 1 \\
D & 0 & 1 & 0 & 1 & 1 \\
E & 0 & 0 & 1 & 1 & 1
\end{array}
$$

(a)

Original term	Associated terms
A	B
B	A, D
C	E
D	B, E
E	C, D

(b)

$$
q = \begin{pmatrix} A = 4 \\ B = 2 \\ C = 1 \\ D = 1 \\ E = 0 \end{pmatrix}
\begin{array}{l} \text{add } B = 2 \\ \text{add } A = 1, D = 1 \\ \text{add } E = \frac{1}{2} \\ \text{add } B = \frac{1}{2}, E = \frac{1}{2} \\ \text{add nothing} \end{array}
\qquad q' = \begin{pmatrix} A = 5 \\ B = 4\frac{1}{2} \\ C = 1 \\ D = 2 \\ E = 1 \end{pmatrix}
$$

(c)

Figure 3-4 Sample process for utilization of term associations. (a) Sample binary term-term similarity matrix for five terms (A through E). (b) Corresponding term associations. (c) Alternative associative indexing strategy. (Add associated terms with weight equal to one-half the original.)

matrix element by 1 whenever the value in the term similarity matrix is greater or equal to K and by 0 when the value is less than K.

A sample binary term-term similarity matrix for five terms, labeled A through E, is shown in Fig. 3-4a. The corresponding term association information is detailed in Fig. 3-4b. Given a particular term vector, such as that labeled q in Fig. 3-4c, it is now possible to add the information about the associated terms with a weighting factor (arbitrarily selected here as one-half of the original weight in the illustration of Fig. 3-4c). It may be noted that in the example one new term has been added to the original vector (E) since its weight is now greater than 0. The weight of several other already existing terms (A, B, and D) has also been altered [32–34].

Term associations and thesaurus classes can be displayed in a variety of formats to help the information system users in formulating the search requests and familiarizing themselves with the vocabulary. One attractive format is based on a graphlike structure where the nodes represent the individual terms and different kinds of lines denote different strengths of association [different magnitudes of the similarity coefficient $SIMILAR(TERM_k, TERM_h)$] between the terms. An excerpt from such a term association map is shown in Fig. 3-5 [35].

One major disadvantage inherent in the use of any thesaurus is the necessity to maintain it. Two different maintenance problems arise. First, the thesaurus may require rebuilding as a result of user interaction with the system. For instance, new queries may be submitted for which the current thesaurus is inadequate, or new user populations and interests may appear which in turn require new vocabulary terms. Second, a thesaurus maintenance system may be needed to accommodate collection growth. When new documents are added to a collection, several updating strategies are possible:

1 The original thesaurus might be left unchanged and used for the expanded collection.

2 New terms derived from the added items might be placed into existing thesaurus categories only.

3 New terms might be placed into separate new classes.

4 The thesaurus might be completely restructured by generating a term classification from the updated vocabulary.

The fourth alternative may be very expensive. Hence it is necessary to consider one of the other possibilities. The available evidence indicates that some performance loss is produced when a thesaurus constructed for an original document environment is later used for an updated collection [36]. Unfortu-

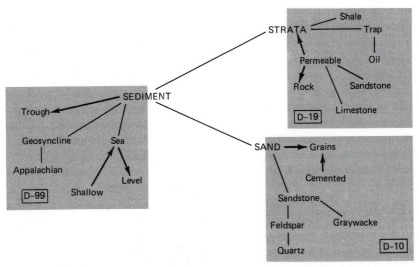

Figure 3-5 Term association map. (Different types of connecting lines denote different strengths of associations between terms). (*Adapted from reference 35.*)

nately, no experimental data are available leading to a clear-cut choice between the second and third alternatives.

Before leaving the subject of automatically generated term associations, it should be mentioned that recall-enhancing expansions of the vocabulary can be generated by using identifiers that are not standard index terms. Specifically, documents exhibiting similarities in bibliographic citation patterns—either references included in the reference lists attached to the documents or citations to the various documents made by other documents—may also reveal similarities in subject content [37,38]. This finding suggests that improved retrieval may be obtained by adding this citation information to documents and query vectors in addition to the normal subject identifiers. Alternatively, the standard subject terms could be replaced by the citation patterns.

One possibility is to lengthen the document vectors by including bibliographic reference indicators to documents outside the collection. Search requests (query vectors) can then be similarly lengthened by adding identifiers of relevant documents designated by the users. One system of that kind is sketched out in Fig. 3-6. The available experimental evidence indicates that substantially better retrieval results are obtainable with the augmented vectors including citations than with standard vectors consisting of subject indicators only. To utilize such a system, it is however necessary to store substantial citation information for the collection, and to obtain information regarding the relevance of documents from the users of the system. The use of bibliographic citations is examined in more detail in Chapter 6.

D Construction of Term Phrases

The recall of a search may be improved by broadening the terms used in query and document specifications and by adding new associated terms. On the other

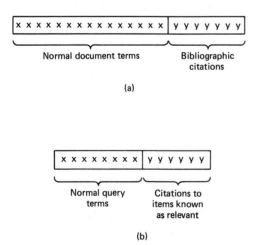

Figure 3-6 Expanded document and query vectors. (a) Expanded document vector. (Each x represents a standard index term, each y a bibliographic reference.) (b) Expanded query vector.

hand, the precision may be improved by using specific terms or by using terms in combination with each other. Terms of high specificity can be identified simply by their concentration in a few documents of a collection, as described earlier. To generate combinations of terms (phrases) one uses two or more terms, say $TERM_k$ and $TERM_h$, with particular occurrence properties, and replaces them by a phrase ($PHRASE_{kh}$). For example, "computer" and "program" may be replaced by "computer program" or "computer programming." One expects the frequency of occurrence of $PHRASE_{kh}$ in the document collection to be smaller than that of $TERM_k$ or $TERM_h$; furthermore, the phrase term will have a more specific interpretation than the individual phrase components.

Various phrase-generation methods are possible, including the use of syntactic language analysis. These methods are used to identify phrases whose components exhibit acceptable syntactic relationships. However, consider first a phrase-generation process based on frequency considerations like those used earlier to generate individual terms. The best phrases (word pairs, triples, etc.) may include terms whose joint frequency of occurrence in the collection is larger than expected, given the frequencies of the individual terms. If PAIR-$FREQ_{kh}$ is the total pair frequency in the collection of $TERM_k$ and $TERM_h$, and $TOTFREQ_k$ and $TOTFREQ_h$ represent the collection frequencies of the individual terms, then the *cohesion* of the term pair may be defined as

$$COHESION_{kh} = SIZE\text{-}FACTOR \cdot \frac{PAIR\text{-}FREQ_{kh}}{TOTFREQ_k \cdot TOTFREQ_h} \qquad (13)$$

SIZE-FACTOR represents a factor related to the size of the indexing vocabulary. Phrases can now be chosen as term pairs with a sufficiently high cohesion factor, subject to certain restrictions.

To utilize the preceding formula, it is necessary to choose an appropriate context for determining when two or more terms co-occur. In principle, it is possible to choose a wide context by declaring that two terms co-occur whenever they are included in a common document. Better (higher-precision) results may be obtainable by restricting the context to terms occurring in the same sentences of particular documents, or in the same sentences but with at most k words occurring between components, or in the same sentences in adjacent word positions, or finally in the same sentences in adjacent word positions and in the correct word order. When the context used to define a phrase is restricted, the phrase detection process becomes more costly because tests must be made to ensure that the various restrictions are obeyed, and this in turn implies that word location information must be stored specifying the positions of the individual words in the sentences. Furthermore, when restrictions are imposed on the phrase formation process, the number of phrases generated for a given item will of course decrease.

In addition to using context for phrase definition purposes, it may also be important to invoke frequency restrictions on one or more of the components of each phrase. As has been stated earlier, the phrase formation process is designed to create specific content identifiers to enhance precision. When rare terms that are already specific in the documents are combined into phrases, the resulting phrase terms may turn out to be overspecific and the retrieval results may deteriorate. Therefore, the phrase formation process should be restricted to include only relatively broad, high-frequency components.

In summary, a reasonable phrase formation method based on statistical word occurrence properties would define a phrase from word pairs with sufficiently high cohesion factors. The phrase components must occur in the same sentences of the document, and at least one component in each phrase should have a document frequency exceeding a stated threshold.

Statistical procedures for the generation of phrase identifiers are often assumed to be unreliable because they lead to the identification of statistically meaningful but syntactically incorrect phrases. Examples show that the statistical methodology leads to unfortunate results, such as, for example, the confusion of "blind Venetian" and "Venetian blind." This particular objection may however not be serious, since among other things these phrases are unlikely to occur in the same documents. Nevertheless, it is important to determine whether more sophisticated linguistic tools might be used to control the automatic indexing process.

The approaches using syntactic and/or semantic analysis features have not met with much success. This is largely because of the technical inadequacy and the excessive cost of the linguistic procedures. However, some advances have taken place in these areas which are mentioned briefly in the next section of this chapter and are covered in more detail in Chapter 7.

It is possible now to propose an automatic indexing process based on simple, well-understood procedures, capable of producing high-performance retrieval results. The word stems occurring in document titles and abstracts are isolated and term weights are computed using either inverse document frequencies [expression (2)] or term discrimination values [expression (9)]. Three classes of terms are then identified. Those in the middle-frequency ranges with positive discrimination values, or frequency characteristics, are used as index terms directly without further transformation. The broad high-frequency terms with negative discrimination values and excessive document frequencies are either discarded or incorporated into phrases with lower-frequency characteristics. Finally the narrow low-frequency terms with discrimination values close to zero are broadened by inclusion into thesaurus categories. The thesaurus class identifiers are then used as index terms for content representation [22,32].

The process is represented schematically in Fig. 3-7 where a document frequency axis is used to arrange the terms into three classes. The terms in the center are used unchanged; the broad terms are subjected to the phrase-formation process, represented by a right-to-left transformation in Fig. 3-7; the narrow, specific terms are incorporated into term thesaurus classes and are represented by the corresponding left-to-right transformation of Fig. 3-7.

The automatic process will produce a large number of content identifiers for each item—typically a hundred terms or more may be automatically as-

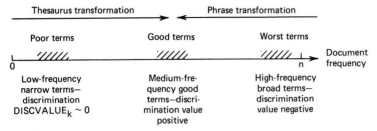

Figure 3-7 Term characterization in frequency spectrum.

signed compared with the half dozen terms used in a manual system. This fact explains in part the high order of performance of automatic indexing systems. Some laboratory evaluation data for automatic indexing strategies are presented in the last section of this chapter.

E Automatic Sentence Extraction

Text processing methods based on a determination of term or sentence importance have been used not only for indexing but also for automatic abstracting purposes. Ideally, given a document represented as natural language text, one would like to construct a coherent, well-written abstract that informs the readers of the contents of the original, or at least indicates whether the full version may be of interest to the reader. In fact, most procedures carry out an extraction process in which the abstract is defined simply as a small set of sentences pulled from the original, which are deemed to be important for purposes of content representation.

The extracting methods used over the years all start with a calculation of word and sentence significance, similar in spirit to the computation of the term weights in automatic indexing [12,39,40]. Criteria for the selection of important terms may be *positional*, involving, the place in the document where a particular term is located (for example, in the summary, title, etc.); they may be *semantic*, involving for example the relationship of this word or sentence to certain other words; or they may be *pragmatic*, such as a system which would consider proper names as highly significant. Furthermore, *statistical weights* based on term frequency or term distribution characteristics may be used in addition to the above criteria.

Given an indication of term significance, it is possible to define the importance of a phrase as a function of the weight of the individual terms and of the distance between the significant phrase components (the number of words between them). Thus if two terms have weights $WEIGHT_i$ and $WEIGHT_j$, respectively, a phrase developed by combining the two terms might be assigned a weight equal to

$$PHRASE\text{-}WEIGHT = \frac{1}{2^{DISTANCE}} (WEIGHT_i \cdot WEIGHT_j) \qquad (14)$$

where DISTANCE equals the number of intervening words. By extension, a significant sentence may be one which contains a large number of significant word groups. A flowchart for a typical sentence extracting process is shown in Fig. 3-8.

Because pure frequency characteristics are not likely to be reliable for either indexing or extracting, a variety of additional criteria have been used experimentally in an effort to obtain more satisfactory extracts. In particular, the word and sentence contexts can be taken into account in determining the *contextual inference* and *syntactic coherence* criteria [41]. Contextual inference means that the context within which a given word or phrase is placed in a document is used in addition to other criteria in an effort to decide on sentence se-

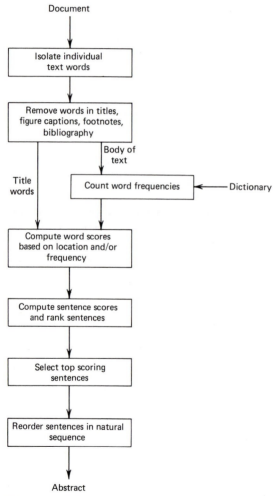

Figure 3-8   Typical sentence extracting system. (*Adapted from reference 39.*)

lection or rejection. Contextual inferences may be based on *sentence or word location* or on the presence of so-called *cue words*. Thus, sentences occurring under certain headings may be particularly important; the same may be true of sentences occurring very early or very late in the paragraph structure. Similarly sentences ending with a question mark are normally rejected, as are certain sentence portions occurring between pairs of commas.

The cue method is based on the presence of positive or negative indicators of sentence value. Thus, the presence of phrases such as "our work," "this paper," and "the present research" is assumed to introduce a statement that should be included in an abstract. Contrariwise, opinions and references to figures or tables that might be identified by "obvious," "believe," "fig. 1," etc., lead to sentence rejection. To operate effectively, the cue method depends on the availability of a dictionary containing the cue words together with indications of their semantic and/or syntactic value. Such a cue word dictionary may be particularly valuable for sentence rejection, as opposed to selection, because rejection can often be based on the presence of a small number of frequently occurring words, whereas selection may depend on longer lists of desirable words.

No matter how sophisticated the extraction process, a set of extracted sentences is not likely to constitute a coherent whole. Even if the extract in fact consists of appropriate topic sentences, the flow of ideas from one sentence to the next is likely to be interrupted because the discourse and reasoning leading to, or following from, the selected sentences is probably absent.

Coherence criteria based on syntactic or semantic considerations can be used to mitigate to some extent the shortcomings inherent in an automatic extracting process. Thus words or phrases indicating intersentence reference can be included in the cue dictionary ("these," "they," "it," "above," "presented earlier," "stated above," etc.), and their presence in a given extract can be used as a clue for inclusion in the abstract of the earlier sentences being referred to. Similarly, if the same important terms occur in adjacent sentences, a presumption exists that the sentences are related, and both should probably be included or excluded [41].

No matter what is done, a stylistically beautiful abstract is not likely to be created automatically because the linguistic difficulties are simply too severe for an effective automatic treatment. For example, the clarification of ambiguous antecedents such as those of certain pronouns is notoriously difficult. Some of the linguistic problems are further discussed in the next section together with other theoretical questions.

The overall conclusion is that automatic abstracting is less developed than automatic indexing and less likely to be used on a production basis in the near future. Abstracts must be placed in a readable natural language context and must obey the normal stylistic constraints. Sets of index terms, on the other hand, are not burdened by stylistic rules. Readable extracts are obtainable without excessive difficulties, but perfection cannot be expected within the foreseeable future.

6 SOME THEORETICAL APPROACHES

*A The Use of Linguistic Methods

It has been mentioned that the absence of syntactic recognition features may cause problems in the construction of indexing phrases capable of reflecting correctly document or query content. Two phrase construction problems, in particular, may be solved by using linguistic tools: first, the coordination of terms in accordance with the available context, and second, the assignment of roles to the phrase components. Given an indexing description such as "hardness, density, titanium, water," it is not clear a priori which qualification (hardness or density) applies to which material (titanium or water); and in "blind, Venetian," blind could presumably function as a qualifying adjective, or alternatively as the governing noun.

The approaches using linguistic methods in information retrieval are really of two kinds: on the one hand, it is possible to use simple methodologies with limited aims such as removing the ambiguity from some noun phrase identifiers; on the other hand, more complex linguistic analysis systems can be utilized but the context in which these systems operate must be limited. In the present discussion, it is possible only to give a very brief introduction; more details are included in Chapter 7 of this volume. A variety of other sources exist describing the use of linguistic methods in retrieval [42–44].

Consider the use of simple syntactic aids for the construction of indexing phrases. Normally, a *context-free phrase structure grammar* is used to obtain for each document, or query sentence, a *parse tree* which shows the syntactic structure of the sentence. A context-free grammar decomposes a sentence into nested and juxtaposed sentence portions, as in the example of Fig. 3-9, where "the man" and "the ball" are identified as noun phrases and "hit the ball" as a verb phrase. Simple phrase structure grammars can be used to recognize many types of noun phrases and prepositional phrases that might constitute useful document identifiers.

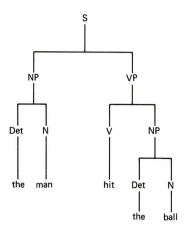

Figure 3-9 Sample context-free phrase structure analysis (S = sentence; NP = noun phrase; VP = verb phrase; Det = determiner; N = noun; V = verb).

Unfortunately, a simplified language analysis system based on context-free grammars exhibits a number of disadvantages. First of all, some sentences whose structure is not of the basic phrase structure type cannot be analyzed by the phrase structure model. Second, a unique analysis pattern is not obtainable for many sentences, but multiple parse trees can be generated—all ostensibly correct according to the grammar in use—without any information that would identify which of those analyses may be semantically acceptable. The notorious sentence "time flies like an arrow" may serve to illustrate a case where at least four reasonable analyses are generated by a typical context-free analysis system [45]:

1 Time passes as quickly as an arrow flies.
2 You should time the flies as quickly as an arrow times the flies.
3 You should time the flies which are similar to an arrow.
4 There exists a species of flies, called "time flies," which are fond of an arrow.

Most important of all, the phrase structure model is not sufficiently rich to make it possible to recognize semantic relationships between sentence components that may not be reflected by some sort of physical juxtaposition of the components in the sentence. Thus a requirement that the phrase components be grammatically related according to the phrase structure model—for example, that the components appear in the same "subtree" within the parse tree— may actually amount to an overspecification, producing an underassignment of phrases for the respective documents. Consider as an example the sentence "people in need of information require effective retrieval systems." In this sample sentence the terms "information" and "retrieval" are not related in the usual noun phrase sense, where "information" is grammatically dependent and modifies the governing element "retrieval." Hence if the indexing rule consisted in requiring a noun phrase or prepositional phrase relationship between phrase components, the phrase "information retrieval" would not be assigned to a document containing this sentence. On the other hand, a frequency-based phrase assignment method of the type covered earlier would correctly generate the phrase "information retrieval."

Various attempts have been made to use simple syntactic analysis systems in actual information retrieval situations. While linguistic methods may eventually prove essential in automatic indexing, the available evidence indicates that the simplified syntactic analysis systems do not yet provide the answer. The frequency-based phrase-generation methods are simpler to implement and are currently more effective [46–50].

At least two possibilities are apparent for helping with the syntactic analysis problems. On the one hand, certain *computer-aided* indexing systems have been proposed where the indexers obtain access to a computer console during the indexing process. In such circumstances, the human operators can intervene at appropriate times during the indexing process. This can be done, for example, by choosing the correct analysis output from among a number of parse trees or by identifying "good" phrases from among a large selection of potential phrases produced by statistical or syntactic procedures [51].

Alternatively, sophisticated linguistic methods are available for carrying out the text analysis. Specifically, syntactic models can be used in which contextual constraints exercised at each level of the analysis are used to restrict the number of syntactic parses [52,53]. These constraints, or restrictions, may be subject matter–specific, or they may depend on the inclusion of semantic data such as "case frames" which identify the (semantic) role of the sentence components.

A conventional parse tree represents the "surface" structure of a sentence, and the results of an initial parsing operation must be subjected to certain transformations before the underlying "deep" (that is, semantic) structure is obtained. The conventional (surface) parse for "John is easy to please" recognizes "John" as the subject of the sentence and "easy to please" as the complement. The deep structure, on the other hand, reflects the meaning of "It is easy for someone (unmentioned) to please John." In that case "John" appears properly as the complement.

Unfortunately the construction of transformational grammars capable of performing the required transformation operations has proved to be too difficult for practical purposes. Indeed, in conventional situations, dozens of possible transformations could in principle be applied at each point to a given surface structure, and no guidance is available for choosing the correct pattern of transformations. Here again substantial progress is evident in recent years, based on the use of restricted areas of discourse and of sufficient context to produce for each sentence only a small number of surface structures, each being subject to only a small number of possible transformations.

It now appears that when the input material is restricted to certain specialized topic areas, limited vocabularies, and limited syntactic patterns, *canonical representations* are obtainable from natural language input. The canonical representations consist of standard forms in which each phrase in the text is assigned a well-defined role, reflecting the full complexity of the syntactic and semantic structures of the text. The canonical forms for the documents can be compared with standard query forms to derive answers to incoming user queries. For the most part, linguistic procedures are incorporated into specialized *question-answering* systems where direct responses are given in answer to search requests, as opposed to answers consisting of document references that must be consulted before direct answers can be obtained [54–58].

In at least two cases, the natural language text of full-length medical records, such as radiology reports and pathology diagnostic reports, has been transformed automatically into standard tabular formats where each text component is identified as to function and meaning. Such tabular formats can then be directly transformed into structured data bases used to generate answers to search requests [59–60]. Such methods may eventually be used in unrestricted automatic indexing environments; however, the linguistic procedures must then possess substantial sophistication, and their application will probably be very costly. It remains to be seen whether this route will actually be pursued in the future.

*B Fragment Encoding

Indexing methods, based on probabilistic considerations, like the previously discussed linguistic methods, offer great promise, although really practical methods applicable on a wide scale have not so far been generated. One line of effort, somewhat tangential to the main developments, is based on the previously mentioned information theoretic considerations relating to the uneven nature of the occurrence frequencies of the standard indexing products. Not only is the number of index terms needed to represent the content of most document collections extremely large—even small collections of a few hundred documents may require several thousand different terms—but many of these terms occur very rarely. Hence their utilization, storage, and maintenance is quite inefficient.

In these circumstances, it is not surprising that the suggestion has been made to replace the normal index words or terms by a small number of artificial entities exhibiting approximately equal occurrence frequencies in the documents of a collection. Specifically, variable length character strings known as "fragments" can be used for indexing instead of full-length words. Normally fragments represent substrings of complete words, or terms. A redundant encoding is often used so that certain characters in the original terms are repeated in several different fragments. For search purposes, a number of different fragments must then be used in a given document or query to replace each original term [61–66].

A variety of encoding procedures can be used to construct a fragment set consisting of more or less equally occurring elements. Consider the following procedure [66]:

    1 A string of n characters is created starting from *each* character of the original text sample; n must be chosen at least as large as the longest fragment expected to occur in the final fragment set.

    2 The character strings are sorted and the frequency of each string is determined.

    3 The frequency of each distinct character string is then compared with a given threshold frequency (the size of the final fragment set is inversely related to the magnitude of the threshold).

    4 Any string whose occurrence frequency exceeds the threshold is selected for inclusion in the final fragment set, and eliminated from the set of strings still under consideration.

    5 Strings whose frequency does not exceed the threshold frequency are shortened by truncation of the rightmost character, the equivalent shortened strings being merged; new frequencies are computed for the shortened strings.

6 Any shortened character string whose frequency now exceeds the threshold is selected for inclusion in the final fragment set, and the procedure is repeated until single character strings are reached.

7 The final fragment set also includes all single character strings.

The original set of index terms must now be mapped into a final fragment set. Various methods suggest themselves such as, for example, the "longest match" algorithm which chooses the longest fragment that matches the beginning (left-hand end) of each term. The longest fragments matching the left end of the remainder of the various words are then successively chosen until the whole text is covered [67]. For efficiency in the final encoding, it is convenient to operate with a total number of fragments equal approximately to a power of 2. Thus, each of 256 fragments can conveniently be represented by an 8-bit code. The fragment encoding for some typical terms is illustrated in Table 3-12.

A thesaurus, or inverted index, giving access to a fragment encoded document set is managed more easily than a standard index, because a dictionary of a few hundred fragments can replace the normal list of many thousands of conventional index terms. However, a "false drop" problem must be contended with in retrieval because certain sets of fragments included in a search request may correspond to several different full index terms. Thus the two fragments RAC and ER can correspond to RAC/ER and also to T/ER/RAC/E, causing documents on terraces to be retrieved when racers are wanted. The seriousness of this problem depends on the actual keyword set used for a particular collection.

A great many automatic text compression methods other than fragment encoding are in use, designed to take advantage of the unequal occurrence probabilities of individual characters and words, and of the redundancies built into the natural language [68]. A description of these methods is beyond the scope of the present discussion.

**C Probabilistic Information Retrieval

Probability theory has also been used as a principal means for modeling the retrieval process in mathematical terms. In conventional retrieval situations, a

Table 3-12 Sample Fragment Encoding

Original term	Fragments
AMINO ACID	AMINO, ACID
BETA HYDROXYLASE	HYDRO, BETA, OXY, YLA, ASE
BETA-HYDROXY LASE	BETA-, -HYDR, LASE, ROX, XY
DICHLOR ACETAT	CHLOR, ACETA, DIC, TAT
HALOGEN	HALO, OGEN
CHLOROFORM	CHLOR, FORM, RO, OF
SULFONAMID	AMID, SUL, FON, LF, NA
IONISATION	ATION, IONI, ISA

Adapted from reference 61.

document is retrieved in response to a query whenever the keyword set attached to the document appears similar in some sense to the query keywords. In this case the document is assumed to be relevant to the corresponding query. More explicitly, since relevance of a document with respect to a query is a matter of degree, one postulates that when the document and query vectors are sufficiently similar, the corresponding probability of relevance is large enough to make it reasonable to retrieve the document in answer to the query.

More formally, the retrieval problem can be expressed as a decision-theoretic process using three basic parameters as follows: P(Rel), the probability of relevance of a record; $LOSS_1$, a loss parameter associated with the retrieval of a nonrelevant or extraneous record; and $LOSS_2$, a loss associated with the nonretrieval of a relevant record. A loss minimizing rule can be devised by noting that the retrieval of an extraneous item causes a loss of $[1 - P(Rel)] \cdot LOSS_1$, whereas the rejection of a relevant item produces a loss of $P(Rel) \cdot LOSS_2$. In these circumstances the total loss is minimized by opting for retrieval of an item whenever

$$P(Rel) \cdot LOSS_2 \geq [1 - P(Rel)] \cdot LOSS_1 \tag{15}$$

Equivalently a discriminant function DISC may be defined, and an item may be retrieved whenever DISC ≥ 0 [69–71], where

$$DISC = \frac{P(Rel)}{1 - P(Rel)} - \frac{LOSS_1}{LOSS_2} \tag{16}$$

A retrieval rule of the kind produced by equation (16) is not useful in practice because the relevance properties of the individual records cannot be divorced from other system parameters. Thus, it becomes necessary to relate the discriminant function to other design parameters, and most notably to the *indexing* process. This can be done by defining two conditional probability parameters:

$P(TERM_i | Rel)$ = the probability of $TERM_i$ occurring in a document given that the document is relevant to a given query

and

$P(TERM_i | Notrel)$ = the probability of $TERM_i$ occurring given that the document is not relevant to the query [71,72].

Using a formula developed by Bayes, a retrieval function P(Rel|Doc) can be obtained, representing the probability of relevance given a document Doc = $\langle$TERM$_1$, TERM$_2$, . . . , TERM$_t\rangle$. In particular,

$$P(Rel|Doc) = \frac{P(Doc|Rel) \; P(Rel)}{P(Doc)}$$

and   (17)

$$P(Notrel|Doc) = \frac{P(Doc|Notrel)P(Notrel)}{P(Doc)}$$

where P(Rel) and P(Notrel) are the a priori probabilities of relevance and nonrelevance of an item, and

$$P(Doc) = P(Doc\,|\,Rel) \cdot P(Rel) + P(Doc\,|\,Notrel) \cdot P(Notrel) \tag{18}$$

If one assumes that the two loss parameters are equal to 1 (LOSS$_1$ = LOSS$_2$ = 1), then the obvious retrieval rule calls for retrieval whenever

$$P(Rel\,|\,Doc) \geq P(Notrel\,|\,Doc) \tag{19}$$

or whenever the discriminant function DISC $\geq$ 1 where

$$DISC = \frac{P(Rel|Doc)}{P(Notrel|Doc)} = \frac{P(Doc|Rel) \cdot P(Rel)}{P(Doc|Notrel) \cdot P(Notrel)} \tag{20}$$

The foregoing rule relates the retrieval of the records to the occurrence characteristics of the terms in both the relevant and the nonrelevant items. For practical application, it is necessary to specify how the probabilities P(Doc | Rel) and P(Doc | Notrel) are to be determined. The problem is twofold in that one must first determine the occurrence characteristics for each term separately, and next the interactions between terms. In most abstract retrieval models the second problem is settled either by considering single-term queries only, where term interactions are of no consequence [71,73], or more drastically by disregarding term interactions altogether, and assuming that terms occur independently of each other in the records of the collection. The first question relating to the individual term occurrences can be handled either by using a probability distribution, such as the Poisson distribution, to characterize the occurrence characteristics of the terms, or by studying the actual occurrences of the terms in a typical sample record collection and applying the findings to other collections at large. (The Poisson distribution is an approximation to the binomial distribution which measures the probability of success in a sequence of success-failure experiments when the number of experiments is large and the probability of success of a given event is small. In the case at hand, the texts under consideration are assumed to be long, the word occurrences are randomly placed in the text, and the probability of occurrence of a particular word is assumed to be small.)

Consider the case where *term independence* is assumed and where the occurrence characteristics are obtained from a sample collection. In such circumstances one can write

$$P(Doc \mid Rel) = P(TERM_1 \mid Rel) \cdot P(TERM_2 \mid Rel) \quad \ldots \quad P(TERM_t \mid Rel) \qquad (21)$$

It remains to determine the probabilities of each term in both the relevant and the nonrelevant items in a collection. Consider a sample collection of N records and assume that R records out of N are relevant to a given query Q and N − R items are nonrelevant. The term occurrence characteristics for a specific $TERM_i$ are listed in Table 3-13.

If one assumes that the term occurrences in the sample record collection of Table 3-13 are typical of the term occurrences at large, one can postulate that $P(TERM_i \mid Rel)$ and $P(TERM_i \mid Notrel)$ representing the probabilities that a given $TERM_i$ occurs in a document, given that the document is respectively relevant and nonrelevant, is equal to

$$P(TERM_i \mid Rel) = \frac{r_i}{R}$$

and

$$(22)$$

$$P(TERM_i \mid Notrel) = \frac{n_i - r_i}{N - R}$$

where r_i represents the number of relevant documents in which $TERM_i$ occurs, and $(n_i - r_i)$ is the number of nonrelevant documents with $TERM_i$.

By inserting the expressions (21) and (22) into expression (20) for the dis-

Table 3-13   Occurrence Table for One Term
(r Relevant Documents Contain Term; n − r Nonrelevant Documents Contain Term; R Relevant Documents Exist in All with Respect to Some Query Q in a Collection of N Documents)

	Relevant	Nonrelevant	
Term present	r	n − r	n
Term absent	R − r	N − n − (R − r)	N − n
	R	N − R	N

criminant function, it is not hard to show that for each query term that matches a given document term, an appropriate term weight is given by

$$\text{TERMREL} = \frac{r/(R - r)}{(n - r)/[N - n - (R - r)]} \tag{23}$$

where r and n − r represent the number of relevant and nonrelevant documents in which the given term occurs. The expression TERMREL, known as the *term relevance,* represents the ratio of the proportion of relevant to the proportion of nonrelevant items in which the term occurs. TERMREL is a term weighting function for the term akin to other term weighting functions (inverse document frequency, term signal, and term discrimination value) previously introduced. It differs from these earlier weighting systems in that the relevant documents to a given query are used to compute TERMREL. Relevance information of particular documents with respect to particular queries may be obtainable in modern on-line information retrieval systems where users have direct access to the system during the course of the retrieval operations [74−76]. The term relevance weights may be most profitably incorporated into these on-line retrieval environments [77−79].

It can be shown that if the terms occur independently of each other, and binary (as opposed to weighted) terms are used to represent the documents, then the optimum query will have terms weighted according to the term relevance factor TERMREL. Furthermore, given a document $D = \langle x_1, x_2, \ldots , x_t \rangle$ and a query $Q = \langle q_1, q_2, \ldots , q_t \rangle$ the best matching function SIMILAR(D,Q) between them is the inner product $\sum_{k=1}^{t} x_k q_k$ previously introduced in expression (11).

Some of the restrictions of the decision-theory model can be removed, for example, by introducing term dependencies [72]. Of more immediate interest may be the utilization of the probabilistic model for automatic indexing purposes. For expository purposes, the indexing problem may be considered to be a classification problem where m subject classes are given, each described by a class term vector. The indexing (classification) task then consists in assigning each document to the class whose subject area most nearly reflects the document description. In indexing terms, the assignment of a document to a subject class may simply imply the use of the corresponding class identifiers to represent individual document content.

In the earlier development, the documents were characterized by the term occurrence probabilities in two classes, the class of relevant and nonrelevant documents, respectively, with respect to a given query. An alternative (classification) context represents a generalization of that used earlier, in that m classes $C_1, C_2, \ldots , C_m$ may be assumed to exist instead of only two. The decision rule now specifies that a document $D = \langle x_1, x_2, \ldots , x_t \rangle$ is assigned to the class for which its probability of occurrence is the largest.

A discriminant function can be constructed as before in terms of the probabilities of occurrence of the individual terms in the various classes. Eventually, each document is assigned to that class which exhibits the largest sum of all the probability values of the various document terms [80–82].

In the previous probabilistic models it was assumed that occurrence frequencies were available to characterize the term occurrences in the various document classes. Unfortunately, in practice, these frequencies are often difficult to generate. An alternative approach may then serve in which a document collection is broken down into homogeneous document classes such that the occurrence properties of the index terms may be characterized by an overall probability distribution with known parameters in each individual document class. In particular, if the terms are assumed to be randomly scattered across the documents within each of the homogeneous classes, the previously mentioned Poisson distribution accurately reflects the term occurrence characteristics.

This fact has been used in many of the early automatic indexing models by noting that the common function words which do not indicate document content exhibit the same occurrence properties in *all* the documents of a collection, and thus are characterized by a single Poisson distribution. The specialty words, on the other hand, that are reflective of document content tend to be clustered in a few documents and a single Poisson formula cannot be used to represent their properties across the documents of a collection. Instead the collection is broken down into subcollections, and the assumption is made that a *different* Poisson distribution applies to a given term in each subclass with different parameters. Several attempts have been made to predict the usefulness of index terms based on an analysis of the term occurrence characteristics in the documents of a collection, followed by a comparison with the Poisson model [71,73,83–86].

7 AUTOMATIC INDEXING EXPERIMENTS

Many observers consider the use of automatic indexing and text processing methods to be acceptable only if substantial advantages can be demonstrated for the automatic system compared with the conventional manual situation, in the form of lower costs, greater speed of operations, or more extensive collection coverage. Unfortunately, it is a fact that comparative tests of indexing effectiveness (and efficiency) must normally be carried out under controlled conditions, using test collections of relatively small size with small sets of test queries. Under these conditions it is not difficult to show that the retrieval effectiveness of many systems operating with automatically assigned content indicators is at least equivalent to that obtaining for manually operated systems. However, it is hazardous to extrapolate test results obtained in a laboratory environment to operational situations possibly involving hundreds of thousands of items. This is particularly true with respect to an evaluation of operating efficiency, as opposed to effectiveness, because the cost or speed of operations in the laboratory reveals little about costs or speeds in practical environments.

A detailed recital of evaluation results in automatic indexing is unlikely to prove conclusive; however, a brief summary of some of the early evaluation studies may provide a useful demonstration of the *relative* effectiveness of various automatic procedures, and an indication of possible future trends. Several different evaluation approaches are possible [87]:

1 Title word studies where an attempt is made to compare index entries derived from document titles with automatically generated terms
2 Studies involving the comparison of automatically generated and manually assigned term or class indicators
3 Retrieval experiments in which the manual or automatic methodologies are actually used in a retrieval environment and an attempt is made to assess the effectiveness in terms of recall and precision

The title word studies conducted for a variety of subject areas such as medicine [88], chemistry [89], or law [90] indicate that for a large proportion of the documents, varying from 60 to 80 percent, some portions of the title are usable directly for indexing purposes. Furthermore, the number of titles which are totally useless in automatic indexing appears to be small in most subject areas—of the order of 10 percent.

These results are reinforced by studies based on a direct comparison between automatically generated sets of terms and their manual equivalents. The coefficient of similarity between manual and automatic index sets may then be taken simply as the proportion of common term assignments (that is, terms present in both the manual and automatic sets) to distinct term assignments that is

$$Q = \frac{C}{A + M - C}$$

where Q is the similarity coefficient between indexing sets, A is the number of distinct terms derived automatically, M is the number of distinct manually assigned terms, and C is the number of common assignments. Various tests of this general type have been performed, and the consensus is that about 60 percent agreement between manually and automatically produced term sets is obtainable [91,92].

While retrieval results based on a direct comparison of content identifiers may be interesting, they prove relatively little in the end, since the terms themselves are not the issue, but rather the retrieval performance obtainable with them. For this reason, the evaluation of *retrieval* results produced by a variety of different indexing methodologies has received considerable attention over the last few years. The first comparison of a conventional, manual indexing system with an automatic text processing system appears to be the one performed by Swanson in the late 1950s [93]. In that instance the manual utilization of a conventional subject-heading index was compared with a system based on words and phrases automatically extracted from the document texts; in addition, a thesaurus was also used to modify the words extracted from the documents. The test results indicate that the average retrieval performance over 50 queries and 100 documents was superior for the system based on automatic text analysis. It may be worthwhile to quote from the conclusions of this early test [93]:

> The apparent superiority of machine-retrieval techniques over conventional retrieval . . . will become greater with subsequent experimentation as retrieval aids for text searching are improved . . . (because) no clear procedure is in evidence which will guarantee improvement of the conventional (manual) system. . . . Thus even though machines may never enjoy more than a partial success in library indexing . . . people appear even less promising.

These original test results were later confirmed by additional experiments in which, for the first time, natural language queries were used instead of manually constructed query formulations [94]. Furthermore, an evaluation methodology very similar to that used to the present day was utilized, in the sense that documents were retrieved in decreasing order of similarity to the queries, the similarity score for an article being computed by summing the weights of those words in the article which coincided with the query words. With such a ranked list of retrieved documents, it is possible to compute recall and precision values following the retrieval of each document (or each nth document) producing a sequence of recall-precision pairs which can be plotted as a curve giving recall against precision, or listed in a table containing average precision values at certain fixed recall points.

Many additional experiments have been performed over the years, designed to evaluate a variety of automatic indexing theories, and in some cases attempts were made to measure large numbers of index language variations [24, 95–97]. The Cranfield and SMART studies are perhaps among the best known. The Cranfield II experiments were designed to measure many linguistic "devices" that are potentially useful for the representation of document content, including synonym dictionaries, hierarchical subject classifications, phrase assignment methods, and others [96,97]. While all indexing tasks were performed manually by trained indexers, the indexing rules were carefully specified and carried out in such a way as to simulate a computer assignment. A collection of 1,400 documents in aerodynamics was used with 279 search requests prepared by aerodynamicists. Three main indexing languages were utilized:

1 The *single terms* were content words chosen from document texts.
2 *Controlled* terms were single terms modified by consulting a manually constructed subject authority list (thesaurus).
3 Simple *concepts* were phrases obtained by concatenation of single terms.

Each of these basic languages was used with a variety of recall-improving procedures (synonym dictionaries, concept associations, term hierarchies, etc.) and precision-improving methods (assignment of weights, specification of term relations).

Somewhat unexpectedly, the retrieval results obtained were apparently counterintuitive, in the sense that the simple uncontrolled indexing language involving single terms produced the best retrieval performance, while the controlled vocabulary and the phrases (simple concepts) furnished increasingly worse results. To quote from Cleverdon [96]:

> The seemingly inexplicable conclusion . . . is that the single term index languages are superior to any other type . . . the single terms appear to have been near the correct level of specificity; only to the relatively small extent of grouping true synonyms (using a synonym dictionary) and word forms (using a suffixing process to generate word stems) could any improvement in performance be obtained. . . .
>
> Of the controlled term index languages that using only the basic terms gave the best performance; as narrower, broader or related terms are brought in . . . the performance decreases. . . .
>
> The simple concept (phrase) index languages were overspecific. . . .

In other words, the conclusion is that, on the average, the simplest indexing procedures which identify a given document or query by a set of terms, weighted or unweighted, obtained from document or query texts are also the most effective. Only the use of synonym dictionaries exhibiting groups of related terms could produce improvements in retrieval performance.

Such a result, if verified in other test environments, is of interest for two reasons: first, the single term indexing process is easier to implement automatically than the more sophisticated, seemingly less effective alternatives; and, second, if the single terms could be shown to operate at the correct level of specificity for the average user query, an automatic indexing process might become competitive in both cost and effectiveness with a manual indexing method.

The verification of the Cranfield results was provided by the extensive evaluation work carried out for some years with the SMART system [98,99]. The experimental, automatic SMART document retrieval system uses a variety of automatic text analysis and indexing methods, including synonym dictionaries, hierarchical term arrangements, statistical and syntactic phrase-generation methods, and the like, to generate sets of weighted content identifiers useful for the retrieval process. Information is retrieved by using a composite vector matching method producing for each query-document pair a coefficient of similarity. A ranking is obtained for the stored items in decreasing order of the query-document similarity, and a variable number of documents can be retrieved as required by the individual requestors. The output is evaluated in terms of recall and precision by processing the same search requests against the same document collections several times, while making selected changes in the indexing procedures between runs as previously explained.

In one extensive set of tests, document collections were used in the fields of computer engineering, aerodynamics, and documentation. A few quotations from the published results may suffice for present purposes [24,87]:

> The order of merit is generally the same for all three collections. . . .
>
> The use of unweighted terms (with weights restricted to 1 for terms that are present, and 0 for those that are absent) is generally less effective than the use of weighted terms. . . .
>
> The use of document titles alone is always less effective for content analysis purposes than the use of full document abstracts. . . .
>
> The thesaurus process involving synonym recognition performs more effectively than the word stem extraction method where synonyms and other word relations are not recognized. . . .
>
> The thesaurus and statistical phrase methods (where phrases are formed by statistical association of terms) are substantially equivalent in overall system performance; other dictionaries, including term hierarchies and syntactic phrases, perform less well.

Thus, the principal conclusions reached by the Cranfield project are borne out by the SMART studies: that computer language devices are not substantially superior to single terms used as indexing devices, and that sophisticated analysis tools are less effective than had been expected. These conclusions are perhaps not surprising, given the fact that a retrieval system is designed to serve a large, sometimes heterogeneous user population. Since users may have different needs and aims, the search requests range from survey or tutorial type questions to very detailed analytical queries. In these circumstances, an excessively specific analysis may be too specialized for most users.

Furthermore, the evaluation process is based on a performance criterion averaged over many search requests. This implies that analysis methods whose overall performance is moderately successful are preferred over possibly more sophisticated procedures which may operate excellently for certain queries but far less well for others. In practice, it may turn out that for each query type, a specific sophisticated analysis will be optimal, whereas for the average query the simpler type of indexing is best.

It remains to apply the evaluation methodology to a comparison of automatic indexing with conventional, manual indexing methods currently used under operational conditions, and to the more advanced, automatic indexing theories based on the term discrimination values and frequency transformations described earlier in this chapter. To answer the first question, certain automatic indexing methods incorporated into the SMART system were utilized together with the exhaustive evaluation work of the operating MEDLARS retrieval system performed at the National Library of Medicine. The MEDLARS system is based on a manual analysis of documents and incoming search requests, and on an exhaustive search of a stored collection of several hundred thousand documents. In the conventional MEDLARS environment, an average recall of 0.577 and an average precision of 0.504 is reported for 300 test queries processed against the complete MEDLARS collection, implying that an average search manages to retrieve almost 60 percent of what is wanted, while only half the retrieved items are not relevant [100].

These results were compared with the automatic indexing methods by applying both types of procedures to a subcollection from the full MEDLARS environment and a subset of the original queries used in the original MEDLARS evaluation. The subcollection was constructed by using for each query one or more documents known to be relevant to the user's needs as entry points to the Science Citation Index (SCI). For each query, 15 new documents were then obtained from the SCI such that each new item cited the original known relevant document. Obviously, such a process produces a set of potentially relevant documents, independent of either of the retrieval systems.

The main retrieval results are summarized in Table 3-14 [101,102]. It can be seen that a deficiency of about 15 percent for the automatic indexing method using word stem extraction techniques (from document abstracts) is reduced to a deficiency of only about 5 percent using the previously mentioned discrimination values to delete negative discriminators. When a thesaurus is used to recognize synonymous and related terms, a small advantage is produced for the automatic indexing process. Other procedures, related to search strategy rather than to indexing, eventually generate an advantage for the automatic system of about 30 percent in recall and precision [102].

It should be noted that the original MEDLARS searches retrieved a total

Table 3-14. Comparison of MEDLARS Controlled Indexing with SMART Automatic Indexing

(Cutoff in SMART Query-Document Similarity Measure Set to Retrieve a Total of 127 Documents)

Analysis method	Cutoff determining number retrieved	Recall	Percent difference from MEDLARS	Precision	Percent difference from MEDLARS
MEDLARS (controlled indexing)	Boolean search (exact match)	0.3117		0.6110	
SMART (word stems with frequency weights)	Query-document similarity 0.2201	0.2622	−16	0.4901	−19
SMART (word stems with discrimination value weighting)	Query-document similarity 0.2109	0.2872	−8	0.5879	−4
SMART (thesaurus)	Query-document similarity 0.3720	0.3223	+4	0.6106	0

of only 127 documents over the 29 test queries, whereas the total number of items determined to be relevant to the query set was equal to 284 documents. Since the threshold in the query-document similarity coefficient used for SMART must be set to retrieve exactly as many documents as MEDLARS had obtained earlier (namely 127), the maximum recall obtainable by either system is 127/284 = 0.4471, obtained when all retrieved items are found to be relevant. This recall ceiling, imposed by the test conditions, accounts for the low recall values obtained by both systems. The precision ceiling (maximum precision obtainable) is of course always equal to 1. One may interpret the results of the foregoing tests as showing that both conventional and automatic indexing methods produce equally good (or equally poor) retrieval results.

The question now arises to what extent the more advanced automatic indexing theories can produce improvements in the performance over the simple frequency-based indexing methods. Consider first the performance of the more refined term weighting system [18–22]. Table 3-15 contains average precision figures for 10 recall points, ranging from 0.1 to 1.0, averaged over 24 user queries for a collection of 425 documents from the world affairs section of *Time* magazine. As previously explained, a recall-precision table may be obtained by choosing various retrieval thresholds, that is, by retrieving a variable number

Recall	Binary weights BIN_{ik}	Term frequency weights $FREQ_{ik}$	Binary with IDF weights $BIN_{ik}/DOCFREQ_k$	Term frequency with IDF $FREQ_{ik}/DOCFREQ_k$
0.1	0.8257	0.7496	0.8085	0.8536
0.2	0.7555	0.7071	0.7741	0.7901
0.3	0.6754	0.6710	0.7114	0.7568
0.4	0.6224	0.6452	0.6328	0.7503
0.5	0.5708	0.6351	0.6218	0.6783
0.6	0.5299	0.5866	0.5673	0.6243
0.7	0.4618	0.5413	0.5124	0.5823
0.8	0.4087	0.5004	0.4384	0.5643
0.9	0.2959	0.3865	0.3374	0.4426
1.0	0.2854	0.3721	0.3188	0.4170

(a)

A. Binary weights BIN_{ik} vs. B. Term frequency weights $FREQ_{ik}$		A. Binary with IDF vs. B. Term frequency with IDF		A. Term frequency $FREQ_{ik}$ vs. B. Term frequency with IDF $FREQ_{ik}/DOCFREQ_k$	
t-test	0.0000	t-test	0.0000	t-test	0.0000
B better than A		B better than A		B better than A	
Wilcoxon	0.0000	Wilcoxon	0.0000	Wilcoxon	0.0000

(b)

Table 3-15 Comparison of binary term weighting with inverse document frequency (IDF) weights (time collection, 425 documents, 24 search requests). (a) Comparison of binary and term frequency weighting with and without inverse document frequency normalization. (b) Statistical significance output for the results of Table 3-15a.

of documents in decreasing order of the query-document similarity, and computing a recall and a precision value for each retrieval threshold. The various recall-precision values can then be plotted on a graph or tabulated as shown in Table 3-15. Detailed methods for the construction of recall-precision tables and graphs are covered in Chapter 5.

It may be seen first of all that an unequivocal result is not obtained for the comparison between binary (BIN_{ik}) and term frequency ($FREQ_{ik}$) weights. In the binary case, the terms are not weighted, whereas a weight proportional to the term occurrence frequency in each document is assigned to each term in the other case. The preferred result is shown in each case by a vertical line in the second and third columns of Table 3-15a. For the collection under study, the binary weights are superior at the low recall end and the term frequency weights at the high recall end. When these basic term weights are combined with an inverse document frequency (IDF) factor proportional to $1/DOCFREQ_k$, the combined weighting system equivalent to $FREQ_{ik}/DOCFREQ_k$ [see expression (2)] is clearly superior. Indeed, the results in the rightmost column of Table 3-15a show improvements ranging from 3 percent at very low recall to over 30 percent at high recall.

Table 3-15b contains t-test and Wilcoxon signed rank test values, giving in each case the probability that the output results for the two runs being compared could have been generated from the *same* distribution of values. Small probabilities—for example, those less than 0.05—indicate that the answer to this question is negative and that the test results differ significantly (hence that one system is clearly superior to the other). The significance figures in Table 3-15b show that for the *Time* collection the method labeled B is significantly better than the A method in all cases. The significance tests used in judging evaluation output are examined in more detail in Chapter 5.

In Table 3-16 the two basic term weighting systems are combined with a term deletion process which eliminates from the document and query vectors those terms deemed to be poor content identifiers. A variety of term deletion procedures are usable in practice [103]. For test purposes two term deletion systems were used to obtain the results of Table 3-16. The first one consists in deleting terms in increasing IDF order, that is, terms exhibiting the highest document frequencies (which may be expected to produce the poorest index terms) are eliminated first. In the other case, terms were deleted in increasing term discrimination order by removing first the terms with the lowest discrimination values. The two runs are labeled IDF CUT and DISC CUT respectively in Table 3-16. For the *Time* collection under study, documents with a document frequency greater than 104 (out of 425 documents) were actually removed to generate the IDF CUT performance. For the DISC CUT performance, the term deletion was restricted to terms with negative discrimination values.

The placement of the vertical bars in Table 3-16 shows that the deletion in inverse document frequency order performs best at low recall, whereas the discrimination value cutoff is best at high recall. A comparison of the results of Tables 3-15 and 3-16 shows that the removal of poor terms produces better re-

Table 3-16   Recall-Precision Results for Term Deletion Methods
(*Time* 425 Collection, 24 Queries)

Recall	Standard BIN_{ik} weights	Standard $FREQ_{ik}$ weights	$FREQ_{ik}$ weights		A. IDF CUT vs. B. Standard $FREQ_{ik}$	A. DISC CUT vs. B. Standard $FREQ_{ik}$
			IDF CUT	DISC CUT		
0.1	0.8257	0.7496	0.8601	0.7911		
0.2	0.7555	0.7071	0.8268	0.7485	t-test	t-test
0.3	0.6754	0.6710	0.7503	0.7362	A better than B	A better than B
0.4	0.6224	0.6452	0.7144	0.7000	0.0000	0.0085
0.5	0.5708	0.6351	0.6872	0.6777		
0.6	0.5299	0.5866	0.6168	0.6350	Wilcoxon	Wilcoxon
0.7	0.4618	0.5413	0.5645	0.5907	A better than B	A better than B
0.8	0.4087	0.5004	0.5017	0.5510	0.0000	0.0127
0.9	0.2959	0.3865	0.4071	0.4177		
1.0	0.2854	0.3721	0.3906	0.4019		

IDF = inverse document frequency
DISC = discrimination value

sults than the composite inverse document frequency weights at low and medium recall points. The statistical significance probabilities on the right-hand side of Table 3-16 show that the improvements obtained with the term deletion process are fully significant.

Table 3-17 includes a comparison of various composite term weighting systems such as those based on inverse document frequency weighting ($FREQ_{ik}/DOCFREQ_k$) [equivalent to expression (2)], on the signal value $FREQ_{ik} \cdot SIGNAL_k$ [expression (6)] and on the discrimination value $FREQ_{ik} \cdot DISCVALUE_k$ [expression (9)]. It may be seen that the composite weights obtained with the inverse document frequency and the discrimination value weights are approximately comparable in efficiency. The results produced by the signal value are substantially less attractive because of the emphasis on low-frequency terms inherent in that weighting system. The two right-hand columns of Table 3-17a demonstrate that the composite weights combined with the elimination of poor terms produces superior precision values at low and medium recall levels. The significance test results of Table 3-17b indicate fully significant performance improvements with an average performance difference ranging from 8 to 15 percent.

A wide variety of phrase-generation methods are potentially useful, as explained earlier. To generate the output of Table 3-18 a simple phrase-generation method was used consisting of phrases obtained from pairs (P) and triples (T) of co-occurring nondiscriminators [104]. Specifically, given three nondiscriminators T_i, T_j, and T_k occurring in a given document abstract, one triple T_{ijk} can be formed as well as three pairs T_{ij}, T_{ik}, and T_{jk}. For the *Time* collection under study an average of 11 phrases were generated by this simple process for each document. Single terms (S), pairs (P), and triples (T) can all be used together (denoted SPT); alternatively, pairs and triples alone can be added to the vec-

Table 3-17 (a)

Recall	Standard term frequency $FREQ_{ik}$ weights	$FREQ_{ik}$ weights with IDF $FREQ_{ik}/DOCFREQ_k$	$FREQ_{ik}$ weights with $DISCVALUE_k$ $FREQ_{ik} \cdot DISCVALUE_k$	$FREQ_{ik}$ weights with $SIGNAL_k$ $FREQ_{ik} \cdot SIGNAL_k$	$FREQ_{ik}/DOCFREQ_k$ with IDF CUT	$FREQ_{ik} \cdot DISCVALUE_k$ with DISC CUT
0.1	0.7496	0.8536	0.8406	0.7212	0.8975	0.8028
0.2	0.7071	0.7901	0.7881	0.7006	0.8315	0.7480
0.3	0.6710	0.7568	0.7197	0.6471	0.7800	0.7286
0.4	0.6452	0.7305	0.6901	0.6229	0.7574	0.6938
0.5	0.6351	0.6783	0.6704	0.6105	0.7372	0.6737
0.6	0.5866	0.6243	0.6176	0.5587	0.6529	0.6349
0.7	0.5413	0.5823	0.5727	0.5263	0.5912	0.5847
0.8	0.5004	0.5643	0.5169	0.4612	0.5481	0.5475
0.9	0.3865	0.4426	0.4208	0.3830	0.4318	0.4259
1.0	0.3721	0.4170	0.4053	0.3593	0.4118	0.4085

(a)

Table 3-17 (b)

	t-test	Wilcoxon
A. $FREQ_{ik}$ weight with IDF $FREQ_{ik}/DOCFREQ_k$	0.0000	0.0000
B. Standard $FREQ_{ik}$	A better than B by 11%	
A. $FREQ_{ik}$ weight with $DISCVALUE_k$	0.0000	0.0000
B. Standard $FREQ_{ik}$	A better than B by 8%	

	t-test	Wilcoxon
A. $FREQ_{ik}/DOCFREQ_k$ with IDF CUT	0.0000	0.0000
B. Standard $FREQ_{ik}$	A better than B by 15%	
A. $FREQ_{ik} \cdot DISCVALUE_k$ with DISC CUT	0.0084	0.0077
B. Standard $FREQ_{ik}$	A better than B by 8%	

(b)

Table 3-17 Composite weighting functions (425 documents, 24 queries). (a) Comparison of composite weighting systems. (b) Statistical significance results for output of Table 3-17a (testing for A better than B).

Recall	$FREQ_{ik}$ control run	Best frequency weighting $FREQ_{ik}/DOCFREQ_k$	Best phrase process PT+SPT	Thesaurus classes	Thesaurus + PT+SPT
0.1	0.7496	0.8536	‖ 0.8860	0.7392	0.8761
0.2	0.7071	0.7901	‖ 0.7984	0.7166	0.7972
0.3	0.6710	0.7568	0.7761	0.6935	‖ 0.7778
0.4	0.6452	0.7305	0.7461	0.6627	‖ 0.7465
0.5	0.6351	0.6783	0.7020	0.6541	‖ 0.7027
0.6	0.5866	0.6243	‖ 0.6563	0.6070	0.6524
0.7	0.5413	0.5823	‖ 0.6010	0.5598	‖ 0.6010
0.8	0.5004	‖ 0.6543	0.5483	0.5111	0.5523
0.9	0.3865	‖ 0.4426	0.4231	0.4091	0.4260
1.0	0.3721	‖ 0.4170	0.4118	0.3950	0.4149

(a)

	t-test	Wilcoxon
A. Thesaurus + PT + SPT phrases	0.6874	0.6833
B. $FREQ_{ik}/DOCFREQ_k$ weights		
A. Thesaurus + PT + SPT phrases	0.4524	0.9657
B. PT + SPT phrases		
A. Thesaurus	0.0000	0.0003
B. Standard term frequency $FREQ_{ik}$		

(b)

Table 3-18 Thesaurus and phrase evaluation. (a) Thesaurus and phrase performance. (b) Statistical significance results for output of Table 4-17a (testing for A better than B).

tors, the corresponding single terms being deleted (PT). When high-frequency nondiscriminators are used for phrase generation, the PT method appears to offer a reasonably high performance standard.

A manually constructed thesaurus designed to group low-frequency terms (terms with a document frequency smaller than 20 out of 425 documents) was also available for experimental purposes with the *Time* collection; the relevant thesaurus class identifiers can be added in each case to the standard document and query vectors.

The performance data are included in Table 3-18 together with the corresponding statistical significance output. It may be seen that for the *Time* collection, the grouping of low-frequency terms into thesaurus classes affords recall improvements over the standard $FREQ_{ik}$ weighting system for all but the lowest recall levels. Moreover, the thesaurus advantage proves statistically significant. The phrase-generation process, however, proved more effective especially at the high precision–low recall end of the performance spectrum. In the middle recall range, the best performance of any of the retrieval runs displayed in Tables 3-15 to 3-18 is obtained by using a combination of the phrase-generation process applied to high-frequency terms with the thesaurus class grouping of low-frequency terms.

The evaluation results presented in Tables 3-15 to 3-18 are indicative of the performance of various sophisticated statistically based automatic indexing methods. Substantial additional work remains to be done in order to determine the optimum indexing system applicable to a particular retrieval environment under given conditions. When no special information is available about a particular collection, the following process will, however, provide a high-quality indexing product:

1 Starting with document abstracts or excerpts, remove common high-frequency words and generate word stems by removing suffixes from the remaining words.

2 Compute the discrimination values of the terms, generate phrases for the high-frequency nondiscriminators with negative discrimination values, and assemble low-frequency nondiscriminators with near-zero discrimination values into thesaurus classes.

3 Compute a weighting factor for each remaining single term, phrase, and thesaurus class, using, for example, the inverse document frequency function [expression (2)].

4 Assign to each document the weighted term vector consisting of single terms, phrases, and thesaurus classes.

In interactive retrieval systems where user information is available during the search process, improved index term assignments may be obtainable as a result of the user-system interaction. The possibility is explored further in Chapter 6.

REFERENCES

[1] E.M. Keen, On the Generation and Searching of Entries in Printed Subject Indexes, Journal of Documentation, Vol. 33, No. 1, March 1977, pp. 15–45.

[2] B.C. Vickery, Techniques of Information Retrieval, Archon Books, Hamden, Connecticut, 1970.

[3] E.M. Keen, On the Performance of Nine Printed Subject Index Entry Types, Research Report, College of Librarianship, Aberystwyth, Wales, September 1978.

[4] F.W. Lancaster, Information Retrieval Systems, Characteristics, Testing and Evaluation, 2nd Edition, Wiley-Interscience, New York, 1979.

[5] W.S. Cooper, Is Interindexer Consistency a Hobgoblin?, American Documentation, Vol. 20, No. 3, July 1969, pp. 268–278.

[6] P. Zunde and M.E. Dexter, Indexing Consistency and Quality, American Documentation, Vol. 20, No. 3, July 1969, pp. 259–267.

[7] M.E. Stevens, Automatic Indexing—A State of the Art Report, National Bureau of Standards, NBS Monograph 91, National Bureau of Standards, Washington, D.C., March 1965.

```
        THE CAMPUS STORE
          "MAIN STORE"
            255-4111
       THANK YOU FOR YOUR
            PATRONAGE


036952  0001  497 1290

1510  0-07-054484-0
  INTRO TO MODERN INFO RETRIEV      65.35
                    Sub Total       65.35
                    Total Tax        5.23
                                  ----------
                         TOTAL     70.58**

Cornellcard # 354116                70.58
NICHOLAS P BOWDEN


14:58  02/05/94  SALE

    SAVE  THIS  RECEIPT
     FOR  RETURNS  OR
          REFUNDS
```

038952 0001 497 1290

1510 0-07-054484-0
INTRO TO MODERN INFO RETRIEV $5.35

Cornellcard # 354116
NICHOLAS P BOWDEN   70.58

14:58 02/05/96 SALE

[8] H.P. Luhn, The Automatic Creation of Literature Abstracts, IBM Journal of Research and Development, Vol. 2, No. 2, April 1958, pp. 159–165.

[9] G.K. Zipf, Human Behavior and the Principle of Least Effort, Addison Wesley Publishing, Reading, Massachusetts, 1949.

[10] H. Kucera and W.N. Francis, Computational Analysis of Present-Day American English, Brown University Press, Providence, Rhode Island, 1967.

[11] H.P. Luhn, A Statistical Approach to Mechanized Encoding and Searching of Literary Information, IBM Journal of Research and Development, Vol. 1, No. 4, October 1957, pp. 309–317.

[12] H.P. Edmundson and R.E. Wyllys, Automatic Abstracting and Indexing—Survey and Recommendations, Communications of the ACM, Vol. 4, No. 5, May 1961, pp. 226–234.

[13] F.J. Damerau, An Experiment in Automatic Indexing, American Documentation, Vol. 16, No. 4, October 1965, pp. 283–289.

[14] K. Sparck Jones, A Statistical Interpretation of Term Specificity and Its Application in Retrieval, Journal of Documentation, Vol. 28, No. 1, March 1972, pp. 11–20.

[15] C.E. Shannon, Prediction and Entropy of Printed English, Bell System Technical Journal, Vol. 30, No. 1, January 1951, pp. 50–65.

[11] S.F. Dennis, Law, Language, Words, Entropy, and Automatic Indexing, unpublished manuscript.

[11] S.F. Dennis, The Design and Testing of a Fully Automatic Indexing-Searching System for Documents Consisting of Expository Text, in Information Retrieval: A Critical Review, G. Schecter, editor, Thompson Book Co., Washington, D.C., 1967, pp. 67–94.

[18] G. Salton, A Theory of Indexing, Regional Conference Series in Applied Mathematics No. 18, Society for Industrial and Applied Mathematics, Philadelphia, Pennsylvania, 1975.

[19] G. Salton and C.S. Yang, On the Specification of Term Values in Automatic Indexing, Journal of Documentation, Vol. 29, No. 4, December 1973, pp. 351–372.

[20] G. Salton and M.E. Lesk, Recent Studies in Automatic Text Analysis and Information Retrieval, Journal of the ACM, Vol. 20, No. 2, April 1973, pp. 258–278.

[21] G. Salton, C.S. Yang, and C.T. Yu, A Theory of Term Importance in Automatic Text Analysis, Journal of the American Society for Information Science, Vol. 26, No. 1, January–February 1975, pp. 33–44.

[22] G. Salton, C.S. Yang, and C.T. Yu, Contributions to the Theory of Indexing, Information Processing 74, North Holland Publishing Company, Amsterdam, 1974, pp. 584–590.

[23] R.A. May, editor, Automated Law Research, American Bar Association, Chicago, Illinois, 1973.

[24] G. Salton and M.E. Lesk, Computer Evaluation of Indexing and Text Processing, Journal of the ACM, Vol. 25, No. 1, January 1968, pp. 8–36.

[25] C.J. van Rijsbergen, Information Retrieval, 2nd Edition, Butterworths, London, 1979.

[26] G. Salton, Automatic Information Organization and Retrieval, McGraw-Hill Book Company, New York, 1968.

[27] J.B. Lovins, Development of a Stemming Algorithm, Mechanical Translation and Computational Linguistics, Vol. 11, No. 1–2, March and June 1968, pp. 11–31.

[28] G. Salton and M.E. Lesk, Information Analysis and Dictionary Construction, in

the SMART Retrieval System—Experiments in Automatic Document Processing, G. Salton, editor, Chapter 6, Prentice-Hall, Inc., Englewood Cliffs, New Jersey, 1971.

[29] K. Sparck Jones, Automatic Keyword Classification for Information Retrieval, Butterworths, London, 1971.

[30] G. Salton, Generation and Search of Clustered Files, ACM Transactions on Data Base Systems, Vol. 3, No. 4, December 1978, pp. 321–346.

[31] R.T. Dattola, Experiments with Fast Algorithms for Automatic Classification, in the Smart Retrieval System—Experiments in Automatic Document Processing, G. Salton, editor, Chapter 12, Prentice-Hall, Inc., Englewood Cliffs, New Jersey, 1971.

[32] G. Salton, Dynamic Information and Library Processing, Prentice-Hall, Inc., Englewood Cliffs, New Jersey, 1975.

[33] V.E. Giuliano and P.E. Jones, Linear Associative Information Retrieval, in Vistas in Information Handling, P. Howerton, editor, Spartan Books, Inc., Washington, D.C., 1963.

[34] M.E. Lesk, Word-Word Associations in Document Retrieval Systems, American Documentation, Vol. 20, No. 1, January 1969, pp. 27–38.

[35] L.B. Doyle, Information Retrieval and Processing, Melville Publishing Company, Los Angeles, California, 1975.

[36] G. Jones and P. Wise, Updating Thesaurus Classifications in Response to Data Base Changes, Scientific Report No. ISR-21, Section XIII, Department of Computer Science, Cornell University, Ithaca, New York, December 1972.

[37] M.M. Kessler, Comparison of the Results of Bibliographic Coupling and Analytic Subject Indexing, American Documentation, Vol. 16, No. 3, 1965, pp. 223–233.

[38] G. Salton, Automatic Indexing Using Bibliographic Citations, Journal of Documentation, Vol. 27, No. 2, June 1971, pp. 98–110.

[39] H.P. Edmundson, Problems in Automatic Abstracting, Communications of the ACM, Vol. 7, No. 4, April 1964, pp. 259–263.

[40] H.P. Edmundson, New Methods in Automatic Extracting, Journal of the ACM, Vol. 26, No. 2, April 1969, pp. 264–285.

[41] J.E. Rush, R. Salvador, and A. Zamora, Automatic Abstracting and Indexing II, Production of Indicative Abstracts by Application of Contextual Inference and Syntactic Coherence Criteria, Journal of the ASIS, Vol. 22, No. 4, July–August 1971, pp. 260–274.

[42] C.A. Montgomery, Linguistics and Information Science, Journal of the American Society for Information Science, Vol. 23, No. 3, May–June 1972, pp. 195–219.

[43] K. Sparck Jones and M. Kay, Linguistics and Information Science, Academic Press, New York, 1973.

[44] F. Damerau, Automated Language Processing, in Annual Review of Information Science and Technology, M.E. Williams, editor, American Society for Information Science, Washington, D.C., Vol. 11, 1976, pp. 107–161.

[45] S. Kuno and A. G. Oettinger, Multiple-Path Syntactic Analyzer, in Information Processing 62, North Holland Publishing Company, Amsterdam, 1963, pp. 128–133.

[46] P. Baxendale, An Empirical Model for Machine Indexing, in Machine Indexing—Progress and Problems, Third Institute on Information Storage and Retrieval, American University, February 1961, pp. 207–218.

[47] W.D. Climenson, N.H. Hardwick, and S.N. Jacobson, Automatic Syntax Anal-

ysis in Machine Indexing and Abstracting, American Documentation, Vol. 12, No. 3, July 1961, pp. 178–183.

[48] F.J. Damerau, Automatic Parsing for Content Analysis, Communications of the ACM, Vol. 13, No. 6, June 1970, pp. 356–360.

[49] D.J. Hillman and A.J. Kasarda, The LEADER Retrieval System, AFIPS Proceedings, AFIPS Press, Montvale, New Jersey, Vol. 34, 1969, pp. 447–455.

[50] G. Salton, Automatic Phrase Matching, in Readings in Automatic Language Processing, D. Hays, editor, American Elsevier Publishing Company, New York, 1966, pp. 169–188.

[51] J. Friedman, A Computer System for Transformational Grammar, Communications of the ACM, Vol. 12, No. 6, June 1969, pp. 341–348.

[52] N. Sager and R. Grishman, The Restriction Language for Computer Grammars of Natural Language, Communications of the ACM, Vol. 18, No. 7, July 1975, pp. 390–400.

[53] W.A. Woods, Transition Network Grammars for Natural Language Analysis, Communications of the ACM, Vol. 13, No. 10, October 1970, pp. 591–606.

[54] G.G. Hendrix, Human Engineering for Applied Natural Language Processing, Fifth International Joint Conference on Artificial Intelligence, M.I.T., Cambridge, Massachusetts, 1977, pp. 183–191.

[55] L.R. Harris, User-Oriented Data Base Query with the ROBOT Natural Language Query System, International Journal of Man-Machine Studies, Vol. 9, 1977, pp. 697–713.

[56] J. Mylopoulos, A. Borgida, P. Cohen, N. Roussopoulos, J. Tsotsos and H. Wong, Torus—A Natural Language Understanding System for Data Management, Fourth International Joint Conference on Artificial Intelligence, Tbilisi, USSR, September 1975, pp. 414–421.

[57] W.J. Plath, REQUEST: A Natural Language Question-Answering System, IBM Journal of Research and Development, Vol. 20, No. 4, July 1976, pp. 326–335.

[58] D.L. Waltz, An English Language Question Answering System for a Large Relational Database, Communications of the ACM, Vol. 21, No. 7, July 1978, pp. 526–539.

[59] G.S. Dunham, M.G. Pacak, and A.W. Pratt, Automatic Indexing of Pathology Data, Journal of the American Society for Information Science, Vol. 29, No. 2, March 1978, pp. 81–90.

[60] R. Grishman and L. Hirschman, Question Answering from Natural Language Medical Data Bases, Artificial Intelligence, Vol. 11, No. 1/2, 1978, pp. 25–43.

[61] H.J. Schek, The Reference String Indexing Method, Research Report, IBM Scientific Center, Heidelberg, Germany, 1978.

[62] E.J. Schuegraf and H.S. Heaps, Query Processing in a Retrospective Document Retrieval System That Uses Word Fragments as Language Elements, Information Processing and Management, Vol. 12, No. 4, 1976, pp. 283–292.

[63] E.J. Schuegraf and H.S. Heaps, Selection of Equifrequent Word Fragments for Information Retrieval, Information Storage and Retrieval, Vol. 9, No. 12, December 1973, pp. 697–711.

[64] M.F. Lynch, Variety Generation—A Reinterpretation of Shannon's Mathematical Theory of Communication and Its Implications in Information Science, Journal of the American Society for Information Science, Vol. 28, No. 1, January 1977, pp. 19–25.

[65] T. Radhakrishnan, Selection of Prefix and Postfix Word Fragments for Data Com-

pression, Information Processing and Management, Vol. 14, No. 2, 1978, pp. 97–106.

[66] I.J. Barton, S.E. Creasey, M.F. Lynch, and M.J. Snell, An Information-Theoretic Approach to Text Searching in Direct Access Systems, Communications of the ACM, Vol. 17, No. 6, June 1974, pp. 345–350.

[67] H.S. Heaps, Information Retrieval—Computational and Theoretical Aspects, Academic Press, New York, 1978.

[68] D. Gottlieb, S.A. Hagerth, P.G.H. Lehot, and H.S. Rabinowitz, A Classification of Compression Methods and Their Usefulness for a Large Data Processing Center, AFIPS Conference Proceedings, Vol. 44, 1975, pp. 453–458.

[69] M. Kochen, Principles of Information Retrieval, Melville Publishing Company, Los Angeles, California, 1974.

[70] W. Goffman, A Searching Procedure for Information Retrieval, Information Storage and Retrieval, Vol. 2, No. 2, July 1964, pp. 73–78.

[71] A. Bookstein and D.R. Swanson, A Decision Theoretic Foundation for Indexing, Journal of the ASIS, Vol. 26, No. 1, January–February 1975, pp. 45–50.

[72] C.J. van Rijsbergen, A. Theoretical Basis for the Use of Co-occurrence Data in Information Retrieval, Journal of the Documentation, Vol. 33, No. 2, June 1977, pp. 106–119.

[73] A. Bookstein and D.R. Swanson, Probabilistic Models for Automatic Indexing, Journal of the ASIS, Vol. 25, No. 5, September–October 1974, pp. 312–318.

[74] F.W. Lancaster and E.G. Fayen, Information Retrieval On-Line, John Wiley and Sons, New York, 1973.

[75] M.E. Lesk and G. Salton, Interactive Search and Retrieval Methods Using Automatic Information Displays, in the SMART Retrieval System, Experiments in Automatic Document Processing, G. Salton, editor, Prentice-Hall, Inc., Englewood Cliffs, New Jersey, 1971, Chapter 25.

[76] G. Salton, Relevance Feedback and the Optimization of Retrieval Effectiveness in the SMART Retrieval System, Experiments in Automatic Document Processing, G. Salton, editor, Prentice-Hall, Inc., Englewood Cliffs, New Jersey, 1971, Chapter 15.

[77] S.E. Robertson and K. Sparck Jones, Relevance Weighting of Search Terms, Journal of the ASIS, Vol. 27, No. 3, May–June 1976, pp. 129–146.

[78] C.T. Yu and G. Salton, Precision Weighting—An Effective Automatic Indexing Method, Journal of the ACM, Vol. 23, No. 1, January 1976, pp. 76–88.

[79] G. Salton and R.K. Waldstein, Term Relevance Weights in On-Line Information Retrieval, Information Processing and Management, Vol. 14, No. 1, 1978, pp. 29–35.

[80] M.E. Maron, Automatic Indexing—An Experimental Inquiry, Journal of the ACM, Vol. 8, No. 3, July 1961, pp. 404–417.

[81] M.E. Maron and J.L. Kuhns, On Relevance, Probabilistic Indexing and Information Retrieval, Journal of the ACM, Vol. 7, No. 3, July 1960, pp. 216–244.

[82] W.B. Croft, A Study of the Effectiveness and Implementation of a Model of Cluster Searching, Research Report, University of Cambridge, Computer Laboratory, 1978.

[83] C.D. Stone and M. Rubinoff, Statistical Generation of a Technical Vocabulary, American Documentation, Vol. 19, No. 4, October 1968, pp. 411–412.

[84] F. Mosteller and E.L. Wallace, Inference in an Authorship Problem, Journal of the American Statistical Association, Vol. 58, No. 302, June 1963, pp. 275–309.

[85] S.P. Harter, A Probabilistic Approach to Keyword Indexing, Part 1. On the Distribution of Specialty Words in a Technical Literature, Journal of the ASIS, Vol. 26, No. 4, July–August 1975, pp. 197–206.

[86] A. Bookstein and D. Kraft, Operations Research Applied to Document Indexing and Retrieval Decisions, Journal of the ACM, Vol. 24, No. 3, July 1977, pp. 418–427.

[87] G. Salton, Automatic Text Analysis, Science, Vol. 168, No. 3929, April 1970, pp. 335–343.

[88] C. Montgomery and D.R. Swanson, Machine-like Indexing by People, American Documentation, Vol. 13, No. 4, October 1962, pp. 359–366.

[89] M.J. Ruhl, Chemical Documents and Their Titles: Human Concept Indexing vs. KWIC Machine Indexing, American Documentation, Vol. 15, No. 2, April 1964, pp. 136–141.

[90] D.H. Kraft, A Comparison of Keyword in Context (KWIC) Indexing of Titles with a Subject Heading Classification System, American Documentation, Vol. 15, No. 1, January 1964, pp. 48–52.

[91] M.E. Stevens and G.H. Urban, Training a Computer to Assign Descriptors to Documents: Experiments in Automatic Indexing, Proceedings of the Spring Joint Computer Conference, Spartan Books, 1964, pp. 563–575.

[92] T.N. Shaw and H. Rothman, An Experiment in Indexing by Word Choosing, Journal of Documentation, Vol. 24, No. 3, September 1968, pp. 159–172.

[93] D.R. Swanson, Searching Natural Language Text by Computer, Science, Vol. 132, No. 3434, October 21, 1960, pp. 1099–1104.

[94] D.R. Swanson, Interrogating a Computer in Natural Language, in Information Processing 62 (Proceedings of IFIP Congress 62), C. Popplewell, editor, North Holland Publishing Co., Amsterdam, 1963, pp. 288–293.

[95] T. Saracevic, An Inquiry into Testing of Information Retrieval Systems, Comparative Systems Laboratory Technical Reports No. CSL: TR-FINAL 1 to 3, Center for Documentation and Communication Research, Case Western Reserve University, Cleveland, Ohio, 1968.

[96] C.W. Cleverdon and E.M. Keen, Factors Determining the Performance of Indexing Systems, Vol. 1: Design, Vol. 2: Test Results, Aslib Cranfield Research Project, Cranfield, England, 1966.

[97] C.W. Cleverdon, The Cranfield Tests on Index Language Devices, Aslib Proceedings, Vol. 19, No. 6, June 1967, pp. 173–194.

[98] G. Salton, editor, the SMART Retrieval System—Experiments in Automatic Document Processing, Prentice-Hall, Inc., Englewood Cliffs, New Jersey, 1971.

[99] G. Salton, editor, Scientific Reports No. ISR-11 to ISR-22, Department of Computer Science, Cornell University, Ithaca, New York, 1966–1974.

[100] F.W. Lancaster, Evaluation of the MEDLARS Demand Search Service, National Library of Medicine, Bethesda, Maryland, January 1968.

[101] G. Salton, A Comparison between Manual and Automatic Indexing Methods, American Documentation, Vol. 20, No. 1, January 1969, pp. 61–71.

[102] G. Salton, A New Comparison between Conventional Indexing (MEDLARS) and Automatic Text Processing (SMART), Journal of the American Society for Information Science, Vol. 23, No. 2, March–April 1972, pp. 75–84.

[103] R.W. Crawford, Negative Dictionary Construction, Scientific Report No. ISR-22, Department of Computer Science, Cornell University, Ithaca, New York, November 1974.

[104] G. Salton and A. Wong, On the Role of Words and Phrases in Automatic Text Analysis, Computers and the Humanities, Vol. 10, No. 2, March–April 1976, pp. 69–87.

BIBLIOGRAPHIC REMARKS

For a review of conventional tools for document indexing see:

B.C. Vickery, Techniques of Information Retrieval, Archon Books, Hamden, Connecticut, 1970.
D. Soergel, Indexing Languages and Thesauri: Construction and Maintenance, Melville Publishing Company, Los Angeles, California, 1974.

Additional basic information on automatic indexing methods may be obtained from the following references:

M.E. Stevens, Automatic Indexing: A State of the Art Report, Monograph 91, National Bureau of Standards, Washington, D.C., March 1965.
G. Salton, A Theory of Indexing, Regional Conference Series in Applied Mathematics No. 18, Society for Industrial and Applied Mathematics, Philadelphia, Pennsylvania, 1975.
L.B. Doyle, Information Retrieval and Processing, Melville Publishing Company, Los Angeles, California, 1975.

EXERCISES

3-1 Explain the significance of each of the following indexing procedures, and determine the effect of each method as a means of enhancing recall and/or precision, respectively:
   a Word stemming process
   b Use of synonym dictionary
   c Use of word location information
   d Use of term weights

3-2 What is the significance of term frequency in the theory of indexing? What is the significance of Zipf's law as a basis for deriving an automatic indexing method? Is the discrimination value of a term related to the occurrence frequency of a term in a document collection? If so, what is the relationship?

3-3 The term relevance factor TERMREL differs from all other term weighting systems in the sense that relevance information must be available for some documents with respect to a given query. Explain the role of relevance information for the computation of the TERMREL weight and give two methods for estimating the required relevance information.

3-4 Consider the following sample document collection:

$$D_1 = (1,0,1,0,0,0)$$
$$D_2 = (3,1,2,1,0,1)$$
$$D_3 = (1,2,3,0,1,0)$$
$$D_4 = (0,1,0,2,1,2)$$
$$D_5 = (1,0,1,4,2,1)$$
$$D_6 = (1,1,0,2,3,2)$$

Generate a term-term similarity matrix similar to that shown in Table 4-10 using one of the term similarity coefficients given in expressions (11) or (12). Choose a threshold value for the term similarity and "expand" the sample documents by adding associated terms to the original term vectors. In what respects do the new expanded vectors differ from the originals?

3-5 Consider the document collection of Exercise 3-4 together with the following query pair

$$Q_1 = (2,0,2,0,0,0)$$
$$Q_2 = (0,0,0,2,0,2)$$

a Exhibit the normal query-document similarity coefficients for all query-document pairs using a vector similarity function such as expressions (11) and (12) in the form SIMILAR (D_i, Q_j). Display the documents in decreasing order of query similarity.

b Compute the discrimination value for each term, and construct updated document vectors using discrimination value weighting.

c Repeat part a using the discrimination value weighting.

d Assuming that D_1, D_2, D_3 are relevant to Q_1 and D_4, D_5, D_6 are relevant to Q_2, compute the term relevance value (TERMREL) for each term and construct updated vectors using term relevance value weighting.

e Repeat part a using the relevance weighting.

f Repeat part a for the "expanded" collection derived in Exercise 3-4.

g Compare the results of parts a, c, e, and f.

The SMART and SIRE Experimental Retrieval Systems

0 PREVIEW

This chapter deals with analysis, file organization, search, and retrieval methodologies that may be used with the advanced information retrieval systems of the future. The SMART system is perhaps the best known of the experimental systems that are not based on a standard inverted file technology. The SMART system design is described in detail in this chapter, including the automatic indexing methods, the clustered file organization, which collects related records into common classes; and the interactive search process which is used to construct improved query formulations based on relevance information supplied by the users to the system.

Various other experimental retrieval systems, including SIRE, also utilize novel features that are not common in conventional retrieval. Some of these extensions are examined at the end of this chapter. The use of local clustering methods and the incorporation of weighted terms in Boolean retrieval are considered in this connection together with additional user feedback and query reformulation methods.

1 INTRODUCTION

Conventional retrieval systems are based for the most part on a common set of principles and methodologies. The documents are normally indexed manually by subject experts or professional indexers using a prespecified, controlled vocabulary; alternatively, some systems use the words included in document texts or text excerpts as index terms. Users or search intermediaries formulate search statements using terms from the accepted vocabulary together with appropriate Boolean operators between terms. The main file search device is an auxiliary, so-called inverted directory which contains for each accepted content identifier and for some of the objective terms a list of the document references, or markers, to which that term has been assigned. In a free text search system, the inverted directory contains the text words from the documents and the references to all documents containing each given word. The documents to be retrieved in response to a given search request are then identified by obtaining from the inverted directory the document reference lists corresponding to each query term, and performing appropriate list comparison and merging operations in accordance with the logical search term associations contained in the query statements. An *exact match* retrieval strategy is used which consists of retrieving all items whose content description contains the term combination specified in the search requests. Furthermore, all retrieved items are considered by the system to be equally relevant to the user's needs, and normally no special methods are provided for ranking the output items in presumed order of goodness for the user.

The existing methodology has certain obvious advantages. In some cases, the indexers and search intermediaries may become expert in assigning useful content indicators to the stored documents and incoming user queries. The retrieval system will then exhibit a high level of effectiveness. The inverted file design also produces rapid response times, because the inverted file manipulations will identify all matching documents before the main document file is ever used. The document file must then be accessed only for those documents which will be shown to the user in response to the query.

The benefits of the conventional retrieval designs are available only under special circumstances, however. In particular, when the indexing and search operations are not carried out consistently by the several intermediaries, the effectiveness of the retrieval operations will suffer. If, for example, one indexer uses "search" when another would use "retrieval," some documents may not be retrieved when wanted. The use of controlled vocabulary lists can minimize this problem, but cannot eliminate it. In practice, the required degree of indexing consistency cannot be guaranteed when similar information items are treated by different indexers and searchers. In such circumstances, the various documents pertaining to a common subject area may be identified very differently, and many of these items may not be retrievable when wanted.

The inverted directory of index terms is most useful in situations where the search vocabulary remains static over long periods of time and is limited to a relatively small number of terms. In such cases, the directory size will remain manageable and relatively little updating may be needed. In practice, the indexing vocabulary is often large, consisting of several tens of thousands of terms for each subject area, and the vocabulary is not stable. The inverted directories to be stored may then become very large, and these directories must be kept up to date when new documents are added to the file or new vocabulary terms are introduced.

The customary library file organization which places in related or adjacent file positions all items that exhibit similar subject content is not followed by the existing inverted file systems. Instead, the main document file is often kept in arbitrary order, and it becomes difficult, given the location of a particular useful document, to determine the location of other related documents. This complicates the file search process, which ideally consists in locating certain useful items, and then proceeding from there to identify additional items resembling the ones found earlier. For the same reason, the inverted file strategy is not well suited to the processing of approximate queries designed to approach a given subject area in small steps, and to the kind of browsing which proves so useful in conventional libraries. Instead, it becomes necessary to formulate complete and specific queries, in the hope of retrieving the entire set of relevant items from the start.

The standard inverted file technology is difficult to change because of the large investments already made in the existing commercial systems. Nevertheless, substantial improvements are possible in the operations of the conventional systems. Thus, in some partly experimental systems, term weighting facilities have been superimposed on the standard Boolean query formulations and inverted file search procedures, leading to the ranking of retrieved documents in accordance with the weights of the matching query and document terms. This makes it possible to present the retrieved documents to the user in decreasing order of the sum of certain term weights. Presumably the user will find it easier to prepare improved query formulations when the items judged by the system to be most relevant are retrieved ahead of other more marginal items.

Systems have also been developed that are based on totally new conceptions of the retrieval task. One of the best known of these, the SMART system, is described in the remainder of this chapter together with certain other nonstandard retrieval system designs.

2 THE SMART SYSTEM ENVIRONMENT

*A Vector Representation and Similarity Computation

The SMART system distinguishes itself from more conventional retrieval systems in the following important respects: (1) it uses fully automatic indexing methods to assign content identifiers to documents and search requests; (2) it collects related documents into common subject classes, making it possible to start with specific items in a particular subject area and to find related items in neighboring subject fields; (3) it identifies the documents to be retrieved by performing similarity computations between stored items and incoming queries, and by ranking the retrieved items in decreasing order of their similarity with the query; and finally, (4) it includes automatic procedures for producing im-

	TERM$_1$	TERM$_2$	...	TERM$_t$
DOC$_1$	TERM$_{11}$	TERM$_{12}$	...	TERM$_{1t}$
DOC$_2$	TERM$_{21}$	TERM$_{22}$	...	TERM$_{2t}$
⋮	⋮			
DOC$_n$	TERM$_{n1}$	TERM$_{n2}$	...	TERM$_{nt}$

Figure 4-1 Term assignment array (n documents, t terms).

proved search statements based on information obtained as a result of earlier retrieval operations [1,2,3,4].

In the SMART system each record, or document, is represented by a *vector* of terms. That is, a particular document, DOC$_i$, is identified by a collection of terms TERM$_{i1}$, TERM$_{i2}$, . . . , TERM$_{it}$, where TERM$_{ij}$ is assumed to represent the weight, or importance, of term j assigned to document i. By "term" is meant some form of content identifier, such as a word extracted from a document text, a word phrase, or an entry from a term thesaurus. A given document collection may then be represented as an array, or matrix, of terms where each row of the matrix represents a document and each column represents the assignment of a specific term to the documents of the collection. A sample term assignment array is shown in Fig. 4-1. In the SMART system, positive term weights are chosen for terms actually assigned to the documents (that is, TERM$_{ij}$ is a positive number when term j actually occurs in document i); and TERM$_{ij}$ is set equal to zero when term j is not present as an identifier of document i.

A particular query, say QUERY$_j$, can be similarly identified as a vector QTERM$_{j1}$, QTERM$_{j2}$, . . . , QTERM$_{jt}$, where QTERM$_{jk}$ represents the weight, or importance, of term k assigned to query j. Instead of insisting on a complete match between all nonzero query and document terms before a document is retrieved by the system, the retrieval of a stored item can be made to depend on the magnitude of a similarity computation measuring the similarity between a particular document vector and a particular query vector as a function of the magnitudes of the matching terms in the respective vectors. A similarity measure often used with the SMART system is the cosine measure, defined as

$$\text{COSINE}(\text{DOC}_i, \text{QUERY}_j) = \frac{\sum_{k=1}^{t} (\text{TERM}_{ik} \cdot \text{QTERM}_{jk})}{\sqrt{\sum_{k=1}^{t} (\text{TERM}_{ik})^2 \cdot \sum_{k=1}^{t} (\text{QTERM}_{jk})^2}} \tag{1}$$

The cosine correlation measures the cosine of the angle between documents, or between queries and documents, when these are viewed as vectors in the multidimensional term space of dimension t. In three dimensions, when only three terms identify the documents, the situation may be represented by the configuration of Fig. 4-2. Each axis corresponds to a different term, and the position of each document vector in the space is determined by the magnitude

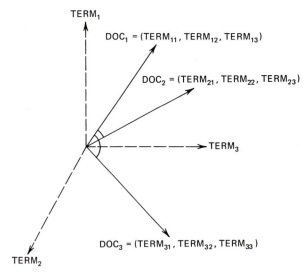

Figure 4-2   Vector representation of document space.

(weight) of the terms in that vector. The similarity between any two vectors is then represented as a function inversely related to the angle between them. That is, when two document vectors are exactly the same, the corresponding vectors are superimposed and the angle between them is zero.

The numerator of the cosine coefficient gives the sum of the matching terms between DOC_i and $QUERY_j$ when the indexing is binary, that is, when $TERM_{jk}$ is assumed equal to 1 whenever term k actually occurs in document i. When the indexing is not binary, the numerator represents the sum of the products of the term weights for the matching query and document terms. The denominator acts as a normalizing factor (by dividing the expression by the product of the lengths of the query and document vectors). This implies that each item is represented by a vector of equal length. If the angle between vectors is small and the normalized vectors are used, the cosine of the angle between the vectors may also be approximated by the distance between the tips of the corresponding vectors.

When a numeric measure of similarity is used for documents and queries, it is no longer necessary to retrieve all documents that exactly contain all the query terms. Instead the retrieval of a document can be made to depend on a particular threshold in the similarity measure or on a specific number of items to be retrieved. Assuming, for example, that a threshold of 0.50 is used, all items are retrieved for which the value of expression (1) is greater than or equal to 0.50; alternatively the top n items may be retrieved, where n is the number of items originally wanted. The retrieved documents may be conveniently presented to the user in decreasing order of their similarity values with the respective search requests. This is of special importance in an interactive retrieval situation where users are directly tied into the retrieval system, because new improved query formulations can then be constructed by utilizing information extracted from previously retrieved documents. Since the first few documents retrieved in response to a search request are those exhibiting the greatest query-document similarity, they are also the ones most likely to be relevant to the users' information needs. Hence they may be most important for query reformulation purposes.

*B Vector Manipulation

The query reformulation process incorporated into the SMART retrieval system is known as "relevance feedback" because relevance assessments supplied by the users for previously retrieved documents are returned to the system and used to construct new query vectors. The reformulated queries can then be compared with the stored documents in a new search operation. The aim is to construct new queries exhibiting a greater degree of similarity with the documents previously identified as relevant by the user than the original queries; at the same time, the new queries are expected to be less similar to the documents identified as nonrelevant by the user than the originals. The assumption is that the reformulated queries will retrieve more items resembling the relevant ones previously retrieved, and fewer items resembling the nonrelevant ones.

The query reformulation process is then based on the following complementary operations:

1 Terms that occur in documents previously identified as relevant by the user population are added to the original query vectors, or alternatively the weight of such terms is increased by an appropriate factor in constructing the new query statements.

2 At the same time, terms occurring in documents previously identified as nonrelevant by the users are deleted from the original query statements, or the weight of such terms is appropriately reduced.

Obviously, the query reformulation process can be carried out automatically by the retrieval system, given only an indication of relevance or nonrelevance of certain previously retrieved items obtained from the user population.

The effect of the relevance feedback operation is represented in the illustration of Fig. 4-3. In Fig. 4-3 and the related diagrams that follow, each document is identified by a point representing the tip of the corresponding vector, and the distance between two points is assumed to be inversely related to the respective cosine similarities between the vectors. Thus when two points appear close together in the space of Fig. 4-3, a substantial similarity exists between the vectors; the reverse is true for two points that appear far apart in the space. In Fig. 4-3, an original query vector (represented by an open triangle) appears with three retrieved documents of which one was identified as nonrelevant and two as relevant. Following the previously mentioned changes in the original query, a new query (the closed triangle) is constructed which appears shifted in the space: the distance to the relevant items is now smaller than be-

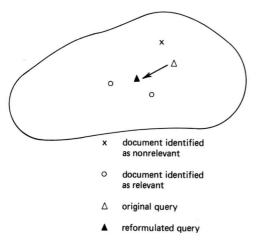

x	document identified as nonrelevant
o	document identified as relevant
Δ	original query
▲	reformulated query

Figure 4-3　Relevance feedback illustration.

fore, and the distance to the nonrelevant one has increased. The relevance feedback process can be repeated several times in the hope of eventually obtaining adequate search output.

The cosine coefficient was introduced earlier to obtain a measure of similarity between a query vector and the various documents in a collection. The same measure also lends itself to the determination of similarities between pairs of documents. Thus, given the term vectors for two documents, DOC_i and DOC_j, the similarity between them may be defined as

$$\text{COSINE}(DOC_i, DOC_j) = \frac{\sum_{k=1}^{t} (TERM_{ik} \cdot TERM_{jk})}{\sqrt{\sum_{k=1}^{t} (TERM_{ik})^2 \cdot \sum_{k=1}^{t} (TERM_{jk})^2}} \qquad (2)$$

By determining the similarity between various pairs of documents, it now becomes possible to construct a *clustered document file*, consisting of classes or clusters of documents such that the documents within a given class exhibit substantial similarities with each other. A clustered file resembles in concept the normal classified document arrangement used in conventional library situations, where items dealing with related subject areas are placed together in a common subject class. The clusters are, however, derived automatically and the construction method may be adapted to the particular collection environment under consideration. Thus, it is possible automatically to construct clustered files incorporating a large number of small clusters or a small number of large clusters; the classes may also overlap in the sense that certain documents may appear in more than one class. This last feature represents a substantial advantage over conventional library classification systems.

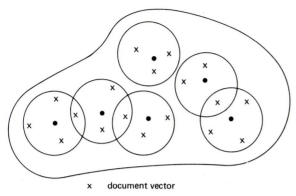

x   document vector

●   centroid vector

Figure 4-4 Sample clustered document collection.

A clustered document file is represented schematically in Fig. 4-4, where each x represents a document vector, and the distance between two particular x's is again assumed inversely proportional to their similarity. The large circular groupings in the figure identify the document clusters. It may be seen that some overlap exists between the clusters: certain documents located near the periphery of some classes actually appear in several classes. In order to render possible the manipulation of a clustered collection, it is convenient to use a special class vector, or *centroid*, to represent a given cluster. The centroids are similar to the centers of gravity of a set of points, and are represented by heavy dots in the illustration of Fig. 4-4. Given a set of m documents constituting a certain document class p, a given centroid vector $CENTROID_p = CTERM_{p1}$, $CTERM_{p2}, \ldots, CTERM_{pt}$ may be computed as the mathematical average of the document vectors included in the pth class. Thus, following the model used in the previous chapter for the construction of term classes, the weight of term k in the centroid for class p can be computed as the average of the weight of term k in all m document vectors incorporated into class p. That is,

$$CTERM_{pk} = \frac{1}{m} \sum_{i=1}^{m} TERM_{ik} \qquad (3)$$

where the summation covers the m documents of class p.

Given a clustered collection of the type shown in Fig. 4-4, a document search is now carried out in two main steps. Each query is first compared with the various centroid vectors by computing the corresponding centroid-query similarity coefficients. For classes whose centroids exhibit a sufficiently high similarity with the query, the individual documents are next compared with the query, using the formula of expression (1), and documents showing sufficiently high similarities with the query are retrieved for the user's attention. Assuming that n documents exist in a collection which is divided into x clusters each containing approximately n/x documents, the number of vector comparisons needed to compare a query with the best cluster is $x + n/x$ (instead of the n comparisons needed in an unclustered file). The number of needed vector comparisons is minimized when the number of clusters x equals $\sqrt{n}$.

For large collections involving many heterogeneous documents, a great many clusters may need to be defined. In that case, the number of required query-centroid comparisons may become excessively large. The search efficiency may then be increased by taking the set of centroids and applying the clustering methodology previously used for the document vectors to compare pairs of centroid vectors. Centroids that are sufficiently similar are then grouped into superclasses identified by supercentroids, as shown in Fig. 4-5, where two superclasses are represented. The file search now requires three steps: first a comparison of the query with the supercentroid vectors; then for some supercentroids, a comparison with the individual centroids included in the corresponding superclusters; finally, for certain centroids, a comparison with the individual document vectors located in the respective document clusters.

The clustered file organization is adaptable to a growing collection environment, because new incoming documents can be treated just like incoming queries. The new items are compared with the existing supercentroids and centroids, and eventually they are included in those clusters for which the document-cluster similarity is sufficiently large. As in the standard inverted file organization, two distinct files are needed for the file search process:

1 The main document file, arranged in order by clusters such that all items included in a common cluster are retrievable in a single access to the main file
2 The auxiliary file of cluster centroids, and supercentroids arranged in a hierarchical tree format where each supercentroid contains pointers specifying the locations of the individual centroids for that superclass, and each centroid in turn points to the locations of the individual document vectors for that class

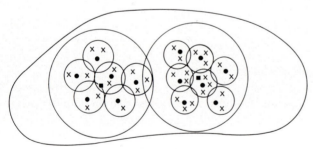

x   document vector

•   centroid vector

■   supercentroid vector

Figure 4-5 Introduction of superclusters.

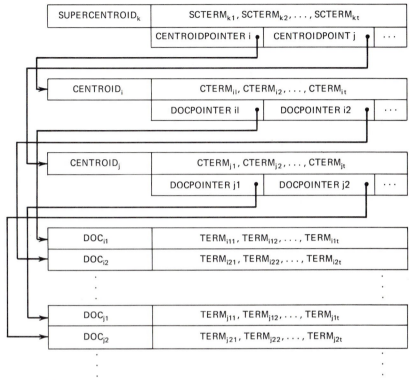

Figure 4-6 Hierarchical vector arrangement for clustered file.

The file arrangement is illustrated in simplified form in Fig. 4-6.

C Vector Generation

Consider now the document indexing process, that is, the method used to construct the document vectors. The basic function of an indexing system is the segregation of the subset of documents relevant to some query from the remainder of the collection. Preferably, all the relevant items might then occur in one or more document clusters, whereas the nonrelevant items would be placed in separate clusters. A situation of this type is shown in Fig. 4-7. Such an ideal document space might be constructed by assigning to the relevant document set the terms utilized by the user population to formulate the corresponding search requests. Unfortunately, it is difficult to know in advance what terms will be considered useful for query formulation purposes, and even in interactive systems where information can be generated about the usefulness of certain terms with respect to certain topic areas, it is still necessary to make the somewhat hazardous assumption that all users interested in specified subject areas would choose the same query terms to express their information needs. Similarly, one would have to assume that all such users would accept the same set of documents as relevant to their queries.

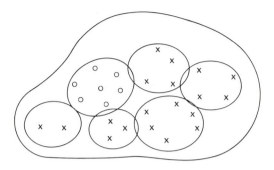

○ relevant document with
   respect to a query

x nonrelevant document
   with respect to a query

Figure 4-7 Ideal document space.

In practice, it is not possible to find a single clustering which is ideal for all subject areas and all users, even given full relevance information in advance. Furthermore, new documents that are added to the collection must necessarily be processed without the use of document relevance information. The best policy may then lead to the use of index terms capable of distinguishing each particular document from the remainder of the collection. This can be achieved by using as a controlling criterion the document frequency of each term in the collection, that is, the number of documents to which a term is assigned. The term discrimination theory examined in the previous chapter indicates that the terms to be preferred are medium-frequency terms that are assigned to a few documents but not to the rest of the collection.

In the SMART system, the text of the document abstracts (or the text of the query statements obtained from the user population) is analyzed automatically. Terms whose document frequency is neither too large nor too small are incorporated directly into the document or query vectors for indexing purposes. Terms whose document frequency exceeds a given threshold are considered too broad and unspecific; they are rendered more specific by being combined with other terms into *term phrases* before assignment to the document and query vectors. On the other hand, terms with a very low document frequency that are assigned to one or two documents only are considered too specific; they can be broadened by grouping them into term classes of the kind found in a *thesaurus* of terms. The thesaurus class identifiers are then incorporated into the term and document vectors instead of the individual rare terms. These operations are described in more detail in the next section, where the SMART procedures are treated more thoroughly.

A simplified flowchart of the SMART processing chain is shown in Fig. 4-8. The processes represented on the left side of the chart consisting of the

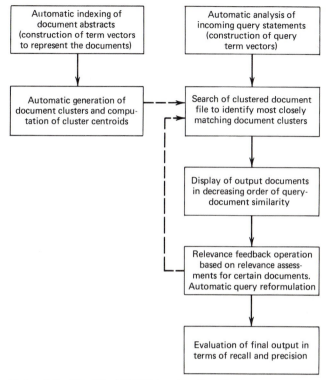

Figure 4-8 Simplified SMART system flowchart.

initial construction of term vectors for the documents and the generation of clustered files are carried out only once, or in any case at infrequent time intervals. The query-processing operations, on the other hand, including the generation of query vectors, the clustered file search, and the relevance feedback operations are performed for each query. Only the query-handling operations need to be done in real time while the user is present.

The SMART system is designed to make available a large variety of experimental methods, including many different automatic indexing procedures, query-document similarity functions, cluster file generation methods, and query-reformulation processes. The system can then serve as a test vehicle to validate the various experimental procedures. For this reason evaluation methods have been incorporated into the system which produce recall and precision information following the retrieval operations.

The following assumptions are implicit in the model used by the SMART environment for the representation of document and query operations:

1   Each document is represented by a particular vector, that is, a particular position in a t-dimensional vector space, where t is the number of permissible terms available for indexing purposes.

2 Each term included in a given document or query vector is assumed to be unrelated (orthogonal) to the other terms, and all terms are considered equally important (except for distinctions inherent in the assignment of weights to the individual terms).

The assumptions are in fact only first-order approximations to the true situation because documents exhibit not only subject content but also extent, or scope. A survey or tutorial text normally has greater scope than a research article. This suggests that the subject matter of a document be represented by a point in a certain location of the subject space as suggested by Figs. 4-3 to 4-5, and that an area of space surrounding the subject points be used to denote scope and extent. The document scope might be determined by using the frequencies with which individual documents are cited in the literature. Thus documents attracting many citations could be assumed to have wide scope.

The second area of simplification in the SMART model is the orthogonality assumption for the various index terms. In the SMART system, each term represents a separate coordinate in the vector space, and no term relationships are assumed to exist. In actual fact, words do not, however, occur independently of each other in the document texts, and neither do the index terms assigned to a collection of items. In recent years, a great deal of work has been devoted to the study of retrieval models which take into account certain term dependencies. These models tend to be complex and difficult to use. The available experimental evidence suggests that the greatest deviations from independence arise for the very rare terms that occur in a few documents only. The discrimination value theory indicates that these terms are not very important for retrieval purposes. For the vast majority of the medium- and high-frequency terms, the independence assumption is not in fact unreasonable.

Perhaps in a few years, some experimental retrieval systems will make provision for the representation of document scope and impact and for the use of term dependencies. At the present time efforts in this direction are in a very preliminary state.

3 SMART SYSTEM PROCEDURES

*A Automatic Indexing

When the SMART system was originally designed in the middle 1960s the experts generally felt that sophisticated language analysis procedures would be required in a machine indexing system to replace the intellect normally applied by the human indexer. Accordingly, the original SMART indexing system was based on the following language analysis tools:

1 Synonym dictionaries, or *thesauruses*, would be used to group the individual terms into classes of synonymous or related terms. When a thesaurus is available, each original term can be replaced by a complete class of related terms, thereby broadening the content description.

2 *Hierarchical term arrangements* could be constructed to relate the content terms in a given subject area. With such preconstructed term hierarchies, the standard content descriptions can be "expanded" by adding to a given content description hierarchically superior (more general) terms as well as hierarchically inferior (more specific) terms.

3 *Syntactic analysis* systems would serve for the specification of the syntactic roles of the terms, and for the formation of complex content descriptions consisting of term phrases and larger syntactic units. A syntactic analysis system can be used to supply specific content identifications, and it prevents confusion between compound terms such as "blind Venetian" and "Venetian blind."

4 *Semantic analysis* systems might supplement the syntactic units by using semantic roles attached to the entities making up a given content description. Semantic analysis systems utilize various kinds of knowledge extraneous to the documents, often specified by preconstructed "semantic graphs" and other related constructs.

The early test results obtained with the SMART system showed that some complicated linguistic methodologies that were believed essential to attain reasonable retrieval effectiveness were in fact not useful in raising performance [5,6]. In particular, the use of syntactic analysis procedures to construct syntactic content phrases and the utilization of concept hierarchies could not be proved effective under any circumstances. It may be that these failures were attributable not to the actual processes themselves but rather to the particular implementations used in the test situations. The fact is that linguistic theories were not sufficiently well understood 15 years ago to permit the construction of effective semantic maps and hierarchical term arrangements, or to design accurate and complete syntactic analysis systems. Some progress has been made in this area in the last few years. However, versatile linguistic methodologies that would be applicable to a wide variety of subject areas are still not easily incorporated into an unrestricted language processing environment at the present time. For this reason the standard SMART indexing procedures are based on simpler language process considerations that are by now well understood. These simple automatic methods can be shown to be superior to conventional indexing methodologies in laboratory test situations [6,7]:

1 The individual words that make up a document excerpt (abstract) or a query text are first recognized.

2 A stop list, comprising a few hundred high-frequency function words, such as "and," "of," "or," and "but," is used to eliminate such words from consideration in the subsequent processing.

3 The scope of the remaining word occurrences is broadened by reducing each word to word stem form; this can be done by using relatively simple suffix removal methods together with special rules to take care of exceptions, as previously explained [8,9].

4 Following suffix removal, multiple occurrences of a given word stem are combined into a single term for incorporation into the document or query vectors.

At this point, the standard query-document vector matching methods introduced in the previous section could be used to identify all documents whose word stem vectors are sufficiently similar to the query vectors. The SMART system retains a much larger number of content indicators than is customary in conventional systems, and the larger number and greater diversity of the terms compensate to some extent for the lack of precision in the term selection. Nevertheless, the foregoing process would provide inferior search results in many cases, because some word stems are obviously more important for the representation of document content than others. Two main operations are needed to transform the word stem vectors into useful term vectors: first a term weight can be assigned to each term reflecting the usefulness of the term in the collection environment under consideration; and second, terms whose usefulness is inadequate as reflected by a low term weight can be transformed into better terms [10–13].

As explained earlier, it is convenient to separate the term weighting task into two parts: first, one must take into account the term characteristics within a given document or document excerpt; second, it is important to consider also the function of the term in the remainder of the collection. The considerations detailed in Chapter 3 favor terms that exhibit high importance in the documents to which they are assigned, as measured, for example, by their occurrence frequencies in the individual documents. At the same time, the best terms must be able to distinguish the documents to which they are assigned from the remainder of the collection; hence their importance factor in the document collection as a whole ought to be low. The importance of a given term k in an individual document i is conveniently measured by the frequency of occurrence in the document $FREQ_{ik}$. The usefulness of the term in the collection as a whole may be reflected by the term discrimination value $DISCVALUE_k$, or alternatively by an inverse function of the document frequency $DOCFREQ_k$ (that is, the number of documents to which the term is assigned). Two possible term weighting functions reflecting the usefulness of term k in document i are

$$WEIGHT_{ik} = \frac{FREQ_{ik}}{DOCFREQ_k} \tag{4}$$

and $WEIGHT_{ik} = FREQ_{ik} \cdot DISCVALUE_k$

Terms with a low weight according to expression (4) could in principle be deleted from the indexing vocabulary. In practice, the deletion of broad, high-frequency terms is likely to cause losses in recall, and the elimination of specific, low-frequency terms may impair the precision. It is then preferable to alter such terms completely. The most obvious methods available for this purpose consist in creating specific *term phrases* incorporating the high-frequency terms that are originally considered too broad, and forming *thesaurus classes* of the low-frequency terms that may be too specific to be used by themselves.

Consider first the phrase-formation process. Ideally, a phrase is a language construct with specific syntactic and semantic properties. Because a full syntactic and/or semantic analysis of document and query texts is not currently possible for normal information retrieval purposes, a simple phrase-formation process must be used. The following phrase-formation criteria are of greatest importance:

1   The phrase components should occur in a common context within the document or query to which the phrase is assigned as a content identifier.

2   The phrase components should represent broad concepts, and their frequency of assignment to the documents of a collection should be sufficiently high.

In the SMART system a phrase is defined as a pair of two distinct word stems not contained on the stop list, such that the components occur in the same sentence within a document or query text, and at least one component has a document frequency in the collection exceeding a given threshold. A more stringent phrase-construction process is obtained by also taking into account the distance in the text between potential phrase components, that is, the number of intervening words between them. The following phrase-construction process can be used in practice:

1   Start with the query and document texts; use a stop list to eliminate common function words; generate word stems by using a suffix deletion process to reduce the original words.

2   Take pairs of the remaining word stems, and let each pair define a phrase provided that the distance in the text between components does not exceed n words (at most n − 1 intervening words), and that at least one of the components of each phrase is a high-frequency term; this frequency cutoff is manipulated to reduce the number of generated phrases to manageable size.

3   Phrases for which both components are identical are eliminated, as are duplicate phrases where all components match an already existing phrase.

4   Phrase weights are assigned as a function of the weights of the individual phrase components; if the term weights are restricted to values between 0 and 1, the phrase weight can be defined as the product of the individual component weights.

The phrase-generation process is illustrated for a sample sentence in Table 4-1. Some of the original words, such as "in," "need," "of," and "require," are deleted following a comparison with the entries contained in a stop list. The remaining words are transformed into word stems: this generates INFORM from "information" and RETRIEV from "retrieval." A maximum distance of four is assumed between phrase components in the text, leading to the generation of the seven phrases listed in Table 4-1c.

The phrase-formation process increases the specificity of the content identifiers attached to queries and documents. The converse operation consists in using thesaurus classes for content identification. A thesaurus contains groupings of similar or related terms into term classes. The use of thesauruses is

> "People in need of information require effective
> retrieval services"

(a)

> "PEOPLE   INFORM   EFFECT   RETRIEV   SERVICE"

(b)

PEOPLE	INFORM	EFFECT	RETRIEV
INFORM	EFFECT	EFFECT	SERVICE
INFORM	RETRIEV	RETRIEV	SERVICE
INFORM	SERVICE		

(c)

Table 4-1 Phrase-generation process. (a) Original sentence. (b) Word stems generated from original sentence. (c) Word pairs (phrases) generated assuming maximum component distance of four.

often advocated for purposes of synonym recognition: when the query specifies "manufacture" and the document contains "production," a term match is obtainable by including both terms in a common thesaurus class. Because the frequency of assignment of a thesaurus class is approximately equal to the sum of the frequencies of the individual terms in the class, thesauruses are most useful for the classification of the low-frequency terms that need to be broadened. Since the automatic term classification (thesaurus) construction methods are all based in one way or another on the computation of similarities between terms, thesauruses are not easily generated automatically. Normally, the term similarities would be obtained by computing similarity coefficients between the term vectors (columns) of the term assignment array (see Fig. 4-1). In effect the similarity between two terms will then depend on co-occurrences of the terms in the documents of a collection. Unfortunately, the terms of most interest for thesaurus construction purposes are those whose overall occurrence frequency in a collection is low. These terms do not co-occur very often in the same documents, and their computed similarity measure must be expected to be very low and may not then furnish an accurate indication of term relationship.

In practice, it becomes necessary either to use a manually constructed thesaurus that obeys the thesaurus construction principles described in the previous chapter, or else to use an automatic thesaurus construction method in which the grouping criteria are relatively weak [14,15]. The well-known *single-link* classification method appears to be most useful in this connection [16]. The single-link process is based on a computation of the term-term similarities for all term pairs. The process then proceeds iteratively as follows:

    1   For each term pair (TERM$_i$, TERM$_j$) whose similarity exceeds a given threshold, an attempt is made to add a third term, TERM$_k$, to the group by computing the similarity between TERM$_k$ and each of the original terms; the new term is added whenever its similarity with *at least one* of the original terms exceeds a stated threshold.
    2   The process is then repeated for term triples, quadruples, etc., by adding a new term whenever its similarity with one of the original terms exceeds the stated threshold.

    An example of this process is shown in Fig. 4-9. The significant term-pair similarities are shown in Fig. 4-9a in tabular form. Figure 4-9b presents the same information in graph form, where the nodes of the graph designate terms, and the branches between nodes represent the corresponding term similarities. The final term clusters are given in Fig. 4-9c. The initial cluster is obtained by first forming the class $\{T_1, T_2\}$. To this are added terms T_3 and T_7 because of the similar term pairs (T_2, T_3) and (T_2, T_7). This produces a new class $\{T_1, T_2, T_3, T_7\}$. This group can be increased to its full size by adding T_8 because of the connection between T_3 and T_8. A second class is formed of terms T_4, T_5, and T_6 in view

(i)(T_1, T_2) (ii)(T_2, T_1) (iii)(T_3, T_2) (iv)(T_4, T_5)

                    (T_2, T_3) (T_3, T_8) (T_4, T_6)

                    (T_2, T_7)

(v)(T_5, T_4) (vi)(T_6, T_4) (vii)(T_7, T_2) (viii)(T_8, T_3)

(a)

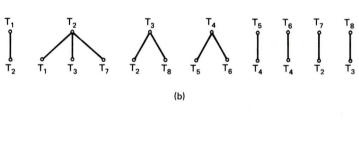

(b)

(c)

Figure 4-9 Single-link cluster example. (a) Initially available term pairs. (b) Corresponding graphical representation. (c) Corresponding single-link clustering.

of the existence of the similar pairs (T_4,T_5) and (T_4,T_6). For the example under consideration the thesaurus classes produced are as follows: $\{T_1,T_2,T_3,T_7,T_8\}$ and $\{T_4,T_5,T_6\}$.

The single-link cluster process requires of the order of n^2 term comparisons to classify n terms, since each term is associated with at most $(n-1)$ other terms. This method has been used to cluster large collections of items [17], and it may be applicable to the general term classification problem because the number of terms does not normally exceed several tens of thousands.

For document clustering, where the file size may comprise hundreds of thousands or even millions of items, less expensive methods may turn out to be more appropriate. A summary of the SMART automatic indexing system is presented in the flowchart of Fig. 4-10.

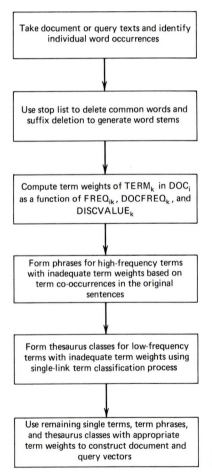

Figure 4-10 Typical SMART automatic indexing process.

*B Automatic Document Classification

It was seen earlier that the preferred file organization in the SMART environment is a clustered collection where the incoming queries are compared first with the centroids of certain document classes and then with the individual documents for those classes whose centroid similarity with the queries is sufficiently large. The clustered file organization lends itself to rapid collection searches and to fast and possibly effective retrieval strategies because all the related documents in a given class are in principle retrievable in a single file access. Furthermore, a clustered file is updated easily, because new documents can be treated like incoming queries in that comparisons with the existing centroids lead to the incorporation of new items into the most closely fitting classes.

The available clustering methods fall into two main types according to whether an initial set of classes already exists or on the contrary new classes must be constructed for a given collection of items. When document sets are to be clustered, a prior classification is not generally available; it is then necessary to construct a new classification for the given set of items. A second clustering criterion distinguishes the *hierarchical grouping* methods which utilize a full document-document similarity matrix specifying the similarity for all document pairs, from the *iterative partitioning* procedures where a rough classification is first generated which is then refined in several steps.

The hierarchical grouping methods which include the previously mentioned clique and single-link procedures are theoretically more satisfying than the alternative partitioning methods because in these methods each item is effectively considered as a possible "seed point" around which a new class is to be built, whereas the classes formed with the iterative partitioning process depend on the strategy used for the initial cluster generation. A form of iterative partitioning is nevertheless used with the SMART system because the number of required document comparisons to cluster n items is of the order of n log n, whereas n^2 comparisons may be needed to obtain the document pair similarities needed by the hierarchical grouping strategies. When the collections are large, a relatively inexpensive clustering method seems essential.

The SMART "single-pass" clustering proceeds in a bottom-up fashion by considering the records one at a time in arbitrary order, while attempting to group them into clusters [18,19]. The first item is initially identified with cluster one. The next item is compared with cluster one and merged with it if found to be sufficiently similar. If the new item is not similar to any already existing cluster, a new cluster is generated. Subsequent items are compared with all existing cluster centroids and entered into classes whenever the centroid similarity is sufficiently large. When a new item is entered into a cluster, the corresponding cluster centroid must be redefined by incorporating terms from the new term vector into the original cluster centroid.

In principle, the single-pass clustering process should serve to assign each item to at least one cluster, and the classification should be complete after one pass through the file. In practice, the resulting classes may not be usable for search purposes without additional refinements. Several problems may arise:

1 The number of clusters produced by the initial pass may become excessively large, implying that a query submitted to the system may have to be compared with a very large number of centroids before access to the individual records is actually obtained.

2 The size of certain clusters may become too large, particularly if a great many records in a collection cover fairly homogeneous subject areas.

3 Alternatively, the cluster size may be very small, and could indeed be limited to a single record in cases where so-called loose records exist that do not match any other records in the collection.

4 The overlap among clusters, that is, the number of items jointly contained in more than one cluster may be too large or too small.

To respond to these eventualities, controls must be introduced to regulate cluster size, cluster overlap, and number of clusters generated, and to handle any "loose" items remaining at the end of the first pass. The loose items actually present no severe problem, since they can naturally be merged with the closest existing clusters. To control the size and the number of clusters, a *cluster splitting* operation is carried out whenever a given cluster size exceeds some preestablished threshold. This is done by generating a term-term similarity matrix for all terms located in the excessively large clusters, and using a new *local* clustering operation to produce two or more new centroids replacing each centroid originally attached to a cluster that had grown too large.

The cluster splitting operation is illustrated in the example of Fig. 4-11 where the assumption is that no class may contain more than four elements. The initial state consists of four clusters, each containing between two and four records. These four centroids are themselves grouped into a supercluster with supercentroid S as shown in Fig. 4-11a. If a new record is added to cluster A, an illegal situation arises, since the cluster size is assumed limited to four elements. The A centroid must then be split thereby creating two new centroids A' and A'' as shown in Fig. 4-11c. At this point the supercluster S is no longer viable since it now contains five elements. This is remedied by splitting S into S' and S'', thereby creating a new hypercluster H included in Fig. 4-11d. The cluster splitting process thus propagates upward in the "cluster tree," starting with the lowest level clusters and moving upward as shown in the example.

A simplified flowchart of the single-pass cluster generation and search process is shown in Fig. 4-12. Generation and search differ in substance only for the lowest-level centroids: during cluster generation a new record must be added to the lowest level of the cluster tree and the cluster splitting routine may need to be invoked; during normal searching, on the other hand, the low-level clusters simply lead to the individual records on the lowest level. The program of Fig. 4-12 maintains a list of centroids to be split. When that list is not empty, the splitting routine is invoked following the placement of each incoming item.

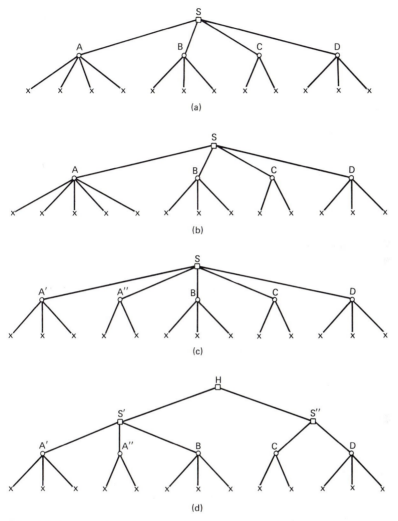

Figure 4-11 Example of cluster splitting process. (a) Initial state of cluster structure. (b) Addition of one more item to cluster A. (c) Splitting cluster A into two pieces A′ and A″. (d) Splitting supercluster S into two pieces S′ and S″.

The cluster generation method may be adapted to special retrieval requirements: when a premium is placed on search precision and the retrieval of nonrelevant items must be avoided, the cluster structure should consist of a large number of small, disjoint clusters on the lowest level of the search tree. When the recall proves more important a smaller number of larger, partly overlapping clusters should prove more effective. Suitable adjustments in the thresholds that control the clustering process can be used to satisfy varying retrieval requirements.

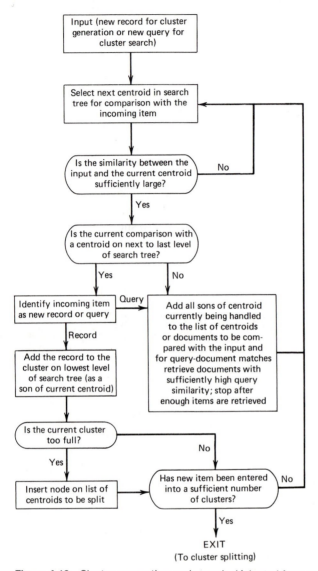

Figure 4-12 Cluster generation and search. (*Adapted from reference 18.*)

*C Relevance Feedback Operations

Most modern on-line search and retrieval environments make provisions for the utilization of flexible search procedures that can generate satisfactory query statements and useful retrieval output in several small steps. An iterative search system is typically implemented by initially submitting a tentative query, and then using system facilities to improve these query statements and the resulting set of retrieved items.

The methods used to construct improved query formulations fall into two broad classes: those which are applied before a file search is actually carried out, and those which depend on the prior retrieval of some retrieved items. In the former case, it is possible to use displayed vocabulary excerpts, term frequency information, and citations to so-called source documents previously identified as relevant by the user to construct improved queries. More specifically, a stored thesaurus of terms can be used to obtain synonym lists for the terms originally included in a search formulation. In addition, frequency data about the number of documents to which a term is assigned can also be stored in the thesaurus to provide an indication of the potential effect of the term for search purposes. When relevant source documents are known in advance, a query might simply be replaced by the terms assigned to such documents in the hope of retrieving additional documents similar to those originally identified as relevant.

An alternative query alteration process is based on the execution of an initial search operation and an initial retrieval of certain stored documents. The display of information relating to these items such as the titles or abstracts of the previously retrieved documents is then used to modify the query statements, normally by adding terms from documents that appear relevant to the user and by deleting terms included in the items that appear useless. This produces new queries whose resemblance to the relevant documents is greater than before while their resemblance to the nonrelevant items is smaller, as suggested in the example of Fig. 4-3. In the SMART system, this process has been called "relevance feedback." It has been shown experimentally that the relevance feedback process can account for improvements in retrieval effectiveness of up to 50 percent in precision for high-recall (broad) searches, and of approximately 20 percent in precision for low-recall searches [20].

Consider first the unrealistic situation where the complete set of relevant documents D_R is known in advance, and hence also the complete set of nonrelevant documents $D_{N-R} = N - D_R$. (In such a case, there is no point in submitting a search request because the known relevant documents can then simply be retrieved from the file without performing a file search.) It can be shown that in such a situation the optimal query which is best able to distinguish the relevant from the nonrelevant documents is a vector obtained by taking the difference between the set of relevant and the set of nonrelevant documents, respectively. More formally, if $TERM_{ik}$ represents the value, or weight, of term k in document i as before, then the average value of term k in the set of R relevant documents is $\left(\frac{1}{R}\right)\left(\sum_{i \in D_R} TERM_{ik}\right)$. Similarly, the average value of term k in the set of $N - R$ nonrelevant documents is $\left(\frac{1}{N-R}\right)\left(\sum_{i \in D_{N-R}} TERM_{ik}\right)$. The value of term k in the optimal query Q_{opt} is then defined as

$$(Q_{opt})_k = C \left(\frac{1}{R} \sum_{i \in D_R} TERM_{ik} - \frac{1}{N-R} \sum_{i \in D_{N-R}} TERM_{ik} \right) \tag{5}$$

where C is a constant [21]

In practice the sets of relevant documents D_R and of nonrelevant items D_{N-R} are not known in advance. However, the relevance judgments obtained from the user population for previously retrieved relevant documents furnish approximations to the sets D_R and D_{N-R}. The assumption is then made that a near-optimal query can be obtained by taking the difference between the sub-sets of relevant and of nonrelevant items known at any particular time. By re-peating the relevance feedback operation several times, and retrieving at each point a new set of documents with an improved query formulation, one may eventually obtain a reasonable approximation to the actual set of relevant and nonrelevant items.

Several formulations are now possible for a new improved query vector Q', starting with an initial query formulation Q and a set $D_{R'}$ of R' documents identified as relevant as well as a set $D_{N'}$ of N' nonrelevant documents, where $D_{N'}$ and $D_{R'}$ are initial representations of the actual set of nonrelevant and rele-vant documents, respectively. First it is possible by analogy to the optimal for-mula of expression (5) to define the new query as simply the difference between the known sets of relevant and nonrelevant items, respectively:

$$Q' = C \left(\frac{1}{R'} \sum_{i \in D_{R'}} DOC_i - \frac{1}{N'} \sum_{i \in D_{N'}} DOC_i \right) \tag{6}$$

DOC_i again represents the vector for the ith document. In formula (6) the infor-mation contained in the original query Q is not used. In practice the original query formulation may contain important information; hence an improved feedback strategy may be produced by using the original query and adding terms from the relevant documents, and/or deleting terms from the nonrelevant ones:

$$Q' = \alpha Q + \beta \left(\frac{1}{R'} \sum_{i \in D_{R'}} DOC_i \right) - \gamma \left(\frac{1}{N'} \sum_{i \in D_{N'}} DOC_i \right) \tag{7}$$

where α, β, and γ are suitable constants. Expression (7) specifies a new query as the vector sum of the old query plus the weighted difference between the average of the known relevant and the average of the known nonrelevant items.

The operations specified by expression (7) are illustrated in the example of Fig. 4-13, where a query Q comprising five terms is shown together with a rele-vant document D_1 and a nonrelevant document D_2. The constants α, β, γ are assumed to take on values of 1, $1/2$, $1/4$, respectively. The new query derived in Fig. 4-13c exhibits increased weights for terms 1 and 3, a decreased weight for term 5, and a new term (term 2) not present in the original query. Correspond-

	Term 1	Term 2	Term 3	Term 4	Term 5
Q = (	5 ,	0 ,	3 ,	0 ,	1)
D_1 = (	2 ,	1 ,	2 ,	0 ,	0)
D_2 = (	1 ,	0 ,	0 ,	0 ,	2)

(a)

$$Q' = Q + \frac{1}{2}\left(\sum_{D_R'} D_i\right) - \frac{1}{4}\left(\sum_{D_N'} \right)D_i$$

$$Q' = (5,0,3,0,1) + \frac{1}{2}(2,1,2,0,0) - \frac{1}{4}(1,0,0,0,2)$$

$$= 5\frac{3}{4}, \frac{1}{2}, 4, 0, \frac{1}{2}$$

(b)

Assume $S(Q,D_i) = \sum_{j=1}^{t} (Q_j, D_{ij})$

$S(Q,D_1) = (5\cdot2) + (0\cdot1) + (3\cdot2) + (0\cdot0) + (1\cdot0) = 16$

$S(Q',D_1) = (5\frac{3}{4}\cdot2) + (\frac{1}{2}\cdot1) + (4\cdot2) + (0\cdot0) + (\frac{1}{2}\cdot0) = 20$

$S(Q,D_2) = (5\cdot1) + (0\cdot0) + (3\cdot0) + (0\cdot0) + (1\cdot2) = 7$

$S(Q',D_2) = (5\frac{3}{4}\cdot1) + (\frac{1}{2}\cdot0) + (4\cdot0) + (0\cdot0) + (\frac{1}{2}\cdot2) = 6\frac{3}{4}$

(c)

Figure 4-13 Relevance feedback operation. (a) Originally available query Q, relevant document D_1, nonrelevant document D_2. (b) Query alteration. (c) Query-document similarities.

ingly, the query-document similarity obtained with the new query Q' is larger than before for document D_1 and smaller than before for D_2.

In practice one finds that the information contained in the relevant documents is more valuable for query reformulation purposes than the terms which originate in the nonrelevant items. The reason is that the set of relevant documents with respect to a given query may be expected to be located in a reasonably homogeneous area of the document space, as in the example of Fig. 4-7. The addition to the query of terms from these relevant items will then produce a definite movement of the query in the direction of these relevant items (see Fig. 4-3). The set of nonrelevant items, on the other hand, is normally much more heterogeneous. The average nonrelevant item may therefore be located almost anywhere in the document space, and subtraction of the corresponding terms

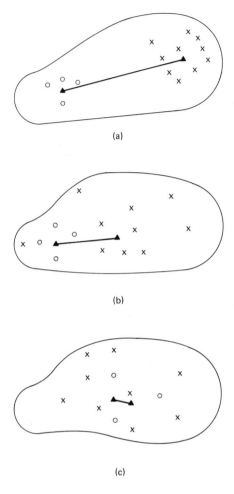

(a)

(b)

(c)

○ relevant document

x nonrelevant document

▲ average item

Figure 4-14 Relevance feedback environment. (a) Ideal relevance feedback situation. (b) Tight relevant document set, but loose nonrelevant set. (c) Intermingled relevant and nonrelevant documents.

removes the query from that area of the space without specifying a definite alternative direction. The feedback equation [expression (7)] should then be used with a smaller weight for γ than for β. Alternatively γ might be specified as 0, thereby creating a *positive feedback* strategy. A third alternative consists in using only a small set of nonrelevant documents by including in the feedback equation only one or two documents—for example, the nonrelevant documents retrieved earliest in a given search (those exhibiting the lowest ranks when the documents are arranged in decreasing order of the query-document similarity).

Since the difference between the average relevant and the average nonrelevant documents is equivalent to the distance between the corresponding vectors in the vector space, it is not surprising that the formal as well as experimental test results show that the retrieval operation is most effective when the relevant documents as well as the nonrelevant documents are tightly clustered, and the difference between the two groups is as large as possible. Such a situation is represented in Fig. 4-14a.

The relevance feedback operation is less favorable in the more realistic case where the set of nonrelevant documents covers a wider area of the space. The corresponding distance between the average relevant and nonrelevant items is much smaller in Fig. 4-14b than in Fig. 4-14a. Finally, the situation is distinctly unfavorable when relevant and nonrelevant are intermixed as shown in Fig. 4-14c. That situation represents a failure of the basic assumption of the SMART document analysis, namely that document content can be represented for retrieval purposes by the term occurrence vectors. Additional information must then be added to the document vectors to distinguish those which are useful from the others. Some approaches to this problem are mentioned in the next section.

The experimental evidence available for relevance feedback indicates that one or two feedback operations are quite effective in raising retrieval performance. Following the second query reformulation a state of diminishing returns sets in and not much further improvement can be expected.

*D Dynamic Document Space

The query alteration process described in the previous subsection was based on information obtained from the user population in the course of the normal retrieval process. In a system where customer intelligence is available, an attempt can also be made to improve the document vector representation (instead of only the query vectors) by incorporating into the document representations new information obtained from the users during the search operations. One possibility consists in adding to the originally available document terms new information derived from relevance assessments furnished by the users in the course of a retrieval operation.

Specifically, when a number of documents retrieved in response to a given query are labeled by the user as relevant, it is possible to render these documents more easily retrievable in the future by making each item somewhat more similar to the query used to retrieve them. Analogously, retrieved documents labeled as nonrelevant are rendered less easily retrievable by being shifted away from the query. Following a large number of such interactions, documents which are wanted by the users will have been moved slowly into the active portion of the document space—that part in which a large number of user queries are concentrated, while items which are normally rejected will be located on the periphery of the space. Eventually, such items could be discarded.

By analogy to the relevance feedback operations, the dynamic document vector alteration can be carried out by constructing a new document representation DOC$'_i$ from the old document representations DOC$_i$ and the terms contained in query Q. The query terms are added to the original document vector using the positive weighting factors α, β, γ, δ, and ϵ:

1 For documents designated as relevant, which must be rendered more similar to query Q:
    a A query term *not* present in the document is added to the document with a weighting factor of α.
    b A query term also present in the document receives increased importance by incrementing its weight by a factor β.
    c A document term not present in the query is decreased in weight by a factor $-\gamma$.
2 For documents designated as nonrelevant which must be rendered less similar to the query:
    a Document terms also present in the query are rendered less important by decreasing their weight by a factor of $-\delta$.
    b Document terms absent from the query are increased in weight by a factor ϵ [22,23].

Several laboratory tests were carried out to test the foregoing dynamic document space alteration methods. In each case, a collection of user queries was first used to generate a modified document space. A new query set, distinct from the original one, could then be processed against both the originally available document space and the modified space. Improvement in recall and precision of from 5 to 10 percent could be detected for the modified space compared with the original space. One would expect that the document vector modification process carried out for a given time period with a particular user population would eventually produce an equilibrium position where documents important to the users could become easily retrievable whereas extraneous documents would be easily rejected. Such a conjecture remains to be verified in practice.

4 AUTOMATIC ENHANCEMENTS OF CONVENTIONAL RETRIEVAL

*A Document Ranking and Term Weighting

Various retrieval systems and procedures have been implemented over the last few years that are based in one way or another on the SMART model [24,25]. Possibly the most useful of these from a practical viewpoint are systems that preserve as much as possible the conventional processing methodology while adding enhancements to simplify the retrieval operations and to improve system effectiveness. The main characteristics of currently existing retrieval technologies are the inverted file organizations and the use of Boolean query formulations. This suggests that improved retrieval services could be obtained by combining the basic inverted file systems with SMART-like ''back-end'' procedures, designed to overcome some of the disadvantages of conventional systems.

Among the methods usable for improving the output produced by conventional file systems are the incorporation of weighted instead of binary terms and the presentation of the retrieved output in decreasing order of the query-document similarity. The generation of *ranked* document output increases user satisfaction and retrieval precision. Furthermore, the ranked retrieval can substantially enhance the chances of success of the relevance feedback process by bringing the relevant items to the user's attention early in the search; this in turn leads to the construction of useful feedback queries.

Ranked retrieval and relevance feedback can in principle be implemented in binary indexing systems where the index terms are either present or absent from the document and query vectors. However, the documents are easier to rank when *weighted terms* are assigned to the queries, and possibly also to the documents, because a composite query-document similarity coefficient can then be computed for each query-document pair based on the weights of matching query-document terms.

In a system such as SMART where each document is represented by a vector of terms and each vector is stored as a complete entity, the use of term weights presents no conceptual problem, because a term weight can simply be listed with each term identification in the corresponding term vector. Thus a particular document i dealing with "fruit" might be listed as

$$DOC_i = (APPLE,4; PEAR,3; \ldots ; PLUM,1)$$

to indicate that the document deals rather more with pears than with plums, and even more with apples. In inverted file systems, the term weighting information must be included in the various inverted lists. Thus the term list for a given term k must now be expanded to include not only the document references for documents to which term k is assigned but also the particular weights for that term in the various documents. A sample inverted file of that kind is shown in Table 4-2.

Given some particular query Q_j, a file organization such as that of Table 4-2 now makes it possible to compute a similarity measure between the query and the document terms. For each term k included in query j, the corresponding term list is extracted from the inverted file, and the weights of terms that occur in both query j and document i are appropriately combined to produce a similarity measure between the given query j and each document that shares

Table 4-2 Typical Inverted Term Lists with Weights

$TERM_1$	$DOC_i, WT_{i1}; DOC_j, WT_{j1}; \ldots ; DOC_m, WT_{m1}$
$TERM_2$	$DOC_i, WT_{i2}; DOC_k, WT_{k2}; \ldots ; DOC_n, WT_{n2}$
$\vdots$	
$TERM_s$	$DOC_j, WT_{js}; DOC_m, WT_{ms}; \ldots ; DOC_p, WT_{ps}$

terms with the query. Consider a query consisting of three terms r, s, and t, and let the similarity measure between the query j and document i be defined as the sum of the products of the matching terms [that is, the numerator of the cosine formula of expression (1)]. To compute the similarity measure between the given query and document, it suffices to enter first the inverted list for term r and pick out $TERM_{ir}$ representing the weight of term r in document i. This leads to the computation of the product $QTERM_{jr} \cdot TERM_{ir}$. A subsequent access to the inverted lists for terms s and t makes it possible to add to the earlier product the terms $QTERM_{js} \cdot TERM_{is}$ and $QTERM_{jt} \cdot TERM_{it}$.

To compute the cosine measure of expression (1) an additional normalization factor consisting of the sum of the squares of all term weights included in each document and each query is needed. This makes it necessary to provide for each document i the factor $\sum_{k=1}^{t} (TERM_{ik})^2$. These factors can be computed in advance for each document and stored in a special "document length" file which is accessed for all documents that have a nonzero similarity with the query. The expanded inverted document reference lists together with the document length file permit the computation of the full cosine similarity measure for all documents sharing one or more terms with the query, followed by the ranking of documents in decreasing order of the query-document similarity.

The SIRE (Syracuse information retrieval experiment) system includes the normal inverted file processing facilities used for the Boolean query operations, as well as the expanded term weighting operations that provide ranked document output [26–28]. The SIRE file organization is shown in Fig. 4-15, and the corresponding processing chain is presented in simplified form in Fig. 4-16. In essence, the SIRE processing chain consists of two main sections. Initially, a Boolean query formulation is processed in the conventional manner. This step identifies all documents whose term assignment precisely matches the query formulation. This subset of documents is then further processed by computing a cosine similarity measure between each document and a "flattened" query consisting of all the original query terms connected by Boolean OR operators. Thus an original query formulated as (A AND B) OR (C AND D) becomes A OR B OR C OR D, or simply the query vector (A,B,C,D).

In the SIRE system the users are not expected to assign weights to the terms. Instead the weight of term k in document i is defined as $FREQ_{ik}$, that is, as the frequency of occurrence of the term in the document. Correspondingly, the document length needed in the denominator of the cosine computation is obtained as the sum of the squares of the individual term frequencies in the document. It is easy to see how the file organization of Fig. 4-15 leads to the proper computation of the cosine measure. A directory to the inverted lists is used to gain access to the document reference numbers and the weights (term frequencies) for all query terms. This produces the numerator of the cosine for each relevant document (each document retrieved by the Boolean query) and the corresponding query. The document length is next obtained for each document from the document length list (Fig. 4-15c). Following the computation of the

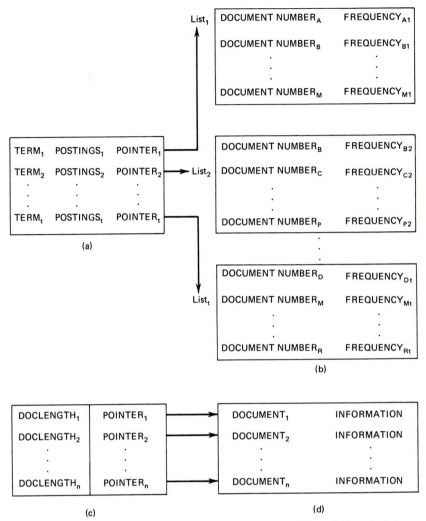

Figure 4-15 SIRE file organization. (a) Directory to inverted lists. (b) Inverted document reference lists. (c) Document length list. (d) Main document file.

query-document similarities, the output information may be extracted from the main document file in decreasing order of the cosine measure by using the file pointers provided for that purpose.

In the SIRE system, the cosine computations and the ranking algorithms are completely divorced from the Boolean retrieval operations. Alternatively, it is possible to give up the Boolean operations completely and process query formulations expressed simply as sets of weighted query terms. In the BROWSER system, a file organization substantially equivalent to that shown in Fig. 4-15 is used together with term weights based on an inverse document

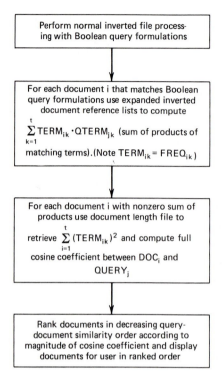

Perform normal inverted file processing with Boolean query formulations

For each document i that matches Boolean query formulations use expanded inverted document reference lists to compute

$$\sum_{k=1}^{t} TERM_{ik} \cdot QTERM_{jk}$$ (sum of products of matching terms). (Note $TERM_{ik} = FREQ_{ik}$)

For each document i with nonzero sum of products use document length file to retrieve $\sum_{i=1}^{t} (TERM_{ik})^2$ and compute full cosine coefficient between DOC_i and $QUERY_j$

Rank documents in decreasing query-document similarity order according to magnitude of cosine coefficient and display documents for user in ranked order

Figure 4-16   SIRE processing chain.

frequency factor [29]. CITE is another system that uses the conventional inverted file technology with term weights, document ranking, and relevance feedback based on the methods described earlier [30].

Another possibility for combining Boolean query processing with term weighting systems is to allow weighted terms directly as part of the normal Boolean formulations. Unfortunately, this approach raises a number of difficult problems, because the normal two-valued logic used to process Boolean queries assumes that a term is either present in or absent from a document or query identification. When the Boolean system is extended to include term weight or importance factors, it becomes necessary to interpret the meaning of compound expressions consisting of weighted terms and Boolean operators such as A_a AND B_b, where a,b represent the weights for terms A and B, respectively. In so doing one would like to define matching functions that resemble the normal Boolean operations and produce equal output for distinct query formulations that are logically equivalent [31,32].

It is possible to design retrieval models that furnish unambiguous retrieval output for weighted Boolean queries. The theory of fuzzy sets provides a model in which the weight of term k in document i represents the degree to which the document is a member of the set of documents indexed by the term k [33]. A weight of 1 then indicates that DOC_i is a full member of the document set indexed by $TERM_k$, a weight of 0 says that the document does not belong to the set, and an intermediate weight designates a partial degree of membership. The effect of compound Boolean expressions can also be defined in the fuzzy set model. Whether weighted Boolean queries will ever become popular in retrieval remains to be seen.

*B   Retrieval through Man-Machine Dialogue and Local Clustering

The previously described relevance feedback process is based on a somewhat rudimentary type of user-system interaction, because the system generates query formulations based on relevance assessments returned by the user for previously retrieved documents. There exist interactive systems where the user is expected to take a much more active role in the retrieval operations. Thus users may be asked to carry out the query reformulations by individually choosing good terms for incorporation into the queries; the corresponding terms may then be chosen from among a set of potentially useful terms displayed by the system. Users may also be asked to assign positive and/or negative weights to the terms considered for incorporation into the query. Finally the users may be asked to assign weights (positive or negative) to displayed documents that may or may not have been retrieved in earlier searches [34].

Relevance judgments can be used as a basis for query reformulation also in conventional retrieval environments where Boolean query statements are used to retrieve documents manually indexed by keywords. The user feedback process devised for the European Community retrieval service consists of the following main steps [35]:

   1   Relevance assessments are obtained for some of the documents retrieved in response to an initial search request.
   2   The set of terms used to index some of the items known as relevant is examined [for example, (A AND B AND C AND D) and also (E AND F AND G)].
   3   Some terms from the query statements chosen under step 2 are removed so as to broaden the resulting search statements [for example, statements (A AND B AND D) and also (E AND F) are constructed].
   4   These shortened queries are used as new search statements to retrieve additional documents; the relevance of some of these newly retrieved documents is then assessed.
   5   For each of the new query statements a "query quality factor" is computed as the ratio between the new relevant items retrieved divided by the new nonrelevant items retrieved.
   6   Those partial queries with sufficiently high query quality factors are chosen and a final feedback query is constructed by inserting OR connectives between the corresponding partial query formulations [for example, the new statement used could be (A AND B AND D) OR (E AND F)].
   7   The newly constructed query is used for search purposes, and the process is repeated if desired.

Additional feedback techniques incorporating slight variations of such a process can easily be devised.

One of the virtues of the relevance feedback and related query reformulation methods is the *local* nature of the operations involved; normally only the previously retrieved documents are used, rather than the whole document set. Such considerations lie at the root of a number of *local clustering* systems designed to improve the final search output. A standard inverted file search is used as a fast preliminary step, and the automatic classification procedures previously described then serve to cluster the (local) set of documents retrieved in response to particular search efforts in the hope of improving the final search output. The corresponding document classes can be used to determine a specific ranking order in which the output items can be brought to the user's attention. By displaying together whole groups of related documents and bringing them to the user's attention simultaneously, the choice of new terms to be incorporated into a feedback query may also be simplified [36].

Local clustering operations can be applied to terms as well as to documents. This produces a *local thesaurus* specifically applicable to each query which is obtained by grouping terms extracted from previously retrieved documents. A typical query reformulation process based on local term clustering might be carried out as follows [37,38]:

1 Relevance assessments are obtained for certain documents retrieved in earlier search operations.

2 Terms from the documents identified as relevant are ranked in decreasing order of relative frequency (frequency of occurrence in the relevant retrieved documents divided by total frequency in the collection), and terms with large relative frequency are used for query reformulation purposes.

3 Alternatively, or in addition, term similarity coefficients may be obtained for pairs of terms occurring in the relevant documents, the size of the coefficients being dependent on common occurrence patterns in the respective documents or document sentences.

4 Terms with large enough similarity coefficients are then clustered, and each original query term is considered as the kernel of a cluster of related terms to be used for query reformulation purposes.

It is not hard to generate extensions and refinements of the local clustering operations previously described. Thus local term association procedures can in principle also incorporate syntactic considerations where syntactic relationships between terms lead to the generation of term groups [39,40]. Document grouping methods, on the other hand, might utilize the similarities not only between the assigned terms but also between bibliographic citations shared jointly by a number of documents [41]. As the use of computers for document processing becomes more widespread, one may expect that the query refinement procedures based on user-system cooperation and on local clustering operations will also become more widespread.

REFERENCES

[1] G. Salton, Automatic Information Organization and Retrieval, McGraw-Hill Book Company, New York, 1968.

[2] G. Salton, editor, The SMART Retrieval System—Experiments in Automatic Document Processing, Prentice-Hall, Inc., Englewood Cliffs, New Jersey, 1971.

[3] G. Salton and M.E. Lesk, The SMART Automatic Document Retrieval System—An Illustration, Communications of the ACM, Vol. 8, No. 6, June 1965, pp. 391–398.

[4] G. Salton, A. Wong, and C.S. Yang, A Vector Space Model for Automatic Indexing, Communications of the ACM, Vol. 18, No. 11, November 1975, pp. 613–620.

[5] G. Salton and M.E. Lesk, Computer Evaluation of Indexing and Text Processing, Journal of the ACM, Vol. 15, No. 1, January 1968, pp. 8–36.

[6] G. Salton, Recent Studies in Automatic Text Analysis and Document Retrieval, Journal of the ACM, Vol. 20, No. 2, April 1973, pp. 258–278.

[7] G. Salton, A New Comparison between Conventional Indexing (MEDLARS) and Automatic Text Processing (SMART), Journal of the ASIS, Vol. 23, No. 2, March–April 1972, pp. 75–84.

[8] J.B. Lovins, Development of a Stemming Algorithm, Mechanical Translation and Computational Linguistics, Vol. 11, No. 1–2, March and June 1968, pp. 11–31.

[9] A. Tars, Stemming as a System Design Consideration, ACM SIGIR Forum, Vol. 11, No. 1, Summer 1976, pp. 9–16.

[10] G. Salton, C.S. Yang, and C.T. Yu, A Theory of Term Importance in Automatic Text Analysis, Journal of the ASIS, Vol. 26, No. 1, January–February 1975, pp. 33–44.

[11] K. Sparck Jones, A Statistical Interpretation of Term Specificity and Its Application in Retrieval, Journal of Documentation, Vol. 28, No. 1, 1972, pp. 11–21.

[12] G. Salton and C.S. Yang, On the Specifications of Term Values in Automatic Indexing, Journal of Documentation, Vol. 29, No. 4, December 1973, pp. 351–372.

[13] G. Salton and A. Wong, On the Role of Words and Phrases in Automatic Text Analysis, Computers and the Humanities, Vol. 10, 1976, pp. 69–87.

[14] G. Salton, Experiments in Automatic Thesaurus Construction for Information Retrieval, Information Processing 71, North Holland Publishing Company, Amsterdam, 1972, pp. 115–123.

[15] K. Sparck Jones, Automatic Keyword Classification for Information Retrieval, Butterworths, London, 1971.

[16] G. Salton, Dynamic Information and Library Processing, Prentice-Hall Inc., Englewood Cliffs, New Jersey, 1975.

[17] W.B. Croft, Clustering Large Files of Documents Using the Single Link Method, Journal of the ASIS, Vol. 28, No. 6, November 1977, pp. 341–344.

[18] R.E. Williamson, Real Time Document Retrieval, Doctoral Thesis, Cornell University, Ithaca, New York, June 1974.

[19] G. Salton and A. Wong, Generation and Search of Clustered Files, ACM Transactions on Data Base Systems, Vol. 3, No. 4, December 1978, pp. 321–346.

[20] E. Ide and G. Salton, Interactive Search Strategies and Dynamic File Organization, in The SMART Retrieval System—Experiments in Automatic Document Processing, G. Salton, editor, Prentice-Hall, Inc., Englewood Cliffs, New Jersey, 1971, Chapter 16.

[21] J.J. Rocchio, Jr., Relevance Feedback in Information Retrieval, in The SMART Re-

trieval System—Experiments in Automatic Document Processing, G. Salton, editor, Prentice-Hall, Inc., Englewood Cliffs, New Jersey, 1971, Chapter 14.

[22] G. Salton, Dynamic Document Processing, Communications of the ACM, Vol. 15, No. 7, July 1972, pp. 658–668.

[23] T. Brauen, Document Vector Modification, in The SMART Retrieval System—Experiments in Automatic Document Processing, G. Salton, editor, Prentice-Hall, Inc., Englewood Cliffs, New Jersey, 1975, Chapter 24.

[24] N.S. Malthouse, Indexgen—Index Term Generation Heuristics, Oak Ridge National Laboratory, Report ORNL-EIS-104, Oak Ridge, Tennessee, June 1978.

[25] Informatics Inc., RADC Automatic Classification On-Line (RADCOL)—User's Manual, Final Technical Report, Rome Air Development Center, Rome, New York, May 1975.

[26] T. Noreault, M. Koll, and M.J. McGill, Automatic Ranked Output from Boolean Searches in SIRE, Journal of the ASIS, Vol. 28, No. 6, November 1977, pp. 333–339.

[27] M.J. McGill, L. Smith, S. Davidson, and T. Noreault, Syracuse Information Retrieval Experiment (SIRE): Design of an On-Line Bibliographic Retrieval System, SIGIR Forum, Vol. 10, No. 4, Spring 1976, pp. 37–44.

[28] M.J. McGill and T. Noreault, Syracuse Information Retrieval Experiment (SIRE): Rationale and Basic System Design, Report, School of Information Studies, Syracuse University, Syracuse, New York, May 1977.

[29] J.H. Williams, BROWSER, An Automatic Indexing On-Line Text Retrieval System, IBM Federal Systems Division Report, Gaithersburg, Maryland, 1969.

[30] T.E. Doszkocs and B.A. Rapp, Searching MEDLINE in English: A Prototype User Interface with Natural Language Query, Ranked Output and Relevance Feedback, Proceedings of the ASIS Annual Meeting, Minneapolis, Minnesota, October 1979, R.D. Tally, editor, Knowledge Industry Publications, White Plains, New York, 1979, pp. 131–139.

[31] A. Bookstein, On the Perils of Merging Boolean and Weighted Retrieval Systems, Journal of the ASIS, Vol. 29, No. 3, May 1978, pp. 156–158.

[32] W.G. Waller and D.H. Kraft, A Mathematical Model of a Weighted Boolean Retrieval System, Information Processing and Management, Vol. 15, No. 5, 1979, pp. 235–245.

[33] A. Bookstein, Fuzzy Requests: An Approach to Weighted Boolean Searches, Journal of the American Society for Information Science, Vol. 31, No. 4, July 1980, pp. 240–247.

[34] R.N. Oddy, Information Retrieval through Man-Machine Dialogue, Journal of Documentation, Vol. 33, No. 1, March 1977, pp. 1–14.

[35] V. Vernimb, Automatic Query Adjustment in Document Retrieval, Information Processing and Management, Vol. 13, No. 6, 1977, pp. 339–353.

[36] D.S. Becker and S.R. Pyrce, Enhancing the Retrieval Effectiveness of Large Information Systems, IIT Research Institute, Report PB 266 008, Chicago, Illinois, 1977.

[37] R. Attar and A.S. Fraenkel, Local Feedback in Full-Text Retrieval Systems, Journal of the ACM, Vol. 24, No. 3, July 1977, pp. 397–417.

[38] T.E. Doszkocs, AID—An Associative Interactive Dictionary for On-Line Searching, On-Line Review, Vol. 2, No. 2, 1978, pp. 163–173.

[39] D.J. Hillman, Customized User Services via Interactions with LEADERMART, Information Storage and Retrieval, Vol. 9, No. 11, 1973, pp. 587–596.

[40] D. Taeuber, CONDOR—Ein Integriertes Datenbank und Informationssystem, Nachrichten für Dokumentation, Vol. 29, No. 3, 1978, pp. 127–130.

[41] H. Small, Cocitation in the Scientific Literature: A New Measure of the Relationship between Two Documents, Journal of the ASIS, Vol. 24, No. 4, July–August 1973, pp. 265–269.

BIBLIOGRAPHIC REMARKS

Many materials dealing with modern information retrieval appear as user manuals and reports issued by the sponsoring organizations. A summary of many existing, advanced systems is included in:

F.W. Lancaster and E.G. Fayen, Information Retrieval On-Line, Melville Publishing Company, Los Angeles, California, 1973.

Additional information about the SMART system can be obtained from:

G. Salton, editor, The SMART Retrieval System—Experiments in Automatic Document Processing, Prentice-Hall, Inc., Englewood Cliffs, New Jersey, 1971.

Advanced bibliographic retrieval services are also examined in various survey papers. The following references may serve as a convenient introduction:

D.B. McCarn and J. Leiter, On Line Services in Medicine and Beyond, Science, Vol. 181, July 27, 1973, pp. 318–324.

T.E. Doszkocs, B.A. Rapp, and H.M. Schoolman, Automated Information Retrieval in Science and Technology, Science, Vol. 208, April 4, 1980, pp. 25–30.

G. Salton, Progress in Automatic Information Retrieval, Computer, Vol. 13, No. 9, September 1980, pp. 41–57.

EXERCISES

4-1 It has been claimed that the generation of ranked retrieval output enhances retrieval effectiveness and user satisfaction.

    a Justify the basic argument.

    b Contrast the methods used to rank documents at the output in the SMART and SIRE systems.

    c Boolean query formulations and inverted file technologies do not ordinarily produce ranked retrieval output; describe two methods that are usable to produce ranked output in a Boolean query environment.

4-2 Relevance feedback and dynamic document space modification are dual operations: in the former the query formulations are enhanced by using terms from previously retrieved documents, and in the latter the document vectors are altered by using terms from queries submitted by the user population.

    a How could relevance feedback and dynamic document space modification be implemented in a retrieval environment based on Boolean query formulations and inverted file technologies; prepare a flowchart-like description for both processes in the new environment.

b Do you feel that relevance feedback and dynamic document space modification are well adapted to an inverted file organization? Carefully explain your reasons.

4-3 Prepare a program to compute the cosine similarity between a given document and query [expression (1)] given the file organization for the SIRE system shown in Fig. 4-15.

4-4 What is the purpose of cluster splitting during the generation of a clustered document collection? In the cluster splitting system represented in Fig. 4-11 a new level of centroids may be created, thereby causing an upward expansion of the cluster tree. Can you think of a cluster splitting method in which the cluster hierarchy expands in a downward direction instead of upward? What are the advantages of both systems of cluster modification for cluster generation and search?

4-5 Consider a sample document collection consisting of six documents, each represented by six terms. Assume that three of the documents are relevant to a given query and three are nonrelevant. Choose the term weights so as to model the situations shown in Fig. 4-14a, b, and c, respectively. Compute the centroid vector for the relevant and the nonrelevant items in each case and show that the distance between the centroids is largest for the case of Fig. 4-14a and smallest for the situation of Fig. 4-14c. What are the consequences in a relevance feedback system?

4-6 What problems arise in implementing a relevance feedback system when a given query does not succeed in retrieving any relevant items? How could one modify feedback equation (7) to handle such a situation?

Retrieval Evaluation

0 PREVIEW

Various automatic retrieval techniques were introduced in the last two chapters that have the potential to alter drastically the current operational retrieval environment. These techniques are not likely to find widespread favor unless their usefulness can be convincingly demonstrated. It is therefore important to understand the problems and techniques involved in the evaluation of retrieval systems and procedures.

This chapter is concerned with the evaluation of retrieval efficiency and effectiveness. Various viewpoints can be taken in evaluating a large system. The text stresses the user viewpoint and examines in detail the various system components which enter into the evaluation task. On the one hand, the system should be able to retrieve a large part of the relevant information contained in the files, while rejecting a large part of the extraneous information; on the other hand, the user effort, time, and cost needed for retrieval should be minimized. The former are characteristics of retrieval effectiveness, often measured by specific values of the recall and precision of the search output. The latter are components entering into an evaluation of search efficiency.

The generation and computation of the recall and precision measures are covered in detail in this chapter together with the computation of various alternative measures of retrieval effectiveness. The best-understood measure of system performance is the cost of using the system. Unfortunately, cost measures are difficult to generate for information retrieval systems. In the end, user satisfaction will depend on a multiplicity of considerations, including the ease with which the system retrieves wanted information, the cost of the system and amount of user effort required in effecting a search, and various human factors such as console design and physical location of the search equipment.

1 INTRODUCTION

To understand the retrieval evaluation problem, it is necessary to examine first the functions of a retrieval system and the various system components. Thereafter, the measures that actually reflect system performance can be introduced.

Information retrieval systems give a user population access to a stored collection of information items. These systems try to locate and retrieve the items as rapidly and economically as possible. The value of the information retrieval system depends on the ability to identify useful information accurately and quickly, the ease of rejecting extraneous items, and the versatility of the methods. Few customers will want a system incapable of retrieving what they want and of rejecting what they do not want. Nor will they want a system that is difficult to handle, slow in furnishing responses, or expensive to use. For these reasons, the evaluation of retrieval systems is of great importance [1–4].

Two kinds of system tests must be distinguished: those concerned with systems *effectiveness*, and those concerned with the *efficiency* of the operations. The effectiveness of an information system is the ability to furnish information services that the users need. On the other hand, efficiency is a measure of the cost or the time necessary to perform a given set of tasks. Ultimately, the viability of a system depends on both the quality and the cost of the operations. A complete evaluation process is then concerned with both effectiveness and efficiency.

There are many reasons for evaluating retrieval systems. For example, one might wish to compare one already existing system with another alternative system. One might also want to determine how system performance changes when some particular system component changes; for example, one could determine the performance changes when the query type is altered or when the subject area is changed. Still another reason is the evaluation of new system components that are considered for inclusion in an existing system. In that case, the operations of the new system could be simulated before a real system is actually built.

The following components are needed in a system test: (1) a detailed description of the system and of its components, or alternatively a model of the system to be examined; (2) a set of hypotheses to be tested, or a particular prototype against which the model is to be measured; (3) a set of criteria reflecting the performance objectives of the system, and measures permitting a quantification of the performance criteria; and finally (4) methods for obtaining and evaluating the data. For example, one might wish to look at the Dialog system and to determine whether the search speed is fast enough to search the data base, the criterion being that maximum allowable response time is 45 seconds, and the evaluation method consisting in asking each user of that data base to measure the response time with a stop watch.

To measure and record system performance, it is desirable to use objective, quantitative criteria. Objective measurements are relatively easy to interpret and are usually free of bias introduced by the evaluator. Objective measurements are obtainable by recording direct observations using questionnaire and interview techniques. Alternatively, some mechanical way may be used to gather the required data. In either case, parameters (that is, constants whose value characterizes the usefulness or worth of a system) must be chosen that are significant for evaluation purposes and are also easily measured and correlated. Some parameters are easily specified—for example, the size of the collection and the system response time. Many other important parameters are interdependent in complex ways—for example, the ability of the system to retrieve useful materials depends on the representation of the documents, the search methods, and the user characteristics. Further, some parameters may not be defined everywhere in the performance range. For example, the ability to retrieve useful items cannot be used when dealing with a document collection that contains no useful documents in a given subject [5–9].

In some circumstances, exact values may be unavailable for certain parameters, or they may be too laborious to supply. For example, the total number of documents in a particular subject area may be unknown and may have to be guessed at using sampling techniques. Probabilistic models are often applicable because many parameters become stable when many observations are made [10]. For example, the average number of relevant items per query or the average number of relevant items retrieved by the system can be estimated either when many documents are matched against a single request or by treating a few documents in many different searches.

2 EVALUATION OF RETRIEVAL EFFECTIVENESS

A System Components

Before a detailed examination of the evaluation parameters can be made, it is necessary to consider briefly the components of an information system and the system environment to determine how system performance is affected by the system environment and operations. The following system components are of concern: acquisitions and input policies, physical form of input, organization of the search files, indexing language, indexing operation, representation of the information items, question analysis, search, and form of presentation of the output [11,12].

Parameters related to the *input policies* include the error rates and time delays experienced in introducing new items into the collection, the time lag between receipt of a given item and its appearance in the file; and the collection coverage, that is, the proportion of potentially relevant information items actually included in the file. The *physical input form*, including document format and document length—title, abstract, summary, or full text—immediately affects the indexing and search tasks, as well as the system economics; and the *organization of the search files* impacts the search process, the response time, the effort needed by system operators, and possibly also the system effectiveness.

The *indexing language* consists of the set of available terms and the rules used to assign these terms to documents and search requests. During the indexing process terms appropriate for the representation of document content are chosen from the indexing language and assigned to the information items in accordance with established indexing rules. Among the parameters that take on special significance in this connection are the *exhaustivity* and *specificity* of the indexing language. An *exhaustive* indexing language contains terms covering all subject areas mentioned in the collection; correspondingly, an exhaustive indexing product implies that all subject areas are properly reflected in the index terms assigned to the documents. A *specific* index language never covers distinct subjects by using a single term, the terms used being narrow and precise.

Retrieval system performance is often measured by using *recall* and *precision* values, where recall measures the ability of the system to retrieve useful documents, while precision conversely measures the ability to reject useless materials. A high level of indexing exhaustivity tends to ensure high recall by making it possible to retrieve most potentially relevant items; at the same time precision may suffer because some marginally relevant items are likely to be retrieved also when many different subject areas are covered by the index terms. When highly specific index terms are used, the precision is expected to be high, since most retrieved items may be expected to be relevant; the converse is true when very broad or general terms are used for indexing purposes because broad terms will not distinguish the marginal items from the truly relevant ones. Thus to obtain high recall an exhaustive indexing is useful in conjunction with an indexing language that provides a variety of approaches to cover the given subject area. To ensure high precision, a highly specific indexing language should be used, and the terms should carry additional content indications such as term weights and relation indications to other terms.

Assuming that the indexing is performed manually by trained persons, the variables affecting the *indexing operation* relate not only to the exhaustivity of the indexing and the specificity of the assigned terms, but also to interindexer consistency, the influence of indexer experience on performance, and the accuracy of the assigned terms.

The *question analysis* and search operations are difficult to characterize. The assignment of terms from the indexing language to information requests, the formulation of meaningful Boolean statements, and the comparison of analyzed requests with the stored information are all complicated tasks. In principle, the content analysis operations are the same for documents and search requests, in the sense that the notions of exhaustivity and specificity are equally as applicable to queries as to documents. Thus, exhaustive query indexing using highly specific terms should produce maximum search recall and precision. In practice, the query processing is often quite distinct from the document indexing because the user is necessarily directly involved in the former but not the latter. In many systems, the query analysis and search operations are therefore delegated to trained experts using appropriate input from the users. Document input, on the other hand, is invariably handled without user input.

The *search operations* are also hard to measure using objective parameters because the role of the user is not well defined in many query formulating environments. Users are rarely asked to state recall or precision requirements, or to evaluate the output products. Yet search strategies need to be devised that respond to the users' specific recall and precision requirements. Among the characteristics that should be included in a measurement of search performance are the type of file organizations used, the type of query-document comparison in use, the effect of the search strategy on system response time and on search performance, and the relevance standards of the system users.

The *form of presentation of the output* is the physical representation of documents found by the system in response to the user's query. The appearance of the output affects the amount of user effort needed to look at the search results and the eventual satisfaction derived from a search. The more complete the form of the output, the easier is the relevance assessment task for the user. On the other hand, as the output is expanded from simple document numbers to full document texts, the time needed to examine the search results also increases.

The foregoing discussion makes clear that the components and parameters of the retrieval system affect the system operations and hence the evaluation results. Each component can be examined separately, or one can compare one entire system with another. In this case the parameters associated with each system are accepted as constant elements in the evaluation. However, one must understand that each of the parameters has an effect on the system, and the importance of each parameter cannot be assessed without taking into account the purposes for which the system is used. This question is discussed further in the next few paragraphs.

B   Evaluation Viewpoints and the Relevance Problem

Information systems may be examined either from the viewpoint of the users or from the viewpoint of system operators and managers. For present purposes, the system managers may be assumed to include all those who influence the policy or the finances of the system, or who are responsible for, or participate in, the actual system operations. Since it is reasonable to assume that an information system exists to meet the needs of its users, the effectiveness criteria of interest to the managers are not unlike those of the users. In particular, the system should meet the user requirements, and failures in the retrieval of relevant materials or in the rejection of nonrelevant items should be minimized. In addition, the managers and to some extent the users are also concerned with the costs and benefits of the system.

Among the many possible evaluation criteria of concern to the user population, six have been identified as critical [13,14]:

1 The *recall*, that is, the ability of the system to present all relevant items

2 The *precision*, that is, the ability to present only the relevant items

3 The *effort*, intellectual or physical, required from the users in formulating the queries, conducting the search, and screening the output

4 The *time* interval which elapses between receipt of a user query and the presentation of system responses

5 The form of *presentation* of the search output which influences the user's ability to utilize the retrieved materials

6 The collection *coverage*, that is, the extent to which all relevant items are included in the system

A list of the criteria of interest to the user population is shown together with the principal related parameters in Table 5-1.

Table 5-1   User Performance Criteria and Related Parameters

User criteria	Selected related parameters
Recall and precision	Indexing exhaustivity (the more exhaustive, the better the recall)
	Specificity of indexing language (the more specific, the better the precision)
	Provisions in indexing language for improving recall (synonym recognition, recognition of term relations, etc.)
	Provisions in indexing language for improving precision (use of term weights, use of term phrases)
	Ability of user population to formulate search requests
	Ability to devise adequate search strategies
Response time	Type of storage device and storage organization
	Query type
	Location of information center
	Rate of arrival of customer queries
	Collection size
User effort	Characteristics of device permitting access to system
	Location of accessing and storage devices
	Availability of help from system staff or aids available from system in nondelegated searches
	Amount of retrieved material
	Type of interaction with system
	Ease of formulation of search requests
Form of presentation	Type of accessing and display device
	Size of stored information file
	Type of output (title, abstract, or full text)
Collection coverage	Type of input device and type and size of storage device
	Ease of content analysis (coverage may be more extensive when content analysis is simple)
	Demand for service (the demand increases with greater coverage)

Of the six user criteria, all but two are relatively easy to measure. The user effort can be expressed in part as the time needed for query formulation, the interaction with the system, and the examination of system outputs. The response time is directly measurable and the form of presentation of the output is easy to state. The collection coverage may present some difficulties if the number of items of interest in a given subject area is unknown. However, consulting published indexes and reference volumes should make it relatively easy to estimate the total number of items that are in fact available from the data base.

This leaves the recall and precision measures. These present the greatest difficulties both conceptually and in practice. An immediate problem in determining the recall and precision is the interpretation of *relevance*. At least two definitions of relevance are possible. An objective view takes into account only a given query and a particular document by stating that

> relevance is the correspondence in context between an information requirement statement (a query) and an article (a document), that is, the extent to which the article covers the material that is appropriate to the requirement statement [15].

That view makes it possible to consider relevance as a logical property between a pair of textual items. It is measurable by the degree to which a document deals with the subject of the user's information need [16,17]. The objective definition of relevance does not take into account the particular state of knowledge of the user during the search operation. A document might be "relevant" even though the user might already have been acquainted with the item before the formulation of the search request, or might have become familiar with the document through earlier search efforts.

A more subjective view of relevance considers not only the contents of a document but also the state of knowledge of the user at the time of the search, and the other documents retrieved or available that the user already knows about. Thus, this notion of relevance depends on the utility of each item to the user. The *pertinent* set of items may then be defined as that subset of the stored items that is appropriate to the user's information need at the time of retrieval [18,19]. Thus a document may be relevant if it deals with the appropriate topic classes but it may not be pertinent if the user is already acquainted with its contents, or if other documents retrieved earlier already cover the appropriate topics. All pertinent items are relevant but not vice versa.

Retrieval effectiveness may be easier to measure by using the objective view of relevance, or topic relatedness, as a criterion for determining relevance than the subjective notion of pertinence. Even in that case, difficulties may arise in assessing the relevance of a document to a query. In borderline cases disagreements may exist among observers about where to place the limit between various grades of relevance, and how to assess the relevance [20,21]. This has led some observers to define relevance in probabilistic terms. In this case relevance is a function of the probability that similarities between the query and document vocabularies will lead a user to accept a given item in response to a particular query [22].

In practice, it is necessary to assume that relevance assessments of documents to queries are available from an external source to the retrieval system if an objective system evaluation is to be accomplished. Hence, a system is judged to be effective if satisfactory evaluation results are obtained using the external relevance criteria.

In the next few sections problems relating to the computation and presentation of the recall and precision measures are examined and alternative retrieval evaluation measures are introduced.

*C The Computation of Recall and Precision

Recall is defined as the proportion of relevant material retrieved, while precision is the proportion of retrieved material that is relevant. In an operational situation, where information needs may vary from user to user, some customers may require high recall, that is, the retrieval of most everything that is likely to be of interest, while others may prefer high precision, that is, the rejection of everything likely to be useless. Everything else being equal, a good system is one which exhibits both a high recall and a high precision.

If a cut is made through the document collection to distinguish retrieved items from nonretrieved ones on the one hand as shown in Fig. 5-1, and if procedures are available for separating relevant items from nonrelevant on the other, the standard recall R' and standard precision P may be defined as

$$R = \frac{\text{number of items retrieved and relevant}}{\text{total relevant in collection}} \tag{1}$$

$$\text{and } P = \frac{\text{number of items retrieved and relevant}}{\text{total retrieved}} \tag{2}$$

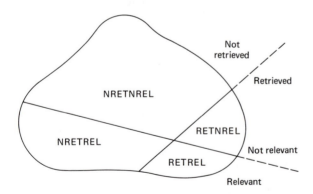

RETREL   : number relevant and retrieved
RETNREL : number not relevant and retrieved
NRETREL : number relevant and not retrieved
NRETNREL: number not relevant and not retrieved

Figure 5-1 Partition of collection.

If relevance judgments are available for each document in the collection with respect to each search request, and if retrieved and nonretrieved material can be unambiguously determined, then the computation of these measures is straightforward [23,24].

In conventional retrieval systems the search requests are presented as Boolean combinations of search terms. The retrieved document set consists of all documents exhibiting the exact combination of keywords specified in the query. That is, each query produces an unordered set of documents that are either relevant or nonrelevant. Hence for each query a single precision and a single recall figure can be obtained. Pairs of recall-precision figures can be compared for two searches i and j, and whenever $RECALL_i \leq RECALL_j$ and $PRECISION_i \leq PRECISION_j$ the results of search j are judged to be superior to those for search i. Unfortunately, problems arise when $RECALL_i < RECALL_j$ and $PRECISION_i > PRECISION_j$ or vice versa $RECALL_i > RECALL_j$ and $PRECISION_i < PRECISION_j$ [25]. In these cases, a judgment of superiority depends on the user's orientation. That is, the user must determine if the principal interest is in recall or in precision, and assess the importance of differences between the recall and precision values. In typical retrieval systems, the recall will increase as the number of retrieved documents increases; at the same time, the precision is likely to decrease. Hence users interested in high recall tend to submit broad queries that retrieve many documents, whereas high-precision users will submit narrow and specific queries.

Some retrieval systems can produce varying amounts of output. A different recall-precision pair can then be obtained for each separate output amount. The finer the division in quantity of output, the greater the number of available recall-precision pairs. For example, the retrieval decision can be based on the number of matching terms between queries and documents. A partial ranking can then be defined for the retrieved document set by first retrieving all items that exhibit at least some arbitrary k matching terms with the query for some judiciously chosen number k. Next all items with k − 1 matching terms are retrieved, followed by those with k − 2 matching terms, and so on down to the items that have no terms in common with the query. In each case the greater the number of matching query terms the higher the rank of the document in the list of retrieved documents. In such a system several different pairs of recall-precision values can be computed depending on the number of matching terms between queries and documents.

In a number of retrieval systems, a ranking is obtained for the retrieved document set by computing a similarity coefficient for each document-query pair. This coefficient reflects the similarities between the corresponding index terms or content representation. The retrieved items are then listed in decreasing order of the query-document similarity coefficients [24]. A pair of recall-precision values can then be computed following the retrieval of each document in the ranked order.

The recall measurement requires knowledge of the total number of relevant documents in the collection with respect to each query. When the size of the document collection is relatively small, it is often possible to obtain relevance judgments for all documents with respect to each query. When the collection sizes are larger, such exhaustive relevance assessments are not normally available. To obtain dependable recall figures, it is then necessary to estimate the total number of relevant documents in the collection. This can be done by sampling techniques. Thus, relevance assessments are made for only a subset of the items in a collection [26]. Alternatively, a given query could be processed using a variety of different search and retrieval methods with the assumption that all relevant documents are probably going to be retrieved by the various searches. The results of the searches are then combined into a single

	Recall-precision after retrieval of n documents		
n	Document number (x = relevant)	Recall	Precision
1	588 x	0.2	1.0
2	589 x	0.4	1.0
3	576	0.4	0.67
4	590 x	0.6	0.75
5	986	0.6	0.60
6	592 x	0.8	0.67
7	984	0.8	0.57
8	988	0.8	0.50
9	578	0.8	0.44
10	985	0.8	0.40
11	103	0.8	0.36
12	591	0.8	0.33
13	772 x	1.0	0.38
14	990	1.0	0.36

(a)

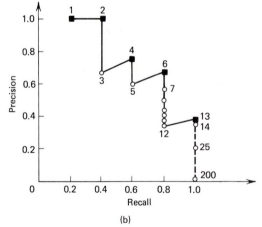

(b)

Figure 5-2 Display of recall and precision results for a sample query. (Collection consists of 200 documents in aerodynamics.) (a) Output ranking of documents in decreasing query-document similarity order and computation of recall and precision values for a single query. (b) Graph of precision versus recall for sample query of Fig. 5-2a.

output list. The list of relevant documents is obtained following a relevance assessment of this single output list.

Consider, as an example of a recall-precision computation, a query which has a total of five relevant documents included in a collection of two hundred documents in aerodynamics. The ranks of the relevant items in decreasing query-document similarity order are shown in Fig. 5-2a as well as the recall and precision values based on these ranks [27]. The recall-precision values are obtained from equations (1) and (2). So if six documents are retrieved including four of the possible five relevant documents, then this produces a recall of $4/5$, or 0.8. The precision is computed as $4/6$ (4 relevant out of 6 retrieved), or 0.67.

Given a set of recall-precision value pairs, such as that in Fig. 5-2a, a recall-precision graph can be constructed by plotting the precision against the recall. The graph for the sample query of Fig. 5-2a is shown in Fig. 5-2b.

Recall-precision graphs, such as that of Fig. 5-2b, have been criticized because a number of parameters are obscured. For example, the size of the retrieved document set and the collection size are not available from the graph [28]. Furthermore, problems arise when producing a continuous graph from a discrete set of points. That is, the value of precision is known exactly for a recall of 0.2 in the example of Fig. 5-2a (1.0), but it is not exactly specified for a recall of 0.4, since the precision varies between 1.0 and 0.67 at that point. Similarly the recall value is specified exactly when the precision is 0.5, but not when it is 1.0. Another problem arises when a number of curves such as the one of Fig. 5-2b, each valid for a single query, must be processed to obtain average performance characteristics for many user queries.

Before defining a single composite recall-precision graph reflecting the average performance of a system for a large number of individual queries, it is convenient first to replace the sawtooth curves for the individual queries, by smoother versions that simplify the averaging process. One possibility consists in using graphs consisting of horizontal line segments such as those shown in Fig. 5-3 for the example of Fig. 5-2. The curve of Fig. 5-3 is obtained by starting

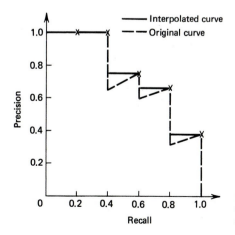

Figure 5-3 Interpolated recall-precision curve for sample query of Fig. 5-2. (Ranks of relevant items are 1, 2, 4, 6, 13.)

at the highest recall value and drawing a horizontal line leftward from each peak point of precision, up to a point where a higher precision point is encountered. The curve of Fig. 5-3 now exhibits a unique precision value for each recall point, and it extends along the scale from a recall of 0 to a recall of 1. For example, at a recall of 0.4 the precision is 1.0 in the graph of Fig. 5-3; however, for any slightly larger value of the recall—say 0.401—the precision has dropped to 0.75. A similar drop in precision from 0.75 to 0.67 occurs as the recall increases from 0.6 to 0.601. The interpolated curve represents the best performance a user can achieve [27].

Given a set of different performance (recall-precision) curves similar to that of Fig. 5-3, corresponding to different user queries, average performance values can be obtained in several different ways. In particular, if $RETREL_i$ is defined as the number of items retrieved and relevant, $RETNREL_i$ is the number retrieved but not relevant, and $NRETREL_i$ is the number relevant but not retrieved for query i, then following the definitions in (1) and (2), the $RECALL_i$ for query i, and the $PRECISION_i$ are defined as

$$RECALL_i = \frac{RETREL_i}{RETREL_i + NRETREL_i} \tag{3}$$

$$\text{and } PRECISION_i = \frac{RETREL_i}{RETREL_i + RETNREL_i} \tag{4}$$

A *user-oriented recall-level average*, reflecting the performance an average user can expect to obtain from the system, may then be defined by taking the arithmetic mean, over NUM sample queries, of expressions (3) and (4):

$$RECALL_{RL} = \frac{1}{NUM} \sum_{i=1}^{NUM} \frac{RETREL_i}{RETREL_i + NRETREL_i} \tag{5}$$

$$PRECISION_{RL} = \frac{1}{NUM} \sum_{i=1}^{NUM} \frac{RETREL_i}{RETREL_i + RETNREL_i} \tag{6}$$

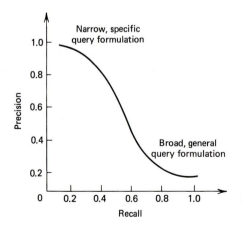

Figure 5-4 Typical average recall-precision graph.

Since the recall and precision values $RECALL_i$ and $PRECISION_i$ for the individual user queries are unambiguously defined as shown in Fig. 5-3, the averages of equations (5) and (6) are also uniquely determined. This makes it possible to compute average precision values at fixed recall intervals, say for recall equal to 0, 0.1, 0.2, . . . , 1.0. In particular, for each query the precision values are computed for the specified 11 values of the recall from 0 to 1.0 in steps 0.1, and equation (6) is used to obtain average precision values over all queries at each of the 11 recall values. The average curve which results has a shape similar to that shown in Fig. 5-4, where the left-hand end corresponds to narrow, specific query formulations where few documents are retrieved and the precision may be expected to be high, while the recall is fairly low. The right-hand end of the curve represents broad, rather general query formulations and hence a large number of retrieved documents.

An alternative *systems-oriented document-level average* is obtained by using the total number of relevant items retrieved by the system over the NUM queries, as well as the total number of nonrelevant items that are rejected. That is, from the NUM original queries, a single hypothetical combined query is built, whose relevant items are defined as the sum of the relevant of all component queries. The document level averages are then defined as

$$RECALL_{DL} = \frac{\sum_{i=1}^{NUM} RETREL_i}{\sum_{i=1}^{NUM} (RETREL_i + NRETREL_i)} \tag{7}$$

$$\text{and } PRECISION_{DL} = \frac{\sum_{i=1}^{NUM} RETREL_i}{\sum_{i=1}^{NUM} (RETREL_i + RETNREL_i)} \tag{8}$$

The averages of equations (5) and (6) give equal importance to each query, while in formulas (7) and (8) the averages depend more on queries with many relevant documents than on those with few relevant items. Consider by analogy a computation of average class size in a university. If there are 10 classes, including 5 with 1 student each and 5 with 99 students each, the *class-level* average size is 50, reflecting the fact that 10 professors teach a total of 500 students, or 50 on average. The *student-level* average size, on the other hand, is 98.02, reflecting the fact that almost all students are in classes with 98 other students. In information retrieval the choice of averaging method depends on whether it is more important to display the average user's result [equations (5) and (6)] or to reflect what happens to the average relevant document [equations (7) and (8)]. If query performance does not depend on the number of relevant documents, the two averages give similar results.

Recall-precision curves may be used to evaluate the performance of information retrieval systems—typically, by computing recall and precision values for two or more systems, or for the same system operating under different con-

Recall	Average precision for 35 queries		Improvement, %
	Word stem	Thesaurus	
0.1	0.7963	0.8788	10.4
0.2	0.6350	0.7567	19.2
0.3	0.5283	0.6464	22.4
0.4	0.4603	0.5577	21.2
0.5	0.4051	0.4912	21.3
0.6	0.3699	0.4470	20.8
0.7	0.3383	0.3893	15.1
0.8	0.2996	0.3287	9.7
0.9	0.2568	0.2726	6.2
1.0	0.2018	0.2093	3.7

(a)

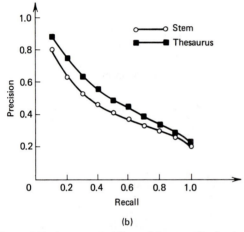

(b)

Figure 5-5 Average recall-precision results for two indexing methods (82 documents, 35 queries). (a) Recall-precision average. (b) Recall-precision graph.

ditions. In these circumstances, the curves produced for systems A and B can be superimposed on the same graph to determine which system is superior, and by how much. In general, the curve closest to the upper right-hand corner of the graph (where recall and precision are maximized) indicates the best performance. A typical example is shown in Fig. 5-5, where the performance of two different indexing systems is shown for a collection of documents in library science averaged over 35 user queries. The "stem" run refers to an indexing process where word stems extracted from the document abstracts are used as index terms to represent document content. In the "thesaurus" run word stems are replaced by "concepts" extracted from a thesaurus representing classes of terms related or synonymous to the original stems. It may be seen from the output of Fig. 5-5 that the average precision of the thesaurus run is between 4 and 22 percent better at the fixed recall points than the word stem run.

Since it is difficult to judge the significance of the differences between two performance curves by citing percentage improvements as in Fig. 5-5, it is helpful to furnish statistical evidence indicating whether a given difference between two averages is in fact significant. Most standard *statistical significance tests* based on paired comparisons will produce statistical evidence giving the probability that differences between the two sets of sample values as great as, or greater than, those observed would occur by chance. When the computed probability is small enough—for example, less than or equal to 0.05—one concludes that the two sets of sample values are significantly different. If, on the other hand, the computed probability is greater than 0.05, the presumption is that the observed differences could have been obtained by chance—that the original pairs of values might in fact have been derived from the same distribution.

The pairs of measurements being compared may typically represent the precision values at some fixed recall level—say, at a recall of 0.1, or at a recall of 0.5—for a set of queries processed by using methods A and B, respectively. The two middle columns of Fig. 5-5a represent an example of this case. Alternatively, the pairs of measurements may represent combined values for several points representing the complete recall-precision curves. Such combined measurements are obtained from the single-valued evaluation measures introduced later in this chapter.

The following assumptions are made for three of the best-known significance testing procedures [29]. The measurements must be obtained independently of each other;

    1 For the *t-test* it is assumed in addition that the differences between the two sets of sample values to be compared are normally distributed.

    2 The *sign test* makes no normality assumptions, and uses only the sign (not the magnitude) of the differences in sample values; thus the computed probability values depend on whether the differences in sample values are mostly positive or negative.

    3 The *Wilcoxon signed rank test* postulates that as differences between pairs increase, significance also increases, but only as these numbers affect the ranking; thus, differences of $-1, 2, -3, 4$, and 20 are equivalent to differences of $-1, 2, -3, 4$, and 5, since only the rank of the ordered differences is important.

Since many sets of recall or precision differences are probably not normally distributed, the less stringent assumptions inherent in the use of the sign test or the Wilcoxon signed rank test may be preferable over those of the better known t-test. A typical set of output data from a sign test process is shown for two search methods A and B in Table 5-2. The table is based on 11 statistics (differences in precision at each of 11 recall values from 0 to 1 in steps of 0.1). For each statistic this table shows the number of queries favoring methods A and B, respectively, and the one-sided probabilities for the test (ignoring ties). The one-sided probabilities represent the probabilities that the sample values could have originated by chance. On the bottom line of Table 5-2 the 11 one-sided tests are combined into a single overall measure. In this case the probabilities measure the chance that method B is not significantly different (better)

Table 5-2   Sign Test for Typical Search Methods A and B
(Average for 42 Queries; Testing for Collection B Better than
for Collection A)

Precision average at recall of	Favoring method			One-sided probabilities
	A	B	Tied	
0	1	7	34	0.0385
0.1	1	7	34	0.0385
0.2	1	8	33	0.0226
0.3	1	13	28	0.0018
0.4	1	15	26	0.0006
0.5	2	17	23	0.0007
0.6	3	20	19	0.0004
0.7	8	16	18	0.0767
0.8	9	17	16	0.0851
0.9	8	18	16	0.0387
1.0	8	18	16	0.0387
Combined	43	156	263	0.0000

Adapted from reference 29.

than A. This is seen to be zero to four decimal places; that is, method B is statistically better than method A.

A majority of the studies undertaken to evaluate the effectiveness of information retrieval systems have used recall and precision measurements to show system performance. Misgivings have been voiced about some of the characteristics of these measures. As a result a variety of alternative methodologies have been proposed. A few developments in this area are examined in the next section.

3   MEASURES OF RETRIEVAL EFFECTIVENESS

A   Measurement Problems

The recall and precision measures introduced earlier are advantageous to the user because they reflect the relative success of the system in meeting various kinds of user needs. Furthermore a particular measurement can be directly interpreted in terms of user experiences. Thus, a precision performance of 0.2 at recall equal to 0.5 implies that the user has obtained one-half of the relevant items in the collection, and that four nonrelevant items have had to be examined for every relevant item that was obtained.

Some qualifying remarks are nevertheless in order in connection with the standard recall and precision measurements. First, it is clear from the basic definitions that recall and precision measurements are normally tied to a given collection of documents and to a given query set. Within such a fixed environment, it is possible to vary the indexing policy or the indexing language or the search methodology and to determine subsequently how these changes may affect the performance of the system in terms of recall and precision. On the other hand, recall and precision must be used with caution in comparing the performance of two entirely different systems based on different document collections, different query sets, and different user populations [30,31].

Consider in particular the changes to be expected in the value of the recall and precision measures when the collection size increases or when the average number of relevant items per query diminishes from one collection to another. In both cases recall and precision can be expected to deteriorate because the number of relevant and retrieved items is not likely to increase in proportion to the size of the collection. Care must then be taken to equate collection and query relevance properties before applying recall and precision measures to the evaluation of different collections.

Another problem arises in connection with the relevance assessments of documents with respect to user queries. Such assessments are needed if the relevant items are to be distinguished from the nonrelevant ones. Some observers maintain that recall and precision measurements apply only to the user environment within which the relevance judgments were first obtained. This is because of the inherent subjectivity of relevance assessments [32]. Fortunately, there exists a good deal of experimental evidence to show that for many of the documents that appear to be most similar to a particular query, and hence are normally retrievable by the search process, very close agreement may be expected from different assessors as to the relevance in each case. This accounts for the fact that while the relevance assessments obtainable from differing evaluators are different for randomly chosen documents, the effect on the resulting recall and precision measurements is relatively small [33]. Furthermore, it is possible to replace the individual opinions about the usefulness of a given document with respect to a given query by global judgments representing a consensus of ideas by several independent judges [34,35].

A third question of interest in using recall and precision measurements is the effect of the query type on the evaluation outcome. In this respect one can distinguish the short *subject-heading* queries in which the topic is expressed as a single short descriptive word string (e.g., "thermal control," "turbulence studies") from *title-length* queries, where a single sentence or title adequately describes the subject area, and from *full-text* queries where a complete paragraph is used to formulate a search request [34]. Different query types may be produced notably in systems where the final query formulations are delegated by the users to trained search intermediaries. Although the short, subject-heading queries will often deal with general topics, whereas the larger full-text queries are sometimes more specific, it is not always true that query length is directly correlated with query specificity. In any case, a system should be tested using a realistic query mix reflecting the query types actually submitted in operational situations.

A last consideration relating to recall and precision computations is the assignment of relevance grades to the documents of a given collection, and the choice of a document rank for output purposes. Under normal circumstances, two relevance assessments are customary: either a document is relevant or it is nonrelevant. In these circumstances, the computation of recall and precision is unambiguous using expressions (1) and (2). If a system uses grades of relevance and the retrieved documents are ranked, several documents may be equally similar to a given query and placed in consecutive location on the output list. However, since the order affects the precision-recall evaluation, techniques are required to compensate for the arbitrary ordering of the equally similar items. One technique is to assign to all these documents a relevance grade equal to the average grade of this set of documents.

In practice, it appears to be a great deal more difficult for the relevance assessors to use many relevance grades than to simply decide between the relevant or partly relevant documents on the one hand and the nonrelevant documents on the other. Furthermore, errors and uncertainties crop up with multiple-category relevance assessments where users are forced to make narrow distinctions between documents that are absolutely relevant, possibly relevant, marginally relevant, or nonrelevant as the case may be. These in fact may outweigh the greater accuracy sought by using the many relevance grades. Nevertheless, various evaluation procedures and parameters have been proposed for use with variable relevance weights and for systems allowing ties in the ranks of the retrieved items. These measures are introduced with additional evaluation criteria in the next section.

*B   Recall, Precision, and Fallout

It was pointed out earlier that recall and precision measurements are directly interpretable by users in terms of search satisfaction. On the other hand, they are sometimes difficult to compute. For example, recall may not be defined because no relevant documents exist in a collection with respect to some query [28,36]. Similarly, precision is undefined when no items are retrieved (the respective measures are computed as 0/0 in each case, which is undefined).

Another deficiency in the use of precision and recall is a lack of parallelism in the properties of the two measures. Assuming that retrieval effectiveness increases with the number of relevant items obtained in answer to a query, and decreases with the number of nonrelevant items retrieved, a measure appears to be needed which reflects the performance for the nonrelevant documents in the same way as recall measures the performance of the relevant. This measure, known as *fallout*, is formally defined using the terminology of Table 5-3 as

$$\text{FALLOUT} = \frac{\text{RETNREL}}{\text{RETNREL} + \text{NRETNREL}}$$
$$= \frac{\text{number of nonrelevant items retrieved}}{\text{total number of nonrelevant in collection}} \tag{9}$$

If the recall is expressed in probabilistic terms as the probability of a document being retrieved given that it is relevant, the fallout is the probability of an item being retrieved given that it is nonrelevant. An effective retrieval system will therefore exhibit maximum recall and minimum fallout.

In a normal retrieval environment, recall, precision, and fallout are not independent of the *generality factor*, defined as the average number of relevant

Table 5-3   Contingency Table

	Relevant	Nonrelevant	
Retrieved	RETREL	RETNREL	RETREL + RETNREL
Not retrieved	NRETREL	NRETNREL	NRETREL + NRETNREL
	RETREL + NRETREL	RETNREL + NRETNREL	RETREL + RETNREL + NRETREL + NRETNREL

items per query included in the collection. Referring to Tables 5-3 and 5-4, one sees that any three of the measures R, P, F, and G automatically determine the fourth. As an example, precision may be determined in terms of recall, fallout, and generality as

$$P = \frac{R \cdot G}{(R \cdot G) + F(1 - G)} \tag{10}$$

However, because the total number of nonrelevant items (RETNREL + NRETNREL) is much larger in practice than the number of relevant (RETREL + NRETREL), any changes in the generality of a collection are likely to affect the fallout less than the precision. In particular, as the generality decreases either because the number of relevant items decreases or because the total collection size increases, the number of relevant retrieved (RETREL) is likely to decrease, but the total number of items retrieved (RETREL + RETNREL) as well as the number of nonrelevant items (RETNREL + NRETNREL) may remain fairly constant. Hence precision will be subject to larger variations than fallout [31]. Furthermore, fallout is unequivocally defined to be zero when no items are retrieved (RETREL + RETNREL = 0), because the number of nonrelevant items in the collection (RETNREL + NRETNREL) may safely be assumed to be nonzero.

These arguments have been used to suggest the replacement of the recall and precision measures by recall-fallout computations. A typical recall-fallout display is shown in Fig. 5-6 for the query previously used as an example in Figs.

Table 5-4   Typical Retrieval Evaluation Measures

Symbol	Evaluation measure	Formula	Explanation
R	Recall	$\dfrac{\text{RETREL}}{\text{RETREL + NRETREL}}$	Proportion of relevant actually retrieved
P	Precision	$\dfrac{\text{RETREL}}{\text{RETREL + RETNREL}}$	Proportion of retrieved actually relevant
F	Fallout	$\dfrac{\text{RETNREL}}{\text{RETNREL + NRETNREL}}$	Proportion of nonrelevant actually retrieved
G	Generality	$\dfrac{\text{RETREL + NRETREL}}{\text{RETREL + RETNREL + NRETREL + NRETNREL}}$	Proportion of relevant per query

n	Relevant	Recall	Fallout
1	x	0.2	0
2	x	0.4	0
3		0.4	0.005
4	x	0.6	0.005
5		0.6	0.010
6	x	0.8	0.010
7		0.8	0.015
8		0.8	0.020
9		0.8	0.025
10		0.8	0.030
11		0.8	0.035
12		0.8	0.040
13	x	1.0	0.040
14		1.0	0.045
20		1.0	0.075
50		1.0	0.225
100		1.0	0.475
200		1.0	0.975

(a)

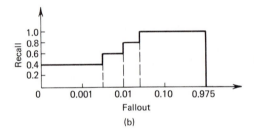

(b)

Figure 5-6 Display of recall and fallout results for sample query of Fig. 5-2. (Collection consists of 200 documents in aerodynamics.) (a) Recall-fallout after retrieval of n documents. (b) Recall-fallout plot.

5-2 and 5-3. The graph of Fig. 5-6 indicates that the fallout is not as easily interpreted by the user as precision. In fact, the two types of effectiveness pairs (recall-precision and recall-fallout, respectively) may well respond to different needs in actual retrieval situations. Since the recall provides an indication of the proportion of relevant actually obtained as a result of a search, while precision is a measure of the efficiency with which these relevant are retrieved, a recall-precision output is *user-oriented*, because the user is normally interested in optimizing the retrieval of relevant items. On the other hand, fallout is a measure of the efficiency of rejecting the nonrelevant in the collection (which in many cases is approximately equivalent to the collection size). For this reason, a recall-fallout display may be considered to be *systems-oriented*, since it indicates how well the nonrelevant are rejected as a function of collection size [37].

The foregoing measures are all based on objective relevance judgments that are independent of the user's prior knowledge of the subject area. Additional measures which depend on the subjective relevance are [27]:

1 The *novelty ratio,* that is, the proportion of items retrieved and judged relevant by users of which they had not been aware prior to receiving the search output

2 The *coverage ratio*, that is, the proportion of relevant items retrieved out of the total relevant known to users prior to the search
3 The *sought recall*, defined as the total relevant examined by users following a search, divided by the total relevant which users would have liked to examine

Many other evaluation measures based on the contingency table display of Table 5-3 have been proposed over the years [19,28,38,39]. Some of these measures use the full information incorporated in the contingency table, as opposed to recall, precision, and fallout that are based on a single column or a single row of the table only. However, most of these measures are not easily interpretable, and it is not likely in these circumstances that they will quickly supplant recall and precision.

**C   Single-Valued Measures

Some observers completely reject the contingency table as a basis for the construction of parameters capable of reflecting retrieval effectiveness. Instead a number of desirable properties are postulated for an ideal effectiveness measure, including in particular the following [40]:

1 The measure should be able to reflect retrieval effectiveness alone, separately of the criteria such as cost.
2 The measure should be independent of any particular retrieval cutoff, that is, of the number of documents retrieved in a particular search.
3 The measure should be expressible as a single number (instead of two values such as recall and precision) which can be put on a scale to give absolute and relative values.

The best known of these single-valued measures is the E measure introduced by Swets [40–43].
To construct the E measure, two distinguishable populations of objects POP_1 and POP_2 are associated with the relevant and the nonrelevant documents with respect to some query. If a parameter r is used to represent some measurable characteristic such as the query-document similarity for each document, the "probability density functions" $FUNC_1(r)$ and $FUNC_2(r)$ with means $MEAN_1$ and $MEAN_2$ and variances VAR_1 and VAR_2 will then indicate how the parameter r behaves for the two populations. That is, $FUNC_1(r)$ represents the probability that a document in POP_1 has value r, and $FUNC_2(r)$ applies similarly to POP_2. A typical graph of these probability density functions is shown in Fig. 5-7.
By choosing a particular value of r—for example, the point r = C—it becomes possible to compute the fraction of each population for which r has a value greater than or equal to C. This is the portion of the area under the probability density curve lying to the right of line r = C. C is in fact a cutoff value such that any item for which $FUNC(r) \geq C$ is retrieved. Since $FUNC_1(r)$ and $FUNC_2(r)$ are associated with the relevant and nonrelevant document popula-

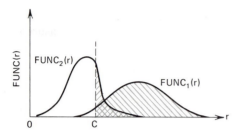

Figure 5-7 Probability density functions for populations POP$_1$ and POP$_2$ comprising the relevant and nonrelevant documents, respectively. (*Adapted from reference 41.*)

tions, respectively, the areas under the density curves to the right of r = C represent, respectively, the proportion of relevant and of nonrelevant documents for which FUNC(r) ≥ C. The first measure is equal to the recall, while the second is equal to the fallout. By plotting the percentages of the populations POP$_1$ and POP$_2$ to the right of the cut C against each other, while varying C, one obtains an *operating characteristic* (OC) curve similar to that shown in Fig. 5-8. If populations POP$_1$ and POP$_2$ are identical with respect to the characteristic r, the operating characteristic is a line running diagonally across the graph. The more different the two populations are from one another the more closely the OC curve will approach the upper left-hand corner of the figure (the 0-100 point of the graph).

Swets plotted the operating characteristics for a large number of retrieval systems using normal probability scales for recall and for fallout. In these circumstances, straight lines are obtained if recall and fallout both show normal distributions with respect to r. Within the limits of experimental error, the lines were all found to be straight, leading to the conclusion that the probability density functions of recall and fallout with respect to parameter r are normal. It follows that recall-fallout performance can be represented by specifying the po-

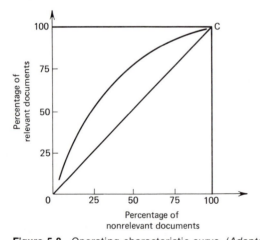

Figure 5-8 Operating characteristic curve. (*Adapted from reference 41.*)

sition of the corresponding straight line. Two typical operating characteristic lines are shown in Fig. 5-9, labeled A and B respectively. Swets' E measure is defined specifically as

$$E = \sqrt{2} \cdot \text{DIST} \tag{11}$$

where DIST is the distance from 0 (see Fig. 5-9) to the operating characteristic curve along the line from point 0 to point R. If the angle of the operating characteristic curve is the same as the diagonal, as it is for line A of Fig. 5-9, that is, the slope of the curve is equal to 1, then the value of E does represent the performance effectiveness. If the angle of the operating characteristic curve is not the same as the diagonal as in line B, then it is necessary to present the slope of the operating characteristic curve as well as the E value.

The main advantage of the (E, SLOPE) measures is that they are derived using a well-known and accepted statistical theory. The disadvantage is that unlike recall and precision, the E and SLOPE measures cannot be translated into a performance characterization as readily by the user population. In practice it is found that values of SLOPE range from 0.5 to 2.0, so that the two values (E, SLOPE) are necessary to express the performance, just as is the case for recall and precision. It should be noted also that the determination of the E measure is based on information equivalent to that contained in a full recall-precision graph. That is, the E value cannot be obtained by using a single retrieval threshold that distinguishes the retrieved from the nonretrieved items of the kind normally available in conventional retrieval situation; a single pair of recall-precision values is, however, computable in that situation.

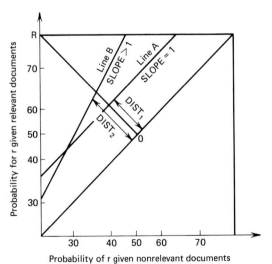

Figure 5-9 Operating characteristics on normal probability scales. (*Adapted from reference 40.*)

Various additional global measures based on established theories—especially probability theory and information theory—have been described in the literature but have not received consideration in practice [44–49]. These measures generally combine aspects of precision and recall in a single expression. One function, based on considerations of measurement theory, uses a special parameter (α) which makes it possible to attach degrees of importance to the recall and precision components [25]:

$$E = 1 - \frac{1}{\alpha(1/\text{PRECISION}) + (1 - \alpha)(1/\text{RECALL})} \tag{12}$$

Large values of the recall and precision measure correspond to small values of the evaluation measure E. For example, assume an α value of 0.50 and recall and precision values equal to 0.50. These parameters produce an E value of 0.50. When the recall remains at 0.50 but precision drops to 0.25, the E value increases to 0.67. On the other hand, if recall remains at 0.50 and precision increases to 0.90, the E value is 0.36.

One composite evaluation measure is independent of the retrieval threshold used to distinguish the retrieved from the nonretrieved items and is applicable to systems that rank the retrieved documents. It is based on considerations similar to those used by Swets, in that the area is computed under a particular form of the recall and precision graph [50,51]. Consider a graph in which the recall of a system is represented along the ordinate and the rank orders of the retrieved documents are plotted along the abscissa. The graph starts at zero and maintains a zero value until a rank is reached corresponding to a retrieved relevant document, at which point the recall jumps to 1/REL (for REL relevant documents included in the system). The recall then stays at 1/REL until the next relevant document is reached, at which point the recall increases to 2/REL, and so on, until the last relevant document rank is reached when the recall reaches its final value of REL/REL or 1.

If this recall step function is plotted on the same graph with a similar function for an ideal system for which the REL relevant documents are ranked 1,2, . . . ,REL, the area between the two step functions can be used as a measure of the recall performance of the system. A typical case is shown in Fig. 5-10 for the query used as an example in Figs. 5-2, 5-3, and 5-6. The ranks of the relevant documents in decreasing similarity order are assumed to be 1, 2, 3, 4, 6, and 13. The difference in area between the ideal retrieval situation and the actual recall curves designated by the tinted area in the example in Fig. 5-10 is given by

$$\frac{\sum_{i=1}^{\text{REL}} \text{RANK}_i - \sum_{i=1}^{\text{REL}} i}{\text{REL}} = \frac{26 - 15}{5} = 2.2 \tag{13}$$

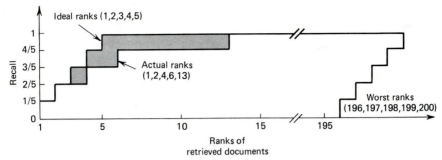

Figure 5-10   Construction of normalized recall measure.

where REL is the number of relevant documents and $RANK_i$ represents the document ranks of the relevant items.

The values for expression (13) range from 0 for the case of perfect retrieval to $N - REL$ for the worst possible case. That is, if the REL relevant documents are ranked 1, 2, 3, . . . , REL, then the value of expression (13) is equal to 0. On the other hand, if the relevant document ranks are $N - REL + 1$, $N - REL + 2$, . . . , N where N is the number of documents in the collection, then the value of expression (13) is equal to $N - REL$. Hence expression (13) can be normalized by dividing by $N - REL$. Finally, subtraction from 1 ensures that the measure equals 1 for the best case and 0 for the worst instead of vice versa. The resulting measure, known as the normalized recall, is then given by

$$RECALL_{norm} = 1 - \frac{\sum_{i=1}^{REL} RANK_i - \sum_{i=1}^{REL} i}{REL(N - REL)} \tag{14}$$

For the case shown in Fig. 5-10, $RECALL_{norm}$ equals 0.989. This reflects the fact that the ranks of the relevant documents deviate very little from the ideal case.

The tinted area in Fig. 5-10 reflects the number of nonrelevant documents that have to be retrieved in order to reach a recall value of 1. Since the latter measure is akin to the fallout, the normalized recall value of expression (14) may in fact be shown to be equivalent to the area under the recall-fallout curve of Fig. 5-6b [42].

An equivalent development for the computation of the normalized area between actual and ideal precision curves leads to a normalized precision measure defined as

$$PRECISION_{norm} = 1 - \frac{\sum_{i=1}^{REL} \log RANK_i - \sum_{i=1}^{REL} \log i}{\log N!/(N - REL)!REL!} \tag{15}$$

Just like ordinary recall and precision, the normalized recall is sensitive to the rank assigned to the last relevant document in the retrieval order, and the normalized precision is sensitive to the rank of the first relevant document in the retrieval order. The normalized measures constitute a summary of the full recall-precision curve; as such they cannot be computed for a single retrieval point corresponding to a single recall-precision pair.

A number of additional single-valued measures also use the differences between the actual ranks of the relevant items retrieved, and either the ideal ranks where all the relevant items are retrieved ahead of any nonrelevant item, or a random system where the relevant items are randomly sprinkled among the nonrelevant. The expected search length [52] and the sliding ratio [53] are two measures of this kind.

Consider first the *expected search length*. Here one assumes that documents are presented to the user in a weakly ordered sequence following an information search—for example, all documents exhibiting NMATCH matching terms with the query would be retrieved before the set with NMATCH − 1 matching terms, and those in turn would precede the set with NMATCH − 2 matching terms, and so on. The *search length* may then be defined as the average number of nonrelevant items that must be scanned by the user before the total number of wanted items is reached.

Consider as an example the case of Fig. 5-11 which includes 3 items in set 1

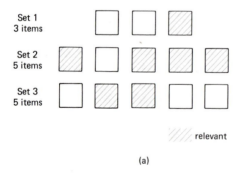

(a)

Number of relevant wanted	Number of sets to be searched	Search length	Average search length
1	1	0, 1, or 2	$1/3 \cdot 0 + 1/3 \cdot 1 + 1/3 \cdot 2 = 1$
6	3	3, 4, 5, or 6	$4/10 \cdot 3 + 3/10 \cdot 4 + 2/10 \cdot 5 + 1/10 \cdot 6 = 4$

(b)

Figure 5-11 Average search length illustration. (a) Partly ordered retrieval output. (b) Average search length computation. (*Adapted from reference 52.*)

and 5 items in each of sets 2 and 3. Set 1 is retrieved before set 2 and set 2 is retrieved before set 3. Within each of the sets the documents are not ranked or ordered. That is, there is no obvious way to order the documents having NMATCH terms in common with the query. The average search length necessary to retrieve 6 relevant items is 4. That is, the searcher will have to examine 4 nonrelevant documents on the average in order to find 6 relevant ones. In particular, since only one relevant item is retrievable from set 1, and 4 more from set 2, it is always necessary to look into set 3 for one additional relevant item to make up the total of 6. The first relevant item in set 3 may be located in position 1, producing a total search length of 3; or in positions 2, 3, or 4, producing search lengths of 4, 5, or 6, respectively. Of the 10 possible ways of distributing two relevant items among 5 positions in set 3, 4 have a relevant item in position 1, 3 more in position 2, 2 more in position 3, and 1 in position 4. This results in the search length computation shown in Fig. 5-11.

Now consider a QUERY and let PREVNREL be the number of nonrelevant documents in all sets preceding the one where the search terminates. If there are REL relevant items in the final set, and if they are put at equal intervals among the NREL nonrelevant documents in that set, then REL + 1 subsequences of nonrelevant documents will normally be created containing NREL/REL + 1 nonrelevant documents each. If one assumes that the request is satisfied at the NUMth relevant item on the last level, the expected search length EXP for QUERY will be

$$\text{EXP(QUERY)} = \text{PREVNREL} + \frac{\text{NREL} \cdot \text{NUM}}{\text{REL} + 1} \tag{16}$$

The expected random search length is obtained by scattering the ALLREL documents relevant to QUERY randomly through the IRREL irrelevant items. It is defined as DESIRED · IRREL/(ALLREL + 1), where DESIRED is the total desired number of relevant. A useful measure is specified as the improvement obtained by the actual case EXP over the random case REXP [51] as follows:

$$\text{EXP(QUERY) REDUCTION} = \frac{\text{REXP(QUERY)} - \text{EXP(QUERY)}}{\text{REXP(QUERY)}}$$

$$= 1 - \frac{\text{PREVNREL} + \dfrac{\text{NREL} \cdot \text{NUM}}{\text{REL} + 1}}{\dfrac{\text{DESIRED} \cdot \text{IRREL}}{\text{ALLREL} + 1}} \tag{17}$$

The *sliding ratio* measure is based on the comparison of two ranked lists of items. One list is the output of an actual retrieval system, and the other represents an ideal system in which the items are ranked in decreasing relevance order [53]. This model is more complex than the ones previously described because it allows the assignment of numeric relevance weights to the documents.

Table 5-5 Sample Computation for Sliding Ratio Measure

Retrieval rank	1	2	3	4	5	
Document number	3	4	5	1	2	Actual
Relevance weight $\text{WEIGHT}_i^{\text{REAL}}$	10	0	8	5	2	system
$\text{SWEIGHT REAL(NUM)} = \sum_{i=1}^{\text{NUM}} \text{WEIGHT}_i^{\text{REAL}}$	10	10	18	23	25	output
Document number	3	5	1	2	4	Ideal
Relevance weight $\text{WEIGHT}_i^{\text{IDEAL}}$	10	8	5	2	0	system
$\text{SWEIGHT IDEAL(NUM)} = \sum_{i=1}^{\text{NUM}} \text{WEIGHT}_i^{\text{IDEAL}}$	10	18	23	25	25	output
$\text{SLIDE(NUM)} = \dfrac{\text{SWEIGHT REAL(NUM)}}{\text{SWEIGHT IDEAL(NUM)}}$	1	0.55	0.78	0.92	1	

Adapted from reference 53.

These replace the usual binary relevance assessments. In an ideal retrieval situation, the documents would be ranked in decreasing order of their relevance weights rather than by a simple precedence of the relevant set ahead of the set of nonrelevant items. Ties in rank and in relevance values between items can be eliminated, for example by assigning to all items in each set the average rank of the items in the set.

The sliding ratio measure SLIDE(NUM) for retrieval cutoff SLIDE may be defined as

$$\text{SLIDE(NUM)} = \frac{\text{SWEIGHT REAL(NUM)}}{\text{SWEIGHT IDEAL(NUM)}} \tag{18}$$

where SWEIGHT REAL(NUM) and SWEIGHT IDEAL(NUM) are the sum of the relevance weights of all items retrieved up to rank NUM in the actual and ideal systems, respectively. A sample calculation is shown in Table 5-5 for five documents which do not exhibit any ties in rank. The value of SLIDE(NUM) at any particular value of NUM shows the ability of the actual system to approximate the retrieval capability of the ideal system. In the limit, as NUM approaches the total number of documents in the collection, WEIGHT REAL(NUM) becomes equal to WEIGHT IDEAL(NUM) and SLIDE(NUM) becomes equal to 1.

The sliding ratio can of course also be used for systems where the relevance weights are restricted to 1 for relevant items and 0 for the nonrelevant. In that case, the ratio approximates the normalized recall and the expected search length.

**D Utility Measure

A property shared by all the measures described in the preceding sections is the fact that only system effectiveness is taken into account. The cost or value of a particular retrieval action has not been considered. Assuming that cost and/or value parameters are available, it is possible to devise retrieval evaluation strategies based on an extension of the standard contingency table as shown in Table 5-6 [54,55]. The data in Table 5-6 show the usual four-way split of the document collection into the number of items relevant and retrieved RETREL, the number of items retrieved and nonrelevant RETNREL, the number of items not retrieved but relevant NRETREL and the number of items not retrieved and not relevant NRETNREL. A value of $VALUE_1$ is assigned to each relevant item that is retrieved, and $VALUE_2$ is assigned to each nonrelevant item that is rejected. Similarly, costs of $COST_1$ and $COST_2$ are associated with nonrelevant items retrieved and with relevant items that are missed.

If the value of the similarity measure between a document DOC and a query QUERY can be expressed as a variable VAR = FUNC(QUERY,DOC), then the *utility* of a given relevant document set DOCSET with respect to some query QUERY at retrieval threshold VAR = THRESHOLD can be expressed as

$$
\begin{aligned}
\text{UTIL(DOCSET,QUERY, THRESHOLD)} = {} & VALUE_1 \cdot RETREL \\
& - COST_1 \cdot RETNREL - COST_2 \cdot NRETREL \\
& + VALUE_2 \cdot NRETNREL
\end{aligned} \tag{19}
$$

or alternatively as

$$
\begin{aligned}
\text{UTIL(DOCSET,QUERY,THRESHOLD)} = {} & \\
VALUE_1 \cdot N \, & \text{Prob\{DOC is relevant and VAR} \geq \text{THRESHOLD\}} \\
- COST_1 \cdot N \, & \text{Prob\{DOC is not relevant and VAR} \geq \text{THRESHOLD\}} \\
- COST_2 \cdot N \, & \text{Prob\{DOC is relevant and VAR} < \text{THRESHOLD\}} \\
+ VALUE_2 \cdot N \, & \text{Prob\{DOC is not relevant and VAR} < \text{THRESHOLD\}}
\end{aligned} \tag{20}
$$

where N is the total number of documents in the system. Expression (20) can be transformed using the probability density functions $FUNC_1(VAR)$ and $FUNC_2(VAR)$ previously introduced in Fig. 5-7. In fact, the area under the density curves to the right of a given threshold represent the probabilities that variable VAR has a value greater than the threshold, given that the documents are relevant and nonrelevant, respectively. By substitution of integrals into expression (20) a useful retrieval threshold is obtained for which the utility of the system is positive.

Table 5-6   Contingency Table with Cost and Value Parameters

	Relevant	Nonrelevant	
Retrieved	v_1 (RETREL)	c_1 (RETNREL)	RETREL + RETNREL
Not retrieved	c_2 (NRETREL)	v_2 (NRETNREL)	NRETREL + NRETNREL
	RETREL + NRETREL	RETNREL + NRETNREL	N

$v_1 = VALUE_1$; $v_2 = VALUE_2$
$c_1 = COST_1$; $c_2 = COST_2$

A substantial literature exists relating to the use of the utility measure for retrieval system evaluation [54–57]. However, until simple methods become available for estimating the cost and value parameters for the individual documents in a collection, the theoretical appeal of this method may outweigh its practical usefulness.

4 EVALUATION OF SYSTEM COST AND EFFICIENCY

A System Tradeoffs

The art of efficiency analysis is not as far advanced as the analysis of system effectiveness. This is because accurate cost data in terms of time, effort, and money spent are difficult to obtain, and because the value of improved information services and the benefits derivable from them is impossible to ascertain in most environments. Furthermore, when identifying information system costs, invariably one is forced to look at noncomparable situations. The cost differences between two systems, such as an automated and a manual one, may not accurately reflect the value of either system. The automated system might, for example, be used for purposes other than information storage and retrieval, or it might be usable on a 24-hour per day basis, whereas a manual system might not. Thus an efficiency evaluation involves a great many intangible factors which may hamper a concrete analysis and render the results unreliable or meaningless.

Nevertheless, it is necessary to consider the cost analysis question. Information systems are not likely to be constructed or installed without some attempt at evaluating their potential efficiency. It is customary to distinguish between *cost-effectiveness* analysis and *cost-benefit* analysis. The former is designed to find the least expensive means for carrying out a given set of operations or to obtain the maximum value from a given expenditure. Cost-benefit analysis requires a systematic comparison between the costs of individual operations and the benefits derivable from them [58–60].

The costs of a system can be divided into the *initial* development *costs* necessary for design, testing, and evaluation; the *operating costs* which are variable and depend on the tasks performed, the personnel used, and the amount of equipment required; and finally, the *fixed costs* for rent, taxes, and other standard items. The benefits obtainable from the information system may be related to decreased costs or increased productivity. Cost savings are difficult to document when manual operations are replaced by automatic ones. It is even harder to measure the benefits of sophisticated information systems which may consist of improved decision making capabilities, increased productivity, stimulation of research capacity, and the like, and the value of these somewhat serendipitous factors is normally impossible to ascertain.

In an information retrieval situation in which the volume of operations—such as number of documents, size and cost of the documents, and average number of queries—is given, the basic alternatives and system tradeoffs relate to the input and document indexing operations on the one hand, and to the information search and output transactions on the other. A particular performance criterion—for example, a given precision level—can normally be attained in many different ways, each of them involving different cost levels. Thus, precision may be raised by using a highly specific indexing vocabulary requiring high indexer proficiency and large indexing costs. Alternatively, the indexing may be performed more casually, but the output might be screened by trained subject experts before presentation to the users, thereby decreasing indexing costs but lengthening search time. Finally, the burden might be shifted to the user, by having customers conduct an interactive search and letting them rephrase the query formulation in the hope of generating better output.

In some cases, it is possible to obtain quantifiable information which relates various system alternatives to the effectiveness or quality of the output product. The following relationships may be cited as examples [7,58,59]:

1 Collection coverage versus expected number of retrievals; normally, a very small proportion of items accounts for a large proportion of all relevant items retrieved; the cost of adding to the collection a large number of the less productive items may thus be difficult to justify in terms of improvements in the output product.

2 Indexing time versus search effectiveness; there is a direct relation between indexing time and indexing exhaustivity and the corresponding expected recall; unfortunately, at high recall, the required indexing time increases much more rapidly than the recall performance, so that diminishing returns set in when the indexing time or exhaustivity exceed a given limit.

3 Specificity of the indexing language and recall-precision balance; normally, a more specific indexing language costs more to develop and produces better precision but may cause losses in recall; obviously, the desirable level of precision and thus the importance of language specificity varies with collection size, high precision being most crucial for very large collections.

4 Equipment complexity versus processing limitations; in general, more sophisticated equipment can produce a greater variety of output products—for example, ranked output consisting of document abstracts, instead of unranked document numbers or titles; on the other hand, more sophisticated processing devices cost more to acquire and to operate and put a greater burden on the system operators, and sometimes on the users.

Even if the various system alternatives are quantifiable in a reliable way, it may be difficult to reach operational decisions because the large fixed costs associated with an implementation may not be easily recoverable by instituting fees for service provided. Until agreement is reached concerning the value and benefits of information services, a cost analysis is not likely to produce the answers by management.

**B   Cost Analysis

There exist two basically distinct approaches to the analysis of the costs of an information system. The first one consists in carefully analyzing the various steps included in an actual processing chain, and in performing direct measurements of the various quantities which enter into the cost picture for a given operation environment. The second consists in generating an abstract model of the system being investigated, and in ascertaining system efficiency by carrying out appropriate simulation studies. In either case, all actual as well as hidden costs ought to be taken into account, including development costs, operating costs, and fixed costs.

Consider first the approach which starts with actual system measurements. As might be expected, volumes of published cost figures may be found in the literature presenting a wide array of measure data [61–64]. In general, the published data are unrelatable to each other, because of differences in the respective environments and in the assumptions made when performing the measurements. However, the published values do make it possible to obtain an idea of the relative expense arising from various processing steps, and occasionally the absolute magnitude of some item—for example, a stated manual cataloging cost of over $10 per item obtained for five large university libraries in 1969— may in itself furnish cause for concern. A unit cost figure is, however, not as useful as an indicator of system efficiency as a calculated cost related to some effectiveness measurement, such as, for example, the cost per citation retrieved by the system or, better still, the cost per relevant citation retrieved [65,66].

A typical efficiency analysis based on initial measurements of *costs, time, and volume* of operations would start with a formal system description, including a specification of the interrelationships between processes, and the generation of basic parameter values relating file sizes, input and output rates, and other operating characteristics. Several functional models of this type exist for libraries and information centers, normally including information acquisition, data encoding or indexing, storage organization, query preparation, information search, output operations, and in some instances also user appraisal and feedback operations leading to query reformulations [67,68].

The statement of time and cost data for equipment, personnel, materials, and procedures, and a specification of the interdependencies between various system parameters then lead to the generation of *performance measurements* which relate system performance to user requirements. The user requirements may be specified in terms of output volume, response time, recall and precision requirements, and the like. If a computer program is used for the computation of the functions, it may be possible to perform measurements for various assumed levels of the parameter values—for example, using different input rates for new materials, and different monthly search volumes. This leads to the generation of different figures of merit for different assumed operating conditions, and to decisions concerning a possible expansion of services or to transformations in the current operating practices.

The cost-time-volume model is valuable in situations where exact system specifications and parameter values are available. In practice these values are usually not available, and when they are, a computation of performance measurements closely tied to current operating characteristics is usually not needed, since the system operations may already be well in hand. In such cases, a more ambitious *system simulation* might be undertaken leading to a theoretical analysis of new concepts and ideas, including system growth studies, error and reliability studies, and comparative evaluations of new system configurations [69,70].

Consider now the specification of actual cost functions. A variety of formulations have been used for this purpose, including some based on cost-benefit comparisons and on the dual use of both efficiency as well as effectiveness criteria [71–74]. One possibility consists, for example, in assuming that costs may be subdivided into four types, including initial costs for development, operating costs for personnel and materials, fixed costs such as rent and taxes, and finally operating returns derived from the sale of products [75]. If the returns are disregarded, development costs are broken down into designing, testing, operating, and reporting, and operating costs are separated into three parts, including clerical, machine, and technical and professional costs, the resulting cost function may be expressed as

$$COST = C(TIME, UNITS)$$
$$= \sum_{i=1}^{FIXED} FIX_i(TIME) + DVLP(TIME) + OPER(TIME, UNITS) \quad (21)$$

where   TIME = unit time
 UNITS = the number of unit operations to be considered
 FIX_i = ith subdivision of the fixed costs in dollars per unit of time
 FIXED = number of subdivisions of fixed cost
 DVLP = development cost in dollars per unit time, amortized as current cost
 OPER = operating cost in dollars per unit time per unit operation
 C(TIME, UNITS) = general cost function varying with time and number of operations

The various factors of equation (21) can be further broken down into individual components. Thus, the operating costs can be expressed as

$$OPER(TIME, UNITS) = UNITS \left[\sum_{j=1}^{CLERICAL} CLER_j(TIME)TIM_{CLRK,j} \right.$$
$$+ \sum_{k=1}^{MACH} MCH_k(TIME)TIM_{MAC,k}$$
$$\left. + \sum_{q=1}^{TECH} TCH_q(TIME)TIM_{TNCH,q} \right] \quad (22)$$

where $CLER_j$ = jth subdivision of the clerical costs in dollars per unit, and time per unit operation (for example, the salary rate of the typists in a certain category)
 CLERICAL = number of subdivisions of clerical cost

MCH_k = kth subdivision of machine costs

$MACH$ = number of subdivisions of machine costs

TCH_q = qth subdivision of technical cost

$TECH$ = number of subdivisions of technical cost

$TIM_{CLRK,j}$, $TIM_{MAC,k}$, and $TIM_{TNCH,q}$ = increments of time used for clerical, machine, and technical operations, respectively

Relationships may also be used between some of the cost components in order to obtain optimum allocations for some of the subunits. Thus the operating cost of individual operations often decreases as the response time is allowed to increase; at the same time the user's "delay cost" increases with time. An optimal response time must then exist, where the operating costs are no longer maximal (as they would be if instantaneous responses were demanded), while the output delay cost is still reasonable [76].

Analogously, search cost could be compared with collection size, where the cost first decreases with increasing file size to some optimal value as the proportion of items that can be stored in internal machine memory increases. Then as the file size increases further, all added items are stored in external, slow access memory, thereby increasing access and search costs. A typical cost curve of this type derivable by appropriate efficiency evaluation methods is shown in Fig. 5-12 [77].

A final cost model to be mentioned is based on a comparison between costs and benefits [78]. Two parameters are defined first, known, respectively, as the benefit to cost ratio BENEFIT/COST, and the PROFIT, equal to BENEFIT − COST. One assumes that the cost COST varies with respect to three parameters: the number of documents $NDOC_F$ in the file, the number of SEARCHES conducted per year, and the number of documents DOCPERSEARCH retrieved per search. All other costs are assumed fixed. A typical annual cost function might then be

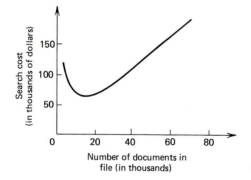

Figure 5-12 Typical cost curve reflecting search cost. (*Adapted from reference 77.*)

$$\text{COST} = \text{FIXED} + \text{MARGE} \cdot \text{NDOC}_F + (\text{FIXEDSEARCH}$$
$$+ \text{VARYSEARCH} \cdot \text{DOCPERSEARCH}) \cdot \text{SEARCHES} \quad (23)$$

where   FIXED = fixed costs
        MARGE = marginal costs of storing an additional item
FIXEDSEARCH = fixed search cost
VARYSEARCH = search cost that varies as a function of the number of output items examined

If one postulates that the benefit derived by a user from a search varies as the fraction of relevant items identified by the search from 0 to 1, then the benefit from a given imperfect search is BENEFIT · VALUE, where VALUE is the fractional user benefit derived from a given search, and BENEFIT is the maximal obtainable user benefit (in dollars). For NUM searches, the yearly benefit is then $\text{BENEFIT}_T = \text{BENEFIT} \cdot \text{VALUE} \cdot \text{NUM}$. In these circumstances the annual net benefit $\text{PROFIT}_T = \text{BENEFIT}_T - \text{COST}_T$ will be

$$\text{PROFIT}_T = (\text{BENEFIT} \cdot \text{VALUE} - \text{FIXEDSEARCH}$$
$$- \text{VARYSEARCH} \cdot \text{DOCPERSEARCH})\text{SEARCHES}$$
$$- \text{MARGE} \cdot \text{NDOC} - \text{FIXED} \quad (24)$$

The simple net benefit model of equation (24) serves only as an approximation to a much more complicated real situation. However when reasonably accurate sample values are used for the various parameters, useful indications may be obtainable from efficiency and effectiveness evaluations reflecting the behavior of the system in the real-life environments that are being investigated.

5 SUMMARY

It should be clear that the most dominant form of evaluation remains the precision-recall curve defined early in this chapter. However, it is also obvious that a great deal of effort has been invested to develop other means of evaluating information retrieval systems. Some of these are reasonably practical even if seldom used, such as fallout, and others are theoretically interesting but almost never used, such as Swets' E.

Difficulties arise in acquiring much of the data required for evaluation. Precision and recall seem to present relatively few conceptual problems, although both depend on the availability of objective relevance assessments of documents with respect to queries. Precision and recall are also readily interpretable in terms of the actual performance of the system, and they may be relatable to cost evaluation by using composite measures such as, for example, the cost per relevant document retrieved.

Since many decisions eventually revolve around system cost, it would be convenient if one could easily measure either the cost or the benefit of a system. Unfortunately, costs and values vary from environment to environment, and the expense associated with a particular system function or operation is often impossible to isolate from the surrounding context. Thus, while some cost evaluation methods have been presented, it must be recognized that the collection of cost data is very difficult. Furthermore, the comparison of costs pertaining to different environments is particularly dangerous.

In the remainder of this book, the evaluation results are based on recall and precision, because these measures remain the standard. In operational retrieval environments, many other factors may, however, prove more important than recall and precision, especially to uninitiated users of the system. Whereas a small improvement in either recall or precision may be completely invisible to the average user, human factor considerations such as ease of use and training required for query submission, output formats, console noise, system reliability, and response time may take on overwhelming importance.

The evaluation measures examined in this chapter make it possible to distinguish well-designed methods from other less effective ones. In the end, acceptable retrieval systems must be easy to use, reliable, effective and inexpensive. All system users look forward to the day when such systems will actually become available for use.

REFERENCES

[1] D.W. King and E.C. Bryant, The Evaluation of Information Services and Products, Information Resources Press, Washington, 1971.

[2] A. Kent, O.E. Taulbee, J. Belzer, and G.D. Goldstein, editors, Electronic Handling of Information: Testing and Evaluation, Thompson Book Co., Washington, 1967.

[3] S. Treu, Testing and Evaluation—Literature Review, in Electronic Handling of Information: Testing and Evaluation, A. Kent, O.E. Taulbee, J. Belzer, and G.D. Goldstein, editors, Thompson Book Co., Washington, 1967, pp. 71–88.

[4] F.W. Lancaster, Evaluating the Effectiveness of Information Retrieval Systems, in Information Retrieval Systems—Characteristics, Testing and Evaluation, 2nd Edition, Chapter 9, John Wiley and Sons, New York, 1979.

[5] C.J. Wessel, Criteria for Evaluating Technical Library Effectiveness, Aslib Proceedings, Vol. 20, No. 11, November 1968, pp. 455–481.

[6] H. Bornstein, A Paradigm for a Retrieval Effectiveness Experiment, American Documentation, Vol. 12, No. 4, October 1961, pp. 254–481.

[7] F.W. Lancaster and W.D. Climenson, Evaluating the Economic Efficiency of a Document Retrieval System, Journal of Documentation, Vol. 24, No. 1, March 1968, pp. 16–40

[8] C.P. Bourne, Review of the Criteria and Techniques Used or Suggested for the Evaluation of Reference Retrieval Systems, Report, Stanford Research Institute, Menlo Park, California, September 1964.

[9] M.B. Snyder, A.W. Schumacher, S.E. Mayer, and M.D. Havron, Methodology for Test and Evaluation of Document Retrieval Systems: A Critical Review and Recommendations, Report to the National Science Foundation, Human Sciences Research Inc., McLean, Virginia, January 1966.

[10] D.W. King and E.C. Bryant, A Diagnostic Model for Evaluating Retrospective

Search Systems, Information Storage and Retrieval, Vol. 6, No. 3, July 1970, pp. 261–272.

[11] T. Saracevic, Linking Research and Teaching, American Documentation, Vol. 19, No. 4. October 1968, pp. 398–403.

[12] F.W. Lancaster, The Functions of Information Retrieval Systems, in Information Retrieval Systems—Characteristics, Testing and Evaluation, 2nd Edition, Chapter 1, John Wiley and Sons, New York, 1979.

[13] C.W. Cleverdon, J. Mills, and E.M. Keen, Factors Determining the Performance of Indexing Systems, Vol. 1—Design, Aslib Cranfield Research Project, Cranfield, England, 1966.

[14] F.W. Lancaster, Criteria by which Information Retrieval Systems May Be Evaluated, in Information Retrieval Systems—Characteristics, Testing and Evaluation, 2nd Edition, Chapter 8, John Wiley and Sons, New York, 1979.

[15] C.A. Cuadra and R.V. Katter, Experimental Studies of Relevance Judgments Report TM-3520, Final Report, Vol. 1, System Development Corporation, Santa Monica, California, June 1967.

[16] T. Saracevic, Relevance: A Review of and a Framework for the Thinking on the Notion in Information Science, Journal of the ASIS, Vol. 26, No. 6, November–December 1975, pp. 321–343.

[17] W.S. Cooper, A Definition of Relevance for Information Retrieval, Information Storage and Retrieval, Vol. 7, No. 1, June 1971, pp. 19–37.

[18] W. Goffman, On Relevance as a Measure, Information Storage and Retrieval, Vol. 2, No. 3, December 1964, pp. 201–203.

[19] W. Goffman and V.A. Newill, Methodology for Test and Evaluation of Information Retrieval Systems, Comparative Systems Laboratory, Report CSL: TR-2, Western Reserve University, Cleveland, Ohio, July 1964.

[20] D.A. Kemp, Relevance, Pertinence and Information System Development, Information Storage and Retrieval, Vol. 10, 1974, pp. 37–47.

[21] S.E. Robertson, The Probabilistic Character of Relevance, Information Processing and Management, Vol. 13, No. 4, 1977, pp. 247–251.

[22] M.E. Maron and J.L. Kuhns, On Relevance, Probabilistic Indexing and Information Retrieval, Journal of the ACM, Vol. 7, No. 3, July 1960, pp. 216–244.

[23] C.W. Cleverdon and J. Mills, The Testing of Index Language Devices, Aslib Proceedings, Vol. 15, No. 4, April 1963, pp. 106–130.

[24] G. Salton, editor, The SMART Retrieval System—Experiments in Automatic Document Processing, Prentice-Hall, Inc., Englewood Cliffs, New Jersey, 1971, Part 3.

[25] C.J. van Rijsbergen, Information Retrieval, 2nd Edition, Chapter 7, Butterworths, London, 1979.

[26] H. Gilbert and K. Sparck Jones, Statistical Bases of Relevance Assessments for the Ideal Information Retrieval Test Collection, Computer Laboratory, University of Cambridge, BL R and D Report 5481, Cambridge, England, March 1979.

[27] E.M. Keen, Evaluation Parameters, in The SMART Retrieval System—Experiments in Automatic Document Processing, G. Salton, editor, Prentice-Hall, Inc., Englewood Cliffs, New Jersey, 1971, Chapter 5.

[28] R.A. Fairthorne, Basic Parameters of Retrieval Tests, Proceedings of 1964 Annual Meeting of the American Documentation Institute, Spartan Books, Washington, 1964, pp. 343–347.

[29] D. Williamson, R. Williamson, and M.E. Lesk, The Cornell Implementation of the

SMART System, in The SMART Retrieval System—Experiments in Automatic Document Processing, G. Salton, editor, Prentice-Hall, Inc., Englewood Cliffs, New Jersey, 1971, Chapter 2.

[30] F.W. Lancaster, Evaluating the Performance of a Large Operating Information Retrieval System, in Electronic Handling of Information: Testing and Evaluation, A. Kent, O.E. Taulbee, J. Belzer, and G.D. Goldstein, editors, Thompson Book Co., Washington, 1967, pp. 199–216.

[31] G. Salton, The "Generality" Effect and the Retrieval Evaluation for Large Collections, Journal of the ASIS, Vol. 23, No. 1, January–February 1972, pp. 11–22.

[32] M. Taube, A Note on the Pseudomathematics of Relevance, American Documentation, Vol. 16, No. 2, April 1965, pp. 69–72.

[33] M.E. Lesk and G. Salton, Relevance Assessments and Retrieval System Evaluation, Information Storage and Retrieval, Vol. 4, No. 4, December 1968, pp. 343–359.

[34] V.E. Giuliano and P.E. Jones, Study and Test of a Methodology for Laboratory Evaluation of Message Retrieval Systems, Report No. ESD-TR-66-405, Arthur D. Little, Inc., Cambridge, August 1966.

[35] R.A. Fairthorne, Implications of Test Procedures, in Information Retrieval in Action, Western Reserve University Press, Cleveland, Ohio, 1963, pp. 109–113.

[36] S.E. Robertson, The Parametric Description of Retrieval Tests, Part I: The Basic Parameters, Journal of Documentation, Vol. 25, No. 1, March 1969, pp. 1–27.

[37] C.W. Cleverdon, Progress in Documentation: Evaluation Tests of Information Retrieval Systems, Journal of Documentation, Vol. 26, No. 1, March 1970, pp. 55–67.

[38] T. Saracevic, An Inquiry into Testing of Information Retrieval Systems, Part I: Objectives, Methodology, Design and Controls, Comparative Systems Laboratory, Report No. CSL: TR-FINAL-1, Case Western Reserve University, Cleveland, Ohio, 1968.

[39] G.F. Romerio and L. Cavara, Assessment Studies of Documentation Systems, Information Storage and Retrieval, Vol. 4, No. 3, August 1968, pp. 309–325.

[40] J.A. Swets, Effectiveness of Information Retrieval Methods, American Documentation, Vol. 20, No. 1, January 1969, pp. 72–89.

[41] B.C. Brookes, The Measure of Information Retrieval Effectiveness Proposed by Swets, Journal of Documentation, Vol. 24, No. 1, March 1968, pp. 41–54.

[42] S.E. Robertson, The Parametric Description of Retrieval Tests, Part 1: The Basic Parameters, Journal of Documentation, Vol. 25, No. 1, March 1969, pp. 1–27; Part 2: Overall Measures, Journal of Documentation, Vol. 25, No. 2, June 1969, pp. 93–107.

[43] M.H. Heine, Design Equations for Retrieval Systems Based on the Swets Model, Journal of the ASIS, Vol. 25, No. 3, May–June 1974, pp. 183–198.

[44] R.R.V. Wiederkehr, Search Characteristics Curves, in Evaluation of Document Retrieval Systems: Literature Perspective, Measurement, Technical Papers, Westat Research Report PB 182710, Bethesda, Maryland, December 1968.

[45] D.W. King and E.C. Bryant, The Evaluation of Information Services and Products, Information Resources Press, Washington, 1971, Chapter 9.

[46] A.R. Meetham, Communication Theory and the Evaluation of Information Retrieval Systems, Information Storage and Retrieval, Vol. 5, No. 5, October 1969, pp. 129–134.

[47] R.H. Shumway, Contingency Tables in Information Retrieval: An Information Theoretic Analysis, in Evaluation of Document Retrieval Systems: Literature Per-

spective, Measurement, Technical Papers, Westat Research Report PB 182710, Bethesda, Maryland, December 1968.

[48] M. Guazzo, Retrieval Performance and Information Theory, Information Processing and Management, Vol. 13, No. 3, 1977, pp. 155–165.

[49] A.E. Cawkell, A Measure of Efficiency Factor—Communication Theory Applied to Document Selection Systems, Information Processing and Management, Vol. 11, No. 8–12, 1975, pp. 243–248.

[50] J.J. Rocchio, Jr., Document Retrieval Systems—Optimization and Evaluation, Harvard University Doctoral Thesis, Report No. ISR-10 to the National Science Foundation, Harvard Computation Laboratory, March 1966.

[51] G. Salton, Automatic Information Organization and Retrieval, McGraw-Hill Book Co., New York, 1968, Chapter 8.

[52] W.S. Cooper, Expected Search Length: A Single Measure of Retrieval Effectiveness Based on the Weak Ordering Action of Retrieval Systems, American Documentation, Vol. 19, No. 1, January 1968, pp. 30–41.

[53] S.M. Pollock, Measures for the Comparison of Information Retrieval Systems, American Documentation, Vol. 19, No. 4, October 1968, pp. 387–397.

[54] W.S. Cooper, On Selecting a Measure of Retrieval Effectiveness, Part I: The Subjective Philosophy of Evaluation; Part II: Implementation of the Philosophy, Journal of the ASIS, Vol. 24, 1973, pp. 87–100, 413–424.

[55] D.H. Kraft and A. Bookstein, Evaluation of Information Retrieval Systems: A Decision Theory Approach, Journal of the ASIS, Vol. 29, No. 1, January 1978, pp. 31–40.

[56] W.S. Cooper, Indexing Documents by Gedanken Experimentation, Journal of the ASIS, Vol. 29, No. 3, May–June 1978, pp. 107–119.

[57] W.S. Cooper and M.E. Maron, Foundations of Probabilistic and Utility Theoretic Indexing, Journal of the ACM, Vol. 25, No. 1, January 1978, pp. 67–80.

[58] F.W. Lancaster, The Cost-Effectiveness Analysis of Information Retrieval and Dissemination Systems, Journal of the ASIS, Vol. 22, No. 1, January 1971, pp. 12–27.

[59] F.W. Lancaster, Cost-Effectiveness and Cost-Benefit Evaluation, in Information Retrieval Systems—Characteristics, Testing and Evaluation, 2nd Edition, John Wiley and Sons, New York, 1979, Chapter 16.

[60] A. Gilchrist, Cost-Effectiveness, Aslib Proceedings, Vol. 23, No. 9, September 1971, pp. 455–464.

[61] F. Alouche, N. Bely, R.C. Cros, J.C. Gardin, F. Levy, and J. Perreault, Economie Générale d'une Chaîne Documentaire Mecanisée, Gauthier Villars, Paris, 1967.

[62] K.W. Webb, W.C. Suhler, G.G. Heller, and S.P. Todd, Jr., Evaluation Models for Information Retrieval and Command and Control Systems (EMIR), IBM Corporation Report, Federal Systems Division, Washington, June 1964.

[63] A Time/Cost Study of Processing Books via Unit Orders and Blanket Orders, Five Associated University Libraries, Newsletter, Vol. 3, No. 4, July 1972.

[64] G. Williams, E.C. Bryant, R.R.V. Wiederkehr, V.E. Palmour, and C.J. Siehler, Library Cost Models: Owning versus Borrowing Serial Publications, Center for Research Libraries, Washington, November 1968.

[65] M.M. Cummings, Needs of the Health Sciences, in Electronic Handling of Information: Testing and Evaluation, A. Kent, O.E. Taulbee, J. Belzer and G.D. Goldstein, editors, Thompson Book Co., Washington, 1967.

[66] C.W. Cleverdon, The Methodology of Evaluation of Operational Information Re-

trieval Systems Based on the Test of Medlars, Cranfield Institute of Technology Report, Cranfield, England, 1968.

[67] C.P. Bourne, G.D. Peterson, B. Lefkowitz, and D. Ford, Requirements, Criteria and Measure of Performance of Information Storage and Retrieval Systems, Final Report to National Science Foundation, Report AD 270 942, Stanford Research Institute, December 1961.

[68] Arthur Andersen and Co., Research Study of Criteria and Procedures for Evaluating Scientific Information Retrieval Systems, Final Report to the National Science Foundation, New York, March 1962.

[69] C.P. Bourne and D.F. Ford, Cost Analysis and Simulation Procedures for the Evaluation of Large Information Systems, American Documentation, Vol. 15, No. 2, April 1964, pp. 142–149.

[70] N.R. Baker and R.E. Nance, The Use of Simulation in Studying Information Storage and Retrieval Systems, American Documentation, Vol. 19, No. 4, October 1968, pp. 363–370.

[71] M.D. Cooper, A Cost Model for Evaluating Information Retrieval Systems, Journal of the ASIS, Vol. 23, No. 5, September–October 1972, pp. 306–312.

[72] B.V. Tell, Auditing Procedures for Information Retrieval Systems, Proceedings 1965 FID Congress, Spartan Books, Washington, 1966, pp. 119–124.

[73] I.J. Good, The Decision-Theory Approach to the Evaluation of Information Retrieval System, Information Storage and Retrieval, Vol. 3, No. 2, April 1967, pp. 31–34.

[74] J. Martyn and B.C. Vickery, The Complexity of the Modelling of Information Systems, Journal of Documentation, Vol. 26, No. 3, September 1970, pp. 204–220.

[75] D.H. Rothenberg, An Efficiency Model and a Performance Function for an Information Retrieval System, Information Storage and Retrieval, Vol. 5, No. 3, October 1969, pp. 109–122.

[76] N.R. Keith, Jr., A General Evaluation Model for an Information Storage and Retrieval System, Journal of the ASIS, Vol. 21, No. 4, July–August 1970, pp. 237–239.

[77] E.C. Bryant, Modeling in Document Handling, in Electronic Handling of Information: Testing and Evaluation, A. Kent, O.E. Taulbee, J. Belzer, and G.D. Goldstein, editors, Thompson Book Co., Washington, 1967, pp. 163–173.

[78] R.R.V. Wiederkehr, A Net Benefit Model for Evaluating Elementary Document Retrieval Systems, in Evaluation of Document Retrieval Systems, Westat Research Report, PB 182710, Bethesda, Maryland, December 1968.

BIBLIOGRAPHIC REMARKS

Many materials covering the evaluation of information retrieval operations and systems appear in the report literature that may not be easy to obtain. Two of the best known of these reports cover the well-known Aslib-Cranfield study and the evaluation of the MEDLARS retrieval service:

C.W. Cleverdon, J. Mills, and E.M. Keen, Factors Determining the Performance of Indexing Systems, Vol. 1—Design, Aslib-Cranfield Research Project, Cranfield, England, 1966.

F.W. Lancaster, Evaluation of the Medlars Demand Search Service, National Library of Medicine, Bethesda, Maryland, January 1968.

The following references contain discussions dealing with theoretical aspects of retrieval system evaluation:

T. Saracevic, Relevance-A Review of and a Framework for the Thinking on the Notion in Information Science, Journal of the American Society for Information Science, Vol. 26, No. 6, November–December 1975, pp. 321–343.
M.E. Maron, editor, Theory and Foundations of Information Retrieval, Drexel Library Quarterly, Vol. 14, No. 2, April 1978.
C.J. van Rijsbergen, Information Retrieval, 2nd Edition, Chapter 7, Butterworths, London, 1979.

The following texts all deal extensively with various aspects of retrieval system evaluation:

F.W. Lancaster, Information Retrieval Systems—Characteristics, Testing and Evaluation, 2nd Edition, John Wiley and Sons, New York, 1979.
A. Kent, O.E. Taulbee, J. Belzer, and G.D. Goldstein, editors, Electronic Handling of Information: Testing and Evaluation, Thompson Book Company, Washington, DC., 1967.
D.W. King and E.C. Bryant, The Evaluation of Information Services and Products, Information Resources Press, Washington, DC., 1971.

EXERCISES

5-1 Consider a retrieval system capable of presenting the output items to the user population in a ranked sequence in decreasing order of presumed usefulness. Consider two particular queries each having 10 relevant documents in a collection. The ranks of the relevant documents for query 1 are 1, 3, 5, . . . ,19, and for query 2 the ranks are 2, 4, 6, . . . ,20.

    a Prepare recall-precision tables and graphs for the two queries similar to those shown in Fig. 5-2 for a sample query.

    b What is the most obvious difference in the evaluation results obtained for the two queries? Do you expect this difference to affect a systems evaluation in which results are averaged over several queries? Why?

    c Prepare recall-precision tables and graphs showing recall-level and document-level averages for the recall and precision results obtained for the two queries.

5-2 The fallout evaluation measure has been called superior to precision for a number of reasons. What are they? Under what circumstances would you prefer to deal with a recall-fallout evaluation instead of a recall-precision output?

5-3 Prepare probability density output and operating characteristic curves similar to those shown in Figs. 5-7 and 5-8 reflecting the performance of the set of relevant items and the set of nonrelevant items, respectively, with respect to some query for the following cases:

    a All relevant items are retrieved ahead of all nonrelevant ones.

    b All nonrelevant items are retrieved ahead of all relevant ones.

    c The relevant items are randomly sprinkled among the nonrelevant ones.

    d The retrieval output follows the pattern specified for queries 1 and 2 of Exercise 5-1.

5-4 Derive the equation for the normalized precision measure given in expression (15).

Furnish a construction for the normalized precision similar to the one given in Fig. 5-10 for the normalized recall.

5-5 Assume that the two queries of Exercise 5-1 are retrieved in groups of three items each, that is, the first three items are retrieved together, followed by the next three items, and so on, until the last items are retrieved. Compute the average search lengths obtained for the two queries, assuming the users wish to retrieve 10 documents in all, 15 documents in all, or 20 documents in all.

Retrieval Refinements

0 PREVIEW

A number of advanced analysis and search techniques have been mentioned in some of the previous chapters, including in particular the use of term weighting methods for indexing and query formulation, the introduction of clustered file arrangements, the dynamic improvement of query formulations using relevance feedback techniques, and the use of bibliographic citations for content identification and retrieval purposes. In the present chapter, these techniques are examined in more detail, and methods are given for implementing the various techniques in retrieval. Wherever possible evaluation results are included showing the usefulness of the various methodologies in retrieval.

Some of the procedures examined in this chapter should prove immediately useful in conventional and experimental retrieval situations. This is the case notably of some term weighting systems that are easy to generate and exceptionally effective, and of the automatic query adjustment systems based on user-system interaction during the course of the search process. Certain other techniques, such as the dynamic document space modification and the automatic thesaurus construction process using pseudoclassification, may prove important in the long run. All the retrieval refinements described in this chapter are conceptually simple and some of them have already been applied in information retrieval under operational conditions.

1 INTRODUCTION

Conventional retrieval operations use Boolean search requests and inverted file systems. A search then produces two distinct document sets: those retrieved in answer to a given query and those not retrieved. Relationships or similarities between individual documents are not utilized and neither are relationships between keywords or query terms. The experimental retrieval systems described in Chapter 4 are more advanced largely because some structure is imposed on the retrieval environment. Thus, by recognizing relationships among the documents of a collection, items which appear to be related can be grouped into affinity classes, to permit browsing and to simplify searches dealing with particular subject areas. By making distinctions among the terms assigned to the documents, some documents—normally those identified by highly weighted terms—can be retrieved ahead of certain others identified by terms of lesser importance. By using the occurrence characteristics of the terms assigned to a collection, it is possible to identify very broad terms assigned to a large proportion of the documents as well as narrow terms assigned to few documents. The former can be rendered less general by combining them into term phrases, and the latter can be broadened by grouping them into thesaurus classes of wider scope.

The foregoing processes produce a greater measure of discrimination among the documents of a collection and among the terms characterizing document content than is customary in conventional retrieval situations. When the documents are clearly distinguished from each other, maximum recall and precision may be obtained for a search, because each particular relevant item may then be retrievable without also retrieving neighboring items that may not be relevant. Furthermore, documents that are distinguished from each other can be ranked for output purposes in decreasing order of the similarity between query and documents. This brings the most important items to the users' attention early in a search when they are most easily used for the generation of improved search formulations in an interactive search mode.

The discrimination operations all depend on the assignment of importance factors, or weights, to the content identifiers used for a document collection, and on the computation of similarity measures between documents, between terms, or between queries and documents. In this chapter, the properties of vector similarity functions are first outlined and some of the applications of term weighting and vector similarity computations previously mentioned for the experimental systems of Chapter 4 are covered in greater detail. This includes the generation of optimum term weights, the construction of document clusters, and the generation of improved query formulations and better document identifications. Normally, the affinities between document vectors are measured by comparing the terms attached to the respective items. In some circumstances, the terms may be replaced by bibliographic citations. In particular, the structure of a document collection might be determined by the citations and bibliographic references relating the items. This possibility is further examined at the end of this chapter.

*2 VECTOR SIMILARITY FUNCTIONS

Consider a collection of objects in which each object is characterized by one or more properties associated with the objects. In information retrieval, the objects might be documents and the properties could be the index terms assigned to the documents. Alternatively, the objects could be index terms, and the properties could be the document identifiers to which the terms are assigned. Each property attached to a given object could be weighted to reflect its importance in the representation of the given object. Alternatively, a property characterizing an item may be considered to carry a weight of 1 when it is actually assigned to an item, or a weight of 0 when the property is not assigned. In the former case one speaks of *weighted* indexing; in the latter case the indexing is *binary*.

The similarity between two objects is normally computed as a function of the number of properties that are assigned to both objects; in addition the number of properties that are jointly absent from both objects may be taken into account. Furthermore, when weighted indexing is used, the weight of the properties appearing in the two vectors may be used instead of only the number of properties.

Consider as an example, two particular objects, say DOC_i and DOC_j, and let $TERM_{ik}$ represent the weight of property (term) k assigned to document i. In binary systems the value of $TERM_{ik}$ is restricted to either 0 or 1. Otherwise, one may assume that the weights vary from some lower limit such as 0 to some predetermined maximum weight for a given collection environment. If t properties are used to characterize the objects, the following property vectors may be defined for two sample objects:

$$DOC_i = (TERM_{i1}, TERM_{i2}, \ldots, TERM_{it})$$
$$DOC_j = (TERM_{j1}, TERM_{j2}, \ldots, TERM_{jt})$$

To compute the similarity between two given vectors, the following vector functions are of principal importance:

1 $\sum_{k=1}^{t} TERM_{ik}$, that is, the sum of the weights of all properties included in a given vector (in this case, the vector for DOC_i).

2 $\sum_{k=1}^{t} TERM_{ik} \cdot TERM_{jk}$, that is, the component-by-component vector product, consisting of the sum of the products of corresponding term weights for two vectors. For binary vectors this reduces to the number of *matching* properties for two vectors (the number of properties with weight equal to 1 in the two vectors).

3 $\sum_{k=1}^{t} \min (TERM_{ik}, TERM_{jk})$, that is, the sum of the minimum component weights of the components of the two vectors.

4 $\sqrt{\sum_{k=1}^{t} (\text{TERM}_{ik})^2}$, that is, the length of the property vector (in this case,

the one for DOC_i) when the property vectors are consider as ordinary vectors.

Consider the following two vectors defined for a system using eight properties:

$$\text{DOC}_i = (3,2,1,0,0,0,1,1)$$
$$\text{DOC}_j = (1,1,1,0,0,1,0,0)$$

The four vector functions introduced earlier are then equal, respectively, to

1 $\sum_{k=1}^{t} \text{TERM}_{ik} = (3 + 2 + 1 + 0 + 0 + 0 + 1 + 1) = 8$

2 $\sum_{k=1}^{t} \text{TERM}_{ik} \cdot \text{TERM}_{jk} = [(3 \cdot 1) + (2 \cdot 1) + (1 \cdot 1) + (0 \cdot 0) + (0 \cdot 0)$
$$+ (0 \cdot 1) + (1 \cdot 0) + (1 \cdot 0)] = 6$$

3 $\sum_{k=1}^{t} \min(\text{TERM}_{ik}, \text{TERM}_{jk}) = (\min(3,1) + \min(2,1) + \min(1,1)$
$$+ \min(0,0) + \min(0,0) + \min(0,1)$$
$$+ \min(1,0) + \min(1,0)$$
$$= (1 + 1 + 1 + 0$$
$$+ 0 + 0 + 0 + 0) = 3$$

4 $\sqrt{\sum_{k=1}^{t} (\text{TERM}_{ik})^2}$

$$= \sqrt{(3 \cdot 3) + (2 \cdot 2) + (1 \cdot 1) + (0 \cdot 0) + (0 \cdot 0) + (0 \cdot 0) + (1 \cdot 1) + (1 \cdot 1)}$$
$$= \sqrt{9 + 4 + 1 + 0 + 0 + 0 + 1 + 1} = 4$$

The expressions under 2 and 3 are based on the manipulation of a particular vector pair; expressions 1 and 4 are single vector functions only. Hence the ordinary vector product (expression 2) and the sum of the minimum components (expression 3) could be used directly to measure the similarity between the vectors. In practice, it is customary to include normalizing factors when computing vector similarities. These factors ensure that the similarity coefficients remain within certain bounds, say between 0 and 1 or between -1 and $+1$. The following similarity measures are all relatively easy to generate and have been used in operational or experimental situations to compute term or document similarities [1,2]:

$$\text{SIM}_1(\text{DOC}_i, \text{DOC}_j) = \frac{2 \left[\sum_{k=1}^{t} (\text{TERM}_{ik} \cdot \text{TERM}_{jk}) \right]}{\sum_{k=1}^{t} \text{TERM}_{ik} + \sum_{k=1}^{t} \text{TERM}_{jk}} \tag{1}$$

$$SIM_2(DOC_i, DOC_j) = \frac{\sum_{k=1}^{t} (TERM_{ik} \cdot TERM_{jk})}{\sum_{k=1}^{t} TERM_{ik} + \sum_{k=1}^{t} TERM_{jk} - \sum_{k=1}^{t} (TERM_{ik} \cdot TERM_{jk})} \tag{2}$$

$$SIM_3(DOC_i, DOC_j) = \frac{\sum_{k=1}^{t} (TERM_{ik} \cdot TERM_{jk})}{\sqrt{\sum_{k=1}^{t} (TERM_{ik})^2 \cdot \sum_{k=1}^{t} (TERM_{jk})^2}} \tag{3}$$

$$SIM_4(DOC_i, DOC_j) = \frac{\sum_{k-1}^{t} (TERM_{ik} \cdot TERM_{jk})}{\min\left(\sum_{k=1}^{t} TERM_{ik}, \sum_{k=1}^{t} TERM_{jk}\right)} \tag{4}$$

$$SIM_5(DOC_i, DOC_j) = \frac{\sum_{k=1}^{t} \min(TERM_{ik}, TERM_{jk})}{\sum_{k=1}^{t} TERM_{ik}} \tag{5}$$

For the two sample vectors previously used as an illustration, the similarity functions SIM_1 to SIM_5 produce the following results:

$$SIM_1(DOC_i, DOC_j) = \frac{2 \cdot (6)}{8 + 4} = 1$$

$$SIM_2(DOC_i, DOC_j) = \frac{6}{8 + 4 - 6} = 1$$

$$SIM_3(DOC_i, DOC_j) = \frac{6}{\sqrt{16 \cdot 4}} = \frac{6}{\sqrt{64}} = \frac{6}{8} = 0.75$$

$$SIM_4(DOC_i, DOC_j) = \frac{6}{4} = 1.5$$

$$SIM_5(DOC_i, DOC_j) = \frac{3}{8} = 0.375$$

The first two coefficients, SIM_1 and SIM_2, are known respectively as the *Dice* and *Jaccard* coefficients. They are widely used in the literature to measure vector similarities. The third coefficient, SIM_3, is the *cosine* coefficient that was introduced earlier in this volume. The cosine is a measure of the angle between two t-dimensional object vectors when the vectors are considered as ordinary vectors in a space of t dimensions. Since the numerator in the cosine expression must be divided by the product of the lengths of the two vectors, long vectors with many terms and hence great length normally produce small cosine similarities. The *overlap* measure, SIM_4, does not have this property because its denominator consists of the lower-weighted terms from the two vectors. In a retrieval environment, the query usually contains low-weighted terms; hence the query-document correlations using the overlap measure SIM_4 will be larger in magnitude than those of the cosine SIM_3.

The last coefficient, SIM_5, is an asymmetric measure; that is the similarity between DOC_i and DOC_j is not in general equal to the similarity between DOC_j and DOC_i. Indeed $SIM_5(DOC_i, DOC_j) = \frac{3}{8}$ whereas $SIM_5(DOC_j, DOC_i) = \frac{3}{4}$. Asymmetric measures are useful to capture the inclusion relations between vectors (vector B is included in vector A if all properties assigned to B are also present in A). The inclusion properties between vectors can be used for the generation of hierarchical arrangements of objects (for example, hierarchical term displays) and for the comparison of queries with documents in retrieval [1].

A great many different similarity measures are discussed in the literature designed to represent the associations between different property vectors. Some of the functions reflect statistical theories, being designed to measure the agreement between two vectors over and above the coincidences that would be expected if the properties were randomly assigned to the vectors [3,4]. In some similarity functions the absence of properties from a vector may be taken into account as well as the presence. For instance the joint absence of a property in two vectors may be weighted differently from the joint presence of a property [5].

All similarity measures exhibit one common property, namely that their value increases when the number of common properties (or the weight of the common properties) in two vectors increases. Measures of vector dissimilarity which are sometimes used instead of similarity measures have the opposite effect. Various evaluation studies exist in which the effect of different similarity measures has been compared in a retrieval environment [1]. The Jaccard [expression (2)] and the cosine measures [expression (3)] have similar characteristics, ranging from a minimum of 0 to a maximum of 1 for nonnegative vector elements. These measures are easy to compute and they appear to be as effective in retrieval as other more complicated functions. Both these measures have been widely used for the evaluation of retrieval functions.

3 TERM WEIGHTING SYSTEMS

A Principal Weighting Strategies

In principle, the retrieval environment is simplest when the information items are characterized by unweighted properties and the indexing operation is binary. In this case, the degree to which a given property (term) may be useful to represent the content of an item is not a consideration. Any property that appears relevant is assigned to the information item and rejected when it appears extraneous. While the indexing is simplified, the task of evaluating the output of a search operation may be complicated because distinctions among the retrieved items, or for that matter among the items that are not retrieved, are more difficult to make for binary than for weighted vectors. When weighted properties are used, a similarity computation between the query and document vectors makes it possible to retrieve the items in strictly *ranked order* according to the magnitude of the query-document similarity coefficients. This should improve the retrieval effectiveness and lighten the user effort required to generate a useful query.

When users, indexers, or search intermediaries manually assign term weights to document and query vectors, the weighting operation is difficult to control. A satisfactory assignment of weights requires a great deal of know-how about the collection and the operation of the retrieval system. For this reason, an effective term weighting operation is probably best conducted by using objective term characteristics automatically to generate term weights.

Several automatic term weighting systems were introduced in Chapter 3 in the discussion on automatic indexing. They are summarized here for convenience:

1 The term frequency (TF) weighting system is based on the notion that constructs (words, phrases, word groups) that frequently occur in the text of documents have some bearing on the content of the texts. Hence the weight of term k in document i, WEIGHT_{ik} might be set equal to the frequency of occurrence of word construct k in document i:

$$\text{WEIGHT}_{ik} = \text{FREQ}_{ik} \tag{6}$$

2 The term frequency system makes no distinction between terms that occur in every document of a collection and those that occur in only a few items. Experience indicates that the usefulness of a term for content representation increases with the frequency of the term in the document but decreases with the number of documents DOCFREQ_k to which the term is assigned. This produces the inverse document frequency (IDF) weighting system:

$$\text{WEIGHT}_{ik} = \frac{\text{FREQ}_{ik}}{\text{DOCFREQ}_k} \tag{7}$$

3 The term discrimination theory depends on the degree to which the assignment of a term to the documents of a collection is capable of decreasing the density of the document space (the average distance between documents). The discrimination value of term k, DISCVALUE_k is obtained as the difference between two measurements of document space density, corresponding to the densities before and after assignment of term k. A typical weighting function for term k in document i is then obtained as

$$\text{WEIGHT}_{ik} = \text{FREQ}_{ik} \cdot \text{DISCVALUE}_k \tag{8}$$

4 The probabilistic indexing theory states that the best index terms are those that tend to occur in the relevant documents with respect to some query. When the terms are assigned to the documents independently of each other, a measure of term value is obtained from the term relevance TERMREL_k. This is the ratio of the proportion of relevant items in which term k occurs to the proportion of nonrelevant items in which the term occurs [expression (23) of Chapter 3]. A weighting system based on the term relevance is thus

$$\text{WEIGHT}_{ik} = \text{FREQ}_{ik} \cdot \text{TERMREL}_k \tag{9}$$

The term frequency, document frequency, and term discrimination theories were previously examined in the discussion dealing with automatic indexing. The term relevance weighting system is theoretically optimal given certain well-specified conditions. However the term relevance factor

$$\text{TERMREL}_k = \frac{r_k/(R - r_k)}{s_k/(I - s_k)}$$

cannot be computed unless relevance assessments are available of the documents with respect to certain queries. In particular, the number of relevant documents (r_k) containing term k, the number of nonrelevant documents (s_k) containing term k, as well as the total number of relevant documents (R) and nonrelevant documents (I) in the collection for some particular query sets must be known in advance.

A similar situation arises for a weighting function based on the *utility* value introduced in the discussion on system evaluation [expression (19) of Chapter 5]. The utility of a search is defined simply as the sum of the values achieved by retrieving relevant items and rejecting nonrelevant ones plus the sum of the costs incurred by retrieving nonrelevant and rejecting relevant items. One may assume that each relevant item that is correctly retrieved increases the usefulness of retrieval by a specified value equal to v_1; similarly each nonrelevant item that is properly rejected increases the system usefulness by a constant value of v_2. Analogously, a constant cost of c_1 is incurred for each nonrelevant item that is retrieved, and a cost of c_2 arises for each relevant item missed by the retrieval system. In these circumstances, appropriate transformations of the utility value introduced in Chapter 5 produce a weighting function, known as the utility weight for a given term k, or UTILITY_k, defined as

$$\text{UTILITY}_k = (v_1 + c_2)r_k - (v_2 + c_1)s_k \tag{10}$$

where r_k and s_k, respectively represent the number of relevant and nonrelevant items containing term k [6]. A corresponding term weighting function for term k in document i is then given by

$$\text{WEIGHT}_{ik} = \text{FREQ}_{ik} \cdot \text{UTILITY}_k \tag{11}$$

The utility and term relevance weighting systems of expressions (9) and (11) may be expected to be more powerful than the alternative weighting schemes based on simple term frequency characteristics [expressions (6) and

(7)]. In the utility and term relevance systems, a distinction is made between term occurrences in the relevant and nonrelevant documents, respectively, whereas in the frequency-based systems the term occurrences are used globally over the whole collection irrespective of occurrences in the relevant and nonrelevant documents. On the other hand, it remains to be seen whether for the relevance-based weighting systems the term weights computed by using relevance data for certain queries and documents will prove robust enough to be applied to new documents and queries for which no prior relevance data are available. Procedures for so doing are suggested in the next section.

*B Evaluation of Weighting Systems

Two collections of documents may serve as examples for the evaluation of the weighting systems introduced earlier. These are the Cranfield collection of 424 documents in aerodynamics, and the MEDLARS collection of 450 documents in biomedicine. Each collection is used with 24 search requests. Table 6-1 contains evaluation output for term frequency weightings (6), inverse document

Table 6-1 Term Utility Weight and Relevance Weight Evaluation
(Average Precision Values for Fixed Levels of Recall from 0.1 to 1.0)

Recall	Term frequency	Inverse document frequency		Utility weight $w = 20r - s$ (actual values)		Relevance weights $w = [r/(R - r)] \div [s/(I - s)]$ (actual values)	
		a	Cranfield aerodynamics collection (424 documents, 24 queries)				
0.1	0.455	0.566	+24%	0.568	+25%	0.571	+25%
0.2	0.410	0.530	+29%	0.540	+32%	0.558	+36%
0.3	0.391	0.476	+22%	0.503	+29%	0.479	+23%
0.4	0.301	0.421	+40%	0.474	+57%	0.479	+59%
0.5	0.280	0.364	+30%	0.416	+49%	0.434	+55%
0.6	0.233	0.301	+29%	0.328	+41%	0.352	+51%
0.7	0.189	0.254	+34%	0.272	+44%	0.324	+71%
0.8	0.155	0.195	+26%	0.211	+36%	0.220	+42%
0.9	0.121	0.150	+24%	0.162	+34%	0.199	+64%
1.0	0.112	0.132	+18%	0.143	+29%	0.164	+46%
			+27.6%		+37.6%		+47.2%
		b	MEDLARS biomedical collection (450 documents, 24 queries)				
0.1	0.543	0.611	+13%	0.676	+24%	0.707	+30%
0.2	0.528	0.601	+14%	0.676	+28%	0.707	+34%
0.3	0.467	0.541	+16%	0.639	+37%	0.705	+51%
0.4	0.421	0.467	+11%	0.609	+45%	0.672	+60%
0.5	0.384	0.438	+14%	0.558	+45%	0.633	+65%
0.6	0.346	0.396	+14%	0.510	+47%	0.616	+78%
0.7	0.316	0.347	+10%	0.459	+45%	0.573	+81%
0.8	0.211	0.245	+16%	0.374	+77%	0.462	+119%
0.9	0.171	0.193	+13%	0.277	+62%	0.354	+107%
1.0	0.120	0.154	+28%	0.204	+70%	0.259	+116%
			+14.9%		+48%		+74.1%

frequency weights (7), utility weights (11), and term relevance weights (9). In each case precision values are shown in Table 6-1 for 10 recall levels varying from 0.1 to 1.0. These are averaged for the 24 search requests. The inverse document frequency weights that are based on frequency characteristics over all documents regardless of relevance produce average precision improvements of about 28 percent for the aerodynamics collections and 15 percent for the biomedical collection over the standard term frequency weights. When the utility weights based on document relevance are used the average advantage in precision increases to 38 and 48 percent, respectively, while an even greater advantage of 46 and 74 percent is obtained for the term relevance weights.

To generate the term relevance and term utility weights $TERMREL_k$ and $UTILITY_k$, respectively, it is necessary to identify the number of relevant and nonrelevant documents r_k and s_k in which the term occurs. Furthermore, for the utility weights, values must be chosen for the value and cost parameters of equation (10). The output of Table 6-1 is based on the assumption that the cost and value parameters associated with the relevant documents (v_1 and c_2) are given a weight equal to 20 times the value and cost parameters associated with the nonrelevant (v_2 and c_1). The utility function of expression (10) is thus computed as $20r_k - s_k$.

The problem of generating the r_k and s_k values was bypassed in the experiments of Table 6-1 by using the actual values found in the two sample collections for these parameters. That is, the unrealistic assumption was made that the characteristics of all terms in the relevant and nonrelevant documents were known in advance for all queries. This, of course, accounts for the excellent performance of the term utility and term relevance weighting systems in the output of Table 6-1.

In practice, the occurrence characteristics of the terms in the relevant and nonrelevant documents are not available before a search is actually conducted. However, the total number of documents $DOCFREQ_k$ to which a given term is assigned is given, and that in turn can be used to estimate the number of relevant documents (r_k) having term k. Note that the document frequency of a term varies from 0 for a term not assigned to any document in the collection to a maximum of N for a term assigned to all N items in a collection. The parameter r_k, on the other hand, varies from 0 for a term not assigned to any relevant items to a maximum of R, the total number of relevant items which exists with respect to a given query. Alternatively R can be interpreted in some circumstances as the number of documents which a user wishes to retrieve in response to a given query.

Normally, the following relationships exist between the total document frequency $DOCFREQ_k$ of a term, and the frequency r_k in the relevant documents:

1   As $DOCFREQ_k$ increases, so will r_k; thus given two terms $TERM_j$ and $TERM_k$, $DOCFREQ_j > DOCFREQ_k$ generally implies $r_j > r_k$.

2   For normal query terms, the number of relevant documents in which a term occurs is relatively larger for lower-frequency terms than for higher-frequency terms; mathematically, one can say that when $DOCFREQ_j > DOCFREQ_k$, one finds that $r_k/DOCFREQ_k > r_j/DOCFREQ_j$. (For example, the one document in which a frequency-one term occurs is more likely to be relevant than the two documents for a term of frequency two.)

Several simple functions can be suggested that conform to these conditions. One possible functional relationship between r_k and $DOCFREQ_k$ for a given term k is shown in the graph of Fig. 6-1. Here for document frequencies between 0 and R, one assumes that a straight-line relation exists between DOCFREQ and r given as $r = (a \cdot DOCFREQ)$ for some constant $a < 1$, and represented by line segment 0A. For frequencies DOCFREQ between R and N, another straight-line relation is assumed expressed as $r = d + (e \cdot DOCFREQ)$ and represented by segment AB. It may be noted that in accordance with assumption 2, the slope of line AB (represented by parameter e) is smaller than the slope of line 0A (parameter a). As a result the proportion $r_k/DOCFREQ_k$ is relatively larger for terms of smaller frequency $DOCFREQ_k$ than for terms of larger frequency. An alternative functional relationship between r and DOCFREQ which also obeys assumptions 1 and 2 is $r = a + b(\log DOCFREQ)$. It can be shown that if the relationship between $DOCFREQ_k$ and r_k is the one represented in Fig. 6-1, the best term weighting function has the shape represented in Fig. 6-2 [7].

In particular, the optimum weight of a term starts with some constant value a for terms of frequency 1. The weight then increases as the document frequency increases to R, the number of relevant documents which a user wishes to retrieve in response to a query. As the document frequency increases still further, the terms become less important and the term weight decreases. Eventually, for terms of document frequency near the number of documents in the data base (N), the weight decays to 0. The frequency spectrum of Fig. 6-2

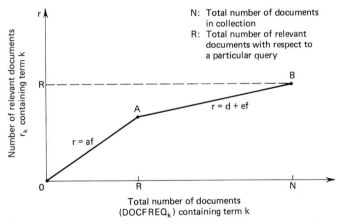

Figure 6-1   Variation of number of relevant documents containing term k with total number of documents containing term k.

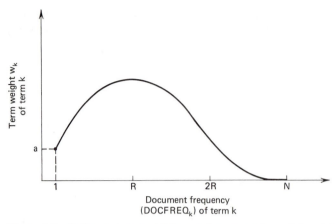

Figure 6-2   Optimum term weighting system assuming relationships of Fig. 6-1.

once again shows that the medium-frequency terms in a collection are the most important for purposes of document indexing.

Consider now the evaluation results obtained for the utility and term relevance weighting schemes where the parameter values for r_k and s_k are no longer assumed to be available, but r_k (and hence $s_k = DOCFREQ_k - r_k$) is obtained by using one of the functional relationships between DOCFREQ and r (for example the one presented earlier in Fig. 6-1). Evaluation results for the term utility and term relevance weighting systems based on estimated r_k values are included in Table 6-2 for the two document collections previously used in Table 6-1. For the utility weights a logarithmic relationship was assumed between r and DOCFREQ [that is, r = a + b log (DOCFREQ) for suitably chosen parameter values a and b]. A hybrid function modeled

Table 6-2   Estimated Term Utility and Relevance Weight Evaluation
(Average Precision Values for 24 Queries at Recall Levels from 0.1 to 1.0)

Cranfield aerodynamics (424 documents, 24 queries)				MEDLARS biomedical (450 documents, 24 queries)			
Utility weight (estimated values)		Relevance weight (estimated values)		Utility weight (estimated values)		Relevance weight (estimated values)	
0.531	+17%	0.552	+21%	0.592	+9%	0.629	+16%
0.501	+22%	0.520	+27%	0.579	+10%	0.629	+19%
0.450	+15%	0.461	+18%	0.511	+9%	0.601	+29%
0.388	+29%	0.421	+40%	0.440	+5%	0.536	+27%
0.332	+19%	0.369	+32%	0.396	+3%	0.512	+33%
0.288	+24%	0.303	+30%	0.333	-4%	0.456	+32%
0.234	+24%	0.259	+37%	0.309	-2%	0.409	+29%
0.184	+19%	0.192	+24%	0.233	+10%	0.296	+40%
0.138	+14%	0.159	+31%	0.186	+9%	0.218	+27%
0.128	+14%	0.131	+17%	0.139	+16%	0.169	+41%
	+19.7%		+27.7%		+6.5%		+29.3%

on the relationship of Fig. 6-1 is used to relate r and DOCFREQ for the relevance weight calculation: in particular, a straight line similar to line segment 0A of Fig. 6-1 (r = a · DOCFREQ) is used for document frequency values up to DOCFREQ = 8; for larger values of DOCFREQ a logarithmic relationship (r = d + e log DOCFREQ) is assumed between r and DOCFREQ.

A comparison between the output of Tables 6-1 and 6-2 indicates that the utility and relevance weighting systems are not as powerful when the parameter values must be estimated than when actual values are available. However the relevance weighting system appears to be more effective than the inverse document frequency even when the relevance parameters are estimated. Since the estimated relevance weights are based purely on the occurrence frequencies of the terms in the documents of a collection, the results of Table 6-2 confirm that substantially more information may be contained in the term frequency data than is normally included in conventional retrieval. Additional work is needed to produce good estimates of term relevance and justification for the curves of Figs. 6-1 and 6-2.

**C Term Weighting in Boolean Query Systems

It was mentioned earlier that systems based on Boolean query formulations are capable of separating a document collection into two parts consisting of the retrieved items on one hand and the rejected (nonretrieved) ones on the other. Additional operations are sometimes carried out for the set of retrieved documents only in order to generate additional discrimination or ranking among these documents. No term weights need to be introduced for this purpose and no changes arise in the interpretation of the normal Boolean operations. The question arises whether the necessary discrimination among documents can be obtained directly by reinterpreting the standard Boolean operations to render them applicable to systems using weighted query terms, and possibly weighted documents.

It is not possible in the present context to examine in detail the questions relating to the processing of weighted Boolean queries [8,9]. It may be sufficient instead to suggest some obvious approaches that lend themselves to a practical implementation. Consider two arbitrary index terms A and B, and let **A** and **B** represent the set of documents indexed by terms A and B, respectively. The Boolean operations normally receive the following interpretation:

1 The query "A OR B" is designed to retrieve the document set $(\mathbf{A} \cup \mathbf{B})$ consisting of documents indexed by term A or by term B or by both A and B.

2 The query "A AND B" retrieves document set $(\mathbf{A} \cap \mathbf{B})$ consisting of documents indexed by both terms A and B.

3 The query "A NOT B" retrieves document set $(\mathbf{A} - \mathbf{B})$ consisting of documents indexed by term A that are not also indexed by B.

Let a and b denote term weights varying from a minimum of 0 to a maximum of 1, and consider an extension of those operations that includes the use of weighted query terms. When the term weight is chosen equal to 1, the normal Boolean operation is implied, whereas a term weight of 0 implies that the corresponding operand may be disregarded. Thus one has

$$A_1 \text{ OR } B_1 \equiv A \text{ OR } B$$
$$A_1 \text{ AND } B_1 \equiv A \text{ AND } B$$
$$A_1 \text{ NOT } B_1 \equiv A \text{ NOT } B$$
and $\quad A_1 \text{ OR } B_0 \equiv A$
$$A_1 \text{ AND } B_0 \equiv A$$
$$A_1 \text{ NOT } B_0 \equiv A$$

When both the document and the query terms are weighted, a weighted Boolean query now receives a simple interpretation. In response to a query such as $A_a \text{ OR } B_b$, the set of retrieved documents consists of those having either term A with a weight at least equal to a or term B with a weight at least equal to b. The retrieved items can be ranked according to the sum of the weights a + b in the documents.

When only the documents are weighted, but not the queries, the full document sets **A** and/or **B** are retrieved using the appropriate Boolean combination, and the ranking applies as before. This situation appears simple to implement in operational retrieval because weights can be assigned to the document terms by the expert indexers, or frequency-based weights can be automatically obtained by the system. To assign weights to the query terms, some input is needed from the users, and reliable term weighting information of this kind may be difficult to obtain.

In the unlikely situation where the query terms alone are weighted but the document terms are not, it appears reasonable to suggest that each weighted query term affects a partial set of documents instead of the full set. Consider as an example, query statements of the form (. . . $((A_a * B_b) * C_c)$. . . . $* Z_z$), where $*$ stands for one of the operators AND, OR, NOT, and where a, b, . . . , z represent weights attached to terms A, B, . . . , Z respectively, such that $0 \le a \le 1$, . . . , $0 \le z \le 1$. The general case involving a multiplicity of binary $*$ operators may be reduced to that of a single binary operator with two operands by assuming that the search process is carried out iteratively, one operator at a time. The problem then consists of interpreting query statements of the form $(A_a * B)$, where $*$ is a binary connective and a and b are the term weights.

The operations of the three Boolean connectives may be described by considering the special case where only one of the two operands carries a weight smaller than 1, that is, where the queries have the form $(A_1 * B_b)$. Extensions to the general case where both query terms carry weights less than unity will then be immediate. Remembering that query term B_0 can be disregarded, whereas B_1 covers the full set **B** of documents indexed by B, it becomes clear that query $A \text{ OR } B_b$ expands the output document set from **A** to **A** $\cup$ **B** as the weight of b increases from 0 to 1. $A \cup B$ comprises the full set of items that are either **A**'s or **B**'s. A query such as (A OR $B_{0.33}$) must then retrieve all the **A**'s plus a third of the **B**'s. Correspondingly, (A AND B_b) shrinks the size of the output from **A** to $A \cap B$, that is, to the set of items that are both **A**'s and **B**'s as b increases from 0 to 1. This suggests that (A AND $B_{0.33}$) covers all the **A**'s that are also in **B** plus about two-thirds of the **A**'s that are not in **B**. Finally, (A NOT B_b) shrinks the output from **A** to **A** – **B**, that is, to the items in **A** that are not also in **B**. The query (A NOT $B_{0.33}$) would then cover all **A**'s that are not in **B** plus two-thirds of the items in the intersection between **A** and **B**.

It remains to determine how the partial set of items that are either included in or excluded from the answering document set is to be identified. The following mode of operation suggests itself:

1 OR operation: as b increases from 0 to 1, the items in **B** not already in **A** that are *closest* to the set **A** are successively added to **A** to generate $A \cup B$ in answer to query (A OR B).

2 AND operation: as b increases from 0 to 1, the items in **A** − **B** that are *farthest* from $A \cap B$ are successively subtracted from **A** until only $A \cap B$ remains in answer to query (A AND B) when b is equal to 1.

3 NOT operation: as b increases from 0 to 1, the items in $A \cap B$ that are *farthest* from **A** − **B** are successively subtracted from **A** until only **A** − **B** remains in answer to query (A NOT B).

To determine the closeness of a particular document to another document or to a set of documents, the similarity coefficients previously introduced to compare queries and documents [expressions (1) to (5)] can be used to obtain affinity indicators between pairs of documents or between a particular document and a set of documents. In the latter case, a typical document C is chosen to represent the given set, such as, for example, the centroid of the document set, and for each document DOC_i, the size of the coefficient $SIM(C, DOC_i)$ is used to indicate whether DOC_i is to be retrieved or not. The computation of a cluster centroid is described in detail in the next section of this chapter.

Consider, as a typical example, the operations for query ($A_{0.33}$ OR $B_{0.66}$) illustrated in Fig. 6-3 together with other examples. The following steps may be used:

1 Compute the centroids of sets **A** and **B**.

2 Remove from set **A** two-thirds of the documents consisting of those exhibiting the largest distance to the centroid of **B**.

3 Remove from set **B** one-third of the documents consisting of those exhibiting the largest distance to the centroid of **A**.

4 The response set is then the union of the remaining items from **A** and **B**

Correspondingly, the output set for query ($A_{0.33}$ AND $B_{0.66}$) (see Fig. 6-3b) is obtained by removing from set **A** one-third of the items not included in the intersection of **A** and **B** and situated farthest from the centroid of **B**; at the same

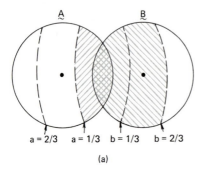

a = 2/3   a = 1/3   b = 1/3   b = 2/3

(a)

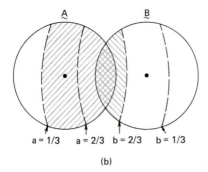

a = 1/3   a = 2/3 b = 2/3   b = 1/3

(b)

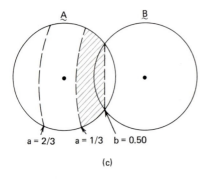

a = 2/3   a = 1/3 b = 0.50

(c)

Figure 6-3 Interpretation of weighted Boolean operations. (a) $(A_{0.33} \text{ OR } B_{0.66})$. (b) $(A_{0.33} \text{ AND } B_{0.66})$. (c) $(A_{0.33} \text{ NOT } B_{0.50})$.

time, one removes from **B** two-thirds of the items that are most removed from set **A**. For the query $(A_{0.33} \text{ NOT } B_{0.50})$ of Fig. 6-3c, two-thirds of the items in **A** are removed from the answer set plus half of the items in the intersection between **A** and **B**.

To summarize, when weighted terms are used for queries that do *not* include Boolean operators, a query-document similarity computation can be used directly to obtain a retrieval value, or ranking, for each document; documents may then be retrieved in decreasing order of their retrieval values. When Boolean operators are included in the queries, a similarity computation is first carried out between certain documents and the centroids, or representatives, of certain document sets. The size of the corresponding similarity coefficients then determines which documents are to be added to (for the OR operation) or subtracted from (for AND and NOT) the basic answering set. The use of term weights in Boolean systems remains to be validated by appropriate retrieval experiments.

4 FILE CLUSTERING

*A Main Considerations

Most information retrieval work is based on the manipulation of large masses of data. The document files to be stored may be extensive, and the vocabularies needed to represent document content may include tens of thousands of terms. In these circumstances, it is useful to superimpose an organization on the stored information in order to simplify file access and manipulation. One way of providing order among a collection of stored records is to introduce a classification, or *clustering*, among the items. Clustering is used to group similar or related items into common classes. In a classified or clustered file, items appearing in a class can be stored in adjacent locations in the file so that a single file access makes available a whole class of items. Such an approach is used in most conventional libraries where the library items are placed on shelves according to their subject content. By browsing among the shelves, the library users can then retrieve a number of different items within a given subject area.

In information retrieval, classification methods are used for two main purposes:

1 To classify the set of *index terms,* or keywords, into term classes according to similarities in the keywords, or according to statistical characteristics of the terms in the documents of a collection

2 To classify the *documents* into subject classes so that related items are accessible to the user population

The *keyword classifications* lead to the construction of thesauruses and synonym dictionaries that can be used for document indexing and query formulation. These may also provide the associative indexing capability previously illustrated in Chapter 3. The *document classifications* on the other hand may serve as devices for the representation of knowledge, and in retrieval they may provide efficient search strategies and effective search results. The efficiency is produced by making it possible for the user to limit the search to specific subject areas. The potential effectiveness of the cluster search process stems from the *cluster hypothesis*, which asserts that closely associated documents tend to be relevant to the same queries [2]. The use of clustered document files may then lead both to high recall and to high precision searches [10].

The following two characteristics are generally considered important for object classifications [11,12]:

1 The classification should be *stable* in the sense that small alterations of the data, because of either the addition of new items or changes in the old ones, should cause only minor alterations in the classification.

2 The classification should also be *well defined* in that a given body of data should produce a single classification or at least one of a small set of compatible classifications.

As it will be seen, the second property is not always present in various heuristic or single-pass classification systems constructed for actual objects. Rather, examples exist where a variety of different classification systems all perform equally well in practical applications. Stability, on the other hand, appears to be essential if a classification is to operate satisfactorily.

Many different methods can be used to cluster a collection of items. If the classification is to perform a useful role, controls must normally be introduced to limit the minimum and maximum number of classes that are generated, as well as the size of the classes and the overlap between classes. Obviously, the number of classes generated should be greater than 1 but smaller than the total number of objects to be classified. It is helpful if the various classes exhibit a roughly comparable size. Further, storage efficiency considerations make it necessary to limit the overlap between classes, defined as the number or proportion of items jointly assigned to two or more classes.

The number, size, and overlap of the classes may be controlled during cluster generation by parameter settings. An example is given in Fig. 6-4 for six items labeled D_1 to D_6. The input to the clustering process is assumed to be a similarity matrix giving similarity measures between all pairs of items as shown in Fig. 6-4a. The clustering process then consists in fixing a threshold T in the similarity coefficients, and grouping all pairs of items whose similarity exceeds the chosen threshold. The illustration of Fig. 6-4b shows that when T = 0.95, no clustering action is possible, and the file consists of 6 unclustered items. As the threshold is lowered to 0.8, three pairs of items can be grouped including (D_1, D_5), (D_1, D_6), and (D_2, D_6); pairs of related items are identified by lines joining the respective items in the graph of Fig. 6-4c. As the threshold value is further reduced to 0.60 and 0.50 additional pairs of items can be joined as shown in Fig. 6-4d and e.

For purposes of the example, one may assume that each cluster of items is defined as a *connected component* in the sense that in a graph representation such as that of Fig. 6-4, a path formed by lines exists from any item to all other items in the cluster. In these circumstances, the illustration of Fig. 6-4 demonstrates that the number of clusters formed decreases and the size of the clusters increases as the similarity threshold is decreased. The number of clusters produced by the four thresholds of Fig. 6-4b to 6-4e is, respectively, 6, 3, 2, and 1.

In information retrieval the cluster processing operation consists in taking an item—for example, a new incoming document or an incoming user query— and comparing it with an existing cluster to determine the affinity of the item with that cluster. This operation is easily carried out by defining for each clus-

	D_1	D_2	D_3	D_4	D_5	D_6
D_1	—	0.3	0.5	0.6	0.8	0.9
D_2	0.3	—	0.4	0.5	0.7	0.8
D_3	0.5	0.4	—	0.3	0.5	0.2
D_4	0.6	0.5	0.3	—	0.4	0.1
D_5	0.8	0.7	0.5	0.4	—	0.3
D_6	0.9	0.8	0.2	0.1	0.3	—

(a)

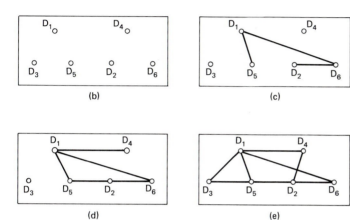

Figure 6-4 Role of threshold in item similarity for cluster formation. (a) Initial item-item similarity matrix. (b) Threshold T = 0.95. (c) Threshold T = 0.80. (d) Threshold T = 0.60. (e) Threshold T = 0.50.

ter a *cluster representative* or *centroid* to represent the class during the cluster manipulations. Comparisons between individual items and the cluster are then performed by computing the item-centroid similarity.

In principle, the centroid of a cluster might be represented by any document located in that cluster. In practice it may be preferable to construct a special centroid vector that is centrally located in the cluster. Typically, the centroid may be defined as the average of the documents in a cluster. That is, the weight of a centroid term is computed as the average of the weights for that term over all items in a cluster, or

$$CTERM_k = \frac{1}{m} \sum_{i=1}^{m} TERM_{ik} \qquad (12)$$

where $CTERM_k$ is the kth term in the centroid, $TERM_{ik}$ is the kth term in the ith document in the cluster, and the cluster contains m documents in all.

A computation such as the one specified by expression (12) produces a centroid vector that is reasonably representative of the items in a cluster. The most heavily weighted terms in the individual documents will be heavily weighted in the centroid. The sample centroid derivation shown in Table 6-3 demonstrates that the two terms 3 and 6 best represent the clustered items. These two terms also receive the highest weight in the centroid. The example of Table 6-3 also shows that the standard centroid computation leads to full centroid vectors with few zero terms even when the individual document vectors are sparse (that is, consist mostly of 0 terms). To improve the storage efficiency of the centroid vectors, it is customary to add a thresholding operation which eliminates centroid terms of excessively low weight. The reduced centroid shown in Table 6-3 is obtained by eliminating centroid terms with weights smaller than 1.

The centroid averaging process suggested in expression (12) may overemphasize the importance of some terms that receive excessively high weights. In some systems the final centroid term weights are therefore determined by using *rank values* rather than actual weights. For example, a weight of 1 can be assigned to the term exhibiting the lowest reduced weight; the next lowest term is given a weight of 2, and so on up until all nonzero terms are accounted for. The rank value process produces term weights of 1 and 2 for terms 6 and 3 of Table 6-3, respectively, replacing the original weights of 3 and 4.

Additional cluster centroid definitions may be used to produce binary centroid vectors with centroid weights restricted to 0 and 1 only. Alternatively, the term weights may be normalized to lie between 0 and 1 by dividing each term weight by the length of the centroid vector [1,2,13]

$$\text{CLENGTH} = \sqrt{\sum_{i=1}^{t} (\text{CTERM}_i)^2}$$

Many cluster generation systems, including the method described in Chapter 4 in connection with the SMART system description, produce a hierarchical cluster tree where large clusters are analyzed and broken down into a number of smaller clusters, which are themselves broken down into still smaller clusters, until finally the lowest level clusters are (figuratively) broken down into individual documents. A typical hierarchical cluster arrangement is shown in Fig. 6-5.

Table 6-3 Cluster Centroid Formation for Three Documents

DOCUMENT$_1$ = (1 , 0 , 3 , 0 , 0 , 4 , 0 , 0 , 0 , 0)	
DOCUMENT$_2$ = (0 , 0 , 2 , 0 , 0 , 3 , 1 , 1 , 0 , 0)	
DOCUMENT$_3$ = (0 , 1 , 7 , 0 , 1 , 2 , 0 , 0 , 1 , 1)	
Standard centroid	= ($\frac{1}{3}$, $\frac{1}{3}$, 4, 0, $\frac{1}{3}$, 3, $\frac{1}{3}$, $\frac{1}{3}$, $\frac{1}{3}$, $\frac{1}{3}$)
Reduced centroid	= (0 , 0 , 4 , 0 , 0 , 3 , 0 , 0 , 0 , 0)
Centroid using rank values	= (0 , 0 , 2 , 0 , 0 , 1 , 0 , 0 , 0 , 0)

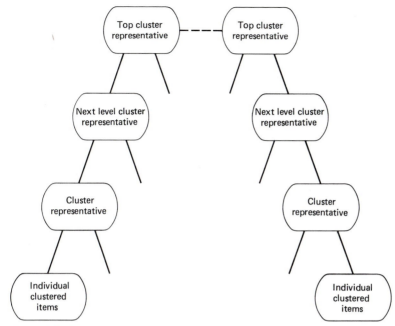

Figure 6-5 Hierarchical cluster arrangement.

A cluster tree such as that of Fig. 6-5 can be searched in many different ways. Intuitively the simplest method consists in proceeding from the top downward in the cluster tree, by comparing the incoming query first with the centroids of the topmost clusters, and continuing downward by next examining the next level of centroids for the clusters that were sufficiently similar to the query. This step is repeated by considering successively smaller clusters until eventually the individual documents in some of the lowest-level clusters are compared with the query. This is a *top-down* cluster search strategy based on the availability of auxiliary files containing all cluster centroids.

An alternative *bottom-up* search strategy may be introduced that uses only the clusters on the next to lowest level of the cluster tree. In that strategy, the incoming queries are compared with the centroids of the lowest-level clusters, and the individual documents included in certain lowest-level clusters are then considered [2,5,14]. The bottom-up search strategy reduces the storage cost for the tree of centroid vectors and may lead to more rapid identification of documents actually relevant to a given query than the top-down search. Furthermore, the likelihood of going down the wrong cluster path and winding up with useless information is reduced when the comparisons with the top centroids are eliminated. Since the number of low-level clusters may, however, be very large, an auxiliary index may be required to gain access to the low-level classes. This index may be conveniently implemented as an inverted file for all low-level centroid terms. A typical search then proceeds by using the individual query terms to access the inverted file of low-level cluster centroids. This leads to the identification of one or more low-level clusters, and these in turn lead to the retrieval of individual documents located in these classes.

Additional details for cluster generation and searching are including in the remainder of this section.

*B Classification Methods

One method for clustering a collection of objects uses similarity (or distance) measurements between each object and each other object in the collection. The objects are grouped into classes when they exhibit sufficiently large similarities or small distances. This process was illustrated earlier in Fig. 6-4, where an item-item similarity matrix was used to generate several cluster arrangements depending on the threshold used.

The clustering methods based on the availability of item-item similarities lead to a variety of *graph-theoretical* grouping strategies. Normally, rules are imposed on the graph obtained by transforming the item-item similarity matrix into a graph as shown in the example of Fig. 6-4. The following restrictions could be imposed on the graph representing the object similarities:

1 The clusters are defined as the *cliques* of the graph, that is, as the groups (maximal subsets) of items for which each item is connected to each other item in the group.

2 The clusters could also be *strings* of items such that item a is connected to b, and b is further connected to c, and so on until no further connected item can be added to the string.

3 The clusters might also be defined as *stars* where some central item is connected to all other items in the group.

4 Finally, the clusters could be *connected components* where an arbitrary path is found between each item in the component and each other item; the *single-link* method described in Chapter 4 is based on the use of connected components.

Consider, as an example, the connection graph of Fig. 6-4e obtained from the item-item similarity matrix of Fig. 6-4a using a similarity threshold of 0.50. The following classes are obtained from Fig. 6-4e for the graph specifications given earlier:

1 For the clique restriction, one finds one clique with three items and five additional cliques each with two items (D_1,D_3,D_5), (D_1,D_4), (D_1, D_6), (D_2, D_5), (D_2,D_6), (D_2,D_4).

2 Several subdivisions into strings are possible for the graph of Fig. 6-4e. Assuming that the strings to be produced are nonoverlapping, the following two strings will cover the graph: (D_3,D_1,D_4) and (D_5,D_2,D_6); another string subdivision would be (D_3,D_1,D_4,D_2,D_5) plus the single-item string (D_6).

3 Various nonoverlapping stars can be generated from Fig. 6-4e such as (D_1,D_3,D_5,D_4) and (D_2,D_6).

4 Finally for the connected component strategy, a single cluster is obtained consisting of all six documents under consideration.

The example of Fig. 6-4 illustrates that even for the graphical clustering methods that exhibit all the theoretically desirable characteristics such as being stable and well-defined, many different cluster structures can be constructed depending on various parameter settings and clustering requirements. The connection pattern between objects is uniquely determined by the threshold chosen for the item-item similarities. However, the final cluster arrangement also depends on the graph representation used to define the clusters, and on additional rules that may be specified concerning the permitted size and overlap of the clusters (the number of items included in a cluster and the number of items jointly assigned to more than one cluster).

The graph-theoretical clustering algorithms tend to be expensive to implement when the number of objects to be grouped is large. In fact, the construction of the item-item similarity matrix alone requires a comparison of each item with each other item, that is, the computation of about $n^2/2$ similarity coefficients for n items. A number of *heuristic clustering* methods have therefore been developed for which the construction of an item similarity matrix is not required.

Most of the heuristic methods are based on the prior availability and subsequent use and refinement of an initial set of clusters. In some cases, the problem under consideration may simply require that a set of new or unknown objects be added to an already existing cluster structure. Alternatively, when initial clusters are not available, some easily identified property of the objects might be used to define an initial set of trial clusters—for example, all objects that have a given property or term in common could be entered into a common trial class. Another possibility consists in taking a small subset of the objects to be clustered and using these to construct a set of so-called core clusters. The remaining parts of the collection that are not originally handled are then subsequently assigned to the existing core clusters.

Assuming the existence of an initial set of clusters, the heuristic methods next proceed by constructing cluster representatives for the existing clusters. The clustering operation itself is again based on similarity measurements between the objects to be clustered and the already existing cluster centroids. A typical iterative cluster refinement process involves the following steps:

1 Compare each document D with all existing cluster centroids, and obtain similarity coefficients $SIM(D,C_k)$ for all clusters in the cluster structure.

2 Determine the cluster for which $SIM(D,C_k)$ is largest for each given document D and place D into that cluster (alternatively, if overlapping clusters are desired, place D into all clusters for which the corresponding centroid similarity is larger than some arbitrary threshold).

3 Recompute the cluster centroids based on the new document assignments, and return to step 1.

4 Stop the process after a fixed number of iterations through steps 1 to 3 or alternatively stop after all document movements from one class to another have ceased.

Such an iterative cluster reassignment process is normally less expensive to perform than the graph-theoretical process described earlier, because the similarity coefficients are not computed for all pairs of items but only for all items with respect to all cluster centroids. If one assumes that log n clusters exist for the n items, the number of centroid-document comparisons is of order n log n (instead of n² as before). However, the heuristic clustering methods are theoretically less satisfying than the graph-based methods because the final cluster structure obviously depends on the initially available cluster arrangement. This undesirable property also characterizes the *one-pass* clustering methods described in Chapter 4. In that case, the documents are processed sequentially one at a time, and each item potentially forms a new class if it does not exhibit sufficient similarities with already existing clusters. The order in which the items enter into the centroid comparison process will then determine the shape of the final clusters.

The two types of classification methodologies can be combined into a single process by using the less expensive n log n process (for example a simple one-pass clustering system) to generate an initial set of trial clusters, and reserving the expensive graph-theoretical method to refine and subdivide each trial cluster. Each trial cluster of size m (m being much smaller than the total collection size n) could then be broken down into several smaller clusters using a graph-theoretical method requiring on the order of m² vector comparisons. Such a hybrid clustering process could generate useful low-level clusters that are as effective as clusters produced by graph-type methods applied to the complete collection.

*C Cluster Search Evaluation

Because of the substantial expense involved in clustering large document collections, a thorough evaluation of cluster search methods has never been performed. Only fragmentary results are available obtained with a few typical clustering arrangements and a few sample document collections [14–17]. In principle, the tradeoff involved in using a clustered document collection for information retrieval purposes, as opposed, for example, to using a standard inverted file, is simple to describe: on the one hand, one may expect that improved recall and precision are obtainable from a search when related documents are collected into common classes because the retrieval of a particular document then automatically leads to the retrieval of additional related items; on the other hand, the clustered organization produces a good deal of systems overhead because of the cost of the clustering operation itself and the requirement to store an auxiliary file of cluster centroids. Furthermore, as will be seen, the comparison of incoming queries with the centroid structure may in fact identify marginal search paths when the centroids appear to be similar to the queries but the corresponding clusters contain few relevant documents.

It was seen in the preceding section that many different methodologies are available to cluster a given document collection. Moreover, given a particular clustering arrangement the comparison of user search queries with the available cluster centroids and the identification of the relevant document clusters can also be carried out in many different ways. Thus given a cluster structure such as the one in Fig. 6-5, one can proceed from the top down, choosing at each level the most likely cluster centroid until eventually the documents in a single cluster on the lowest clustering level are reached. Such a search, known as depth-first, is likely to produce high precision searches that may, however, be deficient in recall. Higher recall may be obtained by following several parallel paths of the cluster structure, leading to the eventual identification of several low-level document clusters. Unfortunately no obvious search strategy exists which will necessarily lead to the retrieval of most useful materials.

One problem arising in cluster searching is the difficulty of obtaining an unequivocal result from a comparison between a user query and a cluster centroid. Normally, an attempt must be made given a particular user query to estimate the probability that a given cluster is a useful cluster. Such an estimate can be based on the frequency of occurrence (or on the weight) of the individual query terms in the corresponding cluster centroid. When the query terms collectively exhibit high occurrence frequencies in a cluster centroid, the presumption may be that the corresponding cluster is useful for retrieval purposes. Unfortunately, the higher level centroids normally represent broad subject classes and the query-centroid comparisons may not identify any particular centroid that is clearly preferable to the other centroids. Such a situation obviously complicates the cluster searching task.

As an example of the efficiencies attainable in cluster searching, consider some sample searches performed for several sets of search requests with a collection of 2,000 documents in computer science. A hierarchical cluster arrangement was generated for the document collection using the one-pass clustering system described in Chapter 4. The hierarchy consisted of four levels, illustrated in the scheme of Fig. 6-5, including 200 clusters on the lowest clustering level with an average of 10 documents each. This arrangement was used with four different search strategies [18]:

1 A standard inverted file search, using an inverted term directory for all terms occurring in the documents of the collection; the documents themselves are entered into the document file in arbitrary order.

2 A standard inverted file search for which the document file is stored in cluster order, that is, one access to the document file retrieves a cluster of related documents.

3 An inverted file constructed for the *centroids* on the lowest cluster level only, providing access to a number of low-level document clusters for each query term.

4 A top-down search of the full cluster hierarchy based on a stored file of all cluster centroids.

The auxiliary inverted term files and the cluster centroid files cannot normally be stored in internal machine memory. In order to carry out the required query-centroid comparisons, it is therefore necessary to transfer various portions of the centroid directory from external bulk storage to internal memory. Such transfers from one type of memory to another are usually carried out for fixed size blocks of data, known as *pages*. For the experiments under discussion, a page is defined as 4,096 characters of storage. A normal page transfer process would transfer into internal storage the particular data page containing the centroid needed at each particular time. To make room for a new page of data, an old page no longer in use must be transferred back to external storage from internal memory. The standard way for doing this is the "least recently used" (LRU) page replacement method which transfers out the page that has remained unused for the longest time.

When only a single page is brought into storage at any one time, a complete disk seek operation is needed for each page (that is, for each centroid) transferred into internal memory. Such a strategy appears ill suited to the processing of hierarchical tree structures, because the need for a particular centroid vector normally implies the simultaneous need for its descendants on a lower level of the tree or for its brothers on the same level of the tree. This suggests that a complete set of centroids ought to be brought into internal memory at the same time, preferably consisting of the originally needed centroid together with its immediate descendants and possibly its brothers. By using a so-called prefetch strategy, the pages containing the descendants or brothers of a given centroid can be prepared for transfer while the initial page is being sought. In these circumstances, a complete disk seek operation is still required for the initial page to be transferred. The pages containing descendant and brother centroids can, however, be transferred at much lower cost amounting to only about one-tenth the time required for a complete disk seek operation.

The file storage requirements for the several search systems are summarized in Table 6-4. The document file itself requires 71 pages of data. The

Table 6-4 Storage Requirements for Cluster Searches
(2,000 Documents in Computer Science; Page Size = 4,096 Bytes)

Standard search using inverted file for document terms	Inverted term index without weights	110	39 pages
	Document file		71 pages
Search using the low-level document clusters only	Inverted index to low-level centroids	84	13 pages
	Document file		71 pages
Full top-down search through cluster hierarchy	Full centroid file (400 terms per centroid)	146	75 pages
	Document file		71 pages

standard inverted term file (using as entries all terms occurring in the documents) uses 39 additional pages. Thirteen pages are needed to store an inverted index for the short centroids on the lowest level of the cluster hierarchy; finally, 75 pages are used to store the full hierarchy of cluster centroids. A cluster storage search using only the low-level centroids appears therefore to produce better storage efficiency than a standard inverted file search or a top-down search through the full store of cluster centroids.

The average search precision and the average number of page faults required to reach a given level of recall using the single-page replacement process are shown in Table 6-5 for three of the four search methods previously described [18]. The averages of Table 6-5 are computed for 23 short Boolean queries containing an average of 4.8 search terms per query. Next to each statistic, Table 6-5 also contains the percentage improvement or deterioration over the standard inverted file search method.

A valid comparison of the search runs can be made only if the total number of retrieved items over the 23 queries is approximately the same for all methods. Since no choice is possible for the number of items retrieved by a

Table 6-5 Short Boolean Queries—Precision and Page Faults
(23 Queries—Separate Relevance Assessments)

Relative recall	Inverted document terms (clustered)	Inverted low-level centroids		Tree search	
		a Average precision comparison			
0.1	0.900	0.406	−55%	0.277	−69%
0.2	0.888	0.406	−54%	0.277	−69%
0.3	0.847	0.403	−52%	0.255	−70%
0.4	0.845	0.393	−53%	0.212	−75%
0.5	0.838	0.388	−54%	0.203	−76%
0.6	0.830	0.385	−54%	0.192	−77%
0.7	0.828	0.356	−57%	0.183	−78%
0.8	0.824	0.346	−58%	0.162	−80%
0.9	0.817	0.329	−60%	0.149	−82%
1.0	0.815	0.329	−60%	0.141	−83%
			−55.7%		−75.9%
		b Average page fault comparison (no prefetch)			
0.1	4.89	3.00	−39%	14.90	+205%
0.2	5.54	3.50	−37%	14.90	+169%
0.3	5.87	4.20	−28%	14.85	+153%
0.4	7.44	4.20	−44%	16.55	+122%
0.5	8.53	4.45	−48%	16.43	+93%
0.6	10.26	4.50	−56%	17.83	+74%
0.7	11.21	4.50	−60%	18.96	+69%
0.8	12.21	4.65	−62%	21.17	+73%
0.9	12.94	4.65	−64%	21.83	+69%
1.0	12.94	4.95	−62%	21.83	+69%
			−50%		+109.6%

conventional Boolean search, that number must necessarily be used as a standard for all methods. For the query collection used in the experiments, a total of 341 documents were retrieved by the conventional inverted file method over the 23 queries. The threshold used for the clustered searches was therefore chosen to retrieve approximately 15 documents per query (15 · 23 = 345).

Separate relevance assessments were available of each document with respect to each query (that is, the inverted file searches were not automatically assumed to produce perfect search output). Furthermore, the recall level exhibited in Table 6-5 is computed separately for each search method rather than globally. That is, relative rather than absolute recall levels are shown, defined as the proportion of relevant items retrieved at a given level out of the total relevant that can be retrieved by each particular method.

The results of Table 6-5 indicate that the full cluster tree search is not competitive with the conventional inverted file process either in precision or in the page fault rate when short Boolean queries are processed. In that case only a few lists of document references must be processed in the inverted file system, corresponding to the few terms included in each query. The cluster tree must, however, always be traversed from top to bottom. The low-level cluster inversion is much more attractive in that case, since only about half as many page faults are needed as in the inverted file process. Both cluster search systems do, however, produce substantially lower precision than the inverted file system.

The amount of work required by an inverted file search increases as the query length and to some extent the number of documents to be retrieved increase. The experimental conditions of Table 6-5 thus favor the inverted file technology. When longer, vector-type queries are processed, the evaluation results become very different. Table 6-6 contains both average precision and average page fault rates averaged over 33 long queries (16.8 terms per query) using page replacement methods with and without prefetch [18].

The results in Table 6-6a show that the standard inverted file search again produces the best search precision. However, the cluster searches are now more competitive than before: the tree search shows a deterioration of 15 percent in precision; for the inverted low-level centroids the precision loss is 19 percent, compared with the earlier losses of 76 and 56 percent, respectively. The page fault rates which apply to the cluster searches conducted for the long queries are much improved over the equivalent runs using the shorter queries. Even with the unfavorable page-at-a-time (no prefetch) page replacement method, the full tree search is nearly competitive with the inverted file list processing. Table 6-6c shows that with a prefetch page replacement, the tree search is 30 percent better than the document inversion.

The results of Table 6-6 indicate that for the long, vector-type queries, a cluster search method seems preferable to the conventional inverted list manipulations. Even more clear-cut results in favor of the top-down cluster search are obtained when a larger number of documents are retrieved in each search than the 15 used in the experiments of Tables 6-5 and 6-6 [18].

Table 6-6 Long Weighted Vector-Type Queries—Precision and Page Faults
(33 Queries; 15 Retrieved Items per Query)

Relative recall	Inverted document terms				Complete tree search	
	Clustered storage	Random storage		Inverted low-level centroids		
		a	**Average precision comparison**			
0.1		0.893		0.783	−12%	0.837	−6%
0.2		0.871		0.746	−14%	0.775	−11%
0.3		0.844		0.702	−17%	0.748	−11%
0.4		0.835		0.679	−19%	0.734	−12%
0.5		0.827		0.664	−20%	0.721	−13%
0.6		0.817		0.656	−20%	0.682	−17%
0.7		0.812		0.623	−23%	0.670	−17%
0.8		0.803		0.612	−24%	0.639	−20%
0.9		0.784		0.610	−22%	0.612	−22%
1.0		0.757		0.582	−23%	0.607	−20%
					−19.4%		−14.9%
		b	**Average page fault comparison (no prefetch)**			
0.1	14.8	15.2	+2%	18.1	+23%	14.9	+1%
0.2	15.7	16.1	+2%	19.4	+23%	17.4	+11%
0.3	17.5	18.2	+4%	22.9	+31%	18.2	+4%
0.4	18.7	19.4	+4%	24.4	+30%	19.2	+3%
0.5	19.9	20.6	+4%	25.9	+30%	21.0	+6%
0.6	21.1	21.8	+4%	28.2	+34%	23.2	+10%
0.7	22.1	23.2	+5%	31.7	+44%	24.5	+11%
0.8	23.2	24.3	+5%	34.7	+50%	26.8	+16%
0.9	24.5	26.0	+6%	36.7	+50%	29.5	+20%
1.0	25.5	27.4	+9%	37.9	+49%	31.8	+25%
			+4.5%		+36.4%		+10.7%
		c	**Page fault comparison (with prefetch)**			
0.1	10.12	10.55	+4%	12.97	+28%	6.44	−36%
0.2	11.00	11.47	+4%	14.02	+27%	7.62	−31%
0.3	12.54	13.29	+6%	17.09	+36%	8.16	−35%
0.4	13.58	14.48	+7%	18.23	+34%	8.76	−35%
0.5	14.80	15.66	+6%	19.59	+32%	9.81	−34%
0.6	15.83	16.84	+6%	21.36	+35%	11.06	−30%
0.7	16.90	18.18	+6%	24.01	+42%	11.87	−30%
0.8	17.87	19.19	+7%	26.28	+47%	13.17	−26%
0.9	19.12	20.78	+9%	27.99	+46%	14.79	−23%
1.0	20.08	22.05	+10%	28.80	+43%	16.06	−20%
			+6.7%		+37%		−30%

**D Automatic Pseudoclassification

It was mentioned earlier that automatic classification techniques can be used to construct affinity classes for either documents or terms. In the former case, the principal aim is to impose structure on the search system in the hope of gaining search efficiencies during the comparison between user queries and stored documents. When *terms* are clustered, the result is a term class arrangement, or thesaurus, that can be used for the construction of expanded search requests and document descriptions by inclusion in the vectors of synonyms and other terms related to those originally available. It is generally accepted that the use of a thesaurus in the indexing and search formulation process can enhance retrieval effectiveness [19,20].

The use of thesauruses in retrieval was briefly illustrated in Chapter 3 as part of the discussion on automatic indexing. Thesauruses are normally constructed manually by subject experts, although automatic classification procedures are usable in principle based, for example, on use of similarity information for term pairs. The similarity between terms might be based on the frequency distribution characteristics of the terms across the documents of a collection. Thus, if two or more terms co-occur in many documents of a given collection, the presumption is that these terms are related in some sense and hence can be included in common term classes. Alternatively, when term distribution information is not available, term classifications can be automatically constructed by adapting an existing document classification and assuming that terms which occur jointly in the document classes could be used to form the desired term classes [21–26].

Even though considerable effort has been devoted to the development of automatic thesaurus construction methods, a really viable thesaurus generation process is still lacking. One problem is the difficulty of identifying representative document collections which could guarantee that the resulting term distribution characteristics would be applicable to other collection environments. Unfortunately, there is no obvious way for obtaining such representative document samples, short of using large comprehensive collections. However, large collections cannot be processed at a reasonable cost. In some studies, term classes have been generated from locally defined, small subcollections of documents, such as the set of documents retrieved in response to a given search request [27]. Whether such procedures will prove generally viable remains to be seen.

Since document retrieval environments normally operate in an on-line mode, permitting users to communicate directly with the retrieval system, the question arises whether information obtained from the user population during the retrieval effort might be used as an aid in constructing term classifications. Such a consideration forms the basis for the so-called pseudoclassification process where the normal use of term frequency information and term probability distributions is replaced by user relevance information of documents with respect to search requests. Since the term classification obtained by a pseudoclassification process depends on particular user queries and specified subject areas, the term classes that are obtained may be applied to other documents in related subjects only if the input data are comprehensive enough to make them applicable to other user groups in different collection environments. The pseudoclassification process is based on the existence of four distinct types of information: (1) a collection of documents in a given subject area, (2) a set of information requests addressed to that collection, (3) a retrieval threshold T which leads to the retrieval of a given document in answer to a particular query whenever a similarity measure between the document and query exceeds T, and (4) a set of user relevance assessments specifying the relevance of individual documents with respect to the available queries [28].

Consider, in particular, a given collection of n documents and m queries in a topic area. The previously specified information can be used to construct two binary n by m matrices specifying the retrieval status and the relevance properties, respectively, for each document-query pair $(DOC_i, QUERY_j)$. Specifically, let VAL and REL represent the *retrieval* and the *relevance* matrices for a given collection of documents and queries. Thus VAL_{ij} may be defined to be equal to 1 whenever DOC_i is retrieved in response to $QUERY_j$, that is, whenever $SIM(DOC_i, QUERY_j) > T$; otherwise VAL_{ij} is set equal to 0. Correspondingly REL_{ij} is defined as 1 when DOC_i is specified as relevant to the $QUERY_j$ and as 0 otherwise. The relevance and retrieval matrices are represented in Fig. 6-6 for typical document and query collections.

Consider now the results of a retrieval operation. It is obvious from the definition of the VAL and REL matrices that four different situations can arise for a given document-query pair $(DOC_i, QUERY_j)$:

1   Both VAL_{ij} and REL_{ij} are defined equal to 1, implying that the relevant document DOC_j is retrieved in response to $QUERY_j$.

2   Both VAL_{ij} and REL_{ij} are defined equal to 0, implying that the nonrelevant document DOC_i is rejected in response to $QUERY_j$.

	$QUERY_1$	$QUERY_2$	$\ldots$	$QUERY_m$
DOC_1	VAL_{11}	VAL_{12}	$\ldots$	VAL_{1m}
DOC_2	VAL_{21}	VAL_{22}	$\ldots$	VAL_{2m}
DOC_n	VAL_{n1}	VAL_{n2}	$\ldots$	VAL_{nm}

VAL =

(a)

	$QUERY_1$	$QUERY_2$	$\ldots$	$QUERY_m$
DOC_1	REL_{11}	REL_{12}	$\ldots$	REL_{1m}
DOC_2	REL_{21}	REL_{22}	$\ldots$	REL_{2m}
DOC_n	REL_{n1}	REL_{n2}	$\ldots$	REL_{nm}

REL =

(b)

Figure 6-6   Retrieval and relevance matrices. (a) Retrieval matrix VAL. (VAL_{ij} implies that DOC_i is retrieved in response to $QUERY_j$.) (b) Relevance matrix REL. (REL_{ij} implies that DOC_i is judged relevant to $QUERY_j$.)

3 and **4** $VAL_{ij} = 1$ and $REL_{ij} =$ or vice versa $VAL_{ij} = 0$ and $REL_{ij} = 1$, implying either that a nonrelevant document is retrieved or that a relevant item is rejected.

From the viewpoint of retrieval effectiveness, cases 1 and 2 represent a favorable outcome, whereas 3 and 4 constitute system failures. A perfect system will produce VAL and REL matrices that are identical, implying that all $(DOC_i, QUERY_j)$ pairs fall into classes 1 or 2, being either correctly retrieved or correctly rejected. Correspondingly, the number of $(DOC_i, QUERY_j)$ pairs falling into classes 3 and 4 may be used as a measure of system inadequacy or failure.

To improve the operations of a retrieval system it is necessary to introduce methodologies capable of shifting some of the $(DOC_i, QUERY_j)$ pairs from classes 3 and 4 to classes 1 or 2, while ensuring at the same time that $(DOC_i, QUERY_j)$ pairs that are already correctly classified are left undisturbed. Two different situations may arise:

3 When a document is incorrectly retrieved ($VAL_{ij} = 1$ and $REL_{ij} = 0$), it becomes necessary to decrease the similarity coefficient SIM with the query so that eventually $SIM(DOC_i, QUERY_j) \leq T$, thus ensuring the rejection of DOC_i in response to $QUERY_j$.
4 On the other hand, for documents that are incorrectly rejected ($VAL_{ij} = 0$ and $REL_{ij} = 1$), the similarity coefficient with the query must be correspondingly increased to achieve $SIM(DOC_i, QUERY_j) > T$, causing the document to be retrieved.

The size of the similarity coefficients for query-document pairs can be altered by introducing refined automatic indexing methods designed to change the original term assignment to queries and documents. Alternatively, sophisticated term weighting strategies could be introduced. A third possibility consists in utilizing term relationship information. This last strategy forms the basis for the pseudoclassification process. Consider in particular a given term classification or thesaurus, in which p different classes are used to group the terms into affinity or similarity classes. The term classification is represented in matrix form in Fig. 6-7. The document and query vectors can now be represented by lengthened constructs as follows

$$DOC_i = (d_{i1}, d_{i2}, \ . \ . \ . \ , d_{it}, c_{i1}, c_{i2}, \ . \ . \ . \ , c_{ip})$$
$$QUERY_j = (q_{j1}, q_{j2}, \ . \ . \ . \ , q_{jt}, c_{j1}, c_{j2}, \ . \ . \ . \ , c_{jp})$$

where d_{ik} represents the assignment of term k to document i and q_{jk} represents the assignment of term k to query j. The elements c_{ik} and c_{jk} represent the term class assignments to the respective vectors. In each case c_{ik} (or c_{jk}) is set equal to 1 whenever class k pertains to document i (or to query j). To increase the size of the similarity measure between a given document-query

	CLASS$_1$	CLASS$_2$	. . .	CLASS$_p$
TERM$_1$	1	0	. . .	1
TERM$_2$	0	1	. . .	1
TERM$_t$	1	0	. . .	0

GROUP =

Figure 6-7 Classification matrix GROUP. (GROUP$_{ij}$ = 1 implies that TERM$_i$ occurs in CLASS$_j$.)

pair, it suffices to place into a common term class two or more terms that did not originally produce a term match in the respective vectors. This operation adds one or more common class identifiers to both vectors, thereby increasing the similarity between them. Analogously, the similarity coefficients can be decreased by appropriately reducing the number of matching term classes.

Consider, as an example, two typical vectors consisting of six terms each (where a 0 entry is used to denote a term that is absent):

DOC$_i$ = (0, 0, lift, propeller, roll, wing)
QUERY$_j$ = (aileron, drag, 0, propeller, 0, wing)

In their original form, two terms (propeller and wing) are present in both vectors. If the document is now assumed to be incorrectly rejected (REL$_{ij}$ = 1 and VAL$_{ij}$ = 0), the size of the matching coefficient can be increased by placing into a term class two or more initially nonmatching terms. Specifically for the two sample vectors, aileron and lift could be placed into a common class k (or alternatively, drag and lift, or roll and aileron, or roll and drag); in each case, the identifier for class k would be added to *both* vectors thereby increasing the similarity between them. For example, placing terms aileron and wing into class k adds the indicator for class k to the DOC$_i$ vector because of the presence of lift in DOC$_i$, and the class k indicator to QUERY$_j$ because of the presence of aileron in the original query vector. This operation on the term classification produces the following lengthened vectors exhibiting one additional matching identifier:

DOC$_i$ = (0, 0, lift, propeller, roll, wing, "class k")
QUERY$_j$ = (aileron, drag, 0, propeller, 0, wing, "class k")

When a document is incorrectly retrieved (VAL$_{ij}$ = 1 and REL$_{ij}$ = 0), the reverse operation is performed and certain terms are removed from the thesaurus classes so as to decrease the number of matching classes assigned to both vectors.

The assignment of terms to classes (or the eventual removal of terms from classes) presents no difficulty in principle when the number of document-term pairs is small and when a large number of thesaurus classes can be introduced. Unfortunately, in practice it is necessary to operate with a large number of (DOC,QUERY) pairs and a restricted number of term classes (small p), and the task consists in constructing the best possible term classification which places a maximum number of (DOC,QUERY) pairs into the correctly retrieved or correctly rejected groups.

Since a given (DOC,QUERY) pair does not occur in isolation in the retrieval system, an operation on the term classification undertaken to help retrieve (or reject) a given document may have unfortunate effects on other documents in the collection. Thus, a given operation such as placement of $TERM_i$ and $TERM_j$ into class k may properly raise the similarity measure for a particular (DOC,QUERY) pair and shift that pair from class 4 to class 1; at the same time that same operation may carry a large number of (DOC,QUERY) pairs out of the 1 and 2 classes and place them into the undesirable 3 or 4 classes. Hence it becomes necessary to check the applicability of a proposed thesaurus operation by determining its effect on all (DOC,QUERY) pairs in the system, and to carry out a given operation only when its overall effect is judged to be beneficial.

The standard pseudoclassification process which is designed to produce an *optimal* term classification in which the maximum possible number of (DOC,QUERY) pairs *satisfy assessment* (that is, belong to classes 1 and 2) is then burdened with a number of substantial disadvantages:

1 To prove the optimality of a given term classification for a particular query and document collection, it is necessary to evaluate each perturbation of the classification by checking its effect on all other (DOC,QUERY) pairs in the system; thus each classification step necessarily involves all (DOC,QUERY) pairs.

2 The sequence in which the individual (DOC,QUERY) pairs are considered and the structure of the term classification available at the beginning of the process may complicate the classification process.

3 A given thesaurus operation may have to be considered many times in a given pass through the (DOC,QUERY) pairs, because although undesirable at a given moment in time, that same operation may be useful at a later time after additional changes have been introduced in the classification.

A variety of heuristic procedures have thus been proposed for the construction of acceptable term classifications. These methods differ from the previously described situation in that convergence of the procedures can normally be proved, but not optimality of the result.

In the standard pseudoclassification method the changes made to the term classification may lead to oscillations because a change once introduced may later have to be reversed. Alternatively, sequences of classification changes may be developed which are repeated indefinitely, so that the process runs forever. To avoid this possibility, on-the-spot global decisions can be introduced to ascertain whether a given operation on the classification should be carried out at any given time. The idea is to process the (DOC,QUERY) pairs in sequence and to make the applicability of a given thesaurus operation dependent only on the (DOC,QUERY) pairs previously processed in the current pass. Furthermore, the whole process must be guaranteed to terminate. The following two strategies have been shown to be effective in practice [29,30]:

1   A proposed change in the term classification is accepted if no *essential* deterioration is produced for any other previously processed document-query pair. By essential deterioration is meant that the document-query similarity for a relevant document currently retrievable is not decreased so far as to render the item nonretrievable; similarly, the correlation measure for a nonrelevant item currently rejected is not increased so much that the item is eventually retrieved.

2   A proposed change in the term classification is accepted if the number of document-query pairs that exhibit improvements as a result of the change exceeds the number of pairs exhibiting deteriorations. Improving means increasing the similarity for relevant documents, and vice versa for nonrelevant items. Deterioration is the reverse of improvement. This strategy uses a global condition in which correctly retrieved or rejected pairs are allowed to cross the retrieval threshold provided only that overall the gains exceed the losses.

Several small-scale evaluations of these strategies were carried out with experimental document collections. In each case, the first strategy appears most effective in increasing the number of (DOC,QUERY) pairs that satisfy the relevance assessment (correctly retrieved or correctly rejected pairs), while the second strategy should be used in order to obtain the best recall and precision results.

The normal pseudoclassification process builds a complete term classification matrix which specifies for each term one or more classes to which the term may be assigned during the course of the operations. However, the term classes themselves are never used for retrieval purposes. Instead relations between *term pairs* are used by adding special identifiers to the document and query vectors whenever a particular term pair is included in a common class. This suggests that the construction of a full-term classification could be replaced by a simple determination of term pair relationships followed by the incorporation of term pair relationship indicators (instead of term class indicators) in the query-document similarity computations. Furthermore, the determination of the relationships between term pairs might depend on the *global occurrence characteristics* of each particular term pair in the documents and queries of a collection. Such considerations have led to the construction of term-term similarity matrices used for pseudoclassification purposes in which the term relationships are derived from the term occurrence frequencies in the documents of a collection [31–32].

Consider, in particular, the collection of term pairs $(TERM_k, TERM_h)$ obtainable from a collection of queries and documents with the property that one of the terms in each pair occurs only in a given DOC_i while the other occurs only in QUERY$_j$ for a given (DOC$_i$,QUERY$_j$) pair. Alternatively, one of the two terms might be assigned to both DOC$_i$ and QUERY$_j$, while the other is assigned to either query or document alone. Such a term pair is called an *acceptable* pair. Clearly a full term match does not exist for an acceptable term pair when a standard vector matching process is used, because the assignment of the two terms differs for the components of a given (DOC$_i$,QUERY$_j$) pair.

If one assumes that the acceptable term pairs occur principally in document-query pairs that already satisfy assessment, that is (DOC$_i$,QUERY$_j$) pairs that are either correctly retrieved or correctly rejected, then no particular action is warranted. On the other hand, if the term pairs occur mainly in (DOC$_i$,QUERY$_j$) pairs for which DOC$_i$ is relevant to QUERY$_j$ (REL$_{ij}$ = 1) but the document is not retrieved (VAL$_{ij}$ = 0), then one might conjecture that a positive semantic relationship exists between the respective terms and that this term relationship has not in fact been taken into account in the query-document match. Analogously, if the term pairs occur in query-document situations where the documents are retrieved even though they are not identified as relevant (REL$_{ij}$ = 0 but VAL$_{ij}$ = 1), then a negative semantic relationship may be assumed to exist between the corresponding terms.

This suggests the following term matching strategy. For each acceptable term pair (TERM$_k$,TERM$_h$) a term relationship factor is computed as a *direct* function of the number of document query pairs containing the term pair for which REL$_{ij}$ = 1 and VAL$_{ij}$ = 0, and as an *inverse* function of the number of document-query pairs containing the terms such that REL$_{ij}$ = 0 and VAL$_{ij}$ = 1. The term relationship factor may then be incorporated into the query-document matching process in an attempt to increase the similarity coefficients for documents that are incorrectly retrieved or incorrectly rejected.

The term relationship factors can be computed in a single pass through the (DOC$_i$,QUERY$_j$) pairs to construct a *term-term relationship* (TTR) matrix of dimension t by t containing for each acceptable term pair (TERM$_k$,TERM$_h$) the corresponding number of (DOC$_i$,QUERY$_j$) pairs for which REL$_{ij}$ = 1 and VAL$_{ij}$ = 0 as well as the number of (DOC$_i$,QUERY$_j$) pairs for which REL$_{ij}$ = 0 and VAL$_{ij}$ = 1. In particular, for a given (TERM$_k$,TERM$_h$) pair (k > h), the below diagonal (k,h)th element of the term-term relationship matrix may be used to store the positive count, Pos(k,h), of term-pair occurrences in (DOC$_i$ QUERY$_j$) pairs for which the term pair is acceptable while the document is incorrectly rejected. Analogously, the above diagonal (h,k)th matrix element stores the negative count, Neg(k,h), of term pair occurrences in (DOC$_i$,QUERY$_j$) pairs where the document is incorrectly retrieved. An appropriate term relationship function T(k,h) for terms TERM$_k$ and TERM$_h$ might be defined as

$$T(k,h) = \frac{Pos(k,h) - a\,Neg(k,h)}{Pos(k,h) + a\,Neg(k,h)}$$

for some constant a.

	Aileron	Drag	Lift	Propeller	Roll	Wing
QUERY$_k$	0	1	0	1	0	1
DOC$_i$	1	1	1	0	0	1
DOC$_j$	1	0	0	1	1	1

(a)

$(DOC_i, QUERY_k)$: $REL_{ik} = 1$, $VAL_{ik} = 0$

$(DOC_j, QUERY_k)$: $REL_{jk} = 0$, $VAL_{jk} = 1$

(b)

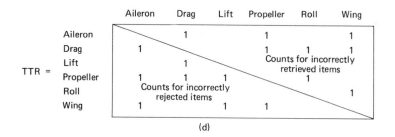

$(DOC_i, QUERY_k)$ { (aileron, drag), (aileron, propeller), (aileron, wing), (drag, lift) (drag, propeller), (lift, propeller), (lift, wing), (propeller, wing) }

$(DOC_j, QUERY_k)$ { (aileron, drag), (aileron, propeller), (aileron, wing), (drag, propeller) (drag, roll), (drag, wing), (propeller, roll) (roll, wing) }

(c)

TTR =

	Aileron	Drag	Lift	Propeller	Roll	Wing
Aileron		1		1		1
Drag	1			1	1	1
Lift		1		Counts for incorrectly retrieved items		
Propeller	1	1	1	1		
Roll	Counts for incorrectly rejected items					1
Wing	1		1	1		

(d)

Term relationship formula	$T(k, h) = \dfrac{Pos\,(k, h) - Neg\,(k, h)}{Pos\,(k, h) + Neg\,(k, h)}$	
Null relationship	*Positive relationship*	*Negative relationship*
T(aileron, drag) = 0	T(drag, lift) = 1	T(drag, roll) = −1
T(aileron, propeller) = 0	T(lift, propeller) = 1	T(drag, wing) = −1
T(aileron, wing) = 0	T(lift, wing) = 1	T(propeller, roll) = −1
T(drag, propeller) = 0	T(propeller, wing) = 1	T(roll, wing) = −1

(e)

Figure 6-8 Term relationship computation. (a) Original term vectors. (b) Relevance characteristics. (c) Acceptable term pairs. (d) Term-term relationship matrix. (e) Term relationship factors.

The single-pass construction of the term-term relationship matrix consists in processing each $(DOC_i, QUERY_j)$ pair in turn, identifying the acceptable term pairs, and increasing the count stored in the (k,h)th or (h,k)th matrix elements depending on whether the term pair $(TERM_k, TERM_h)$ is associated with an incorrectly rejected or an incorrectly retrieved document-query pair [31–32]. An example is given in Fig. 6-8 for two document vectors DOC_i, DOC_j and query $QUERY_k$, where DOC_i is assumed incorrectly rejected and DOC_j incorrectly retrieved. The acceptable term pairs are listed in Fig. 6-8c. The corresponding term-term relationship matrix is given in Fig. 6-8d and the term relationship computations are included in Fig. 6-8e.

It remains to define a vector similarity function incorporating the normal similarities between the term vectors DOC_i and $QUERY_j$, as well as the added term relationships derived from the term-term relationship matrix. Let $SIM(DOC_i, QUERY_j)$ represent the matching function used to compare the DOC_i and $QUERY_j$ vectors, and let $SIM_1(TERM_k, TERM_h)$ and $SIM_2(TERM_k, TERM_h)$ represent similarity functions based on the occurrence counts of positively $[T(k,h) > 0]$ and negatively $[T(k,h) < 0]$ related term pairs, respectively. Then an appropriate composite similarity function could be defined as

$$NEWSIM(DOC_i, QUERY_j) = a_0 SIM(DOC_i, QUERY_j)$$
$$+ \sum_{k,h} a_1 SIM_1(TERM_k, TERM_h)$$
$$+ \sum_{k,h} a_2 SIM_2(TERM_k, TERM_h) \qquad (13)$$

for properly chosen constants a_0, a_1, and a_2, similarity functions SIM, SIM_1, and SIM_2, and acceptable term pairs $(TERM_k, TERM_h)$ contained in the appropriate query-document vectors. The summation signs preceding the second and third terms of expression (13) indicate that the term pair similarity factors need to be summed for all acceptable $(TERM_k, TERM_h)$ pairs contained in a given pair of query-document vectors.

Experimental evaluation results available for small document collections of several hundred documents and several dozen queries show improvements for the composite similarity function NEWSIM over the standard cosine similarity measure ranging from 10 percent in the precision values to over 30 percent in precision for fixed recall levels [32].

5 DYNAMIC QUERY ADJUSTMENT

A General Considerations

Most operational retrieval systems offer an interactive search environment in which users, or search intermediaries, communicate directly with the search system and responses are furnished more or less instantaneously following submission of the search requests. Two kinds of interactive manipulations may be carried out during the course of an information search: the first relates to the submission of queries (search terms) and to the viewing of displayed responses; the other is the construction of the query formulations, sometimes aided by displays of thesaurus contents.

In some of the more sophisticated on-line systems it is possible to list for a given term all alphabetically related terms, or terms included in the same thesaurus category as the original term. In constructing an effective query statement, information about the number of items retrieved in response to earlier query formulations (known as the number of ''hits'') could then be useful; alternatively, the display of portions of retrieved documents or of documents related to those retrieved earlier can also be used for query reformulation purposes. Typically, the number of documents retrieved furnishes some idea about the specificity of the search terms used in the current query formulation: the terms can then be either broadened if the aim is to increase the number of retrieved items, or they can be narrowed in the opposite case. The display of the related search vocabulary or of previously retrieved document texts immediately suggests additional or alternative query formulation possibilities.

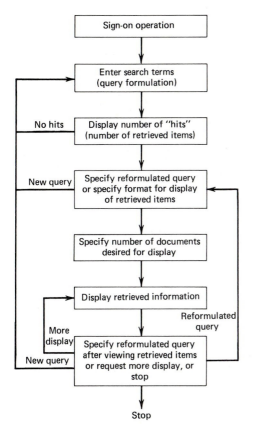

Figure 6-9 Typical interactive retrieval sequence.

Currently available evidence indicates that the query reformulation process is easier to manage by the user when the feedback information utilized for the formulation of query statements consists of previously retrieved document excerpts or surrogates rather than of vocabulary displays [33–36]. This reflects the fact that the display of retrieved documents furnishes indications of how the system has interpreted the user queries, but vocabulary displays do not. However, vocabulary displays can be produced inexpensively before performing any searches at all, but document displays are dependent on a prior search.

The more sophisticated, existing interactive search systems simplify the alteration of query statements by maintaining in storage various stages of earlier query formulations, thereby enabling the user to perform only selective alterations at each step. Appropriate tutorial features may also be used during the search process, including the display of multiple-choice response frames that give the user a choice of processing steps to perform next, as well as backtrack methods capable of returning to earlier displays. A typical interactive search process is illustrated in the chart of Fig. 6-9 [37].

*B Feedback Theory

The query reformulation methods mentioned earlier are designed to generate query statements capable of retrieving the relevant items and of rejecting the nonrelevant ones. When the query modification is carried out manually, the process is difficult to control, first because the characteristics of the relevant and nonrelevant items are known imperfectly, and also because document characteristics are not easily transformed into correct query formulations.

The *relevance feedback* process described in Chapter 4 relieves the user, or search intermediary, by automatically generating new query formulations based on relevance assessments obtained from the users during earlier search operations. More specifically, a newly constructed query will exhibit a high similarity with the document set previously identified as relevant and a low similarity with the nonrelevant document set. Assuming that the set of relevant documents D_R with respect to a query is known, and hence also the set of nonrelevant documents D_{N-R}, the best query Q is one that maximizes a function F defined as the difference between the average query-document similarity for all relevant items and the average query-document similarity for the nonrelevant ones. That is, a query vector Q is wanted which maximizes F, where

$$F = \overline{SIM}_{D_i \epsilon D_R} (Q,D_i) - \overline{SIM}_{D_i \epsilon D_{N-R}} (Q,D_i) \tag{14}$$

$\overline{SIM}$ represents the average similarity coefficient between the query and the set of all documents included in the relevant and nonrelevant document subsets, respectively. When the similarity between vectors is measured by the cosine coefficient, the optimal query has term weights proportional to the difference between the average weights of the terms in the relevant and the average weights of terms in the nonrelevant items [expression (5) in Chapter 4] [38,39, 40].

In practice the relevant and nonrelevant document sets D_R and D_{N-R} are of course not known in advance—if they were, no search would have to be conducted to identify them. Instead a query statement is used to retrieve a number of documents. The user then identifies some subset $D_{R'}$ of relevant items and some subset $D_{N'}$ of nonrelevant items. A new query can then be constructed proportional to the difference between the average of the R' relevant items previously identified and the N' nonrelevant items [expression (6) of Chapter 4]. This query will not, however, perform well unless the subsets $D_{R'}$ and $D_{N'}$ are representative of the actual relevant and nonrelevant sets D_R and D_{N-R} for the given query.

Consider as an example the situation of Fig. 6-10 where the original query is assumed to have retrieved three relevant and four nonrelevant items (located inside the dashed line of Fig. 6-10). The feedback query actually constructed by the normal relevance feedback system (open triangle in Fig. 6-10) will lie in the center of the set of relevant items where the average distance to the relevant is smallest. When that query is actually used for retrieval, a great many nonrelevant items located outside the original retrieval perimeter will then be retrieved. The ideal feedback query (filled triangle in Fig. 6-10) would be situated much closer to a set of relevant items not previously retrieved and farther away from the relevant items retrieved earlier. The retrieval failure illustrated in Fig. 6-10 can be avoided in part by deemphasizing the role of the previously retrieved items in constructing a feedback query and assigning greater importance to the original query statement. In other words, the feedback query is expected to be reasonably close to the original query statement, and in addition, it should exhibit a greater resemblance to the items previously identified as relevant than to the nonrelevant ones. A typical formula used to construct an

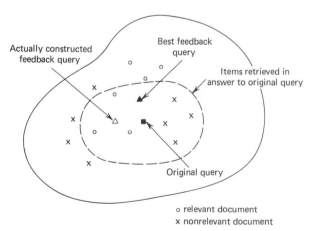

Figure 6-10   Unfavorable relevance feedback situation.

improved query statement Q' from an original query Q, a set of R' documents previously identified as relevant, and a set of N' documents identified as non-relevant is given by

$$Q' = \alpha(Q) + \beta \left(\frac{1}{R'} \sum_{D_i \in D_{R'}} D_i \right) - \gamma \left(\frac{1}{N'} \sum_{D_i \in D_{N'}} D_i \right) \qquad (15)$$

where α, β, and γ are constants, and the terms in parentheses represent the earlier query statement, and the average relevant and average nonrelevant previously identified documents.

The relevance feedback operation is most effective when the relevant documents are tightly clustered and hence exhibit large pairwise similarities, and the nonrelevant documents are also tightly clustered. At the same time the distance between the relevant and nonrelevant items should be large; that is, the similarities between them should be small (see Fig. 4-14a for a schema representing such an ideal document space).

*C Feedback Variations

The relevance feedback process can be implemented in a variety of different processing modes. The formal feedback equation [expression (15)] makes provisions for the incorporation of both relevant and nonrelevant documents in the feedback process. However, the role of the two document types is basically unequal: when the relevant items are used to update the query, certain terms are added to the query and the weight of other terms is increased; the query is then forced to move in the direction where other relevant items may be expected to be located. When nonrelevant items are used for feedback purposes, certain terms are deleted from the query, and other term weights are decreased. The negative feedback operation diminishes the affinity of the query with some items but does not provide alternative directions to control the query movement. Thus a *positive* feedback strategy, where relevant documents are used to update the query serves to construct new queries that will exhibit greater resemblance with the items originally defined as relevant. A *negative* strategy using the nonrelevant items for query updating decreases the query similarity with these nonrelevant items but may not provide a positive direction toward which to move.

The relevance feedback process can then be executed in the following modes [41,42]:

    1 A positive mode where relevant documents are available for feedback purposes
    2 A negative mode where nonrelevant documents are used to update the query
    3 A mixed mode incorporating both positive and negative modes

In each case, the number of documents used to update the query can be varied.

Among the strategies that have been formally evaluated are the standard mixed strategy [equation (15)], a strategy using *all* relevant items that may be available but only *one* nonrelevant document (normally the one retrieved earliest in a search providing ranked output), and a system which emphasizes the original query statement and deemphasizes the role of the feedback documents [the α parameter in expression (15) receives a large weight].

A positive relevance feedback operation is illustrated in the example of Table 6-7. The initial query vector is shown in Table 6-7a. The term weights are listed under the corresponding terms in each case. The updated query (Table 6-7c) contains terms from document 102 originally retrieved and identified as relevant to the query. Two document vectors (numbers 80 and 81) are shown at the bottom of Table 6-7 whose retrieval rank in order of query-document similarity improves from 14 to 7 and from 137 to 6, respectively, as a result of the feedback operation. A comparison of the vectors in Table 6-7b, d, and e reveals that the feedback operation for document 102 is directly responsible for the retrieval improvement of documents 80 and 81.

The positive feedback strategy is obviously not applicable when no relevant documents are retrieved by the original query vector. Furthermore the

Table 6-7 Positive Relevance Feedback Illustration

Vector type	Illustration			
a Initial query vector	airplane 12	available 12	blast 12	dynamic 12
	gust 12	information 12	regime 12	response 12
	subsonic 12			
b Relevant document 102 retrieved with rank 2 (partial vector)	gust 48	lift 48	oscillating 12	penetration 12
	response 24	subsonic 12	sudden 12	
c Query modified by document 102	airplane 12	available 12	blast 12	dynamic 12
	gust 60	information 12	lift 48	oscillating 12
	penetration 12	regime 12	response 36	subsonic 24
	sudden 12			
d Relevant document 80 (improves from rank 14 to rank 7; partial vector)	gust 24	lift 72	penetration 12	sudden 12
e Relevant document 81 (improves from rank 137 to rank 6; partial vector)	lift 84	oscillating 12	sudden 12	

Adapted from reference 13.
Query Q146: What information is available for dynamic response of airplanes to gusts or blasts in subsonic regime?

strategy must fail when dissimilarities are evident in the set of retrieved documents. In that case, the new query is in principle required to approach several different directions at once, and the effect of the feedback operation becomes unpredictable. A negative feedback operation then becomes mandatory.

A comparison of the positive and mixed retrieval strategies indicates that, on the average, the performance of queries that do retrieve some relevant documents in the initial search is not hindered by incorporating some nonrelevant documents in the feedback operation. However, the amount of perturbation in the query vectors is normally larger for the mixed feedback system than for the purely positive one. The mixed strategy must therefore be used with care because of the greater potential for improper query disturbance.

The purely negative feedback strategy is even more difficult to control. Consider the case of Table 6-8, where the most important query term ("data set") is subtracted out because that term happens to have been present in some of the nonrelevant items previously retrieved. Various solutions can be devised which will avoid the predicament illustrated in Table 6-8. One possibility consists in leaving original query terms intact in a negative feedback situation; the updated query will then consist of the original query terms plus additional negatively weighted terms taken from the nonrelevant documents previously retrieved. Alternatively, a thesaurus could be used to add related terms to the original query vector prior to the negative feedback operation. An illustration of such a modified negative feedback system is shown in Table 6-9 for the query previously used as an example in Table 6-8. A comparison of the final query statements shows that the problem exhibited in Table 6-8 is avoided by the process of Table 6-9 [13,42,43].

Several variants of the basic relevance feedback system have been described in the literature. These include a *query splitting* system designed to generate several subqueries from a given original query whenever the set of relevant items retrieved by a given query is not sufficiently homogeneous. Each of the subqueries is then expected to retrieve a different set of relevant items [44]. Another feedback variant, known as "cluster feedback," constructs separate feedback queries from the relevant and/or nonrelevant documents located in different document clusters in a clustered collection [13]. This last process thus performs the feedback operations separately in each document cluster. The feedback refinements remain to be thoroughly evaluated.

Table 6-8   Example of Inadequate Negative Feedback

	Type of vector	Illustration			
a	Initial query vector	available	current	data set	specification
		12	12	12	12
b	Sum of retrieved	access	data set	file list	structure
	nonrelevant documents	48	60	24 24	84
c	Standard negative	available	current	specification	
	feedback result	12	12	12	

Adapted from reference 13.
Query: Please give specification for all currently available data sets.

Table 6-9 Negative Feedback with Related Concepts for Query of Table 6-8

Type of vector	Illustration
a Initial query vector	available current data set specification 12 12 12 12
b Concepts related to "data set" with correlation strength	access bandwidth file interface line list 77 28 50 58 52 47 retrieval sort structure transmission 49 40 49 30
c Related concept vector (top 5 concepts with weight of 24)	access file interface line structure 24 24 24 24 24
d Query vector with related concepts	access available current data set file 24 12 12 12 24 interface line specification structure 24 24 12 24
e Sum of retrieved nonrelevant documents	access data set file list structure 48 60 24 24 84
f Updated query vector (computed by d − e with initial query terms intact)	access available current data set interface −24 12 12 12 24 line list specification structure 24 −24 12 −60

The basic relevance feedback process may be expected to produce between 10 and 20 percent improvement in precision for fixed recall levels. When a second feedback iteration is added, that is, when a modified query is itself modified a second time by a feedback process, additional improvements of a few percentage points may be gained.

An evaluation of the relevance feedback process raises complex problems that are not normally met in the evaluation of single search systems. In particular, it is unclear how documents should be treated that were originally retrieved by a given query and are retrieved once more by the modified feedback query. Some of these documents may well be relevant to the queries. However, a user may not be interested in seeing for a second time items that were already retrieved in an earlier search iteration, and the repeated retrieval of such relevant items should not be included in the recall-precision computations.

Several feedback evaluation systems have been proposed in the literature. The most effective of these known as the "test and control" evaluation, is represented in simplified form in Fig. 6-11 [45]. The idea is to break up a collection into two parts with roughly equal relevance properties. The first subcollection, known as the "test collection," is used in a relevance feedback situation to generate a set of modified feedback queries from the originally available queries. The second, so-called control collection, is then processed in two different searches first against the original queries and later against the modified queries. Recall-precision measurements are used in each case to compare the respective performance. Under experimental conditions, improvements of up to 10 percent in precision for fixed recall levels have been noted for the modified feedback queries compared with the original ones.

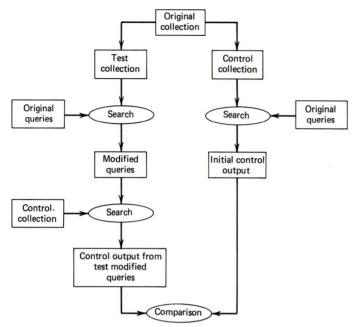

Figure 6-11 Test and control feedback evaluation.

D Dynamic Document Space

It was noted earlier that in some circumstances it becomes useful to modify not only the query statements during the course of the retrieval process, but also the document vectors themselves. For example, when the user population is fairly homogeneous and many queries of the same type are expected to be submitted to the retrieval system, a dynamic document modification process may lead to easier retrieval of relevant documents and a more useful document space for search purposes.

Consider, for example, the document modification system represented in simplified form in Fig. 6-12a. The process consists in modifying the documents retrieved with respect to a given query and identified as relevant by the user so as to render them somewhat more similar to the query that was used to retrieve them. This can be done by adding certain query terms to the various document vectors, or by increasing the weight of query terms that already occur in the document vectors. By making the document vectors more similar to a common query, they are also made more similar to each other. Hence when a new query is submitted that resembles the original one, the modified documents become more easily retrievable.

The document space modification process of Fig. 6-12b is an extension of the earlier one, because documents identified as nonrelevant by the user population are also altered in Fig. 6-12b so as to make these items less similar to the original query, while at the same time, the relevant documents are moved closer to the query as before. In each case, the idea is to perform only minor

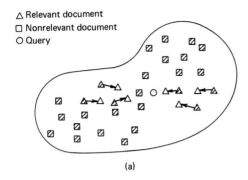

(a)

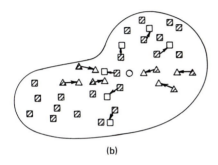

(b)

Figure 6-12 Document space modification. (a) Relevant document modification. (b) Relevant and nonrelevant document modification.

adjustments in the document vectors in response to any particular user-system interaction. Significant document movements will then occur only after a consensus has been reached among several different users concerning the usefulness of particular items in response to a number of different queries. Following many small individual moves of the document vectors, an equilibrium space may eventually be produced where no major additional document alterations occur. Such a conjecture remains to be proved [46].

When the user population of the retrieval system is not sufficiently homogeneous, few queries may be submitted that are similar to each other. In that case, it may not be possible to construct an improved document space. However, a document space modification method may nevertheless be useful in order to handle document *growth and retirement*. In particular, when a collection grows indefinitely through the addition of new items, limitations in the available storage space may make it necessary to retire from the active storage area those items that are least likely to be useful for retrieval purposes. The problem then consists in identifying items as candidates for possible retirement. A number of strategies suggest themselves for this purpose: items may be retired if they have never been retrieved in response to earlier queries or, having been retrieved, if they are always identified as nonrelevant to the respective user queries or if they are always retrieved late in a search.

Some of the foregoing retirement strategies involve a document space modification step, followed by the retirement of items that will have moved to the periphery of the document space. Preliminary evaluations indicate that automatic document retirement methods can usefully be incorporated into a document retrieval system [47].

The concept of document collection modification remains to be tried out in real user environments. In principle, it appears natural that the relationship between items should be altered as science advances, new applications emerge for old ideas, and the use of the collection changes. On the other hand, when changes are introduced into the stored data, searches that are repeated periodically will not necessarily retrieve the same information as before. This loss of stability may be disturbing to some users. Furthermore, the effort to alter the document representations of many items of a transitory nature may hardly be worth the effort. Because of the connection between collection modification on the one hand and collection management (growth and retirement) on the other, the document space modification process may be expected to attract increased attention in the future.

6 CITATION PROCESSING

A Basic Citation Properties

The use of bibliographic references and citations in document processing has not yet been considered. Citations and references between documents are usable for many types of literature studies. References and citations attached to individual literature items may provide alternative expressions of document content. Citation and reference counts can also be used to assess the importance of individual documents or of complete document collections, by assuming that citation frequencies reflect the influence of bibliographic items in a field of study. By extension this argument may also be applied to authors of documents or to selected groups of authors; in particular, author influence might be measured by using the citation frequencies of documents written by a given author. Finally, citations and references can be followed from item to item, and the resulting "network" of papers can serve as a basis for a variety of historic studies and for an examination of the development of individual disciplines [48–53].

A distinction must be made between bibliographic references and citations. A *reference* for a given document is a bibliographic item mentioned in the bibliography of that document. Thus the phrase ''A refers to B'' implies that document B is included as an entry in the bibliography of document A. *Citations* between documents specify additional relationships between bibliographic items. A citation is an inverse reference: when a document A refers to document B, the latter is cited by document A. For a particular document, it is then possible to identify a set of references obtainable by consulting the bibliography of that document, as well as a set of citations made by other documents to the document in question. To identify the citations it is necessary to use a

Luhn

Figure 6-13 Citation terminology: Stiles *refers to* Luhn, or Luhn is *cited by* Stiles. (Luhn is contained in Stiles's reference list.)

Stiles

citation index or, alternatively, to process the reference lists using appropriate sort and merge operations. The dual relationship between references and citations is represented graphically in Fig. 6-13—a reference by an outgoing arrow and a citation by an incoming arrow. When document B refers to document A, B may be expected to postdate A; hence vertical displacement from top to bottom in a citation graph represents increasing time.

The occurrence of bibliographic citations is a comparatively rare phenomenon. For example, about 25 percent of all published papers are never cited at all. Of the archive of citable papers in a particular field of endeavor, about one half are not cited in any given year. Of those that are cited in a particular year, 72 percent are cited once in that year, and 18 percent are cited twice. Thus only about 5 percent of the archive of citable papers is cited at least three times in a given year [54]. From these statistics, it is not difficult to conclude that when a given document attracts many dozens of citations—and, of course, such papers are not hard to find—the very rarity of the phenomenon carries significance. A long list of studies have also shown that citation counts for papers, journals, authors, etc., correlate highly with peer judgments concerning the importance and influence of documents and document authors.

*B   Main Citation Usage

In order to make use of bibliographic reference and citation data, it is first necessary to collect citations for a given corpus of documents. This can be done by taking a number of source documents and following either references or citations to new documents. These new documents can then be used as sources for new searches that discover still other documents. Two possible search strategies are represented graphically in Fig. 6-14.

The search of Fig. 6-14a is a pure citation search which uses as a source a well-known (historical) document in a given area (Luhn). A citation index is then used to identify a number of more recent documents all of which cite Luhn. One of these citing items (Cleverdon) is then used to produce still newer documents which cite Cleverdon (documents Lancaster, Keen, Salton of Fig. 6-14a). The search could continue to cover many generations of documents, thereby using connections between documents over long periods of time.

The search of Fig. 6-14b, on the other hand, covers documents that remain more or less stationary in time. The source document (Luhn) is used as before to uncover the citing items Stiles, Cleverdon, and Sparck Jones. One of these (Sparck Jones) is then used in a backward search by taking the references for Sparck Jones (documents Luhn, van Rijsbergen, Harter) and obtaining further

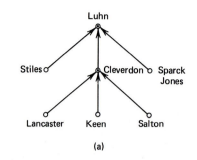

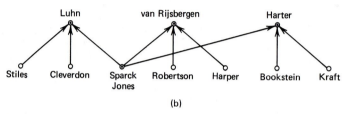

Figure 6-14 (a) Citation search forward in time. (b) Citation search forward and backward.

citations for some of these referenced items. Such a lateral search stays within a relatively narrow time frame, as opposed to the vertical search of Fig. 6-14a.

Citation and reference tracing methods of the kind illustrated in Fig. 6-14 may be used to generate complete citation networks for individual subject areas. Such citation networks are then used as a basis for historical researches of various kinds. A typical citation network is illustrated in Fig. 6-15, where once again downward displacement of the page implies increasing time.

Each reference or citation between two items represents a relationship indicator for the items. However, a direct reference (item A refers to item B) does not imply identity in the subject areas covered by the items. A stronger indication of congruence in subject matter is furnished by the so-called bibliographic coupling and cocitation counts. Two items are coupled bibliographically when they share certain references, that is, when their bibliographies contain various items in common. The coupling strength between two items may in fact be defined as the number of references in common for both items [55,56]. One may expect that when the coupling strength between documents is sufficiently large, the subject matter of the items exhibits strong similarities.

Two documents may also be related by common citation patterns from other documents. In particular, a *cocitation link* is said to relate two items when these items are jointly cited by a third document. The number of cocitations for two documents, that is, the number of documents that jointly cite the two items, is believed to be more significant than the bibliographic coupling strength in pointing to subject matter similarities. Cocitations have thus been widely used to study the development of individual fields of science as well as

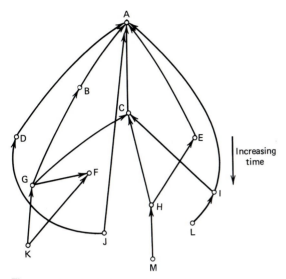

Figure 6-15 Typical citation network.

the structure of science as a whole [57–59]. Figure 6-16 presents a sample contour map in which individual documents are grouped, based in part on the
strength of their cocitation links. In particular, the diameter of the circles
around each document is related to the total number of citations attracted by
the documents and hence to the importance of the documents. The distance
between two documents, on the other hand, is inversely related to the cocitation strength between them, that is, the closer the items in the map, the higher

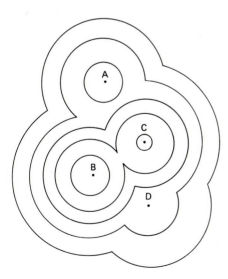

Figure 6-16 Typical contour map based
on cocitations.

the number of cocitations between them. Maps such as that of Fig. 6-16 have been constructed at different periods in time for certain subject areas thereby describing the development of a given field of study [50,59].

If citations and references attached to documents carry subject significance, it appears reasonable to use them for content representation in addition to, or instead of, the normal index terms. In particular, if the citation and reference patterns are known for a collection of documents, a particular document could be represented by a bibliographic attribute vector of the form

$$\text{DOC}_i = (r_{i1}, r_{i2}, \ldots, r_{in}, c_{i1}, c_{i2}, \ldots, c_{im}) \tag{16}$$

where r_{ij} is an identifier representing the jth reference attached to DOC_i and c_{ik} the kth citation to the document. The normal vector similarity computations between pairs of documents or between queries and documents, can then be performed using the standard term vectors or alternatively, the bibliographic attribute vectors of expression (16). The two vector forms can also be combined by adding the bibliographic information to the normal index terms.

Studies in which bibliographic indicators have replaced the standard terms and keywords for content identification have shown that bibliographic indicators represent more specific content identifications than normal keywords [55, 60,61]. Furthermore, precision improvements have been noted in searches carried out with bibliographic vectors replacing the normal term vectors [62]. In some retrieval environments the bibliographic identifiers may be immediately available as a by-product of the computer composition of the documents, whereas the terms and keywords might have to be generated by a more or less complicated indexing process. One may expect an increased utilization of bibliographic data for retrieval purposes in the immediate future [63].

7 SUMMARY

The standard information retrieval operations may be refined by using sophisticated automatic indexing methods that are capable of assigning weighted, instead of binary, terms to the documents of a collection. The term weights may be based on the term occurrence characteristics in the documents of a collection—for example, terms occurring mostly in documents identified as relevant to the user queries may receive higher weights than terms occurring in the nonrelevant documents.

Improved search efficiency may be obtained by clustering the document collection and placing into common classes all documents that appear to be sufficiently similar to each other. Various automatic classification methods are available for this purpose, and efficient top-down or bottom-up cluster search methods have been devised.

The manipulation of weighted query and document terms also leads to methods for generating improved query statements based on information obtained from the user population in the course of the retrieval operations. The relevance feedback operations have been shown experimentally to lead to substantial improvements in retrieval effectiveness. Relevance information obtained from the users about the importance of certain documents in the collection can also lead to improvements in the document descriptions themselves, and to modern collection management strategies capable of accommodating growing or shrinking document collections. Furthermore, relevance data are needed for the construction of improved term weighting measures: indeed the relevance feedback process represents an obvious possibility for the estimation of the term relevance factor. Finally, relevance information may be used to generate trial or starting clusters in various heuristic clustering systems.

Improvements in search and retrieval performance may be obtainable by incorporating bibliographic citations instead of only content terms in the document descriptions. There are indications that at a time when document texts are increasingly available in machine-readable form, the latter possibility may be especially attractive.

REFERENCES

[1] G. Salton, Automatic Information Organization and Retrieval, McGraw-Hill Book Company, New York, 1968.

[2] C.J. van Rijsbergen, Information Retrieval, 2nd Edition, Butterworths, London, 1979.

[3] H.E. Stiles, The Association Factor in Information Retrieval, Journal of the ACM, Vol. 8, No. 2, April 1961, pp. 271–279.

[4] M.E. Maron and J.L. Kuhns, On Relevance, Probabilistic Indexing and Information Retrieval, Journal of the ACM, Vol. 7, No. 3, July 1960, pp. 216–244.

[5] W.B. Croft, Organizing and Searching Large Files of Document Descriptions, Doctoral Thesis, University of Cambridge (England), 1978.

[6] H. Wu and G. Salton, A Term Weighting Model Based on Utility Theory, in Information Retrieval Research, R.N. Oddy, S.E. Robertson, C.J. van Rijsbergen and P.W. Williams, editors, Butterworths, London, 1981, pp. 9–22.

[7] C.T. Yu, K. Lam, and G. Salton, Term Weighting in Information Retrieval Using the Term Precision Model, Journal of the ACM, Vol. 29, No. 1, January 1982, pp. 152–170.

[8] A. Bookstein, Fuzzy Requests: An Approach to Weighted Boolean Searches, Journal of the ASIS, Vol. 31, No. 4, July 1980, pp. 240–247.

[9] A. Bookstein, On the Perils of Merging Boolean and Weighted Retrieval Systems, Journal of the ASIS, Vol. 29, No. 3, May 1978, pp. 156–158. pp. 156–158.

[10] W. Goffman, An Indirect Method of Information Retrieval, Information Storage and Retrieval, Vol. 4, No. 4, December 1968, pp. 361–373.

[11] N. Jardine and R. Sibson, A Model for Taxonomy, Mathematical Biosciences, Vol. 2, No. 2–3, May 1968, pp. 465–482.

[12] K. Sparck Jones, Some Thoughts on Classification for Retrieval, Journal of Documentation, Vol. 26, No. 2, June 1970, pp. 89–101.

[13] G. Salton, Dynamic Information and Library Processing, Prentice-Hall, Inc., Englewood Cliffs, New Jersey, 1975.

[14] W.B. Croft, A Model of Cluster Searching Based on Classification, Information Systems, Vol. 5, No. 3, 1980, pp. 189–195.

[15] G. Salton, Cluster Search Strategies and the Optimization of Retrieval Effectiveness, in The Smart Retrieval System, G. Salton, editor, Prentice-Hall, Inc., Englewood Cliffs, New Jersey, 1971, Chapter 10.

[16] R.T. Grauer and M. Messier, An Evaluation of Rocchio's Clustering Algorithm, in The Smart Retrieval System, G. Salton, editor, Prentice-Hall, Inc., Englewood Cliffs, New Jersey, 1971, Chapter 11.

[17] R.T. Dattola, Experiments with a Fast Algorithm for Automatic Classification, in The Smart Retrieval System, G. Salton, editor, Prentice-Hall, Inc., Englewood Cliffs, New Jersey, 1971, Chapter 12.

[18] G. Salton and H. Wu, A Comparison of Inverted File Searching with Cluster Tree Search Operations, Technical Report, Computer Science Department, Cornell University, Ithaca, New York, 1981.

[19] C.W. Cleverdon and E.M. Keen, Factors Determining the Performance of Indexing Systems, Aslib Cranfield Research Project, Volumes 1 and 2, Cranfield (England), 1968.

[20] G. Salton and M.E. Lesk, Computer Evaluation of Indexing and Text Processing, Journal of the ACM, Vol. 15, No. 1, January 1968, pp. 8–36.

[21] V.E. Giuliano and P.E. Jones, Linear Associative Information Retrieval, in Vistas in Information Handling, P. Howerton, editor, Spartan Books, Rochelle Park, New Jersey, 1963.

[22] B. Litofsky, Utility of Automatic Classification Systems for Information Storage and Retrieval, Ph.D. dissertation, University of Pennsylvania, Philadelphia, Pennsylvania, 1969.

[23] A.R. Meetham, Graph Separability and Word Grouping, Proceedings of 1966 ACM National Conference, Association for Computing Machinery, New York, 1966, pp. 513–514.

[24] K. Sparck Jones, Automatic Keyword Classification for Information Retrieval, Butterworths, London, 1971.

[25] G. Salton, Experiments in Automatic Thesaurus Construction for Information Retrieval, Information Processing-71, North Holland Publishing Company, Amsterdam, 1972, pp. 115–123.

[26] P.K.T. Vaswani and J.B. Cameron, The NPL Experiments in Statistical Word Associations and Their Use in Document Indexing and Retrieval, Computer Science Report No. 42, National Physical Laboratory, Teddington, England, April 1970.

[27] R. Attar and A.S. Fraenkel, Local Feedback in Full-Text Retrieval Systems, Journal of the ACM, Vol. 24, No. 3, July 1977, pp. 397–417.

[28] D.M. Jackson, The Construction of Retrieval Environments and Pseudoclassification Based on External Relevance, Information Storage and Retrieval, Vol. 6, No. 2, June 1970, pp. 187–219.

[29] C.T. Yu, A Formal Construction of Term Classes, Journal of the ACM, Vol. 22, No. 1, January 1975, pp. 17–37.

[30] C.T. Yu, A Methodology for the Construction of Term Classes, Information Storage and Retrieval, Vol. 10, Nos. 7/8, July/August 1974, pp. 243–251.

[31] C.T. Yu and V.V. Raghavan, Single-Pass Method for Determining the Semantic Relationship between Terms, Journal of the ASIS, Vol. 28, No. 5, November 1977, pp. 345–354.

[32] V.V. Raghavan and C.T. Yu, Experiments on the Determination of the Relation-

ships between Terms, Proceedings of First Annual SIGIR Conference, Association for Computing Machinery, New York, May 1978, p. 150.

[33] M.E. Lesk and G. Salton, Interactive Search and Retrieval Methods Using Automatic Information Displays, AFIPS Conference Proceedings, Vol. 34, Montvale, New Jersey, 1969, pp. 435–446.

[34] R.N. Oddy, Information Retrieval through Man-Machine Dialogue, Journal of Documentation, Vol. 33, No. 1, March 1977, pp. 1–14.

[35] C. Vernimb, Automatic Query Adjustment in Document Retrieval, Information Processing and Management, Vol. 13, No. 6, 1977, pp. 339–353.

[36] J.H. Williams, Jr., Functions of a Man-Machine Interactive Information Retrieval System, Journal of the ASIS, Vol. 22, No. 5, September–October 1971, pp. 311–317.

[37] P.C. Mitchell, J.T. Rickman, and W.E. Walden, SOLAR—A Storage and On-Line Automatic Retrieval System, Journal of the ASIS, Vol. 25, No. 5, September–October 1973, pp. 347–358.

[38] J.J. Rocchio, Jr., Relevance Feedback in Information Retrieval, in The Smart Retrieval System—Experiments in Automatic Document Processing, G. Salton, editor, Prentice-Hall, Inc., Englewood Cliffs, New Jersey, 1971, Chapter 14.

[39] G. Salton, Relevance Feedback and the Optimization of Retrieval Effectiveness, in The Smart Retrieval System—Experiments in Automatic Document Processing, G. Salton, editor, Prentice-Hall, Inc., Englewood Cliffs, New Jersey, 1971, Chapter 15.

[40] J.J. Rocchio, Jr., Document Retrieval Systems—Optimization and Evaluation, Report ISR-10 to the National Science Foundation, Harvard Computation Laboratory, Cambridge, Massachusetts, March 1966.

[41] E. Ide, New Experiments in Relevance Feedback, in The Smart Retrieval System, G. Salton, editor, Prentice-Hall, Inc., Englewood Cliffs, New Jersey, 1971, Chapter 16.

[42] E. Ide and G. Salton, Interactive Search Strategies and Dynamic File Organization, in The Smart Retrieval System, G. Salton, editor, Prentice-Hall Inc., Englewood Cliffs, New Jersey, 1971, Chapter 18.

[43] J. Kelly, Negative Response Relevance Feedback, in The Smart Retrieval System, G. Salton, editor, Prentice-Hall Inc., Englewood Cliffs, New Jersey, 1971, Chapter 20.

[44] A. Borodin, L. Kerr, and F. Lewis, Query Splitting in Relevance Feedback Systems, in The Smart Retrieval System, G. Salton, editor, Prentice-Hall Inc., Englewood Cliffs, New Jersey, 1971, Chapter 19.

[45] Y.K. Chang, C. Cirillo, and J. Razon, Evaluation of Feedback Retrieval Using Modified Freezing, Residual Collections, and Test and Control Groups, in The Smart Retrieval System, G. Salton, editor, Prentice-Hall, Inc., Englewood Cliffs, New Jersey, 1971, Chapter 17.

[46] T.L. Brauen, Document Vector Modification, in The Smart Retrieval System—Experiments in Automatic Document Processing, G. Salton, editor, Prentice-Hall, Inc., Englewood Cliffs, New Jersey, 1971, Chapter 24.

[47] K. Sardana, Automatic Document Retirement Algorithms, Scientific Report No. 22, Section 12, Computer Science Department, Cornell University, Ithaca, New York, 1974.

[48] E. Garfield, Citation Indexing—Its Theory and Applications in Science, Technology and Humanities, John Wiley and Sons, New York, 1979.

[49] D.J. deSolla Price, Networks of Scientific Papers, Science, Vol. 149, No. 3683, 1965, pp. 510–515.

[50] E. Garfield, Citation Measures as an Objective Estimate of Creativity, Current Contents, No. 34, August 16, 1970, pp. 4–5.

[51] J.R. Cole and S. Cole, The Ortega Hypothesis, Science, Vol. 178, No. 4059, October 27, 1972, pp. 368–375.

[52] E. Garfield, Citation Analysis as a Tool in Journal Evaluation, Science, Vol. 178, No. 4060, November 3, 1972, pp. 471–479.

[53] J.H. Westbrook, Identifying Significant Research, Science, Vol. 132, No. 3435, October 18, 1960, pp. 1229–1234.

[54] D.J. deSolla Price, The Citation Cycle, in Key Papers in Information Science, B. C. Griffith, editor, Knowledge Industry Publications Inc., White Plains, New York, 1980, pp. 195–210.

[55] M.M. Kessler, Comparison of Results of Bibliographic Coupling and Analytic Subject Indexing, American Documentation, Vol. 16, No. 3, July 1965, pp. 223–233.

[56] M.M. Kessler, Bibliographic Coupling between Scientific Papers, American Documentation, Vol. 14, No. 1, January 1963, pp. 10–25.

[57] E. Garfield, ISI Is Studying the Structure of Science through Cocitation Analysis, Current Contents, No. 7, February 13, 1974, pp. 5–10.

[58] H. Small and B.C. Griffith, The Structure of Scientific Literature, I. Identifying and Graphing Specialties, Science Studies, Vol. 4, 1974, pp. 17–40.

[59] H. Small, Co-citation in the Scientific Literature: A New Measure of the Relationship between Two Documents, Journal of the ASIS, Vol. 24, No. 4, July–August 1973, pp. 265–269.

[60] E. Garfield, Science Citation Index—A New Dimension in Indexing, Science, Vol. 144, No. 3619, May 8, 1964, pp. 649–654.

[61] E. Garfield, The Citation Index as a Subject Index, Current Contents, No. 18, May 1, 1974, pp. 5–7.

[62] G. Salton, Automatic Indexing Using Bibliographic Citations, Journal of Documentation, Vol. 27, No. 2, June 1971, pp. 98–110.

[63] E. Garfield, ISI's On-Line System Makes Searching So Easy Even a Scientist Can Do It: Introducing METADEX Automatic Indexing and ISI/BIOMED Search, Current Contents, No. 4, January 26, 1981, pp. 5–8.

BIBLIOGRAPHIC REMARKS

Additional coverage of query formulation and query modification in information retrieval is provided by

H.S. Heaps, Information Retrieval—Computational and Theoretical Aspects, Academic Press, New York, 1978.

G. Salton, Dynamic Information and Library Processing, Prentice-Hall, Inc., Englewood Cliffs, New Jersey, 1975.

Clustering algorithms are examined in many texts. The second reference below (Hartigan) provides actual computer programs for several clustering methods and the third (Sparck Jones) specializes in term classification

P.H.A. Sneath and R.R. Sokal, Numerical Taxonomy: The Principles and Practice of Numerical Classification, W. H. Freeman, San Francisco, California, 1973.

J.A. Hartigan, Clustering Algorithms, John Wiley and Sons, New York, 1975.

K. Sparck Jones, Automatic Keyword Classification for Information Retrieval, Butterworths, London, 1971.

A thorough coverage of citation processing is provided by

E. Garfield, Citation Indexing—Its Theory and Applications in Science, Technology and Humanities, John Wiley and Sons, New York, 1979.

EXERCISES

6-1 Consider the following similarity matrix between objects

	1	2	3	4	5	6	7	8	9
1	0	0	1	0	1	1	1	0	0
2	0	0	0	0	0	0	0	0	1
3	1	0	0	0	1	0	1	0	0
4	0	0	0	0	0	1	0	1	0
5	1	0	1	0	0	0	0	0	0
6	1	0	0	1	0	0	0	1	0
7	1	0	1	0	0	0	0	0	0
8	0	0	0	1	0	1	0	0	0
9	0	1	0	0	0	0	0	0	0

a Find all the cliques.

b Find all the connected components.

c State the algorithm used to determine the clusters using a single-link method.

d Give a list of desirable clustering properties for a document collection leading to an effective and/or efficient retrieval system. Under what circumstances would it be preferable to use cliques rather than connected components to search a collection of objects, and vice versa? What are the tradeoffs between the two methods?

e Do the cliques listed under part a exhibit the desirable properties listed under part d? Same question for the connected components listed under part b. If not, how could the cliques or the connected components be modified to produce an improved classification?

6-2 What is the main idea behind the pseudoclassification process? What are the differences between a standard term classification and the notion of pseudoclassification? Would you expect the results of a pseudoclassification to remain unchanged when the user population of a retrieval system changes?

6-3 How can a citation index be used in retrieval? Suppose the cocitation strength were available for all document pairs in a collection of documents. How could that fact be utilized to design an effective retrieval service? Are there obvious similarities between the use of citations and the use of pseudoclassification in retrieval?

6-4 Consider the document output obtained for a given query by an initial search and a feedback search based on user relevance assessments for the top three retrieved items.

	Initial search			Feedback search	
	Rank	**Document number**	**Relevant**	**Document number**	**Relevant**
Initially	1	680		425	x
retrieved	2	425	x	430	
	3	430		129	x
	4	129	x	680	
	5	320		529	
	⋮	⋮	⋮	⋮	⋮

a Compute the recall-precision pairs following the retrieval of each document for both searches.

b Are the differences in recall-precision measures reflective of the improvements actually obtained by the feedback process?

c Design a feedback evaluation system which emphasizes the retrieval of relevant items not previously seen by the user.

d Use the sample search to compare the new feedback evaluation derived under part c with the original evaluation under part a.

6-5 Consider the following document collection indexed by three terms A, B, and C:

	D_1	D_2	D_3	D_4	D_5
A	1	0	1	0	1
B	1	1	0	0	1
C	0	1	0	1	0

a Exhibit the documents retrieved by the following queries

(A OR B) AND C
(A AND B) OR C
A NOT B

b How many documents would you expect to retrieve using the following weighted Boolean queries for the sample collection?

$A_{0.33}$ OR $B_{0.66}$
$A_{0.33}$ AND $B_{0.66}$
$A_{0.33}$ NOT $B_{0.50}$

c Do any common documents appear in the responses to the three weighted Boolean queries of part b? Carefully explain your reasoning.

Natural Language Processing

0 PREVIEW

The documents and user queries under consideration in information retrieval are often available as natural language formulations. It is important therefore to be aware of the automatic methods currently used to process natural language texts. This chapter describes the state of the art in the automatic processing of natural language material with emphasis on applications in information retrieval.

The various levels of linguistic methods are examined first and the role of linguistic methods in information retrieval is described. This is followed by a general examination of modern language understanding systems. The components of language processing systems are then covered in detail with emphasis on the syntactic process which is of greatest interest in information retrieval. The main features of several grammatical models are described, including phrase structure grammars, transformational grammars, and augmented transition network grammars. This is followed by a discussion of applications of syntactic analysis in information retrieval.

The full scope of language understanding may not be needed in information retrieval. Language understanding is, however, an essential component in the design of question-answering systems. The chapter closes with a description of linguistic methods useful for question answering. The structure of knowledge representation systems is covered and the language processing component of certain well-known experimental question-answering systems is described to provide an example of the potential of the currently available automatic language processing techniques.

1 COMPONENTS OF NATURAL LANGUAGE SYSTEMS

A Interest in Natural Language Processing

This chapter is devoted to a study of the problems which arise when natural language data are processed by computers. In particular, the main approaches to natural language processing are covered, and an attempt is made to provide a state-of-the-art view of different efforts in this area.

One may want to question the wisdom of examining linguistic procedures in an information retrieval context, particularly when the material in the earlier chapters makes it clear that linguistic methods play only a minor role in retrieval at the present time. The fact is however that a large part of the information stored in bibliographic retrieval systems consists of natural language data, and that many users would prefer, given the choice, to approach a retrieval system by using natural language formulations of their information needs. Furthermore, even if the currently usable language processing techniques appear inadequate for full utilization under operational retrieval conditions, there is always the hope that new developments may render the linguistic techniques more attractive in the future.

Precisely what does one expect to gain in using linguistic approaches in the retrieval context? The most immediate aim is surely the possible use of free language formulations by retrieval system users, both for the submission of initial query statements and for the various interactive processes in which queries or documents are adjusted based on information obtained from the user population. The use of natural language search statements could raise the efficiency as well as the effectiveness of the retrieval operations by making possible the formulations of precise requests that correctly reflect user needs and by simplifying the user-system interactions.

A second application of natural language processing is the use of complex analysis techniques for the content representation of the input documents. Indeed, when the analysis system is confined to the use of single words for the content description of queries and documents, a user query dealing with "computational complexity" and indexed by the terms "compute" and "complex" is just as likely to cover extraneous topics such as "computation with complex numbers" as the actual subject area of interest. Of course, phrases can be automatically assigned to documents and search requests by using term co-occurrence statistics and word adjacency operators; but the statistical techniques are imperfect. In particular, they do not distinguish between cases such as "blind Venetian" and "Venetian blind." However, if accurate linguistic techniques were usable to combine single terms into meaningful larger units, then complete *structured index descriptions* might be generated consisting, for example, of noun-verb-noun combinations or of sentence units of even larger scope. Substantial improvements in text analysis and hence in retrieval should result.

Another important problem in retrieval is the construction of synonym dictionaries and thesauruses in which related words are grouped into affinity classes. Under current conditions thesauruses are constructed manually, or automatically by using word co-occurrence information. However, if linguistic descriptions were available to characterize the individual text units, a thesaurus class might be defined as the set of words occurring in similar contexts in the documents of a collection.

In addition to the free-language query submission and automatic indexing applications, a variety of extensions to the normal information retrieval process come easily to mind in which sophisticated language analysis techniques based on the use of deductive and contextual information obtainable from texts would play a major role. The following possibilities may be cited in this connection [1–5]:

1   Automatic question-answering systems might be designed where the system is expected to give explicit answers to incoming search requests (''What is the boiling point of water?'' Answer: 100 degrees Celsius), as opposed to merely furnishing bibliographic references expected to contain the answer.

2   Automatic abstracting systems could become practical where the document texts are automatically reduced to abstract-length excerpts that inform the reader about the content of the corresponding documents.

3   Foreign language documents could be treated automatically making it possible, for example, to extend the automatic indexing techniques to include documents originally available in languages other than English.

4   Sophisticated treatment of the full text of natural language documents could be considered as required, for example, for text analysis and text concordance generation.

Because of the difficulties that are inherent in a complete linguistic analysis of natural language texts, many of these problems are currently approached by creating a simplified situation—for example, by restricting the allowable discourse area to a narrow topic slice, or by imposing limitations on the variety of natural language forms that are actually handled by the system. These restrictions might be given up in the future, assuming sufficient gains in understanding the natural language phenomena.

B   Levels of Language Processing

It is customary to recognize several different levels of language processing. These may be characterized as the phonological, morphological, lexical, syntactic, semantic, and pragmatic levels.

The *phonological* level deals with the treatment of speech sounds as needed, for example, for the handling of speech understanding or speech generation systems. This level of linguistic processing is not of immediate interest in the retrieval context and is not discussed further in this volume.

The *morphological* level of linguistic processing is concerned with the processing of individual word forms and of recognizable portions of words. The recognition and removal of word suffixes and prefixes and the generation of word stems (used earlier to enhance search recall) are based on morphological knowledge.

The *lexical* level deals with the procedures operating on full words. In information retrieval this covers operations such as common word deletion, dictionary processing of individual words, and the replacement of words by thesaurus classes. In syntactic parsing applications where an attempt is made to obtain a structural description of a sentence, a preliminary lexical operation normally identifies a set of linguistic features (for example, noun, adjective, preposition, etc.) for each text word to be used later in the main syntactic analysis process.

The *syntactic* level is designed to group the words of a sentence into structural units such as prepositional phrases, and subject-verb-object groupings that collectively represent the grammatical structure of the sentence. A syntactic analysis is normally based on the surrounding structure in which the individual words are embedded in a sentence and on the use of syntactic features characterizing the individual words. Most currently available syntactic analysis systems are sufficiently advanced to permit the recognition of the principal structural characteristics of English text.

The *semantic* level adds contextual knowledge to the purely syntactic process in order to restructure the text into units that represent the actual meaning of a text. Thus a syntactic analysis for the utterance "John is easy to please" would designate "John" as the subject of the sentence, whereas the semantic process would designate "John" as the complement, as indicated by the semantic interpretation, "It is easy for someone (unnamed) to please John." A variety of such preestablished semantic characterizations of the terms are normally used to obtain satisfactory semantic interpretations.

Finally, the *pragmatic* level uses additional information about the social environment in which a given document exists, about the relationships that normally prevail in the world between various entities, and about the world-at-large to help in the text interpretation. For example, knowledge of the size of pigs and pens, respectively, and of the normal habitat of pigs permits an unambiguous interpretation of the sentence, "The pig is in the pen."

The morphological and lexical operations were examined in Chapter 3 as part of the automatic indexing operations. The principal interest in the present discussion is then confined to the syntactic, semantic, and pragmatic levels of linguistic processing.

In dealing with the various linguistic procedures, one must consider the degree to which the individual levels are easily recognized and independent of each other. Unhappily this question, like so many others in language processing, is controversial. All knowledgeable observers agree that automatic language processing raises complicated issues, that the use of the context in which individual words occur is essential for automatic text interpretation, and that syntax and semantics are related in that semantic knowledge is needed to avoid ambiguities in the syntax, whereas syntactic information helps in producing useful semantic output [6].

Unfortunately, beyond the general realization that the language analysis task is difficult, there is little agreement about how to handle the job. It is unclear which levels of language processing are most important and how the corresponding techniques are best applied. One school of thought points to the fact that human processes are highly integrated and concludes that a language analysis system must necessarily be based on the global use of many different approaches at each point in the process:

> Understanding is a completely integrated process; the idea of building modular systems (where, for example, the syntactic phase is isolated from the semantic) has hampered advances in parsing, because the full range of our knowledge should obviously be available to help disambiguate, find appropriate word senses, and just as importantly help us know what to ignore [7].

This viewpoint is supported by the fact that in some of the existing question-answering systems dealing with restricted topic areas, a sophisticated syntactic analysis system proves unnecessary, since the few semantic patterns accepted by these systems are completely understood and procedures to handle these patterns can be provided in advance.

Many other observers prefer the modular viewpoint of language analysis. This uses a large dictionary storing linguistic features for the words in the language, and a grammar designed to produce a rigorous analysis of the possible sentences in the language. A semantic analysis system is then added to transform the syntactic output into formalized units of meaning. Most people still feel that a syntactic analysis system is essential when unrestricted natural language input is processed [8]. Since the syntax alone can be helpful in certain retrieval tasks, whereas the semantic processing is not as yet well understood, a good deal of emphasis is placed on syntax in the present chapter.

C Language Understanding Systems

The earliest uses of computers for language processing date back to the 1950s when programs were written that could translate short excerpts of text from one language to another—often from Russian or German into English [9,10]. Substantial effort was invested in the construction of mechanized dictionaries useful for the translation of large unrestricted texts. But when these dictionaries were actually put to the test by using them on large samples of input, it turned out that the translation task became too difficult. New programs had to be written to take care of problems that had not been met in considering the earlier text samples, and the new modifications interfered with the earlier programs which were originally thought to be adequate. When it proved impossible to reach a steady-state condition after some 10 or 15 years of work, the machine translation work was generally given up in favor of more fundamental work in language analysis and understanding [11].

Thus small text samples were intensively studied in an attempt to determine all the information contained in or derivable from the sample, and systems were built that could automatically answer direct questions dealing with the specific and restricted topic areas covered by particular text samples. Unfortunately, the lessons learned earlier through the machine translation work had to be learned all over again: while it was comparatively simple to deal with 250-word text samples and 300-word dictionaries, the extensions to larger portions of the language were neither assured nor forthcoming even after substantial effort.

While the general understanding of how human beings analyze language has been increased by recent psychological experiments, it has not been possible so far to translate this understanding into automatic programs that can satisfactorily process large samples of unrestricted natural language texts [12].

The early approaches to language analysis tended to be word-oriented. Each word was assumed to represent one or more well-defined units of meaning, and when words were combined the available grammars more often than not produced a number of acceptable output analyses. For example, given standard dictionary entries for the words ''time'' and ''flies'' as

Time: singular noun or transitive verb
Flies: plural noun or transitive verb or intransitive verb

many standard grammatical analysis systems would produce at least two acceptable results for the sentence, ''Time flies'':

1 A declarative statement in which ''time'' is interpreted as a noun subject of the sentence and ''flies'' is the intransitive verb
2 An imperative sentence where ''time'' is interpreted as a transitive verb and ''flies'' is the plural noun complement

The first interpretation is of course the one normally assumed whereas the latter must be termed semantically improbable because flies are not the type of insects that are normally timed. For longer sentences, such as for example the well-known ''Time flies like an arrow,'' the number of acceptable syntactic outputs could be much larger than two.

Refinements were introduced into the early syntactic analysis systems in the form of transformations defined on the standard syntactic output. Thus given an accepted syntactic interpretation for the sentence ''John hit the ball'' another acceptable analysis would be produced for the passive form ''The ball was hit by John.'' Formally defined transformations could then account for equivalences between active and passive moods, and between declarative and the corresponding interrogative forms of a sentence.

Even though the complexity of the syntactic analysis systems grew rapidly, it became clear that many issues of syntactic "well-formed-ness" were not explainable by syntax alone, and that a sentence-by-sentence analysis based purely on syntax was not sufficient to analyze many texts. For example, it is not possible using simple syntactic considerations to explain the fact that the sentence "John and his sister went to Paris" is acceptable, whereas "John's sister and he went to Paris" is not.

Clearly some semantic features must be incorporated in the syntactic process before a sentence can finally be interpreted. For example, by recognizing semantic usages for ambiguous words such as "ball," and taking into account the context in which a given word occurs, it becomes possible to produce correct interpretations for sentences such as "He played with the ball" and "He went to the ball" [13].

One direct link between syntax and semantics is provided by the introduction of *case grammar* [14]. In case grammar a sentence is considered as a tense-less *proposition* consisting of a verb and related noun phrases and embedded sentences, plus a *modularity* specifying tense, mood, and aspect. By using a dictionary to store partial semantic characterizations, or *cases*, for each noun, and then classifying the verbs according to which cases could be related to them, one could then specify the permissible patterns in the language by using a finite set of relations between verbs and nouns (also known as *case frames*). Typical cases for nouns are agent (A), object (O), instrument (I), indirect object (D), and so on. Typical case frames for the word "write" could be

(A)—with (I)
(A)—(O)
(A)—to (D)
(A)— (O) to (D) with (I)

as in "The author writes with a pen," "The author writes a letter," "The author writes to his publisher," "The author writes a letter to his publisher with a pen." It was found experimentally that a relatively small number of case frames could account for a vast number of different sentences in the language. The case frames could also effectively constrain the accepted utterances to include meaningful sentences only.

In recent years, most of the interest in computational linguistics has been devoted to the integration of various linguistic approaches into complete language processing systems. A complete language processing system of the kind useful in information retrieval can then be viewed as a three-part structure [1]:

1 First a standardized, formal representation is constructed of the meaning of each sentence or unit of discourse; typically units of meaning are extracted for each component from a dictionary, and the components are then assembled into a formal sentence representation using the constraints imposed by the syntax.

2 This formally restricted input is then compared with a stored *knowledge base* in order to augment the initial descriptions and to identify additional relationships between entities.

3 Finally, a desired task is performed which uses the combined information provided by the available input augmented by the stored knowledge; for example, inference procedures may be used to derive and formulate answers to requests for information.

A feeling exists that knowledge may be organized around *conceptual entities* such as objects, relations, events, and scenes, with associated descriptions and procedures. Given such conceptual structures the reasoning process—for example, the process needed to generate answers in response to incoming queries—consists in a matching and recognition process. The objects and events provided at the input (for example, the incoming user queries) are compared against stored knowledge structures. Then special "reasoning strategies" including inferencing capabilities are used to derive a desired output. Many people feel that the information included in the stored knowledge structures should be clustered so that similar objects may appear in close proximity. In this way related elements can share common properties and the comparison and search process in the knowledge base may be simplified [15].

Beyond these general perceptions about knowledge representation, there is no agreement about what structures are actually needed and how they are to be represented in an operational system. One unsolved problem concerns the usefulness of representing knowledge by a small number of *primitive* concepts. If useful semantic primitives could be identified, the construction and manipulation of the knowledge base would be substantially simplified. All processes could then be reduced to the manipulation of only those primitive entities for which specific rules would be established.

In the so-called conceptual dependency model only six conceptual categories are recognized, including real world objects, real world actions, attributes of objects, attributes of actions, times, and locations. These categories are related in only 16 different ways [16]. In situations where the number of primitive concepts is small, the reasoning and inferencing processes are relatively simple. Since only a small number of entities are available in each category, the possible events that may occur can be established and stored in advance. For example, five "acts" are allowed in conceptual dependency describing physical actions that people can perform (termed "propel," "move," "ingest," "expel," and "grasp"). For each act, a small set of inferences is defined as true with varying degrees of certainty when the particular act occurs.

Many people, however, do not believe that it is possible or realistic to represent knowledge using semantic primitives. Instead it is suggested that human beings use a variety of redundant descriptions to represent each object, and that the particular description used in a given instance depends on circumstances. The holistic view of knowledge representation is based on a redundant characterization of each object consisting in part of comparisons with other objects. When enough comparisons with other objects are stored, a given entity is then assumed to be completely described. A table might, for example, be characterized in part by saying that it is more similar to a chair than to a lamp. As more information is obtained about an object, the new data are simply added to the existing descriptions.

Regardless of one's views about the primitive components in a knowledge base, it becomes necessary to make a choice about the structures actually used to represent knowledge and the types of knowledge to be represented by them. Two principal structural representations are described in the literature. The first is the semantic graph or *semantic net* [17]. Such a graph consists of nodes and of branches, or links connecting certain pairs of nodes. In a semantic graph the nodes are used to represent the main concepts of interest, including objects, events, assertions, actions, abstractions, and functions, as well as attributes and characteristics of objects. Links between nodes identify hierarchical and contextual relations between the concepts, as well as other special information relating to the concepts. The nodes of a particular semantic net might, for example, represent the individual members of a given family, and the links between pairs of nodes could identify the relationship between certain members of the family, such as husband-wife or father-son. Other nodes representing properties of certain persons, such as age, profession, or marital status, could be linked to the nodes representing the corresponding persons. The hierarchical arrangement of topic classes contained in a conventional library classification system represents a form of semantic net in which the relationships between concepts is restricted to hierarchical inclusion.

The other type of knowledge structure that is much discussed is variously known as a "frame," "script," or "schema" [6,18,19]. A frame is a complicated data structure, typically representing a complex object such as a living room, a birthday party, or a restaurant. In particular, the frame would include the collection of knowledge associated with the concept being represented, including both the information that is always true of a given environment—for example, the fact that a restaurant contains tables and chairs, and customers eating food—and also information that may be true only in particular instances —for example, that a certain person would be located in a certain restaurant. A frame may be viewed as an extended notion of *case*, in the sense that the frame circumscribes an area of discourse by defining a context within which certain things are allowed to happen.

A script is a frame that also contains the timing sequence in which events are expected to happen. Certain portions of the script could store events that might be expected to happen—for example, that after having eaten in a restaurant, the customer is expected to pay the bill. In addition prescriptions of what would happen if the expectations were not confirmed could also be stored—for example, the fact that a customer who refused to pay the bill would be asked by the restaurant owner to wash dishes.

Given a stored collection of frames or scripts, the process of understanding a new statement implies that the new information must fit with the collection of knowledge already stored. In particular, the interpretation of a sentence would depend on the contents of certain frames, and might also lead to the modification of certain frames in accordance with the new available knowledge. Since the frames specify sequences of events, a comparison of a particular event with the knowledge stored in the frames makes it possible to draw inferences. Thus, the inference might be that the customer who does not pay the bill at the restaurant forgot a wallet or lost it, or that it was stolen.

At the present time, the specific structure of a frame is not completely understood, and no established methods exist for searching collections of frames, updating the stored information, and drawing appropriate inferences. Nor is there any agreement about what stored knowledge base is actually needed and how this store should be represented. There is, however, agreement that a complete language processing system must be based not only on linguistic techniques (such as lexical analysis, parsing, and the application of semantic rules) but also on a large variety of stored knowledge about the particular topic and the situation being discussed. Further the generally available ''common sense'' know-how about time, events, states, actions, motivations, and beliefs must be available. A complete automatic language understanding system will not become practical until satisfactory solutions are provided for the construction and manipulation of the required knowledge structures.

Fortunately, a good deal can be accomplished in various applications areas, including information retrieval in particular, without totally mastering the language understanding problem. The remainder of this chapter is concerned with language processing methods that might actually be used in various practical situations.

2 LANGUAGE PROCESSING AND INFORMATION RETRIEVAL

Before describing the language processing methods to be used in information retrieval, it is important to point out that a variety of views have been expressed concerning the importance of linguistic methods in information retrieval. On the one hand, some individuals are convinced that to retrieve items ''about'' certain subjects, it is necessary to use all available facts pertaining to these items. This operation necessarily requires an analysis of meaning which is not substantially different in information retrieval from other areas of language understanding. In particular, a desirable indexing, or content analysis, approach would then consist of translating the document or query into some formal language consisting of concepts and relationships between the concepts. This introduces the notion of a semantic network and of translations from one language (the input) to another (the formalized index descriptions). Necessarily then, it is argued the full power of language processing tools is needed in information retrieval [20].

To support this view, one can point to the growing use of semantic tools in analyzing linguistic structures—semantic markers are increasingly included as entries in dictionaries and thesauruses, and relationship indicators specified in semantic nets are usable to form phrases and to disambiguate terms. Even when complete networks with semantic relationships are not available, some syntactic tools such as the previously mentioned case grammar utilize word identifiers (agent, object, instrument) that have semantic connotations.

The opposite view about the importance of language analysis in retrieval comes to very different conclusions. In particular, a good deal of evidence points to the importance and usefulness of statistical, probabilistic, or vector space techniques of the kind discussed in Chapters 3 and 4 for both indexing and classification. On the other hand, no comparable evidence now shows that linguistic methods are effective in retrieval. The reason may be that a fundamental difference exists between information retrieval on the one hand and certain other language processing tasks on the other. In retrieval one needs to render a document retrievable, rather than to convey the exact meaning of the text. Thus, two items dealing with the same subject matter but coming to different conclusions are treated identically in retrieval, that is, either they are both retrieved or they are both rejected. In a question-answering or language translation situation, these documents would of course be treated differently. This amounts to a qualitative difference between document retrieval on the one hand and question-answering or language translation systems on the other. For example, to answer a specific question about an apple it is helpful to have some detailed knowledge about apples. To retrieve documents about apples, it may be unnecessary to understand precisely what the concept of apple actually entails. Instead, it may be sufficient to detect rough similarities between documents and concepts—for example, it might be enough to know that an apple is more similar to a pear than to an elephant. The notion of vector matching and vector similarity computation was used extensively in the earlier chapters for classification and retrieval purposes.

This view of information retrieval rejects the notion that information retrieval is simply an early stage of more refined question answering [21]. Question answering makes it necessary to understand the topic area in order to permit the generation of inferences leading to specific answers. Information retrieval, on the other hand, simply provides references to the users designed to fill an information need. To quote from Sparck Jones:

> The whole idea of meaning representation is dubiously relevant to document retrieval in anything like its present form . . . one can get quite good (retrieval) results with simple terms and weights [22].

This is not to say that some well-established linguistic procedures could not lead to improvements in retrieval effectiveness. This idea is further explored in the next few sections.

3 SYNTACTIC ANALYSIS SYSTEMS

Among the many kinds of syntactic analysis systems, three stand out as especially important: the phrase structure grammars, which are believed to model

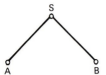

Figure 7-1 Rewrite rule S → A + B.

form. The simple rewrite rule (1) would appear in tree form as shown in Fig. 7-1. In the direct sentence generation system, the *derivation tree* for sentence 1 would then appear as shown in Fig. 7-2. On the other hand, when the grammar (4) is used to generate sentence 1, the derivation tree appears as in Fig. 7-3. The tree of Fig. 7-3 is more complicated than that of Fig. 7-2, but it tells something about the structure of the sentence. In particular, Fig. 7-3 exhibits the *constituent phrases* of the sentence—for example, the fact that "the" and "man" go together to form the noun phrase "the man." For this reason a tree of the type shown in Fig. 7-3 is known as a "phrase structure tree," or "phrase marker," and a grammar such as (4) is known as a "phrase structure grammar" [23–25].

A phrase structure grammar is used to exhibit the constituent phrases of the sentences. In the case of sentence 1 the constituent structure is represented as

((the man) (hit(the ball)))   (5)

which corresponds quite well to one's intuition about this sentence. That is, a segmentation such as

((the) (man hit the) (ball))

would be curious because the initial "the" is obviously associated with "man," etc. A good grammar should then produce a constituent structure which conforms to linguistic intuition.

A grammar such as that of expression (4) is known as a "context-free" phrase structure grammar because the nonterminal symbols of the left-hand side of the rewrite rules can be replaced by the right sides of the rules regardless of the context in which these symbols may appear. That is, no contextual restrictions apply to any rewrite rule.

Consider now the sentences.

19. john phoned mary
20. john phoned up mary
21. john phoned mary up

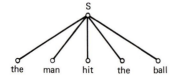

the   man   hit   the   ball   **Figure 7-2** Direct sentence generation.

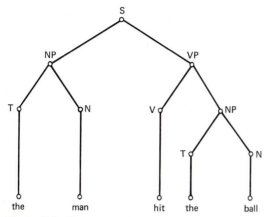

Figure 7-3 Phrase structure sentence generation.

The word "up" is dependent on "phoned," and "phoned up" intuitively is a constituent phrase. The first two sentences, 19 and 20, are easily handled by the context-free grammar:

$$
\begin{aligned}
S &\rightarrow NP + VP \\
NP &\rightarrow john \mid mary \\
VP &\rightarrow V + NP \\
V &\rightarrow phoned \mid phoned + up
\end{aligned}
$$

(6)

But to handle sentence 21, one needs additional rules such as

$$
\begin{aligned}
VP &\rightarrow V' + NP + PART \\
V' &\rightarrow phoned \\
PART &\rightarrow up
\end{aligned}
$$

(7)

Use of (7) produces the phrase marker of Fig. 7-4, corresponding to the consti-

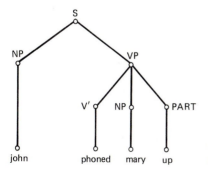

Figure 7-4 Phrase marker for "John phoned Mary up."

tuent structure (john(phoned mary up)). Intuitively "phoned mary up" is a constituent, but a context-free phrase structure grammar is unable to exhibit the phrase. This shows that context-free grammars do not reflect the full complexity of the language. In this case, they cannot handle *discontinuous constituents* such as "up" in "phoned up."

Another problem is due to the agreement expected in the number of subject and verb. Consider the following grammar:

$$
\begin{aligned}
S &\rightarrow NP + VP \\
NP &\rightarrow T + N \\
T &\rightarrow \text{the} \\
N &\rightarrow \text{man} \,|\, \text{men} \,|\, \text{ball} \,|\, \text{balls} \\
VP &\rightarrow V + NP \\
V &\rightarrow \text{have} \,|\, \text{has}
\end{aligned}
\tag{8}
$$

This generates sentences such as "the man has the ball" or "the men have the ball." Unfortunately, the grammar also generates "the man have the ball," "the men has the ball," and so on. This problem can be fixed by making distinctions between singular and plural noun phrases, labeled NP_s and NP_p, respectively, and between singular and plural verb phrases and verbs, denoted VP_s, V_s, VP_p, and V_p.

A new grammar can now be generated that will ensure agreement in number between subject and verb:

$$
\begin{aligned}
S &\rightarrow NP_s + VP_s \,|\, NP_p + VP_p \\
NP_s &\rightarrow T + N_s \\
T &\rightarrow \text{the} \\
N_s &\rightarrow \text{man} \,|\, \text{ball} \\
NP_p &\rightarrow T + N_p \\
N_p &\rightarrow \text{men} \,|\, \text{balls} \\
VP_s &\rightarrow V_s + NP_s \,|\, V_s + NP_p \\
V_s &\rightarrow \text{has} \\
VP_p &\rightarrow V_p + NP_s \,|\, V_p + NP_p \\
V_p &\rightarrow \text{have}
\end{aligned}
\tag{9}
$$

The new grammar (9) can now distinguish between the two trees of Fig. 7-5.

Problems such as the discontinuous constituents and the subject-verb agreement led to the development of more powerful grammars than simple phrase structure systems, including in particular the transformational grammars.

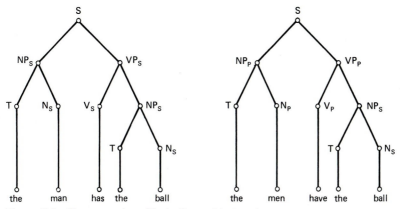

Figure 7-5 Phrase markers illustrating subject-verb agreement.

B Transformational Grammars

The basic innovation in the transformational grammars is the introduction of *context-sensitive* rewrite rules of the type

$$w \; A \; x \rightarrow w \; \gamma \; x \tag{10}$$

where A is a nonterminal variable of the grammar and γ is a string of terminal or nonterminal characters. The rule specifies that when the variable A appears in the context w and x (that is, is preceded by w and followed by x, where either w or x might be unspecified), then A can be replaced by the string γ.

A context-sensitive rewrite rule could be added to grammar (6) to generate sentence 21 as follows:

$$\text{phoned} + \text{up} + \text{NP} \rightarrow \text{phoned} + \text{NP} + \text{up} \tag{11}$$

leading to the following progression of transformations for the generation of sentence 21:

$$
\begin{aligned}
S &\rightarrow NP + VP \\
&\rightarrow john + VP \\
&\rightarrow john + V + NP \\
&\rightarrow john + phoned + up + NP \\
&\rightarrow john + phoned + NP + up \\
&\rightarrow john + phoned + mary + up
\end{aligned}
\tag{12}
$$

Subject-verb agreement can similarly be handled by introducing contextual symbols sing and pl, standing for singular and plural, and rewrite rules such as

$$N \rightarrow \underline{man} \,|\, \underline{ball}$$
$$V \rightarrow \underline{have}$$
$$\underline{sing} + \underline{have} \rightarrow has$$
$$\underline{pl} + \underline{have} \rightarrow have$$
$$\underline{man} + \underline{sing} \rightarrow man \qquad (13)$$
$$\underline{man} + \underline{pl} \rightarrow men$$
$$\underline{ball} + \underline{sing} \rightarrow ball$$
$$\underline{ball} + \underline{pl} \rightarrow balls$$

where the underline under <u>man</u>, <u>ball</u>, <u>have</u> indicates that these are nonterminal symbols covering varying forms of the corresponding terms.

A more convincing argument for the need for transformational grammars can perhaps be made by giving examples of related sentences that intuitively ought to be handled by a practical grammar:

22.   Chomsky proved the theorem
23.   the theorem was proved by Chomsky
24.   Chomsky did not prove the theorem
25.   did Chomsky prove the theorem?
26.   was the theorem proved by Chomsky?
27.   the theorem was not proved by Chomsky
28.   did not Chomsky prove the theorem?
29.   was not the theorem proved by Chomsky?

It is obvious that all these sentences can be generated from the first one by suitable sequences of transformations, including in particular active-passive, positive-negative, and declarative-interrogative transformations. A feature list for the eight sentences is shown in Table 7-1.

Assuming that sentence 22 can be generated by a rule such as

$$S \rightarrow NP_1 + V + ed + NP_2$$

where NP_1 and NP_2 denote specific instances of particular noun phrases, it is easy to devise context-sensitive transformation rules that will generate the transformed sentences:

Active-passive:
$$NP_1 + V + ed + NP_2 \rightarrow NP_2 + was + V + ed + by + NP_1$$
Positive-negative:
$$NP_1 + V + ed + NP_2 \rightarrow NP_1 + did \; not + V + NP_2$$
Declarative-interrogative:
$$NP_1 + V + ed + NP_2 \rightarrow did + NP_1 + V + NP_2$$

Table 7-1 Feature List for Sentences 22 to 29

Active	Positive	Declarative	Sentence number
√	√	√	22
x	√	√	23
√	x	√	24
√	√	x	25
x	√	x	26
x	x	√	27
√	x	x	28
x	x	x	29

The remaining rules, such as passive-interrogative or negative-interrogative, are equally simple to generate.

The language analysis, or *recognition* process, using a phrase structure grammar is straightforward since it consists in a sequential application of the rewrite rules to the initial sentence symbol (S), and terminates when the complete sentence of terminal symbols has been generated and no nonterminals remain.

The recognition process using a transformational grammar is more complex. A transformational grammar may be separated into two parts. The first is known as the *base component* of the grammar that generates the so-called deep structure of a sentence reflecting the actual syntactic and semantic interpretation of the input. Second, there is the *transformational component* that operates on the output of the base component and generates the *surface structure* of the sentence reflecting the actual phonetic representation. The sentence *generation* process using a transformational grammar is outlined in Fig. 7-6. Sentences that are semantically identical but structurally different will exhibit the same deep structure but different surface structures [26].

To utilize a transformational grammar for the analysis of natural language input, it is necessary to reverse the process of Fig. 7-6 as follows:

1 A standard parsing system is used first to obtain one or more trees exhibiting the *surface* structure of the input.
2 *Reverse* transformations must then be applied to the surface structures to obtain the underlying *deep* structure.

This process must be repeated for each initial surface tree and for all alternative intermediary trees obtained when more than one reverse transformation applies.

Unfortunately, while the number of transformations that produce a surface structure from the underlying deep structure is normally small, this is not true when the process is reversed. Experience indicates that the reverse process ex-

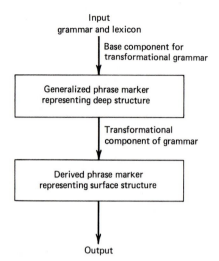

Input
grammar and lexicon

Base component for
transformational grammar

Generalized phrase marker
representing deep structure

Transformational
component of grammar

Derived phrase marker
representing surface structure

Output

Figure 7-6 Sentence generation using transformational grammar.

plodes except when the number of generated surface trees is very small or when enough information is provided for each node in the surface trees to select only those inverse transformations that are likely to lead to correct deep structures. There is some hope that for sufficiently restricted topic areas appropriate statements of surface structure/deep structure relations might be generated so as to render a transformational analysis useful in practice [8,27].

**C Augmented Transition Network Grammars

The augmented transition network (ATN) grammars offer all the facilities inherent in transformational grammars. In addition their structure is sufficiently simple to render a practical application reasonable. As a result, ATN grammars have been chosen for incorporation into most practical language processing systems [28–30].

Several grammatical systems including the ATN operations are based on the notion of a *finite state machine* represented as a graph. A finite state graph consists of *nodes* and *branches* between certain pairs of nodes. Each node symbolizes a state of the machine, and the branches represent transitions from one state to another. A transition from state A to state B takes place when the symbol attached to branch AB occurs at the input.

Consider as an example the simple finite state graph of Fig. 7-7. The start is assumed to be in state S. If the next input symbol is "a," a transition is made from S to state Q_1. If the initial input symbol is not "a," the recognition process fails because no other path is provided for leaving state S. Assuming that the first symbol is in fact an "a," two possibilities are open in state Q_1: either the next input symbol is a "b," in which case the machine stays in state Q_1, or the recognition process ends at the pop exit. The pop marker does not represent a new state but simply designates a compulsory exit from the graph. When the pop is reached after the last input symbol has been read, the input is *ac-*

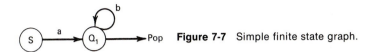

Figure 7-7 Simple finite state graph.

cepted, that is, a correct analysis has been obtained. It is clear from the graph of Fig. 7-7 that the only sentences actually accepted are of the form abbb . . . b, also written ab^n for some value of $n \geq 0$.

Machines such as that of Fig. 7-7 are not capable of accepting all context-free languages. Suppose, however, that a collection of graphs were available and that it were possible to jump from one graph to another by labeling certain branches with the start state of some graph. An example of such a network is given in Fig. 7-8. It may be seen that once arrived in state Q_1, the current status can be saved and the graph can be started again at state S. A *push-down store*, or *stack*, is used to store the current status before proceeding back to the beginning state. A stack uses a last-in first-out discipline, very much like the usual stack of plates in a cafeteria line. That is, only the top item is accessible (the one last placed onto the stack). In the example of Fig. 7-8, the branch in state Q_1 is labeled push S to indicate that the current state (Q_1) is "pushed" onto the stack before going back to state S, unless a "b" is recognized at the input, in which case the alternative transition to state Q_2 would be made without going back to S.

When the pop symbol is reached and the stack is empty, the input is accepted. If the stack is not empty when a pop is reached, the top symbol is read from the stack and a return is made to the state from which the original push occurred. It can be verified that the graph of Fig. 7-8 accepts the input sentence $a^n b^n$ for $n > 0$, that is, a string of a's followed by a string of the exact same number of b's. Such a sentence is context-free.

Consider as an example the input aabb. The details of the analysis are presented in Table 7-2. The first "a" is recognized, causing a transition from S to Q_1. Before returning to S to accept the second "a," the current state (Q_1) is stored in the stack. When the second "a" is read from the input, a second transition occurs from S to Q_1. When the first "b" is read, a transition is made to Q_2 from where the pop exit is reached. Since the stack is not empty, the stack contents reveal that a return to state Q_1 is in order which now makes possible the acceptance of the final "b" symbol.

In practical transition networks, there may be ambiguity in the node labels. That is, from a given state several possible transitions to other states may be possible. Then it is wise to arrange the possible paths according to the probability that a given path will lead to a correct acceptance of the input. The most

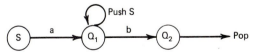

Figure 7-8   Finite state graph recognizing context-free languages.

**Table 7-3   Recognition Process of "The Tall Man in the Stetson Is John Wayne"
Using Grammar of Fig. 7-10**

Current state		Input string remaining to be recognized	Stack contents
1	S	the tall man in the Stetson is John Wayne	—
2	NP	the tall man in the Stetson is John Wayne	S(NP)
3	Q_6	tall man in the Stetson is John Wayne	S(NP)
4	Q_6	man in the Stetson is John Wayne	S(NP)
5	Q_7	in the Stetson is John Wayne	S(NP)
6	PP	in the Stetson is John Wayne	S(NP)Q_7(PP)
7	Q_9	the Stetson is John Wayne	S(NP)Q_7(PP)
8	NP	the Stetson is John Wayne	S(NP)Q_7(PP)Q_9(NP)
9	Q_6	Stetson is John Wayne	S(NP)Q_7(PP)Q_9(NP)
10	Q_8	is John Wayne	S(NP)Q_7(PP)Q_9(NP)
11	Pop	is John Wayne	S(NP)Q_7(PP)Q_9(NP)
12	Q_{10}	is John Wayne	S(NP)Q_7(PP)
13	Pop	is John Wayne	S(NP)Q_7(PP)
14	Pop	is John Wayne	S(NP)
15	Q_1	is John Wayne	—
16	Q_4	John Wayne	—
17	NP	John Wayne	Q_4(NP)
18	Q_8	Wayne	Q_4(NP)
19	Q_8	—	Q_4(NP)
20	Pop	—	—
21	Q_5	—	—
22	Pop	Accept	—

input word is recognized (that is, when a transition is completed) an appropriate terminal node of the tree is created. When a pop is reached, the currently active subtree is attached to the node representing the next higher level subtree to which the process now returns. The tree building process for the sample sentence of Table 7-3 is illustrated in detail in Fig. 7-11.

The problems previously mentioned for the standard context-free phrase structure grammars are of course still present with transition networks of the type illustrated in Fig. 7-10. In particular the grammar could equally well accept the sentence "the tall man in the Stetson are John Wayne." This kind of problem can be taken care of by a larger grammar of the same type which distinguishes plural noun phrases (P.NP) from singular noun phrases (S.NP), plural verbs (P.V) from singular verbs (S.V), and so on. This solution produces an unwieldy grammar and requires a great deal of backtracking.

The solution is to use an *augmented* transition network grammar which adds to the basic apparatus a set of *storage registers*, tests on the content of the storage registers, and *actions* consisting either of storage register settings or of structure building operations that change the structure of the output tree. The storage registers are used principally to store information about the number or type of a noun or the tense of a verb. For example, when analyzing "the tall

Figure 7-11 (*opposite*)   Tree building process for sample sentence of Table 7-3.

Line number in Table 7-3	Line number in Table 7-3

1

S

2

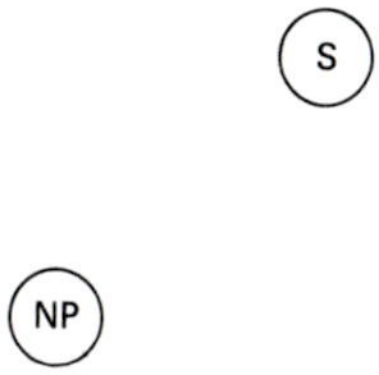

S

NP

3

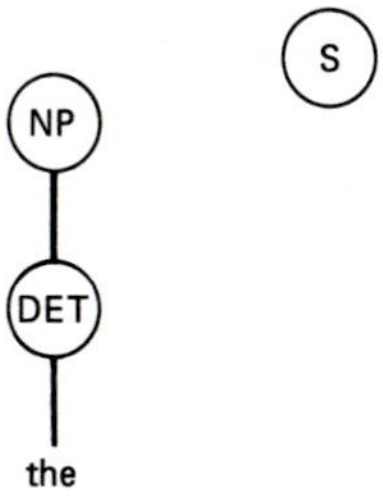

S

NP

DET

the

4

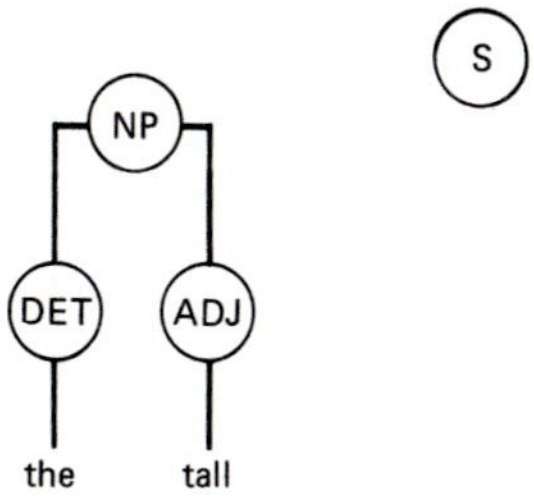

S

NP

DET ADJ

the tall

5

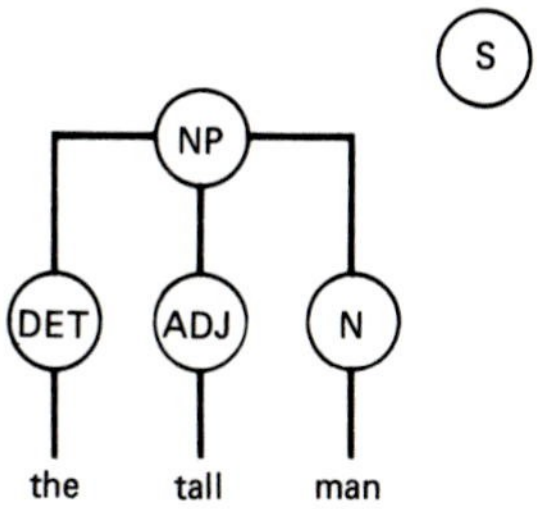

S

NP

DET ADJ N

the tall man

6

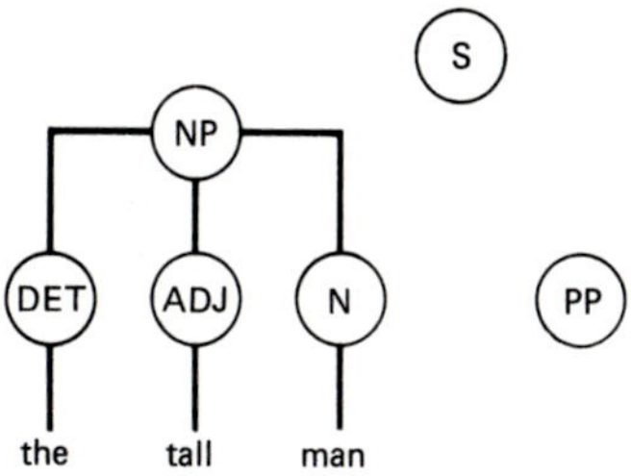

S

NP

DET ADJ N

the tall man

PP

7

S

NP

DET ADJ N

the tall man

PP

PREP

in

8

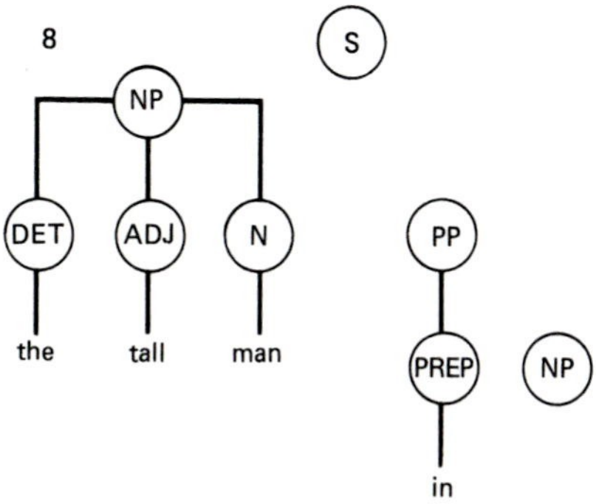

S

NP

DET ADJ N

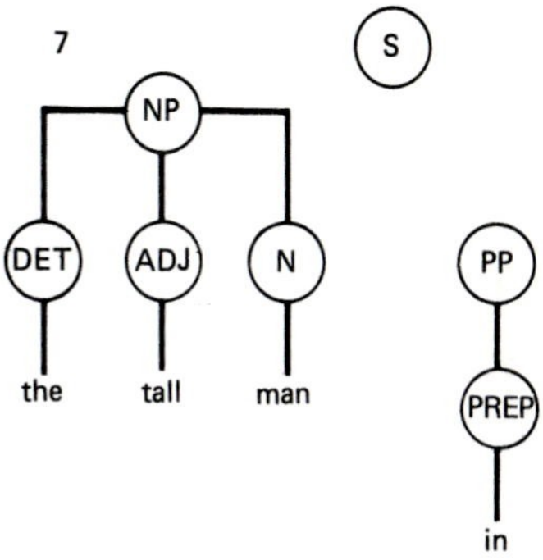

the tall man

PP

PREP NP

in

(*Continued*)

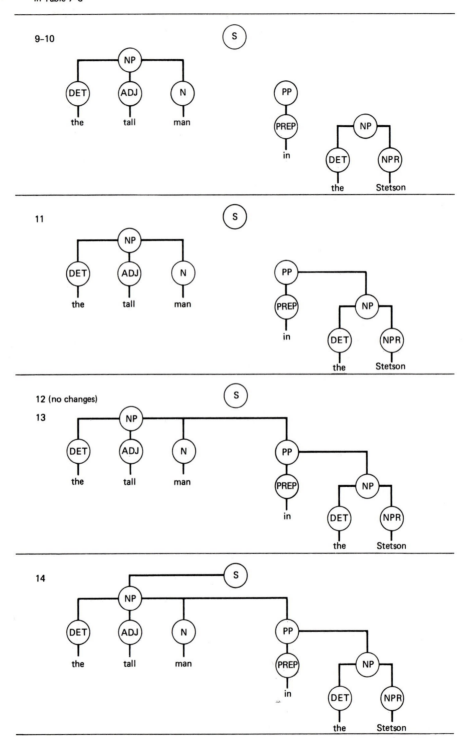

15 nothing changes
16

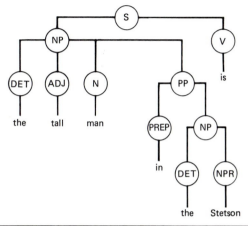

19

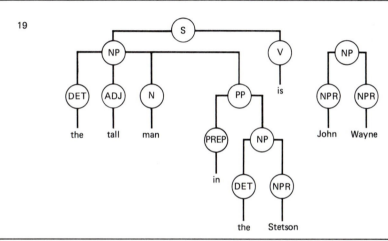

20 final tree

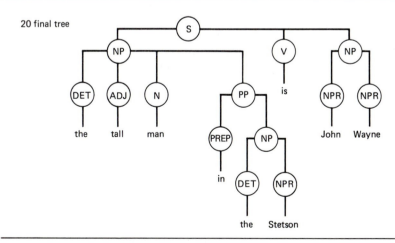

man," a "singular" identifier is stored in a register to specify the number of "man." Later on when the verb is analyzed, a test is performed prior to making the corresponding transition on the graph to ensure that the number of the verb currently being processed is the same as the number of the noun previously stored away in the register. The result is that the fragment "is John Wayne" would be accepted whereas "are John Wayne" would be rejected.

The structure building operations may be quite complex as required, for example, to rearrange a phrase structure tree following the analysis of a passive sentence. Alternative grammatical analysis systems have been suggested including some that scan a sentence in right-to-left instead of left-to-right order, some based on simultaneously following several analysis paths instead of backtracking when an ambiguity is detected, and some where the input is scanned many times instead of only once. Many people feel that ATN grammars are simpler to deal with operationally than other syntactic formalisms. Several of the question-answering systems mentioned later in this chapter use ATN grammars to handle the syntactic analysis part.

4 SYNTACTIC ANALYSIS IN INFORMATION RETRIEVAL

Syntactic analysis methods can be used in standard bibliographic retrieval systems in two main ways: on the one hand, a syntactic identification may enhance the indexing operation by making possible the assignment to the documents and queries of syntactically correct phrases replacing the single terms that are normally used. On the other hand, it may be possible by using syntactic approaches to obtain a more detailed view of the document contents, leading to directed retrieval activities that would take into account individual document portions such as sentences and paragraphs.

The latter possibility has led to the so-called passage retrieval, where attempts are made to retrieve individual passages or sentences of documents rather than complete documents only [31–33]. Passage retrieval is based on the analysis of the full text of documents, the aim being to retrieve either *answer reporting* passages, that is, passages from which an answer to a question can effectively be inferred, or alternatively *answer indicative* passages which indicate that the same document also contains an answer reporting passage. Passage retrieval may be advantageous because answers to questions could be immediately available instead of merely references to answers.

The basic idea in passage retrieval is the construction of detailed queries followed by the retrieval of all passages that contain all aspects of the query. A syntactic analysis system might be used to control the detailed comparison between queries and document passages. In addition, a thesaurus that expands the original query by including synonyms and other related words is also needed.

Connected passages might also be retrieved by choosing appropriate answer reporting, or answer indicative passages, and then adding follow-up sentences starting with connecting terms, such as "however," "these," or "on the other hand." The follow-up sentences should also exhibit additional matches with the query. In tests performed with experimental collections, the passage retrieval technique produced fairly high recall results exceeding 60 percent in many cases [31–32].

A possibly more immediate use of syntactic techniques in information retrieval is provided by its application to the indexing task, and particularly to the choice of noun phrases or prepositional phrases for indexing purposes. One possibility consists in using a simplified syntactic analysis that assigns one or more syntactic markers to each text word, and defining an indexing phrase as consisting of sets of contiguous words representing a specified sequence of syntactic markers [34–37].

One particular technique for the detection of indexing phrases uses the following basic indexing procedure [34–35]:

1 A *recognition* dictionary is used to assign *one* of 16 possible syntactic categories to each word (one particular category identifies the corresponding word as a "throw-away" word to be disregarded).

2 A *format* dictionary stores a total of 77 permissible syntactic formats for the phrases to be assigned to the text; these formats range in complexity from a single noun (N) to a sequence of five nouns (ZZZZZ) none of which is sufficiently meaningful to be permitted to stand alone.

3 The indexing cycle consists in accumulating sequences of non-throwaway words of up to five words from the input, the length of a sequence being determined by the occurrence of delimiters such as punctuation signs. The syntactic markers corresponding to the input words are obtained from the recognition dictionary, and the format dictionary is used to determine whether the input sequence of markers corresponds to one of the permissible formats in the dictionary. If so, the corresponding phrase is accepted as an indexing phrase. If no match occurs with one of the stored formats, the candidate phrase is shortened by deletion of one word and the operation is repeated.

In tests comparing this simple automatic indexing process against a conventional manual indexing method, slightly lower recall but slightly higher precision were obtained for the machine process compared with the manual methodology, indicating again that conceptually quite simple automatic methods can be competitive with the conventional manual procedures [36].

An alternative method of generating indexing phrases consists, of course, in performing a full syntactic analysis of a text, or text excerpt such as an abstract, and in assigning those phrases as index terms whose components exhibit specified syntactic relations between them [38]. Such a process was used in an early implementation of the SMART system in the hope of avoiding ambiguities of the "Venetian blind" versus "blind Venetian" type.

In the SMART system, a dictionary of *criterion trees* was used to record the allowable syntactic patterns between phrase components. A criterion tree is a structure including term specifications, syntactic indicators, and syntactic relations obtaining between certain terms. A typical criterion phrase specifica-

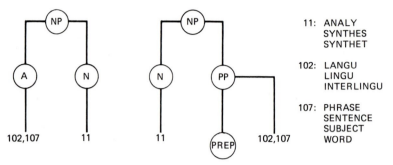

Figure 7-12 Sample criterion phrase specification.

tion is shown in Fig. 7-12. The example of Fig. 7-12 exhibits the syntactic relations which are specified between the word classes. Each word class is given a numeric code (11, 102, and 107 in the example), and a dictionary is used to substitute one or more actual words or word stems for each class. The left-hand tree of Fig. 7-12 covers phrases such as language analysis, linguistic analysis, and interlingual synthesis. The right-hand tree represents analysis of words, synthesis of language, analysis for sentences, etc.

The flexibility of the criterion tree process stems from three main characteristics:

1 Word stems rather than individual words are used in the dictionary as class entries; a single word stem represents many words.
2 Class numbers, rather than words or word stems are attached to the nodes of the syntactic trees.
3 A variety of syntactic connection patterns is provided between the word classes.

As a result, a small criterion tree dictionary can account for a large number of potential indexing phrases.

When the criterion tree dictionary is used for indexing purposes, the index terms and phrases are generated using the normal indexing process. A context-free phrase structure grammar is then used to determine the syntactic structure of the indexing phrases. Finally, a check of the preconstructed criterion tree dictionary reveals whether the actual syntactic pattern in the phrases matches an entry in the tree dictionary. If so a phrase is accepted; otherwise it is rejected.

The existing experimental evidence unfortunately shows that the criterion tree dictionary does not operate as well as expected [39]. In fact, the statistical phrase construction methods described in Chapters 3 and 4 would normally outperform the syntactic phrase procedures. Since the syntactic processing is expensive to perform, there is obviously no point in going that route unless substantial improvements in recall and precision are obtainable. The disappointing results of the early tests may be due to two principal causes:

    1 A phrase structure grammar was used to perform the syntactic analysis, rather than a more sophisticated transformational or ATN grammar; it is conceivable that a more refined syntactic process could provide more accurate retrieval results.

    2 The syntactic restrictions imposed on the indexing phrases are often very confining, with the result that satisfactory phrases are rejected because the components do not obey the preestablished restrictions.

An example may be used to illustrate the second argument. The loosest kind of syntactic connection between two or more phrase components is a requirement to have the components appear in a common subtree of the syntactic phrase marker. Unfortunately, even such a loosely formulated syntactic restriction will cause the rejection of some phrases that appear essential for content identification. Consider a sentence such as "Experts in *linguistics* may study sentence generation and *analysis*." Most syntactic analysis systems would not place the terms "linguistics" and "analysis" into a common subtree, and hence the phrase "linguistic analysis" would not be assigned to a document containing that sentence, even though no other phrase would appear to be more pertinent.

    The conclusion is that the role of linguistic methodologies in general and of syntactic analysis in particular is still unresolved for information retrieval. Before reaching a final conclusion in this area, it is wise to wait for the appearance of more sophisticated language analysis methods that are at the same time sufficiently efficient to permit incorporation into operational retrieval frameworks. Such methods should then be thoroughly evaluated to determine their actual value in information retrieval.

5 LINGUISTIC METHODS IN QUESTION ANSWERING

**A Knowledge Representation

While some question exists about the usefulness of language processing in information retrieval, most experts feel that the linguistic methodology cannot be bypassed in question-answering systems. It is not possible in the present context to examine in detail the components and structure of modern question-answering systems. A brief look at some of the more notable features must suffice.

    Consider first the problem of knowledge representation. It was seen earlier that stored knowledge structures are needed in many language processing systems. They are required both for the representation of knowledge in the topic area under discussion and also to supply "common sense" knowledge that is normally available to human beings.

    Before examining the various types of knowledge structures, it may be useful to look briefly at some of the characteristics of question-answering systems. Such systems may be considered to be extensions of the normal data base management and document retrieval systems in the following sense:

1   The data records used as a basis for question answering may in principle be more general and of greater scope than those common in business processing or in bibliographic retrieval. In any case, they are not normally restricted to the simple tabular format common in data base systems, or to the processing of bibliographic records alone.

2   The queries allowed in question answering are also more general than those common in data base systems or in document retrieval. In data base systems the normal query specifies the values of certain attributes attached to the records—for example, a request for personnel records could refer to items whose profession equals engineer, whose age is 33, with length of service exceeding 10 years. In document retrieval, queries consist of keyword identifiers possibly interconnected by Boolean operators. In question-answering systems, on the other hand, a greater variety of queries may be allowed. For ease of interaction one would also like to allow natural language queries, and furnish natural language answers.

3   External knowledge intrudes because the answering process in a question-answering system depends on a knowledge of the social context and on the prevailing conversational framework in addition to the normally required subject knowledge. In particular, the problem of determining the *focus* of a query plays a role in general question answering, when it does not normally in data base management or in document retrieval. That is, in question answering it becomes necessary to decide why users are asking a question in addition to ascertaining what they want to know before formulating an answer. (A user who asks, "Why did you fly to Stockholm?" does not want a reply stating "because it was too far to walk," even though such an answer might be formally correct.)

The knowledge structures needed to cope with this expanded environment normally take the form of *semantic nets*. These consist of *nodes* to represent the concepts, events, characteristics, and values of interest in a system, as well as *branches* specifying the relationships between nodes. The branches may be labeled with "case" labels, such as agent, object, instrument, source, or destination, to simplify the interpretation of the graph [40–45]. A typical semantic network representing the operation of bolting two objects together using nuts and bolts is shown in Fig. 7-13. The branches of Fig. 7-13 designate timing information as well as whole-part and subset-superset relationships.

A wide variety of semantic nets has been introduced in the literature. Two main types may be distinguished, the *logical* networks and the *conceptual* networks. In the logical network, the graph is interpreted as a logical statement about properties holding for various entities. The basic primitives in a logical network are *predicates* defined for the entities under discussion. A predicate is a logical function of one or more variables producing a truth value (true or false) when the variables are replaced by appropriate actions, objects, instruments, and so on.

Typical predicates defined for a given area of study could be "is a member of," "is the father of," "is a prime number." When the variable *slots* in a predicate are filled with appropriate entities, a predicate becomes a *proposition*,

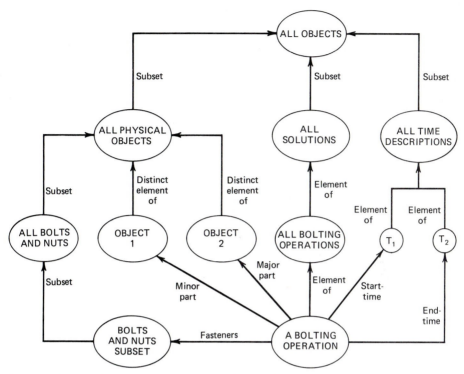

Figure 7-13 Sample semantic network (describing a bolting operation using nuts and bolts to connect two objects). (*Adapted from reference 46.*)

that is, a statement with a truth value. Typical propositions involving the predicates introduced earlier are "John is the father of Mary," "17 is a prime number," "x is a member of class y." Figure 7-14 illustrates the logical net representation of a sample proposition.

Two or more distinct propositions can be combined into a compound proposition using logical relationships, such as the Boolean connectives AND, OR, NOT. Thus, given two propositions such as "x is a member of y" and "y is a member of z," a new proposition would be stated as "x is a member of y AND y is a member of z." More generally, using a logical model, a semantic network can be provided with a precise semantic interpretation, and with the inference rules and procedural steps necessary to construct answers in response to certain questions. In other words, since the components of the logical net include all the apparatus of the *predicate calculus*, the question-answering process effectively becomes a theorem-proving task guided by precise logical rules.

Consider a query such as "is x a member of z?" Given the stored propositions, "x is a member of y" and "y is a member of z," the compound proposition "x is a member of y AND y is a member of z" is generated. From this the formal inference rules may be usable to derive a new proposition "x is a member of z" which can then be used to answer the question affirmatively.

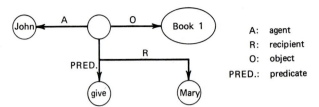

Figure 7-14 Typical representation of a proposition as a logical network, "Agent (John) gives object (book 1) to recipient (Mary)." (*From reference 47.*)

It is clear that given a proper choice of predicates and logical characteristics describing the data, a wide variety of different kinds of information can be represented. For example, normal index terms, values of attributes, as well as hierarchical and other relationships between entities may be represented. A logical network could then serve as a specification of the semantic and/or syntactic characteristics of many types of records, including commercial files, document collections, and other kinds of artifacts.

However, for some purposes the logical framework may be somewhat confining for the representation of general knowledge. It may then be convenient to allow for more general *conceptual networks*, where once again the nodes represent the basic concepts and entities of interest. The relationships between concepts represented by the branches are then essentially open-ended. A variety of relationships represented by portions of conceptual semantic nets are presented in Fig. 7-15.

In one formalism, the following components are recognized [45]:

1 *Concepts* that are considered as the essential constants or parameters of the world
2 *Events* that represent the actions which occur in the topic area under consideration
3 *Characteristics* that are used to modify concepts, events, or other characteristics
4 *Values* that represent the attributes attached to individual records such as a particular weight of a person or an address of an individual

In many semantic networks a distinction is made between *generic* concepts that represent abstractions or classes of events, from particular instances of events. A generic statement such as "physical objects carry a weight" would then be treated differently than a specific instance such as "Joe Smith weighs 150 pounds."

Among the operations that must be defined for semantic nets are the basic *search* functions that relate individual instances to characterizations on the generic level. *Node-creating* operations can add information to a network. *Network transformation* rules alter the network in accordance with newly available information, or combine individual events, concepts, and characteristics into sequences of events, or *scenarios*. The network transformations and exten-

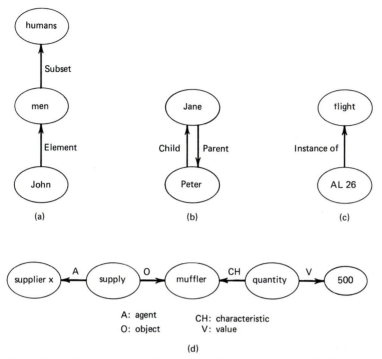

Figure 7-15 Typical relationships included in semantic nets. (a) "John is a member of the human species." (b) "Peter is the son of Jane." (c) "AL 26 is a flight." (d) "Supplier × supplies 500 mufflers."

sions may then serve a role in content representation similar to that previously mentioned for frames, scripts, or schemes.

The basic problem with the current perceptions of knowledge representation is that they lack *uniformity*. In other words, no *accepted* theory of knowledge representation exists. Many of the structures appear to be produced by ad hoc definitions. Rules used to manipulate the structures are sometimes uncertain and inadequately motivated. The structures are thus hard to extend to new discourse areas or to altered processing environments. Since an adequate theory of knowledge representation is essential for question-answering purposes, it is not surprising that the question-answering problem still lacks a general solution.

B Question-Answering Environment

From what has already been said it should be clear that a number of quite sophisticated processing steps are required in order to produce direct answers to questions. At the least, it is necessary to thoroughly comprehend the subject area under discussion. In addition the context surrounding the question-answering interplay must be understood. Finally, a complete language analysis system capable of transforming user-formulated queries into answers to questions must be available.

Most existing question-answering systems perform tasks of substantial sophistication in a restricted semantic environment. Typically, a microworld is chosen in which only a small number of entities and a small number of relations are recognized. This automatically implies that the dictionaries which specify the syntactic and semantic properties of the concepts are of limited size, and that the syntactic and semantic patterns that occur (or that are allowed to occur) are also restricted to those of a well-defined domain of discourse. Alternatively, a larger area of discourse may be tolerated, or the dependence of the syntactic and semantic systems on the discourse area may be less rigid, provided that the resulting ambiguities can be resolved externally, possibly by interaction with the user during the course of the question-answering process [48].

In many systems the more difficult problems in language analysis are disregarded. The system may not, for example, include methods for the interpretation of conjunctions (and, or, but, etc.), the proper resolution of quantification (all, every, each, some, etc.), the handling of anaphoric expressions (where pronouns are used to refer to antecedents in the text that may be ambiguous), the processing of ellipses (where parts of the text are omitted because the intended meaning is clear from the context), and the interpretation of polysemantic words, such as "base," whose meaning must be clarified by the context.

Typically, a special-purpose environment is chosen where many of the aforementioned difficulties can be bypassed. Examples are the use of special kinds of texts such as pathology data and medical diagnostic summaries [49–52] or of formatted data structures such as occur in data base management [53–59]. In either case, the conversion of an information request into a formalized statement of user needs may be simpler to carry out than in totally unrestricted question-answering environments.

The language analysis features incorporated into some existing question-answering systems are described in the remainder of this chapter.

*C Linguistic Features in Question Answering

One of the earliest operational question-answering systems was LSNLIS, designed to answer questions about chemicals and rock samples brought back from the moon by the astronauts [53–54]. Like other existing question-answering systems, the LSNLIS system is characterized by a discrete knowledge area and by circumscribed user interests. The system is modular in that the syntactic component is separated from the semantic interpretation, and that in turn is distinct from the data base retrieval component, as seen in Fig. 7-16.

The user queries are first subjected to a standard syntactic analysis using an ATN grammar. The semantic rules are tightly bound to the subject matter and are designed to produce formal representations of the meaning of the queries. These formal representations are then compared with the stored data

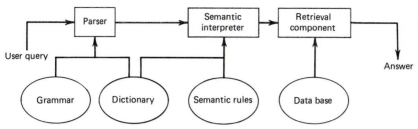

Figure 7-16 Basic operations of the LSNLIS system.

base consisting of information about the composition of the various rock samples found on the moon, the amount of material found of each type of mineral, the location where each sample was found, and so on. Eventually, appropriate answers are extracted from the data base.

The semantic interpretation rules constitute possibly the most interesting part of the system. Two types of information are used as input, consisting first of portions of the syntactic phrase markers produced by the syntactic analysis, and second of certain semantic features attached to the terminal nodes of the syntactic trees (that is, semantic classification data for some of the words in the query texts).

Consider, as an example, the semantic interpretation rule "author of" presented in detail in Fig. 7-17. The input consists of two syntax tree excerpts identified, respectively, as S:NP-V and S:V-NP, representing the usual subject-

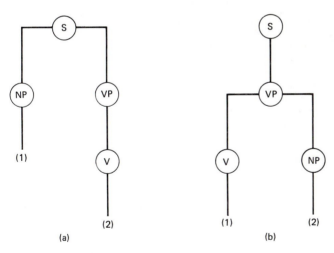

(S:NP-V ((1) PERSON))
AND (S:V-NP ((2) DOCUMENT) ((1) EQU WRITE))
THEN (1) NP-V AUTHOR OF (2) V-NP

(c)

Figure 7-17 Semantic interpretation in the LSNLIS system. (a) Subject-verb tree—S:NP-V. (b) Verb-object tree—S:V-NP. (c) Semantic rule "author of."

verb and verb-object components. Assuming that the dictionary processing reveals that the word attached to node (1) of the subject-verb tree is a member of the class of "persons," that is, an animate human being, while nodes (1) and (2) of the verb-object tree correspond, respectively, to some form of the word "write" and to a member of the class of "documents," the conclusion is that node (1) of the NP-V tree is the "author of" node (2) of the V-NP tree. The rule of Fig. 7-17 then makes it possible to answer questions such as "who wrote document x?" or "list the authors writing documents that concern rock samples."

Many of the existing question-answering systems are based on an organization similar to LSNLIS in the sense that the syntactic information produced by an ATN analysis is used with semantic information attached to the nodes of the syntactic tree (for example, information about the "cases" of the concepts attached to certain nodes) to derive the semantic interpretations of the user queries. When the queries to be handled by the system are tightly circumscribed and the discourse area is well defined, the number of different syntax trees and the variety of the needed semantic interpretation rules often proves sufficiently small to permit the construction of practical question-answering systems.

Because of the restricted discourse areas, many of the semantic ambiguities arising in the language-at-large are effectively eliminated in the practical question-answering environment. Thus the word "sample" in the LSNLIS context may safely be assumed to refer to a lunar sample without further analysis. Nevertheless, a substantial amount of effort can be spent to adapt the question-answering environment to the sometimes sloppy habits of the users. Thus, some systems include routines for spelling correction, ellipsis substitution, and the resolution of pronoun reference [55–57]. Ellipsis in the question-answering context normally implies that the user proposes a series of questions without repeating all components. The user might state: "identify all samples in which glass was found"-- "what about chromite?" and the system would interpret the second part as "identify all samples in which chromite was found." Pronoun reference is normally resolved by looking for a likely referent in the preceding context. Thus "identify the composition of all samples containing glass—list *their* identification numbers" would be interpreted as "list the identification numbers of all samples containing glass."

A substantial amount of work has also gone into the perfection of the dialogue between system and user during the question-answering process. In some systems a clarifying dialogue is in fact initiated with the user when an ambiguity arises. The hope is that the user will resolve the ambiguity by letting the system know which of several alternatives may be correct. The same strategy can be used to get the user to certify the correctness of a final interpretation of the query by the system. If the user returns a "yes," the system proceeds to the retrieval phase; a "no," on the other hand, would mean that the user's interest was misinterpreted. The user would then submit a new formulation of the query [57–59].

Several question-answering systems utilize a syntactic analysis component that is not based on the ATN formalism. The REQUEST system, for example, is based on a transformational grammar [27], and the LSP project uses a "string analysis" system [50–52]. The latter is noteworthy because its somewhat formalized input, consisting of reports on medical test results or medical diagnostic summaries, makes it possible to reduce the sentences of natural language text to a tabular format which serves as a basis for the retrieval component. The system includes

1 A syntactic analysis component
2 A system of transformations to regularize the syntactic structure of each sentence
3 A reduction of the text to tabular format
4 A retrieval component that uses the entries in the columns of the tables to answer user queries.

A typical tabular format for an excerpt of a diagnostic report is shown in Table 7-4. Such a table might not be easily generated for general texts that do not exhibit the kind of stereotyping and uniformity of language that apparently occurs in some scientific disciplines.

In several question-answering systems, the linguistic processing is not as tightly bound to the domain of discourse as expected. Inevitably, a substantial amount of ambiguity must then be accepted, because restrictive semantic rules are no longer included in the process. The ROBOT system uses a relatively general system of linguistic processing, initially based on an ATN grammar [60]. The tight semantic interpretation rules are then replaced by an interesting verification system that uses the stored data base itself to help in the disambiguation of concepts that require elaboration.

Specifically, given a query such as "list the names of all Chicago secretaries," the system will search the data base to determine whether "Chicago" might be an attribute of secretary. When "Chicago" is discovered as a component of the address of some secretaries, the query is reinterpreted to mean "list the names of all secretaries located in Chicago." A request for "green Fords," where "green" is listed both as a color and as the name of a person, and Ford identifies the name of a person or alternatively an automobile manufacturer, is eventually interpreted correctly because the data base contains entries only for records where car manufacturer equals Ford, and car color equals green, whereas no records exist in the data base for the other three possible interpretations.

An alternative to using the data base for semantic verification consists of building an elaborate knowledge component into the question-answering system. This knowledge system in the form of scripts or frames can then be used not only for query interpretation but also for the generation of answers to questions [61,62]. The answer generation problem in unrestricted question-answering systems presents many unresolved problems. The obvious answer to a

Table 7-4 Tabular Format for Typical Diagnostic Summary

"Patient first had sickle cell anemia diagnosed at age 2 years when he complained of leg pain; he was worked up and diagnosis was made."

	Conjunction	Patient	Treatment			Patient state			Time	
			Instrument	Verb medical	Verb pattern	Body part	Sign	Diagnosis	Prep.	Reference point
1.		patient		first had diagnosed				sickle cell anemia	at	age 2 years
2.	when	he			complained of	leg	pain			
3.		he		was worked up						
4.	and			diagnosis was made						

Adapted from reference 51.

question is almost never adequate—for example, a simple yes/no answer to a user query will be found confining in most instances. Instead users look for answers that take into account the focus of the questions and offer appropriate elaborations and rationalizations. The time is not yet at hand when knowledge encoded in frames or scripts can be used efficiently for the interpretation of queries and the generation of system responses in unrestricted automatic question-answering systems [63].

6 SUMMARY

It has become evident in recent years that an unrestricted automatic natural language information system must necessarily incorporate a complete language understanding system. The latter in turn should be based on an acceptable theory of language, and on prestored knowledge covering the area of discourse under consideration, the general world knowledge normally assumed, and the psychological context of a given interaction in question answering.

Since these basic cornerstones of a full language processing system are not close to being under control, the choice on the part of practitioners interested in making use of language processing tools is twofold. On the one hand, an attempt can be made to use sophisticated linguistic tools in a restricted discourse area where the semantic difficulties can be resolved by the context and much of the ambiguity is automatically absent. This is the path followed by researchers who design question-answering systems in restricted topic environments. On the other hand, some of the language processing tools that appear to be well understood—notably syntactic analysis—could be used to improve the effectiveness of some classes of information systems. The use of syntactic methods in information retrieval may become attractive before long, especially in automatic indexing applications to control the phrases assigned to documents and queries for content identification. Syntactic analysis systems could also be useful for incorporation into full-text processing systems—for example, for automatic abstracting and passage retrieval.

Current indications are that more comprehensive linguistic theories may be needed before sophisticated language processing tools will actually be usable in many general-purpose automatic information systems.

REFERENCES

[1] T.R. Addis, Machine Understanding of Natural Language, International Journal of Man-Machine Studies, Vol. 9, No. 2, March 1977, pp. 207–222.

[2] K. Sparck Jones and M. Kay, Linguistics and Information Science, Academic Press, New York, 1973.

[3] C.A. Montgomery, Linguistics and Information Science, Journal of the ASIS, Vol. 23, No. 3, May–June 1972, pp. 195–219.

[4] K. Sparck Jones and M. Kay, Linguistics and Information Science—A Postscript, in Natural Language in Information Science, D.E. Walker, H. Karlgren and M. Kay, editors, FID Publication 551, Skriptor, Stockholm, 1977, pp. 183–192.

[5] F.J. Damerau, Automated Language Processing, in Annual Review of Information Science and Technology, Vol. 11, M.E. Williams, editor, American Society for Information Science, Washington, DC., 1976, pp. 107–161.

[6] G. Silva and C.A. Montgomery, Knowledge Representation for Automated Understanding of Natural Language Discourse, Computers and the Humanities, Vol. 11, No. 4, July–August 1977, pp. 223–234.

[7] R.C. Schank, M. Lebowitz, and L. Birnbaum, An Integrated Understander, American Journal of Computational Linguistics, Vol. 6, No. 1, January–March 1980, pp. 13–30.

[8] N. Sager, Computational Linguistics, in Natural Language in Information Science, D.E. Walker, H. Karlgren, and M. Kay, editors, FID Publication 551, Skriptor, Stockholm, 1977, pp. 75–100.

[9] A.G. Oettinger, Automatic Language Translation, Harvard University Press, Cambridge, Massachusetts, 1960.

[10] Y. Bar Hillel, Language and Information, Addison-Wesley Publishing Company, Reading, Massachusetts, 1964.

[11] Automatic Language Processing Advisory Committee, Language and Machines, National Academy of Sciences, Publication 1416, Washington, DC., 1966.

[12] D.E. Rumelhart, Introduction to Human Information Processing, John Wiley and Sons, New York, 1977.

[13] J.J. Katz and J.A. Fodor, The Structure of Semantic Theory, Language, Vol. 39, No. 2, 1963, pp. 170–210.

[14] C.J. Fillmore, The Case for Case, in Universals in Linguistic Theory, E. Bach and R.T. Harris, editors, Holt Rinehart and Winston, New York, 1968, pp. 1–88.

[15] D.G. Bobrow and T. Winograd, An Overview of KRL—A Knowledge Representation Language, Cognitive Science, Vol. 1, No. 1, January 1977, pp. 3–46.

[16] R.C. Schank, Conceptual Dependency Theory, in Conceptual Information Processing, Chapter 12, North Holland Publishing Company, Amsterdam, 1975, pp. 22–82.

[17] N.V. Findler, editor, Associative Networks—Representation and Use of Knowledge by Computers, Academic Press, New York, 1979.

[18] M. Minsky, A Framework for Representing Knowledge, in The Psychology of Computer Vision, P. Winston, editor, McGraw-Hill Book Company, New York, 1975, pp. 211–277.

[19] R.C. Schank and R.P. Abelson, Scripts, Plans, Goals and Understanding, Lawrence Erlbaum Associates, Hillsdale, New Jersey, 1977.

[20] J.C. Gardin, On the Relation between Question-Answering Systems and Various Theoretical Approaches to the Analysis of Text, in The Analysis of Meaning, M. MacCafferty and K. Gray, editors, Aslib, London, 1979, pp. 206–220.

[21] S.E. Robertson, Between Aboutness and Meaning, in The Analysis of Meaning, M. MacCafferty and K. Gray, editors, Aslib, London, 1979, pp. 202–205.

[22] K. Sparck Jones, Problems in the Representation of Meaning in Information Retrieval, in The Analysis of Meaning, M. MacCafferty and K. Gray, editors, Aslib, London, 1979, pp. 193–201.

[23] N. Sager, Syntactic Analysis of Natural Language, in Advances in Computers, Vol. 8, Academic Press, New York, 1967, pp. 153–188.

[24] S. Kuno and A.G. Oettinger, Multiple-Path Syntactic Analyzer, in Information Processing—62, North Holland Publishing Company, Amsterdam, 1963, pp. 306–311.

[25] S. Kuno, Automatic Syntactic Analysis, in Seminar in Computational Linguistics,

A.W. Pratt, A.H. Roberts, and K. Lewis, editors, Public Health Service Publication 1716, Government Printing Office, Washington, D.C., 1968, pp. 19–41.

[26] N. Chomsky, Aspects of the Theory of Syntax, MIT Press, Cambridge, Massachusetts, 1965.

[27] W.J. Plath, REQUEST: A Natural Language Question-Answering System, IBM Journal of Research and Development, Vol. 20, No. 4, July 1976, pp. 326–335.

[28] R. Grishman, A Survey of Syntactic Analysis Procedures for Natural Language, American Journal of Computational Linguistics, Vol. 13, No. 5, 1976, Microfiche 47.

[29] W.A. Woods, Transition Network Grammars for Natural Language Analysis, Communications of the ACM, Vol. 13, No. 10, October 1970, pp. 591–606.

[30] M. Bates, The Theory and Practice of Augmented Transition Network Grammars, in Natural Language Communication via Computers, L. Bolc, editor, Lecture Notes in Computer Science, Springer Verlag, Berlin, 1978, pp. 191–260.

[31] J. O'Connor, Retrieval of Answer Sentences and Answer Figures by Text Searching, Information Processing and Management, Vol. 11, No. 5/7, 1975, pp. 155–164.

[32] J. O'Connor, Data Retrieval by Text Searching, Journal of Chemical Information and Computer Sciences, Vol. 17, 1977, pp. 181–186.

[33] I. Steinacker, Indexing and Automatic Significance Analysis, Journal of the ASIS, Vol. 25, No. 4, July–August 1974, pp. 237–241.

[34] P.H. Klingbiel, Machine Aided Indexing of Technical Literature, Information Storage and Retrieval, Vol. 9, No. 2, February 1973, pp. 79–84.

[35] P.H. Klingbiel, A Technique for Machine-Aided Indexing, Information Storage and Retrieval, Vol. 9, No. 9, September 1973, pp. 477–494.

[36] P.H. Klingbiel and C.C. Rinker, Evaluation of Machine-Aided Indexing, Information Processing and Management, Vol. 12, No. 6, 1976, pp. 351–366.

[37] J.M. Carroll, W. Fraser, and G. Gill, Automatic Content Analysis in an On-Line Environment, Information Processing Letters, Vol. 1, No. 4, June 1972, pp. 134–140.

[38] G. Salton, Automatic Phrase Matching, in Readings in Computational Linguistics, D.G. Hays, editor, American Elsevier Publishing Company, New York, 1966, pp. 169–188.

[39] G. Salton, The SMART Automatic Document Retrieval System—An Illustration, Communications of the ACM, Vol. 8, No. 6, June 1965, pp. 391–398.

[40] R.J. Brachman, What's in a Concept: Structural Foundations for Semantic Networks, International Journal of Man-Machine Studies, Vol. 9, No. 2, March 1977, pp. 127–152.

[41] J.R. Abrial, Data Semantics, in Database Management, J.W. Klimbie and K.I. Kofferman, editors, North Holland Publishing Company, Amsterdam, Holland, 1974, pp. 1–60.

[42] J.W. Sowa, Conceptual Graphs for a Data Base Interface, IBM Journal of Research and Development, Vol. 20, No. 4, July 1976, pp. 336–357.

[43] G.G. Hendrix, Encoding Knowledge in Partitioned Networks, Technical Note 164, Stanford Research Institute, Menlo Park, California, June 1978.

[44] H.J. Schmid and J.R. Swenson, On the Semantics of the Relational Data Model, ACM SIGMOD Conference Proceedings, Association for Computing Machinery, New York, 1975, pp. 211–223.

[45] N. Roussopoulos and J. Mylopoulos, Using Semantic Networks for Data Base

Management, Proceedings of the Conference for Very Large Data Bases, Association for Computing Machinery, New York, 1975, pp. 144.

[46] B.J. Grosz, The Representation and Use of Focus in Dialogue Understanding, SRI Technical Note 151, Stanford Research Institute, Menlo Park, California, July 1977.

[47] N. Cercone, Morphological Analysis and Lexicon Design for Natural Language Processing, Computers and the Humanities, Vol. 11, No. 4, July–August 1977, pp. 235–258.

[48] T. Winograd, Understanding Natural Language, Academic Press, New York, 1972.

[49] G.S. Dunham, M.G. Pacak, and A.W. Pratt, Automatic Indexing of Pathology Data, Journal of the ASIS, Vol. 29, No. 2, March 1978, pp. 81–90.

[50] N. Sager, Sublanguage Grammars in Science Information Processing, Journal of the ASIS, Vol. 26, No. 1, January–February 1975, pp. 10–16.

[51] R. Grishman and L. Hirschman, Question Answering from Natural Language Medical Data Bases, Artificial Intelligence, Vol. 11, 1978, pp. 25–43.

[52] N. Sager and R. Grishman, The Restriction Language for Computer Grammars of Natural Language, Communications of the ACM, Vol. 18, No. 7, July 1975, pp. 390–400.

[53] W.A. Woods and R.M. Kaplan, The Lunar Sciences Natural Language Information System, Report No. 2265, Bolt Beranek and Newman, Cambridge, Massachusetts, September 1971.

[54] W.A. Woods, R.M. Kaplan, and B. Nash-Webber, The Lunar Sciences Natural Language Information System, Report No. 2378, Bolt Beranek and Newman, Cambridge, Massachusetts, 1972.

[55] G.G. Hendrix, E.D. Sacerdoti, D. Sagalowicz, and J. Slocum, Developing a Natural Language Interface to Complex Data, ACM Transactions on Database Systems, Vol. 3, No. 2, June 1978, pp. 105–147.

[56] W.A. Martin, Some Comments on EQS, A Near Term Natural Language Data Base Query System, Proceedings ACM 1978 Annual Conference, December 1978, pp. 156–164.

[57] D.L. Waltz, An English Language Question Answering System for a Large Relational Data Base, Communications of the ACM, Vol. 21, No. 7, July 1978, pp. 526–539.

[58] E.F. Codd, R.S. Arnold, J.M. Cadiou, C.L. Chang, and N. Roussopoulos, Rendezvous: Version 1, Report RJ 2144, IBM Research Laboratory, San Jose, California, January 1978.

[59] E.F. Codd, Seven Steps to Rendezvous, Report RJ 1333, IBM Research Laboratory, San Jose, California, January 1974.

[60] L.R. Harris, User Oriented Database Query with the ROBOT Natural Language Query Sytem, International Journal of Man-Machine Studies, Vol. 9, 1977, pp. 697–713.

[61] D.G. Bobrow, R.M. Kaplan, M. Kay, D.A. Norman, H. Thompson, and T. Winograd, GUS—A Frame-Driven Dialog System, Artificial Intelligence, Vol. 8, No. 2, April 1977, pp. 155–173.

[62] W. Lehnert, Problems in Question Answering, Sixth International Conference on Computational Linguistics, Ottawa, Canada, 1976.

[63] B. Shneiderman, Software Psychology: Human Factors in Computer and Information Systems, Winthrop Publishers, Cambridge, Massachusetts, 1980.

BIBLIOGRAPHIC REMARKS

The following references can be used to obtain an overview of several linguistic techniques used in automatic information processing:

L. Bolc, editor, Natural Language Communication via Computers, Lecture Notes in Computer Science, Springer Verlag, Berlin, 1978.

R. Rustin, editor, Natural Language Processing, Courant Computer Science Symposium No. 8, Algorithmics Press, New York, 1973.

The following references provide a deeper view of various methods currently used for knowledge representation:

D.G. Bobrow and A. Collins, editors, Representation and Understanding, Academic Press, New York, 1975.

N.V. Findler, editor, Associative Networks—Representation and Use of Knowledge by Computers, Academic Press, New York, 1979.

R.C. Schank and R.P. Abelson, Scripts, Plans, Goals and Understanding, Lawrence Erlbaum Associates, Hillsdale, New Jersey, 1977.

Problems arising in interfacing linguistic techniques and information retrieval are covered in the following references:

K. Sparck Jones and M. Kay, Linguistics and Information Science, Academic Press, New York, 1973.

D.E. Walker, H. Karlgren, and M. Kay, editors, Natural Language in Information Science, FID Publication 551, Skriptor, Stockholm, 1977.

EXERCISES

7-1 In Chapter 4, four different grammatical interpretations were given for the sentence, "Time flies like an arrow."
   a List the various facts of world knowledge that appear to be needed in a language analysis system capable of recognizing the sample sentence.
   b Assuming that a context-free grammar is used for recognition purposes, generate a set of semantic rules based on the stored knowledge that are capable of eliminating the extraneous analyses (leaving only the correct interpretation) when added to the normal context-free recognition process.

7-2 Explain the similarities and differences between a context-free grammar, a context-sensitive grammar, a transformational grammar, and an ATN grammar. What do the initials ATN stand for? Explain the function of the concepts represented by the A, T, and N, respectively.

7-3 Consider a TN grammar capable of recognizing character strings consisting of A's and B's only. Generate a TN grammar that accepts all input strings exhibiting an equal number of A's and B's regardless of the ordering of the letters, and rejects all other strings. Thus AABB, ABAB, the null string, etc., would be accepted; however, AAB, ABABC, A, etc., would be rejected.

7-4 Consider the following segment of a phrase structure grammar for English:

> (1) S → NP + VP
> (2) VP → V
> (3) NP → DET + ADJ* + N

The asterisk * following ADJ indicates that a variable number of adjectives are acceptable.

a Draw a transition network corresponding to the three rules.

b Show the individual steps needed to recognize the sentence "The big gray hippo wallows."

c How can the grammar and network be extended to accept the sentences "The big gray hippo wallows mightily" and "The big gray hippo mightily wallows"?

d Illustrate the recognition of one of the earlier sentences by giving the phrase markers corresponding to each step of the recognition process.

7-5 Consider the first two paragraphs of the current chapter.

a Choose indexing phrases (noun phrases, prepositional phrases) to represent the content of these paragraphs.

b Generate a set of criterion phrases together with the corresponding thesaurus (as in Fig. 7-12) to represent the phrases specified under part a.

c Specify the noun-phrase portion of a context-free grammar capable of recognizing the corresponding phrases in conjunction with the criterion phrase dictionary of part b.

d How would you extend the criterion phrase dictionary and the grammar to handle the content of the third paragraph of this chapter, in addition to the first two paragraphs? What does this imply about the ease of extending limited linguistic recognition systems to wider subject areas?

Chapter 8

Access to Information: Hardware and Software Approaches

0 PREVIEW

This chapter examines special-purpose devices and methodologies useful in storing and accessing collections of information items. A number of conventional storage devices such as cards, disks, and tape are introduced first. This leads to the description of more specialized hardware systems that may be used in obtaining rapid access to stored data, including parallel and associative processors and special-purpose "back-end" search processors. The chapter ends with an examination of the main procedures available for accessing and processing data bases consisting of stored texts. The principal file access methods are described, and various text matching procedures are covered which make it possible rapidly to identify portions of text that match a given query statement. Additional advanced hardware developments that may enhance the design of future information retrieval systems are included in Chapter 10.

1 CONVENTIONAL STORAGE DEVICES

This chapter is concerned with the machines and procedures that are especially designed for the processing and retrieval of bibliographic and textual information. A historical perspective is presented in the first section followed by a description of specific devices for the manipulation of large data bases and the processing of large quantities of text.

Modern data processing activities as we know them have their origin long ago, starting most likely with the beginnings of formal trade between individuals. When a person is involved in trade, an essential skill is the ability to decide on the worth of the item being traded in relation to the item being received. For example, ancient traders were expected to know or keep track of how many cattle were required in exchange for a husband or wife [1]. As the complexity of trading grew, the need for record keeping and for mechanisms to track and process information led to the invention of various systems of symbols (for example, the Arabic numbers 1, 2, 3, . . . , 10) and of operations which could be performed on those symbols (such as addition or comparison for equality). The complexity and the speed of these processing operations has increased over time to meet growing demands. Processing aids, such as the abacus, were soon developed that furnish greater processing speed and increase human abilities to master complex problems.

Among the most noticeable advances in information processing were the greatly enhanced capabilities for performing numerical computations [2]. As an example, the analytical engine developed by Babbage in 1834 was specifically designed to aid the military purposes of Great Britain by calculating the trajectories of cannons and other firearms [3]. The modern computing era began during the Second World War when automatic computing equipment was used in Great Britain for the decoding of encrypted messages, and in the United States for the calculation of ballistic firing tables. The interest in the automatic storage and retrieval of bibliographic and textual information existed from the beginning because of the large available information collections, and the difficulties of dealing with textual materials by conventional methods.

A Punched Cards

A major innovation of concern in information retrieval occurred with the use by Herman Hollerith of punched card techniques to process the data collected for the 1890 census. Hollerith proposed using one or more paper cards for each individual responding to the census and encoding all responses by punching holes into these cards at precise locations. He then designed mechanical devices to ''look at'' prespecified locations on the cards to determine if a hole had been punched. The number of holes could then be automatically tabulated. Hollerith used a linear scan of the set of cards which looked at the same location in every record to determine whether a specific value was present. Hollerith's idea was enormously successful. In fact, punched cards have remained an important medium for the storage of information through most of the history of computers. Figure 8-1 shows a contemporary punched card of the Hollerith design.

Punched cards can be ''read'' by commercially available readers at speeds of around 1,000 cards per minute. If a data base of a million characters were stored on cards, this data base would require about 12.5 minutes to read.

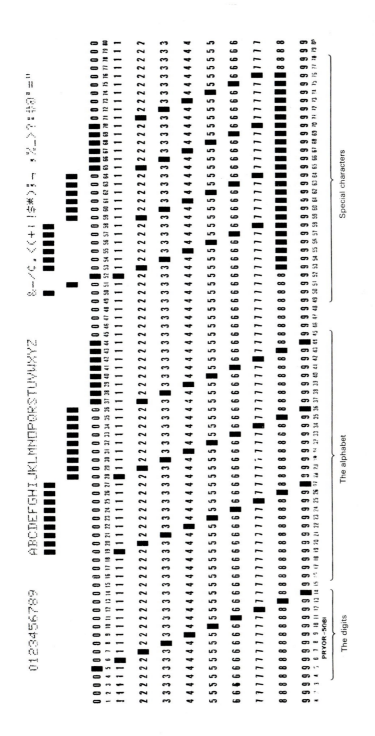

Figure 8-1 Punched (Hollerith) card.

Other storage media have been developed that prove to be more efficient, more reliable, and more cost effective than punched cards. Among these are the magnetic tapes, disks, and drums. Random access storage devices such as core or semiconductor memories have also been developed to provide rapid access to information. These devices are briefly introduced in the remainder of this section.

B Magnetic Tape

The magnetic tape devices used with computers resemble the home tape recorder. Information is stored along the length of the tape on a number of *tracks*. The stored information can then be recovered by "replaying" the tape. Each character of information is represented by a sequence of magnetic spots stored across the width of the tape. All the spots (bits) pertaining to a single character are processed together when a character is added to, or removed from, the tape. The digital characters are commonly packed together along the length of the tape at the rate of 1,600 or 6,250 characters per inch of tape. A typical magnetic tape device is shown in Fig. 8-2.

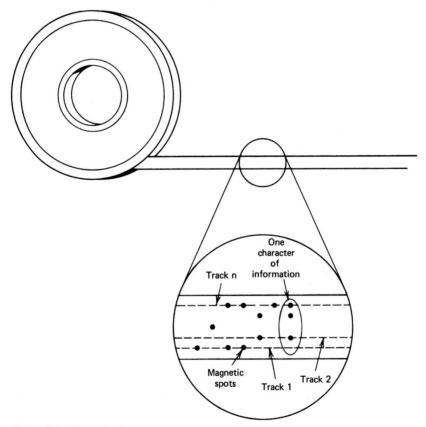

Figure 8-2 Magnetic tape.

Since the information is stored on a magnetic tape in sequential order, it is necessary to scan the tape from the beginning in order to find a specific unit of information. Such a sequential search is potentially very slow. For example, if one million characters are stored in records of 1,000 characters at a density of 1,600 characters per inch using a $3/4$-inch gap between records, and if the tape reading speed is 125 inches per second, about 11 seconds are needed to read the tape. Furthermore, before any tape can be read, it is usually mounted on a tape drive by a human operator. This operation may take a minute or more, depending on the circumstances. Tape storage is, however, inexpensive: a tape reel holding 180 million characters at a density of 6,250 characters per inch may cost as little as $11.

C Magnetic Disks

If a magnetic tape appears similar to a home recording tape, then a magnetic disk resembles a phonograph record. Information is stored on a platter capable of retaining a magnetic image. This platter has concentric rings with information sequentially stored on any one ring (track). To find information on a single platter, one needs to know which track to examine and where on that track the information is stored. Information is placed on a magnetic disk by means of a *read-write* head. In many disk devices one read-write head is used per disk face; that is, if information is kept on both sides of the disk, two read-write heads may be used. To locate a specific item of information, the read-write head is moved to the appropriate track and the information is read as it passes in front of the read head. An alternative to the moving read-write head is to have a read-write head for every track of a disk. This *head per track* arrangement eliminates mechanical movement (a slow process).

The magnetic disk is a direct access device because it is not necessary to scan past *all* preceding characters of information to get to a desired unit of information. Rather it is possible to go directly to a desired track on a particular disk. A track may store between 7,000 and 13,000 characters. A standard disk arrangement consists of a group of disks arranged on a single shaft. Current capacities of disk packs are in the range of 300 million characters of information. A typical disk pack is represented in Fig. 8-3.

Information can be read from magnetic disks at the rate of 100,000 characters per second. Thus about 10 seconds is needed to read a data base of one million characters. However, since it is not necessary to examine all records sequentially on the disk, the time required to locate a specific item may be much less than is required for a tape. Disk storage is, unfortunately, much more expensive than an equivalent quantity of tape storage. Disk packs may or may not be removable from the disk drives. Removable packs may cost about $600. Nonremovable packs are less expensive; when they are used, auxiliary tapes may serve for off-line storage.

A recent innovation in disk technology is the small, soft, 5- to 8-inch, *floppy disk*. A floppy disk is easily carried or mailed because it weighs only a few ounces, and it is not harmed by a certain amount of bending or mistreat-

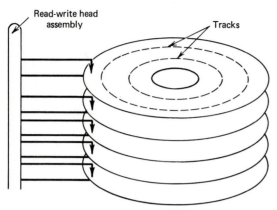

Figure 8-3 Disk pack with access mechanism.

ment. Floppy disks storing about one million characters may cost as little as $1 per disk. They can store anywhere from 1,000 to 3,000 or more characters per track, with access speeds of about $^1/_2$ second. Floppy disks are currently used as the main bulk storage medium in many mini- and microcomputers.

D Random Access Storage Devices

Locating stored information items or transferring information from storage to the computer processing unit tends to be comparatively slow on most computer systems. This is true particularly when mechanical motion is involved, as exemplified by the movement of a tape or the spinning of a disk. Devices that require no mechanical movement for reading or writing tend to be faster. For each such device, the time needed to read or write an item may be the same for all items, no matter where located in storage. For this reason, such devices are known as random access devices.

Random access devices, such as core or metal oxide semiconductor (MOS) memories, tend to be expensive, although prices are declining rapidly. At the present time a storage array for one million characters may cost about $6,000. Compared with disks and tapes, these devices provide only limited storage capacities. That is, the capacity of a disk may be stated in billions of characters, while the core and semiconductor memories may provide several millions of characters only. Random access devices are useful because they are very fast; one can find a specific item very quickly. A typical core storage device is shown in Fig. 8-4. Information is stored in small rings, or cores, that are magnetized in one direction or the other. The cores are arranged on a plane, and several core planes may be stacked one on top of the other. The access to the information stored in a core array is accomplished by sensing the direction of the magnetism measured by the resistance to a prespecified current.

The reading rate for core storage is about five times greater than for disk devices. To read a data base of a million characters requires 2 seconds for core devices compared with the 10 seconds needed for disks. In many systems, the performance of core or MOS memories is enhanced by using still faster and

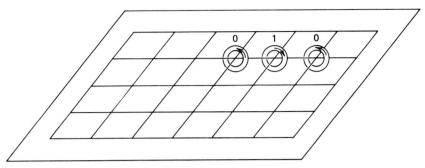

Figure 8-4 One plane of magnetic core storage.

more costly *cache* memories that speed up the transfer between core and the central processing units of the machines.

E Data Cell

In many applications a need exists for a mechanism that stores very large quantities of information in a cost-effective manner. A data cell is, in effect, a combination of magnetic tapes and small magnetic drums. As shown in Fig. 8-5, this device uses cells containing large strips of magnetic tape. Each cell and each

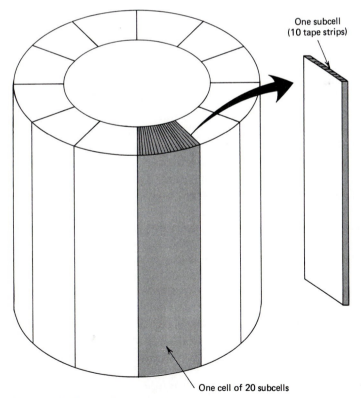

Figure 8-5 Data cell storage device.

strip of tape within a cell is individually addressable. When a tape strip is selected for reading or writing, it is wrapped around a small rotating drum; the
information on the tape can then be read as the drum rotates. Billions of characters of information can be stored on a data cell rather inexpensively. Unfortunately, the data cell exhibits relatively slow speed because of the mechanical
motion required to (1) find the particular cell, (2) find the particular strip of tape
in the cell, and (3) load the tape strip on the drum.

As one would expect, the mechanical motion involved in the operation of
the data cell makes this a relatively slow device. However, once a particular
tape strip has been located and loaded, the device is capable of operating at
speeds corresponding to the drum rotation time. Thus a one million character
data base will require 27.5 seconds to read if the tape strip is to be located,
loaded, and read.

F   Access to Storage

While storage devices are often capable of storing large quantities of information, any manipulation of the stored information will traditionally occur within
the central processing unit of the computer. Hence a communications path
must be provided between each storage device and the central processing unit
of the computer system. Most central processing units have a much greater
speed than the storage devices to which they are attached. It is therefore necessary to speed up the information transfer by developing holding areas (buffers)
from which the information can be read more rapidly than from the storage devices themselves and by establishing intermediate processing devices (channels) which can open and close appropriate paths, translate the information if
necessary, ensure that information is channeled to the proper location, and no-
tify the central processing unit that a particular transfer process is complete.

Figure 8-6 shows the communication processes in a computer system
equipped with a variety of communications devices. The multiplexor channel
interleaves information from a number of slower devices such as card readers
and punches. That is, it takes advantage of the inherent slowness of the devices
by selecting messages from a variety of active devices for transmission to the
central processor. If a storage device is relatively fast, it is more efficient to
select and transmit all the messages from that one device before working on the
information from some other device. A selector or burst channel is therefore
used with the faster storage devices. The tape and disk control units are used to
turn the individual devices on or off and to process the information being transformed.

In many situations a specific item of information will be needed from a data
base. More often than not the process required to access this item will interrupt
whatever else the computer may be doing at that time. Processing resumes
when the item is located and transferred to the central processing unit. If the
operations are reasonably efficient and the required data bases are small, such a
processing mode may prove acceptable. For instance, many microcomputer

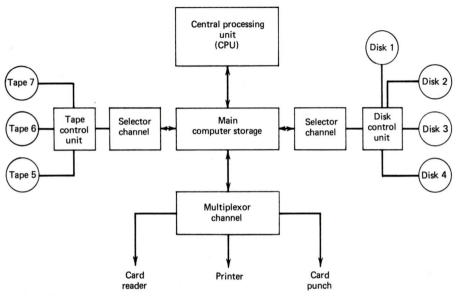

Figure 8-6 Typical computer system with input-output and storage.

systems use tape cassettes for storage; information can be transferred from the cassettes at the rate of 30 characters per second. Accessing a data base of 1,250 characters (about 250 English words or 1 printed page of text) will require 41.66 seconds. Such a time frame may be acceptable to the computer hobbyist, but it may prove unacceptable to a scientist. In many practical situations, stored data bases of a million characters are common. The accessing process described earlier could then stretch to many hours.

The use of buffers and channels will, of course, speed up the process. However, even when additional facilities are provided for increased access speed, the program design and the form used to store the data often determine the speed of the information system. In particular, even if the computer system were capable of performing computations in a few billionths of a second, the true processing time would be much slower if the machine were forced to wait for periodic input from the data base.

A second significant feature of most computer systems is the necessity of knowing the actual storage location of a given information item before that item can be retrieved. That is, in order to find information records on a particular topic the location of the corresponding information records must be known, or else the location must be deducible from available data. If the location information is not immediately available, auxiliary index files, such as the inverted files, are used. It would be easier and less expensive if a system were able directly to find the needed records without concern for location. Presumably there would then be no need for inverted files or other indexes to locate the information. This possibility is discussed below under Associative Processors.

2 HARDWARE ENHANCEMENT OF RETRIEVAL

A   Microprocessors and Processing Chips

For many years attempts have been made to design the ultimate information retrieval aid. Such a device may be expected to furnish direct answers to incoming user queries, formulate educated guesses when questions cannot be answered unequivocally, maintain and update personal files and appointment schedules, and perform computations on stored data as well as translations and other transformations on natural language text. The device itself is often pictured as being pocket-sized, requiring little energy to operate, and capable of processing unlimited quantities of information of many kinds.

The basic idea of such a "memory extender" (Memex) is now over three decades old, and information professionals have been striving to design that type of retrieval engine for a long time [4,5]. In its full scope, the memory extender remains outside the realm of practical possibilities for the immediate future. The enormous technological strides which have been made during the last decade at least in the hardware area may, however, lead one to conclude that the time when the full Memex can actually be constructed is fast approaching.

Without a doubt the most significant trend over the past few years has been the impressive decrease in both the size and the cost of existing electronic hardware devices together with a simultaneous increase in processing capability. Complete *microprocessors* are currently implemented on small silicon plates, or *chips*, each chip including tens of thousands of active processing elements (transistors) on a plate measuring substantially less than 1 inch square. Microprocessors are now so inexpensive to manufacture that they are incorporated into many devices intended for home use: they have been used in particular to control automobile systems, microwave ovens, and video tape equipment, and they provide the basic processing capability in many toys and games sold to children and adults.

A microprocessor implementation takes many different forms. In its simplest form, only the chip itself is provided, which includes storage space to save short programs and some data, as well as an arithmetic unit and a sequence control unit to handle the program decoding. If a keyboard is added for manual input and a digital readout register, one obtains a programmable device. Handheld models capable of text and numeric processing that will fit into one's pocket can be acquired for a few hundred dollars at the present time.

When substantially more internal storage capacity is furnished, typically for 32,000 characters of data, and one or two soft (floppy) disks are added for external storage together with keyboard input and cathode ray tube display, the cost of the system jumps to $2,000 to $5,000. Such a system is then usable for text and program editing, messaging, and many tasks needed in a question-answering situation. For full information retrieval usage, an output printer becomes mandatory, as well as a large (hard) disk for bulk storage of several million characters of text. The latter alone may add about $5,000 to the system cost, so that a full information retrieval configuration may cost between $10,000 and $15,000 at current prices [6–9]. The microprocessor characteristics are summarized for three typical systems in Table 8-1.

In principle, theoretical limits exist for some technological advances. However, these limitations are not expected to affect the continued gains in the performance/cost ratio of existing electronic devices for many decades. Furthermore, the conditions under which microcomputer components are currently being developed lead to predictions for increasing parallelism in the process organization and to the existence of "overkill" capacity in the equipment. More specifically, since the individual integrated circuits incorporated in a computing device are expensive to generate initially because of the human skill needed in the design effort but, once designed, are inexpensive to produce in large quantities, it may be economically advantageous to produce components that are rather more sophisticated than may be required for a particular application. The resulting electronic components may then be sufficiently versatile to be used in many different capacities.

Such a deliberate overdesign implies that each chip might be used to carry out input/output manipulations, file management, memory management, interrupt processing, and other information transfer and processing operations. If each function is assigned to a separate hardware component, a parallel processing capability of the kind mentioned later in this chapter results, where several kinds of arithmetic operations are overlapped with data fetch and input/output operations. In an information system environment, separate processors could then be assigned to distinct system operations, and the functions of each processor might be optimized within the context of the total system design [10].

One problem to be faced when new machine architectures are introduced is the need to convert existing applications programs to the new system environment. The conversion problem becomes particularly onerous when large-

Table 8-1 Microprocessor Configurations

Configuration	Typical use	Cost

Handheld calculator
  Digital readout
  Input keyboard
  Several dozen storage registers
  Arithmetic unit
  Automatic sequence control
	Small programs and
	  calculations
		$100–$300

Minimal processor
  16- to 32-bit address
  32,000 characters of data storage
  2 to 5 microseconds add time
  Floppy disks for storage
  Cathode ray tube display
	Word processing capability
	  Text editing
	  Program editing
	  Indexing
	  Cataloging
		$2,000–$5,000

Full microprocessor configuration
  Printer added to minimal processor
  Hard disk for bulk storage
	Information retrieval
	  Inverted file processing
	  Output printing
		$10,000–$15,000

scale changes in the machine architecture are involved such as those inherent in switching from a largely sequential processing chain to a parallel processing system. When the applications programs are originally written in some high-level programming language, automatic translation programs may be available to perform the required conversion. Programs written to take particular advantage of the existing hardware organization, such as machine language or assembly language programs, must, however, be converted by time-consuming intellectual procedures.

In summary, the processing technology is becoming increasingly miniaturized; at the same time, a trend exists toward special function architectures where separate, sophisticated modules are devoted to specialized functions. This may, in time, lead to a fine tuning of individual system components and to the use of components that precisely fit a particular problem situation. The time is rapidly aproaching when large classes of users will be able to access small, inexpensive computers capable of satisfying sophisticated computational and data processing requirements.

B General Characteristics of Retrieval Hardware

It was suggested earlier that small personalized machines are becoming increasingly common. If these devices are to prove useful in information retrieval, it becomes necessary to provide an interface with the large data bases that exist in various locations. Furthermore, user terminals must be available that are capable of displaying the retrieved information in a user-friendly manner.

The standard available display terminals can currently exhibit 24 lines of text at any one time, exclusive of illustrations. Because of the low resolution of the current displays, it is not possible to view full document pages in a conventional typeset format. Hence the standard display equipment is not well suited for the retrieval of full document texts. High-resolution terminals are coming into use that are capable of displaying full typeset pages with illustrations, allowing 60 lines of readable text. One may expect that good-quality color graphics can eventually be added, allowing displays of document output that the users will actually be happy to see displayed on a screen. At the present time, high-resolution displays capable of controlling the display from local memory inside the terminal are costly—somewhere between $10,000 and $20,000. These costs should decline as the equipment becomes more widespread. The wide availability of small, personal machines with high-resolution display equipment will greatly enhance the usefulness of the existing, automatic retrieval services.

It has been stated that the ideal information retrieval system should have the capacity to store between one billion and one trillion characters. The system should also be of low cost, and it should be capable of finding the stored data in a time period acceptable to a user waiting at a terminal for a response [11].

These represent stringent requirements. For example, if one assumes that the data base consists of 1 billion characters and if a computer were to process 100,000 characters per second (about as fast as information can be read from a contemporary disk), then a user could wait for 2.7 hours for a response. Thus, either the size of the search files must be drastically reduced or some mechanism must be found for accessing these large quantities of data in a more reasonable time frame.

The standard solution to this problem consists in building auxiliary index files that identify subsections of the main files containing the information of interest to particular users. Alternatively, the use of *special-purpose search and storage* architectures may prove useful to process large information files. These special-purpose devices are in principle capable of processing data independently on a stand-alone basis. More commonly, they are attached to one or more general-purpose host machines. Each user can then access a general-purpose machine—possibly a personal minicomputer or a common large host machine—while delegating the actual search function to the special-purpose device attached to the host machine(s).

The following types of special-purpose search equipment can be distinguished:

1 *Smart peripheral* devices such as disks or drums whose normal function is the storage of information. By adding special processing hardware to the disks, information might be selected, checked, and processed right in the storage device, thereby allowing a good deal of processing to take place in parallel, and avoiding much unnecessary transfer to and from the central processing unit of the general-purpose computer(s).

2 The functions of the smart peripherals can be expanded by adding other processing capabilities, thereby creating special *back-end data base processors* connected to the general-purpose host machine. The general-purpose (host) machine normally controls the data base processor and handles transfers of information between machines; the back-end machine is charged with special-purpose tasks such as information search and special data base computations [12].

3 A number of special-purpose search computers could also be interconnected by operating in a *network mode*. The data stored in a given machine might then be accessed by other machines in the network whenever this may be required by the data base process.

In discussing each special computer configuration, it is convenient to make distinctions based on the number of processing units available and on the type of information search provided. In particular, a search conducted directly in a mass storage device may be distinguished from a search conducted indirectly in a buffer or intermediate storage area [13].

When a special-purpose search computer is used, the search is initiated by the special-purpose machine in response to a request received through a host computer system as shown in Fig. 8-7. The information is examined by the special computer to determine what items should be retrieved. Records that pass the retrievability criteria are then passed on to the host computer system. Sig-

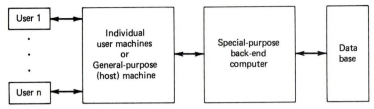

Figure 8-7 Back-end computer use for data base processing.

nificant efficiencies are achieved when the quantity of data that must be scanned in response to each query is large, because the host computer can attend to other work while the search operation takes place on the special-purpose machine.

   If the special-purpose processor is integrated directly into a mass storage device, the system is then capable of a direct search. That is, the central processing unit would receive a request which is then passed along to the special mass storage device. This device will search through its data base and return to the central processing unit only those items of information meeting the retrievability criteria.

   A number of different special-purpose computer configurations are discussed in the remainder of this section. In each case, the potential importance of the device for information retrieval is briefly mentioned.

C Parallel Processors

Multiple processor devices come in two main designs. The first is based on a number of parallel but independent processing units. Such a configuration may include several central processing units, each unit being capable of a wide range of functions. For instance, two different processing units may each be searching different portions of a collection as illustrated in simplified form in Fig. 8-8. The units may independently be able to determine the potential usefulness of the various documents to a user query. Alternatively, each processor might carry out different operations on the same data base in parallel, such as, for example, word stemming, thesaurus transformation, and query-document similarity calculations. By using several processors, the processing time for a full data base of information items may be decreased according to the number of processors in use [14].

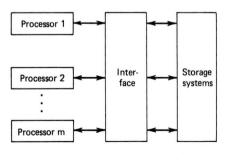

Figure 8-8 Use of separate parallel processors.

Multiple processors of this design are now in limited use in information retrieval environments. In order to increase processing efficiency through the use of multiple, independent processors, it is necessary to identify different procedures that can be carried out simultaneously on different portions of the data base. In information retrieval the complexity of the operations renders the specification of parallel procedures difficult, and it is not obvious that several processors can be kept occupied simultaneously for long periods of time.

Consider a query formulation such as (TERM$_1$ and (TERM$_2$ r TERM$_3$)). Such a query may be processed in three steps as follows:

1 Use the processors in parallel to retrieve the information items associated with TERM$_1$, TERM$_2$, and TERM$_3$. This step takes advantage of the parallel capability.

2 Perform a set union operation for the sets associated with TERM$_2$ and TERM$_3$. This is a sequential process that might be carried out on a single processor.

3 Perform a set intersection operation with the result of step 2 and the set of items retrieved by TERM$_1$. This is another sequential process.

It is clear from this sequence that the advantages of the parallel processing in step 1 may be outweighed by the extra cost and complexity due to the presence of the multiplicity of processors. In general, the number of processors to be used in a multiprocessor system should be determined by a cost-effectiveness measure. That is, one would like to be assured that each additional processing unit will actually serve to increase the efficiency of information processing.

*D Associative Processors

The second design for parallel processing consists in using an associative processor containing several processing units. In this case, however, each processing unit carries out exactly the same process as every other processor at each instant in time. The name associative processor is derived from the associative array (matrix) storage area in which the processing of the information occurs. Each row of this matrix is designed to accept an individual item of information, and the contents of all rows are processed simultaneously. For example, each row may be loaded with a unit of information (such as a different query term) to be compared with a desired value. Each item will then be compared at the same instant with the desired value and all items meeting the desired search criteria will be identified simultaneously.

Figure 8-9 shows the operation of an associative processor searching for the value BLUE among several units of text. The desired value is placed in the comparand register in a specific set of character positions to be searched. The locations to be searched in the array processor are identified by placing 1s in the appropriate positions of a mask register. The positions identified by 0s in the mask register (that is, positions 1 to 4 and 9 to 24 in the example of Fig. 8-9) are ignored in the search. When a comparison is made for a particular term,

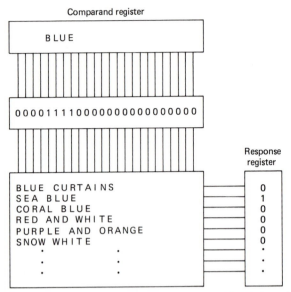

Figure 8-9 Array processor search for term BLUE (specified as positions 5 through 8 of a 24-element row).

such as BLUE, the entire list of data elements is compared simultaneously. Each matching data element is identified in the response register by the appearance of a 1 [15].

Instead of performing parallel search operations, associative processors could also be used to perform arbitrary parallel computations on all elements of the associative array. Thus, in a vector oriented system such as the SMART system, a device that could perform simultaneous calculations between a set of document vectors and a query vector would have great advantages over a system in which the calculations are carried out one document at a time. For example, the calculation of the similarity between a query in the comparand register and each document in the associative array might be performed in the following way:

1 Load the document vectors into the associative store.
2 Load the query vector into the comparand register.
3 Set the mask register so that the character positions correspond to the locations of the weights of the individual query terms.
4 Instruct the associative processor to perform a sum of product operations for the elements of the query vector with each element of all document vectors.

The last step will simultaneously multiply each term weight of the query vector with each term weight of corresponding terms in the document vectors. The resulting products are then summed and placed in the response register. The result corresponds to the numerator of the cosine similarity between the query and each document vector stored in the associative array. Note that three of the four steps in this process are concerned with setting up the associative processor prior to the actual vector computations.

The advantages of associative processing are numerous. Note specifically that there is no need to be concerned with the location in storage of a desired item until the item has met the desired search criteria. Note also that one may conduct partial searches for terms such as BL*E, where the third character identified by an asterisk is not specified. No preliminary processing is needed since the data are examined by content rather than location. There is therefore no need to prespecify the location of documents by using an index.

Unfortunately, the use of associative processing also entails many disadvantages. A large problem is simply the necessary transfer of information into the associative processor. This is normally carried out as a sequential process which is thus relatively slow. Second, the location in which a given term value appears in the associative processor must be specified precisely. Third, the cost of associative processing equipment is high, and the existing associative memories are small.

An example of an associative array processor is the Staran, developed by Goodyear Aerospace. The original design was intended for the processing of images [16]. This design has already been shown to be useful in data base management environments.

Staran is composed of 32 separate matrices (arrays), each matrix consisting of 256 rows and 256 columns. If one assumes that each character requires 8 columns of matrix storage, then each matrix can store a maximum of 8,192 characters, or 256 rows of 32 characters each. All the matrices are connected to a single comparand and a single mask register. Each matrix does, however, have its own response register. An operation may be conducted on all the matrices simultaneously. Figure 8-10 shows the basic architecture of a system which includes a Staran associative processor.

For information retrieval one sees immediate application of a device such as Staran to provide a parallel search of an inverted index. This can be done by loading all the terms included in the inverted index in the associative array of

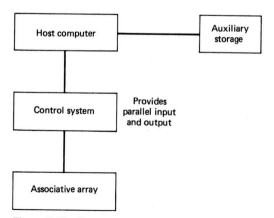

Figure 8-10 Staran organization.

the Staran and passing the query terms through the comparand register. When a match is obtained between a query term and a term stored in the array, the corresponding list of document identifiers may become immediately available. In such an application, the tradeoff is between the high cost of associative processing compared with the cost of the contemporary software methods used to perform inverted file manipulations.

*E Fast Computations Using Array Processors

Many computer applications areas are distinguished chiefly by the need for substantial computational power. For example, in signal processing, large masses of data are received as a continuous stream from external devices, such as radar or satellite equipment, and must be processed and "cleaned up." In such circumstances, the need for fast internal computation becomes overwhelming. To respond to this demand, special processors, known as "array processors" (AP), have been developed that provide very fast arithmetic operations and work in conjunction with a general-purpose computer (the host computer) to which they are attached. The computational APs are not to be confused with the associative processors used mostly for searching that were described previously [17,18].

Array processors are normally implemented as specialized high-speed floating-point machines (that is, they perform computations on floating-point numbers) working in parallel with their host computer. No character manipulation or input-output facilities are normally provided. The computational power of APs is due to two main features:

1 Parallel functional units: instead of including all arithmetic and logical functions of the processor in a single "arithmetic and logical unit" as is done in standard computers, the various functions of the central processing unit are split up into separate functional units that can all operate in parallel; thus in an array processor it is possible to perform an addition in the adder, and also a multiplication in the multiplier, and also a fetch operation to retrieve an item of data from memory, and also an instruction decoding operation, all these operations being carried out in parallel using separate functional units.

2 Pipelined functional units: some units of the array processor are *pipelined* to speed up the processing of a single function, notably addition and multiplication; this means that a given operation is carried out in steps, or stages, in such a way that a given processing unit can effectively carry out several operations at the same time, provided each operation is in a separate stage. A pipelined processing unit, such as a multiplier, consisting of three stages is shown schematically in Fig. 8-11. Three operations (multiplications) can in principle be carried out in the multiplier at the same time: the first multiplication that was started earliest is in stage 3 in the illustration of Fig. 8-11, the second multiplication started one stage later is in stage 2, and the third started most recently is in stage 1. After each time unit the pipelined processor advances by one stage; that is, a new operation can be started in each unit of time if the pipeline is filled, the results of the operation being available three stages later.

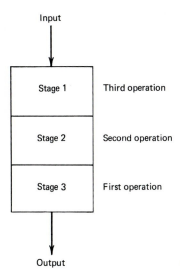

Input

Stage 1	Third operation
Stage 2	Second operation
Stage 3	First operation

Output

Figure 8-11 Pipelined processing unit.

Because of the limited set of functions provided, the cost of AP processing is low (typically $40 per hour) compared with the cost of a large standard computer (typically $1,000 per hour).

When an array processor is coupled to a general-purpose (host) computer as shown in Fig. 8-12, all input-output, program setup, and data base operations are normally carried out by the host. Computational tasks can, however, be assigned to the AP after transfer by the host of relevant instructions and data into the array processor. The AP then executes its program while the host waits or performs other tasks unrelated to what is going on inside the AP. When the AP finishes its task, a "device interrupt" is sent to the host; the host then reads the results out of the AP, and processing continues.

Whether it pays to use an AP with a host computer depends on whether the savings obtained by executing a routine in the AP outweigh the costs of communicating programs and data between host and AP. The following factors appear important in this connection:

1 The data manipulations should be executable as floating-point arithmetic rather than as address, character, or integer manipulations.

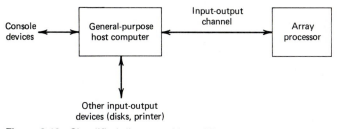

Figure 8-12 Simplified diagram of host-AP system.

2 The application should include long computations to justify the required host overhead and data transfer time.
3 The program to be executed should be small.
4 The data required by the AP should be easy to select.

Information retrieval appears, at first, to furnish a poor application for APs because of the large data base to be processed and the many data transformations as opposed to arithmetic operations to be performed. On the other hand, it is obvious from the material in the preceding chapters that the computational requirements are certainly not negligible in many information retrieval processors. Examples are the computation of similarity coefficients between vectors, the generation of term weighting functions such as the term discrimination and term relevance values, the generation of cluster centroids for clustered document collections, and the computation of recall-precision factors.

Consider, as an example, the computation of the cosine function between DOC_i and $QUERY_j$ defined as

$$COS(DOC_i, QUERY_j) = \frac{\sum\limits_{k=1}^{t} TERM_{ik} \cdot QTERM_{jk}}{\sqrt{\sum\limits_{k=1}^{t} (TERM_{ik})^2 \cdot \sum\limits_{k=1}^{t} (QTERM_{jk})^2}}$$

Looking only at the numerator of the cosine function, the following operations appear to be executable in parallel on an array processor of the type illustrated in Fig. 8-13:

1 The *multiplication* of the vector element $TERM_{ik}$ with the element $QTERM_{jk}$
2 The *addition* of the previous factor $TERM_{i,k-1} \cdot QTERM_{j,k-1}$ to the sum of the previous $k - 2$ products
3 The *memory fetching* operation required to extract terms $TERM_{i,k+1}$ and $QTERM_{j,k+1}$ from memory

In these circumstances, the parallelism of the AP unit appears to be immediately useful. Detailed analyses of the use of parallel computing facilities in information retrieval remain to be carried out [19].

*F   Content Addressable Segment Sequential Memory (CASSM)

The content addressable segment sequential memory (CASSM) was designed and built at the University of Florida as a general-purpose device, of benefit to all nonnumeric applications including information retrieval. The basic CASSM design is presented in Fig. 8-14. The CASSM design provides a number of distinct *cells*, each cell consisting of a storage unit and a separate processing unit. During a search operation, the various cells operate in parallel, and all the pre-

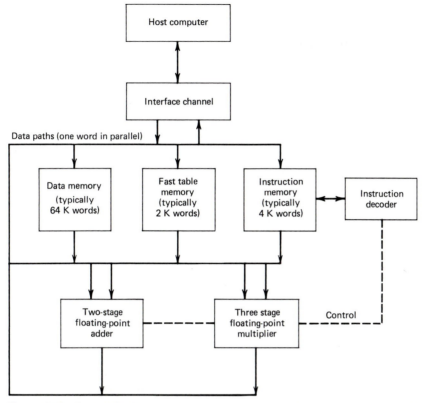

Figure 8-13 Typical floating-point array processor (constants, data, and instructions are kept in separate memories; multiplier and adder are pipelined; integer arithmetic, instruction decoder, adder, and multiplier are separate functional units).

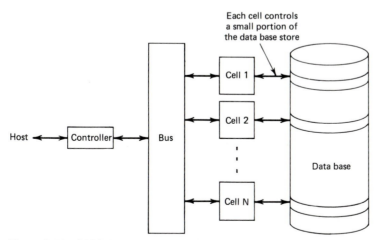

Figure 8-14 CASSM system organization. (*Adapted from reference 13.*)

liminary processing needed to choose the items to be retrieved is done in the CASSM device rather than the host machine. The actual implementation of the CASSM prototype was carried out on a special disk modified to include reading and writing units for each track of the disk [20].

An initial assumption of the CASSM design is that the entire data base will reside within the CASSM device used for data base storage. Thus, as the size of the data base increases, the storage and processing facilities of CASSM must also increase. A given data base may of course be spread over several cells.

CASSM is intended for use with a general-purpose computer acting as a "smart" peripheral device. The general-purpose computer accepts the user's commands or requests, translates these to a set of CASSM instructions, and passes these instructions to CASSM. The special-purpose device then carries out the instructions, all cells executing an instruction simultaneously.

Execution of an instruction on CASSM is broken down into three phases: (1) the instruction phase in which an operation is sent to each cell of CASSM, (2) an execution phase in which the instruction is carried out, and (3) a deactivation phase in which the current operation is removed. Each phase requires one rotation of the disk, but because CASSM is designed to carry out the three operations concurrently, one complete operation actually takes place per revolution.

A search for a specific item of information requires that the item pass a test qualifying it as a potential record of interest. That is, CASSM keeps track of the types of records it stores and checks to see if a record is of the proper type. If the record passes this test, the appropriate field within a record is located and its value examined. Only if all these conditions are satisfied will a record be retrieved.

For example, a data base may contain information on both automobiles and owners of automobiles. A search for the records for silver automobiles will therefore require:

1   A test of the record type to isolate the automobile records
2   Location of the color field for all automobile records
3   Retrieval of the record if the value of the color field is equal to SILVER

Note that this process is conducted for all records in the data base during the single revolution of a disk (about $1/60$ second).

CASSM is an experimental device and as such exists only as a prototype and simulator. The design is limited by the necessity to store the entire data base on the device. It is not clear whether the processing efficiencies could be maintained if a data base were to be loaded into CASSM in small segments in several different loading operations.

*G   Relational Associative Processor (RAP)

The relational associative processor (RAP) was developed at the University of Toronto as a device for the processing of information specified by a relational data base model (see Chapter 9). RAP, like CASSM, is a smart peripheral de-

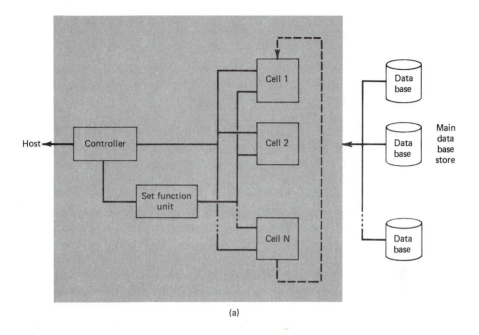

(a)

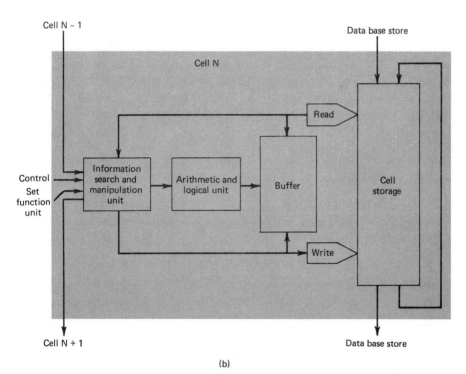

(b)

Figure 8-15   The RAP system. (a) RAP system organization. (b) RAP cell organization.

vice subdivided into cells. Each cell is capable of searching and manipulating data. The cells are interconnected as shown in Fig. 8-15a so that a cell may either manipulate data directly in its own storage or may indirectly manipulate the data in other cells. Each cell contains a buffer to connect the cell processing unit to the data base, as well as an arithmetic and logical unit and a separate search and manipulation unit as shown in Fig. 8-15b.

If the data base is small enough to fit within the cell storage areas, then RAP may be considered to be a multiple processor using direct searches. When the data base is too large for the cell storage, then the search is indirect since the necessary data must first be transferred from the main data base store. The latter case is more general; hence RAP is considered a multiple processor indirect search device.

RAP requires the general-purpose computer to interact with the user for query or command processing. These must be translated by the general-purpose device before they are sent to RAP. In operation, each cell operates simultaneously with all other cells by processing the data stored in its memory. Each information unit which meets the search criteria is then sent to a set function unit for potential integration with the results from other cells. For example, the set function unit may count the number of information items meeting the search criteria. The information items eventually selected are delivered to the general-purpose computer for presentation to the user or for further processing [21–23].

When the data base is large, RAP is used in conjunction with conventional disk drives. A section of the data base is moved to a RAP cell at each stage of operation. That is, a large data base such as the motor vehicle data base for a state government would of necessity be searched in many segments to isolate the SILVER automobiles.

The RAP operations require that all the information on one track of a disk be of the same type. That is, the automobile records would be distinct from the driver records. Thus, the search for the SILVER automobiles will not require a test of the driver records. The process needed to search for SILVER automobiles will therefore require the following steps:

1   Locating the automobile records
2   Loading the automobile records onto RAP
3   Isolating the color field
4   Retrieving the records with color field equal to SILVER

*H   Data Base Computer (DBC)

The data base computer was designed at Ohio State University to manipulate very large data bases using currently available technology. The DBC is assumed to be connected to a large general-purpose computer for direct interaction with the user. The retrieval operations are divided into two cycles, including first the functions that access the data (the data loop) and the functions associated with the structure of the information (the structure loop) as shown in Fig. 8-16.

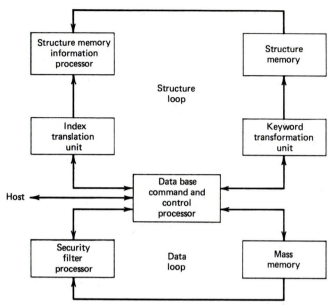

Figure 8-16 Data base computer organization.

The functions are accomplished by independent modules working on a continuous stream of data (a pipeline architecture). The central module of the DBC is the data base command and control processor. This element receives requests from the general-purpose computer system, translates these requests to commands for the various functional components of the DBC and controls the functions of the individual components. When the commands have been executed, the data base command and control processor delivers the requested information to the general-purpose computer.

The structure loop is composed of four functional units. Together these four functions translate a request into a set of physical locations to be searched. The physical locations are, in fact, blocks of mass storage which contain the information items. The data loop has two functional units which access and check the information items before they are sent to the general-purpose computer.

The structure loop first decodes keywords into one or more file names and fields within the file which must be searched. This is accomplished in the keyword transformation unit. This translation produces code numbers designating the addresses of the individual search terms.

The structure memory is, in fact, an inverted file for the data base. An entry consists of a code number and a series of three numbers of the form

LOGICAL POINTER, CLUSTER NUMBER, SECURITY SPECIFICATION

where (1) the logical pointer identifies a block of information items that are potentially relevant, (2) the cluster number is assigned to a record at the time it is entered into the data base and identifies subsets within blocks, and (3) the security specification is a simple attribute which is checked prior to the retrieval of any information.

The results from the structure memory module are then passed to the structure memory information processor. This device performs Boolean and logical operations. These operations are performed in a manner similar to that described for the inverted file operations in Chapter 2. The results of these operations are sets of logical identifiers. These identifiers are passed on to the index translation unit, which translates them from logical pointers to the physical addresses of the data items.

If the information is to be directly retrieved, the data base command and control processor passes the physical addresses identified by the index translation unit on to the mass memory. The mass memory also performs Boolean and logical operations in order to identify the actual information items to be retrieved. In comparison the structure loop determines which blocks of memory are to be examined. The mass memory unit selects the appropriate block of storage and tests the individual information items to determine which of these qualify for retrieval.

Once the specific information items have been selected, the security filter processor sorts the items into a desired order and performs final security checks to ensure that the user is qualified to receive the items [24,25].

A user request for silver colored automobiles from a data base which includes both automobiles and licensed drivers might be conducted as follows:

1 The keyword SILVER is passed through the keyword transformation unit. This converts SILVER into a code which can be used to search the structure memory.

2 The structure memory is searched for all entries with this value. This search is conducted in parallel across all entries. The result is a set of addresses of blocks of records in which at least one record contains the desired value.

3 In this simple search there is no necessity to combine sets so the structure memory information processor simply passes the addresses on to the index translator unit.

4 The index translator unit is used to convert the logical addresses to specific disk cylinder addresses. These physical addresses are then passed to the data base command and control computer.

5 The mass memory device (usually a disk) is used to scan the individual blocks identified by the physical addresses. Each record is scanned for the value of its color field, and those equal to SILVER are selected and sent to the security filter, back to the data base command and control processor, and finally back to the host computer.

I Other Special-Purpose Devices

Several devices were described in the preceding subsections that are capable of performing the entire information retrieval process, or at least major portions of the process. One can, however, also consider the development of more specialized ''black boxes'' that perform more restricted functions. An especially onerous operation is the comparison of lists of items that becomes necessary to determine the ''hits'' when Boolean queries are processed with inverted files. Indeed the lists of documents corresponding to two search terms must then be merged using set union and set intersection operations when the terms are related by OR and AND operators, respectively. When the document lists are long, the list processing operations become expensive.

In these circumstances special list merge networks may be useful in which many of the required operations are carried out in parallel. Consider, in particular, two lists of n entries each. When a single comparison unit is available capable of comparing an entry on list 1 with an entry on list 2, at least n sequential comparison operations are needed to traverse the lists. Alternatively, one can conceive of n comparison units all working in parallel using different elements of the input lists: the first entry of list 1 might then be compared with the first entry of list 2 using compare unit 1; the next entries of the two input lists are treated in compare unit 2, and so on until the last (nth) elements of the lists are processed in compare unit n.

The outputs of the initial set of comparisons might be fed in pairs to n/2 additional compare units all working in parallel, followed by n/4 more compare units on the next level, and so on down to a single unit that compares the final two elements. When such a network of comparison units is used, the n-element input lists can be ''traversed'' in log n steps, instead of the n steps needed for the single compare unit. Various devices of this type have been proposed and tested in experimental systems [26–28].

Another possibility for effecting savings in retrieval consists in optimizing the available query statement before initiating a search operation. A query preprocessing system could then be built, designed to check the query for syntactic errors, to reduce the Boolean statements to minimal form, to pretest the queries against a small data base, and to evaluate the usefulness of some search terms prior to the actual search operation [29]. In situations where information queries are submitted by users unfamiliar with the retrieval operations a query preprocessing system might well pay for itself in improved efficiencies when the final searches are actually conducted.

As an extension of the previously mentioned special-purpose devices, one might conceive of a whole array of separate devices each designed to optimize a particular operation such as text scanning, search of inverted indexes, list merging, and query reformulation. Such an organization might then constitute a powerful, but probably also expensive, retrieval configuration [30].

3 TEXT ACCESS METHODS

*A Dictionary Search Methods for Static Files

In the preceding section various hardware devices were described that may be useful to store and retrieve large information files. This section examines specific file accessing methods that are of special importance in a bibliographic retrieval system dealing with natural language texts. The first and most important task concerns the search of a dictionary or index to find the entries corresponding to particular query terms. For example, given a library catalog in which the items are arranged in alphabetical order according to author name, one may want to find the entries corresponding to particular authors. Alternatively an inverted index file must be searched to determine the location of the lists of document identifiers corresponding to particular query terms.

Linear Scan   Certain file access methods were introduced in Chapter 1. The present treatment stresses accessing methods that are particularly useful in a dynamic file environment where file additions and deletions must be processed together with information retrieval requests. The most obvious file accessing method that can be used to find a record identified by a particular search term consists in performing a *linear scan* of the complete file, one record at a time. This method can be used no matter how the file is ordered. However the traversal time of the complete file will be excessive when the file is large (of order n for a file of n records). A linear scan is therefore not normally usable in practice.

Binary Search   The next possibility consists in using an access technique that eliminates from further consideration at each search step not just one single record as in a linear search, but a whole section of the file. The well-known *binary search* described in Chapter 1 is a case in point where an ordered file is

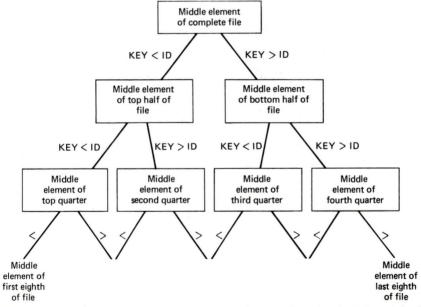

Figure 8-17 Implicit tree organization of binary search. (Search proceeds to left of node when KEY < ID and to right of node when KEY > ID.)

searched by eliminating one-half of the file still under consideration at each search step. In a binary search the query term, also known as the "key," is first compared with the record in the middle of the file. If the search key is identical with the identifier (ID) attached to the middle record, an acceptable record has been found. Otherwise, one next proceeds to the middle of the top half of the file if the key is smaller than the record ID, or to the middle of the bottom half if the search key is larger than the record ID. This process of dividing the file into two halves continues until an appropriate record is found.

The binary search may be described graphically by a tree as shown in Fig. 8-17. The elements of the ordered file which are compared with the search key are represented by the tree nodes. Whenever the value of the search key is smaller than the current record identifier, the left path is chosen from the node; conversely the right path is chosen if the search key value exceeds the value of the record ID. It is known that tree search strategies of the type illustrated in Fig. 8-17 are much faster than linear scans (of order log n instead of n as before) [31–32].

A study of the binary search strategy shows that the method used to compare the search key with a given record identifier is precisely the same at each tree node. The only difference in procedure occurring from one node to the next in the search tree is a redefinition of the portion of the file to be considered in the search. Let BEG and END designate the addresses of the first and last elements of the file, respectively, and let the address of the middle element be defined as MID = [(BEG + END)/2]. The binary search strategy for a given file F may then be summarized by the four steps of Table 8-2. Assuming that the search of the complete file is expressed by using parameters (KEY, BEG, END, FILE F), then the left path of the search tree leads to a new search with parameters (KEY, BEG, MID − 1, FILE F). That is, the end of the file is now assumed to be the record immediately preceding the middle record of the file. Moving to the right in the search tree means that the search is next carried out with parameters (KEY, MID + 1, END, FILE F). That is, the beginning of the file is now defined as the record immediately following the middle element. A process like the binary search that is carried out by repeating the same program with only a change of the parameters used is known as a "recursive" process. Recursion is an important concept in computing because the automatic equipment is especially useful when the same process can be repeated many times.

Table 8-2   Outline of Binary Search Program

		BIN SEARCH (KEY, BEG, END, FILE F)
1. If	ID[MID] = KEY	Search ends because the wanted element has been found
2. If	ID[MID] > KEY	Repeat binary search with parameters (KEY, BEG, MID − 1, FILE F)
3. If	ID[MID] < KEY	Repeat binary search with parameters (KEY, MID + 1, END, FILE F)
4. If	BEG > END	Stop the search because no entry exists in file equal to KEY

BEG: address of first element of subfile
END: address of last element of subfile
MID: address of middle element of subfile
ID[k]: identifier of kth record

Estimated Entry Search   In the binary search, the next record identifier to be compared with the search key is chosen at each point from the middle of the remaining subfile. In many cases, it is possible to make a guess about the position of a file element when its identifier is known. For example, when a normal dictionary is used to find the word RETRIEVAL, one would certainly not begin by opening the dictionary somewhere in the middle. Rather one might look about two-thirds of the way down because a term starting with the letter R would occur toward the end of the file. The same is true when trying to find someone's name in the telephone book or a given bibliographic citation in a library card catalog.

When a guess can be made about the likely position of a given record in an ordered file, the binary search can be replaced by an *estimated entry* search, which is similar to a binary search except for the computation of the next record element to be considered in the search. When good guesses are made about the position of a wanted record, an estimated entry search will be faster than a binary search (but still of order log n for a file of n items).

Direct Access Search   If one knows or can compute the exact position in which a wanted record appears in the file, the file can be accessed directly. A search of order 1 is then carried out instead of order n for a linear scan, or order log n for a tree search. A well-known direct search method, already discussed at length in Chapter 2, is the *indexed search*, where an auxiliary index is used containing the addresses of the records corresponding to a given search key. Obviously, there is no need to conduct the search of the main file in these circumstances, since the needed addresses are obtained from the index. Assuming that the index search can be performed free of charge—a very unrealistic assumption—only one (order 1) file access is required in the main file to retrieve the wanted item.

It was mentioned earlier that the creation of an index may be costly because any auxiliary file must be stored and maintained. An alternative well-known direct file access process, known as a "hashing," or "scatter storage," replaces the use of auxiliary indexes by a computation or transformation of the search key into a storage address where the corresponding records are stored.

One of the problems arising with the use of a hashing system is the choice of the hashing function used to transform the search keys into appropriate memory addresses. In general the number of possible search keys is very large, whereas the memory space available to store the corresponding record identifiers (known as the "hash table") is small. Hence it is necessary to transform a large number of possible keys into a small number of memory addresses. The transformation should be done in such a way that the available memory space is evenly used; that is, each memory address should have an equal chance of storing a given record. Furthermore, clusters of records exhibiting nearly equal keys should be broken up—for example, records corresponding to the search keys HOP and HOPE should not be mapped into the same address.

Two of the best-known hashing methods are the multiplication and divi-

Table 8-3   Typical Hashing Method Using Key Multiplication

(Assumed Hash Table Size is 64 Positions)

Record M: Key 11 01 <u>01 00</u>
  Key squared 1 0 1 0 1 <u>1 1 1 1 0 0</u> 1 0 0 0 0
  Decimal address corresponding to $(1\ 1\ 1\ 1\ 0\ 0)_2$ equals
         $32 + 16 + 8 + 4 + 0 + 0 = \underline{60}$
Record N: Key 11 01 01 01
  Key squared 1 0 1 1 0 <u>0 0 1 0 0 1</u> 1 1 0 0 1
  Decimal address corresponding to $(0\ 0\ 1\ 0\ 0\ 1)_2$ equals
         $0 + 0 + 8 + 0 + 0 + 1 = \underline{9}$

---

sion hash functions. In the multiplication method the key is multiplied by itself (squared) and the middle digits of the product are used as a record address; in the division method, the key is divided by a prime number and the remainder after division is transformed into the needed address [33]. A sample key transformation using the multiplication method is shown in Table 8-3 for two nearly equal keys using an assumed hash table size of 64 (equal to 2^6) memory positions. The two keys are 11010100 and 11010101, respectively, corresponding to the letters M and N in the well-known EBCDIC coding system. The keys differ in the rightmost binary digit only. The squaring operation produces 16-digit binary products. In the example, the middle six binary digits are then transformed into one of 64 memory addresses by conversion to decimal form. The record corresponding to key M in Table 8-3 will be located in position 60 of the hash table, whereas key N is transformed into position 9.

A hashing system (unlike a binary search scheme) can gracefully accommodate situations where several records exhibit the same key, because a complete *bucket* of records can be associated with each hash table address, rather than a single record only. A bucket provides space for several records, but even when larger buckets are used, *collisions* are unavoidable for most hash functions. A collision occurs when two or more distinct keys are transformed into the same record address. Collisions will complicate the retrieval process, because the record identifiers found in the designated buckets must be checked before the corresponding records are actually retrieved from the file. Furthermore, collisions may lead to *overflow* conditions when not enough space exists to accommodate all the records that must be located in a particular bucket. Various provisions can be made to handle the overflow: a second hashing operation can produce a new overflow bucket address located in a secondary hash table; alternatively, a pointer system can be provided to designate for each bucket the addresses corresponding to any overflow records. Overflow problems produce efficiency losses in the hashing system because extra memory accesses are then required to retrieve the needed records.

*B   Dictionary Search Methods for Dynamic Files

Dynamic and Extensible Hashing   The basic hashing or scatter storage method described up to now supports searches involving single keys in a static file with few file additions or deletions. Sequential searches that handle the records in some specified order are difficult to carry out in a hashed file, because the records are scattered throughout the storage area. The scattering of the records also destroys any natural clustering properties of the records. For example, records identified by the terms CAT and CATS will not be found adjacently, even though this might be useful in certain applications.

When the file grows and the original hash table size m becomes too small, it is necessary to rehash the whole file using a larger hash table size, say of size 2m. The rehashing operation is onerous because all file records must now be moved in storage. For this reason *dynamic* or *extensible* hashing systems have been introduced which avoid overflow conditions and the repositioning of records when the file size grows [34–36]. Various schemes have been proposed: in general an auxiliary index is interposed between the key terms and the final record addresses in the main file. The hashing operation is then used to identify an address in the index rather than in the main file, and each index position in turn points to the main file addresses of the corresponding records. Instead of changing the main file configuration as new records are added, the index is made to grow; thus when a given bucket overflows, the corresponding index entry is changed to produce two entries, corresponding to two new buckets replacing the single original bucket. Similarly, when the file shrinks, two or more buckets can be merged into a single bucket by appropriate transformations in the index. When the index is used as the hash table instead of the main file, an even use of the index space corresponds to an even use of the full memory space in the standard hashing system.

Dynamic Tree Search   It was mentioned earlier that the basic binary tree search is not easily adapted to dynamic file conditions. Since the file must be maintained in ordered sequence according to key values, an insertion of a new record into its proper place may cause the displacement of half the records in the file. Furthermore the tree traversal operation needed to locate the next record identifier to be matched against the query may be expensive to perform. Indeed for a file of n records, the binary tree exhibits $\log_2 n$ levels, and hence $\log_2 n$ different record identifiers must be compared with the query key. Since a new disk seek operation may be needed for each record identifier, the standard binary tree operation will be expensive to carry out for large files.

This suggests that a tree search could be more efficient when the number of levels in the search tree is small. The height of the tree, that is, the number of tree levels, can be reduced by packing more than one key value (record identifier) into each node of the tree. Furthermore some file growth can be accommodated by leaving space in each tree node for new key values corresponding to new records added to the file. The best known of the dynamic search trees obeying these specifications is the so-called B-tree [37–39].

In a B-tree of order d, the root node at the top of the tree contains at least one key value and two pointers to the next tree level corresponding to keys that are smaller and larger, respectively, than the original key value. Each node other than the root contains at least [d/2] key values and at most d key values. The number of pointers to the next tree level is one larger than the number of keys at the corresponding node. A typical B-tree of order 4 is shown in Fig. 8-18. Each node of the sample tree can in principle accommodate four different terms, although as few as two terms may actually be used. The number of pointers to the next tree level varies therefore between 3 and 5. The natural (alphabetic) order of the keys is maintained because the pointer to the left of a given term is used to find smaller terms than the given key value (that is, occurring earlier in the alphabetic sequence), whereas the right pointer locates larger terms that are higher in the alphabetic order. For example, the left pointer from NETWORK locates CATALOG, HARDWARE, and MORPHEME, whereas the right pointer locates REVIEW and SYNONYM.

A B-tree search is carried out like a binary tree search except that all record identifiers located at a given node are compared with the available key values and the appropriate left or right pointers are chosen depending on the outcome of the key comparisons. For example, when the B-tree of Fig. 8-18 is searched with the query term FILE, the left pointer is taken from node A, followed by the pointer located between CATALOG and HARDWARE from node B (because FILE is larger than CATALOG, but smaller than HARDWARE), followed by the pointer between ENCYCLOPEDIA and GRAMMAR from node E, and so on.

Since all key values stored in a given node are obtainable in one file access, the maximum number of file accesses is of order $\log_d n$ for a file of n items, corresponding to the height of the tree. New keys can be added to or deleted

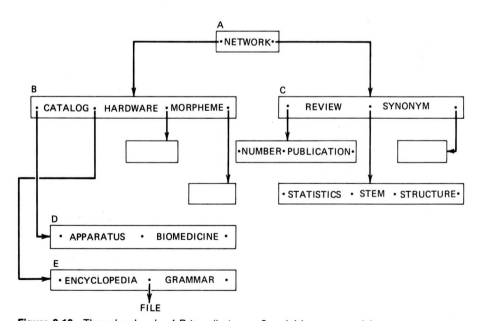

Figure 8-18   Three-level order 4 B-tree (between 2 and 4 keys per node).

from a particular node so long as the basic size restrictions are obeyed. However, when a new key value is added to a node of size d, an illegal node of size d + 1 is created. This situation is handled by splitting a node of size d + 1 into two nodes of size at least equal to [d/2]. Such a splitting operation is shown in Fig. 8-19 for a B-tree of order 4. The assumption is that the term CLASS must be added to node B of the tree of Fig. 8-19a. Since this node already contains four terms, it is split into two pieces, and a new separating term is added to the father node on the next higher tree level (node A of Fig. 8-19b). Because the father node has now grown in size by one term, it may itself have to be split. The node splitting operation may thus propagate upward along the levels of the tree, the maximum number of splitting operations being equal to the height of the B-tree.

The reverse node merging operation may become necessary when terms are deleted from a given node. This situation is illustrated in Fig. 8-20 where the term ENCYCLOPEDIA is deleted from the B-tree of Fig. 8-18. An undersized node is then produced containing only one term (node D of Fig. 8-20). This node is merged with its brother (node C of Fig. 8-20) and the term CATALOG, which is no longer necessary to distinguish the merged nodes, migrates downward by one level. The father node may then become undersized and may in turn have to be merged with a brother. The node merging operation like the earlier splitting operation may thus migrate upward along the B-tree levels.

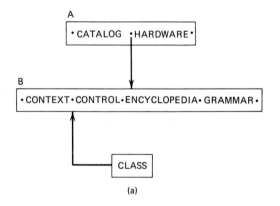

(a)

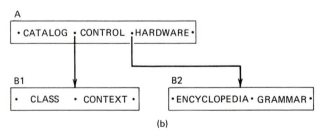

(b)

Figure 8-19 Node splitting operation for B-tree of order 4. (a) Initial condition prior to insertion of CLASS. (b) Condition following bucket splitting after insertion.

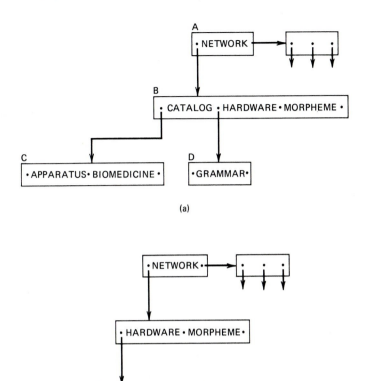

Figure 8-20 Node merging operation following term deletion. (a) Initial state following deletion of ENCYCLOPEDIA. (b) Final state following deletion of ENCYCLOPEDIA.

A search of a B-tree of order d is of order $\log_d n$ for a file of n records. The node insertion and deletion operations are also of order $\log_d n$, since each operation may affect at most one node on each tree level. A B-tree implementation requires more memory space than the conventional hashing system, because the key values and pointer structures must be kept in storage in order to be used. A B-tree search is also more time-consuming than a standard hashing operation—typically by a factor of 3 or 4; but the B-tree search is much faster than a binary search by a factor of 10 or more. Because of the simple way of reorganizing the B-trees following insertion and deletion of key values, the B-tree search system has become the standard for the implementation of dictionary and index search systems in dynamic file environments.

Many other search tree systems have been proposed to handle special situations. In the well-known *digital search trees*, or *tries*, each node of the search tree is associated with a portion of a key value rather than with a whole key. In many cases, a small number of tree levels may then be used to accommodate key values of widely varying length. For example, only three trie levels are

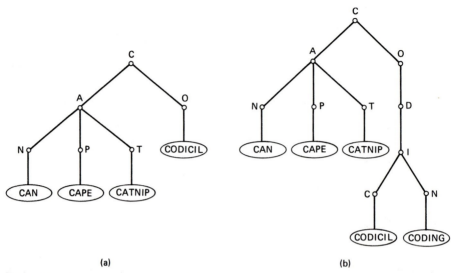

Figure 8-21 Digital search trees. (a) Initial digital search tree. (b) Digital search tree follow-ing addition of CODING.

needed to distinguish the terms CAN, CAPE, CATNIP, and CODICIL, assuming that a node is associated with a single key character, as shown in Fig. 8-21a. The basic trie structure may change drastically when new terms are added as shown in the example of Fig. 8-21b illustrating the addition of the term COD-ING. However procedures exist for optimizing the representation of digital search trees and for handling term additions and deletions [33,40–41].

*C Multiple Key Dictionary Search

All the foregoing dictionary access methods are usable for single key searches where only one query key is present. Single key searches are relatively simple to implement because the existing one-dimensional storage devices can easily accommodate a file maintained in order according to the single (one-dimensional) key values. In practice, search requests may include many different keys. For example, one wants to retrieve all the bibliographic records pertaining to a given author *and* published in a given year, or all the records dealing with INFORMATION as well as with RETRIEVAL.

The standard access methods, with the exception of systems maintaining dense (inverted) indexes for each possible key value, are difficult to adapt to multikey searches. In principle, one can maintain auxiliary indexes covering a combination of several search terms. For example, given three search terms A, B, or C, one could maintain seven distinct indexes covering the records pertaining to the keys A, B, and C separately, as well as to the possible term combinations A and B, A and C, B and C, and A and B and C. When a larger number of individual terms are present, the number of term combinations is however very large, and the task of identifying the most productive term combinations is difficult [42].

Another possibility consists in using a *superimposed coding* system, where each individual term is encoded by a binary number and the logical union of the various component codes designates the term combination. For example, assuming that CHOCOLATE, NUTS, and VANILLA are identified by codes 100010, 001001, and 100001, the query term CHOCOLATE CHIP COOKIE (assumed to be composed of CHOCOLATE, NUTS, and VANILLA) is represented as 101011 equal to $100010 \vee 001001 \vee 100001$ [33].

The superimposed coding system was introduced for retrieval in the well-known edge-notched card systems some 40 years ago. These systems are unfortunately afflicted by the "false drop" problem, where a given code combination retrieves many spurious records. Certain term codes may also be included in other term code combinations. In the previously used example, the term VANILLA is already included in the combination of CHOCOLATE and NUTS. A longer treatment of term coding systems is unhappily beyond the scope of this discussion.

D   Text Scanning Machines

In addition to the standard dictionary or index searches where table entries corresponding to particular keywords or terms must be identified, it may also be necessary in a bibliographic retrieval system to scan linear texts in order to determine whether a given phrase or query pattern occurs in the text, and if so where. Indeed, it was noted in Chapter 2 that some conventional retrieval systems include options for a so-called string search in which the query terms are directly compared with document texts or text excerpts. In these circumstances, no indexes or auxiliary files need be maintained. Unfortunately, a full text scan is normally slow and hence inappropriate for on-line searching. Special methods and devices have, however, been developed to speed up the text search process [43–47].

One particular text search device is based on the idea also incorporated into RAP and CASSM and previously illustrated in Fig. 8-8, in that several search modules are used to process different portions of the stored texts under the supervision of a master control computer. Each search module is attached to a mass storage device such as a disk. When a command is issued by the master control computer to initiate a text search, each search module begins a sequential search of its portion of the stored texts. The text read by a search module is continuously compared with the query statements. When a document is found that satisfies a particular query statement, a report is sent to a master control computer which may either directly report the discovery to the user or accumulate the information for inclusion in a summary report to the user. To gain speed, the queries can be batched and responses can be generated simultaneously for many different queries.

The actual search process may be broken into two parts: (1) term detection and (2) query resolution. Term detection is concerned with the location of query words or pattern in the stored data base. Query resolution is the process of determining if the combination of matches found by the term detection pro-

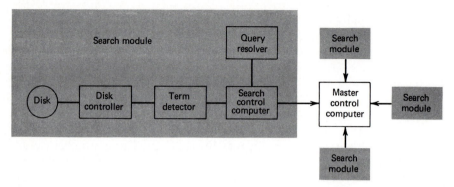

Figure 8-22 Information retrieval machine-searcher organization (several search units attached to single master control).

cess matches the term combination specified in the user's query. For example, a user may specify that two particular terms must appear in the same document (a Boolean AND operation). Additional search facilities may include term combinations based on all the Boolean operators previously discussed, as well as on word proximity, and sentence and paragraph inclusion specifications.

A typical search module for a text scanning machine could then be based on the use of four special units: a disk controller, term detector, search control unit, and query resolver, as shown in the diagram of Fig. 8-22. The search control unit carries out data transfer operations, communications between the term detector and the query resolver, and the general overall control operations for the search module. The disk controller oversees all access operations to the disk and the stored information. Equipment of the type represented in Fig. 8-22 can scan text at rates of up to 1 million characters per second using a single search module only.

**E   String Matching Using the Finite State Automaton Model

A key element in a text scanning system is the term detector which must necessarily operate rapidly if large quantities of text are to be processed under operational conditions. The most simple-minded text scanning system possible is based on a character-by-character comparison of a given query (key) pattern with a text excerpt (string). The basic procedure consists in comparing the first character of the query pattern with the first character of the text string. If these first characters match, the second characters are compared, and so on. If any pair of characters does not produce an exact match, the standard procedure is to shift the query pattern over by one character position and to restart the matching procedure. This becomes expensive because the matching process must start over near the beginning of the input pattern many times. For example, given

query pattern   AAAB
text string   AAAAAAB

16 character comparisons are required before it becomes clear that the four input characters match the last four characters of the text string. In general because of the backtracking and restart characteristics of the standard text scanning method, up to m · n character comparisons may be required in the worst case in order to match a query pattern of length m against a text string of length n.

Fortunately, more sophisticated approaches to the text scanning problem exist. Algorithms have been devised that operate in linear or even sublinear time—that is, the number of character comparisons needed does not exceed (and in fact may be substantially smaller than) the number of characters in the query and text strings, instead of the square of that number as in the earlier example [48–50]. These algorithms analyze the query pattern (that is, the query terms) prior to the actual search operation and construct auxiliary modules or tables to control the actual character comparisons used to match the query patterns with the text strings.

A favorite term detection process is based on the concept of the *finite state automaton* (FSA) which was introduced in Chapter 7 as a controlling element in the augmented transition network grammars [26,48,51]. An FSA is a conceptual machine composed of five basic elements:

1   I—a set of input symbols acceptable to the automaton
2   S—a set of states
3   R—a set of rules which determine the next state of the automaton given its current state and an input symbol
4   B—a beginning state (an element of S)
5   F—a set of (one or more) final states (elements of S)

It will be remembered from the preceding chapter that the operation of a finite state automaton is representable in diagram form by using nodes (circles) to represent the individual states and branches (edges) between the nodes to represent transitions between states. A symbol attached to each branch then represents the element of the set of acceptable input symbols causing the particular transition from one state to the next. Figure 8-23a shows a finite state automaton with a beginning state 1 and a final state 4. The input symbols accepted by the FSA are assumed to be the letters of the alphabet, and the sample automaton of Fig. 8-23a "accepts" the input string WIN.

The automaton of Fig. 8-23a handles the string WIN no matter where that string occurs in the text; that is, the automaton does not discriminate between SWINE, WIND, TWIN, and WIN. Furthermore, no instructions are given in Fig. 8-23a about what happens when the input does not contain the exact letter string W followed by I followed by N. Clearly, a usable FSA capable of detecting complete words in running text must be able to detect word delimiting, or interword characters, such as blanks that might occur between words; furthermore, instructions must be provided about what is to happen when an expected character is not received at the input. The complete automaton needed to de-

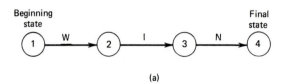

(a)

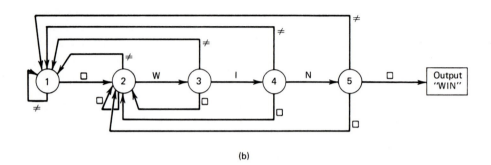

(b)

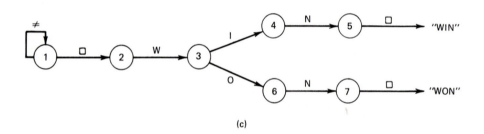

(c)

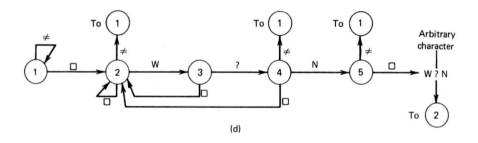

(d)

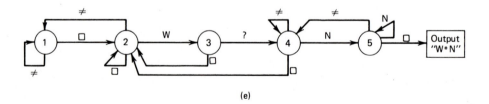

(e)

tect the word WIN is shown in Fig. 8-23b. An interword delimiter is indicated in that figure by a □, and an arbitrary character other than one attached to a labeled branch leaving a given state is designated by ≠. When the string □WIN□ occurs at the input, the traversal of the automaton from beginning state 1 to final state 5, and then back to state 2, is straightforward. If the input consists of □WON□, the normal transitions would occur from state 1 to states 2 and 3. At that point, the input character is an O; the three branches out of state 3 are labeled I, □, and ≠, respectively. Since the letter O is neither I nor □, the ≠ exit is taken from state 3 back to 1, where the automaton is now prepared anew to recognize □WIN□. The recognition process also fails for the input □WINTER□, because the path taken from state 5 returns to state 1 rather than back to state 2 via the output label "WIN."

A single automaton can be built for the detection of several query words. The graph of Fig. 8-23c presents an FSA capable of detecting WIN and WON. The alternative exits back to state 2 when a □ occurs, or back to state 1 for the occurrence of any character other than one already attached to a branch (≠), are omitted in Fig. 8-23c. The full construct including the upper (≠) and lower (□) exits is similar to that of Fig. 8-23b.

The automaton of Fig. 8-23c could be simplified by eliminating one state, if the string W?N were to be recognized, where ? represents exactly one arbitrary character. The corresponding automaton is shown in Fig. 8-23d. Note that the label ? is not identical with ≠, since ? represents any character other than □, whereas ≠ represents the default exit taken for any character other than one attached to a label. The automaton of Fig. 8-23d recognizes WAN, WIN, WON, or for that matter WNN, WZN, etc.

Suppose that one were interested in recognizing patterns such as WIN, WON, WOMAN, WOMEN, or in general the sequence W*N where * represents any character string of arbitrary length. The automaton needed for this purpose is no more complicated in principle than the one used for the recognition of "WIN" in Fig. 8-23b; it is shown in Fig. 8-23e. The main difference between Fig. 8-23e and b lies in the recognition of the arbitrary string of "don't care" characters. This requires a redefinition of the default state chosen when a specifically labeled character does not occur as expected. In the example of Fig. 8-23e the initial default state is state 1. That is, if the input consists of SIN instead WIN, one returns to state 1 from state 2 when the S occurs at the input instead of the expected W. After state 4 is reached following the input of characters □, W, and ?, the default state for ≠ characters is now changed to state 4. At that point the W has already been recognized, and any arbitrary string ending in N is now acceptable following the W. A slight complication arises for strings that include several N's following the initial W, as in WINN, or WIN-

---

Figure 8-23 (*opposite*)   Finite state automata used for string recognition. (a) Basic automaton for detection of WIN. (b) Complete automaton for detection of WIN. (c) Automaton for detection of WIN and WON. (d) Automaton for detection of W?N. (e) Automaton for detection of W*N.

		□	≠	W	I	N
	1	2	1	1	1	1
	2	2	1	3	1	1
Current	3	2	1	1	4	1
state	4	2	1	1	1	5
	5	2	1	1	1	1

Figure 8-24 Tabular representation specifying new state given current state and input symbol for finite state automaton of Fig. 8-23b.

NIN. The appropriate pointers to handle these cases are included in the graph of Fig. 8-23e.

A general finite state automaton can be defined for any user-specified string of symbols. The state transitions may be represented in each case by a table using the current state as input and specifying the corresponding next state for each acceptable input symbol. An example is shown in Fig. 8-24 for the automaton of Fig. 8-23b. The tabular representation of the finite state automaton can be used for rapid comparisons of an arbitrary incoming text with query terms previously encoded into the automaton.

In principle a separate automaton can be used for each individual term in a query. Several automata can also be combined for the detection of groups of terms and of contiguous terms. Thus, two given automata A and B could each search for a distinct term. The results of the comparison for A and B might be passed on to a new automaton C. When the two search terms are not expected to occur contiguously in the input text, the search results are directly passed on to the output device. Otherwise, automaton C is used to verify the text contiguity condition. The organization of the several finite state automata is illustrated in Fig. 8-25 [47–49].

The main problem encountered in the use of finite state automata for text scanning purposes is the need to build and maintain the transition structures for each incoming query. When new queries are continuously submitted to a retrieval system, the overhead inherent in the construction of the transition matrices may lower the efficiency of the process for operational use. On the other hand, if the query set remains constant over long periods of time—such as in systems for the selective dissemination of information—the state transition matching process is straightforward and efficient.

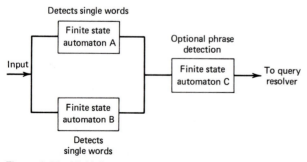

Figure 8-25 Multiple term detection using finite state automaton.

Various other efficient text scanning methods have been developed in the last few years [49–50]. The Boyer and Moore method is one of the most attractive ones. It is briefly described in the next subsection.

**F   The Boyer and Moore String Matching Method

Like the previous FSA string detection system, the Boyer and Moore (BM) method depends on a prior analysis of the query pattern [50]. Specifically to use the BM process it is necessary to construct an auxiliary table including the positions in the pattern for all individual characters, as well as for all contiguous character strings consisting of more than one character.

Consider, for example, the input

```
1   2   3   4   5   6
B   A   N   A   N   A
```

A character position number may be used to designate the place of each character in the pattern. The pattern analysis would note that character B occurs in position 1, character A in positions 2, 4, and 6, and character N in positions 3 and 5. Furthermore the pair AN occurs in positions 2, 3, and 4, 5; NA occurs in 3, 4, and 5, 6; ANA occurs in positions 2, 3, 4, and 4, 5, 6; and so on. The position information is used later to determine the place where a matching operation must be restarted once a mismatch between characters has occurred.

The BM algorithm proceeds by first comparing the rightmost (rather than the leftmost) character in the pattern with a particular character in the string. If a match is found, a left shift is made and the character to the left of the rightmost pattern character is treated. A string pointer is used to designate the string character that must currently be matched with the given pattern character. This pointer is moved left by one character position when a match occurs; when a character mismatch occurs, the string pointer is moved to the right so as to designate the next string character to be compared with the rightmost pattern character. The principal complexity in the BM algorithm consists in determining exactly the pointer shift (in number of string characters to be skipped) in the event of mismatch.

Two principal rules are used to specify the permissible pointer shift when a mismatched character is detected:

1   When a mismatched string character is detected, an attempt is made to find that string character elsewhere in the pattern, and to determine the pattern shift necessary to achieve coincidence (known as the Δ_1 shift); should the string character not occur in the pattern at all, a shift by the whole length of the pattern is in order.

2   When a portion of the pattern matches some substring in the text, an attempt is made to find a repeating occurrence in the pattern of the originally matching subpattern; the shift needed to bring the new occurrence of the subpattern in coincidence with the matching substring is known as the Δ_2 shift.

In order to detect a complete match between a query pattern and a pattern of the text string, the conditions giving rise to the Δ_1 and Δ_2 shifts must both be satisfied, because a mismatched string character must eventually find a match in the pattern (hence the Δ_1 shift), and an already matching part of the pattern must again be matched following a pointer shift operation (hence the Δ_2 shift). At each point in the matching process it is then appropriate to execute a shift equal to the maximum between Δ_1 and Δ_2.

Consider the following query pattern and text string:

```
         1 2 3 4 5 6 7 8 9
Pattern: c b a a b c a b c
String:  a b c d e f a b c a b c d e f a b c . . .
                       ↑ √ √ √
```

After a successful comparison between the ninth (last), eighth and seventh characters, a mismatch is found in the sixth character position. At this point, two pattern shifts are possible. Consider the Δ_1 shift first: Since the mismatched string character f occurs nowhere in the pattern, the pattern can be shifted all the way beyond the f character position, producing the following new situation:

```
Pattern:           c b a a b c a b c
String:  a b c d e f a b c a b c d e f a b c . . .
                                       ↑
```

The Δ_2 shift is determined by finding a new occurrence of the matching subpattern abc in positions 7 to 9. Since the abc subpattern is repeated in pattern positions 4 to 6, a shift of 3 will maintain the match with the originally matching substring:

```
P:         c b a a b c a b c
S: a b c d e f a b c a b c d e f a b c
           √ √ √       ↑
```

Since the largest possible pointer shift is most advantageous, the Δ_1 shift is executed in the case under consideration. A full example of the BM process is included in Fig. 8-26 [52].

It is easy to see that the number of required character matches between strings and patterns will decrease as the differences between the text string and query patterns increase (that is, as fewer string characters occur in the pattern) and as the pattern exhibits fewer repeating portions. Normally, the number of character mismatches is much larger than the number of character matches. In such a case, the number of character comparisons will be substantially less that the text string length, and the BM process will prove particularly efficient. A disadvantage of the BM process is that embedded "don't care" characters occurring in the middle or at the end of the query patterns are difficult to handle.

```
        1 2 3 4 5 6
P :  B A N A N A
S :  I - W A N T - T O - F L A V O R - N A T U R A L - B A N A N A S
                ↑
```

(a) T≠A and T does not occur in pattern : shift by pattern length.

```
P :          B A N A N A
S :  I - W A N T - T O - F L A V O R - N A T U R A L - B A N A N A S
                ↑
```

(b) L≠A and L does not occur in pattern : shift by pattern length.

```
P :              B A N A N A
S :  I - W A N T - T O - F L A V O R - N A T U R A L - B A N A N A S
                      ↑
```

(c) N≠A, but N occurs in pattern; to bring N in coincidence with next occurrence in pattern, Δ_1 shift = 1.

```
P :                B A N A N A
S :  I - W A N T - T O - F L A V O R - N A T U R A L - B A N A N A S
                        ↑ √ √
```

(d) NA matches NA, but -≠A; next occurrence of NA in pattern is in positions 3 and 4 of pattern; to bring matching parts in coincidence Δ_2 shift = 2; since nonmatching string character does not occur in pattern, can shift pattern beyond -; that is Δ_1 shift = 4

```
P :                  B A N A N A
S :  I - W A N T - T O - F L A V O R - N A T U R A L - B A N A N A S
                          ↑ √
```

(e) A matches A, but R≠N and R does not occur in pattern; Δ_2 shift = 2 to reach next occurrence of A in pattern; Δ_1 shift = 5 to shift beyond R.

```
P :                      B A N A N A
S :  I - W A N T - T O - F L A V O R - N A T U R A L - B A N A N A S
                              ↑
```

(f) N≠A, Δ_1 shift = 1 to reach next occurrence of N in pattern.

```
P :                        B A N A N A
S :  I - W A N T - T O - F L A V O R - N A T U R A L - B A N A N A S
                                ↑ √ √ √
```

(g) ANA = ANA but B≠N; for next occurrence of ANA in pattern Δ_2 shift = 2; for next occurrence of nonmatching string character B, Δ_1 shift = 2.

```
P :                          B A N A N A
S :  I - W A N T - T O - F L A V O R - N A T U R A L - B A N A N A S
                                  √ √ √ √ √ √
```

(h) Complete match.

Figure 8-26 Sample pattern match using BM process.

Don't care conditions occurring at the beginning of the queries do not, however, pose any special problems.

In operational environments, a decision on what process to choose for text matching purposes must depend on a comparison between the programmed string matching methods and the previously described special-purpose hardware devices or information retrieval machines that may be available for use.

4 SUMMARY

The purpose of this chapter has been to present actual information retrieval hardware devices and processing methods and to mention some new possibilities for information retrieval implementation in a changing technological environment. Technological changes have raised the possibility of greatly increased processing efficiencies. One of the most significant of these changes is the movement of some of the processing power to specialized data storage devices. That is, through the use of smart peripherals, the quantity of information that must be transferred from one storage device to another may be reduced. Information is examined where it is stored, and only that portion passing the initial screening is actually transferred for additional processing.

Second, there is interest in the development of specific devices for certain information retrieval tasks. Each step in the information retrieval process may be analyzed and special devices may help to carry out the individual steps. The result may be a series of special-purpose devices that collectively constitute a powerful retrieval system.

In addition to the special-purpose hardware, efficient data structures and file access procedures have been introduced which perform dictionary and index table searches in a dynamic file environment with a minimum of file rearrangement. The dynamic hashing and B-tree file search procedures are especially attractive in this connection.

Finally, new text matching methods implemented by hardware or by software programs can now be used for a fast scanning and detection of character patterns in running texts. These text scanning systems may in time be used to find answers to queries by a direct examination of the texts rather than by the conventional inverted file processing.

Whether these developments will find favor with the users and managers of retrieval systems ultimately depends on their economic viability as well as on their ease of use and effectiveness. One may expect results from practical tests of the new methodologies within the next few years.

REFERENCES

[1] W. Durant, The Story of Civilization: Part 1, Our Oriental Heritage, Simon and Schuster, New York, 1954.
[2] W.L. Schaaf, editor, Our Mathematical Heritage: Essays on the Cultural Significance of Mathematics, Collier Books, New York, 1963.

[3] M. Bohl, Information Processing, 2nd Edition, Science Research Associates, Chicago, Illinois, 1976.

[4] V. Bush, As We May Think, Atlantic Monthly, Vol. 176, No. 1, 1945, pp. 101–108.

[5] L.C. Smith, ''MEMEX'' as an Image of Potentiality in Information Retrieval Research and Development, Third International Information Retrieval Conference, Cambridge, England, June 1980.

[6] N. Knottek, Mini and Microcomputer Survey, Datamation, Vol. 24, No. 8, August 1978, pp. 113–124.

[7] T.C. Chen, Computer Technology and the Database User, IBM Corporation, Research Report RJ-2316, San Jose, California, August 1978.

[8] P.W. Williams, The Potential of the Microprocessor in Library and Information Work, Aslib Proceedings, Vol. 31, No. 4, April 1979, pp. 202–209.

[9] A.D. Pratt, The Use of Microcomputers in Libraries, Journal of Library Automation, Vol. 13, No. 1, March 1980, pp. 7–17.

[10] F.G. Withington, Beyond 1984: A Technology Forecast, Datamation, Vol. 21, No. 1, January 1975, pp. 54–73.

[11] B. Parhami, A Highly Parallel Computing System for Information Retrieval, Proceedings of the Fall Joint Computer Conference, AFIPS Press, Montvale, New Jersey, 1972, pp. 681–690.

[12] R.S. Rosenthal, The Data Management Machine—A Classification, Proceedings of Third Workshop on Computer Architecture for Non-Numeric Processing, Association for Computing Machinery, New York, May 1977, pp. 35–39.

[13] O. Bray and H.A. Freeman, Data Base Computers, Lexington Books, Lexington, Massachusetts, 1979.

[14] C.C. Foster, Computer Architecture, Encyclopedia of Computer Science, A. Ralston and C.L. Meek, editors, Petrocelli/Charter, New York, 1976, pp. 263–268.

[15] P.B. Berra, Data Base Machines, ACM SIGIR Forum, Vol. 12, No. 3, Winter 1977, pp. 4–22.

[16] K.E. Batcher, STARAN Series E, Proceedings of the 1977 International Conference on Parallel Processing, August 1977, pp. 140–143.

[17] A.L. Robinson, Array Processors: Maxi-Number Crunching for a Mini Price, Science, Vol. 203, 12 January 1979, pp. 156–160.

[18] C.N. Winningstad, Scientific Computing on a Budget, Datamation, Vol. 24, No. 10, October 1978, pp. 159–173.

[19] G. Salton and D. Bergmark, Parallel Computations in Information Retrieval, in Lecture Notes in Computer Science, Vol. 111, W. Handler, editor, Springer Verlag, Berlin-New York, 1981, pp. 328–342.

[20] G.P. Copeland, C.J. Lipovski, and S.Y.W. Su, The Architecture of CASSM: A Cellular System for Non-Numeric Processing, Proceedings of the First Annual Symposium on Computer Architecture, Association for Computing Machinery, New York, December 1973, pp. 121–125.

[21] P.J. Sadowski and S.A. Schuster, Exploiting Parallelism in a Relational Associative Processor, Proceedings of the Fourth Workshop on Computer Architecture for Non-Numeric Processing, Association for Computing Machinery, New York, August 1978, pp. 99–109.

[22] S.A. Schuster, H.B. Nguyen, E.A. Ozkarahan, and K.C. Smith, RAP2—An Associative Processor for Data Bases and Its Application, IEEE Transactions on Computers, Vol. C-28, No. 6, June 1979, pp. 446–458.

[23] S.A. Schuster, H.B. Nguyen, E.A. Ozkarahan, and K.C. Smith, RAP2—An Asso-

ciative Processor for Data Bases, Proceedings of the Fifth Annual Symposium on Computer Architecture, Association for Computing Machinery, New York, April 1978, pp. 52–59.

[24] D.K. Hsiao and K. Kannan, The Architecture of a Database Computer—A Summary, Proceedings of the Third Workshop on Computer Architecture for Non-Numeric Processing, Association for Computing Machinery, New York, May 1977, pp. 31–34.

[25] D.K. Hsiao, K. Kannan, and D.S. Kerr, Structure Memory Designs for a Database Computer, Proceedings of the ACM '77 National Conference, Association for Computing Machinery, New York, October 1977, pp. 343–350.

[26] L.A. Hollaar, Text Retrieval Computers, Computer, Vol. 12, No. 3, March 1979, pp. 40–50.

[27] L.A. Hollaar, A Design for a List Merging Network, IEEE Transactions on Computers, Vol. 28, No. 6, June 1979, pp. 406–413.

[28] W.H. Stellhorn, An Inverted File Processor for Information Retrieval, IEEE Transactions on Computers, Vol. C-26, No. 12, December 1977, pp. 1258–1267.

[29] S.E. Preece, Design for a Modular Query Pre-Processor System, Proceedings of the Annual Meeting of the American Society for Information Science, American Society for Information Science, Washington, DC., 1974.

[30] L.A. Hollaar and D.C. Roberts, Current Research into Specialized Processors for Text Information Retrieval, Proceedings of the 4th International Conference on Very Large Data Bases, September 1978, pp. 270–279.

[31] C.E. Price, Table Look-up Techniques, Computing Surveys, Vol. 3, No. 2, June 1971, pp. 49–65.

[32] W.A. Burkhard and R.M. Keller, Some Approaches to Best-Match File Searching, Communications of the ACM, Vol. 16, No. 4, April 1973, pp. 230–236.

[33] D.E. Knuth, The Art of Programming, Vol. 3: Searching and Sorting, Addison Wesley Publishing Company, Reading, Massachusetts, 1973.

[34] M. Scholl, New File Organizations Based in Dynamic Hashing, ACM Transactions on Database Systems, Vol. 6, No. 1, March 1981, pp. 194–211.

[35] R. Fagin, J. Nievergelt, N. Pippenger, and H.R. Strong, Extendible Hashing—A Fast Access Method for Dynamic Files, ACM Transactions on Database Systems, Vol. 4, No. 3, September 1979, pp. 315–344.

[36] P. A. Larson, Dynamic Hashing, BIT, Vol. 18, 1978, pp. 184–201.

[37] D. Comer, The Ubiquitous B-Tree, Computing Surveys, Vol. 11, No. 2, June 1979, pp. 121–137.

[38] J. Nievergelt, Binary Search Trees and File Organization, Computing Surveys, Vol. 6, No. 3, September 1974, pp. 195–207.

[39] R. Bayer and E. McCreight, Organization and Maintenance of Large Ordered Indexes, Acta Informatica, Vol. 1, No. 3, 1972, pp. 173–189.

[40] E.H. Sussenguth, Jr., The Use of Tree Structures for Processing Files, Communications of the ACM, Vol. 6, No. 5, May 1963, pp. 272–279.

[41] E. Horowitz and S. Sahni, Fundamentals of Data Structures, Computer Science Press, Woodland Hills, California, 1976.

[42] V.Y. Lam, Multiattribute Retrieval with Combined Indexes, Communications of the ACM, Vol. 13, No. 11, November 1970, pp. 660–665.

[43] A. El Masri, J. Rohmer, and D. Tusera, A Machine for Information Retrieval, Proceedings of the Fourth Workshop on Computer Architecture for Non-Numeric Processing, Association for Computing Machinery, New York, August 1978, pp. 117–120.

[44] D.C. Roberts, A Specialized Computer Architecture for High Speed Text Searching, Second Workshop on Computer Architecture for Non-Numeric Processing, Association for Computer Machinery, New York, 1976.

[45] R.M. Bird, J.B. Newsbaum, and J.L. Trefftzs, Text File Inversion: An Evaluation, Proceedings of the Fourth Workshop on Computer Architecture for Non-Numeric Processing, Association for Computing Machinery, New York, August 1972, pp. 42–50.

[46] R.M. Bird, J.C. Tu, and R.M. Worthy, Associative/Parallel Processors for Searching Very Large Textual Data Bases, Proceedings of the Third Workshop on Computer Architecture for Non-Numeric Processing, Association for Computing Machinery, New York, May 1977, pp. 8–16.

[47] D.C. Roberts, A Specialized Computer Architecture for Text Retrieval, Proceedings of the Fourth Workshop on Computer Architecture for Non-Numeric Processing, Association for Computing Machinery, New York, August 1978, pp. 51–59.

[48] A.V. Aho and M.J. Corasick, Efficient String Matching: An Aid to Bibliographic Search, Communications of the ACM, Vol. 18, No. 6, June 1975, pp. 333–340.

[49] D.E. Knuth, J.H. Morris, and V.R. Pratt, Fast Pattern Matching in Strings, SIAM Journal of Computing, Vol. 6, No. 2, June 1977, pp. 323–350.

[50] R.S. Boyer and J.S. Moore, A Fast String Searching Algorithm, Communications of the ACM, Vol. 20, No. 10, October 1977, pp. 762–772.

[51] R. Haskin, Hardware for Searching Very Large Text Databases, Proceedings of Fifth Workshop on Computer Architecture for Non-Numeric Processing, Association for Computing Machinery, New York, March 1980, pp. 49–56.

[52] G. Salton, Automatic Information Retrieval, Computer, Vol. 13, No. 9, September 1980. pp. 41–56.

BIBLIOGRAPHIC REMARKS

The following texts contain introductory descriptions of information technologies:

M.Bohl, Information Processing, 2nd Edition, Science Research Associates, Chicago, Illinois, 1976.This is a good introduction to computer systems, providing a large number of illustrations for easy visualization of the various devices and their uses.

J.G. Burch, Jr., and F.R. Strater, Jr., Information Systems—Theory and Practice, 2nd Edition, Hamilton Wiley Company, Santa Barbara, California, 1979. The appendix to this text provides an excellent short introduction to information technologies.

More advanced descriptions of computer hardware are included in:

D.P. Siewiorek, C.G. Bell, and A. Newell, Computer Structures: Principles and Examples, McGraw-Hill Book Company, New York, 1982, 926 pages.

H.W. Gschwind and E.J. McCluskey, Design of Digital Computers—An Introduction, 2nd Edition, Springer Verlag, New York, 1975.

G.A. Korn, Minicomputers for Engineers and Scientists, McGraw-Hill Book Company, New York, 1973, 303 pages.

The development of information technologies for applications such as information retrieval is often covered in workshop proceedings such as those on Computer Architecture for Non-Numeric Processing published by the Association for Computing Machinery. Many of the developments from these conferences are synthesized in a single text:

O. Bray and H.A. Freeman, Data Base Computers, Lexington Books, Lexington, Massachusetts, 1979.

A variety of journals regularly cover new hardware development, including in particular the journals published by the Computer Society of the IEEE (Institute of Electrical and Electronics Engineers). Of particular interest is the readable *Computer,* and the more technical *IEEE Transactions on Computers.* Software procedures useful for dictionary access and text processing often appear in literature published by the Association for Computing Machinery, notably the *Communications of the ACM* and the *ACM Transactions on Database Systems.*

EXERCISES

8-1 In information processing the main file characteristics, such as file size and record contents, normally determine the storage medium used to maintain the records as well as the file access methods. Thus, a file of 100 bibliographic records each described by author name, document title, journal name, volume number, date of publication, pagination, and short abstract may best be accommodated on a set of 3 by 5 index cards that are manually searched to find a given item. Card storage is inexpensive; the file is easily updated, and rapid file searches are possible when the file size is small. As the file grows, a manually accessed card file necessarily becomes less advantageous. Describe the desirable characteristics of an automatic device capable of storing and manipulating each of the following files:
  a A file of 1,000 bibliographic records organized sequentially according to the alphabetic ordering of the title. The file is moderately active—that is, a fair number of searches are conducted; but the volatility is low—there are few additions and deletions.
  b A file of 1,000,000 records stored in random order. The file is very active but of low volatility.
  c A file of 1,000,000 records stored in random order.The file is active as well as volatile.
  d A file of 1,000,000,000 records stored in random order. The file is moderately active, but with relatively few additions and deletions.
8-2 As the technology used to store a given file of records changes, conversion costs are incurred in the changeover from one medium to another. For example, the conversion of a manual file into a computer-based file may entail a costly keypunching operation to transfer the original information onto punched cards from where the information can in turn be transferred onto tape or disk. Identify the problems and costs incurred in the following changes of storage technology for a given file of records:

     a Magnetic tape to magnetic disk

     b Magnetic disk to associative array storage

     c Magnetic disk to data base computer

8-3 Changes in storage technology may produce advantages in the accessing and file updating operations. Identify the benefits obtained from the file conversions listed in Exercise 8-2.

8-4 Describe in flowchart form the complete process used to answer the following queries:

     (1) TERM A AND TERM B

     (2) TERM A NOT TERM B

     (3) TERM A WITH TERM B   (WITH $\equiv$ in same sentence as)

     Assume that the following storage technology is used to store the corresponding file of records:

     a An associative array processor such as the Staran

     b The data base computer

8-5 Three main characteristics may be identified that are of primary importance in information retrieval:

     a The file searches should be efficient as well as effective.

     b The user interface should permit a relatively effortless interaction between user and system.

     c The storage medium should accommodate files of substantial size.

     Describe methods and techniques capable of accommodating these various aims. Are there limitations indicating that the stated requirements cannot all be met simultaneously by a single system?

8-6 Consider three retrieval systems with the following sets of keywords:

     a BAT, CAT, HAT, MAT, SAT

     b FAIR, FAITH, FALL, FAME, FAN, FANCY

     c HE, SHE, HER, HERE, THERE, SHEAR

     For each keyword system, construct a system of finite state automata capable of recognizing the various keywords in a text scanning system. Can you think of a method whereby a single set of states is used to store repeating portions of the various keywords—for example, the ending AT in part a or the sequence FA in part b?

8-7 Use the Boyer-Moore method to compare the keyword FANCY with the document title "FANATIC FANNY FARMER STRUCK MY FANCY." Show all steps and explain each of the required character shifts. How many character comparisons are needed to obtain a complete match?

Data Management Systems

0 PREVIEW

Bibliographic information retrieval systems have a good deal in common with other information systems, such as question-answering and data base management systems. Information retrieval and question answering share a common interest in natural language processing. The bond between information retrieval and data base management is provided by the common storage structures — both types of systems use inverted file directories — and the common processing strategies. The design and operations of data base management systems are examined in this chapter.

The main characteristics of the several types of information systems are summarized first, followed by a description of the principal features of data base management systems. The three well-known data base models known as the relational, hierarchical, and network models are introduced. Certain query-processing strategies are then examined that may help in extracting relevant information from the data base in answer to incoming user queries. Finally, the use of data base management systems for the preservation of data quality is described, including the data security and integrity provisions that are often used, and the restart and recovery techniques that can be invoked when system failures occur.

The chapter closes with a brief discussion of the problems arising when several users are allowed to use a data base management system concurrently, and when the stored files are distributed among several cooperating, remotely located sites.

1 TYPES OF INFORMATION SYSTEMS

A Information Retrieval and Question Answering

The previous chapters dealt primarily with document retrieval systems, designed to retrieve bibliographic references in answer to queries submitted by the user population. In that context, the term "information" receives the specialized interpretation of data derived from texts or bibliographic items. Ideally, information retrieval systems can retrieve many different kinds of products for the user, including full bibliographic citations for the retrieved items, abstracts, lists of assigned keywords, contract and project numbers, references to other documents, or even full document texts. The expectation is that many of the retrieved documents will contain elements that directly respond to the user's information needs. Indeed, the success of the existing bibliographic retrieval systems indicates that these systems are used as an important source of information by many users.

Unfortunately the existing systems are restricted in many ways: most importantly, users are not given direct facts in answer to any question, but rather obtain information that may lead to answers; second, the existing systems confine themselves to the retrieval of document citations or document excerpts only. That is, following the document retrieval step, most systems do not provide additional automatic aids to process or interpret the retrieved data. Instead, the users are left entirely to their own devices when it comes to interpreting and utilizing the retrieved information.

In actual fact, many user queries require data from a variety of sources. This may include normal bibliographic references and also nonbibliographic data of many kinds such as product information, marketing data, technology forecasts, business data, information about federal rules and regulations, legal decisions, and industrial or manufacturing summaries. As it happens, data bases covering these and many other classes of information already exist in the field, but the methods needed to coordinate the various data sources and to provide simple and compatible accessing procedures are not available [1].

It is likely that most information system users are interested in facts, rather than in documents that need to be studied before the needed information can be extracted. One possibility for simplifying the user's task in this respect consists in breaking up each document into small pieces—for example, individual chapters, pages, paragraphs, or even sentences—and in retrieving the individual pieces rather than full documents only. The work on *passage retrieval* that was briefly mentioned in Chapter 7 constitutes a step in that direction. If this approach were to be effective, it might become necessary to analyze the document content sufficiently deeply to be able to characterize the various text portions and to point out differences and relationships between them. Furthermore, the full document texts must also be stored to provide the needed passage retrieval capability.

Passage retrieval is attractive because the basic retrieval process used for full document retrieval, including the file organization, query formulation, and user-system interaction methods, may remain unchanged. On the other hand, the information input and analysis tasks are now vastly more complicated, and the resulting system may be too expensive to use. In the final analysis, passage retrieval may constitute a step in the right direction so far as the user is concerned, but the ability to answer questions by citing specific facts included in the data base is still lacking.

The *question-answering* systems mentioned in Chapter 7 are specifically designed to provide direct answers to questions; however, the earlier discussion indicated that the construction of unrestricted question-answering systems was not a likely prospect for the visible future. Not all relevant facts could possibly be stored in any particular system, nor could all the needed relationships between stored facts be identified in advance. Necessarily then, a viable question-answering system would operate with a restricted data base using procedures for refining the available information as needed by deducing new facts from already available information and supplementing the description of incompletely specified items by extraneous knowledge.

Simple deductive systems can be built that are capable of answering many questions for which the direct answer is not initially contained in the data base. Thus, given the facts that "Joe Smith is an employee" and that "All employees are at least 18 years old," an answer generating system could be built to handle correctly a question such as "Is Joe Smith at least 18 years old?" However, more complicated situations are easy to imagine where even sophisticated systems would soon become stymied. Consider, for example, a knowledge base consisting of the following sentences:

Joe Smith is an employee.
87 percent of all employees are union members.
Joe Smith voted in the last election.

It is obvious that the question "Is Joe Smith a union member?" cannot be answered unequivocally. However, if one knew that Smith's job classification entails compulsory union membership, an answer might be provided. Alternatively, if it were known that a union election had recently been held, the system could answer "yes" with reasonable confidence, assuming that information was available to the system about labor unions and elections and the interactions between them.

In the earlier examples, potential ambiguities—for example, the distinction between political elections and union elections—were deliberately disregarded. Unfortunately, linguistic ambiguities are unavoidable and effective disambiguation or interpretation methods are not readily available. It is not surprising then that practical question-answering systems have been based on highly simplified world pictures where only a small number of facts are used, the description of all items is unambiguous and complete, and the relationships between the items are prespecified. In such situations, direct answers can be provided to a wide variety of questions. The so-called data base management systems are the most widely used and most successful systems in this class. They are examined in the remainder of this chapter.

B Data Management Systems

Data management systems exhibit many similarities with standard information retrieval systems: a stored data base is generated and maintained, and information searches are conducted resulting in the retrieval of portions of the stored data in answer to user queries. The distinguishing characteristic in data management systems is the definite structure of the stored information: instead of dealing with natural language texts as in document retrieval, or with arbitrary facts as in question answering, uncertainties and ambiguities are eliminated by using only information items whose structure is severely restricted and completely specified. In particular, data management systems normally process files of data described by a small set of prespecified *attributes*. For example, a file of personnel records may be identified by the names of the people involved, the addresses, the age of each person, the job classifications, and the yearly salaries for each person. Each attribute may be expected to carry only one of a small number of specific *values*—for example, the age attribute may range in value from 18 to 65 for the employees in question. A particular record in the file can then be described by citing the specific values taken on by the attributes for that particular record. Thus the person named Smith might be specified as

(NAME = Smith; ADDRESS = 110 Main St.; AGE = 25;
JOB CLASS = 123; SALARY = 19,500)

It is obvious that in such an environment many of the most difficult retrieval problems can be bypassed, including in particular the choice of the indexing language, and the content analysis and indexing operations themselves. Furthermore, by assuming that each item is completely and unambiguously described by the chosen *attribute values* (the values of the available attributes), the type of processing to be carried out is also limited. In particular, one would want to compare the attribute values specified in a user query with the attribute values characterizing the stored data in the hope of retrieving all records whose attribute values match a given set of query attribute values, or all records whose attribute values fall within a certain range (for example, all persons whose age is between 25 and 35). In addition, data base management systems may be designed to perform simple numeric processing tasks, such as determining counts of the number of records obeying a particular specification—for example, the number of books published in a given year, or by a particular publisher; or obtaining averages, such as the average cost of the books published in a given year.

It is easy to see that systems exhibiting the capabilities outlined above fulfill many immediate needs in a variety of different circumstances: it becomes possible to choose rapidly from a list of employees all those qualified for a given job, or from a set of military personnel all those currently present in a given geographic area and able to take on a particular task. Similarly, one can obtain manufacturing components from a parts inventory obeying particular specifications, or identify mail items that need to be routed in a given direction, or airline flights scheduled for specified routes.

Systems capable of performing tasks of that kind are known as *data base management systems* (DBMS). They are enjoying great popularity and widespread use at the present time [2–5]. Certain data base systems have been adapted for specialized use by particular user classes. *Management information systems* (MIS) are essentially data base management systems that include additional computational features thought to be of interest to managers. Thus, given sales figures covering certain periods of time, a trend analysis could be carried out using an MIS that would project these figures into the future [6–9].

Management information systems extend the processing capabilities of standard data base management systems in a direction useful to management personnel. In the so-called *decision support systems* (DSS) the aim has been to extend the basic file processing routines by adding capabilities from other areas of computer application including, for example, graphic data processing, pattern matching, and artificial intelligence. The aim in this case is to provide in an easily accessible form the large diversity of resources normally thought to be needed for decision making purposes.

Consider as an example the person responsible for the design of school bus routes in a given community. Such a person requires information about the number of school-age children living in particular areas, the number and type of available school buses, the distances between various points on prospective routes, and the schedules followed in various schools. In addition to this standard information that could be provided by conventional data base management systems, other less tangible, but potentially equally important data might also be used to solve the routing problem. This could include information about peak traffic loads, icy road conditions, and traffic light placement. Information might also be useful concerning the composition of voting districts in the community, and the expected opposition from the parents to some of the proposed bus routes. Once a particular routing is tentatively chosen, the ideal decision support system would provide simulation capabilities, complete with graphic output displays, through which the progress of the various buses could be monitored in a dry-run situation in the hope of detecting problem areas before final decisions are actually reached.

Completely flexible decision support systems are not currently used in practice, but beginnings have been made in many application areas including medicine, banking, and airline management [10–15]. Most existing systems lack the ability to use information from many different sources, and in addition provide only limited processing aids. The chart of Fig. 9-1 exhibits relation-

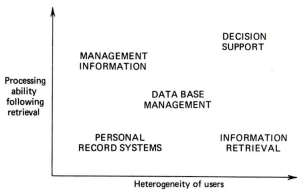

Figure 9-1 Characteristics of several information systems.

ships between various types of information systems based on the type of user that is likely to be attracted to the system and the processing ability following an initial retrieval action. Whereas normal bibliographic retrieval systems must serve many different user types but provide little processing support beyond retrieval, the reverse is true of management information systems. Decision support systems are demanding on both accounts, which explains why such systems are not yet widely used.

The data base management systems, by constrast, are widely used and have achieved great sophistication with considerable theoretical background. They share the main file structures and search methodologies with bibliographic retrieval, and they provide processing facilities that are also of interest in the bibliographic retrieval environment. The data base management systems will be studied in the remainder of this chapter.

2 THE STRUCTURE OF DATA BASE MANAGEMENT SYSTEMS

A Basic Concepts

It was mentioned earlier that many of the harder problems arising in information retrieval are avoided in data base management because of the simpler, more structured nature of the data being manipulated. On the other hand, the missing content analysis and other text processing operations are replaced in the DBMS by a greater concern for *user friendliness* and *data quality*, and by the inclusion of sophisticated methods for processing and updating the data base. In a typical bibliographic retrieval system, ordinary users are not allowed to change the stored data. This contrasts with a DBMS, where much of the design complexity is associated with the data manipulations and the available methods for introducing changes to the stored information. Furthermore, data base systems are designed to be used by nonexperts, and great care is taken to insulate the users from the details of the processing system, and by extension to ensure that users cannot interfere with each other. This implies that in addition to providing the normal search and retrieval capability, the system is also charged with various access control tasks and with the preservation of data integrity and correctness.

A data base management system exhibits three main components: first a *data base* consisting of a variety of files broken down into individual records together with the accessing and file maintenance operations performed on the files; second, a *communications* system that provides the interface between the system users and the automatic system, including also the message handling, editing, and output display functions; and finally, a *transaction management* system that is charged with the scheduling of jobs received from the various users, the access control to the files, the handling of concurrent operations for tasks that may be carried out simultaneously, and the implementation of restart and recovery procedures following system failure.

The following features, which are present in most data base management implementations, render such systems attractive to the user populations [16–21]:

1 The user application programs can normally be written without detailed know-how of the methods used to represent and organize the data in storage, and without regard to the particular procedures used to access the data. In other words the user programs exhibit *physical data independence* because they do not depend on the actual implementation methods used by the data base management system.

2 Attempts are also made to provide *logical data independence* in the sense that the user programs may effectively be independent of the internal structure of the data base objects and of the various relationships which may be defined between objects.

3 High-level language facilities are often provided to help the users in submitting queries to the system and in specifying the required file processing operations.

4 Data quality may be maintained by having the user supply validation statements concerning the characteristics of files and data items—for example, a specification of the range of values that may be acceptable for specific attributes—and letting the system automatically provide error checks designed to verify the validation assertions.

5 Restart facilities are provided charged with maintaining correct processing sequences when failures occur by having the system record the status of current conditions at appropriate intervals and using backup facilities to resume the programs after corrections based on the recorded status information.

6 *Security* provisions may be incorporated in the form of privacy transformations and access controls to ensure that the stored information is not misused or misappropriated.

To translate the high-level process specifications into specific machine operations and to provide the data independence mentioned earlier, it is necessary to store a detailed description of the file structures actually used and of the structure of the individual records included in each file. This description of the data and file representations is known as a *schema*. Various schema types may

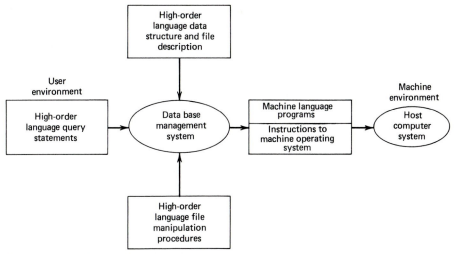

Figure 9-2   Environment for typical data base management system. (*Adapted from reference 21.*)

be distinguished, including the *external* or *user schema* utilized by individual customers to specify the structure of their own data, a *conceptual schema* which is common for all users and serves to supply the required data independence, and finally a machine or *internal schema* used to represent the actual physical data structures that are needed by the system to carry out the file processing operations.

Normally high-level "data description" languages are provided by the data base management system to help the system users in specifying the individual user schemas. Once a schema is specified by the user, the translation of the external schema into the internal form used by the programs is then completely left to the system. In performing the program setup and translation operations,

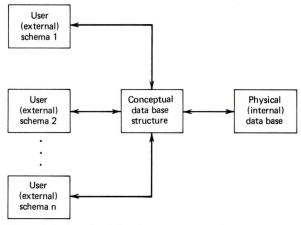

Figure 9-3   Levels of data base representation.

the system normally uses a stored *data dictionary* which records the description of all objects in the system, including the files and corresponding file schemas, the user terminals and their identifications and characteristics, the individual users and their status and file access authorizations, and the particular transactions or file manipulations that actually need to be carried out.

The structure of a typical data base management system from the user's viewpoint is shown in Fig. 9-2, and the relationship between the various file descriptions is summarized in Fig. 9-3.

B Structure of Information Items

To describe the individual operations of a data base management system, it is necessary to consider in more detail the structure of the information which needs to be manipulated. The utilization of special information structures constitutes in fact a principal characteristic distinguishing conventional bibliographic retrieval from data base management: specifically, the information used in bibliographic information retrieval is normally assumed to be unstructured, and the data elements are often self-describing in the sense that it is easy to distinguish author names from publishers or document titles. In a data base management environment the individual record elements are not self-describing, and a definite record structure is either assumed or implied.

Consider as an example the components of a typical bibliographic record used by the INSPEC retrieval service and represented in Table 9-1. This record includes three types of identifiers, including the objective terms such as author, journal, or page numbers; the content identifiers consisting in Table 9-1 of freely chosen terms and terms extracted from a controlled vocabulary arrangement; and finally the title and abstract of the document. In addition to the structure implied by this list, a great deal of syntactic and semantic structure is inherent in the language of the title and abstract; furthermore, the chronological relationship which exists between the actual article and the bibliographic references attached to the item can be used to define explicit hierarchical relations between articles.

In actual fact, the linguistic structure built into a bibliographic record is not normally used in information retrieval. The terms and keywords are nearly al-

Table 9-1 Components of Bibliographic Record Used by INSPEC Service

Title of item	Number of references
Author name(s)	Classification codes
Author affiliation(s)	Controlled index terms
Publication identification	Free index terms
Volume, issue, or part number	Type of article or treatment
Date of publication	(for example, bibliography
Page numbers	or literature survey,
Language of publication	general or review article)
Full text of abstract	

ways assumed to be independent of each other, and the language analysis methods needed to exhibit the linguistic structure of title and abstract are expensive to carry out and not sufficiently reliable for practical use. In data base management the situation is very different because structure is deliberately built into the records and used in retrieval.

To describe the structure of the information items in a data base system, it is convenient to distinguish the *entities* being manipulated from the *attributes* characterizing the entities. The normal distinction between the two depends on the role they play in a particular retrieval environment: entities are data objects that have an independent life of their own, and as such they constitute the elements of principal interest for the user of the retrieval system; attributes, on the

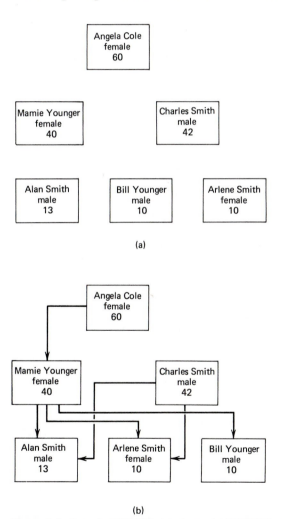

Figure 9-4 Sample PERSON data base. (a) PERSON entities identified by attributes NAME, SEX, AGE. (b) PERSON entities with specified parent-child relations.

other hand, exist only because they are assigned as identifiers to the defined entities. The choice of appropriate entities and attributes to be used in a given data base system is a matter of substantial difficulty for the data base designer, and data elements used as attributes in one context may well be defined as entities in another. For example, the entity STUDENT may be characterized by the attribute TEACHER who is responsible for a particular class in which the student is registered; on the other hand, a TEACHER may constitute a separate entity identified by separate attributes. A typical entity class consisting of persons identified by attributes NAME, SEX, and AGE is shown in Fig. 9-4a. The actual values of the attributes characterizing the individual persons are included in Fig. 9-4.

It is customary in DBMS environments to define two types of *relationships* between entities, including the generic or *hierarchical inclusion* relationships where some entities are general or governing types of entities and others are narrower and thus dependent on the more general ones. In that case, a hierarchical, tree-type arrangement can be used to represent the relationships such that the governing entities are placed above the corresponding descendants in a two-dimensional graph. Typical hierarchical relationships are whole/part and parent/child relationships. The parent/child relationships defined for the data base of Fig. 9-4a are identified in Fig. 9-4b by vertical pointers (arrows) to the hierarchically inferior child.

The other type of relationship between entities includes the nonhierarchical relationships for which an unambiguous governing-descendant characterization cannot be used. Many different types of nonhierarchical relationships may be used in particular cases, including, for example, cause/effect relationships (as between "poison" and "death") and actor/acted upon relationships (as between "pilot" and "plane"). To represent nonhierarchical relationships, *networks* instead of tree structures must normally be used where the pointers once again represent connections between related entities. A typical example is shown in Fig. 9-5 for the entity types PILOTS, EMPLOYEES, PLANES, and DEPARTURES. The pilots have a flight capability, being certified to fly certain planes; at the same time the pilots are also employees of an airline company. The airline assigns certain employees to particular departures, each departure representing a flight leaving at a certain time and date with a particular routing. Obviously a plane must also be assigned to each departure. Relationships such as those illustrated in Fig. 9-5 cannot be represented by a hierarchical tree arrangement [22,23].

For efficient implementation, relationships between entities are often classified according to how many entities of one type may be associated with the entities of another type. Thus there may be one-to-one (1:1) relationships as between PLANES and DEPARTURES, a particular unique plane being normally assigned to each given departure. Alternatively the relationship may be many-to-one (n:1) as between STUDENTS and CLASSROOM, where many students are assigned to a given class, or many-to-many (n:m) as between PROJECTS and EMPLOYEES, where one project occupies many employees but one employee may be assigned to many projects.

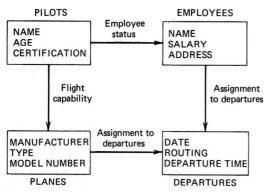

Figure 9-5 Typical nonhierarchical relationship in data base.

In the data base, the relationships between entities are normally represented by *pointers* included as identifiers for a given entity, and representing the addresses of the related entities. Thus in the example of Fig. 9-4, the record for Mamie Younger includes three pointers, one each to specify the addresses used to store the record for Alan Smith, Arlene Smith, and Bill Younger. The use of physical address pointers simplifies the handling of information requests in which entity relationships play a role, such as, for example, "Give the name and age of all descendants of Mamie Younger" or "Are there any pilots less than 30 years old that earn over $50,000?"

Only relationships between entities have been discussed up to now. However, explicit or implied relationships can also be recognized between attributes of entities. Thus semantic relations of many kinds are definable between attributes, such as, for example, the relationship between a person's age and his occupation (elementary school children are normally less than 15 years old, whereas plumbers or welders are over 15). Another type of relationship between attributes depends on whether the values of certain attributes may or may not be the same for distinct records of a collection. Consider, for example, a personnel file and assume that the social security (SS) number uniquely identifies each person in the file. In these circumstances, it is clear that if two records happen to be identified by the same SS number, then necessarily the age attribute must also be the same, because the two records then represent the same person. Technically speaking, one says that a *functional dependency* exists between the social security number of a person and the age of that person, or the SS number functionally determines the age.

Semantic relationships and functional dependencies between attributes are usable in file design and to verify the correctness of the data, as will be seen later.

*C The Relational Data Base Model

Depending on the kind of relationships that are explicitly used in the data manipulations, it is customary to distinguish three abstract data base models, known, respectively as the relational, the hierarchical, and the network models. As the names indicate, the hierarchical and network retrieval models are based, respectively, on hierarchical and network types of relationships between the entities. In the *relational data base model* no explicit relationships are defined between entity types, and no pointers are actually stored. Instead, the relationships between the entities must be derived before they can be used in answering the queries. Because of the absence of directly specified relationships, the relational model is conceptually easy to deal with, but the processing needed to retrieve the records wanted in response to a given query may be quite complex [24,25].

A *relation* is simply a table representing the records in a given file in such a way that each record, also known as a *tuple*, is identified by an ordered set of attribute values. In other words, each record corresponds to a particular row of the table, and all rows are assumed to be distinct and of the same length. The order in which the rows appear in the table is immaterial and so is the order of the columns. Each column corresponds to a particular attribute characterizing the records, the column entries being the values of that attribute for the various records. A sample relation is shown in Table 9-2 representing a collection of students.

Each relation is characterized by its *relation scheme,* which is simply the ordered list of attribute names used to identify the records. The relation scheme for the sample relation of Table 9-2 is RELSCHEME (NAME, NUMBER, CLASS, CREDITS, ADDRESS, CITY). Some attributes or subsets of attributes can be used uniquely to identify the records included in a given relation. These are known as *candidate keys* or simply keys. Normally, one of the candidate keys, known as the *primary key,* is actually selected to represent the records. For the relation of Table 9-2 all the attributes except for CLASS are candidate keys. The student number (which certainly uniquely identifies a given student) could be used as the primary key.

A particular data base normally includes relations corresponding to a number of different relation schemes. The list of relation schemes characterizing a given data base is known as a *relational data base scheme*. A typical example is shown in Fig. 9-6 for a data base dealing with employees, managers, and projects. When a query is processed which requires information from more than one relation, it must be possible to relate the record information included

Table 9-2   A Sample Relation

Name	Number	Class	Credits	Address	City
Brindle	01764	SOPH	60	264 First St.	New York
Camino	25611	FRESH	20	11 A St.	Kansas City
Daniel	43799	SENIOR	100	1011 Main St.	Kingston
Katzer	77084	GRAD	130	2146 Meadowbrook	Philadelphia
McGill	37340	SOPH	45	1819 Edgemont	Washington
Noreault	19450	SOPH	48	12 Ackerman	Syracuse
Salton	30981	GRAD	110	2365 Meadowlark	Cambridge
Waldstein	47592	JUNIOR	90	12 Woodsy Ave.	Ithaca

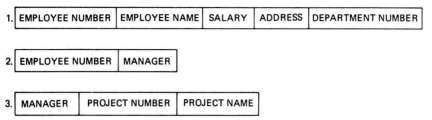

Figure 9-6 Sample relational data base scheme.

in one relation with the information contained in some other relation. In the absence of pointers to relate corresponding records, the record relationships are obtainable indirectly if some of the attributes characterizing the records are included in more than one of the relation schemes that make up a given data base. In other words, the pointer structures used in the hierarchical and network data base models are replaced in the relational model by redundancy in the stored attributes.

For the sample relational data base scheme of Fig. 9-6 the EMPLOYEE NUMBER is included in both the first and the second relation schemes, and the attribute MANAGER is included in the second and third relation schemes. Thus by choosing entries in the first and second relations corresponding to a common employee number, one can identify the manager corresponding to a given employee. An additional search in the third relation for the manager record corresponding to a given manager included in the second relation determines the project to which a given employee is assigned.

In addition to interrogating a data base, typical relational database operations include the insertion of records into a relation, as well as the deletion and the modification of stored records. The required operations may be summarized by use of a *relational algebra* that manipulates relations [25]. The following operations are of main interest:

1 Given two homogeneous relations in which the records are identified by the same number and the same types of attributes, the *union* of the two relations is a new relation containing all the distinct tuples contained in either of the original ones. Given relations R and S shown in Fig. 9-7a and b, respectively, the union R ∪ S is shown in Fig. 9-7c. The record (Adams, 25, New York) appears only once in the union, even though it is contained in both R and S, because duplicated tuples are not allowed in a relation.

2 The *difference* between two homogeneous relations contains all tuples from the first relation that are not also contained in the second one. The difference R − S appears in Fig. 9-7d.

3 A *selection* operation can be used to choose certain *rows* of a relation, depending on conditions imposed on the values of certain attributes. The general notation used to choose certain tuples from a relation R is SELECT$_F$(R), where F is a formula expressing a condition. Figure 9-7e shows the relation SELECT$_{(NAME = ADAMS)}$(R) consisting of all records in R whose NAME attribute is "Adams."

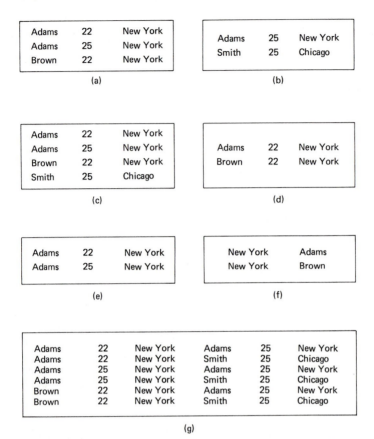

Adams	22	New York
Adams	25	New York
Brown	22	New York

(a)

Adams	25	New York
Smith	25	Chicago

(b)

Adams	22	New York
Adams	25	New York
Brown	22	New York
Smith	25	Chicago

(c)

Adams	22	New York
Brown	22	New York

(d)

Adams	22	New York
Adams	25	New York

(e)

New York	Adams
New York	Brown

(f)

Adams	22	New York	Adams	25	New York
Adams	22	New York	Smith	25	Chicago
Adams	25	New York	Adams	25	New York
Adams	25	New York	Smith	25	Chicago
Brown	22	New York	Adams	25	New York
Brown	22	New York	Smith	25	Chicago

(g)

Figure 9-7 Relational algebra. (a) Relation R. (b) Relation S. (c) Relation R ∪ S. (d) Relation R − S. (e) Relation SEL$_{(NAME\ =\ ADAMS)}$(R). (f) Relation PROJ$_{3,1}$(R). (g) Relation R × S.

4 The converse of a select operation is known as a *projection*. In a projection, certain columns are chosen from an original relation to form a new relation, care being taken as usual to eliminate any row duplications that may result. The order in which the columns appear in the projected relation may be altered as part of the project operation. Figure 9-7f contains a relation PROJECT$_{3,1}$(R) obtained by taking column 3 followed by column 1 from the original relation R. The deletion of the second attribute eliminates the distinction between the first two tuples of R; a single tuple (New York, Adams) thus replaces the two original tuples in the projected relation. Project operations are useful to break down large complex relations into several smaller and simpler ones.

5 The *Cartesian product* R × S of two relations R and S is a new relation consisting of all possible unique tuples obtained by taking a tuple from R followed by a tuple from S. The length of the rows in R × S is equal to the sum of the length of tuples in R plus the length of tuples in S. Relation R × S is shown in Fig. 9-7g. Unless duplicate tuples are generated, the number of rows in

R × S is equal to the product of the number of tuples in R and S. The Cartesian product operation can be used to construct a single large relation from two or more smaller ones.

The five basic operations of the relational algebra can be used to generate additional operations that may be useful. Thus the intersection of two relations R ∩ S is defined as R − (R − S); that is, it consists of all tuples in R that are not only in R. Of particular interest is the *join* operation in which a single relation is formed from two initially given relations based on certain conditions of equality or inequality among the attribute values included in the relations. Two types of join operators may be distinguished known as the *natural* (or unrestricted) join and the *restricted* (conditional) join. Both of these operations are effectively special cases of the Cartesian product operation, and they are used to construct larger relations from smaller ones.

The restricted join is a product operation where conditions are imposed on the values of attributes from the original relations. The notation T $\underset{(B<D)}{JOIN}$ V used in Fig. 9-8f implies that the joined relation consists of the tuples which result by taking a tuple from relation T followed by a tuple from relation V with the added condition that the value of attribute B in relation T be smaller than the value of attribute D in relation V. A restricted join is then equivalent to a Cartesian product followed by a select operation. The restricted join is illustrated in Fig. 9-8f for the relations T and V shown in Figs. 9-8d and e. The first tuple in the joined relation (1,2,3,3,1) is obtained by juxtaposing the first tuple

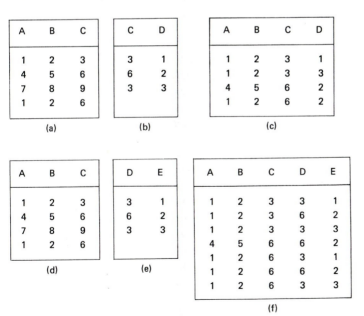

Figure 9-8 Join operations. (a) Relation T. (b) Relation U. (c) Natural join (unrestricted) T JOIN U. (d) Relation T. (e) Relation V. (f) Relation join T $\underset{(B<D)}{JOIN}$ V.

from T and the first tuple from V [(1,2,3) and (3,1), respectively]. In that case, the value of attribute B in relation T (2) is clearly smaller than the value of attribute D in V (3).

For the *unrestricted or natural join,* the assumption is that certain attributes in the relations to be joined cover the same domain of values, that is, certain columns in the two relations represent values for the same attribute. Such a situation exists for relations T and U of Fig. 9-8a and b where attribute C is repeated in both relations. The unrestricted join is then similar to the restricted join except that the join condition is assumed to be the equality of the components for the columns representing identical attributes. For the example of Fig. 9-8 the operation T JOIN U is then equivalent to the restricted join T JOIN$_{(C = C)}$ U . In addition one copy of each duplicated column resulting from the join operation is eliminated in the natural join. In the example of Fig. 9-8c only one copy of column C is maintained instead of the two produced by the normal join operation.

The natural join is used when items are wanted for which the components are initially stored in different relations. Thus given the relational data base scheme of Fig. 9-6, a natural join of relations 1 and 2 produces a list of employees together with the corresponding managers. Similarly a natural join of relations 2 and 3 produces a list of managers followed by the corresponding employee numbers, project numbers and project names.

Sample retrieval operations using the relational model are examined later in this chapter.

*D   The Hierarchical Data Base Model

The relational data base model is conceptually very simple, because each file is represented by a table with homogeneous rows consisting of a specified number of attribute values. To obtain answers to information requests, a great deal of work may, however, become necessary to manipulate the relations, including, for example, the previously mentioned join and Cartesian product operations. In addition, large relations may have to be maintained in which certain attribute values are repeated many times. This last solution reduces the number of needed join operations but entails substantially increased storage costs. Thus by maintaining a single relation consisting of the list of managers together with the corresponding employee names one avoids the join between relations 1 and 2 of Fig. 9-6. In the large, single relation, the name of the manager is repeated once for each corresponding employee.

The choice between operational complexity and increased storage cost inherent in the relational model may be avoided by complicating the storage structures through the introduction of pointers connecting different types of records. In the hierarchical model the assumption is that a natural hierarchy is definable where a large number of narrow entities can conveniently be related to a small number of broader entities, that are in turn relatable to still broader entities, and so on, until a single global entity remains at the top of the hierarchy. For example, individual citizens live in cities that are grouped into counties which in turn are located in states, and so on. A typical hierarchical arrangement of *record types* is shown in Fig. 9-9a. When a many-to-one relationship exists between a given type of record (record type) A and a second record type B, the records of type A are considered hierarchically inferior to those of type B. Hence in the hierarchical arrangement type A would be listed below type B.

In the example of Fig. 9-9, the assumption is made that each postal region contains many post offices each of which in turn serves as a center for many postmen; furthermore each postman services many postal patrons. In the actual file arrangement a hierarchically superior entity can be stored together with all the inferior entities to which it is related. This is suggested in the illustration of Fig. 9-9b. One possible physical implementation for such a system is the pointer chain of Fig. 9-9c, where the record for postman A *points to* (gives the address of) the record of patron a, which in turn points to the next patron ser-

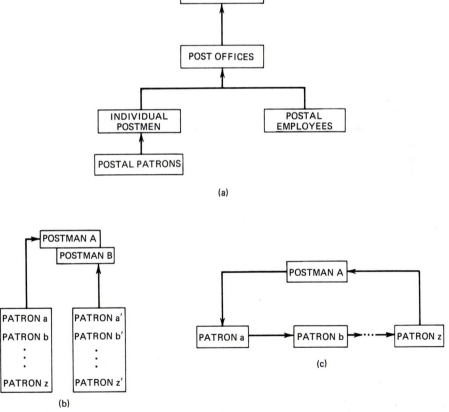

Figure 9-9 Hierarchical data base system. (a) Hierarchical arrangement of record types. (b) Many-to-one relationship between record types. (c) Pointer chain arrangement.

viced by the same postman (patron b), and so on, down to the last patron, whose record then points back to postman A to complete the chain.

Obviously such an arrangement makes it easy to retrieve the set of postal patrons corresponding to a given postman. More generally, in the hierarchical data base system the file structure is accessed in a top-down manner by starting at the top of the hierarchy and proceeding downward in the tree structure until all desired items are found.

When a tree structure is usable to represent the relationships between record types in a natural way, a hierarchical data base system affords an efficient implementation of the search and retrieval problem. Unfortunately, hierarchies appear restrictive in many situations. Consider, for example, the data base of Fig. 9-6 used earlier as an example. If one assumes that each manager handles many projects and many employees, one obtains the structure shown in Fig. 9-10a. The structure of Fig. 9-10a makes it difficult to relate employees and projects. If one were interested in the set of employees assigned to the various projects, one could create a second set of employee records placed below the project information, as shown in Fig. 9-10b. In that case, some of the employee information would be duplicated in the file system.

Suppose now that some employees are assigned to many projects. In that case, a many-to-one relation exists between projects and managers as well as between projects and employees, corresponding to the structure of Fig. 9-10c. Such a structure is not allowed in a hierarchy because the PROJECT records now have two hierarchically superior record types. This can be avoided by creating a second tree to be added to the tree of Fig. 9-10b. Such a tree is shown in Fig. 9-10d. The combination of the two trees of Fig. 9-10b and d is now usable to represent all the necessary relationships for the original data base of Fig. 9-6. For obvious reasons a solution which consists in the use of several partly overlapping hierarchies is not ideal, because a great deal of the stored information must be duplicated and jumps are necessary from one tree to another to gain access to appropriate portions of the data base.

Much duplication in the stored data can be avoided by introducing additional pointer systems to be used together with the normal physical pointers. Consider, for example, the tree structure of Fig. 9-10a, and assume that it becomes necessary to add data indicating that some employees are assigned to many projects. In other words, the projects records are considered to be hierarchically inferior not only to the manager records but also to the employee records. This could be done by adding as a new tree the structure of Fig. 9-10d necessitating the duplication of certain project as well as certain employee information. The duplication can, however, be avoided by using a new set of so-called logical pointers connecting employees to the projects to which they are assigned. The PROJECT file then becomes a logical child (logically inferior) to the logically superior employee file. This is shown in Fig. 9-11a, where the logical pointers are symbolized by dashed connections.

The logical pointer system effectively introduces nonhierarchical relationships into the data base system without abandoning the basic hierarchical struc-

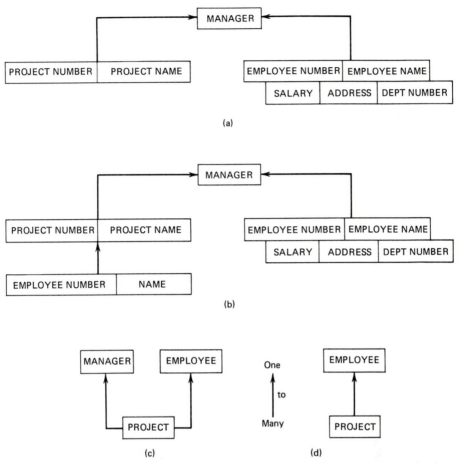

Figure 9-10 Relationships between record types. (a) Sample hierarchical structure for data base of Fig. 9-6. (b) Altered structure accounting for many-one relation between employees and projects. (c) Hypothetical relationship between record types. (d) Structure reflecting assignment of employees to many projects.

ture. In the example of Fig. 9-11b the dual pointer system provides two kinds of siblings for the PROJECT file: the physical siblings consisting of sets of projects directed by the same manager, and the logical siblings consisting of projects to which a given employee is assigned in common. An example of this situation is shown in Fig. 9-11b, where projects a, b, and c are physical siblings since they are all managed by the same manager, whereas projects a and d are logical siblings because employee 1 is assigned to both projects.

One more problem must be mentioned concerning the representation of many-to-many relationships between types of records. It was seen earlier that the normal hierarchical arrangement accommodates only many-to-one and one-to-one relationships. Many-to-many relationships do occur in many situations, and provisions must be made for them in an effective data base system. Con-

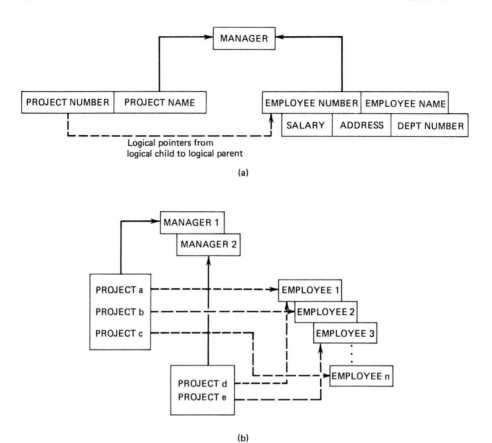

Figure 9-11 Logical pointer structure. (a) Hierarchical data base with logical pointer arrangement. (b) Pointer arrangement illustrating physical and logical connections.

sider again the sample data base of Fig. 9-10b, where the many-to-one relationship between employees and projects is represented by physical pointers. If the logical pointers already used in Fig. 9-11a to relate the PROJECT and EMPLOYEE records were added to the structure of Fig. 9-10b, a method would be provided to represent the many-to-many relationship between projects and employees. In that case, the many-to-many relationship is replaced by two many-to-one relationships, one of them being implemented by logical pointers as shown in Fig. 9-12a.

An alternative, more direct way for implementing many-to-many relationships between two record types consists in creating a third record type representing the intersection between the two original types of records. The many-to-many relationship can then be represented by conventional many-to-one pointers between each of the original record types and the newly defined intersection records. For the example under discussion, the intersection records could specify the percentage of time each employee spends on a particular project. The logical structure of the resulting data base is shown in Fig. 9-12b

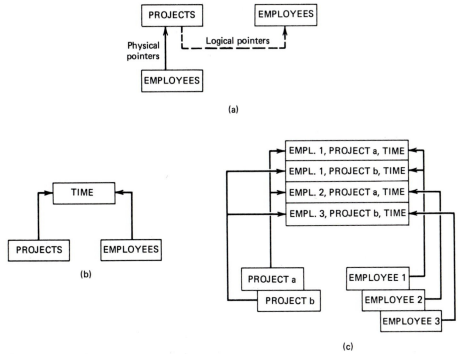

Figure 9-12 Implementation of many-to-many relationships in hierarchical systems. (a) Implementation of many-to-many relationship using logical pointers. (b) Use of intersection records. (c) Sample data base for structure of part b.

where TIME records are used to represent the intersection. A short example, showing the pointer structure used for two projects and three employees, is included in Fig. 9-12c.

The use of logical in addition to physical (hierarchical) pointers and of intersection record types adapts the hierarchical data base model to most processing requirements. The usefulness of the hierarchical structure is not diminished by the alterations because the hierarchy always controls the record access. Specifically, each record is stored together with its descendants (the other records to which it is related by a many-to-one relationship), and each descendant is stored in turn with its own descendants. Access to the tree structure is obtainable by using the records located at the *root* of the tree, that is, at the top of the tree in the illustrations. For the hierarchy shown in Fig. 9-9a, access must be obtained by first looking at the file of postal regions, which in turn gives access to certain post office records from where one can get to individual postmen or postal employee records. An example of an access implementation is shown in Fig. 9-13.

In the illustration of Fig. 9-13 an index is provided to access the records constituting the root, that is, the records of type A. The descendants of each particular record of type A, say a_i, are then stored sequentially after a_i in tree accessing order. The accessing order used in the example of Fig. 9-13 is known as "preorder," where the root is listed first for each subtree, followed by the leftmost child which is in turn followed by its leftmost child if there is one. When no further children are available, the next sibling to the right of the most recent child is taken up, and so on until the tree is exhausted. For the subtree starting at the root record a_{10}, the preorder list contains in order a_{10}-b_1-b_2-d_1-d_2-c_1-c_2.

To find a particular record in the tree the index is first consulted to find a particular record among the root records. From there the pointers are followed to the corresponding list of child records. This list is then scanned until the wanted record is found. Since the number of child records may be variable, and the initial ordered arrangement may change as records are added and deleted, it is prudent to provide overflow storage in addition to the primary storage area for the lists of records. Records that do not fit into the primary area are then pushed into the overflow area, which is connected to the primary storage by pointers as shown in Fig. 9-13c.

The access arrangement illustrated in Fig. 9-13 is known as the hierarchical indexed sequential access method (HISAM). It is used in the well-known Information Management System (IMS) implemented by IBM [16,26,27]. In the HISAM access method, immediate access is obtained only to certain records of the root of the tree; the remaining records are then located by a sequential scanning process. A faster (but more expensive) accessing method consists in providing pointers to access the individual descendants of each root record. This is done in the hierarchical direct access method (HIDAM). In the HIDAM organization, individual pointers would thus connect each pair of adjacent records in

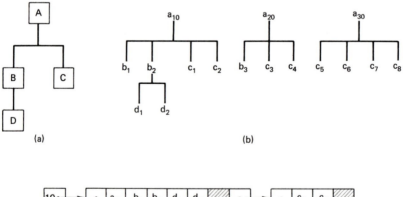

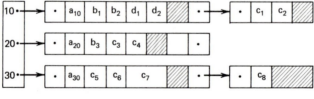

Figure 9-13 Typical hierarchical indexed sequential access method (HISAM). (a) Basic structure. (b) Sample data base. (c) Indexed sequential storage arrangement.

the access path (for example, in the data base of Fig. 9-13 from a_{10} to b_1, from b_1 to b_2, from b_2 to d_1, and so on). A hashing method could also be used to access the records located at the root of the tree instead of the special index shown in Fig. 9-13. In that case, one obtains a direct hierarchical access system (HDAM). Because the popular IMS data management system is based on hierarchical data structures, the hierarchical model has been widely accepted as a basis for data base operations.

*E The Network Data Base Model

The network data base model has been intensively studied over many years and has been sanctioned by official groups charged with the standardization of automated data processing activities [28–30]. More specifically, a special group of experts known as the Data Base Task Group (DBTG) was set up some years ago by the Conference on Data Systems Languages (CODASYL) in order to study and propose standards for data base processing. Since the parent CODASYL committee had earlier been responsible for the development of the well-known Common Business Oriented Language (COBOL), the DBTG eventually proposed a model for data base management, known as the DBTG proposal, which is designed to operate with COBOL. The DBTG proposal uses a network data structure and has served as the basis for the design of several network data base systems; the IDS/II system designed by Honeywell Information Systems is a typical example [31].

The underlying idea behind both the hierarchical and the network data base models is the need for easy manipulation of different types of records. The pointer systems are designed to make it easy to "travel" from a particular record occurrence to the set of related records. It was seen earlier that the principal relationship between different record types used in the hierarchical model was a many-to-one correspondence between a set of records of some particular type and a single record of some other type. The simple many-to-one relationship also forms the basis for the network model, but in that model the allowable patterns of many-to-one relations are more flexible than in the hierarchical case. For example, in a network model, several different many-to-one relationships can be defined from a single record type, say, A, to various other record types B, C, D, etc. The structure of Fig. 9-10c that is disallowed in the hierarchical model is specifically permitted in a network implementation. On the other hand, the direct use of many-to-many relationships is still prohibited because of the resulting complications in the pointer structures. Intersection record types may again be used for the substitution of many-to-one relationships for the original many-to-many relationship, as explained earlier.

The greater complexity of the allowable relationships in the network model simplifies the navigation in the data base, that is, the movement from one record type to another as required to generate answers to certain queries. On the other hand, the file access becomes more complicated. Consider, as an example, a set of suppliers of certain goods, and a set of clients that order these goods. A many-to-many relationship is definable between the supplier records and the goods records because one supplier may furnish many different items, while a single item may be obtained from several suppliers. Analogously, a many-to-many relationship also exists between the client records and the goods records because once again a client buys many items while one item may be bought by many clients. This situation is represented schematically in Fig. 9-14a.

Since the many-to-many relationships are not directly representable, two new record types can be introduced: the first one, labeled "quantity," provides the quantity of a certain item ordered by a particular client; and the second, known as "price," can state the price for an item obtained from a particular supplier. Using the three basic record types and the two intersection record types, the two many-to-many relationships of Fig. 9-14a are now replaceable by four many-to-one relationships as shown in Fig. 9-14b.

The structure of Fig. 9-14b is obviously not a hierarchy and could not therefore be directly used in a hierarchical system. In a hierarchical system it would be necessary to break up the structure into several trees following duplication of the intersection records. In a network system, a direct implementation is possible by using, for example, pointer chains of the kind shown in Fig. 9-9c to represent the many-to-one relationships. In the terminology used by the Data Base Task Group, the set of records included in a particular pointer chain, consisting of a particular single record of type A and of the number of related records of type B, is known as a "data base set." (The term "set" as used here is not to be confused with the conventional mathematical meaning of that term.) The single record of type A to which the other records in a data base set are related is a member of the *owner* type of records, the other records of type B are included in the *member* record type. In Fig. 9-14b, the intersection record types (that is, quantity and price) are "member" types, whereas clients, goods, and suppliers are "owner" types.

A typical implementation using pointer chains to represent the data base sets is shown in Fig. 9-14c for the earlier example of Fig. 9-14b. It is easy to see that the pointer chains can be followed from any particular record to any other related record. However, the structure is substantially more complicated than a comparable hierarchical implementation. To avoid errors in a search, it is necessary to control the traversal process when using the overlapping pointer structures. In the DBTG proposal this is done by means of so-called currency pointers which identify the last record of each record type that was accessed at each particular point, as well as the last accessed record in each data base set.

A detailed evaluation of the effectiveness and efficiency of the various data base models is not possible at present. Some general remarks may suffice. The relational system appears superior from the viewpoint of the casual user. Only a single construct must be understood, and that construct consists of simple tables. Furthermore, high-level languages are available to manipulate the tables. For small data base problems, the relational model appears obviously preferable.

On the other hand, as the data base grows in size, the efficiency of the pro-

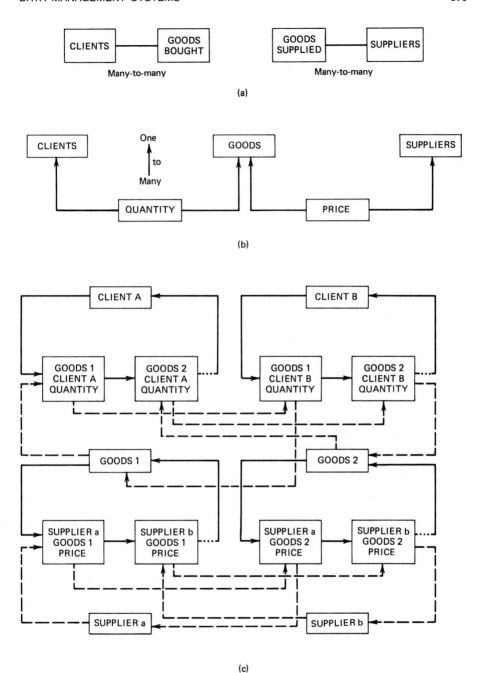

Figure 9-14 Network data base implementation. (a) Two many-to-many relationships. (b) Four many-to-one relationships for data base of part a. (c) Pointer chain implementation for relationships of part b.

cessing operations becomes important. In that case, the explicit relationship indicators (pointers) or the use of separate indexes affording access to various groups of records may become essential. In particular, in the hierarchical and network systems, the pointers allow direct access to sets of related records, whereas in the relational system these relationships and the corresponding access paths may first have to be established before they can be used. Unfortunately, the pointer structures and the implementation of complex many-to-many relationships between record types are more difficult to deal with than a simple table; as a result a substantial burden is placed on the programming staff charged with setting up the data base system.

At the present time, most commercial applications are based on the hierarchical or network data base models. The conceptually simpler relational model has, however, been studied intensively in recent years, and various theoretical advantages have been claimed for that model [32]. Furthermore the slow sequential scan of all the records included in a given relation may be avoided by providing auxiliary indexes that offer access to groups of related records. Because of its greater conceptual simplicity and ease of use, one may expect that the relational model will become solidly established as a tool for data base manipulations in the visible future.

3 QUERY PROCESSING

*A Query Language Types

A great deal of work has been devoted to the construction of data base query languages. Since data base systems are designed for use by business-oriented persons rather than by computer experts, a main consideration is user friendliness and transparency of the operations. In particular, great importance is attached to the use of high-level query languages which reflect the overall user's intent rather than the computer operations that may be required to obtain any particular result. Unhappily, the use of high-level query languages entails a good deal of extra work in transforming the user statements into programs acceptable by the computer. Furthermore, the efficiency of the programs resulting from such a transformation may leave something to be desired. A tradeoff thus exists between the use of low-level programming-type query statements that may be hard to formulate but lead to efficient search and retrieval specifications, and the use of high-level user-friendly query formulations that may lead to slower, more expensive retrieval processes.

The query languages used in data base environments must provide for more processing alternatives that those commonly used in bibliographic retrieval. Whereas the latter need only specify how to retrieve documents, a DBMS query language also permits the user to ask for calculations on the stored numerical data and for the retrieval of computed information derived from the originally stored data. In principle, it might be useful to provide the full scope of the unrestricted natural language for the formulation of data base queries. For reasons outlined earlier, a natural language analysis system is still too complex and expensive for use in most commercial applications. However, restricted natural language features are being included in some data base query languages, as will be seen [33–39].

In some situations, the problem of whether a high-level (user-friendly) or a low-level (programming-type) query language is to be used never arises. Only a very high-level querying capability can, for example, serve in a department store to provide information to masses of untrained customers about the location of various kinds of merchandise. In principle, a game of "twenty questions" might be played by confronting the customers with question sequences in the hope of eventually leading them to the desired information. Specifically, as each question is proposed, the user provides a yes/no answer which then triggers the next query. A typical query sequence of this kind is shown in Table 9-3.

Since it is difficult to design efficient sequences of simple yes/no queries that will lead to correct final responses in a small number of steps, a faster process is the so-called menu approach, where the user is confronted with an enumeration of different available alternatives. The choice of a particular alternative will then lead to a further display containing a more refined list of possibilities. Eventually, the user obtains the desired information without further question. The menu approach serves as a basis for the operation of certain electronic news services where news items are displayed at individual user stations to specific customers upon demand [40].

A typical menu display suitable for a department store information system is illustrated in Fig. 9-15. In that case, the user first chooses item 3 (women's wear) from the number of alternatives offered, followed in the next display frame by item 4 (shoes), eventually leading to a response locating the shoe department on floor 2 section C. It should be pointed out that while the menu approach may rapidly lead to a final answer, the system is not foolproof. In fact, users may find it difficult to make a proper choice among the offered alternatives; and once the wrong path is followed, all subsequent displays in the current sequence will be unhelpful. Consider, for example, a user interested in fluids used to wash automobiles. This user might decide to follow the sequence

Table 9-3 Sample Query Sequence

Query	User response
Purchase item?	Yes/no
	√
Clothing?	Yes/no
	√
Appliances?	Yes/no
	√
Kitchen appliances?	Yes/no
	√
Major kitchen appliances such as stoves, dishwashers?	Yes/no
	√
Answer: Floor 5 Section B	

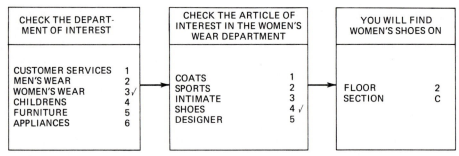

Figure 9-15 Menu display suitable for department store inquiry system.

starting with automobile supplies only to find later that cleaning agents were actually classified under household rather than automobile supplies. The design of transparent classification systems leading to unambiguous menu sequences is not a task that is currently well understood.

The menu approach is most successful when it is used by people who may be expert in a particular subject area without, however, being knowledgeable in computer processing. In that case the kind of erroneous choice previously illustrated can be avoided and proper responses may be obtained without training the users in the formulation of queries or the search methodologies. Typical examples that come to mind are populations of medical doctors where the retrieval system might furnish diagnostic aids based on menu displays of symptom lists. Alternatively, the menu system could be used by lawyers for statute or case law searching, by chemists dealing with the properties of chemical compounds, and by other professional groups operating in restricted topic areas with a well-defined terminology.

The use of *tabular querying* methods is related to menu querying but provides somewhat greater flexibility in the permissible query formulations and in the specification of processing sequences. In that case an electronic questionnaire properly filled in and submitted through the automatic display equipment replaces the normal query formulation process. A sample tabular query is contained in Table 9-4 for a data base dealing with hazardous chemicals. The user in this case is interested in the chemical names and the manufacturers of toxic

Table 9-4   Sample Tabular Query

Property or specification	Relation	Value	Output	Operation number
CHEMICAL FORM	=	GAS		1
LETHAL DOSE FOR 50%	≥	10 PARTS/MILLION		2
PRODUCTION	≥	1000 KG/YEAR		3
1, 2	AND			4
4, 3	AND			5
CHEMICAL NAME			PRINT	
COMPANY NAME			PRINT	
COMPANY ADDRESS			PRINT	

gases for which the lethal dose to 50 percent of the exposed population is at least 10 parts per million and the production is at least 1,000 kilograms per year. In the formulation of Table 9-4 the three basic requirements (that is, the chemical form, the lethal dose, and the production amount) are effectively "anded" together to produce the final query.

The well-known Query-by-Example (QBE) system is a commercial tabular querying system specially adapted to the relational data base model [41]. In QBE, a relation (file) to be operated upon during the search process must first be displayed in raw form on the user console by drawing a table showing the relation name at the head of column 1 and the attribute names identifying that relation as heads of subsequent columns. A typical frame for the display of a given relation is shown in Table 9-5. In a real case, the first row of the table would be automatically filled in with the correct relation and attribute names.

To operate on a displayed relation, the user fills in the various columns of the table with appropriate instructions and values of attributes. In QBE, two kinds of values are distinguished: those taken literally, where the value shown is directly used as an operand, and those used as samples to designate unknown values of corresponding attributes. In the examples that follow, sample values are underlined, whereas actual values are written without underline.

To retrieve the name and employee numbers for all records contained in the EMPLOYEES file, one first requests a display of the EMPLOYEES relation and then fills in the attribute columns corresponding to employee name and number with the command PRINT (P.) followed by a dummy value. The result is shown in Table 9-6a. When the query formulation involves more than one relation, the frames for all required relations must be displayed, and the relationships between the values of corresponding attributes must be appropriately specified. Consider as an example, the query formulation shown in Table 9-6b. This display involves the EMPLOYEES and the MANAGER relations. The first part of Table 9-6b is identical to Table 9-6a. The second part qualifies the names of the employees actually wanted to those whose manager is "Smith."

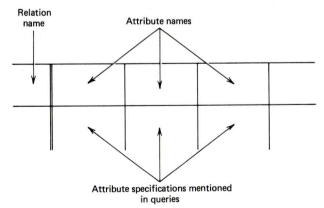

Table 9-5 Display of relation framework in the query-by-example system.

EMPLOYEES	EMP. NUMBER	EMP. NAME	SALARY	ADDRESS	DEPT. NUMBER
	P. 123	P. BROOKS			

(a)

EMPLOYEES	EMP. NUMBER	EMP. NAME	SALARY	ADDRESS	DEPT. NUMBER
	P. 123	P. BROOKS			

MANAGER	EMP. NUMBER	MANAGER NAME
	123	SMITH

(b)

EMPLOYEES	EMP. NUMBER	EMP. NAME	SALARY	ADDRESS	DEPT. NUMBER
		SMITH	X		
	P. 123	P. BROOKS	> X		

(c)

Table 9-6 Query-by-example query formulations. (a) Print the names and numbers of all employees. (b) Print the names and numbers of all employees whose manager is Smith. (c) Print the names and numbers of employees whose salary exceeds Smith's.

Note that the name "Smith" is to be taken literally which accounts for the lack of underlining in the table. In Table 9-6b, the *same* dummy employee number (namely, 123) is used in the EMPLOYEES and the MANAGER relations to indicate that the employee names to be retrieved are precisely those managed by "Smith." Relationships between attribute values other than equality can be specified by using appropriate quantifiers as shown in the example of Table 9-6c, where the request covers the names and numbers of all employees whose salary is at least as large as some unknown value x, x being specified as Smith's salary. Even though the QBE system can be used to formulate queries of substantial complexity, the basic features can be mastered rapidly by untrained users.

In addition to the table languages, several higher-level query languages have been proposed in which English keywords are used to specify the role of files and attributes. The SEQUEL language is a typical example which is also designed to operate in a relational framework [42,43]. The basic construct in SEQUEL is the SELECT-FROM-WHERE specification, where the SELECT part specifies the attributes actually wanted, the FROM portion identifies the relation in which these attributes occur, and the WHERE clause introduces an expression characterizing the attribute values previously named. In many cases, a SEQUEL formulation can be immediately understood without further clarification or instruction. Thus the formulation

SELECT   EMP. NAME, EMP. NUMBER
FROM   EMPLOYEES
WHERE   SALARY $\geq$ 10,000
AND   DEPT = 123

requests names and numbers of employees included in the EMPLOYEE relation such that the value of the SALARY attribute equals at least 10,000 and the DEPARTMENT is specified as department 123.

Attributes from several relations can be used by nesting the SELECT-FROM-WHERE clauses. In particular, the expression following the WHERE statement can itself introduce a new relation. Thus, the names of employees whose manager is SMITH may be requested in the following way:

SELECT   EMP. NAME, EMP. NUMBER
FROM   EMPLOYEES
WHERE   EMP. NUMBER IS IN
         SELECT EMP. NUMBER
         FROM   MANAGER
         WHERE   MANAGER NAME = 'SMITH'

The keywords "IS IN" introduce a second relation, which restricts the values of the employee numbers to only those managed by Smith.

A language such as SEQUEL uses linguistic constructs for query specification. The English words are, however, used in a specialized sense with unambiguous syntactic and semantic properties. Higher-level query languages also exist in which the English-like specifications are replaced by mathematical formulas. The so-called relational calculus is a case in point, where the wanted records are identified by a given variable name, and a mathematical expression involving the variable is then used to characterize the records actually wanted [44]. Thus, if the variable t is used to identify the records under consideration, and R and S are names of relations, the specification $\{t \mid R(t) \lor S(t)\}$ requests the retrieval of all records that are contained either in relation R or in relation S.

In addition to the higher-level nonprocedural languages, it is of course also possible to use lower-level programming-type languages where the actual procedures needed to carry out the retrieval operations are directly specified. The *relational algebra* previously introduced in Fig. 9-7 is an example where join, project, and select operations correspond directly to particular relational operations. For example, given two relations containing attributes A and B and attributes C and D, respectively, the following expression in the relational algebra is used to obtain the values of attribute A for all the records for which the value of attribute B in the first relation equals the value of attribute C in the second, and the value of attribute D is "Smith."

$$\text{PROJECT}_A(\text{SELECT}_{B=C \text{ AND } D='\text{SMITH}'}(AB \times CD)) \tag{1}$$

Assuming that the two relations are the previously used EMPLOYEES and MANAGER relations, and the four attributes A, B, C, D correspond, respectively, to employee names, employee numbers, employee numbers, and manager names, the query of expression (1) once again requests the names of all employees whose manager is "Smith." The difference between the procedural formulation of expression (1) and the previous formulations is the direct operational specification of expression (1), consisting in this case of a Cartesian product joining the two relations, followed by a selection, which is followed in turn by a projection.

In some operational environments, several different query facilities are provided to serve different user classes. This is the case, for example, in the Laboratory Animal Data Bank available through the National Library of Medicine which is searchable by experimental scientists with a menu approach or by information professionals with programming knowledge using a programming-type query language [45,46]. The idea is that the information professionals charged with operating the system will find it worthwhile to study the file structure and the relationships between attributes in order to be able to propose efficient query formulations. On the other hand, the file search itself constitutes only an incidental part of the activities for the experimental scientist. In that case there is no immediate need to learn the command structure of the retrieval system or the file organization actually used to store the characteristics of laboratory animals.

The use of a high-level nonprocedural query manipulation language is particularly important in management information systems and decision support systems where few users have programming knowledge [47–49]. In such situations English-like query languages are often considered to be essential because the user is then removed from the details of the processing system to the greatest possible extent. The same motivation lies behind the work in natural language query formulations in some question-answering environments.

*B Processing Strategies

All the data base query languages mentioned earlier contain features for processing, summarizing, maintaining, and updating the stored information files in addition to the formulation of actual user queries. The following types of operations are particularly important:

1 File modification commands such as insert, delete, and modify
2 Arithmetic capabilities such as addition and subtraction
3 Assignment and print commands used to assign new or computed

values to the attributes of certain records and to print out information contained in the records

4 Aggregate operations used to obtain global values for the records stored in a given file, including average, sum, maximum, and minimum values

When the files to be processed are small and the contents remain static over long periods of time, the search and updating processes are not of much consequence. In that case, a sequential scan through the whole file might be used to process each stored record sequentially in order to carry out the necessary operations. Unfortunately, in most real situations the files are neither static nor small. As the number of records becomes larger, the number of terms needed to identify these records will also grow, and a sequential scan that processes all records sequentially one at a time becomes too slow and too costly for practical use. Typically, indexes are then created which can be used to isolate certain portions of the file without touching the remainder of the stored information. An inverted index similar to that introduced earlier for bibliographic records can then be used to identify all the records containing particular values of certain attributes. The corresponding records can also be retrieved rapidly if they are clustered, that is, stored contiguously in the main file.

As the number of terms used to identify the stored records or the number of clusters used to partition the collection grows, the single index can in turn be broken down into a hierarchy of indexes including successively fewer entries. The highest-level index is then used to provide access to a more detailed lower-level index which gives access in turn to still more detailed indexes, until in time some of the records stored in the main data file are eventually identified. This is the method used in the cluster tree search where successively smaller groupings of records are determined until at the end a few records included in a common low-level centroid are obtained.

The hierarchy of indexes and the main records file must be searched and maintained efficiently under addition, deletion, and modification of the contents. When related records are connected by pointers, additions and deletions can be handled by simple changes in the pointer arrangements as shown in Fig. 9-16a and b respectively. Eventually as more and more local changes are made a complete reorganization of the storage area becomes necessary. Such a reorganization will "compact" the space by storing in adjacent positions items that actually belong together and by plugging the holes left by deleted records.

File reorganizations may involve alterations at the conceptual level that require changes in the file schema. This is the case when the hierarchical or network arrangement is altered or when changes are made to the attribute lists that identify certain record types. Alternatively changes may be made at the physical level, for example, by creating a new level of indexing, or by changing the accessing method used to retrieve the records from storage. In either case, the file reorganization can be carried out by copying the data base to auxiliary storage and performing the necessary modifications off-line. Eventually the corrected version is then reloaded into the main store following the updating oper-

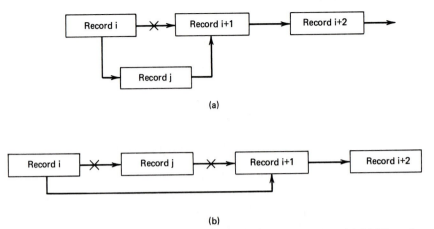

Figure 9-16   Pointer changes used for record addition and deletion. (a) Addition of record j between record i and record (i + l). (b) Deletion of record j from chain.

ation. Alternatively, the corrections can be performed in place, while other operations proceed normally. In that case, it becomes necessary to block access to portions of the data base while the revisions are carried out. While special methods have been devised that minimize the difficulties inherent in data base updating and maintenance, any reorganization may be expected to require substantial resources especially when the size of the data base is large [50,51].

In addition to the file organization and file modification processes, attention must also be paid to the efficiency of the search and retrieval operations. A good deal is known about the tradeoffs involved, for example, in creating and maintaining an auxiliary index compared with the larger search cost incurred when an index is not available. Unfortunately, it is not possible in the present context to examine these efficiency problems in detail. Some observations relating to the search process used for the relational data base model will suffice for present purposes [52–54].

The basic problem in query optimization consists in determining a reasonable order for executing the operations necessary to retrieve the stored records in response to a particular query formulation. The term "reasonable" implies that the grossest inefficiencies should be eliminated whenever possible. The optimization problem is of special importance for relational data base queries because the easy access paths provided by the pointer structures between records are not always available in that system. In fact, unless special precautions are taken, typical query language expressions may produce very inefficient processing sequences in a relational environment.

Consider, as an example, the query formulation of expression (1) involving two relations consisting of employee name and employee number (attributes A and B) on the one hand, and employee number and manager name (attributes C and D) on the other. The first operation specified in expression (1) is the Cartesian product (AB × CD). This involves a single scan of the first relation; however, for *each* record in relation 1, all records in the second relation must be scanned to generate the single relation involving the four attributes ABCD. Assuming that the number of records in the two relations is n_{AB} and n_{CD}, respectively, the number of records that need to be scanned is thus equal to $n_{AB}(1 + n_{CD})$. Obviously the generation of a Cartesian product such as the one specified in expression (1) is expensive for large relations.

More generally, it is obvious that relational operations designed to generate large relations from smaller ones should be avoided, whereas on the contrary the transformation of large relations into small ones should be preferred. This implies that Cartesian products as well as joins and relational union operations should be replaced whenever possible by select, project, or relational intersection; in any case, the expensive operations should be delayed in the hope of reducing the scope of these operations.

It turns out that for the query of expression (1), the product operation is totally unnecessary. Indeed only the attribute values corresponding to certain employee numbers are to be retrieved in that case, rather than the complete set of records involving all attributes. More specifically, the following transformations are possible for the query formulation of expression (1):

1 Since the selection operation [$\text{SELECT}_{D=\text{'SMITH'}}(AB \times CD)$] involves only the records in the second relation, the SELECT operation can be migrated inside the product, thereby obtaining a reduced query specification as follows:

$$\text{PROJECT}_A(\text{SELECT}_{B=C}(AB \times \text{SELECT}_{D=\text{'SMITH'}}CD)) \tag{2}$$

The Cartesian product is now much less costly, since only a few of the CD records (those corresponding to manager Smith) are involved.

2 The condition $\text{SELECT}_{B=C}$ which follows the Cartesian product converts that product into a natural join operation between AB and the selected records from CD. The new query statement thus becomes

$$\text{PROJECT}_A \left(AB \underset{B=C}{\text{JOIN}} (\text{SELECT}_{D=\text{'SMITH'}} CD) \right) \tag{3}$$

Various methods can be used to execute the join operation. A multiple scan of the relations is always possible: typically for each element (record) of relation 1 it is necessary to scan the second relation in order to find all possible elements that meet the join conditions. This requires as many complete scans of relation 2 as there are elements in relation 1. The multiple scanning can be avoided by constructing an index for the attributes of the second relation that are needed in the join operation. When an index is available, the elements of relation 2 corresponding to each element in relation 1 are immediately identified without further scanning. Another possibility consists in sorting the two relations according to the values of the attributes needed in the join prior to the actual joining operation. This makes it possible to carry out the join operation by performing a single scan of both relations. Assuming that relation 1 has n entries and relation 1 has m entries, the multiple scan requires n × m file access operations. If the two relations were sorted and then merged, the number of operations will be n log n and m log m for the sorting, and m + n for the final merging. A comparison of n × m with n log n + m log m + n + m shows that the latter is preferable except when the file sizes are trivially small.

Whether it is worthwhile to construct an index on the join attributes or to sort the relations prior to joining depends on the size of the relations, the difficulty of the indexing or sorting operations, the size of the internal memory used in the system under consideration, and the frequency with which a given join operation must be carried out.

The following general optimization rules are useful under most operational conditions:

1 Perform all selection operations as early as possible since the effect is a reduction in the size of the relations.
2 Preprocess the files before performing a join by creating an index on the join attributes, or by sorting where indicated.
3 Assemble sequences of selections or sequences of projection operations into a single selection or a single projection; a sequence of these operations can be executed in a single scan of the relation.
4 Combine projection operations with other binary operations involving several relations to decrease the number of attributes that need to be processed.
5 Combine selection operations with a prior Cartesian product to generate a join, a natural join being generally less expensive to perform than a Cartesian product.

A substantial effort has been devoted to the optimization of the query processing function in some of the modern relational data base systems [32,52–54]. The alternative hierarchical and network systems which provide fast access paths for the most important record combinations may nevertheless be preferred to an optimized relational system in many circumstances.

4 DATA QUALITY

A Integrity and Security

The preservation of data correctness is considered of great important in many data base environments. Several sources of errors are of interest: the accidental introduction of incorrect data resulting from clerical input errors or from common programming errors, and the malicious modification of information. The problem of data base protection takes on two main aspects: the *security* or *access control* mechanism which is designed to ensure that users will access only that portion of the data base which they are actually entitled to see, and the preservation of *data integrity*, which is designed to protect the data from nonmalicious errors such as the introduction of attribute values that are semantically inconsistent (such as EMPLOYEE AGE = 139), or the use of duplicate key values for different records.

The security problem is normally attacked by assigning to each user a *password* designed to identify all legitimate users for access purposes. The passwords are presumed to be known only to individual users and to the system itself. In addition to the compulsory use of passwords before obtaining system access, each user is expected to identify those portions of the data base that are actually needed for each particular application. This may be done by introducing a separate *subschema* for each user in which all system objects required by that particular user are properly defined. The assignment of particular system objects to particular users implies that users receive their own *view* of the data base. Furthermore by restricting the individual users to their own user views — for example, managers to the records covering their own department only — the data objects may be protected from involuntary misuse to some extent. In particular, programming errors which force users to access portions of the data base for which they have no use can then be easily detected.

Certain *physical* protection mechanisms also exist, including especially *data encryption* methods designed to transform the data into a form which cannot be recognized by unauthorized persons. Encryption methods can be used prior to storing the data to ensure that the contents of a data base will not be revealed to unauthorized users. On the other hand, encrypted files may be difficult to sort and to access by means of standard index files.

Methods may also be available which provide *authorization* to individual users to perform certain operations. In the query-by-example system, users may be individually authorized to perform specific operations on particular files (relations), including insertion (I.), deletion (D.), updating (U.), and printing (P.). Tabular displays similar to those shown in Table 9-6 can be used to specify the necessary authorizations. The first sample authorization of Table 9-7 allows any user to read records for employees whose salary does not reach 10,000. In Table 9-7b, a specific person (J. Doe) is authorized to update the salary of a specific record.

The available security mechanisms may be expected to prevent many erroneous alterations of the data base. On the other hand, no currently available security device will permanently foil a persistent transgressor with sufficient imagination and know-how [55–57].

An important aspect of data base preservation is the preservation of data *integrity*. In many situations restrictions can be placed on the characteristics or values of certain attributes that must be observed if the data environment is to appear "sensible." For example, the value of currently used postal zip codes in the United States is less than 100,000 and greater than 00600; the length of employee names is less than 30 characters; and the age of active employees is less than 100. Integrity constraints of many kinds can be declared in advance to be enforced by the system at convenient points in time. A given constraint may, for example, be verified each time an affected record is updated, or each time the record is accessed.

EMPLOYEES	EMP. NUMBER	EMP. NAME	SALARY
AUTR(P.) <u>BROOKS</u>	<u>123</u>	<u>SMITH</u>	< 10,000

(a)

EMPLOYEES	EMP. NUMBER	EMP. NAME	SALARY
AUTR(U.) J. DOE	123	SMITH	<u>10,000</u>

(b)

Table 9-7 Authorization mechanism in query-by-example. (a) Authorization for anyone to read employee names and numbers provided salary is less than 10,000. (b) Authorization for J. Doe to update the salary of employee Smith.

In the QBE system, integrity constraints are declared by means of tabular displays similar to those used for authorizations. An example is shown in Table 9-8, which specifies that during record insertion and updating, the salary figure for any employee must necessarily amount to at least $5,000.

In addition to using direct integrity constraints declared for specific record attributes, the integrity of the data may also depend on preserving certain implied relationships between attributes. A good deal of attention has been devoted in recent years to the development of a data base design theory based on the use of attribute relationships. This design theory is most developed for the relational data base model, and depends in large measure on the specification and use of *dependencies* of various kinds between attributes. The most important dependency type is the *functional* dependency, which guarantees that the values of certain attributes are identical for different records under the assumption that the values of certain other attributes are also the same. Formally one says that attribute B *functionally depends* on attribute A (or A functionally determines B) if no two records can have a different value for attribute B, assuming that the value is identical for attribute A. Functional dependency may be denoted by drawing an arrow from the determining toward the functionally dependent element, that is, $A \rightarrow B$. It is clear that if an attribute is a candidate key for a given relation, then necessarily the other attributes will be functionally dependent on that key.

Consider, as an example, a STUDENT relation whose relational scheme is (STUDENT NAME, STUDENT ADDRESS, COURSE, GRADE). If the student names are all distinct, then the names may function as a key. It is then clear that

STUDENT NAME $\rightarrow$ STUDENT ADDRESS

since the same student cannot have two different addresses. Similarly the combination of the student name and the course number in which the student is

EMPLOYEES	EMP. NUMBER	EMP. NAME	SALARY
CONSTR(I.U.)			> = 5,000

Table 9-8 Integrity declaration in query-by-example.

enrolled will determine a unique grade

STUDENT NAME, COURSE → GRADE

The functional dependencies, once determined, can be used directly for integrity checking by verifying that all dependencies are valid at all times. In addition, the dependencies are useful for the generation and use of relations in *normalized* form. The normalization process is generally carried out by decomposing each relation into component parts that are conceptually simpler than the original. The simpler normalized form is attractive because certain difficulties that may arise for nonnormalized relations as a result of data insertion or deletion are absent for the normalized case [58–60].

Consider, as an example, the STUDENT file introduced earlier. Because the values of all attributes must be specified for each record in the relational model, it is impossible to enter into the file the names and addresses of students who are not enrolled in a course. Alternatively, the names of students who drop their only course are also lost. If the basic STUDENT relation were replaced by two smaller relations called NAME FILE and GRADE RECORD, respectively, the update problems mentioned earlier would not exist. Specifically if the two new relations are defined as

NAME FILE(STUDENT NAME, STUDENT ADDRESS)
GRADE RECORD(STUDENT NAME, COURSE, GRADE)

the original relation can be reconstructed and the names of unenrolled students are preserved.

Three principal normal forms are described in the literature, known, respectively, as the *first, second,* and *third normal forms* (1NF, 2NF, and 3 NF). The first normal form characterizes a relation in which each component of each record is not further decomposable; that is, each attribute represents a nondecomposable entity. The relation used as an example in Table 9-2 is certainly in 1NF, assuming that the components of the address attribute (for example, the street number) are not meaningful by themselves.

A relation is in 2NF if it is in 1NF and if every attribute that is not a key is *fully* dependent on each key attribute. That is, the so-called partial dependencies are disallowed where a given attribute is dependent on a portion of a key attribute. In the relation R identified by the scheme R(CITY, STREET, ZIP) the combination of (STREET, ZIP) is a key, but one actually observes that the zip code by itself determines the city (although not vice versa). Hence the functional dependency

$$ZIP \rightarrow CITY$$

represents a partial dependency on a key attribute.

A relation is in 3NF if it is in 2NF and no nontrivial *transitive* dependencies are present. A transitive dependency between attributes A, B, and C implies that $A \rightarrow B$ and $B \rightarrow C$, but $B \nrightarrow A$. (The latter condition is needed because if $A \rightarrow B$ and $B \rightarrow A$, then attributes A and B would be equivalent and the transitivity property would become trivial.) For the previously used STUDENT relation one observes

$$
\begin{aligned}
\text{STUDENT, COURSE} &\rightarrow \text{STUDENT} \\
\text{STUDENT} &\rightarrow \text{ADDRESS} \\
\text{STUDENT} &\nrightarrow \text{STUDENT, COURSE}
\end{aligned}
\tag{4}
$$

Hence the relation is certainly not in 3NF. Assuming that the combination (STUDENT, COURSE) is used as a key, the relation is also not in 2NF because of the partial dependency STUDENT $\rightarrow$ ADDRESS. Update anomalies can occur for nonnormalized relations, as previously illustrated for the STUDENT relation. This accounts for the interest in normalization and relational decomposition.

The decomposition of relations into component parts would not be useful if methods were not available for reconstructing the original by rejoining the components without loss of information. A so-called lossless join decomposition of relations is possible under well-defined conditions. In particular, it is known that any relation has a lossless join decomposition into third normal form preserving all the original dependencies between attributes [20]. For example, the relation R(STUDENT, ADDRESS, COURSE, GRADE) has a lossless pair decomposition into R_1(STUDENT, ADDRESS) and R_2(STUDENT, COURSE, GRADE) because R may be recovered by the unrestricted join R_1 JOIN R_2 using the equivalence of the student names as a join condition.

Substantial advances are continually being made in the development of data base theories, for example through the introduction of new normal forms such as the fourth or Boyce-Codd normal form (BCNF) and the use of new types of dependencies between attributes such as the so-called multivalued dependencies [61]. One may expect that these theoretical activities will substantially affect the design characteristics of the data management systems in the future.

**B Concurrent Data Base Operations

It has been implicit in the foregoing exposition that the programs used to access the data base operate independently of each other and that provisions are made for preventing interference between activities that may take place concurrently. In most data base environments the concurrent execution of many transactions (processes) is the rule rather than the exception. For example, an automated airline reservations system simultaneously receives hundreds of different inquiries all of which must be answered by consulting the same data base. The main interference problem does not of course arise from reading the data because in that case the integrity of the data is not normally compromised. Problems do, however, arise when modifications are made to the stored information in a multiuser environment. In the airline reservations system, methods must thus be available to prevent the simultaneous sale by different agents of the same airplane seat to different prospective passengers.

The basic methodology used to prevent interference between different transactions consists in applying a *locking mechanism* to a specific portion of the data base before a given transaction is to introduce modifications to the data. The lock is used to prevent other transactions from accessing the same data until the lock is removed. A transaction involving a lock mechanism thus consists of five basic steps:

Locking a portion of the data base
Reading the original data
Modifying the data
Writing the modified data
Unlocking the data base

A special *lock manager* serves in most data base systems to assign and record all existing locks, and to prevent access to locked portions of the data base [62–64].

When a locking mechanism is used to control access, special care must be taken to avoid undesirable side effects. Assuming, for example, that several transactions are waiting to access a given locked portion of the data base, the next transaction to be given access following release of the lock must not be chosen arbitrarily because some transactions could then be made to wait forever. Such a condition, known as ''livelock,'' can be avoided, for example, by providing access on a first-come first-served basis.

A possibly more serious situation arises when two or more transactions are *deadlocked* because they each demand access to data locked by other transactions. The following order of operations leads to a deadlock situation:

1 Transaction 1 : lock data base A
2 Transaction 2 : lock data base B
3 Transaction 1 : request lock on data base B
4 Transaction 2 : request lock on data base A

In this example, the first two steps are carried out normally because different portions of the data base are affected by the locking requests for the two transactions. At step 3, transaction 1 is asked to wait because transaction 2 currently holds a lock on data base B. At step 4, transaction 2 will similarly come to rest because another lock has already been placed on data base A. From this point on, both transactions will obviously wait forever.

Various solutions are available for preventing deadlock. For example, each transaction may be asked to request all the needed locks at the same time, at which point either the locks are all granted simultaneously or they are all rejected. Alternatively, the locks affecting a particular set of data bases may all have to be placed in some particular preestablished order. For example, if data base A necessarily precedes data base B in the established order, then the lock requests for transaction 2 are not admissible. Instead of preventing deadlock, the system can simply detect deadlock, and later *roll back* some of the transactions involved and cancel their effect on the data base. Rollback and recovery methods are mentioned later in this chapter. In general, rollback is less satisfactory than deadlock prevention because some users may then be forced to reenter a transaction that had already been started.

Even when livelock and deadlock operations are successfully avoided, the concurrent execution of different processes may still lead to unwanted interference problems. In effect the concurrent transactions must be interleaved in such a way that the end effect is the same as if the transactions were executed separately and independently of each other. The latter condition is known as ''serializability.'' In situations where several data base transactions can be executed concurrently, a *scheduler* included in the data base system is charged with the resolution of potential conflicts between transactions. More specifically, the scheduler imposes a *protocol* on each transaction restricting the sequences of steps that a transaction may execute. Assuming that the established protocols are followed by all transactions, the scheduler will then produce a serializable schedule.

One kind of protocol which is known to guarantee serializability is the *two-phase locking protocol* which specifies that for each transaction all locking operations must precede all unlocking operations. The two-phase protocol may lead to deadlock; however, assuming that deadlock prevention methods are also used, the two-phase requirement will allow the scheduler to produce a processing order that is equivalent to that of a serial schedule. In a serial schedule, the transactions are completely independent of each other.

An example of a serial schedule is shown in Table 9-9a, where all the operations for transaction 2 precede those for transaction 1. A serializable, but not serial, schedule is shown for the same operations in Table 9-9b. It may be seen that for each transaction all locking operations precede all unlocking operations. However, the schedule of Table 9-9b is equivalent to the serial schedule of Table 9-9a where all of transaction 2 precedes all of transaction 1. A nonserializable schedule for the transactions is given in Table 9-9c. In the example of Table 9-9c, the locks on data base B cannot be placed in such a way that operation 6 of transaction 1 may precede operation 7 of transaction 2. The effect of transaction 2 on data base B is in fact lost in the schedule of Table 9-9c, because the old values for data base B are read at step 6 in Table 9-9c, whereas

Table 9-9   Illustration of Two-Phase Locking Protocol

Transaction 1	Transaction 2
a Serial schedule for two transactions	

Transaction 1	Transaction 2
	1. Read data base A
	2. Perform operations on A
	3. Write modified A
	4. Read data base B
	5. Perform operations on B
	6. Write modified B
7. Read data base B	
8. Perform operations on B	
9. Write modified B	
10. Read data base C	
11. Modify C	
12. Write modified C	

Transaction 1	Transaction 2
b Serializable schedule for two transactions	
1. Lock C	
	2. Lock A,B
3. Read data base C	
	4. Read data base B
5. Operate on C	
	6. Operate on B
7. Write modified C	
	8. Write modified B
	9. Unlock B
10. Lock B	
11. Read data base B	
	12. Read data base A
13. Operate on B	
	14. Operate on A
15. Write modified B	
	16. Write modified A
17. Unlock B,C	
	18. Unlock A

Transaction 1	Transaction 2
c Nonserializable schedule for two transactions	
1. Read data base C	
	2. Read data base B
3. Modify C	
	4. Modify data base B
5. Write data base C	
6. Read data base B	
	7. Write data base B
8. Modify B	
	9. Read data base A
10. Write modified B	
	11. Modify A
	12. Write data base A

the new modified values are read at that point by transaction 1 in Table 9-9a and b.

**C   Restart and Recovery Methods

It was seen earlier that deadlock conditions can be eliminated by ''rolling back'' or undoing certain transactions and letting others proceed normally. To be able to go back in time and reverse the effect of certain transactions, it is necessary to store information regarding the effect on the data base of the various operations, and the order in which these operations are executed. The normal method used for this purpose consists in maintaining a *journal* or *log* which records all the operations that may have to be undone or repeated in case of trouble [65]. In particular, whenever an item in the data base is updated, inserted, or deleted, a record describing the particular modification is added to the log. When the system malfunctions, or crashes, for one reason or another, the log can be consulted and the data base can be restored by rolling back the system to a consistent state existing at some point prior to the malfunction. From that point on the various operations can then be repeated.

In general, the information in the log is used to undo the effect of transactions that had affected the state of the data base prior to the crash. On the other hand, incomplete transactions whose results had not yet been recorded in the data base can be ignored during rollback and may simply be repeated when a restart of operations is ordered.

To limit the amount of information in the log that needs to be consulted during the recovery process, it is customary to keep periodic summaries of the state of the data base in the form of *backup copies* and *journal checkpoints*. A backup copy of the data base is a complete copy produced at infrequent intervals representing a consistent data base state. Typically a backup copy might be produced once a day. When all else fails, the backup copy can be read in and all operations may be resumed at that point. A journal checkpoint represents a summary of the state of the transactions at a given point in time. The checkpoint information consists of lists of active transactions together with appropriate status information for each transaction. Checkpoint information is recorded in the log with reasonable frequency. When a crash occurs, each entry in the log is analyzed back to the last previous checkpoint to determine its effect. In addition the checkpoint information identifies transactions that need to be undone and/or repeated.

To simplify the restart and recovery operations it is customary to recognize a *commit* point for each transaction when the transaction must be regarded as being *completed*. This implies that all operations included in the transaction are terminated and the results have been entered in the log. If a crash occurs following commitment, the effects will survive the crash, even though the newly altered information may not yet have been entered into the data base. The log specifically distinguishes committed from uncommitted transactions. Commitment of a transaction should be reflected to users who must know when they can safely assume that the transaction need not be reentered in case of later trouble. Until the commit point is reached, a transaction can always be aborted by canceling or backing out of the transaction.

A so-called two-phase commit policy, not to be confused with the two-phase locking protocol is often followed which minimizes the problems inherent in crash recovery. Two main rules are followed:

1 No transaction can actually write into a data base before it has committed.

2 No transaction can commit before all its effects on the items in the data base have been entered into the log.

Assuming that the two-phase locking protocol is used in addition to this commit policy, and that unlocking operations occur only following commitment, it becomes impossible for any transaction to read values in the data base provided by uncommitted transactions.

When the two-phase commit policy is followed, uncommitted transactions may simply be disregarded in a crash situation because these transactions could certainly not have affected the data. On the other hand, committed transactions must be redone following the rollback operation. When the two-phase commit or some equivalent policy is not used, the recovery process is much more difficult because uncommitted transactions might then have changed the data base and other transactions might have read values written by these uncommitted transactions. The original changes to the data base introduced by the uncommitted transactions must then be undone, and so must the transactions that had read values from these transactions. This effect can propagate indefinitely and render the recovery process impossible to carry out in an effective manner. Even when an appropriate commit policy is used to distinguish transactions that must participate in the recovery process from others that can be ignored, any crash recovery procedure is costly to implement and requires substantial system resources.

**D Distributed Data Bases

The assumption has been made up to this point that the data base under consideration is centrally managed, although of course the users might be geographically dispersed and various transactions might be executed concurrently. In actual fact many systems exist involving several different computers and a number of different data bases located in a variety of different places. In such a circumstance one speaks of a *distributed* data base system. Possibly the best-known operating distributed data base system is the worldwide airline reservations system: each participating airline uses its own data base located near its particular headquarters location; common protocols are, however, used which control the operations when information involving more than one data base is needed to answer a given query [66–70].

The usefulness of distributed data base operations has become increasingly obvious because of the popularity of the many small minicomputer systems. These systems can obviously be used to control local data bases and to perform operations of interest in local environments. Furthermore, when data are needed that are not locally available, the local computers can address requests to a network of other machines and other data bases located in various remote places.

A distributed data base environment complicates the systems organization and the resulting data base operations. A decision must first be made about the allocation of the files to the various locations, or *nodes*, of the data base network. A particular file could be kept in some unique, central place; alternatively it could be *partitioned* by allocating the various file portions to several different nodes. Finally, the file or certain file portions could be *replicated* by storing copies in several places. The use of partitioned files may reduce the number of messages and requests circulating from node to node assuming that the file portions of interest at a particular site are locally stored. When the data files are replicated, the message traffic between nodes may be substantially reduced. In fact, a tradeoff exists between the extra storage used by the data replication and the increased speed of operations resulting from the reduced communications load between the nodes.

In a distributed data base system the need for the basic physical and logical data independence is expanded to include also *location* and *replica transparency*. Location transparency implies that the user programs are independent of the particular location of the files, while replica transparency extends the transparency to the use of an arbitrary number of copies.

Once a particular file environment is created, procedures must be available for executing the various transactions and furnishing results to the requesting parties. A given transaction might be run locally; alternatively, various remote points might be asked to carry out the operations followed by the routing of responses to the originating points. The latter strategy involves a good deal of overhead in handling the message queues that may be formed at various points in the network.

It goes without saying that all operations must be carried out in a distributed environment in such a way that data integrity and consistency are maintained. This implies that special locking and update strategies must be used to ensure that all copies of a given data base are properly updated. Specifically, all files must be locked before updating, the locks must be held until the end of a given transaction, and file alterations must be broadcast through the network to all replicas before the end of the transaction. Special transaction commit policies have been invented for this purpose in distributed systems. Specifically, a transaction coordinator is named for each transaction, and the coordinator alone is empowered to commit a given transaction after querying the participating sites concerning their individual readiness to commit.

It is obvious from what has been said that the distributed data base environment creates a host of complications. Because of the current widespread use of computer networks and the increasing availability of on-line access to computational facilities by a wide range of users, the organization and operations of distributed data base systems have become popular areas of investigation for researchers in the computer field.

5 SUMMARY

The questions of interest in data base management coincide to a large extent with those arising in all information retrieval environments: they involve the management of interactive multiuser systems including efficient accessing, search, and retrieval procedures, and user-friendly query formulation and output display methods. By restricting the information to be processed in data base management to well-defined, homogeneous entities, characterized by a small number of unambiguous attribute values, the indexing and content-analysis problems met in other retrieval environments are avoided. The emphasis is placed instead on the processing of mixed queries often involving partly numeric data whose values need to be compared or manipulated arithmetically before answers can be generated to the available queries. High-level procedures and languages may then be available in a data base management system for defining, organizing, processing and accessing the structured data. In addition, a data base system normally maintains data quality and security, and ensures that the user programs are insulated from the details of the logical and physical system implementation.

The strength of the data management area is the wide applicability in many different user environments, and the large number of utilities and system resources that are often furnished, including crash protection, deadlock detection, automatic construction of secondary indexes and hashing systems, integrity checks, access authorization management, and transaction concurrency and distributed data facilities. The weaknesses of the existing systems arise from the small number of well-defined operations that are implemented efficiently often at the expense of complicating operations that do not fit the standard model. Efficient access paths are normally provided for programs that use the available data structures, pointer systems, and record grouping properties of the files. When the existing facilities are not suited to the given processing requirements, the execution of the operations becomes cumbersome and time-consuming. In the relational system tradeoffs exist between the use of decomposed relations in normalized form where the integrity and correctness of the data are easily ensured, and the extra work involved in rejoining the normalized relations when necessary.

One may expect that increasing efforts will be made in the immediate future to eliminate some of the restrictions inherent in existing data management implementations. Eventually, the existing data base operations may be converted into truly flexible decision support and question-answering environments.

REFERENCES

[1] R. N. Landau, J. Wanger, and M. C. Berger, Directory of Online Databases, Vol. 1, No. 3, Cuadra Associates, Santa Monica, California, Spring 1980, p. 72.

[2] C. Mader and R. Hagin, Information Systems: Technology, Economics, Applications, Science Research Associates, Chicago, Illinois, 1974.

[3] I. Benbasat and R. Goldstein, Data Base Systems for Small Business : Miracle or Mirage, Data Base, Vol. 9, No. 1, Summer 1977, pp. 5–8.

[4] J. P. Fry and E. H. Sibley, Evolution of Data-Base Management Systems, Computing Surveys, Vol. 8, No. 1, March 1976, pp. 7–42.

[5] R. Ashany and M. Adamowicz, Data Base Systems, IBM Systems Journal, Vol. 15, No. 3, 1976, pp. 253–263.

[6] W.M. Zani, Blueprint for MIS, Harvard Business Review, Vol. 48, November–December 1970, pp. 95–100.

[7] G. B. Davis, Management Information Systems: Conceptual Foundations, Structure and Development, McGraw-Hill Book Company, New York, 1974.

[8] J. C. Emery, An Overview of Management Information Systems, Data Base, Vol. 5, No. 2–4, December 1973, pp. 1–11.

[9] S. L. Alter, How Effective Managers Use Information Systems, Harvard Business Review, Vol. 54, November–December 1976, pp. 97–104.

[10] E. D. Carlson, J. L. Bennett, G. M. Giddings, and P. E. Mantey, The Design and Evaluation of an Interactive Geo-Data Analysis and Display System, Information Processing '74, North Holland Publishing Company, Amsterdam, 1974, pp. 1057–1061.

[11] P. Berger and F. Edelman, IRIS: A Transaction Based DSS for Human Resources Management, Data Base, Vol. 8, No. 3, Winter 1977, pp. 22–29.

[12] R. Davis, A DSS for Diagnosis and Therapy, Data Base, Vol. 8, No. 3, Winter 1977, pp. 58–72.

[13] C. F. Starmer and R. A. Rosati, A DSS for Managing Patients with a Choice Illness, Data Base, Vol. 8, No. 3, Winter 1977, pp. 51–57.

[14] E. R. McLean and T. Riesing, MAPP: A DSS for Financial Planning, Data Base, Vol. 8, No. 3, Winter 1977, pp. 9–14.

[15] R. L. Klaas, A DSS for Airline Management, Data Base, Vol. 8, No. 3, Winter 1977, pp. 3–8.

[16] C. J. Date, An Introduction to Data Base Systems, 3rd Edition, Addison Wesley Publishing Company, Reading, Massachusetts, 1981.

[17] D. C. Tsichritzis and F. H. Lochovsky, Data Base Management Systems, Academic Press, New York, 1977.

[18] G. Wiederhold, Database Design, McGraw-Hill Book Company, New York, 1977.

[19] D. Kroenke, Database Processing: Fundamentals, Modeling, Applications, Science Research Associates Inc., Chicago, Illinois, 1977.

[20] J. D. Ullman, Principles of Data Base Systems, Computer Science Press, Potomac, Maryland, 1980.

[21] C. T. Meadow, Analysis of Information Systems, 2nd Edition, John Wiley and Sons, New York, 1973.

[22] M. E. Senko, Data Structures and Data Accessing in Data Base Systems: Past, Present, Future, IBM Systems Journal, Vol. 16, No. 3, 1977, pp. 208–257.

[23] M. E. Senko, Information Systems: Records, Relations, Sets, Entities and Things, Information Systems, Vol. 1, 1975, pp. 3–13.

[24] D. D. Chamberlin, Relational Data-Base Management Systems, Computing Surveys, Vol. 8, No. 1, March 1976, pp. 43–66.

[25] E. F. Codd, A Relational Model of Data for Large Shared Data Banks, ACM Communications, Vol. 13, No. 6, June 1970, pp. 377–387.

[26] IBM Corporation, Information Management System—General Information Manual, IBM Report GH 20-1260, White Plains, New York, 1975.

[27] W. C. McGee, The Information Management System IMS/VS, IBM Systems Journal, Vol. 16, No. 2, 1977, pp. 84–168.

[28] R. W. Taylor and R. L. Frank, CODASYL Data-Base Management Systems, ACM Computing Surveys, Vol. 8, No. 1, March 1976, pp. 67–103.

[29] CODASYL, Database Task Group Report, Association for Computing Machinery, New York, April 1971.

[30] T. W. Olle, The Codasyl Approach to Data Base Management, John Wiley and Sons, New York, 1978.

[31] C. W. Bachman, On a Generalized Language for File Organization and Manipulation, Communications of the ACM, Vol. 9, No. 3, March 1966, pp. 225–226.

[32] M. M. Astrahan, M. W. Blasgen, D. D. Chamberlin, K. P. Eswaran, J. N. Gray, P. P. Griffiths, W. F. King, R. A. Lorie, P. R. McJones, J. W. Mehl, G. R. Putzolu, I. L. Traiger, B. W. Wade, and V. Watson, System R: A Relational Approach to Database Management, ACM Transactions on Database Systems, Vol. 1, No. 2, June 1976, pp. 97–137.

[33] L. R. Harris, User Oriented Database Query with the ROBOT Natural Language Query System, International Journal of Man-Machine Studies, Vol. 9, 1977, pp. 697–713.

[34] D. L. Waltz, An English Language Question Answering System for a Large Relational Database, Communications of the ACM, Vol. 21, No. 7, July 1978, pp. 526–539.

[35] E. F. Codd, R. S. Arnold, J. M. Cadiou, C. L. Chang, and N. Roussopoulos, Rendezvous Version 1: An Experimental English-Language Query Formulation System for Casual Users of Relational Data Bases, IBM Research Report RJ 2144, IBM Research Laboratory, San Jose, California, January 1978.

[36] G. G. Hendrix, E. D. Sacerdoti, D. Sagalowicz, and J. Slocum, Developing a Natural Language Interface to Complex Data, ACM Transactions on Database Systems, Vol. 3, No. 2, June 1978, pp. 105–147.

[37] P. Dell 'Orco, V. N. Spadavecchia, and M. King, Using Knowledge of a Data Base World in Interpreting Natural Language Queries, Information Processing 77, North Holland Publishing Company, Amsterdam, 1977, pp. 139–144.

[38] J. Mylopoulos, P. A. Bernstein, and H. K. T. Wong, A Language Facility for Designing Database-Intensive Applications, ACM Transactions on Database Systems, Vol. 5, No. 2, June 1980, pp. 185–207.

[39] S. C. Shapiro and S. C. Kwasny, Interactive Consulting via Natural Language, Communications of the ACM, Vol. 18, No. 8, August 1975, pp. 459–462.

[40] J. Martyn, Prestel and Public Libraries: An LA/Aslib Experiment, Aslib Proceedings, Vol. 31, No. 5, May 1979, pp. 216–236.

[41] M. M. Zloof, Query-by-Example: A Database Language, IBM Systems Journal, Vol. 16, No. 4, 1977, pp. 324–343.

[42] D. D. Chamberlin, M. M. Astrahan, K. P. Eswaran, P. P. Griffiths, R. A. Lorie, J. W. Mehl, T. Reimer, and B. W. Wade, Sequel 2: A Unified Approach to Data Definition, Manipulation and Control, IBM Journal of Research and Development, Vol. 20, No. 6, November 1976, pp. 560–575.

[43] D. D. Chamberlin and R. F. Boyce, SEQUEL: A Structured English Query Language, Proceedings of ACM SIGFIDET Workshop, Ann Arbor, Michigan, May 1974, pp. 249–264.

[44] E. F. Codd, Relational Completeness of Database Sublanguages, in Proceedings of ACM/SIGMOD Conference on Data Models, R. Rustin, editor, Association for Computing Machinery, New York, 1974, pp. 64–98.

[45] National Library of Medicine, Instructions to the Laboratory Animal Data Bank, Memorandum to LADB Users, Bethesda, Maryland, January 14, 1980.

[46] National Library of Medicine, Laboratory Animal Data Bank—Fact Sheet, Bethesda, Maryland, August 1980.

[47] K. D. Eason, Understanding the Naive Computer User, The Computer Journal, Vol. 19, No. 1, February 1976, pp. 3–7.

[48] T. P. Gerrity, Jr., Design of Man-Machine Decision Support Systems: An Application to Portfolio Management, Sloan Management Review, Vol. 12, No. 3, Winter 1971, pp. 59–75.

[49] H. T. Gibson, Determining User Involvement, Journal of Systems Management, August 1977, pp. 20–22.

[50] N. C. Shu, B. C. Housel, R. W. Taylor, S. P. Ghosh, and V. Y. Lum, Express: A Data Extraction, Processing and Restructuring System, ACM Transactions on Database Systems, Vol. 2, No. 2, June 1977, pp. 134–174.

[51] G. H. Sockut and R. P. Goldberg, Database Reorganization—Principles and Practice, ACM Computing Surveys, Vol. 11, No. 4, December 1979, pp. 371–395.

[52] P. A. V. Hall, Optimization of Single Expressions in a Relational Data Base System, IBM Journal of Research and Development, Vol. 20, No. 3, May 1976, pp. 244–257.

[53] J. M. Smith and P. Y. Chang, Optimizing the Performance of a Relational Algebra Database Interface, Communications of the ACM, Vol. 18, No. 10, October 1975, pp. 568–579.

[54] S. B. Yao, Optimization of Query Evaluation Algorithms, ACM Transactions on Database Systems, Vol. 4, No. 2, June 1979, pp. 133–155.

[55] C. Wood, E. B. Fernandez, and R. C. Summers, Data Base Security: Requirements Policies and Models, IBM Systems Journal, Vol. 19, No. 2, 1980, pp. 229–252.

[56] R. Fagin, On an Authorization Mechanism, ACM Transactions on Data Base Systems, Vol. 3, No. 3, September 1978, pp. 310–319.

[57] D. D. Chamberlin, J. N. Gray, and I. L. Traiger, Views, Authorization and Locking in a Relational Data Base System, Proceedings National Computer Conference 1975, AFIPS Press, Montvale, New Jersey, 1975, pp. 425–430.

[58] E. F. Codd, Further Normalization of the Database Relational Model, in Proceedings ACM/SIGMOD Conference on Data Models, R. Rustin, editor, Association for Computing Machinery, New York, 1974, pp. 33–63.

[59] C. Delobel and R. O. Casey, Decomposition of a Data Base and the Theory of Boolean Switching Functions, IBM Journal of Research and Development, Vol. 17, No. 5, September 1973, pp. 374–386.

[60] C. Delobel, Normalization and Hierarchical Dependencies in the Relational Data Model, ACM Transactions on Data Base Systems, Vol. 3, No. 3, September 1978, pp. 201–222.

[61] R. Fagin, Multivalued Dependencies and a New Normal Form for Relational Databases, IBM Transactions on Data Base Systems, Vol. 2, No. 3, September 1977, pp. 262–278.

[62] D. D. Chamberlin, R. F. Boyce, and I. L. Traiger, A Deadlock Free Scheme for Resource Locking in a Database Environment, Information Processing 74, North Holland Publishing Company, Amsterdam, 1974, pp. 340–343.

[63] K. P. Eswaran, J. N. Gray, R. A. Lorie, and I. L. Traiger, The Notions of Consistency and Predicate Locks in a Database System, Communications of the ACM, Vol. 19, No. 11, November 1976, pp. 624–633.

[64] R. H. Thomas, A Majority Consensus Approach to Concurrency Control for Multiple Copy Databases, ACM Transactions on Database Systems, Vol. 4, No. 2, June 1979, pp. 180–209.

[65] J. S. M. Verhofstad, Recovery Techniques for Database Systems, Computing Surveys, Vol. 10, No. 2, June 1978, pp. 167–195.

[66] H. Lorin, Distributed Processing: An Assessment, IBM Systems Journal, Vol. 18, No. 4, 1979, pp. 582–603.

[67] A. L. Scherr, Distributed Data Processing, IBM Systems Journal, Vol. 17, No. 4, 1978, pp. 324–343.

[68] J. N. Gray, Notes on Database Operating Systems, Operating Systems—An Advanced Course, R. Bayer, R. M. Graham, and G. Segmuller, editors, Springer Verlag, New York, 1978, pp. 393–481.

[69] J. B. Rothnie Jr., P. A. Bernstein, S. Fox, N. Goodman, M. Hammer, T. A. Landers, C. Reeve, D. W. Shipman, and E. Wong, Introduction to a System for Distributed Databases (SDD-1), ACM Transactions on Database Systems, Vol. 5, No. 1, March 1980, pp. 1–17.

[70] P. A. Bernstein, D. W. Shipman and J. B. Rothnie, Jr., Concurrency Control in a System for Distributed Databases (SDD-1), ACM Transactions on Database Systems, Vol. 5, No. 1, March 1980, pp. 18–51.

BIBLIOGRAPHIC REMARKS:

At the present time the data base area is very active. New texts appear every year, new journals are created regularly, and the literature is rapidly expanding. The following texts cover the theory and practice of data base management systems:

D. Kroenke, Database Processing: Fundamentals, Modeling, Applications, Science Research Associates, Inc., Chicago, Illinois, 1977.

C. J. Date, An Introduction to Data Base Systems, 3rd Edition, Addison Wesley Publishing Co., Reading, Massachusetts, 1981.

J. D. Ullman, Principles of Data Base Systems, Computer Science Press, Potomac, Maryland, 1980.

The text by Date emphasizes the hierarchical database systems, whereas Ullman examines mainly the relational systems.

The following texts deal largely with data structures and file access methods:

E. Horowitz and S. Sahni, Fundamentals of Data Structures, Computer Science Press, Woodland Hills, California, 1976.

G. Wiederhold, Database Design, McGraw-Hill Book Company, New York, 1977.

Several review articles cover the history and the general context of data base management systems including:

J. P. Fry and E. H. Sibley, Evolution of Data-Base Management Systems, Computing Surveys, Vol. 8, No. 1, March 1976, pp. 7–42.

M. E. Senko, Data Structures and Data Accessing in Data Base Systems: Past, Present, Future, IBM Systems Journal, Vol. 16, No. 3, 1977, pp. 208–257.

I. Benbasat and R. Goldstein, Data Base Systems for Small Business: Miracle or Mirage, Data Base, Vol. 9, No. 1, Summer 1977, pp. 5–8.

The latter is a nontechnical general review addressed to business managers.

The following articles provide an introduction to the conceptual data base models:

E. F. Codd, A Relational Model of Data for Large Shared Data Banks, ACM Communications, Vol. 13, No. 6, June 1970, pp. 377–387.

R. W. Taylor and R. L. Frank, CODASYL Data Base Management Systems, ACM Computing Surveys, Vol. 8, No. 1, March 1976, pp. 67–103.

T. W. Olle, The CODASYL Approach to Data Base Management, John Wiley and Sons, New York, 1978.

D. D. Chamberlin, Relational Data-Base Management Systems, Computing Surveys, Vol. 8, No. 1, March 1976, pp. 43–66.

Many journals contain material in the data base management area, including periodicals covering the practical aspects addressed to relatively nontechnical audiences such as:

Computerworld
Data Base
Datamation
Harvard Business Review

Additional more technical and theoretical material is contained in the following journals:

ACM Transactions on Database Systems
IBM Systems Journal
Information Systems
Information Technology: Research and Development
Journal of Systems Management

EXERCISES

9-1 Use the chart of Fig. 9-1 to place the following types of information systems in appropriate positions. Explain your choice in each case.

    a Question-answering systems

    b Public libraries

    c Private industrial or special libraries

    d Poison control centers
    e Automated inventory control systems
9-2 Consider a data base management system designed to maintain the student-course records needed by the faculty and administration in a particular school. Specify the types of records that must be included in the system and design a user (external) data base schema as well as the conceptual and the internal data base schemas.
9-3 Given the two relations M and N, carry out the following operations in the relational algebra:

A	B	C
One	Sine	Plus
Two	Cosine	Plus
Three	Tangent	Minus
Seven	Cotangent	Minus

Relation M

C	D	E
Plus	Sine	Seven
Minus	Sine	Two
Plus	Tangent	Three
Minus	Cotangent	Two

Relation N

    a The Cartesian product $N \times M$
    b The natural join M JOIN N
    c The restricted join $N \underset{B \neq D}{\text{JOIN}} M$
    d The projection $\text{PROJ}_{3,1} N$
9-4 List the advantages and disadvantages of each of the three main data base models including the relational, hierarchical, and network models. What mechanisms are available to obtain file access to data bases organized according to the various model specifications? How does one search the stored data in each model?
9-5 Why is it useful to make special provisions to implement many-to-many relationships in some data base systems? How are many-to-many relationships implementated in relational, hierarchical, and network systems?
9-6 Design relational, hierarchical, and network data bases that include the following relationships between record types
    a Managers responsible for many projects
    b Managers responsible for many employees
    c Employees assigned to many projects
    d Projects carried out by many employees
Describe how the three data base organizations would be used to retrieve the names of all employees that report to several managers, and the number of managers responsible for more than one project.
9-7 List the various circumstances that render necessary the protection of data bases against unauthorized access. What methods can be used to provide the required protection, and how do these methods operate?
9-8 Why is it necessary to protect the integrity of the stored data in a data base management system? What methods are available for integrity preservation? In which way are integrity considerations used in specifying the structure of relational data base systems?

Chapter 10

Future Directions in Information Retrieval

0 PREVIEW

This concluding chapter considers new developments which may be expected to affect the information retrieval world in the not too distant future. In a few years the text entry problem will have been solved either by using character recognition equipment to recognize textual materials or through the widespread use of word processing. It will also be possible to store full documents digitally or in microform, and to use automated graphics equipment to handle illustrations and pictures. Various advanced technologies that may be helpful for the processing of full documents are briefly introduced. This is followed by a summary of theoretical approaches for the representation and analysis of document content, including fuzzy set theory, term dependency analysis, and composite document representations. A number of sophisticated automatic document processing systems are also described that will be capable of processing full documents and of servicing large user populations.

Eventually paperless electronic systems may be created which will offer a wide variety of individually tailored information services to the users. Such systems could include many facilities that are not yet currently available, including natural language recognition, graphics processing, speech recognition, and inexpensive point-to-point communications.

1 INTRODUCTION

The material contained in the previous chapters covers the existing theory and practice in information retrieval, as well as various extensions that could in principle be implemented at once in the proper environment. This last chapter deals with new ideas and technologies that may be just beyond the current state of the art. Technological innovations are mentioned which should significantly alter the search and retrieval process as it exists today, and theoretical developments are discussed that may provide new insights into the information search and retrieval functions.

One of the characteristics of the existing operational retrieval systems is the large investment in manpower and resources necessary to provide even relatively simple retrieval services. The design and implementation of retrieval programs constitute major tasks in themselves; in addition, substantial resources must be devoted to the generation or acquisition of the data bases to be manipulated and searched. In these circumstances, even minor adjustments in procedures require careful consideration; more far-reaching innovations are often out of the question because of the large resources that are required. This may explain the tendency among many observers to think of the ideal retrieval facility as a simple extension of the currently existing systems and procedures. Thus a good deal of attention is devoted to the implementation of sophisticated user-system interfaces permitting users and search intermediaries to carry out the retrieval operations without some of the limitations that hamper the existing search efforts. From time to time new search protocols are proposed for conducting iterative searches in such a way that earlier search results are utilized to formulate improved query statements usable in subsequent search operations. The relevance feedback process described earlier is an example of such a system. Efforts are also made to extend the retrieval operations to several different data bases while merging the respective search output.

The future directions in information retrieval may be considered by reviewing theories that are currently under active consideration and in studying technologies that are likely to be prevalent in the foreseeable future. The theories of most interest deal with natural language processing systems using extended representations of information content. The new technologies include special processing "chips," microprocessors, optical character readers, optical memories, and micrographic devices. One may expect that new theoretical developments could in time be coupled to the new technologies, leading to the implementation of flexible, new user support systems capable of controlling many different file processing activities. Sooner or later, the conventional information processing systems may be replaced by "paperless" systems in which machine-readable entities are processed instead of hard-copy products, and all information flow operations are carried out electronically.

It is premature to submit a definitive design of the information system of the future. However, it is not too early to study the developments that may be expected to form the basis for the design of the information handling systems of the future.

2 TECHNOLOGICAL DEVELOPMENTS

A Automatic Document Input

The existing information retrieval systems have enjoyed increasing popularity in the last few years. As more and more items are added to the files, one may expect that an ever larger proportion of the population will become interested in using the automatic search and retrieval facilities. Unfortunately, many of the items that need to be added to the files are not currently available in a form which allows incorporation into existing data bases. In principle, it is possible to charge a typist, keypuncher, or data entry clerk with the task of converting paper documents into machine-readable form. An exceedingly proficient typist might produce errorless copy at the rate of 100 words per minute. This would generate 192 double-spaced pages of machine-readable text in an 8-hour working day, assuming no coffee breaks, lunch hours, errors, or corrections. A more reasonable rate for experienced typists may be 50 typed pages per day. As a mechanism for information input into an automated retrieval system, such a process is inconvenient and labor-intensive, particularly if one considers that the data input operation constitutes a second typing operation, following initial document preparation in many cases.

Fortunately, the data input problem may be on the way to a solution. A typing operation may still be initially required to create the original documents. This typed copy is now increasingly produced with equipment capable of capturing the information in machine-readable form. *Word processing machines* are used in many places to produce edited, machine-readable text that can be converted into a final printed product. In the foreseeable future, one may expect that increasing quantities of text will become available in a format acceptable for input to automated information retrieval systems [1–3].

The word processing concept was initially introduced as a means of simplyifying certain secretarial tasks—notably the typing of multiple copies of letters. A standard typewriter would be used supplemented by a paper or magnetic tape storage unit. The information being typed by the human operator could then be punched out or recorded automatically on the auxiliary storage equipment. When additional copies of previously typed materials were needed, the recorded tape could be used as input without additional keyboarding.

At the present time, far more sophisticated word processing stations are used, including the following components:

1   A keyboarding unit
2   A storage unit, often consisting of a floppy (soft) disk capable of storing, inexpensively, between 50 and 1,000 pages of text

3 A video display unit capable of displaying any page of stored or typed text

4 A print unit that can print out a final ouput product

5 A connection to a computer or to communications lines capable of joining several word processing stations.

The enhanced word processing equipment can now be used not only for the basic typing and further reproduction of text but also for changing, revising, and editing text. The video display unit is particularly helpful in this respect because appropriate editing commands can be supplied from the keyboard. Final copies of text can also be obtained, in a format ready for printing. Furthermore, the materials generated by word processing can be disseminated to the recipients electronically using the available communications lines. Word processors could then function as originating and receiving stations in an electronic mail system. Since a large proportion of the correspondence in a business organization is internal to the company itself, it is not hard to see that electronic word processing systems can in principle take over the vast majority of the routine communications in an office. The effect of word processing on the publishing and information retrieval world is equally far-reaching: the multiple typing operations normally needed to produce final versions of books and documents may soon be a thing of the past; instead the word processor output can be used to drive automatic typsetting equipment, and the material stored in word processors can be taken over directly by an information storage and retrieval system.

Word processing machines do not of course help in converting materials that may already be available in standard, printed form, nor do they solve the input problem for users who may not have access to machine-readable input that may already exist elsewhere. In that case it may be useful to consider *character reading* equipment using optical reading methods to convert printed information directly to machine-readable form. Optical character readers are now available that convert text printed in a variety of type fonts to machine-readable form at a rate of about 80,000 characters per hour, producing over 500 double-spaced pages in a standard 8-hour day [4].

Character readers do not require coffee breaks; however, the existing devices are error-prone, the quality of the output being dependent on the characteristics of the printed input. For example, the input character "t" represented in Fig. 10-1 may be interpreted as a "c" by a standard optical character reader when the upper portion of the character is misformed or exhibits less contrast than the lower portion of the character. The most sophisticated available character reading equipment is now able to recognize correctly about 90 percent of the characters, and about 70 percent of the full words, contained in arbitrary printed input texts. When a machine-aided, human posteditor is added to "clean up" the output of the character recognition system, close to 100 percent correct output may be produced.

The postediting process is typically carried out as a two-step process:

Figure 10-1 Typical input to character reading equipment.

1 An automatic process is used to highlight each character falling below a given threshold of recognition acceptability.

2 A manual character replacement phase then allows a human operator to correct the output of the optical recognition system.

The automatic highlighting process determines a level of certainty for each character as a function of the degree of agreement between features recognized in the input and the patterns stored by the recognition system. Thus, for the character "M" represented in Fig. 10-2 the recognition characteristics may include certain identified vertices as well as line segments (vectors) with appropriate directions.

Given an input character such as the one used as an example in Fig. 10-3, it may be seen that only the vector information matches. Such a character may then be recognized as an "M" with a certainty level of $4/7$, or 0.571. Assuming that the threshold for acceptable characters is 0.75, the corresponding input would be submitted to a human operator for appropriate action during the postediting phase. Obviously, the postediting task increases the cost and decreases the efficiency of the character recognition process.

The recognition process described earlier may furnish a serviceable solution to the text input problem. Alternatively, a training system could be used where the characteristics of some sample input are used by the system to set appropriate recognition procedures capable of handling new text whose features are similar to that of the training sample. Unfortunately, some aspects of the text input problem are still not treated satisfactorily. A few text characters may be left unrecognized even when a human editor is available, because the

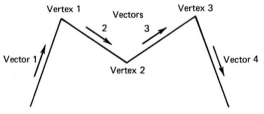

Figure 10-2 Recognition characteristics for letter "M."

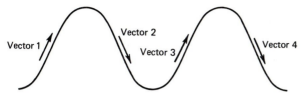

Figure 10-3   Character recognized as "M" with certainty level of 0.571.

recognition threshold may be erroneously met for misinterpreted characters. Thus, the input of Fig. 10-1 may be recognized as a "c" without ever being shown to the editor. Second, special portions of the text, such as author names, document titles, and descriptive indexing information, may require separate treatment from the remainder of the text, and the character recognition equipment may not necessarily be adapted to the identification of these special text elements. Finally, the equipment does not treat pictorial and graphical portions of documents that may also need to be processed. Special graphics equipment is needed to handle illustrations and pictures.

An automatic character recognition system might also be supplemented by an automatic *voice input* system. With such a system, information could be dictated, or read, directly to an automated typewriter or display input equipment, thereby eliminating the distinction between readability and machine readability. Some voice input systems already exist, for example, children's games are sold which properly recognize spoken input words such as "stop," "right," "left," or "go," provided the words are properly uttered in isolation. Certain computer systems in fact accept up to 1,000 individually specified words.

Unfortunately, a substantial distinction must be made between the recognition of distinct spoken words in a given language uttered by speakers to which the equipment has been properly adapted, and the recognition of normal running speech in arbitrary dialects by unknown speakers [5]. A solution to the latter problem appears to be as difficult as the natural language analysis problems previously discussed in Chapter 7. Whether the remaining character recognition problems can be handled effectively in the foreseeable future to solve the information input problem without any keyboarding remains to be seen.

B   Optical Storage

In addition to the input problem, the storage problem is a primary concern in information retrieval. In situations where only limited data classes are processed—for example, in systems where the retrieval activity is based on document citations and keywords only—the conventional magnetic disk technology normally proves satisfactory. Magnetic devices are erasable and lend themselves easily to most file updating and maintenance requirements. Furthermore auxiliary index files can then be constructed and maintained to guarantee reasonably rapid access to individual information items.

In many cases, it may, however, be desirable to access or display for the user's attention copies of the full contents of articles. In that case it becomes necessary to handle different type sizes, pictorial information, signatures and graphical data. A photographic or other optical storage medium may be needed that is capable of storing digital as well as video information. Videodiscs, holograms, and micrographic storage devices are of main concern in this connection.

Videodiscs   A videodisc is a picture storage device that can be connected to the home television set. If it is used in the home, the videodisc can provide a color TV movie for the $15 purchase price of the disk. The player for the videodisc was priced at approximately $500 in 1981, but this price may decrease in time. The importance of the videodisc for information retrieval is not necessarily to keep the viewer entertained but rather to store large quantities of information at little cost [6,7].

Consider first the manner in which information is stored on a videodisc. Figure 10-4 shows graphically the method of "burning" information representations onto the disk. As information is received as input, it is translated through a series of electronic devices to control parameters which guide a laser beam. The beam in turn creates pits in the surface of a rotating master disk. These pits may then be "read" to reproduce the information.

Videodiscs are not currently capable of rewriting. That is, once the information is put onto the master disk, it cannot be erased and rewritten. However, duplicates of the master disk may be created. This process is similar to creating

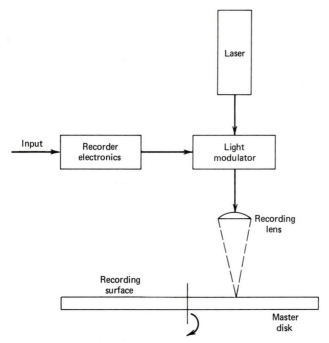

Figure 10-4   Videodisc recording.

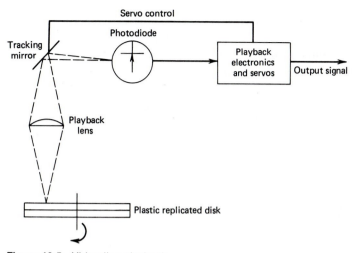

Figure 10-5 Videodisc playback.

duplicate copies of phonograph records. One rotation of the videodisc (one track) produces one visual image (one television picture). There are 54,000 concentric tracks on most current videodiscs. In the more sophisticated videodisc readers, these tracks may be accessed in any order. Figure 10-5 represents the system used to recover the information from the videodisc. Note that the playback system uses reflected laser light to encode the information.

Initial work with videodiscs indicates that 10 billion bits or approximately 1 billion characters of information may be stored on a single disk. Reproductions of a videodisc in quantities of about 1,000 will cost less than $20 per disk. This includes the cost of the disk and of the reproduction process but not of the information contained on the disk. Thus, given a data base of information items each averaging 1,000 characters, 1 million of these records can fit on a videodisc. In addition, work is currently underway to increase the capacity of a single videodisc to 10 billion characters.

An unknown factor is the error rate associated with the stored information. For the home entertainment application that is not important; however, for the storage of digital information it may be critical. That is, if one watches a TV picture and a single blue dot suddenly turns red for $1/30$ second, there is little concern. However, if that mistaken blue dot is the difference between CANCEROUS and NOT CANCEROUS in a medical data base, then it could amount to catastrophic error. Mechanisms for assuring the integrity of digitally encoded information on videodiscs remain to be worked out as of this writing. When this problem is resolved, the videodisc technology may actually produce significant changes in the processing of large data bases with periodic updates. Using videodiscs may, for instance, reduce the need for large communication networks to remote data bases. Instead, institutions such as the National Library of Medicine may simply mail periodic updates of their data bases to geographically dispersed sites. These sites will own inexpensive videodisc readers attached to inexpensive computers for immediate and reliable access to the information.

Additional applications may also become economically attractive. For example, if it were feasible to store digital information on the videodiscs in addition to pictorial data, the combination of the two might be applicable to the storage of museum information, photography retrieval, etc. In addition, one may also opt to intersperse audio information among the recorded video and digital information. Time and thought will be required to ensure the success of the videodisc technology in the information retrieval environment.

Holographic Devices   Another approach for information storage consists in using holographic devices. A hologram is a picture showing a three-dimensional object. The hologram is created by illuminating an object with laser-generated light from two angles. As the light reflected from the object hits one of the laser beams (the reference beam) an interference pattern is created. This pattern is recorded on film as the hologram. The recording operation is represented in Fig. 10-6. When a laser beam is passed through the hologram, it is deflected so that a viewer perceives the original object as shown in Fig. 10-7.

An interesting feature of holographic recording is that the holographic image is literally dispersed across the entire hologram. That is, if a hologram is cut in half and illuminated, the entire object may still be perceived. The resolution of the object is reduced, however.

If the object photographed by the holographic device is replaced by a digital pattern representing characters or other digitally encoded data, then the digital data will also be redundantly stored in the hologram. Reproduction of the data requires that the display of the hologram be focused on a photodetector device to convert the picture back to digital signals.

Holographic storage of information is "safe." Because of the natural re-

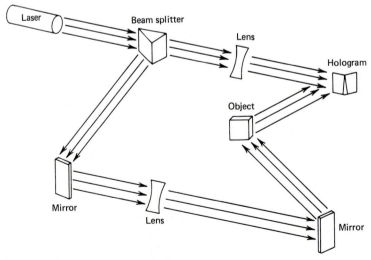

Figure 10-6 Holographic recording.

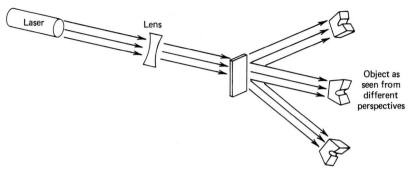

Figure 10-7 Holographic viewing.

dundancy, a substantial portion of the hologram may be destroyed without actually losing the information. The hologram is also capable of huge quantities of storage. It has been stated that a single 4 by 6 inch piece of film can hold up to 20,000 individual holograms or 20 million characters of information. A device for reading this information may cost as little as $5,000 [8].

The holographic storage devices, like the videodiscs, are not capable of rewriting. However, reproduction costs of $1 or even less for a 4 by 6 inch film (fiche) is possible, and as for videodiscs, holograms may be interspersed with video images, making new applications a real possibility.

Micrographic Storage   Micrographic storage devices, such as microfilm or microfiche, provide another solution to the storage problem of bulk materials in retrieval. Micrographic devices have been available for many years and have proved to be cost effective in many applications [9]. Micrographic storage, like video equipment, is used to store vast quantities of information, the storage efficiency being achieved by using a substantial size reduction (typically by a factor of 24) for the recorded information. A standard 4 by 6 inch microfiche thus normally stores 98 pages of digital or pictorial information.

Unfortunately, the microform technology does not easily permit erasing or modification of the recorded information. Its application in information retrieval is normally found in situations where the existing file remains largely unchanged, and new film or fiche is used when additional documents are to be incorporated into the file. An additional disadvantage of this equipment is the substantial discomfort felt by many users when confronted by this technology. The size reduction renders necessary the use of special reading equipment which magnifies the recorded information before viewing by the user. Most people would prefer hard-copy document output that can be carried around and directly manipulated to the somewhat remote microforms.

For storage and retrieval purposes special fiche storage devices are used from which a particular fiche can be extracted on demand. It is customary to use the fiche number as the main identification, although in principle, the contents of a particular fiche can be specified by using conventional keywords and index terms. However, since a single fiche may contain many pages of disparate material in addition to pictures and graphs, the full content of a fiche is not easily captured by standard methods. A particular fiche extracted from the storage device may be automatically sent to a microfiche reader for viewing purposes. Alternatively a microfilm copy can be made for the user's personal attention, or paper copies can be produced of certain documents using a micro-form-to-hard-copy conversion device.

A typical document processing system using micrographics equipment is shown in Fig. 10-8. Optical character recognition equipment is provided in the illustration for input purposes using the semiautomatic process previously described in which a human operator resolves input ambiguities using a special editing terminal. A combined magnetic and optical storage system is then used for storage and retrieval. Specifically, a standard search is conducted using the document content descriptions stored on conventional disk equipment. Assuming that the standard search produces the location identifications (fiche numbers) of the corresponding full document texts, the corresponding fiches can then be extracted from the fiche storage device for further processing.

In the combined magnetic and optical storage system of Fig. 10-8, the microfilm processing system is completely mechanized. Furthermore, all the graphics equipment is currently in existence and can be bought off the shelf [10]. However, the physical movement of the microforms from the storage area to the viewing position requires a mechanical transport device which is cumbersome and expensive. More generally, the marriage between the magnetic and graphic storage technologies represented in the system of Fig. 10-8 is somewhat forced. Different accessing keys are used in the two systems and the pictorial portion of the information stored on the microforms is not directly used in retrieval. For this reason, systems such as the one represented in Fig. 10-4 will not provide long-range solutions to the existing information retrieval problem.

Efforts have recently been made to permit a digitization of micrographic images following a normal optical scan. That is, as each image is scanned, the images are converted into digital form; the converted image can then be displayed on a normal cathode-ray tube display screen, or entered into computer storage. The perfection of these techniques may solve the interface problem between the micrographic and digital storage equipment and produce a harmonious system involving both technologies [11].

Following a description of certain novel retrieval theories, various extended information systems are considered whose design is based in part on the microprocessing, character reading, and graphics equipment previously mentioned. Such extended systems may then provide a solution to the existing information problems.

3 INFORMATION THEORIES AND MODELS

A Natural Language Processing

In attempting to predict the design of future information systems, it appears best not to concentrate on the existing retrieval practice but to identify features that are generally considered desirable but are currently beyond the state of the

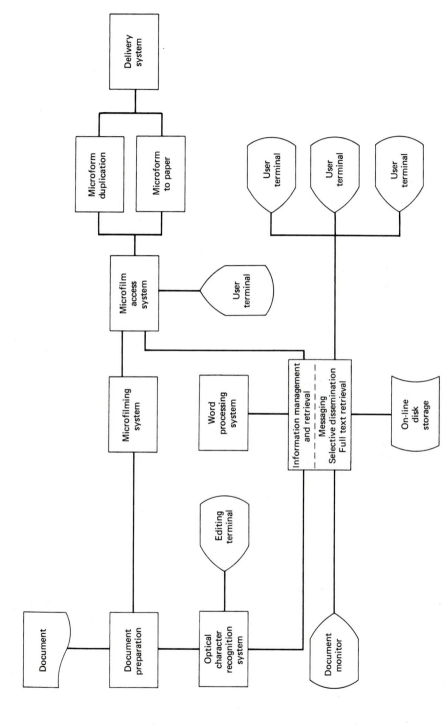

Figure 10-8 Document management system using micrographics.

art. Without a doubt, the most immediately important problem of this kind is the understanding and processing of the written and spoken natural language [12]. If user queries could be submitted using a conventional, natural language formulation, and texts could be automatically analyzed, abstracted, translated where necessary, and properly classified according to the document content, then the main difficulties which currently hamper the information system user would automatically disappear. No longer would it be necessary to worry about the design of controlled indexing languages; the need for well-trained, consistent indexers no longer arises; and the burden currently placed on users and search intermediaries in the formulation of useful queries is lifted.

Unfortunately, the discussion in Chapter 7 on natural language processing indicates that the free manipulation of unrestricted natural language data is not a likely prospect for the foreseeable future. In particular, no agreement exists about the best way for formalizing document content, about the world knowledge (above and beyond the specialized knowledge in a given subject area) that may be needed to understand texts and interpret natural language statements, and about reasoning strategies, inferences, and deductions that may be needed in order actually to respond to user inquiries [13–14].

The approach in information science has been to use specialized techniques in an attempt to provide at least some linguistic input to the standard document analysis and retrieval process [15–16]. Methods have notably been developed for recognizing and assigning noun phrases as document and query identifiers, and syntactic techniques have been used for dealing with individual document sentences instead of complete documents [17–20].

The primary difficulty in natural language processing is due to the flexibility and by extension the ambiguity of most languages. Many ways exist for expressing the same thought; hence it is easy in principle to generate documents and to formulate information requests. At the same time, a given utterance may receive many different interpretations depending on the context in which it appears; hence it is difficult to generate definite or unique interpretations of natural language materials. The approach mentioned earlier in the discussion on character recognition can be followed by considering the use of semiautomatic language analysis methods. That is, the machine might automatically identify potential ambiguities, and a human operator could then attempt to resolve them [21–22].

Various other techniques have been used in information retrieval in attempting to cope with the language ambiguity problem. In the vector processing model, special weights are attached to the terms that identify documents and search requests, reflecting the degree of importance of each term or the degree of certainty with which the term describes the document content. Global similarity computations between weighted term vectors are then used to indicate the relationship between pairs of documents or between queries and documents [23–24]. Thus, the degree of affinity between two items can vary depending on the certainty or interpretation of the respective content identifiers.

Somewhat similar characteristics are exhibited by the fuzzy set and probabilistic approaches to retrieval that are briefly introduced in the next few paragraphs.

**B Fuzzy Set Theory

The basic idea in fuzzy set theory is that elements or entities can be assigned to sets to varying degrees. That is, instead of either including an element in a given set or excluding it from the set, a *membership function* is used to express the degree to which the element is a member of the set. This concept is of interest in language processing, and by extension in information retrieval, because the assignment of individual words to meaning categories is a fuzzy process; so is the assignment of documents to concept categories, and hence also the retrieval of documents in answer to certain queries [25].

In language processing, various attempts have been made to use the fuzzy set approach to model linguistic vagueness, ambiguity, and ambivalence. For example, given a set of well-defined meaning categories, the total meaning of a given word might be expressed as a weighted combination of the membership functions of that word in various meaning classes. Linguistic quantifiers ("most," "some," "a few") and hedges ("sort of") might also be described by using fuzzy measurements of some kind [26–28].

In information retrieval, the fuzzy set approach can be used to classify the documents into fuzzy affinity classes and also to control the actual retrieval process. Consider first a document DOC and a particular term A. If **A** denotes the "concept class" of all items dealing with the subject denoted by A, then the membership function of document DOC in set **A** may be denoted as $f_A(DOC)$. In the usual terminology $f_A(DOC)$ represents the weight of term A in document DOC. Given a number of concept classes **A, B, . . . ,Z** representing various subject areas, it is now possible to identify each document by giving its membership function with respect to each of the concept classes, that is,

$$D = (f_A(DOC), f_B(DOC), \ . \ . \ . \ ,f_Z(DOC)) \tag{1}$$

Expression (1) thus takes the place of the normal term vector used in the vector processing model of retrieval.

Given document representations of the kind shown in expression (1), all the usual vector processing operations are now expressible as fuzzy set operations. In particular, the distance (or similarity) between two documents or between a document and a query may be obtained as a function of the differences in the membership functions of the two items in corresponding concept classes. Specifically, given T different concept classes, the *fuzzy distance* between documents DOC' and DOC" might be computed as

$$d(DOC',DOC'') = \sum_{x \epsilon T} (f_x(DOC') - f_x(DOC''))$$

or alternatively

$$d(DOC', DOC'') = \sqrt{\sum_{x \in T} (f_x(DOC') - f_x(DOC''))^2}$$

Ranked retrieval is achieved by retrieving the documents in order of increasing fuzzy distance from the query.

One attractive feature of the fuzzy set approach is the possibility of extending the definition of the membership function from single terms to combinations of terms. Thus, given the membership functions of document DOC with respect to terms A and B, the following rules apply for Boolean combinations of terms [25]:

$$\begin{align}
f_{(A\ AND\ B)}(DOC) &= \min(f_A(DOC), f_B(DOC)) \\
f_{(A\ OR\ B)}(DOC) &= \max(f_A(DOC), f_B(DOC)) \\
f_{(NOT\ A)}(DOC) &= 1 - f_A(DOC)
\end{align} \tag{3}$$

It is easy to verify that the fuzzy set rules of expression (3) satisfy the normal rules of Boolean algebra when $f_A(DOC)$ and $f_B(DOC)$ are restricted to the values 0 and 1. The fuzzy set retrieval model thus represents an extension of the normal Boolean retrieval system to the case where the assignment of weighted identifiers is possible for the documents but not for the queries.

Since the vector space model effectively supplies term weights for both the documents and the queries, the fuzzy set model is in a sense intermediate between a conventional Boolean query system where no term weights are allowed and a vector processing system. The attractions of the fuzzy set model are its compatibility with the standard Boolean query processing system and the interpretation of the fuzzy weights as linguistic indicators of term ambiguity or ambivalence. A number of attempts have been made to use fuzzy set models in retrieval; however, the resulting systems have never been evaluated, and the linguistic relationship has not so far been exploited [29–34].

**C Term Dependency Models

The flexibility and ambiguity characteristics of the natural language are reflected in the fuzzy set retrieval model where terms and other content identifiers apply to some degree in particular cases. A different approach consists in using as a measure of term importance values expressing the likelihood that a given term occurs in a particular environment, or the likelihood that the term should be assigned to a given document. Such *probability measures* can be used as term weights, and the documents can then be retrieved in ranked order according to the probability of relevance to the given queries.

Given a particular document identified by a binary term vector $x = (x_1, x_2, \ldots, x_t)$ the optimal retrieval rule in the probabilistic model consists in first evaluating $P(x)$, the probability of occurrence of x in a relevant document, and $Q(x)$, the probability of occurrence of x in a nonrelevant document, and then in retrieving the document represented by x whenever $P(x) > Q(x)$ [35–36]. The actual values of the probabilities $P(x)$ and $Q(x)$ depend on the occurrence probabilities of the individual terms $x_1, x_2, \ldots, x_t$ in the relevant and nonrelevant documents of a collection, respectively.

It was mentioned earlier that under the assumption that the terms are assigned independently to the documents of a collection, the probabilistic retrieval model produces an optimal term weighting function TERMREL, known as the "term relevance," representing the logarithm of the proportion of relevant documents in which a term occurs, divided by the proportion of nonrelevant items in which the term occurs [37–38]. The normal linguistic intuition makes it clear, however, that words or concepts do not occur in the language independently of each other. Hence one may expect that retrieval models that are based on the term independence assumption will not reflect reality very accurately. A more realistic treatment would take into account various similarities and dependencies between the terms.

In the fuzzy set model of retrieval, the notion of term dependence is directly built in, in that many terms may be assigned to common concept classes and somewhat different membership functions may be used to reflect differences between them. In probabilistic retrieval the same effect is obtainable by computing *term dependence* probabilities as a function of the probability of co-occurrence of several terms in the documents of a collection, compared with the occurrence probabilities of the individual terms alone.

In fact, exact formulations for the occurrence probabilities $P(x)$ and $Q(x)$ of a given document vector x in the relevant and nonrelevant documents of a collection are provided by the Bahadur-Lazarsfeld expansion (BLE). This expansion takes into account the occurrence probabilities of the individual terms x_i, as well as all dependencies between term pairs, triplets, and all higher-order dependencies [39,40]. The correct retrieval strategy then consists in using the BLE expansion to compute the probabilities $P(x)$ and $Q(x)$, and in retrieving a document represented by x whenever the expression $\log[P(x)/Q(x)]$ is sufficiently large. Unfortunately this method is not immediately usable in practice because an exponential number of pairwise and other higher order dependencies exist between the terms, and because no obvious way is provided for estimating all the required probabilities.

Various techniques suggest themselves for constructing approximations to the exact process. One possibility consists in using a *tree dependence* model where each term is allowed to be dependent on only one other term [37,41,42]. Another approach consists in using the BLE expression in a suitably truncated form. A possible measure of pairwise term dependence is given for two sample terms x_i and x_j as

$$I(x_i, x_j) = \sum_{\substack{x_i=0,1 \\ x_j=0,1}} P(x_i, x_j) \log \frac{P(x_i, x_j)}{P(x_i)P(x_j)} \tag{4}$$

where $P(x_i, x_j)$ is the joint probability of occurrence of both terms x_i and x_j in the documents of a collection, $P(x_i)$ and $P(x_j)$ are the individual occurrence probabilities of the two terms, and the summation is taken over the four combinations of values obtained by assuming values of 0 or 1 for both x_i and x_j [39]. Since the probability of occurrence of a given document vector x [that is, $P(x)$ and $Q(x)$] must be computed separately for the relevant and nonrelevant documents of a collection, the probability values in the term dependence expression (4) must also be obtained separately for the relevant and the nonrelevant documents of a collection. That is, expression (4) may be assumed to be valid for the relevant documents, and a similar expression with Qs replacing all the Ps would apply to the nonrelevant items.

A realistic method for estimating these probabilities consists in using the *relevance feedback* strategy introduced in Chapter 6. In relevance feedback, tentative search requests are first submitted to a retrieval system; the relevance or nonrelevance of initially retrieved items is then used to generate improved query formulations that are more similar to the documents identified earlier as relevant than the original queries, and less similar to the documents identified as nonrelevant. The reformulated queries are then processed in a second search operation in the expectation that additional useful items may be retrieved. The query reformulation process may be repeated until the user is satisfied with the retrieval results [43–45]. If the relevance feedback process is used for a given document collection over some period of time, relevance information should eventually be obtainable for a substantial number of documents. This implies that the occurrence characteristics of a large number of terms in the relevant and nonrelevant retrieved documents should become known.

It remains then to estimate the occurrence probabilities of the terms in the relevant and the nonrelevant documents of a collection by looking at the corresponding occurrence probabilities in the *relevant retrieved* and in the *nonrelevant retrieved* items, respectively. If $P(x_i)$ and $Q(x_i)$ denotes the occurrence probability of term x_i in the relevant and nonrelevant items of a collection, the estimated values could be obtained as

$$P(x_i) \text{ estimated} = \frac{\text{number of relevant and retrieved items containing term } x_i}{\text{number of relevant and retrieved items}}$$

$$Q(x_i) \text{ estimated} = \frac{\text{number of nonrelevant and retrieved items containing term } x_i}{\text{number of nonrelevant and retrieved items}}$$

(5)

The probability estimation methods of expression (5) have been used experimentally with good success [41,45]. However, conclusive evidence about the usefulness of including term dependencies in retrieval is still lacking. In particular, practical methods remain to be worked out for choosing a small number of the most important term dependencies, and for actually generating the corresponding term dependence factors used in the probability formulas.

*D Composite Document Representations

The fuzzy set and probabilistic retrieval models constitute enhancements of the conventional retrieval environment in the sense that term ambiguities and term dependencies are taken into account. Another, even more fundamental question, concerns the proper choice of the initial, basic concepts to be used for the representation of document content. In principle, the vocabulary included in query and document formulations must be used as a basis for the choice of content identifiers. However, it is not clear a priori how many basic concepts ought to be used, and how these concepts are to be defined.

One possible approach consists in taking an indexed document collection in which term vectors are used to represent the various documents, and in performing a *factor analysis* to derive the few independent concepts from the larger class of initially available terms. Unfortunately, a factor analysis process is expensive to carry out, and becomes impractical when more than a few hundred documents and queries are involved.

A more efficient method for generating a set of independent basic concepts may be obtained by first choosing a set of *core documents* from a sample document collection, the core being selected in such a way that core items have no common terms. The assumption is then made that the full concept space corresponds to the space initially defined by the core documents. Specifically, the documents outside the core are processed one at a time, and an appropriate place is found in the initial core concept space for each term included in these documents. That is, each of the new terms is defined as a combination of the originally chosen concepts [46,47]. Various methods can be used for defining the mapping of the new terms into the original concept space. So far, no conclusive information is available about the effectiveness of this type of process.

In addition to document content represented by the standard content terms, or keywords, documents may also be characterized by *scope,* or *extent;* survey articles tend to have greater scope than research notes dealing with specific technical subjects. Documents also carry various degrees of *influence;* many articles are effectively "lost" in the sense that they are unknown and are never referred to by other items in the literature; other documents become famous and serve as starting points for additional developments. Individual documents may also be characterized by citing other items in the literature that may exhibit similar or related information content. For example, a document dealing with a legal problem may be explicated by citing related cases covering legal precedents; similarly, a religious article may be better understood by adding references to authorized interpretations of the text.

This suggests that the normal vector representations of document content in which a term represents a particular content identifier be extended to cover these other factors. In particular, a document might be identified by using three types of identifiers:

1 Normal content terms including single words, phrases, and thesaurus categories

2 Factual or objective identifiers covering proper names of authors, publishers, dates, language of publication, and so on

3 Interpretational identifiers representing related documents designating scope, influence, and other interpretations

It has been suggested that the interpretational aspect of document content be represented by citations to other related bibliographic items [48,49].

A particular document might thus be represented as

$$D = (d_1, \ldots, d_k, o_{k+1}, \ldots, o_n, c_{n+1}, \ldots, c_t) \tag{6}$$

where d_f represents the weight of the fth content term, o_m represents the mth objective identifier, and c_p represents the pth citation to a related document.

Instead of using simple bibliographic citations to related documents for content representation, the *cocitation strength* could be used, defined as the degree to which two particular documents are cited in common [50].

The extended vector representations can be utilized in retrieval experiments by introducing *composite matching* coefficients to measure the similarity between a document and a query as a combination of the similarities for the various classes of identifiers [51]. The similarity SIM(D,Q) between a document D and query Q might then be computed as

$$\begin{aligned}
\text{SIM}(D,Q) = \ &\alpha[\text{content identifier similarity}] \\
&+ \beta[\text{objective term similarity}] \\
&+ \gamma[\text{citation similarity}]
\end{aligned} \tag{7}$$

for suitable weighting factors α, β, and γ. Much work is still required in the future for the generation and evaluation of useful extended content representations and composite query-document comparison methods.

4 ADVANCED INFORMATION SYSTEMS

A Mixed Information Retrieval Systems

Bibliographic retrieval is concerned with the processing of books and documents, available generally in natural language form. In many situations, even the most advanced bibliographic retrieval system will not satisfy the users' needs. Consider, for example, the problem of determining whether a particular chemical substance is toxic, that is, proves harmful to human beings who come in contact with it. In that case, textual data must be coordinated with numeric information produced by tests conducted with the substance in question. The user will thus require various resources in order adequately to resolve the toxicity question, including bibliographic information related to the chemicals, health effects, production processes, chemical uses, and so on. In addition experimental output and test information are needed about the production and use of chemicals, and about the known hazards of related substances as they affect populations in certain geographic areas.

The factual information relating to chemical characteristics and hazards differs from normal textual data in the sense that the *values* of specific attributes are important rather than the attributes themselves; furthermore, these values require analysis instead of simple retrieval. Data base management systems are normally designed to offer storage and retrieval capabilities for stored numeric information, as well as data analysis capabilities to perform statistical computations and to produce output summaries.

The chemical toxicity problem may then be attacked by supplying a variety of resources including in particular those contained in data management as well as bibliographic retrieval systems. More generally, an increasing need exists in many situations for sophisticated information systems capable automatically of coordinating related information from many sources. For example, an article dealing with the development of a chemical information system by a specific chemical company might be supplemented by information about the governmental regulations affecting data required from chemical companies, and by articles dealing with the availability of other chemical information systems, or articles written by the same author or citing the original article.

A system capable of pulling together many different but related resources would obviously expand the user's knowledge of a given problem by supplying a particular piece of information, as well as the context for this information. The ultimate information system is thus often conceived as a *network* of different information facilities including bibliographic retrieval, data base management, data analysis, citation indexing, and text processing systems. In order to utilize such a network effectively, the user ought to understand the capabilities of each resource and the interactions between them. System aids could be provided in the form of catalogs of available facilities, sample search protocols, lists of search commands and their effects, tutorial sequences, and so on.

Of particular interest in this connection are common interface systems which would permit the user to formulate in a common language information requests which are to be submitted to many different information systems. It is then up to the interface system to convert the original user statements into the different internal languages required by the various resources [52]. Common interface systems are helpful in that they render it unnecessary for users to concern themselves with the internal details of many different information systems. Of even greater interest might be systems that could themselves decide, given a particular query, which of many resources should be called upon to furnish the answer. In this mode, the system "knows" the capabilities of different resources and decides how best to use the available facilities to answer a given search request.

The design of such intelligent information systems is still somewhat beyond the state of the art. However, considerable advances are being made in developing special-purpose systems that facilitate access to many different resources and relieve the user from the operational details that must normally be mastered before file access can be obtained [53–55].

B   Personal Computing and Paperless Information Systems

A special class of information system that has been much in the news in recent times is designed to mechanize the paper handling routines normally taking place in office environments. An extension of these *office automation* systems are the so-called paperless information systems from which the hard-copy paper products are eliminated [56,57].

Until recently the supply of paper was plentiful and the printing operation was inexpensive. As a result the production of large journals and the bulk mailing of heterogeneous materials to large classes of recipients appeared justified. Printing and paper costs have been increasing steadily in recent years. At the present time, it appears much more important to target the disseminated information precisely to recipients who are actually likely to be interested in receiving each item. This results in the production of smaller, more specialized journals, and eventually in the replacement of journals by electronic distribution systems where individual items are distributed only to specially intended receivers.

The following main points are often cited in support of the paperless information systems of the future:

1   The volume of material to be processed and stored is becoming too large to be handled by a full-text, hard-copy paper system.

2   The materials of interest to any one person are becoming increasingly fragmented over many files, books, and journals, and the time available for finding and selecting the interesting portions is limited.

3   The cost of paper publication continues to increase at precipitous rates, in part because the publishing industry is labor-intensive and has not so far fully benefited from automation.

4   The conventional publication system continues to experience increasing delays in publishing research materials in part because the work force that originates the materials increases while at the same time the scope of many journals is constricted by rising costs and decreased subscription income.

5   An increasing proportion of the information materials is initially available in machine-readable form produced as a by-product of word processing or automated typesetting systems.

A situation is then postulated in which users, including office workers, scientists, technical personnel, and so on, have access to personal on-line console terminals. These terminals would be used to receive text, compose letters and documents, search for stored information, seek answers to factual questions, build information files, converse with colleagues by sending and receiving messages, receive mail, and generally conduct many kinds of information processing activities. Many different files could be maintained in such a system, including personal files accessible to the owner alone, mail files for incoming and outgoing messages, central files belonging to a given organization, and external files such as those maintained by outside information banks and libraries. A summary of various files and file operations of interest in such an environment is contained in Table 10-1.

Table 10-1   File Operations and Files for Typical Office Automation System

Typical operations	Typical files involved
Information search	Text files in digital form
Information retrieval	Text files in microform medium
Storage of new information	Personal files including personal data, addresses, comments, personal bibliographies
Refiling of old information	
File maintenance	
Data computations	
Text and letter composition	Mail files including data and status of incoming and outgoing messages
Text processing including correction, editing, hyphenation, justification, and so on	Central business files including information and status of stored correspondence
Communications, that is, sending and receiving of messages	External files such as generally accessible library files
	Master index files giving access to other files

In an automated file processing system a particular information item may be contained in several different files, for example, in certain publicly accessible files as well as in a variety of private files. Users may be allowed to use their own access points (content identifiers, keywords, etc.) to find a particular item, and different access conditions may obtain for the different users. Nevertheless each item need be stored only once assuming that index files are available to translate the different types of content descriptions into pointers referring to a given common storage location.

The obvious advantages of an automated, personal file processing system include the possibility rapidly to access a large variety of information products, including possibly the full text for many items, the convenience of being able to maintain and search private and public files at various levels of specificity and complexity, and the saving in space and paper handling.

The trend toward personal computing is accelerated by the recent startling advances in VLSI (very large scale integration) technology which makes possible the construction of powerful small computers coupled to large inexpensive storage devices (32-bit microprocessors with 128,000 bytes of storage) at costs not much in excess of $1,000 [58]. (See Table 10-2.) This technology makes it possible to expand computer services by simply furnishing small machines to large classes of potential users. This possibility is especially attractive in view of the increasing availability of personalized information services variously known as teletext or viewdata, where prestored information is disseminated on demand to individual recipients [59], and by advances in communications and networking that may in time allow the transmission of large masses of data using novel technologies such as fiber optics transmission lines [60].

The use of small, individual computers avoids some of the resource allocation problems which complicate life when a single large computer is used to service large user classes. Furthermore, users may prefer being ''in charge'' of their own machines, instead of having to contend with the restrictions normally imposed by computing center rules and regulations.

Table 10-2   Microprocessor Configurations

Configuration	Typical use	Typical cost

Handheld calculator
  Digital readout
  Input keyboard
  Several dozen storage registers
  Arithmetic unit
  Automatic sequence control
	Small programs and
	  calculations
		$50–$200

Minimal processor
  16–32 bit address
  32,000 to 128,000 characters of data
    storage
  2 to 5 microseconds add time
  Floppy disks for storage
  Cathode ray tube display
	Word processing capability
	Text editing
	Program editing
	Indexing
	Cataloging
		$1,000–$5,000

Full microprocessor configuration
  Printer added to minimal processor
  Hard disk for bulk storage
	Information retrieval
	Inverted file processing
	Output printing
		$10,000–$15,000

On the other hand, the future paperless systems also raise difficult legal and social problems that have not so far been adequately considered: for example, methods must be worked out for safeguarding the interests of a variety of parties in the information chain, including authors, publishers, information product vendors, and so on. At the present time royalty payments are not made when a user withdraws an item from a conventional library. An automated system with point-to-point communication facilities is, however, equivalent to an unrestricted, universal photocopying system, where anyone can easily obtain all stored materials. This possibility beclouds the future of the publishing industry and of the conventional library systems [61]. A good deal of thought must also be given to the role of the existing copyright legislation that protects ownership of information, as well as to the financial arrangements that must be made between the parties involved in the electronic communications system and to the provisions required for safeguarding the information stored in the publicly available files.

One may expect that many of the objections to the institution of paperless information systems will eventually disappear as the automatic systems become more sophisticated and more user-friendly. In time, a large proportion of the manual transactions currently performed with paper systems should be carried out automatically with electronic counterparts. And even if some paper products were to be maintained indefinitely, a more rational and hopefully more convenient information handling system will surely be instituted to serve the growing number of information users.

5   CONCLUSION

After reading some of the foregoing material, it will be obvious that a wealth of information and know-how exists about the theory and practice of information retrieval. Many insights relating to the information retrieval problem are obtainable by studying elements of related areas such as decision theory, artificial intelligence, software engineering, information theory, combinatorial mathematics, linear algebra, computational linguistics, pattern recognition, scene analysis, and logic. Viable solutions to the information problem will eventually be found by combining results derived from these various disciplines.

Many challenges lie ahead for researchers and practitioners in information retrieval. First, the knowledge and technology already available ought to be incorporated into the existing retrieval system implementations. The brief summary of technological and theoretical developments contained in this chapter indicates how much can already be done to improve the current information handling facilities. Second, there is a continued need for more basic work in various areas where progress has been relatively lacking, such as language processing, voice recognition, graphics storage and display, and the performance analysis of existing or projected systems.

There is little doubt that the pressures of organizations and individuals who demand a more effective utilization of information will continue to increase. The importance of timely and useful information necessary to carry out almost any task continues to grow, and the penalties in time, effort, and money to be paid when information resources remain unused or poorly used are fast increasing. A continued need then exists for high quality work in information retrieval and for the training of individuals knowledgeable in the various aspects of information handling. It is hoped that this text will make a modest contribution toward that aim.

REFERENCES

[1] J. Whitehead, Word Processing: An Introduction and Appraisal, Journal of Documentation, Vol. 36, No. 4, December 1980, pp. 313–341.

[2] R.M. Woelfle, The Impact of Word Processing on Engineering Communications, IEEE Transactions on Professional Communications, Vol. PC-23, No. 4, December 1980, pp. 159–163.

[3] J.C. Lawlor, What Can WP Do for Managers, in Information Choices and Policies, Proceedings of the ASIS Annual Meeting, American Society for Information Science, Vol. 16, Washington, D.C., 1979, p. 355.

[4] M.J.F. Poulsen, Optical Character Readers, Encyclopedia of Computer Science, A. Ralston and C.L. Meek, editors, Petrocelli/Charter, New York, 1976, pp. 1017–1022.

[5] A. Newell, J. Barnett, J.W. Forgie, C. Green, D. Klatt, J.C.R. Licklider, J. Munson, D.R. Reddy, and W.A. Woods, Speech Understanding Systems, North-Holland/ American Elsevier, London, 1973.

[6] K. S. Winslow, Videodisk in Your Future, Educational and Industrial TV, May 1975, pp. 21–22.

[7] P.B. Schipma and D.S. Becker, Text Storage and Display via Videodisk, Proceedings of the ASIS Annual Meeting, Vol. 17, American Society for Information Science, Washington, D.C., 1980, pp. 103–105.

[8] T.H. Maugh II, Holographic Filing: An Industry on the Verge of Birth, Science, Vol. 201, August 1978, pp. 431–432.

[9] National Micrographics Association, 1978-1979 Guide to Micrographic Equipment, Vols. 1 and 2, 7th Edition, New York, 1979.

[10] C.F.J. Overhage, Plans for Project Intrex, Science, Vol. 152, No. 3725, May 20, 1966, pp. 1032–1037.

[11] G. McMurdo, The Interface between Computerized Retrieval Systems and Micrographic Retrieval Systems, Journal of Information Science, Vol. 1, 1980, pp. 345–349.

[12] National Technical Information Service, Natural Language Processing, Special Bibliographies, Vols. 1 and 2, 1964-77 and 1978-79, Springfield, Virginia, 1980.

[13] T.R. Addis, Machine Understanding of Natural Language, International Journal of Man-Machine Studies, Vol. 9, No. 2, March 1977, pp. 207–222.

[14] G. Silva and C.A. Montgomery, Knowledge Representation for Automated Understanding of Natural Language Discourse, Computers and the Humanities, Vol. 11, No. 4, July–August 1977, pp. 223–234.

[15] K. Sparck Jones and M. Kay, Linguistics and Information Science, Academic Press, New York, 1973.

[16] C.A. Montgomery, Linguistics and Information Science, Journal of the ASIS, Vol. 23, No. 3, May–June 1972, pp. 195–219.

[17] R. Grishman, A Survey of Syntactic Analysis Procedures for Natural Language, American Journal of Computational Linguistics, Vol. 13, No. 5, 1976, Microfiche 47.

[18] W.A. Woods, Transition Network Grammars for Natural Language Analysis, Communications of the ACM, Vol. 13, No. 10, October 1970, pp. 591–606.

[19] J. O'Connor, Retrieval of Answer-Sentences and Answer-Figures from Papers by Text Searching, Information Processing and Management, Vol. 11, Nos. 5/7, 1975, pp. 155–164.

[20] J. O'Connor, Data Retrieval by Text Searching, Journal of Chemical Information and Computer Science, Vol. 17, 1977, pp. 181–186.

[21] P.H. Klingbiel, A Technique for Machine-Aided Indexing, Information Storage and Retrieval, Vol. 9, September 1973, pp. 477–494.

[22] P.H. Klingbiel and C.C. Rinker, Evaluation of Machine-Aided Indexing, Information Processing and Management, Vol. 12, No. 6, 1976, pp. 351–366.

[23] G. Salton, The Smart Retrieval System—Experiments in Automatic Document Processing, Prentice-Hall Inc., Englewood Cliffs, New Jersey, 1971.

[24] G. Salton, Dynamic Information and Library Processing, Prentice-Hall Inc., Englewood Cliffs, New Jersey, 1975.

[25] L.A. Zadeh, Fuzzy Sets, Information and Control, Vol. 8, No. 3, 1965, pp. 338–353.

[26] L.A. Zadeh, Fuzzy Logic and Its Application to Approximate Reasoning, Information Processing 74, North-Holland Publishing Company, Amsterdam, 1974, pp. 591–594.

[27] J.A. Goguen, The Logic of Inexact Concepts, Synthese, Vol. 19, 1968-69, pp. 325–373.

[28] G. Lakoff, Hedges—A Study in Measuring Criteria and the Logic of Fuzzy Concepts, English Regional Meeting of the Chicago Linguistic Society, Chicago, Illinois, 1972.

[29] T. Radecki, Mathematic Model of Information Retrieval Based on the Concept of a

Fuzzy Thesaurus, Information Processing and Management, Vol. 12, No. 5, 1976, pp. 313–318.

[30] A. Bookstein, Weighted Boolean Retrieval, Proceedings ACM-BCS Conference on Research and Development in Information Retrieval, in Information Retrieval Research, R.N. Oddy, S.E. Robertson, C.J. van Rijsbergen, and P.W. Williams, editors, Butterworths, London, 1981.

[31] A. Bookstein, Fuzzy Requests: An Approach to Weighted Boolean Searches, Journal of the ASIS, Vol. 31, No. 4, July 1980, pp. 240–247.

[32] D.A. Buell and D.H. Kraft, A Model for a Weighted Retrieval System, Journal of the ASIS, Vol. 32, No. 3, May 1981, pp. 211–216.

[33] W.G. Waller and D.H. Kraft, A Mathematical Model of a Weighted Boolean Retrieval System, Information Processing and Management, Vol. 15, No. 5, 1979, pp. 235–245.

[34] V. Tahani, A Fuzzy Model of Document Retrieval, Information Processing and Management, Vol. 12, 1976, pp. 177–187.

[35] M.E. Maron and J.L. Kuhns, On Relevance, Probabilistic Indexing and Information Retrieval, Journal of the ACM, Vol. 7, No. 3, 1960, pp. 216–244.

[36] A. Bookstein and D.R. Swanson, A Decision-Theoretic Foundation for Indexing, Journal of the ASIS, Vol. 26, No. 1, 1975, pp. 45–50.

[37] C.J. van Rijsbergen, A Theoretical Basis for the Use of Cooccurrence Data in Retrieval, Journal of Documentation, Vol. 33, 1977, pp. 106–119.

[38] S.E. Robertson and K. Sparck Jones, Relevance Weighting of Search Terms, Journal of the ASIS, Vol. 23, No. 3, 1976, pp. 129–146.

[39] R.O. Duda and P.E. Hart, Pattern Classification and Scene Analysis, John Wiley and Sons, New York, 1973.

[40] C.T. Yu, W.S. Luk, and M.K. Siu, On Models of Information Retrieval, Information Systems, Vol. 4, No. 3, 1979, pp. 205–218.

[41] D.J. Harper and C.J. van Rijsbergen, An Evaluation of Feedback in Document Retrieval Using Cooccurrence Data, Journal of Documentation, Vol. 34, No. 3, September 1978, pp. 189–206.

[42] S.E. Robertson, C.J. van Rijsbergen, and M.F. Porter, Probabilistic Models of Indexing and Searching, ACM-BCS Conference on Research and Development in Information Retrieval, in Information Retrieval Research, R.N. Oddy, S.E. Robertson, C.J. van Rijsbergen, and P.W. Williams, editors, Butterworths, London, 1981.

[43] J.J. Rocchio, Jr., Relevance Feedback in Information Retrieval, in The Smart System—Experiments in Automatic Document Processing, G. Salton, editor, Prentice-Hall, Englewood Cliffs, New Jersey, 1971, Chapter 14.

[44] E. Ide and G. Salton, Interactive Search Strategies and Dynamic File Organization in Information Retrieval, in The Smart System—Experiments in Automatic Document Processing, G. Salton, editor, Prentice-Hall, Englewood Cliffs, New Jersey, 1971, Chapter 18.

[45] H. Wu and G. Salton, The Estimation of Term Relevance Weights Using Relevance Feedback, Department of Computer Science, Cornell University, Ithaca, New York, 1980.

[46] M.B. Koll, WEIRD—An Approach to Concept-Based Information Retrieval, SIGIR Forum, Vol. 13, No. 4, Spring 1979, pp. 32–50.

[47] M.B. Koll, Information Retrieval Theory and Design Based on a Model of the User's Concept Relations, ACM-BCS Conference on Research and Development in

Information Retrieval, in Information Retrieval Research, R.N. Oddy, S.E. Robertson, C.J. van Rijsbergen, and P.W. Williams, editors, Butterworths, London, 1981.

[48] G. Salton, Automatic Indexing Using Bibliographic Citations, Journal of Documentation, Vol. 27, No. 2, June 1971, pp. 98–110.

[49] E. Garfield, Citation Indexing, John Wiley and Sons, New York, 1979.

[50] H.G. Small, A Co-Citation Model of a Scientific Specialty: A Longitudinal Study of Collagen Research, Social Studies of Science, Vol. 7, 1977, pp. 139–166.

[51] R. Knaus, A Similarity Measure on Semantic Network Nodes, Paper presented at the Annual Meeting of the Classification Society, Gainesville, Florida, 1978.

[52] R. Marcus and J. Reintjes, Computer Interfaces for User Access to Heterogeneous Information Retrieval Systems, Massachsuetts Institute of Technology, Electronic Systems Laboratory Report ESL-R-739, Cambridge, Massachusetts, April 1977.

[53] R.A. Winter, T. Lozano-Perez, and B.O. Marks, An Overview of the Chemical Substances Information Network, Computer Corporation of America, Technical Report No. CCA-79-20, Cambridge, Massachusetts, September 1979.

[54] D. Eastlake III, T. Lozano-Perez, and D. Low, Design of Version I Prototype Chemical Substance Information Network, Computer Corporation of America, Technical Report No. CCA-80-6, Cambridge, Massachusetts, June 1980.

[55] M. Bracken, J. Dorigan, and J. Overbey, Chemical Substances Information Network, MITRE Corporation, Technical Report MTS-7558, McLean, Virginia, June 1977.

[56] C.A. Ellis and G.J. Nutt, Office Information Systems and Computer Science, ACM Computing Surveys, Vol. 12, No. 1, March 1980, pp. 27–60.

[57] F.W. Lancaster, Toward Paperless Information Systems, Academic Press Inc., New York, 1978.

[58] D.P. Bhandarkar, The Impact of Semiconductor Technology on Computer Systems, Computer, Vol. 12, No. 9, September 1979, pp. 92–98.

[59] J. Martyn, Prestel and Public Libraries: An LA/Aslib Experiment, Aslib Proceedings, Vol. 31, No. 5, May 1979, pp. 216–236.

[60] L.M. Branscomb, Information: The Ultimate Frontier, Science, Vol. 203, January 12, 1979, pp. 143–147.

[61] G. Salton, Suggestions for Library Network Design, Journal of Library Automation, Vol. 12, No. 1, March 1979, pp. 39–52.

BIBLIOGRAPHIC REMARKS:

Two kinds of materials suggest themselves as additional sources for information on the future of information retrieval. The first consists of reviews outlining the current state of the art and including also short-term projections for the future. Such material can be found in certain conference proceedings and in some of the widely circulated journals in the computer field. There exist yearly proceedings of a Conference on Office Automation sponsored by the American Federation of Information Processing Societies (AFIPS). The Institute of Electrical and Electronics Engineers (IEEE) and the Association for Computing Machinery (ACM) jointly sponsor a yearly conference on Very Large Data Bases. Conference proceedings are also available covering many computer technologies of interest such as microprocessors and computer graphics. The journals that regularly include reviews and projections into the future of information science include Computerworld, Datamation and the ACM Computing Surveys.

Another type of article takes a more frankly visionary approach. In that area it is however necessary to distinguish materials with a science-fiction approach from articles exhibiting a solid technical foundation. The following articles or books are certainly worth reading:

V. Bush, As We May Think, Atlantic Monthly, Vol. 176, No. 1, 1945, pp. 101–108.
J. G. Kemeny, A Library for 2000 A.D., in Management and the Computer of the Future, M. Greenberger, editor, MIT Press, 1962, pp. 134–178.
F. W. Lancaster, Toward Paperless Information Systems, Academic Press Inc., New York, 1978.
J. C. R. Licklider, Libraries of the Future, MIT Press, Cambridge, Massachusetts, 1965.
G. Salton, Dynamic Information and Library Processing, Prentice-Hall Inc., Englewood Cliffs, New Jersey, 1975, Chapter 10.

Name Index

Subject Index